www.wadsworth.com

www.wadsworth.com is the World Wide Web site for Wadsworth and is your direct source to dozens of online resources.

At *www.wadsworth.com* you can find out about supplements, demonstration software, and student resources. You can also send email to many of our authors and preview new publications and exciting new technologies.

www.wadsworth.com
Changing the way the world learns.®

Free study resources for your American History course—*available online!*

Primary source documents, video and audio clips, activities, and self-quizzing—all FREE to you when you purchase this text!

American Journey Online

http://ajaccess.wadsworth.com

FREE access with every new copy of the text!

American Journey Online comprises 16 primary source collections that capture the landmark events and major themes of the American experience—through images and the words of those who lived it. Discover hundreds of rare documents, pictures, and archival audio and video, along with essays, headnotes, and captions that set the sources in context. Full-text searchability and extensive hyperlinking make searching and cross-referencing easy.

Also Available:
***American Journey Online*
User's Guide with Activities**
This helpful resource is available on the home page of **http://ajaccess.wadsworth.com** and at the Book Companion Web Site (**http://history.wadsworth. com/americanpast7e**). It is also available as a print resource (ISBN 0-534-17433-7).

Book Companion Web Site

At the Wadsworth American History Resource Center

http://history.wadsworth.com/ americanpast7e

At the Book Companion Web Site for this text, you'll find a wide variety of study aids that will help you make the most of your course! These features include:

Chapter outlines and summaries • Tutorial quizzes • Flashcards • Glossary • Simulations—interactive, detailed accounts paired with critical thinking and multiple choice quizzes • **American Journey Online** activities and video exercises • An *At the Movies* feature that provides descriptions, critical thinking questions, and Web links for major films throughout American history • Crossword puzzles • The U.S. Image Bank, featuring images and maps that can be put into multimedia presentations • Interactive maps with questions • Primary sources • and much more!

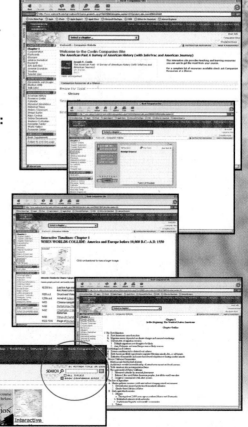

To access the Book Companion Web Site, simply visit the URL listed above or click on "Student Book Companion Sites" at the Wadsworth History Resource Center home page (**http://history.wadsworth.com**). Click on your book cover, and you're there!

You can also find your Book Companion Site with the easy-to-use search feature, located in the top right hand corner of the American History Resource Center home page. Simply type in "Conlin," select "Book Companion Web Sites," and click on "Go."

THE AMERICAN PAST

A Survey of American History
Volume I: To 1877

SEVENTH EDITION

JOSEPH R. CONLIN

THOMSON

WADSWORTH

Australia • Canada • Mexico • Singapore • Spain • United Kingdom • United States

THOMSON
WADSWORTH
PUBLISHER: Clark Baxter
SENIOR DEVELOPMENT EDITOR: Margaret McAndrew Beasley
ASSISTANT EDITOR: Julie Yardley
EDITORIAL ASSISTANT: Eno Sarris
TECHNOLOGY PROJECT MANAGER: Jennifer Ellis
EXECUTIVE MARKETING MANAGER: Caroline Croley
MARKETING ASSISTANT: Mary Ho
ADVERTISING PROJECT MANAGER: Tami Strang
PROJECT MANAGER, EDITORIAL PRODUCTION: Kimberly Adams
PRINT/MEDIA BUYER: Doreen Suruki
PERMISSIONS EDITOR: Sarah Harkrader

PRODUCTION SERVICE: Orr Book Services
TEXT DESIGNER: Sue Hart
PHOTO RESEARCHER: Lili Weiner
COPY EDITOR: Mark Colucci
ILLUSTRATOR: ElectraGraphics, Inc.
COVER DESIGNER: Lisa Devenish
COVER IMAGE: *Go West,* circa 1885. Reprinted with permission from Hulton Archive/Getty Images.
COMPOSITOR: Thompson Type
PRINTER: Quebecor World/Versailles

Printed in the United States of America
2 3 4 5 6 7 07 06 05 04 03

For more information about our products, contact us at:
Thomson Learning Academic Resource Center
1-800-423-0563
For permission to use material from this text,
contact us by:
Phone: 1-800-730-2214
Fax: 1-800-730-2215
Web: http://www.thomsonrights.com

Library of Congress Control Number: 2003107884

Student Edition: ISBN 0-534-62137-6

Instructor's Edition: ISBN 0-534-10557-2

Wadsworth/Thomson Learning
10 Davis Drive
Belmont, CA 94002-3098
USA

Asia
Thomson Learning
5 Shenton Way #01-01
UIC Building
Singapore 068808

Australia/New Zealand
Thomson Learning
102 Dodds Street
Southbank, Victoria 3006
Australia

Canada
Nelson
1120 Birchmount Road
Toronto, Ontario M1K 5G4
Canada

Europe/Middle East/Africa
Thomson Learning
High Holborn House
50/51 Bedford Row
London WC1R 4LR
United Kingdom

Latin America
Thomson Learning
Seneca, 53
Colonia Polanco
11560 Mexico D.F.
Mexico

Spain/Portugal
Paraninfo
Calle/Magallanes, 25
28015 Madrid, Spain

To the Memory of
J.R.C. (1917–1985)
L.V.C. (1920–2001)

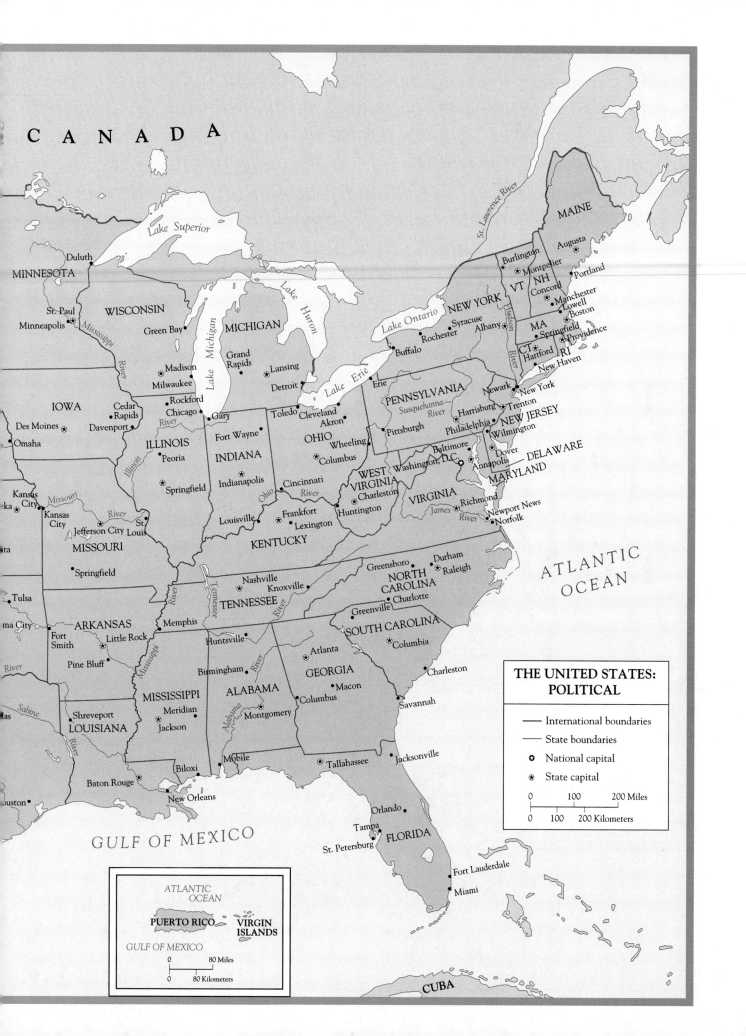

CANADA

MINNESOTA

Duluth

St. Paul
Minneapolis

WISCONSIN

Lake Superior

Green Bay

Lake Michigan

Madison
Milwaukee

Rockford

IOWA

Cedar
Rapids

Chicago
Gary

Des Moines
Davenport

Omaha

ILLINOIS

Peoria

Springfield

Kansas
City

Missouri River

Kansas
City

Jefferson City
MISSOURI

St.
Louis

Springfield

Tulsa

ma City

ARKANSAS

Fort
Smith

Little Rock

Pine Bluff

River

Sabine River

LOUISIANA

Shreveport

MISSISSIPPI

Meridian
Jackson

Baton Rouge

ouston

New Orleans

Biloxi

MICHIGAN

Grand
Rapids

Lansing

Detroit

Lake Huron

Fort Wayne

INDIANA

Indianapolis

Toledo

OHIO

Cleveland
Akron

Columbus

Wheeling

Lake Erie

Erie

Cincinnati

Ohio River

Louisville

Frankfort
Lexington

KENTUCKY

Huntington

WEST
VIRGINIA

Charleston

Nashville
Knoxville

Tennessee River

TENNESSEE

Memphis

Mississippi River

Huntsville

Birmingham

ALABAMA

Alabama River

Montgomery

Mobile

Columbus

Atlanta

GEORGIA

Macon

Tallahassee

Lake Ontario

Rochester
Syracuse

Buffalo

Albany

PENNSYLVANIA

Susquehanna River

Pittsburgh

Harrisburg

NEW YORK

St. Lawrence River

MAINE

Augusta

Burlington
Montpelier

VT

NH

Concord

Portland

Manchester
Lowell
Boston

MA

Springfield
Providence

Hudson River

CT
Hartford

RI

New Haven

Newark
Trenton

New York

NEW JERSEY

Philadelphia

Wilmington

Dover

DELAWARE

Baltimore

Washington, D.C.

Annapolis

MARYLAND

VIRGINIA

Richmond

James River

Newport News
Norfolk

Greensboro

Durham
Raleigh

NORTH
CAROLINA

Charlotte

Greenville

SOUTH
CAROLINA

Columbia

Charleston

Savannah

Jacksonville

ATLANTIC
OCEAN

Orlando

Tampa

St. Petersburg

FLORIDA

Fort Lauderdale

Miami

GULF OF MEXICO

CUBA

**THE UNITED STATES:
POLITICAL**

—— International boundaries

—— State boundaries

⊙ National capital

✳ State capital

0   100   200 Miles

0   100   200 Kilometers

ATLANTIC
OCEAN

PUERTO RICO   **VIRGIN
ISLANDS**

GULF OF MEXICO

0   80 Miles

0   80 Kilometers

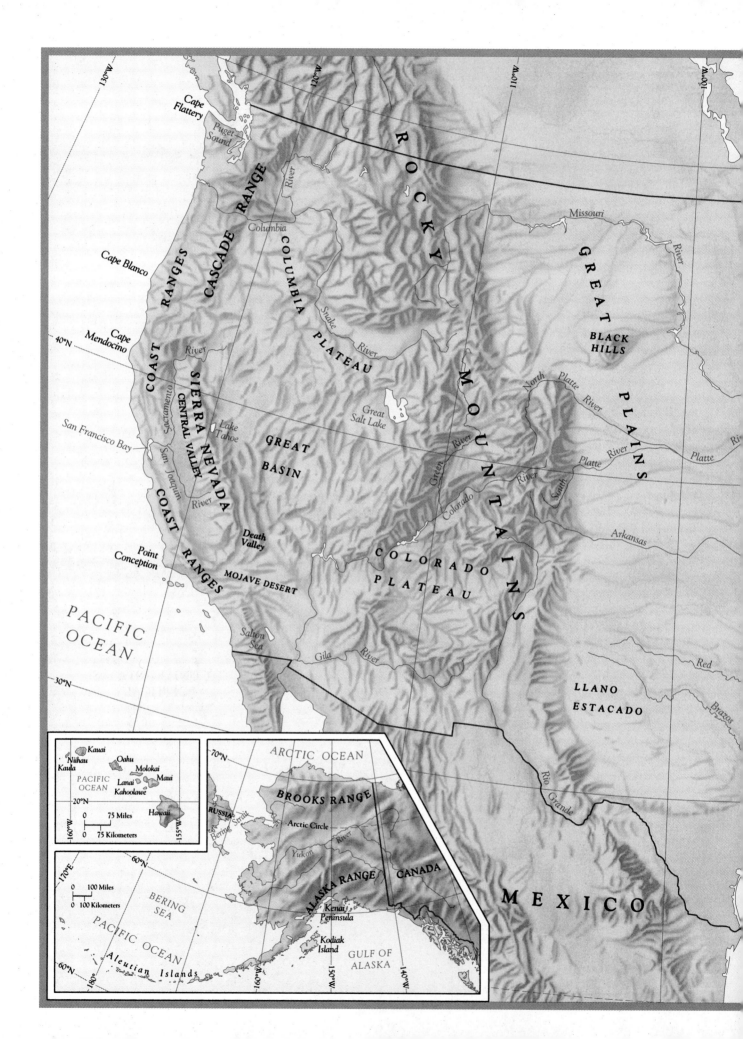

130°W

120°W

110°W

100°W

Cape
Flattery

Puget
Sound

R O C K Y

Missouri

Columbia

River

C O A S T

R A N G E S

C A S C A D E   R A N G E

Cape Blanco

C O L U M B I A

P L A T E A U

M O U N T A I N S

G R E A T

Snake

River

P L A I N S

Cape
Mendocino

40°N

C O A S T

S I E R R A   N E V A D A

River

CENTRAL VALLEY

**BLACK
HILLS**

Sacramento

San Francisco Bay

Lake
Tahoe

Great
Salt Lake

North

Platte

River

San Joaquin

G R E A T

B A S I N

Green

River

Platte

River

South

R A N G E S

River

Death
Valley

Colorado

River

Platte

Arkansas

Point
Conception

MOJAVE DESERT

C O L O R A D O

P L A T E A U

**PACIFIC
OCEAN**

Salton
Sea

Red

30°N

Gila

River

L L A N O

E S T A C A D O

Brazos

Rio

Grande

M E X I C O

Kauai

Niihau

Oahu

Kaula

Molokai

PACIFIC
OCEAN

Lanai

Maui

Kahoolawe

20°N

0   75 Miles

Hawaii

0   75 Kilometers

160°W

155°W

70°N

ARCTIC OCEAN

BROOKS RANGE

RUSSIA

Arctic Circle

River

Yukon

CANADA

Bering Strait

60°N

ALASKA RANGE

170°E

0   100 Miles

Kenai
Peninsula

0   100 Kilometers

**BERING
SEA**

Kodiak
Island

**GULF OF
ALASKA**

PACIFIC OCEAN

60°N

Aleutian   Islands

180°

170°W

160°W

150°W

140°W

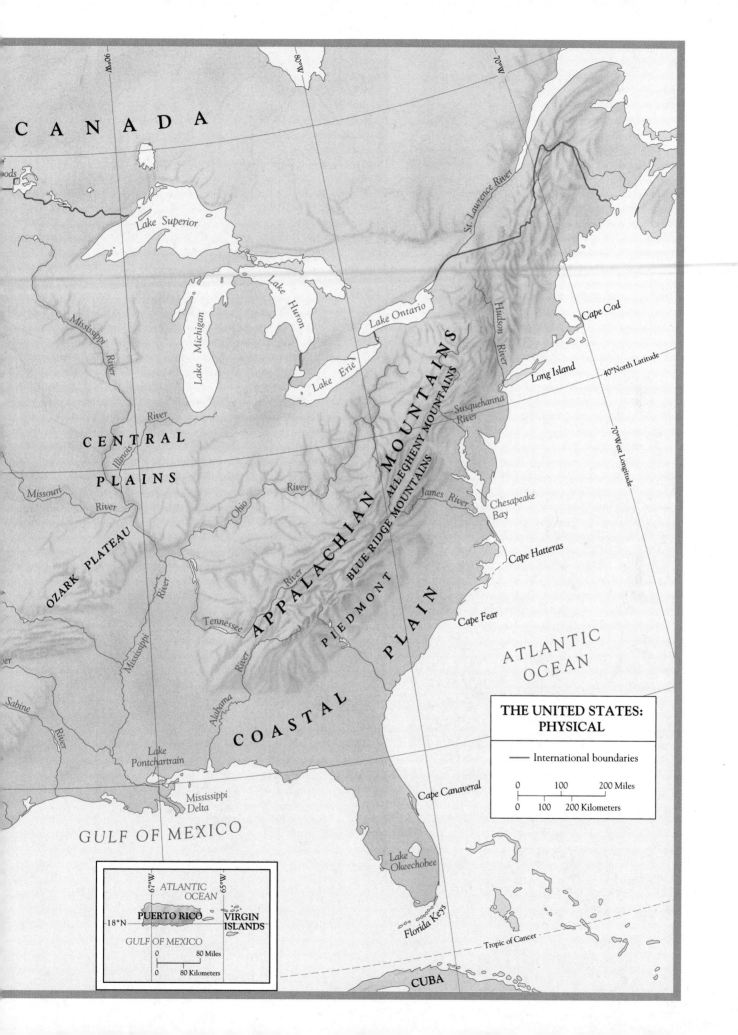

CANADA

Lake Superior

Lake Michigan

Lake Huron

Lake Ontario

Lake Erie

Mississippi River

St. Lawrence River

Hudson River

Cape Cod

Long Island

40°North Latitude

70°West Longitude

Susquehanna River

CENTRAL

Illinois River

PLAINS

Missouri River

James River

Chesapeake Bay

Cape Hatteras

APPALACHIAN MOUNTAINS

ALLEGHENY MOUNTAINS

BLUE RIDGE MOUNTAINS

Ohio River

OZARK PLATEAU

River

Tennessee River

PIEDMONT

Cape Fear

ATLANTIC OCEAN

Mississippi River

River

Alabama River

Sabine River

COASTAL PLAIN

Lake Pontchartrain

Mississippi Delta

THE UNITED STATES: PHYSICAL

—— International boundaries

| 0 | 100 | 200 Miles |
| 0 | 100 | 200 Kilometers |

Cape Canaveral

GULF OF MEXICO

Lake Okeechobee

Florida Keys

Tropic of Cancer

ATLANTIC OCEAN

67°W   65°W

18°N **PUERTO RICO**   VIRGIN ISLANDS

GULF OF MEXICO

| 0 | 80 Miles |
| 0 | 80 Kilometers |

CUBA

Brief Contents

Table of Contents

List of Maps

Preface

The photograph of the westward-bound wagon train on Volume I captures well the vastness of the country to be crossed to Utah, California, or Oregon by the tens of thousands who made the journey during the 1840s and 1850s.

The seventh edition of *The American Past* is a newer book than any version since the first: a new publisher, a new look, a more thorough rewrite of the previous edition, and more new material. I doubt that there is a paragraph that has escaped at least a polishing. I have completely rewritten large sections of most of the chapters.

The seventh edition is a lot less hefty than the sixth or, for that matter, the fifth. For about a decade, I have seen survey textbooks, including *The American Past,* grow too big. Some seem more closely related to the unabridged dictionary sitting on a stand in a corner of the library than to the kind of book that students can carry with them in bags slung over their shoulders. An equally painful consequence of textbooks' runaway growth has been the runaway price tags on them. I trust the "streamlined" *American Past* will provide some budgetary as well as physical relief.

I have slimmed down the seventh edition by, first of all, eliminating pure ornament: the bells, whistles, fuss, feathers, and curlicues that are nice enough in a book but add heft and cost to it. We excised 50 pages simply by reducing chapter openers from two-page spreads to a single page. I have forsaken illustrations-for-the-sake-of-a-picture, a few maps that, upon reflection, were superfluous, and chronologies and charts so dense in data that not a student in a hundred is apt to look at them. Expanding the book's trim size has helped reduce the number of pages while maintaining an attractive layout.

I have not dropped a single subject essential to understanding how the United States and the American people got to be the way they are. Nor have I stripped down the treatment of ideas difficult to grasp so that they are inadequately explained. In fact, I have added discussions of topics new to this edition when new research seemed sufficiently basic and convincing to belong in a survey course textbook.

Nevertheless, the total length of the narrative, as well as the size of the book, has been reduced. This was possible because I subjected my prose to a closer and more rigorous editing than I did when revising previous editions. It was an interesting exercise: dismaying when I discovered how verbose I had been just a few years ago; an occasion of jubilation when I realized that while reducing the size of the book, I was also writing a clearer and livelier presentation of American history than I had in six previous tries. Setting aside great literature, there are few passages of prose in the English language that cannot be improved by deleting words. (I believe I have identified four words in the Gettysburg Address that Lincoln might have stricken had the train to Gettysburg been delayed for half an hour.)

My ambition for *The American Past* has, from the first, been to write a book not for research historians, or even for history majors, but for college freshmen and sophomores who intend to become accountants, ecologists, engineers, nurses, psychologists, retailers, webmasters, and zookeepers—students who may be "taking the survey" for reasons other than "history is my favorite subject." I believe that a sense of history—some knowledge of their past—makes such students, if not better accountants, ecologists, and so on, then better citizens and even fuller human beings.

Years at the front of lecture halls, however, taught me that few students can be persuaded that this is so; they must be seduced into it. That, I think, is best accomplished not with flash, dash, and gimmickry. A history textbook attempting to compete with glossy advertisements for SUVs, reality television, and video games is as foolish a venture as the history department softball nine demanding a franchise in the National League. Students have to be wooed to a love of history, or just an appreciation for it, by good lectures, intelligently guided classroom discussion, and a textbook they find enjoyable to read and, therefore, do read.

Narrative is the kind of prose most people find enjoyable to read. Nonspecialists are turned off by turgid explication, compartmentalization, and dissection of minutiae. So narrative is the way I do it. I incorporate into the "story" economic, diplomatic, technological, and other developments when they move the "plot" along, rather than stacking them up in disembodied blocks of information unrelated to the information in the blocks atop or below them. This is particularly important, I think, when working with the relatively recent research of historians of racial and ethnic minorities, gender, and the environment. To treat African Americans, Hispanics, postcontact Indians, women, and children as if they were not part of the flow of American history, but bystanders to be dealt with in another room, is to demean them posthumously—quite as insultingly as they were demeaned in other eras. A textbook is a peculiar sort of book, but a history textbook should be a *book,* not a cluttered collage of snippets.

During the more than two decades that *The American Past* has been in print, I have heard from many professors—perhaps close to 200—who have assigned the text to their classes. It has been gratifying that even some of the annoyed correspondents closed their letters with a comment something like

"My students really like *The American Past.* They actually read it!"

That has been the idea and remains the guiding principle behind the seventh edition.

NEW TO THE SEVENTH EDITION
Streamlined Text and Updated Research

The seventh edition narrative has been tightened, which has reduced the length of the text about 10 percent. And, throughout, I have woven into the story pertinent material from my reading of recent scholarship.

New Map Captions

For the first time, I have written explanatory captions for the maps—"pointers" to help readers locate the significant features of each map. I have added some new maps where they would enhance a point in the text (see, for example, Chapter 20). In Chapter 51, there is a new multi-election electoral vote map that illustrates the significant party shift in presidential elections in the final decades of the twentieth century. I have also eliminated a few maps that seemed to add nothing to the narrative (for example, electoral vote maps of landslide victories when there was no sectional pattern of voting).

Illustrations

Many illustrations are new with this edition. I have written new captions for all of them to make the historical signifi-cance clear and so that they serve a pedagogical purpose, rather than simply breaking up the type with a decoration.

"How They Lived" Features

I have written about 15 new "How They Lived" features, placing one in each chapter. In response to reviewer feedback, I have dropped the biographical boxes ("Notable People"), replacing them with new "How They Lived" features, which instructors say they find more useful. These features deal with "slices of life," mostly social history: for example, piracy (Chapter 6), road building (Chapter 14), a ward heeler's day (Chapter 26), smoking (Chapter 32), hobos and tramps (Chapter 35), fads and sensationalism (Chapter 40), drugs (Chapter 48), changing sexual mores (Chapter 49).

Sidebars

There are about a hundred new sidebars highlighting information that is too interesting (or amusing) to pass up but that, if related in the narrative, would interrupt the "conversational" flow of the book.

Revisions to Coverage

Topics that are new with the seventh edition, or those that I have expanded or altered my take on (almost always because of persuasive research I have read since the sixth edition), include fresh material about pre-Columbian Indians in Mesoamerica (Chapter 1) and precontact Indians in what is now the United States (Chapter 5). There is some new material on slave rebellions (Chapters 6 and 18) and rather a lot on family history and the role of gender relations in American development (Chapters 6, 10, 36, and 46). There is new material on Jefferson (Chapters 11 and 12), technology (Chapter 14), crime (Chapter 17), the illegal African slave trade (Chapter 19), and immigration and nativism (Chapters 22, 29, and 51). I have introduced information new to me in just about every chapter dealing with twentieth-century political history, particularly in Chapters 42, 43, 45, and, of course, the final chapters, some of which qualifies as news as well as history.

Evolving Interpretations

One's own historical politics changes over the years. If there existed a person who cared to read the chapters about the Jacksonians and the Whigs in all seven editions of *The American Past* (Chapters 14–16 in this edition), such a drone would discover that I have, albeit slowly, "crossed the aisle" from Andrew Jackson's benches to those of the Whigs. I am sitting there now, in this edition, perhaps closer to Henry Clay and the border state Whigs than to the New Englanders.

There are other eras in which, if my sympathies have not so radically changed, I have come to see both sides of the division with greater balance: colonial governors versus colonial assemblies (Chapters 6 and 7), Federalists versus Jeffersonians (Chapters 11 and 12), and agrarians versus business Republicans (Chapter 32). My assessment of the progressives is still in flux; in any case, I have looked at them differently in this edition (Chapters 34–36 and 38) than I did in the sixth.

A Note on Contemporary History

A comparable mellowing in writing about very recent history—about people and events of which I first read in the newspapers—is due not to a greater certainty, as in the instance of Jackson and the Whigs, but to a rampant uncertainty. I realize that I was dead wrong in some positions I took as a citizen and as a voter, but I am not yet convinced that the other side in those times was quite in the right.

As Margaret Beasley, my editor at Wadsworth Publishing, knows painfully well, I do not much like writing recent history precisely because of this lack of certainty and perspective. Still, in the final chapters, I have resisted the *World Almanac* technique of merely piling up names, facts, and dates—that would mean abandoning the liveliness of the first nine-tenths of the book. So the final few chapters of this edition are rewritten, drawing on previous editions only for phrasings I still like and insights I still think valid. If a reader of these chapters exclaims, "Wrong, wrong, wrong!" I can respond only, "You're probably right, right, right."

ACKNOWLEDGMENTS

I appreciate the comments and suggestions I've received from teaching historians who have read and critiqued chapters of the text:

George Alvergue, Lane Community College
Scott Carter, Shasta College
Richard H. Condon, University of Maine at Farmington
Stacy A. Cordery, Monmouth College
Linda Cross, Tyler Junior College
Barry A. Crouch, Gallaudet University
William Marvin Dulaney, College of Charleston
Carla Falkner, Northeast Mississippi Community College
George E. Frakes, Santa Barbara City College
Thomas M. Gaskin, Everett Community College
Joan E. Gittens, Southwest State University
John E. Hollitz, Community College of Southern Nevada
Robert R. Jones, University of Southwestern Louisiana
Martha Kirchmer, Grand Valley State University

Milton Madden, Lane Community College
Patricia L. Meador, Louisiana State University, Shreveport
Angelo Montante, Glendale Community College
Jack Oden, Enterprise State Junior College
Emmett Panzella, Point Park College
Richard H. Peterson, San Diego State University
Nancy L. Rachels, Hillsborough Community College
Michelle Riley, Del Mar College
William Scofield, Yakima Valley Community College
Richard S. Sorrell, Brookdale Community College
Ronald Story, University of Massachusetts
Daniel C. Vogt, Jackson State University
Loy Glenn Westfall, Hillsborough Brandon Community College
Donald W. Whisenhunt, Western Washington University
Lynn Willoughby, Winthrop University
Larry Wright, Inver Hills Community College

For helping me in the preparation of this revision, I must first name research librarian *ne plus ultra* Marilyn Grande Murphy. She does not answer queries more quickly than a silicon chip does, but she answers them better. Since I have been residing in "the sticks" for several years now, I have realized how important it was to me earlier in life to be able to walk to a good library in 15 minutes and browse the stacks. Now, when the phone lines are working, the Internet is a godsend, but it is not the same thing. I have also learned in recent years to appreciate that it was a very lucky day when I made the acquaintance of Ms. Murphy and she let me have her email address.

Lisa Devenish designed the covers for the three volumes in which *The American Past* is published, and created a first impression on which, indeed, I would not mind the book being judged.

Margaret McAndrew Beasley was the developmental editor for the seventh edition, as she was for the sixth. Once again, she managed me in my most irritable and frustrated moments with a cool, good-humored virtuosity that, when I reflect on it, was dazzling. Perhaps I could have done better; I doubt it.

I am also grateful to Clark Baxter, publisher for history; Kim Adams, production project manager; John Orr, freelance project editor; Lili Weiner, freelance photo researcher; Caroline Croley, executive marketing manager; and the Wadsworth sales team—all for their respective roles in the process of delivering *The American Past* to you.

1

DISCOVERIES

Indians, Europeans, and America 15,000 B.C.– A.D. 1550

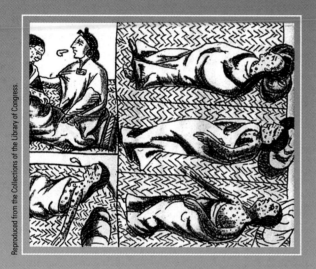

Reproduced from the Collections of the Library of Congress.

I feel a wonderful exultation of spirits when I converse with intelligent men who have returned from these regions. It is like an accession of wealth to a miser. Our minds, soiled and debased by the common concerns of life and the vices of society, become elevated and ameliorated by contemplating such glorious events.

Peter Martyr

Broken spears lie in the roads;
We have torn our hair in our grief.
The houses are roofless now,
And their walls are red with blood. . . .
We are crushed to the ground;
We lie in ruins.
There is nothing but grief and suffering
in Mexico and Tlateloco.

Anonymous Aztec poet

HUMANITY ORIGINATED IN East Africa. From there, people migrated south, west, and north, colonizing Africa, Asia, and Europe—but not the Americas for a geological epoch. Even isolated Australia was populated 20,000 years before a human footprint was impressed in American mud.

The date of the first discovery of America is disputed, but it was likely about 15,000 years ago, when Asian hunters crossed from Siberia to what is now Alaska. They walked, which is impossible today, when 56 miles of frigid sea—the Bering Strait—separate Asia and America. Fifteen thousand years ago, however, the earth was locked in an ice age. Temperatures everywhere were far lower than they are today. Much of the earth's water was frozen in the polar ice caps and in glaciers larger than our nations. Consequently, sea level was about 400 feet lower than it is today. Our beaches were inland, miles from the surf. Vast tracts of sea bottom today were dry, including the floor of the Bering Strait, now 180 feet below the surface. A rather high "land bridge," a hundred miles wide, connected Siberia and Alaska. This was the route traveled by the first discoverers of America.

They did not know they were discovering a "new world." They were nomads checking out the territory, as nomads do, or chasing dinner—herds of caribou?—or fleeing enemies. In as few as a thousand years, however, waves of these immigrants colonized two continents, advancing their frontier, on average, a mile a month. They were the ancestors of the people we call "Indians" or "Native Americans."

THE FIRST COLONIZATION

The Paleo-Indians (*old* Indians) were a *pre*historic people, and so their story is beyond the compass of historians. Historians study the past in the written words the people of the past have left us. They can tell us nothing of human beings who lived, loved, begat, hated, and died before there was writing. To know about *pre*historic (preliterate) people, we must turn to archaeologists, linguists, and folklorists, scholars who sift particles of information, like gold dust, from the gravel of artifacts—things human beings made—from the structure of language, and from tales passed by word of mouth from one generation to the next.

The pictures these men and women sketch are fuzzier than the portraits historians can draw from their written documents. As a Chinese saying has it, "The palest ink is clearer than the best memory." Still, faint is better than blank. Without folklore and analysis of language, oral tradition, and artifacts, the American past would not begin until A.D. 1492, a bit more than 500 years ago. It was then that Europeans, who scribbled endlessly of their achievements, follies, and sins, discovered the Western Hemisphere for themselves, inundating it with their numbers. Thanks to archaeology, linguistics, and folklore, we can pencil in a more ancient heritage.

Diversity

The Paleo-Indians knew no more of agriculture than of alphabets. When they crossed to America, there was not a farmer on the planet. Like all people of their day, the first Americans lived by hunting, fishing, and gathering. They took from nature the makings of their meals and clothing, their shelter, tools, and weapons. They were nomads because there was no alternative to wandering. In all but the lushest environments, even small communities soon exhaust the food that can be hunted and gathered near a fixed abode. Home was where the food was.

By the time the mystery of agriculture was first unlocked in the Middle East about 8,000 B.C., the Paleo-Indians had lost contact with the Eurasian landmass. A global warming 2,000–3,000 years earlier melted the massive glaciers of the Ice Age and reduced the size of the polar ice caps. Sea level rose, drowning the land bridge between Siberia and Alaska.

Paleo-Indian ways of life diversified rapidly. The Americas were uncrowded, and wandering tribes found it easy to split up when their numbers grew too large for the range or when chiefs had a falling out. Soon enough, the vastness of America and the diversity of its climates and land forms isolated the scattered Paleo-Indians from one another, resulting in a dizzying variety of cultures.

Indian languages, for example, once just a handful, multiplied until there were at least 500 of them. Tribes living in harsh environments continued to survive precariously into historic times on what they could hunt, snare, net, gather, and grub. Other Indians learned to farm, producing the surplus of food that, as in the Middle East, India, and China, made the emergence of civilization possible. The Native Americans who learned to *produce* food, rather than depending on nature to provide it, lived in Mesoamerica (meaning "between the Americas": that is, Mexico and Central America) and in Peru.

Some Indians had mastered only primitive tool making when, after 1500, they were dazzled (and crushed) by European technology. Others perfected handcraft to a level of refinement unattained in Africa, Asia, or Europe.

Some Native Americans left no more mark on the land than the remains of campfires and garbage dumps that we need space-age technology in order to identify. By contrast, the labor force of the "Mound Builders" of central North America was sufficiently large and disciplined that they heaped up massive earthen structures that have survived the ages. One great mound, in the shape of a bird, was 70 feet in height, an edifice as impressive and durable as a Mesopotamian ziggurat. In Ohio, two parallel Mound Builder "walls" ran 60 miles from Chillicothe to Newark. Some scholars believe that Cahokia, in Illinois across the Mississippi from St. Louis, had a population of 30,000.

The Indians' closeness to nature made them canny in lore based on observation and on trial and error. For example, the effects of more than 200 natural medicines in use today were known in prehistoric America. Given the isolation of the Indians from the process of cultural diffusion—the ongoing exchange of ideas and techniques—in the "Old

Did Paleo-Indians Wipe Out the Mastodons?
Mastodons, hairy elephants larger than today's, once flourished in North America. They became extinct a few thousand years after the first discovery of America. Did the Paleo-Indians destroy them? They did hunt mastodons; spear points have been found in fossilized mastodon skeletons. Elsewhere in the world, Stone Age people destroyed species: saber-toothed tigers in Europe, any number of brightly plumed birds in New Zealand. Zoologists point out that if hunters kill only slightly more of a species than are born each year, the species will disappear in a few centuries. With single births after a long gestation period, mastodons may well have been one of the earliest species to be wiped out by human beings.

▲ *The Mayans, and the Aztecs after them, built many-storied pyramids of heaped earth faced with stone, quite as formidable as the ziggurats of Mesopotamia. They were symbols of power, and many were used as temples where captives were sacrificed to the gods. Some anthropologists believe that the "Mound Builders" of the American Midwest were recalling Mesoamerican pyramids in building their heaped earth monuments.*

World" of Asia, Africa, and Europe, the first Americans' achievements, in so short a time, are astonishing.

Mesoamerican Civilization

In Guatemala, Belize, and southern Mexico, Indians made the intellectual leap that signals the birth of civilization. Olmecs, Toltecs, and Mayans farmed so productively that they supported a populous and highly organized society in which many individuals could work at tasks other than farming. Just as the ancient civilizations of Asia did, the Mesoamericans developed a system of writing with which they carved records in stone and composed "books" on processed strips of cactus fiber similar to the papyrus of ancient Egypt.

Alas for historians, after 1500 a zealous Spanish bishop condemned these writings as "superstition and lies of the devil." So effective was his command they be burned that only three Mayan literary works survive. But inscribed rock proved too much for censors. Carved writings are abundant in Mesoamerica, and in recent decades, experts have learned to read them. They provide us with a chapter of American history long assumed to be lost.

At one time or another, some 40 cities dotted Mesoamerica. Several were home to 20,000 people. By A.D. 500, Teotihuacán, founded about the time of Christ near present-day Mexico City, was home to 125,000. These cities were governed by an aristocracy of priests and warriors who directed the construction, at the center of each city, of at least one pyramid-shaped earth-and-stone temple. The pyramid at Chichén Itzá rose 18 stories.

The Mayans were superb mathematicians and astronomers. They discovered the use of the zero, a breakthrough achieved in only one other world culture, India. They timed the earth's orbit around the sun as accurately as any other astronomers of their era and applied their findings to an accurate calendar.

War and Religion

The Mesoamerican rulers took little interest in the empire building that obsessed Old World elites. Each city-state was an independent entity with a limited hinterland. Not that the Mesoamericans were peaceable folk. Far from it. They were chronically fighting with their neighbors, for their religion compelled war. Their gods (jaguarlike beings, eagles, serpents, the sun) thirsted for human blood.

In solemn public rituals, noblewomen made symbolic blood sacrifice by drawing strings of thorns through punctures in their tongues. Their brothers and husbands drew the barbs through their foreskins. The blood that fell from their wounds was absorbed into strips of fiber that were burned, dispatching the sacrifice in smoke to the heavens.

But symbolic blood sacrifice was not enough for the Mesoamerican deities. They also demanded that priests throw young women into pits to die and that they drag other victims to the tops of the pyramids, where, using stone knives, the priests tore their hearts, still beating when the operation was correctly performed, from their breasts. Thus the chronic war: The Mesoamericans needed prisoners for sacrifice.

MAP 1:1 Mayan Civilization   The Olmecs, among whom Mesoamerican civilization originated, lived in southern Mexico. The Mayans, who succeeded rather than displaced them, were centered to the east in present-day Yucatán, Guatemala, and Belize.

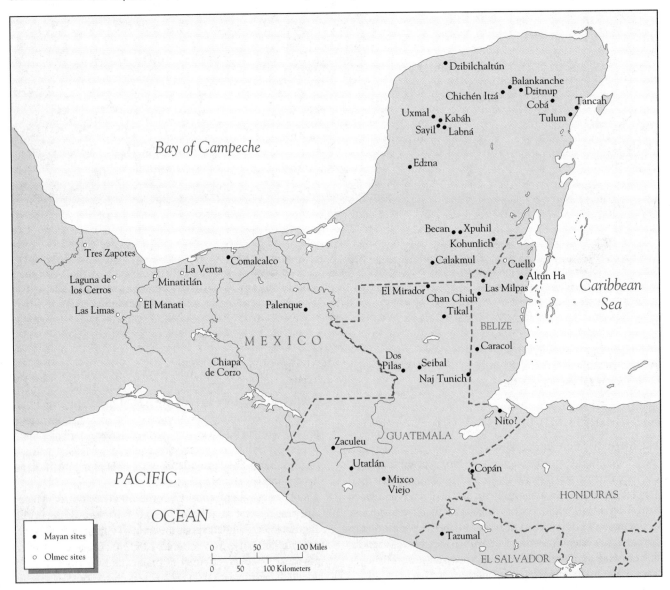

Locked in a Circle of Time

It is impossible to say how Mesoamerican civilization would have evolved had it not been destroyed by technologically superior Europeans. History is what happened, not what might have been. However, there are indications that, about 600 years before Cortés landed at Vera Cruz, Mesoamerican civilization went into a "stall," ceasing to "progress" in the Western sense of the word. One of the Mayans' greatest achievements, their complex system for marking the passing of time, may provide a clue as to why.

Mayan priests were excellent astronomers. Their solar calendar was close to perfect, counting 365 days in a year. Because there are no seasons in the tropics, however, and because even the rainy season in Mesoamerica was erratic and unpredictable, the solar year was of less interest to the Mayans than it was to makers of calendars elsewhere.

So the Mayans devised other calendars, some not yet understood. Two of these were tied into the solar year, and with one another, as the means of dating events. There was a 13-day cycle and another, called *tzolkin,* of 260 days: 20 × 13 = 260 (the basis of Mayan mathematics was 20 rather than 10). If one pictures the three cycles as cogs meshing with one another, a 13-cog

© Copyright The British Museum

wheel within a 260-cog wheel within a 365-cog wheel, no single alignment of cogs would be repeated for 18,980 days, or 52 solar years on the button.

The complexity of the calculation shows the sophistication of Mayan mathematics. However, the beauty of their cycles within cycles also locked the Mayan mind into a rigidly circular view of time. The Mayans seem to have believed that each day was a repetition of the day 52 years earlier, and 104 years and 156 years earlier. Each 5,200 years, they believed (introducing the factor of 10?), the universe was destroyed and created anew. Time passed, but there was no "progress"—just a return of things to where they had already been and would be again.

Such a worldview was ill adapted to cope with the unimaginably unexpected. Hurricanes worried the Mayans more because of their unpredictability than because of their destructiveness. How infinitely more troubling must it have been for their cultural heirs, the Aztecs, to learn of the arrival of huge seagoing canoes, white-skinned men with hairy faces, suits of iron, horses, and cannons blasting thunder and death from afar? Mesoamerica's cultural foundations may themselves have been a Spanish ally.

Cultural Cul-de-Sac?

Elsewhere in the world, city-states made war in order to conquer and then exploit their neighbors. Along with the misery they caused, the empires they built—Persia, Rome, China, Islam—advanced the march of civilization. However, the bloodlust of the Mesoamerican gods meant that the Mayans made war not to foster material and, consequently, cultural *progress* (a word unique to Western civilization), but to stand still. Mesoamerican genius and energies were devoted to rounding up people to kill so as to stay on the right side of the gods and avoid a fate worse than that with which they contended when heaven was in a good mood.

Conservatism was not good to the Mayans. By 1500, most of their cities were abandoned. The Spaniards who swooped down on Mesoamerica found the great pyramids smothered in tropical vegetation. Most of those they conquered, including the Mayans, lived in small villages. The Mesoamericans visited the ruins of the once great cities only for religious functions.

What happened? Some scholars think that the Mesoamericans warred themselves into collapse. They point to the massive stone heads the Olmecs sculpted and then buried, as if to hide them from enemies. Others think that the Mesoamerican cities were rendered unlivable by soil depletion. In order to support a large urban population, farmers must produce a large surplus of food. But the soil of the tropical forest is easily exhausted by intense cultivation. Whatever the explanation, by 1500, Mesoamerican civilization was thriving only to the northwest of the Mayan heartland, in the valley of Mexico—the land of the Aztecs.

The Aztecs

The Aztecs (who called themselves the "Mexica") were newcomers in Mesoamerica, emigrating from the north during the 1200s. Their culture then was primitive compared to that of the Toltecs, who had brought civilization to Mexico. However, like the Turks who overran the Arab world and the Manchus who made China their own, the Aztecs recognized

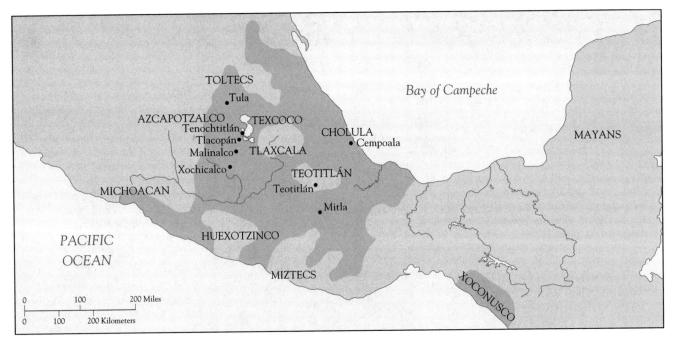

MAP 1:2 Mexico Under the Aztecs, 1519 The sway of the Aztecs—their tributary states—extended to both coasts of Mexico.

a better way of living when they conquered one. Carving out an enclave on the shores of Lake Texcoco about 1325, they embraced Mesoamerican civilization.

Within a century, the Aztecs dominated Mexico. They directly governed few other peoples. By 1500, however, tribute—"protection money," insurance against attack—in the form of grain, cloth, lumber, skins, feathers, and gold, rolled in from as far away as the Pacific and Gulf coasts. The Aztecs put this wealth to work, building one of the world's most splendid cities, Tenochtitlán. By 1500, it covered six square miles and was home to 200,000. One plaza, the site of a market, accommodated 50,000 sellers and buyers. Surrounded by Lake Texcoco, the Aztec capital was superbly defended. Only three narrow causeways, broken here and there by drawbridges, connected Tenochtitlán to the mainland, where other peoples dwelled. Thirty-foot granite walls could not have made a city more secure.

Blood and Gore

The greatest temple in Tenochtitlán was a pyramid with a base 200 feet square. Two dizzyingly steep staircases climbed to altars 200 feet above the street. The steps were stained black with dried blood, for the Aztecs too practiced human sacrifice. Indeed, Huitzilopochtli, a god who accompanied the Aztecs from the north, demanded 10,000 hearts in an ordinary year. In 1478, a year Huitzilopochtli was more agitated than usual, priests in cloaks of human skin and stinking of gore (they were forbidden to wash or to cut their hair) sent 20,000 volunteers and captives to their doom in four days. The emperor Ahuitzotl, so it was said, slaughtered 80,000 to dedicate a new temple. (Such astronomical fig-

ures are difficult to credit; but the point of the Aztec chroniclers who claimed them is clear enough.)

Bad years afflicted the Aztecs all too often during the late 1400s and early 1500s. Their calendar, inherited from the Mayans, implied that a catastrophe was in the works. Omens of all sorts, from natural calamities to female spirits wailing in the streets, had nerves on edge. No one was more anxious than the emperor Moctezuma II, whose reign began in 1502. It has been suggested that, psychologically, he and the Aztecs were ready prey for enemies who devoted their resources not just to staying on the right side of their gods, but to exploiting the new and the strange wherever they found it.

EUROPE: DRIVEN, DYNAMIC, EXPANSIVE

On October 12, 1492, on a beach in the Bahamas, a thousand miles east of the Aztecs, a band of rugged men, mostly Spaniards, waded ashore from three small ships. They named their landfall San Salvador, or "Holy Savior." Their leader was a redheaded Italian about 40 years of age. To his Spanish crew he was Cristóbal Colón, to us Christopher Columbus. To the Arawak, the Bahamians who welcomed Columbus, he represented a bizarre world unlike anything they had imagined.

Christopher Columbus

Falling to his knees, as pious as any Aztec priest, Columbus proclaimed San Salvador the possession of the queen who had financed his voyage, Isabella of Castile, and her hus-

Other Discoverers

Columbus was not the first outsider to touch on America after the Ice Age. The Inuit (Eskimos), seafaring Arctic hunters, regularly landed on both sides of the Bering Strait. Possibly, like the Styrofoam floats from Japan that wash up on our Pacific beaches today, Japanese fishermen survived being blown eastward to the Americas. Certain themes in Indian art tantalize archaeologists as "Asian."

There are a number of legends about pre-Columbian explorers in America. Olmecs told of black people in Central America; some see Negroid features in the famous Olmec stone heads. A Chinese document of 200 B.C. tells of Hee Li, who visited a land to the east he called "Fu-Sang." About A.D. 700, Irish bards began singing of St. Brendan, a monk who sojourned far to the west of the Emerald Isle in a land "without grief, without sorrow, without death."

There is nothing mythical about Vikings from Greenland who, about A.D. 984, established a colony at L'Anse aux Meadows, Newfoundland, which they called "Vinland." They traded with the locals, the "skraelings," for furs. Relations soured, however, and the Indians attacked. Curiously, for the Vikings were the terror of Europe, the skraelings paralyzed them with fear. One assault was repulsed only when a pregnant woman, Freydis, disgusted by the trembling men, seized a sword and chased the skraelings away by slapping it on her breasts and, no doubt, having a thing or two to say. Freydis then had the cowards of Vinland killed, personally murdering their women, after which she and her followers returned to Greenland.

band, Ferdinand of Aragon, the first rulers of unified Spain. Columbus would tell them that the trees were "the most beautiful I have ever seen." He "found no human monstrosities, as many expected." "On the contrary," he said, "among all these peoples good looks are esteemed." Columbus wrote that the Arawak were "very generous," that they did not "know what it is to be wicked, or to kill others, or to steal." He added that it would be easy to enslave them.

Some Spaniards would try to enslave the natives of the New World. For the moment, however, Columbus inquired politely of the Arawak about the location of Japan and China. Those fabulous countries, not the balmy but poor Bahamas, were the places for which he was looking.

The historical development of the America we know, begins with Christopher Columbus and the second significant discovery of America. Our origins as Americans, whatever our genetic inheritance, lay not on the pyramids of Mexico, but in the churches, state chambers, and counting houses of western Europe, in a culture that was to impress itself not only upon the Americas but upon the world.

Motives

To Columbus, San Salvador was an outlying island of "the Indies," the collective name Europeans gave to the mysterious, distant East, which included Cipango (Japan), Cathay (China), the Spice Islands (Indonesia), and India itself. Thus Columbus bestowed upon the inhabitants of the Americas the name that has stuck to their descendants to this day—Indians.

Columbus had sailed from Spain with the idea of finding a feasible sea lane to the Indies. In part, he was driven by religion. A devout Roman Catholic, Columbus believed God had selected him to carry the gospel of Christ to the lost souls of Asia. There were worldly motives too. Columbus longed for personal glory. Like the artists, architects, and scholars of the Renaissance, he craved recognition as a great individual. If obsession with self is tawdry and disagreeable in our own time, individualism was once one of the forces that made the culture of western Europe so dynamic.

Another such force was greed. Columbus wanted money. He meant to get rich doing business with (or conquering and enslaving) the peoples he encountered. Gold and silver were always in season, of course. "Gold is most excellent," Columbus wrote. "He who has it does all he wants in the world, and can even lift souls up to Paradise." Gold and silver paid for the Asian gems and porcelains that rich Europeans coveted, the fine cotton cloth of Syria and the silks of China, and tapestries and carpets that were beyond the craft of European weavers. Then there were the exotic drugs, dyes, perfumes, and especially the spices of the Indies—cinnamon from Ceylon, Indonesian nutmeg and cloves, Chinese ginger, and peppercorns from India—luxuries that made life more pleasant, something more than a struggle for survival on earth and salvation after death. Columbus asked the Arawak about precious metals practically before the Bahamian breezes had dried the surf from his stockings.

Teasers

Europe's interest in the exotic East was fueled by the *Letter of Prester John*. The ostensible author, John, a Christian king and priest, claimed to "reign supreme and to exceed in riches, virtue, and power all creatures who dwell under heaven." He was contacting Christian Europe in order to form an alliance and "wage war against and chastise" the Muslims who were enemies to both parties.

It was a hoax. No one fitting the description of Prester John dwelled in Asia. Nor were there the red and green lions he mentioned. Still, the prospect of a powerful Christian friend with whom to catch the Muslims in a pincers (and from whom to buy the goods of the Indies) overcame the skepticism of many Europeans.

The Voyages of Sir Marco Polo also included absurdities, such as snakes wearing eyeglasses. But the book was no hoax. Marco Polo of Venice was real, and he lived in China for many years. His contention that the exquisite Asian porcelains, silks, tapestries, and spices Europeans bought cost a pittance in China was true. More than any other document, Polo's *Voyages* convinced the explorers of the fifteenth century that betting their lives on voyages to the East might mean fabulous riches.

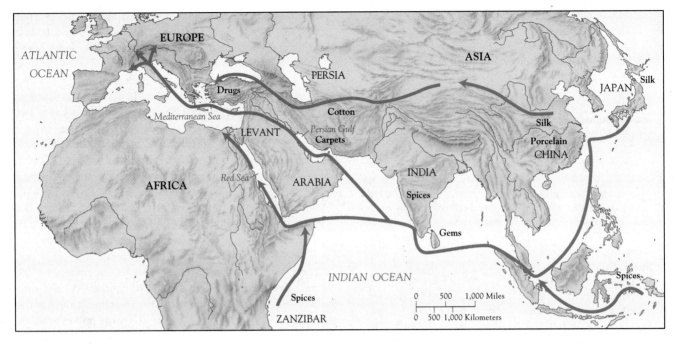

MAP 1:3 European Trade with Asia and Africa   Asian and East African goods—luxuries in Europe—were transported by land and sea as many as 8,000 miles.

High Overhead

The goods of the Indies had trickled into Europe since the days of the Roman Empire. From adventurers who traveled to East Asia, Europeans learned that luxuries expensive to them were abundant and cheap in the East. Crusaders, knights who briefly ruled parts of the Levant (present-day Lebanon, Syria, and Israel), enjoyed firsthand the richer lifestyle of the Muslims there.

The crusaders were driven back to Europe, but they continued to covet the goods of the East, which the triumphant Muslims were happy to sell them. These textiles, gems, perfumes, and spices were carried by ship through the Indian Ocean and Persian Gulf or Red Sea, or they were brought overland in caravans to the eastern end of the Mediterranean Sea: the Levant, Constantinople (Istanbul), Egypt. They then made their way to Europe in the vessels of powerful Italian city-states, most notably Venice and Genoa. Italian merchants were Europe's middlemen, the wholesale distributors who sold the spices and the rest to retailers all over the continent.

By the time the luxuries of the Indies reached the castles of Spain and the market towns of France, they were expensive indeed. The cost of transport alone was prodigious. The pepper that enlivened an English baron's stew may have traveled as far as 8,000 miles on donkey back. The trade routes passed through the lands of predatory Central Asian tribes or, if the pepper came by sea, through the haunts of East African pirates. Merchants had either to pay for safe passage or hire toughs of their own to battle the locals. Either way, the cost was, as always, passed on to consumers.

The Unpopular Middleman

The Levantines took a handsome profit. They were not in business for the glory of Allah and the service of humanity. The Christian Italians added their markup, shrugging off imprecations that they were gougers. Today, the magnificent Renaissance cathedrals and palaces the Italian merchant princes built are an inspiration to the world. In the time of Columbus, the glories of Italy also aroused resentment among the consumers whose purchases of Asian goods made the construction of these grand buildings possible.

In western Europe, envy of Italian wealth fathered the dream of finding a route to the Indies that bypassed the Mediterranean Sea, which Italian navies controlled. The prince whose sailors could eliminate the Italian middlemen would stop the flow of his country's wealth to Italy. Indeed, such a prince could imagine his subjects displacing the Italians as Europe's wholesalers of Asian products. As for the navigator who found this new route to the Indies, he could expect an opulent reward. Columbus was just one of several Italian sailors who went to Portugal, Spain, England, and France looking for financial backing.

PORTUGAL AND SPAIN: THE VAN OF EXPLORATION

Portugal and Spain were first to search for a new route to the Indies. The map reveals one reason this should have been so. Both countries face the Atlantic, Portugal entirely so. Additionally, Portugal and Spain were Europe's first unified nation-states, shaking off feudalism—a political system in which power was fragmented in many hands—and creating a powerful central government. Such a government, unlike a gaggle of squabbling feudal barons, was capable of accumulating the vast resources needed for world exploration and could find the will to undertake it.

Iberian Nationalism

France and England were well along in the process of national unification at the end of the 1400s. Both countries were to be major players in the overseas expansion of Europe. But Portugal was a unified nation by 1400. Its kings had come to the fore by driving out the Moors, Muslim Arabs and Berbers having roots in what is now Morocco.

Prince Henry, the third son of King John I, turned Portugal's attention to the Atlantic. Leading a life as ascetic as a monk's, he was a stay-at-home (which is ironic, given his nickname, "Henry the Navigator"). He left Portugal only once, on a military expedition across the narrow Strait of Gibraltar. But Henry was obsessed by the sea and far-off lands, both known and imagined. He sent 15 maritime expeditions down the western coast of Africa to buy gold and slaves from black kingdoms west and south of the Sahara. Under his aegis, the Portuguese colonized Madeira, 350 miles off the coast of Africa, in 1418; and the Azores, Atlantic islands 900 miles west of Portugal, in about 1427.

Henry also sponsored an exploration "research and development center" at Sagres in southern Portugal. Mariners were brought there to share their experiences with mapmakers and scholars who studied ancient travel accounts. Together they speculated, sometimes fantastically, sometimes brilliantly, about world geography. When sailors complained of the contrary winds off Cape Bojador that had turned Arab seamen back from "the green sea of darkness," Portuguese shipwrights developed a vessel that bested them—the caravel. Caravels could be rigged with the triangular lateen sails of the Mediterranean, which made it possible to beat against the wind, or with the large square sails of northern Europe, which pushed ships at high speed when the winds were cooperating. Caravels required relatively small crews, so they could be provisioned for longer voyages than other vessels. Caravels were "the best ships in the world and able to sail anywhere," said Luigi da Cadamosto, an Italian in Prince Henry's service.

Portugal's Route to Asia

Henry the Navigator died in 1460, but his legacy lived on. In 1488, a ship commanded by Bartholomeu Dias returned to Portugal after reaching the Cape of Good Hope, at the foot of the African continent. This was the corner to be turned. There would be clear sailing to the Indies by way of rounding Africa.

Not for 10 years would another Portuguese, Vasco da Gama, actually reach the Indian port of Calicut, toting up profits twenty times the investment in his voyage. Portugal then built a commercial empire consisting of small trading posts stretching from West Africa to the Persian Gulf and Macau in China. The single Portuguese holding in the Americas, Brazil, was the consequence of a mishap befalling Pedro Cabral, bound for Asia by da Gama's route, in 1500. Cabral's caravel was blown so far west it touched on the eastern bulge of the South American continent, thus accidentally establishing Portugal's claim to Brazil.

Portugal's African and Asian trade enriched the nation. As early as 1503, peppercorns sold in Lisbon for one-fifth the price the Levantines charged merchants from Venice and Genoa. The Portuguese had bypassed and undercut the Italian middlemen with a vengeance.

Long before 1503, Portugal's success in tracing the African coast had the effect of killing any interest King John II might have had in "the enterprise of the Indies," a

Oceanica Classis

▲ *Columbus commanded three ships on his voyage of 1492. The* Niña *and the* Pinta *were caravels, which Columbus preferred to his flagship, the* Santa Maria, *depicted here in a drawing of 1493. The caravels were nimble sailers; the* Santa Maria, *slow and hard to handle. Its value was that it could carry far more provisions than the* Niña *and* Pinta.

lumbus was commissioned Admiral of the Ocean Sea, quite an exalted title. He was granted extensive authority over any lands he discovered and a generous share of any profits to be made. He was outfitted with two caravels, the *Niña* and the *Pinta,* and a clumsier, larger carrack, the *Santa Maria.* The total cost of the expedition was $14,000 (in today's money), which was small potatoes: Isabella and Ferdinand spent that much entertaining a distinguished visitor for a week.

Frustration

Four times Columbus crossed the Atlantic bearing letters of introduction addressed to the emperors of China and Japan (and letters with blanks in which he could fill in names). Four times he returned after Indians told him no, sorry, they had never heard of such persons. Each time he returned to Spain, Columbus told Isabella and Ferdinand that after one more try, he would surely "give them as much gold" and "all the spices and cotton" they needed.

To the day of his death in 1506, Christopher Columbus insisted that he had reached some of the 7,448 islands Marco Polo said lay off the coast of Asia. Sustained for a lifetime by a dream, he could not admit that his voyages pointed in quite another direction.

Indeed, it dawned only slowly on the Spaniards, who actually settled San Salvador, Cuba, and Hispaniola (present-day Haiti and the Dominican Republic), that they were living not in Asia but in a "new world" previously unknown to Europeans. When they faced this reality, many fell to cursing the lands Columbus discovered as obstacles in the way to Asian riches. Cuba and Hispaniola were notorious for bloody quarrels among the frustrated treasure seekers there.

scheme presented to him by Christopher Columbus. Residing in Portugal since 1476, Columbus argued that the best way to get to East Asia was not by hugging the African coast and battling those damnable winds. The best route was due west across the Atlantic. John II entertained this notion for several years but then dismissed Columbus, calling him "a big talker, full of fancy and imagination."

Spain's Decision to Go West

Columbus took his proposition to Spain. He met plenty of ridicule there too. Scholars at the University of Salamanca described his plan as "vain, impracticable, and resting on grounds too weak to merit the support of the government." But Columbus had influential friends as well as mockers. After Dias found the southern tip of Africa for Portugal, Isabella and Ferdinand grew more interested in the Atlantic. They paid Columbus a modest annuity, just to keep him around.

In 1492, when Isabella and Ferdinand captured the last Moorish stronghold in Spain—the preoccupation of their reign—Columbus was making noises about taking his enterprise to France or England. Isabella decided to take a chance, and, suddenly, events moved with remarkable dispatch. Co-

Why "America"? Why Not "Columbia"?

Columbus cannot complain about the fact that his discovery was not named Columbia after him. He never admitted he had visited anywhere but "the Indies."

America was named for Amerigo Vespucci, another Italian, who twice voyaged to the New World. If Columbus was a medieval man, Vespucci was a modern. Vespucci wrote of his voyages, "Rationally, let it be said in a whisper, experience is worth more than theory," a principle Columbus defied. Marveling at the American animals unknown in Europe, Vespucci noted that "so many species could not have entered Noah's ark," a heresy of which the pious Columbus was incapable.

It was Vespucci who first declared in print that it was a "new world" across the Atlantic. In 1507, a German cartographer, drawing the first map to show the Americas as separate from Asia, named this new world for Amerigo in the Latin of his given name, feminine because the names of the continents of Africa and Asia were of feminine gender.

In the late nineteenth century, a descendant, Signora America Vespucci, petitioned the United States Congress for payment for the 400 year use of her ancestor's name. She did not collect.

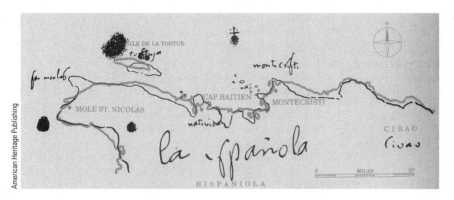

◀ *Columbus's greatness as a navigator is recognized. Not so well known is the fact that he was a superb mapmaker. His sketch of the northwest coast of Hispaniola (present-day Haiti), done by observation aided only by primitive methods of measuring distance, is close to perfect.*

In 1513, an expedition led by Vasco Núñez de Balboa aggravated the disappointment. Balboa crossed the Isthmus of Panama. It was only 40 miles wide at one point, but the isthmus festered with disease. From a mountain, Darien, Balboa looked down on another great ocean, the Pacific. The implication was obvious: Asia might be far indeed from where Balboa stood. In 1519, an expedition commanded by Ferdinand Magellan confirmed the suspicion. A Portuguese sailing for Spain with five ships and 265 men, Magellan found a strait to the Pacific through the southern tip of South America, which now bears his name. He was killed in the Philippines, but one of his vessels, commanded by Juan Sebastián de Elcaño and manned by only 18 wretched survivors, struggled back to Europe.

At hideous cost, it was a magnificent achievement—the first voyage around the world. But the Magellan–de Elcaño route was no trade route. Adverse winds and currents in the Strait of Magellan meant it could take months just to get from the Atlantic to the Pacific. (Columbus crossed the entire Atlantic in just four weeks.) Until almost the end of the age of sail, ship's masters avoided rounding South America from the Atlantic.

Poor Bargain

International politics contributed to Spanish frustration. In 1493, to head off conflict between Spain and Portugal, the pope, in *Inter Caetera,* divided all the world's lands not "in the actual possession of any Christian king or prince" between the two nations. The pope's line of demarcation ran from the North Pole to the South Pole, a hundred leagues (about 300 miles) west of the Azores. The next year, in the Treaty of Tordesillas, the Portuguese persuaded Isabella and Ferdinand to move the line farther west (thus laying the legal grounds for Portuguese settlement of Brazil after 1500). Wherever the line was drawn, Spain was shut out of all Asia but the yet undiscovered Philippines.

Until 1521, the Spanish in the New World thought of Tordesillas as a bad bargain. Their share of the world's non-Christian wealth was nothing like the loot the Portuguese were raking in on their side of the Tordesillas line. The Spanish were stuck with steamy, mosquito-plagued islands where there was no spice, no cotton, no silk, and very little gold.

THE SPANISH EMPIRE

Then, in 1519, pretty much the worst of years in Spanish America, an extraordinary soldier landed on the coast of Mexico with 508 soldiers, 200 Indians, several Africans, seven small cannons, 16 horses, and dozens of war dogs—gigantic mastiffs trained to kill. What this motley party found and did in Mexico brought an end to Spanish grumbling.

Cortés in Mexico

Bearded Hernán Cortés was not the first Spaniard to land in Mexico. Gonzalo Guerrero, shipwrecked in the Yucatán in 1511, became a military leader of the Mayans, helping them to drive out other Spanish adventurers. Like Columbus, however, Cortés was the discoverer who made a difference. He landed at Vera Cruz. After sending word to Cuba of his intention to march to Tenochtitlán, he burned the ships that had brought his army to Mexico. They would conquer or die.

Cortés was attacked by the Tabascans of the coast. The Spaniards, with their cannons, horses, and dogs easily defeated them, losing only two men. The shrewd Cortés then offered the Tabascans an alliance against their tribal enemies inland. He would repeat this procedure—victory in battle, peace, alliance—with every Indian people he confronted on his march to Tenochtitlán. Totomacs, Tlaxcalans, Tolucans, and Cholulans—all joined him to fight the Aztecs, whom everybody detested and no one could defeat. The Mexican battle tactic was to charge the enemy line, trying to break through and turn the flanks. In such a melee, with both sides carrying the same weapons, total victory was difficult. However, when the Spaniards added horses, war dogs, and firearms to the stew, they made decisive victory possible. At the same time, without the numbers his Indian allies provided, ten or more to each Spaniard, Cortés might have ended up as obscure a historical character as Gonzalo Guerrero.

Mexican religion played into Cortés's hands. An Aztec legend held that a fair-skinned deity named Quetzalcoatl would one day emerge from the east to rule Mexico. Moctezuma II feared Cortés to be this god. According to one of his advisers, the emperor "enjoyed no sleep, no food . . . Whatsoever he did, it was as if he were in torment." Reaching

▲ *An Aztec artist drew this picture of Moctezuma II, Cortés, Malinche (Cortés's Mexican mistress and translator), and armored conquistadores proceeding to Tenochtitlán when the Aztecs welcomed the Spaniards. Apparently, a Spaniard altered the painting, depicting Cortés and Malinche in European style.*

Tenochtitlán on November 8, 1519, Cortés was actually welcomed into the city where he promptly made the emperor his hostage.

Aztec nobles soon realized that the Spaniards were less than divine. Cortés ordered a stop to human sacrifice. What god would do such a thing? When soldiers stumbled on a store of jewels, silver, and gold, "as if they were monkeys, the Spanish lifted up the gold banners and gold necklaces. . . . Like hungry pigs they craved that gold." With perverse truth, Cortés told Moctezuma, "I and my companions suffer from a disease of the heart which can be cured only with gold."

Conquest

The Aztecs rebelled, and the Spaniards barely managed to fight their way out of the city. Half of them and perhaps 4,000 Tlaxcalans were killed. With their lives in the balance, the Spaniards nevertheless insisted on carrying eight tons of treasure on their retreat.

But it was the Aztecs, not the Spanish, who were doomed by Mexican gold. Cortés gathered new Indian allies and Spanish reinforcements from Cuba. He returned to Tenochtitlán, besieged the city for 80 days, and conquered it brick by brick. About 15,000 people were killed on the final day of the battle, August 13, 1521.

Hernán Cortés won not just a great battle; he won a ready-made empire. He and his lieutenants inserted themselves at the top of Aztec society in place of the nobility they had exterminated. They lived off the labor of the masses as the Aztec nobles and priests had done. Only rarely has one people been able to set itself up over another with such ease. The already centralized Aztec political structure and the submissiveness of the common people made it possible for the Spaniards to rule with minimal resistance.

The Conquistadores

The conquest of Mexico revived Spanish interest in the New World. There was a rush to the Americas as thousands of all classes packed into ships to search for Mexicos of their own. These young men (and a few not so young) called themselves "conquistadores"—conquerors. In a generation, they subdued an area several times the size of Europe.

Rarely has history shaped a people for conquest as Spanish history shaped the conquistadores. Because much of Spain is mountainous, agriculture never satisfied the ambitious. Because the Christian Spanish associated trade with Moors and Jews, whom they despised, the upper classes shunned commerce. The worldly role of the hidalgo, the Spanish male with pretensions to nobility, was to fight.

He was a caballero, a knight. The bravery and fortitude of the conquistadores under daunting conditions awes us to this day. The other side of their military character, their ruthlessness and cruelty, has also been remembered.

Spain's zealous Roman Catholicism factored into its extraordinary achievement. Because the national enemy had been of another faith, Spanish nationalism and Roman Catholicism were of a piece. Like their Muslim foes, the Spaniards believed that a war for the purpose of spreading true religion was by its very nature a holy war. Death in such a war was a ticket to paradise. It was a belief that made for soldiers nonchalant about death and therefore chillingly formidable.

Such cultural baggage would curse Spain in centuries to come. When the American gold and silver were spent, Spanish disdain for agriculture, trade, and other productive labor contributed to the nation's impoverishment. In the sixteenth century, however, reckless bravery and religious fanaticism were superbly calculated to conquer a whole new world.

Exploration North and South

After the news of Mexico reached Spain, King Charles I (better known as Emperor Charles V) encouraged additional conquests by promising conquistadores the lion's share of the gold and silver they won. (The king got one-fifth.) He also granted land to his subjects, and *encomiendas,* the legal right to force the Indians who lived on the land to work for them. It was not slavery, but, in practice, the distinction was fine.

Only one conquistador's find rivaled that of Cortés. In 1531, an aging illiterate, Francisco Pizarro, led 168 soldiers and 62 horses high into the Andes Mountains of South America. There he found the empire of the Incas, 3,000 miles in extent, tied together by roads Pizarro called unmatched in Christendom, and rich in gold and silver. Bolder than Cortés, for reinforcement was not an option, Pizarro was also an artist of treachery. He captured the Inca emperor Atahualpa, whose person was so sacred to the Incas that 80,000 Inca soldiers were paralyzed. For eight months, they brought Pizarro a ransom of gold that filled a room 22 feet long by 17 feet wide. Then, Pizarro had Atahualpa murdered, and defeated the bewildered Incas.

No other explorer found much gold and silver, least of all those who ventured into what is now the United States. Between 1539 and 1542, Hernando de Soto (who had been with Pizarro) wandered our Southeast in a fruitless search for riches. He was buried by his soldiers in the Mississippi River. Only half the mourners at his funeral got back alive to the West Indies.

During the same years, Francisco Coronado trekked extraordinary distances in the Southwest. His quest was for the "Seven Cities of Cíbola" among which, according to an imaginative priest, Fray Marcos de Niza, was "the greatest city in the world . . . larger than the city of Mexico." Coronado's 1,500 men found only dusty adobe villages. "Such were our curses that some hurled at Fray Marcos," wrote one soldier, "that I pray God may protect him."

Spanish America

No matter. For more than a century, Mexican and Peruvian gold and silver made Spain the richest and most powerful nation of Europe. By 1550, the equivalent of $4.5 million in precious metals was crossing the Atlantic each year; by 1600, $12 million. Not for another century would this river of riches dry to a trickle. American wealth financed the cultural blossoming of Spain as well as huge armies to do the king's bidding. By the end of the 1600s, Spain's empire stretched from Florida to Tierra del Fuego at the foot of South America.

Over so vast an area, economy and society varied immensely. Generally, however, the ownership of land in Spanish America was concentrated in the hands of a small group of *encomenderos* who lived off the labor of Indians in peonage or black Africans in slavery. Government was centralized in the hands of viceroys (vice kings). The Roman Catholic Church exercised great power, mostly for the good, trying to protect those on the bottom from the rapacious upper classes.

The empire flourished. Before more than a handful of other Europeans slept overnight in the New World, Spain boasted 200 towns and cities, and two universities, in the Western Hemisphere. The majority of Spain's American subjects were Indians, whose fate was not pleasant. It has been estimated that there were at least 5 million Mexicans in 1500. In 1600, there were 1 million.

The Black Legend

It can seem a wonder that any Native Americans survived. Indeed, the evils they suffered and the possibility of their extinction was the message of Catholic priests who took up their cause. "I am the voice of Christ," Father Antonio de Montesinos told conquistadores who had come to doze through mass, "saying that you are all in a state of mortal sin for your cruelty and oppression in your treatment of this innocent people."

A conquistador who became a Dominican friar, Bartolomé de Las Casas, devoted his life to lobbying the Spanish king for laws protecting the Indians. The Spaniards treated them, Las Casas said, "not as beasts, for beasts are treated properly at times, but like the excrement in a plaza." His scorching

▲ *This woodcut portrayal of Native Americans was carved in Germany about 1500, almost certainly by someone who never saw an Indian. Note the Indians' European features and the fact that they are rendered as cannibals. Of all the tribes confronted by Europeans by 1500, only the Caribs of the West Indies ate human flesh.*

description of conquistador cruelty, *A Brief Relation of the Destruction of the Indians,* was overblown. Las Casas was a propagandist; propagandists exaggerate. But *A Brief Relation* was not fantasy; the *leyenda nera,* the "black legend" of Spanish cruelty, was not legend in the essence of its message.

The *encomenderos* should not be seen as devils. In the context of the sixteenth century, their atrocities were close to routine. It was an era of indifference to suffering, and callousness was not a European monopoly. The depravity was Asian, African, and Native American too, and it was exercised not only on those of different races. Warfare in Europe meant unmitigated horror for peasants caught in the paths of marauding armies. The bloodiness of Mesoamerican religion has already been noted. Africans devised devilishly ingenious tortures without any tutoring from outsiders.

Many more Indians died of pick and shovel than at sword point. The Arawak of the Caribbean, for example, were a physically delicate people who died off within a few generations under the hard labor they were forced to perform. The Indian population of Hispaniola in 1492 was at least 200,000; in 1508, 60,000; in 1514, 14,000. By 1570, only two small native villages survived on the island.

THE COLUMBIAN EXCHANGE

The collision of worlds occasioned by Columbus's voyage established a biological pipeline between landmasses that had drifted apart 150 million years before human beings appeared on earth. Some species had flourished in both worlds:

oaks, dogs, deer, mosquitoes, the virus that causes the common cold. There were, however, a large number of animals and plants in the Americas that were new to the first Europeans to arrive. And they brought with them flora and fauna unknown to the Indians.

Impact on America

Native American mammals were generally smaller and less suited for meat and draft than Old World livestock. The Aztecs had only five domesticated animals: the turkey, Muscovy duck, dog, bee, and another insect. The Incas had only the guinea pig, llama, and alpaca. So the Spaniards were quick to import hogs, cattle, sheep, and chickens along with European grasses to feed them (plus about 70 percent of the plants we know as weeds). Not only did the arrival of these creatures alter the ecology of the New World—profoundly—but the Indians introduced to them soon came to depend on them. Even those native peoples who escaped Spanish conquest were glad to raid the newcomers' flocks and herds. The wool-weaving art that is intimately identified with the Navajo of the American Southwest was refined when the Navajo domesticated European sheep.

The people of Mexico were initially terrified by the sight of a man on horseback. It reinforced their briefly held delusion that the Spaniards were gods. Even after the Indians recognized that horses were ordinary beasts, however, the Spanish equestrian monopoly gave the conquistadores an immense advantage in battle. Within two centuries, runaway, then feral, horses migrated as far as the Great Plains

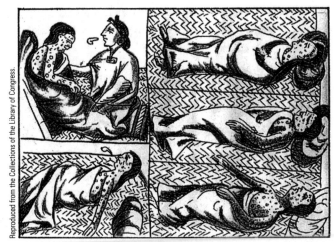

▲ *An Aztec depiction of victims of the Old World disease that killed more Native Americans than any other—smallpox—which wiped out whole peoples in the Americas. Europeans died of smallpox too, but not in the numbers Indians did. Some Europeans survived epidemics thanks to resistance passed down through millennia of "living with" the disease.*

'Taters and Tomaters

Europeans took slowly to potatoes and tomatoes. In the face of evidence to the contrary, many clung to the belief that potatoes were an aphrodisiac and tomatoes were poisonous. It was 300 years before the white potato became a staple in the country with which we most associate it, Ireland.

Tomatoes were grown in Europe as ornamental plants by 1500. Some people must have eaten the fruits from the start, but generations of medical authorities warned so frantically of dire effects that, as late as 1820, one Robert G. Johnson could gather a crowd looking forward to seeing him collapse in agony, when he announced he would eat a tomato on the courthouse steps in Salem, New Jersey. He ate. He lived.

of North America. There they became the basis of several cultures that never heard of Spain. The Sioux, Comanche, Pawnee, Apache, Nez Percé, Blackfoot, Crow, and other tribes of the plains, previously agricultural peoples, captured the mustangs and became peerless horsemen independent of European example.

Among the valuable "green immigrants" from Europe were grains such as wheat and barley, citrus fruits, and sugar cane. Mexico was exporting wheat to the West Indies by 1535. It is difficult to picture the West Indies without sugar cane. Columbus himself introduced lettuce, cauliflower, citrus fruits, figs, and pomegranates to America. Within a few decades after his death, bananas (from Asia) and watermelons (from West Africa) were being cultivated in the New World.

Impact on the World's Food Supply

If America contributed few food animals to the world's larders, American plant foods revolutionized European, African, and Asian diets. Maize (Indian corn), an American native, astonished Europeans by the height of its stalks and size of its grains. Cultivation of the crop spread to every continent, increasing the food supply and contributing to the rapid increase in population that characterizes the last 500 years of human history.

The sweet potato became a staple in West Africa, where it was introduced by slave traders. (The yam, superficially similar, was already established there.) Beans, squash and pumpkins, peppers, strawberries (there was a European strawberry, but it was inferior to the American), vanilla and chocolate, wild rice, and tomatoes are American foods that were unknown in Europe, Africa, and Asia.

It is estimated that of 640 food crops grown in Africa today, all but 50 originated in the Americas. Manioc (tapioca), also of American origin, is today the staple for 200 million people in the tropics. The white ("Irish") potato, a native of the Andes, provides basic sustenance for even greater numbers. Curiously, the white potato was slow to make an impact. It took 250 years for its cultivation to spread from Peru to Spain and, from there, across the temperate zone from Ireland to China.

Many national cuisines depend on foods of American origin for their zest, particularly the tomato and the extraordinary variety of chili peppers that have been developed from a Mexican forebear. Think of Hungarian paprika. Think of Italian sauces for pasta. These, as well as tobacco, were contributed to the Old World by the New.

Disease

The most tragic of the intercontinental transactions was in microscopic forms of life. Many diseases for which Europeans, Africans, and Asians had developed resistance were unknown to Native Americans before 1492. Smallpox, measles, influenza, bubonic and pneumonic plague, tuberculosis, typhus, and cholera were as foreign to the Americas as horses and Spaniards. Biologically, the Indians had not learned to "live with" these killer diseases.

Why were they absent? Scholars note that all of these diseases initially spread to human beings from domesticated

VD

It has been suggested that syphilis was not carried from America to Europe but was a mutation of yaws, a disease long (and still) endemic in tropical Africa. If so, the timing and the place of the mutation in Europe—1493 in Cádiz—is a coincidence without peer. The case for an Old World origin of syphilis is very weak. The only evidence pointing toward it is the similarity of the yaws microbe and the syphilis microbe.

The evidence for an American origin is mostly circumstantial—when and where syphilis first appeared in Europe—but powerfully so. And there is more than circumstance: Indications of syphilis have been found in pre-Columbian human bones in America but never in bones buried in Africa, Asia, or Europe before 1493.

animals–sheep, goats, cattle, buffalo, pigs, and fowl. The Native Americans had few such domesticates. They hunted herd animals, but they did not, like Europeans, Africans, and Asians, live in close proximity to them. The rarity of large cities in America also explains the absence (so far as we know) of virulent epidemic disease in pre-Columbian America. Smallpox, measles, and the other terrible diseases Europeans brought on their ships are "crowd diseases." Highly infectious, once they were introduced to a dense population, they savaged it. If, before Columbus, similar afflictions appeared in the Americas, they died out for lack of crowds in which to spread.

Old World diseases were catastrophic in America. Transplanted Europeans and Africans suffered badly enough when epidemics swept through the colonies, but the Indians died in heartrending numbers. Bacteria and viruses killed far more Native Americans than did swords or even forced labor.

America's microbic revenge was venereal disease. Europeans first identified syphilis as a new disease in 1493, in Cádiz, Spain, the port to which Columbus returned after his first voyage and released his crew. Syphilis was next noted in Naples, where several of Columbus's crewmen went as soldiers. It spread at terrifying speed throughout the world, following the trade routes. What better agents for spreading a sexually transmitted disease worldwide quickly than seamen and the prostitutes who were their chief sexual partners?

Europeans, Africans, and Asians reacted to syphilis as Indians reacted to measles and smallpox, diseases previously unknown to them. Symptoms were severe, and death came quickly. About 10 million people died of syphilis within 15 years of Columbus's voyage. Only later did the disease take on the slower-acting form in which it is known today and in which American Indians now know smallpox, measles, and the rest.

for FURTHER READING

The most exciting and productive research in American history in recent years has been about pre-Columbian Mesoamericans. Most of this material is in scholarly journals, yet to be synthesized in a book for general readers. However, Brian M. Fagan, *Kingdoms of Gold, Kingdoms of Jade: The Americas Before Columbus,* 1991, presents much of it very well. Also see the relevant sections of Alvin M. Josephy Jr., *America in 1482: The World of the Indian People Before the Arrival of Columbus,* 1991. On Mayan art and religion, see Linda Sechele and Mary Ellen Miller, *The Blood of Kings,* 1986.

Daniel J. Boorstin, *The Discoverers: A History of Man's Search to Know His World and Himself,* 1985, is a fine historian's best work; volume 2 provides a superb narrative and analysis of the adventure of European discovery. Jared Diamond, *Guns, Germs, and Steel: The Fates of Human Societies,* 1997, is a largely persuasive geographical explanation of why, among other things, it was Europeans, and not Indians, Africans, or Asians, who surged into the unknown in the 1400s.

A biography of Columbus by Samuel Eliot Morison, *Admiral of the Ocean Sea,* 1942, is a classic and well worth a read despite many valid revisions of Morison's vision. There was a deluge of books about Columbus published in the early 1990s to coincide with the five hundredth anniversary of his discovery. Almost all of them (and several theatrical films) seem to have been inspired by the belief that the discovery was at best a big mistake and, more

likely, one of history's most evil chapters. If one had nothing nasty to say about Columbus in 1992, one said nothing at all.

The most readable of these "politically correct" books is Kirkpatrick Sale, *The Conquest of Paradise,* 1990. Even though Columbus is portrayed as a fool when he is not a fiend, the book is based on exhaustive research and is replete with contemporary accounts of the horrors the discovery meant for the American natives. An exception to the phenomenon of 1992 is William D. Phillips Jr. and Carla Rahn Phillips, *The Worlds of Christopher Columbus,* 1992, a thoughtful and incisive study.

On the conquest of Mexico, see a classic in the grand literary tradition of the nineteenth century, William H. Prescott, *History of the Conquest of Mexico,* 1873. For the story told from an Aztec perspective, see Leon Lopez-Portilla, *The Broken Spears,* 1962. On Spanish America, see James Lockhart and Stuart B. Schwartz, *Early Latin America,* 1983; Mark A. Burkholder and Lyman L. Johnson, *Colonial Latin America,* 1990; and Donald J. Weber, *The Spanish Empire in North America,* 1990.

Alfred E. Crosby, in *The Columbian Exchange: Biological and Cultural Consequences of 1492,* 1972, and in *Ecological Imperialism: The Biological Expansion of Europe,* 1986, was the first to explore discovery and exploration on this elemental level. William Cronon, *Changes on the Land,* 1983, is a superb example of environmental history.

 ## AMERICAN JOURNEY ONLINE AND INFOTRAC® COLLEGE EDITION

Visit the source collections at http://ajaccess.wadsworth.com and http://infotrac.thomsonlearning.com, and use the Search function with the following key terms to explore documents, images, audio and video clips, articles, and commentary related to the material in this chapter:

Aztecs	Hispaniola	Tenochtitlán
Christopher Columbus	Lake Texcoco	
Hernán Cortés	Maya	

Additional resources, exercises, and Internet links related to this chapter are available on *The American Past* Web site: http://history.wadsworth.com/americanpast7e.

HISTORY ONLINE

American Indians of the Pacific Northwest
http://memory.loc.gov/ammem/award98/wauhtml/aipnhome.html
Multi-formatted site dealing with some of North America's most prosperous tribes.

The Columbus Navigation Homepage
www1.minn.net/~keithp/
Excellent look at many aspects of Columbus's achievements.

The Aztecs/Mexicas
www.indians.org/welker/aztec.htm
Thoroughgoing multi-media examination of Aztec culture.

Spanish Exploration and Conquest of Native Americans
www.floridahistory.com
About the explorations of de Soto and Coronado.

2

SETTLEMENT ACROSS THE SEA

The Idea, the Failures, Success 1550–1624

North Wind Picture Archives

Where every wind that rises blows perfume,
And every breath of air is like an incense.
> Francis Beaumont and John Fletcher, English poets

The nature of the Country is such that it Causeth much sickness, and the scurvy and the bloody flux, and divers other diseases, which maketh the body very poor, and Weak. . . . We are in great danger, for our Plantation is very weak, by reason of the death, and sickness. . . . I have nothing to Comfort me, nor there is nothing to be gotten here but sickness, and death.
> Richard Frethorne, settler in Virginia

ENGLAND'S CLAIM TO a piece of America dated from 1497, when King Henry VII, impressed by Columbus, agreed to fund John Cabot, yet another Italian navigator looking for a backer, to look for the sea route to Asia that eluded Columbus. It eluded Cabot too, but he touched on Newfoundland and Nova Scotia, claiming them and adjacent properties for Henry.

The French monarchy showed little interest in the New World until 1523, when one of King Francis I's privateers (in effect, pirates contracted by the king) captured a Spanish ship carrying Mexican gold. Startled by so pretty a prize, Francis sent his Italian, Giovanni Verrazano, across the Atlantic. Verrazano claimed much of the eastern coast of North America for France.

The pope scolded Francis, reminding him that, in *Inter Caetera,* he had granted the world's non-Christian real estate to Portugal and Spain. Francis dipped his pen in sarcasm and asked to see the provision in Adam's will that entitled the pope to bestow such gifts.

ENGLAND'S SLOW TURN TOWARD AMERICA

Adam's will or not, Spain enjoyed a near monopoly of the Americas for a century. Other nations envied the Aztec and Inca riches that poured into Spain during the 1500s—Spain's *siglo de oro,* or "golden century"—but none was up to challenging Spanish might. Only late in the *siglo de oro*, under Queen Elizabeth I, did England, cautiously, act on John Cabot's claims.

▲ *John Cabot (Giovanni Caboto) of Venice believed, like Columbus, that Asia could be reached by sailing west across the Atlantic. After news of Columbus's crossing reached England, Henry VII came up with the money Cabot had been seeking. In 1497, Cabot reached North America and claimed it for England. The king rewarded Cabot with an income of £20 a year for life, which Cabot collected once. Cabot disappeared during a second voyage in 1498.*

The Protestant Reformation

The sixteenth century was a time of religious turmoil in Europe, the era of the Protestant Reformation. During the years Cortés was shattering the Aztecs, a German monk, Martin Luther, shattered the unity of western Christendom. While Coronado searched for the Seven Cities of Cíbola in the scorching Southwest, a French lawyer in rainy Geneva, John Calvin, was laying the foundations of a dynamic religious faith that would profoundly shape American history.

In 1517, Luther published an attack on several doctrines and practices of the Roman Catholic Church. Called to account by the Holy Roman Emperor, Charles V (King Charles I of Spain, soon to be flooded with Aztec gold), Luther denied the authority of the pope to determine true religion. The only source of God's word, Luther declared, was the Bible.

In a short time, large parts of Germany, Scandinavia, and the Netherlands embraced the new teachings. Many ordinary folk were disgusted by the moral laxity common among Catholic priests. German princes were attracted to Luther's Protestantism because, if they broke with the Roman pope, they could seize church lands, which accounted for a quarter to a third of Europe.

Spain remained Catholic. So did England's Henry VIII, crowned in 1509. He condemned Luther in a scholarly book, *Defense of the Seven Sacraments*. An appreciative reader, Pope Leo X honored Henry as "Defender of the Faith."

The Church of England

The title proved to be high irony, for in 1527, Henry himself broke with Rome. He had no quarrel with Catholic doctrine and ritual. But Henry was determined to dissolve his marriage to a Spanish princess, Catherine of Aragon, who, after a history of babies dead in womb or cradle, was at the end of her childbearing years. There was a daughter, Mary. But these were days when monarchs still joined their soldiers on the battlefield. Henry believed that for his Tudor dynasty to survive, he must have a son, a king. Then there was Cupid. Henry was in love with a comely young flirt of the court, Anne Boleyn, who wanted a wedding ring, not a mistress's pillow.

Popes tended to be supportive when kings had problems of this sort. However, Pope Clement VII feared the wrath of Charles V (who was Catherine of Aragon's nephew) more than he wanted to help out Henry. He refused to annul the king's marriage, whereupon Henry had Parliament declare papal authority invalid in England. The king, according to the Act of Supremacy, was head of the Church of England.

Like the German princes, Henry confiscated the lands of the monasteries and nunneries in England. He sold them to ambitious subjects for whom owning land meant prestige. Thus did a clever king fill his treasury and create a class of well-to-do landowners whose place in society depended on the independence from Rome of the Church of England. History would rank Henry VIII as a jewel of the age of monarchy were it not for a gluttony that transformed him into a grotesque figure and a ruthlessness that carried him through six wives, two of whom he divorced and two of whom he beheaded.

A Changing Church

Henry VIII did not much alter religious practice and church government in England. His reformation had few consequences in the daily lives of common people. But people in power have discovered before and since that tinkering with an established order, however delicately, often liberates a spirit of debate and innovation that becomes tumultuous and revolutionary. That happened in England.

A true Protestantism germinated within the Church of England during the reign of Edward VI, Henry VIII's only son. Alas for the reformers who called the shots for Edward (he was a boy of just 16 when he died in 1553), Edward's successor was his older half sister, Mary Tudor, the daughter of Catherine of Aragon. Mary was a zealous Catholic who had seethed for two decades over her mother's humiliation. Now queen, she married her cousin, Prince Philip of Spain, soon to be known as "His Most Catholic Majesty." Then, Mary alarmed even Philip by the ardor with which she rooted out Protestants in her court. Mary also persecuted Protestants among ordinary people, as well as sixteenth-century methods allowed. Three hundred were executed, earning the queen the unflattering nickname of "Bloody Mary."

Had Mary been a better politician, lived a long life, and borne a child to succeed her, England might have been eased back into the Catholic Church. Like her brother Edward, however, Mary sat on the throne for a very short time. She died in 1558, childless.

English Protestants who had fled to Geneva (home of the most radical of the Protestant reformers, John Calvin) returned to England. They became known as Puritans because they spoke of "purifying" the Church of England of Catholic beliefs and practices such as statues in churches, the burning of incense in religious services, and the authority of bishops. The Puritans found justification for none of these things in the Bible, their only religious authority.

THE ELIZABETHAN AGE: SEEDBED OF COLONIZATION

Mary's successor, Elizabeth I, was one of the shrewdest politicians ever to wear a crown. The daughter of Anne Boleyn, she was a survivor. To have been alive and kicking in 1558, she had to be wily. Her father beheaded her mother as an adulteress and witch when Elizabeth was 3. When Elizabeth was 14, the English church embraced Protestantism under Edward VI, and English foreign policy took an anti-Spanish turn. Elizabeth went along. When she was 20, England returned to Rome under Bloody Mary and became an

ally of Spain. Elizabeth went along. Now queen at 25, she was well practiced in the arts of concealing her true sympathies. She knew how to cajole the schemers who crowded the royal court, pushing wildly different views of religious truth and foreign policy. She also knew how to bide her time.

Thus, when Spain's Philip II proposed marriage, Elizabeth waffled. To wed His Most Catholic Majesty would surely set English Protestants to plotting against her. However, to humiliate Philip by rejecting him abruptly might well plunge England into a war with Spain, for which the island nation was not prepared. Flirtatious when circumstances demanded, regally aloof when it served her purposes, Elizabeth seemed to say yes to Philip, then no, then maybe. In fact, she said nothing at all. She wore Philip down and won time to determine the best direction. Elizabeth took her royal duties seriously.

Sea Dogs

Elizabeth's American policy was also devious. During the first two decades of her reign, she tacitly recognized Philip's claim to all the Americas. By the late 1570s, however, Elizabeth first tolerated, then quietly encouraged, a restless, swashbuckling fraternity of Spaniard-hating sea captains who meant to chip away at Philip's empire.

The most daring of these "sea dogs" (the name comes from a shark common in English waters) was a slave trader who aspired to more respectable work, Francis Drake. In 1577, Drake set sail in the *Golden Hind*, rounded South America by the Strait of Magellan, and attacked unfortified Spanish ports on the Pacific. Defenses there were moot—no ship of any nation except Spain had ever plied those waters.

If the pickings were easy, Drake correctly reckoned that Spanish warships awaited him in the Atlantic. Instead of returning the way he had come, Drake sailed north to California, reconditioned the *Golden Hind*, and struck west across the Pacific. His expedition was only the second to circumnavigate the globe.

During the same years, another sea dog, Martin Frobisher, sailed three times to Newfoundland, looking for a likely site to plant a colony and find gold. There was to be no settlement, and the thousand tons of "gold ore" Frobisher proudly brought back to England turned out to be worthless rock. In 1578, Elizabeth quietly licensed two half brothers, Humphrey Gilbert and Walter Raleigh, to establish an English settlement in any land "not in the actual possession of any Christian prince."

In winking at these operations, Elizabeth played her usual game. Officially, she appeared to acquiesce to Spain's New World monopoly. In fact, she was challenging it, discreetly; but by 1580, she abandoned discretion. Drake had returned to England, the *Golden Hind* so stuffed with Spanish treasure that it listed dangerously, a few degrees from capsizing. The profit on the voyage was 4,700 percent. Coveting her royal share of the loot and knowing that Philip II's patience was exhausted anyway, Elizabeth boarded the ship and knighted Drake.

Makeup

Some portraits of Elizabeth I show a clownlike face, as white as paper and overlaid with bright splotches of rouge, with no eyebrows—every hair had been plucked. When older, the queen did indeed wear such unsubtle makeup and dyed her hair a brilliant red. In part, no doubt, her face painting represented the impulse to fiddle with one's appearance, which is found in every culture and must be described as the nature of the species. But the queen also had a political motive for her makeup. With no eyebrows to arch and her face encased in lard encrusted with chalk, she presented her company with an immovable mask. As she wished to do, she betrayed no emotion, neither approval nor anger nor surprise, no matter what a courtier or foreign ambassador said to her.

▲ *For years, Queen Elizabeth pretended that Francis Drake was on his own in his raids on Spanish colonial settlements. (He would have been hanged as a pirate had he been captured.) However, when Drake returned from his voyage around the world, the* Golden Hind *so laden with Spanish gold and silver that it was barely floating, the queen boarded the ship and knighted Drake. There would be no more pretending.*

Lost Colonies

Gilbert and Raleigh tried to be the first English colonizers of America but failed. In 1583, Gilbert built an outpost in Newfoundland, but the descent of the northern winter persuaded him to flee south. Sailing south, his two ships were caught in a nasty storm. A bold old sea dog to the end, Gilbert shouted

his last recorded words across the waves to his second ship: "We are as near to heaven by sea as by land."

The next year, Raleigh's scouts recommended the Chesapeake Bay as a more likely site for a colony. The climate was mild, the soil rich, and the Chesapeake was far enough from Spanish St. Augustine in Florida to seem safe from Spanish attack. Knowing how to flatter the right people, Raleigh named the country Virginia after Elizabeth, the "Virgin Queen" (she never married). In 1587, he shipped 91 men, 17 women, and 9 children there to settle it.

Uncooperative winds blew the expedition to Roanoke Island in what is now North Carolina. The sandy, wooded island was not as well advantaged as any number of other sites on the Chesapeake. Still, Roanoke might have succeeded had it not been three long years before the settlers were resupplied. When Raleigh's agents finally returned in 1590, they found Roanoke's buildings abandoned. The word "CROATOAN" was carved on one of the structures in "fayre Capitall letters."

This was a good sign. Governor John White had instructed the colonists that if they left Roanoke, they were to leave the name of their destination in such a way. If they

Spanish Virginia

The Spanish did not ignore the lands north of St. Augustine. In 1526, about 500 colonists, including 100 slaves, began to build a settlement at the mouth of the Pee Dee River in what is now South Carolina. The slaves rebelled and escaped. Only 150 Spaniards survived to limp back to Hispaniola.

In 1571, a few Jesuit priests established a mission in Virginia, not far from which the English would found their first successful colony 35 years later. They converted several high-ranking Powhatan Indians to Catholicism, or so they thought. The Powhatan killed the missionaries.

▲ *John White, the governor of Roanoke, was an artist who painted the land and its native inhabitants so that Walter Raleigh could use the paintings in his unending quest for financial backers. Here, White depicted a man and woman in the village of Secotan (North Carolina) dining on boiled corn kernels. The Indians boiled food by dropping heated rocks into watertight baskets. Understandably, they coveted the iron pots of the English, which could be set directly on a fire.*

were *forced* to leave, they were to punctuate their message by carving a cross. There was no cross with "CROATOAN," so White concluded that the colony had relocated on Croatan Island near Cape Hatteras. There, White's entourage wandered the woods, discharging muskets and singing English songs to assure any who might be hiding that they were not Spaniards, but to no avail. There was no trace of the Roanoke settlers.

What happened? Some historians believe that the settlers, finding life on Roanoke untenable, joined friendly Lumbee Indians on Croatan. A century later, after the Lumbee had moved to the interior of North Carolina, some members of the tribe were observed to be fair skinned and blue eyed, with a number of English words in their language.

BEGINNINGS OF EMPIRE

Raleigh was slow to resupply Roanoke because of financial problems, for which he had a genius. It was not easy to convince tightfisted Elizabethan investors to pump money into enterprises "without sure, certayne, and present gayne." More important, in 1588 and 1589, England was preoccupied with a threat to the kingdom itself. Philip II, furious with Drake and other sea dogs, had assembled a fleet of 130 ships with which to invade England.

The Spanish Armada

The Spanish Armada (armed fleet) of 1588 was a disaster. Designed to transport 30,000 troops, its ships, built for the Mediterranean, were awkward on the swells of the Atlantic.

The Armada was outmaneuvered in the English Channel by small, quick English pinnaces. Regrouping in the harbor of Calais in France, the Armada was savaged by fire ships, old vessels the English lathered with tar, stuffed with gunpowder, set aflame, and sailed (unmanned) into the midst of the Spanish fleet.

The next year, returning home by rounding the British Isles to the north, the Armada was beset by storms. Only half of the ships, and just a third of Philip's soldiers, made it back to Spain. The Elizabethans may be excused for suggesting that God had lined up on their side. They called the storms that finished off the Armada "the Protestant Wind." They told each other that "God himselfe hath stricken the stroke, and ye have but looked on."

Whatever God's opinion in the matter, the sea dogs had demonstrated that Spain was not invincible. As the *siglo de oro* drew to a close, England, France, the Netherlands, and even Sweden were ready to chance colonies in America.

Promoters

The sea dogs demonstrated that the English could challenge Spain. Some Elizabethan landlubbers promoted the idea that the English *should* establish colonies. The most energetic was Richard Hakluyt, a bookish but by no means parochial, minister of the Church of England. Hakluyt rummaged tirelessly through the libraries of Oxford and London, collecting and publishing hundreds of explorers' accounts of the geography, resources, and attractions of America. His masterwork, *The Principal Navigations, Voyages, Traffiques, and Discoveries of the English Nation*, came out between 1598 and 1600.

In his books and in conversations with moneyed men, Hakluyt argued that investment in American colonies would infallibly produce a profit, add to England's prestige, and "enlarge the glory of the gospel." He lived until 1616, long enough to be a shareholder in the first permanent English settlement in America.

Sir Walter Raleigh continued to promote colonization too. He survived until 1618, but he was not as lucky as Hakluyt. After a lifetime sinking his and others' money in colonial debacles, the dashing soldier, poet, and personal favorite of Queen Elizabeth ran afoul of her successor, James I. Raleigh spent the last 13 years of his life imprisoned in the Tower of London.

Other writers, like advertisers of every era, played down the dangers and risks of investing in colonies, puffed up the attractions, and simply lied through their teeth. Virginia, they said, rivaled "Tyrus for colours, Balsan for woods, Persia for oils, Arabia for spices, Spain for silks, Narcis for shipping, the Netherlands for fish, Pomona for fruit and by tillage, Babylon for corn, besides the abundance of mulberries, minerals, rubies, pearls, gems, grapes, deer."

Hard Economic Facts

Some boosters emphasized the possibility that English conquistadores might stumble on gold and silver mines as the Spanish had or find the water passage to Asia that the Span-

Philip's subjects spent and spent on their luxuries. Philip spent on his endless wars. Their profligacy ensured that one day Spain would be the poorest nation in western Europe.

Easy Come, Easy Go

Instead of devoting American gold and silver to the improvement of agriculture, Spain purchased much of its food abroad, impoverishing its own farmers. Fisheries were neglected in favor of buying fish from others. Philip II's attempt to encourage the manufacture of textiles, leather, and iron goods at home was thwarted by the cheaper costs of imports. Even the majority of Spain's dreaded soldiers were, in fact, German and Italian mercenaries.

The result? Gold and silver dribbled out of Spain as quickly as they were shipped in. American loot ended up in countries with no mines in America but with a class of canny, grasping merchants and hustling manufacturers. Other nations did the final count of the Spanish doubloons. They included enemies of Spain quite glad to make whatever the Spanish would buy and to transport whatever the Spanish wanted shipped. Even the hated Drake easily found Spanish buyers for slaves he had stolen from other Spaniards.

Every transaction left Spain poorer and her enemies richer. England and Holland, Spain's bitterest foes, would fight one another to determine which of them would bleed the Spanish. In the Treaty of Utrecht in 1713, England took as the spoils of victory not territory but the *asiento de negros,* a license to sell 4,000 Africans into slavery in the Spanish colonies each year.

Surplus Population

Another circumstance encouraging interest in colonies was the widespread anxiety that there were just too many people in England. The population of England had soared during the 1500s, largely because of a decline in the incidence of mortal disease. But food production and opportunities for employment had not kept pace with the population explosion.

Some believed that the "enclosure movement" was at fault. That is, raising sheep was more profitable than farming land in small plots. So wealthy landowners, and even villagers who owned land in common, converted separate little fields into large pastures, which they enclosed with hedges as fences. Tending sheep required a fraction of the labor force that tilling the land did. Consequently, villagers who lost their rights to farm the land were sent packing.

Some of these surplus people wandered the countryside in gangs. They worried villagers and gentry alike with their begging, bullying, and theft. The boldest of them waylaid travelers on lonely stretches of highway. Other refugees congregated in cities, forming a half-starved and apparently hopeless underclass that, like the poor of all ages, was a source of disease, crime, and disorder. "Yea many thousands of idle persons," Hakluyt wrote, "having no way to be set on work . . . often fall to pilfering and thieving and other lewdness, whereby all the prisons of the land are daily pestered and stuffed full of them."

▲ *As a young man, Sir Walter Raleigh was a "favorite" of Queen Elizabeth; that is, he was kept around for his conversation and was indulged financially. Artful flattery was a favorite's favorite tool. Raleigh, tirelessly promoting colonization projects, named Virginia for Elizabeth, the "Virgin Queen."*

ish had not. Others pictured American outposts from which sea dogs would sally forth to seize Spanish ships and raid Spanish ports. Hakluyt described dozens of likely harbors and coves suitable to such enterprises.

But an economy could not be built on piracy. Moreover, although it was expensive to protect treasure fleets from raiders—20 warships to defend 20 merchantmen carrying gold and silver—it could be done, and the Spanish did it. More persuasive to sober English capitalists, there were signs by 1600 that Spain's American gold and silver mines were not unmitigated blessings. True, Spain's fabulous wealth enabled grandees at home to purchase whatever they desired, enjoy a style of life that was the envy of Europe's elite, and pay huge armies to terrorize the continent. It was also true, however, that Spain's *hidalgos*, like Miguel Cervantes' fictional Don Quixote, assumed that their inherent nobility and matchless bravery were quite enough on which to build the future.

King Philip II was no Don Quixote. Humorless, hard-working, unimaginative, ascetic, and invariably dressed in black, Philip thought in the longest of terms—eternity. His parents' coffins sat in his living quarters to remind him of his own mortality. Philip understood that the mines of Mexico and Peru had bottoms, that the gold and silver would run out. So he tried to promote industry and trade to provide for his beloved Spain when the easy money was gone. He failed.

Common Seamen

They were small men by our standards; few seamen of the age of discovery and colonization topped five and a half feet. But they were as tough as the oaken ships they sailed. Most were teenagers or men in their early 20s, and reaching maturity did not guarantee a long life. The odds that anyone who survived childhood diseases would die before the age of 35 were overwhelming. They were worse for men who went to sea.

If the sixteenth-century sailor survived shipwreck and battle, he faced hazards on his own vessel. He might be killed by a crewmate in a fight over a triviality. He might die being punished. Discipline on the high seas was immediate and brutal as an object lesson for the crew. Flogging was as regular as rain. Keelhauling (dragging a man underwater the length of the hull, where, if he did not drown, his body was shredded by barnacles—shellfish that clung to the vessel) was not common but was far from unusual. After a mutiny, Magellan beheaded one ringleader, quartered another alive, and marooned a third on a desert island. When he pardoned the other mutineers, they were so grateful that they became Magellan's most loyal followers.

Finally, the common seaman risked not only landlubber diseases; he ran a high risk of contracting scurvy, a vitamin C deficiency. It can be prevented and even reversed by a diet of fruits and vegetables. At sea, however, the menu did not include such foods because they were perishable. Meals consisted of salt beef, rock-hard biscuits, water, and wine. The officers ate slightly better. The onions, garlic, and dried fruit in their larders doubtless explains the lower incidence of scurvy among them.

A sailor's labor was heavy. Seamen hauled heavy canvas up and down masts, with pulleys as their only mechanical aid. Merely holding the ship on course was heavy work. The crude tiller pitted the seaman's strength against the forces of wind and ocean currents. Every ship leaked and had to be pumped by hand constantly—frenziedly during storms.

Ships on long voyages had to be refitted regularly—"serviced." A ship in danger of sinking because of the weight of the barnacles on its hull was sailed to a beach where it was careened (turned on its side). The barnacles were then scraped off, and the hull was recaulked with rope and pitch. If the captain decided that the sails needed to be rearranged, seamen virtually rebuilt the ship above deck. The small crew was kept hopping, repairing sails and lines, and scrubbing the decks with vinegar and salt water. But boredom was more likely than overwork to cause discontent.

Why did men choose such a life? First, *choose* is not quite the right word. Most sailors were born in seaports, literally bred to the life. Their options were few. A portion of the seamen were forced on the ships. Columbus's crew was put together in part by drafting convicts. For several centuries to come, shorthanded captains made up their crews by waylaying ("shanghaiing") hapless young men.

Finally, for all its dangers and discomforts, the sea offered a remote but alluring chance for social and economic advancement. Although some of the great captains of the era were, like Magellan, born into the upper classes, others, like Columbus, worked their way up. Columbus first shipped out as a boy, perhaps only 10 years old, and was illiterate until he was 30. Yet he became an intimate of royalty. Many conquistadores first came to the New World as common seamen and lived to become wealthy landowners. Even the lowliest can dream.

One response to England's population problem was a chilling criminal code. In the seventeenth and eighteenth centuries, a wretch could be hanged for the pettiest of crimes—for the theft of a rabbit from a gentleman's hutch. When the poor were so numerous and desperate, it was easy to believe that only the constant threat of the gallows kept them from running amok.

Or the pestering poor could be sent abroad. To Hakluyt and others, colonies were social safety valves. People who were economically superfluous and socially dangerous at home could, by the alchemy of a sea voyage, become cheerful consumers of English products and suppliers of the raw materials that England needed. "The fry of the wandering beggars of England," Hakluyt said, "that grow up idly, and hurtful and burdensome to this realm, may there be unladen, better bred up, and may people waste countries to the home and foreign benefit, and to their own more happy state."

Indeed, the desperation of the English living in huts of "stickes and turfes" made many glad to go overseas. As for those who found the idea unattractive, the "Bloody Code" served nicely as an incentive. North America was better than the noose. It is estimated that during the first century and a half of English settlement in the New World, one colonist in ten (about 50,000 total) had been convicted of a crime and "transported" as punishment. They were usually minor crimes, but not always. Some of today's country club families claiming ancient American lineage were surely "founded" by rapists, aficionados of mayhem, and murderers.

Private Enterprise

Colonies were financed and organized by private concerns that were forerunners of the modern corporation. These merchant-adventurer companies ("adventurer" refers to the adventuring, or risking, of money) were developed before the colonial era in response to the expense and risks of overseas trade.

It was neither cheap nor a sure thing to send a ship packed with trade goods out to sea. Pirates, warships of hostile nations, and storms and shoals waited to do many vessels in, and they did. Therefore, instead of gambling his entire fortune on a single ship, an investor joined with others in ownership to divide the risks. If a ship owned by such a company was lost, individual shareholders lost money, felt sorry for themselves, and, being human, looked for a way to blame someone else for their misfortune. But they were not ruined. They had not sunk everything they had into the venture. And they likely owned shares of other ships that would return at a profit.

Such capitalists covered themselves at home by securing charters from the Crown granting them special privileges in the business in which they were involved. Thus, the Muscovy Company, founded in 1555, had a chartered monopoly of the importation of furs and forest products from Russia. The most famous and successful of these protocorporations was the East India Company. Founded in 1600, it actually governed large parts of India for a century and a half.

When James I was persuaded that American colonies were a good idea, he chartered similar companies to do the job. In 1606, the king authorized a company in the port of Plymouth to "plant" a colony on the American coast between 38 and 45 degrees north latitude. The London Company was granted the same privilege between 34 and 41 degrees.

The tracts overlapped, but the two companies were forbidden to set up within 100 miles of one another. The buffer zone was designed to avoid rivalries that, in the Spanish West Indies, had sometimes turned violent. The 100-mile no-colony zone also hurried the two companies along: The first to arrive in America had the pick of sites.

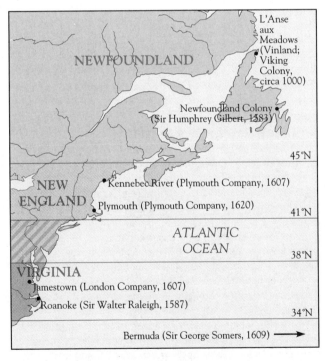

MAP 2:1 The English in America, 1583–1607 Raleigh, Gilbert, and other early colonizers ranged the North American Coast from Newfoundland to just short of Spanish Florida in their efforts to plant a successful English colony. The first successes were in the two regions known as "New England" and "Virginia." Note the zone in which both the London Company and Plymouth Company were authorized to settle, on the condition that their colonies be at least 100 miles apart.

JAMESTOWN

In August 1607, the Plymouth Company established Fort St. George on a bluff above Maine's Kennebec River. Like Humphrey Gilbert's people in Newfoundland a few decades earlier, the 45 colonists found the Maine winter disagreeable. Nevertheless, when Raleigh Gilbert arrived with a resupply ship the next year, he found "all things in great forwardness." Then, at summer's end, Gilbert learned that he had inherited the family fortune; his childless brother back in England had died. Who needed Fort St. George? The entire contingent returned home with the happy heir.

The First Families of Virginia

The London Company had better luck in Virginia, if 15 years of suffering and wholesale death can be called lucky. In May 1607, Captain Christopher Newport brought three ships into Chesapeake Bay and landed his passengers on a peninsula on the James River (named for the king). Roanoke was on Newport's mind. He would select no island that could be surrounded by Spanish ships. Instead, he picked a peninsula that could be defended against Indians almost as easily as an island. Captain John Smith, a soldier who remained in Jamestown, as the fortified village they built was called, said that Newport's choice was "a verie fit place for the erecting of a great citie."

This was nonsense. Jamestown was surrounded by brackish, malarial swamp, poorly suited to crops. Two centuries later, when the town ceased to serve as a center of government, just about everyone living there gladly moved out.

But Jamestown's limited agricultural prospects were not important to Newport, Smith, or the London Company. The first Virginians were not expected to be self-sufficient. Their assignment was to look for gold and to buy goods from the local Indians that would sell for a profit in England. And, preposterously, several Polish glassmakers (probably refugee Polish Brethren—Protestants fleeing persecution at home) were to set up a workshop in which to practice their craft. The first Virginians arrived with some illusions.

Pocahontas

Not long after landing in Virginia, John Smith was taken prisoner by the Powhatan. According to Smith—and he was more than willing to make a story up—he was seconds away from having his skull crushed by war clubs when Chief Powhatan's 12-year-old daughter, Matoaka, also known as Pocahontas ("the playful one"), begged the chief to spare Smith's life.

Pocahontas was playful. Naked, she visited Jamestown and turned cartwheels in the tracks that passed for streets. In 1614, Pocahontas became a Christian and married John Rolfe. She bore a son, but both his parents died when he was still a lad—Pocahontas in 1617 while visiting England, Rolfe in 1622 when Pocahontas's uncle attacked Jamestown.

Survivors

Mere survival was a struggle. Raw wilderness proved too much for the English. They had no experience as foragers. They could not compete as hunters and gatherers with the Powhatan Indians, for whom extracting a living from nature was at the heart of their culture. In January 1608, a fire destroyed what was left of the provisions the Jamestowners had brought with them. Hunger, as John Smith wrote, "forced many to flee for reliefe to the Savage Enemy."

In the language of the Powhatan, Virginia was called Tsenahkommaka ("densely populated land"). At about 40,000 in 1607, the Native American population of the Chesapeake region may have reached a point at which the Indians themselves were suffering food shortages. The introduction of 200 new residents may have been just too much for Virginia. Once the Jamestowners' numbers declined to a few dozen, they did manage to hang on. If they survived on such things as oysters, snakes, and mushrooms, that is what foraging is all about.

John Smith had a distinguished military record. The Virginians might have lived by raiding Indian farms, and when desperate, they tried. But the Powhatan Confederacy held the preponderance of power. Had they decided to wipe out the interlopers during Virginia's first years, they could have done so in a weekend. Jamestown may have survived destruction because relief ships arrived annually with manufactured goods the Indians learned to covet.

Then there was disease. Malaria, dysentery, typhoid fever, scurvy, and plain enervating apathy took a devastating toll. In 1607, 144 Englishmen landed at Jamestown. The next year, 38 were alive. In 1608 and 1609, 500 new colonists arrived. By 1610, Jamestown's population was 60.

Unpermissive Society

Smith, who rivaled Raleigh as a publicist, credited his military discipline with saving the colony. In fact, Smith's no-nonsense control—he executed one settler for making a dinner of his wife—probably did avert complete disintegration. But Smith was less than beloved. His successor as governor, George Percy, called him "an Ambitious unworthy and vayneglorious Fellowe."

Thomas West, Baron De La Warr, named governor in 1610, also enforced a rigorous discipline, this time aimed at making the colony self-sufficient in food. Settlers were marched to work in the fields as if they were troops. Troublemakers and the merely idle were dealt with swiftly and harshly. De La Warr and his successors, Thomas Dale and Thomas Gates, prescribed the death penalty for dozens of offenses, including individual trade with the Indians and killing a domestic animal without permission. Virginians were whipped for throwing wash water into the streets or carrying out "the necessities of nature" within a quarter mile of the fort. Under this authoritarian rule, fields were expanded, and "earth-fast" houses (what we call "pole buildings": buildings with no foundations) were erected.

Virginia expanded along the banks of the James, but mortality remained high. Between 1610 and 1618, 3,000 new settlers arrived. In 1619, the population of Virginia was 1,000. Between 1619 and 1623, 4,000 settlers arrived. In 1624, the population of Virginia was 1,300.

The "Stinking Custom"

If the Virginians had found no way to make money, the London Company would surely have written off the colony as a big mistake. But the colonists did find profit growing tobacco, a native American plant that Columbus had brought back to Europe on his first voyage to the New World.

Smoking got off to a bad start in Europe. The first addict, Rodrigo de Jerez, was jailed by the Spanish Inquisition for seven years because of his habit. But Rodrigo was the wave of the future. Slowly, inexorably, the practice of "drinking" tobacco smoke spread. The lure of the exotic—the trendy—is always potent among the leisured classes. And some European physicians seized on tobacco as a miracle drug, prescribing it liberally to their patients and calling it "the holy, healing herb," "a sovereign remedy to all diseases."

When Jamestown was founded, the Spanish West Indies provided just about everyone's weed. The Powhatan grew their own, but John Rolfe, a Virginian with the habit, found the local tobacco "poore and weak and of a byting taste." Securing seed from Trinidad, Rolfe experimented in his garden in 1612. In 1614, he had more than enough for his own pipe and shipped four barrels of the leaf to England. The reception was sensational. In 1617, Virginia exported 10 tons of tobacco at a profit of three shillings a pound! In 1618, the shipment was 25 tons—and by 1628, 250 tons! The price at

Thank You for Not Smoking

Both James I and his son, Charles I, disapproved of tobacco. James called it "a custom loathesome to the eye, harmful to the brain, dangerous to the lungs, and in the black stinking fume thereof, nearest resembling the Stygian smoke of the pit that is bottomless." That was in 1604, before there was a single English colony, let alone a colony flourishing by growing tobacco.

However, as late as 1631, when Virginia was booming thanks to tobacco, Charles I commanded an earl to limit tobacco cultivation on his estate because of "the great abuse of tobacco to the enervation of the body and of courage."

Neither father nor son was willing to take a cut in income in order to stifle the habit. When a giant hike in James I's tax on tobacco resulted in a sharp reduction in imports, and therefore in the tobacco duties he collected (what did he expect?), he slashed the tax to a payable level.

At least two colonies founded later than Virginia enacted antismoking measures. Connecticut tried to license smokers; only those who were prescribed tobacco for reasons of health could apply. Massachusetts briefly forbade smoking *outdoors*—not for moral reasons but to prevent fires.

▲ *When tobacco boomed in Virginia in the 1610s, the inhabitants of Jamestown planted every available square inch of the town with the crop, roadways included.*

which tobacco sold explains this amazing growth. In the early seventeenth century, ordinary tobacco brought the equivalent in today's money of $17 a pound, and the finest grades, $100 a pound.

Who Shall Till the Fields?

Emigrants hurried across the Atlantic. The very streets of Jamestown were planted with tobacco. A colony recently starving now neglected food production in order to cultivate a weed to be burned. Authorities lamented that the settlers' "greediness after great quantities of tobacco causeth them" not to "build good homes, fence their grounds, or plant any orchards." In "An Acte for Tradesmen to Worke on Theire Trades" in 1632, the Virginia Assembly commanded gunsmiths and naylers, brickmakers, carpenters, joyners, sawyers and turners . . . to worke at theire trades and not plant tobacco."

Mostly, it was a losing effort. A carpenter could make a living. A farmer could tend a thousand tobacco plants plus four acres of maize, beans, and squash—enough to support a household of five. It did not require a gift for higher mathematics to calculate what the income from 10,000 or 50,000 tobacco plants would mean.

Land was abundant, rich, seemingly endless, and available for a pittance. The problem was labor. Who would work

for another in a country that offered so extraordinary an opportunity to get rich? The Jamestowners enslaved Indians. However, unlike the Indians of Mexico, the natives of Virginia were alien to intensive, disciplined labor. At the first opportunity, they disappeared into the forest, which to them was not howling wilderness but home.

In 1619, a Dutch ship tied up at Jamestown and paid for the tobacco it took aboard with "20 and odd Negroes," probably seized from a slave trader bound for the Spanish West Indies. Soon, human cargoes from Africa and the West Indies arrived regularly in Virginia. In 1660, there were 900 black Virginians in a population of 25,000. Only after 1700, however, would African Americans be the backbone of the workforce. During the seventeenth century, ambitious Virginians made the transition from toiling farmer to comfortable planter by importing white servants from England.

Under the "headright system" instituted in 1618, each head of household who came to Virginia was granted 50 acres of land for each person whose fare across the Atlantic he paid. Thus, a family of five secured 250 acres upon disembarking. Virginians or Englishmen with cash to spare could amass larger estates by recruiting emigrants from among the masses of England. In return for their transportation to Virginia, these people signed contracts binding themselves to labor for their master without pay for a number of years, usually seven. Thus was Virginia peopled, thus the tobacco grown.

Massacre

For 15 years, the English coexisted with the Powhatan Confederacy. Many held the Indians in contempt, comparing them to the "savage Irish," whom the English detested. Red and white regularly skirmished, although the fights were more brawls than battles. The aged head of the Confederacy, Chief Powhatan, did not view the enclave of pale-skinned outsiders as much of a threat, and he was fascinated by the firearms, woven cloth, pots, pans, and mirrors they offered in trade. In 1614, when John Rolfe married Powhatan's daughter, Pocahontas, something of a détente was inaugurated.

Then Powhatan died, to be succeeded as chief by his brother, Opechancanough, an altogether different character. Opechancanough had nearly been killed by John Smith in 1609, and he recognized what many Indians after him were to learn, always too late: The once tiny, starving white enclaves with interesting things to sell were growing in size, strength, and confidence, and pushing hungrily into the Indians' ancestral lands.

In March 1622, Opechancanough struck. He and his warriors entered Jamestown as if to trade or chat. Suddenly, they attacked, killing the founding father of the tobacco business, John Rolfe, and 346 others. About a third of Vir-

▲ *Visiting England in 1616, Pocahontas sat for this portrait in finery befitting the wife of a prosperous tobacco merchant, which her husband, John Rolfe, was fast becoming.*

▲ *The Jamestown Massacre of 1622 was unexpected, sudden, and terrifying. The start of it probably looked much as this artist rendered it, but the killing continued until 300 Virginians were dead.*

ginia's white population died, a catastrophe. But it was not enough in a place where fortunes were being made. The survivors bandaged their wounds, refused Opechancanough's offer to trade kidnapped women for peace, and retaliated with their superior weapons, sorely punishing the Powhatan. Other Indians were tricked into a peace parley at which as many as 200 were poisoned. Some Virginians called for a kind of genocide, "a perpetuall warre without peace or truce [to] roote out from being any longer a people, so cursed a nation, ungratefull to all benefitte, and incapable of all goodnesse." By 1625, it is estimated, the number of Powhatan was reduced from 40,000 to 5,000.

After one last Indian offensive in 1644, the Powhatan were driven into the interior. In 1669, 2,000 of them were counted. By 1685, apparently, the people and culture were extinct. The pattern of white–Indian relations that would be repeated for more than two and a half centuries had been drawn in the mud of Jamestown.

A Royal Colony

The London Company was also a casualty of the massacre of 1622. Although some planters and merchants were getting rich from tobacco, the company itself never recorded a profit. Citing this failure and the massacre, King James I revoked the company's charter in 1624 and took direct control of Virginia. The House of Burgesses, a legislative assembly of 22 members elected by landowners and established in 1619, continued to function. But the king appointed a governor empowered to veto its actions. Virginia was, thus, the first English colony, the first colony in which there was significant self-government, and the first royal colony directly administered by the Crown.

OTHER BEGINNINGS

By 1622, the English in Virginia were not the only Europeans living in what is now the United States. Before the seventeenth century was 10 years old, both the Spanish and the French had registered their presence in what is now the United States.

French America

In 1562, a French adventurer named Jean Ribault tried to launch Charlesfort, near what is now Port Royal, South Carolina. Like Roanoke, Charlesfort simply evaporated. Two years later, René Goulaine de Ladonnière took 300 colonists to Florida, close by the spot where Ponce de León began his explorations. The settlers were Huguenots, Puritan-like Protestants. They planned to use Fort Caroline as a base from which to raid Spanish treasure ships.

The colony was vexed by Indian troubles and the refusal of the aristocrats there to work with their hands. However, it was destroyed in 1565, when it was attacked by a Spanish expedition led by Pedro Menéndez de Avilés. Florida's history did not have a pretty beginning. When Menéndez discovered that the French he had captured were Protestants, he had them hacked to death.

French interest in America shifted north. In 1608, an extraordinary sailor, Samuel de Champlain (he made 12 voyages to the New World!), founded Quebec on a site on the St. Lawrence River that had been claimed for France in 1535. The next year, in company with Huron Indian allies, Champlain was exploring the lake in New York and Vermont that now bears his name when he stumbled on a party of Iroquois, old enemies of the Huron. At the request of the Huron, the French turned their muskets on the Iroquois. It was their introduction to European military technology and the beginning of long intertribal wars in which the French and English would play major roles.

New France, the St. Lawrence river basin, having no cash crop like tobacco, grew slowly. In 1627, there were but 100 French there; in 1663, only 3,000. In some ways, Quebec was a religious and cultural center: A college was founded there in 1635 (a year before Harvard, the first college of the English) as well as an Ursuline convent school for Indian girls. But mostly, Quebec was a rude, uncomfortable trading post where Indians exchanged hides and furs for decorative trinkets, blankets, textiles, iron tools and implements, guns, and brandy.

Hispanic Beginnings

In 1565, before destroying Fort Caroline, Pedro Menéndez de Avilés established St. Augustine, Florida, between the Matanzas and San Sebastian Rivers. In 1586, Sir Francis Drake sacked the town, but St. Augustine recovered. It is the oldest surviving European settlement (by 42 years) in what is now the United States.

In 1609, two years after the founding of Jamestown, a party of Spaniards hiked the banks of the Rio Grande almost to its source in the Sangre de Cristo Mountains of New Mexico. There they founded Santa Fe, from which traders tapped the numerous Indians of the country for furs, hides, and small quantities of precious metals, while Franciscan missionaries sallied out to win the Indians' souls. By 1630, they claimed to have baptized 86,000 Pueblo, Apache, and Navaho Indians.

Santa Fe is the oldest seat of government in the United States. (St. Augustine was administered from Cuba.) By 1609, however, the Spanish empire had reached the limits of its capacity to expand. Except for England's minuscule trading posts on Hudson Bay, founded much later, Santa Fe remained the remotest European town of any size in North America, isolated by colossal distance from the imperial center of Mexico. Like the French in Canada, the Spanish in Santa Fe would not contribute to American culture as dominant forces but only in their responses to the great English experiment in settlement that had its beginnings in Virginia.

FURTHER READING

The historical literature dealing with the background of England's colonial era is vast. G. R. Elton, *England Under the Tudors*, 1974, is a good overview. For social and "mental" context, see Peter Laslett, *The World We Have Lost*, 1965. Specifically related to English interest in North America are Carl Bridenbaugh, *Vexed and Troubled Englishmen*, 1968; A. L. Rowse, *Elizabethans and America*, 1959; and Keith Wright, *English Society, 1580–1680*, 1982.

Fixing on important incidents are Thomas E. Roche, *The Golden Hind*, 1973; Garrett Mattingly, *The Armada*, 1959; Karen Ordahl Kupperman, *Roanoke: The Abandoned Colony*, 1984; and David B. Quinn, *Set Fair for Roanoke*, 1985. Relevant biographies include Paul Johnson, *Elizabeth I*, 1974; P. L. Barbour, *The Three Worlds of Captain John Smith*, 1964; Stephen J. Greenblatt, *Sir Walter Raleigh*, 1973; and James A. Williamson, *Sir Francis Drake*, 1975.

On early Virginia, see Carl Bridenbaugh, *Jamestown, 1544–1699*, 1980; Alden Vaughan, *Captain John Smith and the Founding of Virginia*, 1975; and Edmund S. Morgan, *American Slavery, American Freedom*, 1975. On the Indians of the region,

see Gary Nash, *Red, White, and Black*, 1982; Thad W. Tate and David W. Ammerman, eds., *The Chesapeake in the Seventeenth Century*, 1979; and Peter Wood et al., *Powhatan's Mantle: Indians in the Colonial Southeast*, 1989. See also the relevant chapters of the following books by James Axtell, our most accomplished and reliable recent historian of Indians: *The European and the Indian*, 1981; *The Invasion Within: The Contest of Cultures in Colonial America*, 1985; and *After Columbus: Essays in the Ethnohistory of Colonial North America*, 1988.

General works (also relevant to subsequent chapters of this book) include Charles M. Andrews, *The Colonial Period of American History*, 1934–1938; Daniel Boorstin, *The Americans: The Colonial Experience*, 1958; Wesley F. Craven, *The Southern Colonies in the Seventeenth Century*, 1949; Jack P. Greene and J. R. Pole, eds., *Colonial British America*, 1984; Curtis E. Nettels, *The Roots of American Civilization*, 1938; John E. Pomfret with Floyd Shumway, *Founding the American Colonies*, 1970; and Clarence Ver Steeg, *The Formative Years*, 1964.

  ## AMERICAN JOURNEY ONLINE AND INFOTRAC COLLEGE EDITION

Visit the source collections at http://ajaccess.wadsworth.com and http://infotrac.thomsonlearning.com, and use the Search function with the following key terms to explore documents, images, audio and video clips, articles, and commentary related to the material in this chapter:

Jamestown
John Smith
Martin Luther
Pocahontas
Powhatan
Richard Hakluyt
Sir Walter Raleigh

Additional resources, exercises, and Internet links related to this chapter are available on *The American Past* Web site: http://history.wadsworth.com/americanpast7e.

HISTORY ONLINE

Discourse of Western Planting
http://odur.let.rug.nl/~usa/D/1501-1600/hakluyt/plant.htm
Extracts from Richard Hakluyt's published promotions of English colonies in North America. These were the arguments with which men like Hakluyt and Raleigh approached investors.

Jamestown
www.gov.colo/Jthanout/JTbriefs.html
Well-selected variety of information about the Jamestown colony.

3

ENGLISH AMERICA

The Thirteen Colonies
1620–1732

> We must be knit together in this work as one man; we must entertain each other in brotherly affection . . . we must uphold a familiar commerce together in all meekness, gentleness, patience and liberality; we must delight in each other, make other's conditions our own, rejoice together, mourn together, labor and suffer together.
>
> John Winthrop

> They differ from us in the manner of praying, for they winke [close their eyes] when they pray because they thinke themselves so perfect in the highe way to heaven that they can find it blindfold.
>
> Thomas Morton

IN 1608, 125 MEN, WOMEN, and children left the English village of Scrooby, made their way to Hull, and took a ship to Holland, where they settled in the "fair and beautifull citie" of Leiden.

They were quiet in their travels because they were breaking the law. Going abroad without royal permission was forbidden. The Scrooby villagers were willing to risk punishment because they were being persecuted for their religious beliefs. They were members of a small sect called "Separatists" because they believed that Christians who were "saved"—elected for salvation by God—should worship only in the company of other such "saints," separate from those who were damned. This belief earned them the hostility of the Church of England, to which all the English were expected to adhere, and of the king, who was the head of the church.

The Separatists are better known to us as the Pilgrims. Their leader for a generation, William Bradford, called them that because they did a good deal of wandering, as if on a pilgrimage, in search of a place they might live godly lives unmolested.

NEW ENGLAND COLONIES

The Pilgrims were not molested in Leiden; the Dutch tolerated most forms of worship. In fact, Leiden was a bit too free and easy for the straitlaced Pilgrims. They fretted that their children were absorbing a casual attitude toward parental authority, "getting the reins off their necks," and embracing the juvenile misbehavior for which the Dutch were notorious. Moreover, like the children of foreigners before and since, the sons and daughters of the Pilgrims were growing up as much Dutch as English. The Pilgrims may have disliked the intolerance of the English crown, but they were also English to the core themselves, as ethnocentric as any Chinese, Ghanaian, or Powhatan Indian.

Plymouth Plantation

Virginia's success, apparent by 1620, helped provide a solution to the Pilgrims' dilemma. The bonanza profits from growing tobacco on the Chesapeake rekindled the enthusiasm of the Plymouth Company, which had failed to develop a colony in Maine in 1607.

The trouble was that Virginia's prosperity lured most would-be emigrants there. The Plymouth Company could not find settlers for an entirely new colony at least a hundred miles north of Jamestown. Then, Sir Edwin Sandys, a major shareholder, had an idea. He won the consent of James I not to persecute the Separatists if they relocated to America.

In 1620, the Leiden exiles returned to England just long enough to board two small America-bound ships, the *Mayflower* and the *Speedwell*. The *Speedwell* leaked so badly it turned back, thus missing the opportunity to enshrine its name in American history books. The *Mayflower* was herself none too seaworthy but survived a rough passage longer than that of Christopher Columbus a century earlier.

A hundred colonists disembarked at the southern end of Massachusetts Bay. They built "Plymouth Plantation" on the site of Pawtuxet, an Indian village that had been wiped out by disease, probably brought by European fishermen, several years earlier. The Pilgrims regarded the fact that their settlement was ready made, with fields ready to plow, as a sign that God approved of their mission. He had "cleared" an already developed land of people so that his saints might dwell on it. He did not send a mild winter, however. Half the settlers died of malnutrition or disease before the spring of 1621.

Then came another positive sign, "a special instrument sent of God": Tisquantum, or Squanto, an Indian who spoke English, wandered into the colony. A native of Pawtuxet, Squanto had been kidnapped in 1605 and taken to England. He made his way to Virginia with John Smith in 1614, was

▲ *A contemporary reconstruction of Plymouth when the settlement was several years old. "Streets" are wide enough for an ox or horse, but not a wagon. Dooryards were fenced not for privacy—there was little—but to keep hogs out of gardens.*

Plimouth Plantation, Inc. Photographer, Gary Andrashko.

kidnapped by Spaniards but escaped, and, six months before the founding of Plymouth, returned to Pawtuxet to find it abandoned. This well-traveled man, far more cosmopolitan than the Pilgrims, nonetheless adopted them as his tribe. He was an invaluable member of their community. He guided

The "Fun" Colony

"Merrymount," now Quincy, a few miles from Plymouth, is a colony forgotten. In 1623, a curious character named Thomas Morton arrived at Plymouth and persuaded some of his fellow passengers to join in a colony where they would be, in the words of Plymouth governor Bradford, "free from service, and . . . trade, plante, & live togeather as equalls."

According to Bradford, Morton presided over a riotous style of life. The Merrymounters were frequently drunk and "set up a May-pole, drinking and dancing aboute it many days togeather, inviting the Indean women, for their consorts, dancing and frisking together, (like so many fairies, or furies rather,) and worse practices."

Also aggravating, Morton stole Indian trade from Plymouth by offering firearms for furs and hides. This worried Governor Bradford because the Indians were better hunters than the whites "by reason of ther swiftnes of foote, & nimblnes of body" and because the guns could be turned against the colony. He sent Captain Miles Standish and a small force to arrest Morton. There was no battle because, according to Bradford, Morton and his friends were too drunk to resist. The only casualty was a Merrymounter who staggered into a sword and split his nose.

Morton was put on an island to await the next ship bound for England. Indian friends brought him food and liquor and helped him escape; he returned to England on his own and denounced the Pilgrims. Neither he nor the Pilgrim fathers were punished. If authorities then had known the phrase "can of worms," they would surely have applied it to the squabble.

Increasing and Multiplying

Nearly half of Plymouth's settlers died during the colony's first winter. Just two of the survivors more than made up for the loss within their own lifetimes.

John Alden and Priscilla Mullins arrived on the *Mayflower* and married soon thereafter. (The wedding was immortalized two centuries later by Henry Wadsworth Longfellow.) The Aldens both lived into their 80s. They had 12 children, of whom 10 survived to adulthood. Eight of these Aldens married and, together, had at least 68 children—more people than died in Plymouth in 1620–1621. The Aldens' great-grandchildren, a few of whom they lived to know, numbered 400, or four times the original population of the colony.

▲ *This rendition of Captain Miles Standish distastefully observing the antics at nearby "Merrymount" was based on the depiction of the settlement by Plymouth governor Bradford. The Merrymounters had to have taken an occasional break from partying; Thomas Morton, the head of the "colony," competed with the Pilgrims in buying furs from the Indians.*

the newcomers about the country, taught them native methods of fishing and cultivation, and, according to Governor William Bradford, asked for prayers so that "he might goe to the Englishmen's God in Heaven."

Self-Government

Squanto was a better citizen than many who arrived on the *Mayflower.* Even before landing, Pilgrim elders like Bradford and William Brewster, and the colony's military officer, Captain Miles Standish, grew nervous that, once ashore, the "strangers" among them—that is, the non-Separatists— would defy their authority. Several had said as much during the voyage. Worse, the grumblers had a legal justification for going their own way. The site of Plymouth lay outside the tract of land assigned to the Pilgrims in the Plymouth Company charter. Therefore, the legal authority the charter vested in the leaders of the expedition was shaky.

To reassert that authority, 41 of the passengers signed the Mayflower Compact while still aboard ship. The document began by asserting the party's enduring loyalty to "our dread Sovereign Lord King James" (whose instructions as to the location of the colony they were flouting). The signers then bound the settlers together in a "Civil Body Politik" for the purpose of enacting and enforcing laws. The Mayflower

Compact is memorable because of its implicit principle— that a government's authority derives from the consent of those who are governed. King James got his ceremonial due. However, the signers of the compact, who were a majority of the adult males, also stated that the right to make laws in the colony was based on the fact that the majority consented to be subject to those laws.

Early Plymouth was, in fact, a rather democratic place. Almost every male head of household was a shareholder in the company and could, therefore, vote to elect the governor. (William Bradford held the post for 30 years.) Important questions were resolved by vote. Such broad and active participation of the people in government was found in few places anywhere in the world.

Subsistence Economy

Plymouth was also autonomous of England for most practical purposes. The Crown interfered little in the colony's internal affairs. This was a consequence of the fact that the Pilgrims never came up with a moneymaker like John Rolfe's tobacco plants. Simply put, the colony failed to arouse the interest of influential Englishmen (or much of anyone) back home. Furs purchased from the Indians provided Plymouth some income with which to buy goods from

English merchants. Fishing for cod helped. But Plymouth was just a tiny, distant community of subsistence farmers. The Pilgrims raised enough food to live. Indeed, after the first terrible winter, they thrived. But no one got rich tilling New England's rocky soil or salting codfish for export.

The dearth of profits discouraged the owners of the Plymouth Company. By 1627, they agreed to sell their shares to the settlers. Although it took 15 years to pay them off, the sale had the effect of transferring control of Plymouth Plantation to those who lived there. Plymouth remained a self-governing commonwealth until 1691, when it was absorbed into its younger but much larger neighbor, Massachusetts Bay.

Massachusetts Bay

Virtual self-government was half accidental in Plymouth. Had a Pilgrim plowman turned up a vein of gold ore in his cornfield, the king would have royalized the colony, as he seized Virginia in 1624.

In the most important colony of New England, by way of contrast, self-government was the consequence of well-laid plans meticulously carried out. There were no starving times in Massachusetts Bay, established in 1630 some 40 miles north of Plymouth. The founders of the Massachusetts Bay colony worked out the fine details of their migration long before they weighed anchor. Provisions and supplies were abundant for the thousand people who made up the first wave of settlement. Within a few months, Massachusetts was home to seven towns!

By design, the settlers were a fair cross section of English society. They were of both sexes, more or less balanced in numbers, and of all ages and social classes up to the rank of lady and gentleman. There were skilled artisans and professionals among them, most notably, well-educated ministers of God; there were farmers and laborers. Only nobles were missing from the mix.

The founders of Massachusetts Bay intended to create, quite literally, a *new* England based on the society they knew at home. In just one major particular did the colonists reject old-country ways. Although they called themselves members of the Church of England, they abhorred the church's practices. New England was to be a truly godly commonwealth such as the world had not known since the days of the apostles.

To ensure they were able to create, shape, and control their Zion, the settlers brought with them the charter of the Massachusetts Bay Company, the legal justification of their right to self-government. Shareholders in the company who chose to stay in England sold out to those who went to America. There would be no company directors back home to question decisions made in Massachusetts.

Puritan Beliefs

These cautious, prudent people were the Puritans. Their religion was Calvinist. Like the Separatists, they were disciples of the theologian John Calvin, who believed that human nature was inherently depraved, that all men and women bore the guilt of Adam and Eve's original sin. In the words of a Massachusetts poet, Anne Bradstreet, man was a "lump of wretchedness, of sin and sorrow."

If God were just, and nothing more, all sons and daughters of Eve would be damned to hell for eternity because of their sinful nature. Since God was all good, there was nothing that sin-stained men and women could do to earn salvation. From such corrupt actors, no act of charity, no act of faith, no sacrifice, no performance of a ritual could possibly merit divine approval.

Was there then no hope? In fact there was, and in the Puritans' hope for the next world lies the key to understanding the kind of society they built in this one. For God was not merely just, he was also infinitely loving. He made a gift of grace to some people. These were the "elect," his "saints." No one deserved the gift of grace. No one earned it. Saints were by nature as corrupt as the damned multitudes who surrounded them. God's love, and it alone, was the reason they were predestined to join him in paradise.

In return for the gift of grace, the elect bound themselves to a covenant (contract) with God. They would enforce God's law in the community in which they lived. If they failed to keep their part of the bargain, if they tolerated sin within their community, the Puritans believed, God would punish them as severely as he had punished his chosen people of the Old Testament, the ancient Hebrews.

Errand in the Wilderness

It is not quite correct, therefore, to say that the Puritans came to America in order to worship as they pleased. First of all, the Puritans were a powerful minority in England. Although some were harassed, others worshiped pretty much as they pleased on the fens of Lincolnshire and the Yorkshire moors. One of their most respected ministers, John Cotton, had been the pastor of St. Botolph's in old Boston, said to be the largest parish church in England. Cotton was no wild-eyed

---

Hypocrites?

"We are decendid," wrote humorist Artemus Ward in 1872, "from the Puritans, who nobly fled from a land of despitism to a land of freedim, where they could not only enjoy their own religion, but prevent everybody else from enjoyin' his."

Ward was witty, but mistaken to imply that the Puritans were hypocrites. They did persecute religious practices other than their own; they hanged several Quakers. But they never claimed to have set up in America in the cause of religious toleration. Nineteenth-century Americans saddled them with that reputation. Puritans forthrightly said that other forms of worship were abominations. As Thomas Shephard of Cambridge wrote in 1645, "Toleration of all upon pretence of conscience I think God my soul abhors it." The Puritans were intolerant, but they were not hypocrites.

---

creature of the fringe, hiding in a hedge from persecutors. He was a man of status and respect.

It is more accurate to say that the Puritans came to America because they were not at all pleased with the way non-Puritans were worshiping in England. They wanted to remove themselves from "the multitude of irreligious, lascivious, and popish persons" in the old country. Their "errand into the wilderness" of Massachusetts was to *purify* the Church of England. Thus their name.

To Puritans, the Church of England was violating the covenant, thus courting divine punishment. "I am verily persuaded," wrote John Winthrop, the soon-to-be governor of Massachusetts, "God will bring some heavy affliction upon this land."

In Massachusetts, the Puritans believed, they would escape God's wrath because there they would honor the covenant. For years, some Puritan leaders harbored the illusion that the English would look across the Atlantic at them, see by their splendid example the errors of their own ways, and invite the Puritan fathers home to escort England into righteousness. "We shall be as a citty on a hill," Winthrop wrote, a beacon of inspiration.

A Commonwealth

The Puritans believed in community, that individuals should support one another in life's spiritual quest and in its material concerns too. In the godly commonwealth, in Winthrop's words, "every man might have need of [every] other, and from hence they might be knit more nearly together in the bond of brotherly affection."

There was little patience in such a community for individualism and none for eccentricity. The Puritans enforced a strict code of moral and social behavior on everyone, saint and sinner alike. Because God punished a community that tolerated sinners, and not just the sinners, the Puritans were swift and harsh with what are today called "victimless crimes," or acts we do not regard as crimes at all. The most ordinary of Puritans understood this principle that can bewilder twenty-first-century Americans. When, in 1656, a simple girl named Tryal Pore confessed that she was guilty of fornication, she said that "by this my sinn I have not only done what I can to Poull Judgement from the Lord on my selve but allso upon the place where I live."

The same sense of community moved Puritans to point out to their neighbors when they were doing wrong. Judge Samuel Sewall of Massachusetts was not thought to be a busybody when he visited a wig-wearing relative to tell him that his hairpiece was sinful. Sewall was seen as looking after his kinsman's soul. The man liked his wig too much to give it up, but he did not tell Sewall to mind his own business. He argued only as to whether wearing a wig really was a sin.

Blue Laws

The law books of Massachusetts and other New England colonies were filled with regulations that, in our day, would be considered outrageous or ridiculous. God commanded that the Sabbath be devoted to him. Therefore, the Puritans forbade on Sundays activities that on Wednesday or Thursday might be perfectly in order: working, sports, "idle chatter," whistling, and even "walking in a garden." Some things appropriate in private were forbidden in public. In 1659, a sea captain named Kemble returned from a voyage of three years. He kissed his wife on the threshold of their home and was sentenced to sit in the stocks for two hours for "lewd and unseemly behaviour."

A woman who was a "scold," guilty of "Exorbitancy of the Tongue in Raling and Scolding," was humiliated on the ducking stool—she was tied to a chair on a seesaw-like lever and dunked repeatedly in a pond to the merriment of onlookers. Unsurprisingly, attendance at church was obligatory. In Maine in 1682, Andrew Searle was fined five shillings "for not frequenting the publique worship of god" and for "wandering from place to place upon the Lords

▲ *A few hours sitting in the stocks—public humiliation—was a fairly common punishment in early New England for minor offenses, especially violations of "Blue Laws." A variation was the pillory, in which the offender stood, head and hands similarly locked in place. Laughter and mockery on such occasions were tolerated; physical abuse of offenders was not.*

days." More serious crimes, such as theft, arson, assault, and wife beating, were punished with a flogging or branding.

As far as capital crimes were concerned, the New England Puritans were far more "liberal" than Old England was. Because the Bible was their guide in crime, as in much else, the Puritans reserved the death penalty for only those offenses that were punished by death in the Bible: murder, treason, witchcraft, incest, sodomy (homosexuality), "buggery" (bestiality), adultery, and blasphemy.

Not that hanging was mandatory for those convicted of these crimes. Between 1630 and 1660, fewer than 20 people were executed in Massachusetts: four murderers, two infanticides, three sexual offenders (including Thomas Granger, who coupled with "a mare, a cow, two goats, five sheep, two calves, and a turkey"), two witches, and four Quakers (members of a religious sect believed to "undermine & ruine" authority). It appears that only one adulterous couple, Mary Latham and James Britton, were hanged. Other adulterers were granted mercy—and a lesser punishment—or acquitted by juries because they did not want the miscreants executed. Connecticut enacted the death penalty for a child who struck or cursed his parents, but it was not enforced. When Joseph Porter was brought to court for calling his father "a thief, liar, and simple ape shittabed," and insulted the judge too, his conviction was thrown out on appeal.

The Puritans believed that social distinctions were divinely decreed. "Some must be rich, some poore," said John Winthrop—not some *are* rich, some poor. It was therefore an offense for people of lesser class to ape the fashions of their betters. In Connecticut in 1675, 38 women were arrested for dressing in silk. Obviously, the offenders could afford their finery, but their social standing in the community did not justify their wearing it. Another law forbade people of modest station to wear silver buckles on their shoes. Such adornments were "fit" only for magistrates and ministers.

A Well-Ordered Society

Between 1630 and 1640, 21,000 English men and women settled in New England. Most were family farmers. Indentured servants, the backbone of Virginia's labor force, were fewer in the North. Slaves of African origin were exotic until after 1700.

New England's authorities retained close control of the expansion of their colonies. Newly arrived groups were allotted land for towns of 50 to 100 families. Each family was granted fields for tillage, a woodlot for fuel, and the right to keep animals on the village common, which was just that— a pasture for common use. Social status in Old England determined just how much land a family was granted.

When newcomers settled too far from the town center to find meetinghouse and common convenient, the township's lands were divided into communities independent of one another. When a township grew overcrowded, some of its people moved west and north, sometimes as individuals but usually as members of a new community with authority from the colony to establish a new town.

Puritan Names

Many Puritans named their children from the Old Testament, not only after the great figures—Adam, Noah, Deborah, Judith—but after obscure characters whose names may have rung as discordantly in most Puritan ears as the names of people today who were named by "hippie" parents: Ahab, Zerubbabel, Abednego, and so on.

Others made a statement with an infant's name. Increase Mather, a prominent minister, was named from the biblical injunction, "Increase, multiply, and subdue the earth." Records have revealed no one named Multiply or Subdue, but there is a Fight the Good Fight of Faith Wilson, a Be Courteous Cole, and a Kill-Sin Pemble. Other notable names include The Lord Is Near, Fear-Not, Flee Fornication, and Job-Raked-Out-of-the-Ashes.

A couple named Cheeseman were told their infant was going to die during childbirth. Not knowing the child's sex, they baptized it "Creature." Creature Cheeseman fooled the midwife and lived a long life with her unusual moniker.

Not too much should be made of these names. Only 4 percent of Puritans were saddled with them. A boy was likelier than today to be named just plain Bill. About half of the girls in records of Puritan baptisms were bestowed only three rock-solid English names: Sarah, Elizabeth, and Mary.

Such firm social control enabled the Puritans to create one of the most literate populations in the world. In 1642, Massachusetts required parents to teach their children how to read. In 1647, townships of 50 families or more were required to support a school; towns of 1,000, a Latin (secondary) school. The Puritans had a college to train ministers, Harvard in Cambridge, Massachusetts, as early as 1636.

THE EXPANSION OF NEW ENGLAND

The rapid growth of population in Massachusetts and Puritan insistence that everyone in the community conform to God's law as the elite defined it prompted the founding of Rhode Island, Connecticut, and New Hampshire within a few years of the founding of Massachusetts itself.

Troublesome Roger Williams

Rhode Island and Providence Plantations, still the long official name of the smallest state, was founded by a brilliant and cranky minister named Roger Williams. In Massachusetts in 1631, he quarreled with Governor John Winthrop (who admired him) and other overseers almost before he was tucked into in his new bed.

Williams was the strictest sort of Puritan, and his demanding conscience, as rigorous with himself as with others, led to his banishment from Massachusetts Bay. He agreed with mainstream Puritans that most people were damned, that only a few were saved. But just who were these

▲ *New England's pioneers did not live in log cabins. That durable American institution was introduced by Swedes and Finns living on the Delaware River. New Englanders built framed houses sided with clapboards like this home constructed in Dedham, Massachusetts, in 1637. Frame construction required a sawmill and skilled artisans, both of which the well-organized Puritans had from the start.*

elect? The establishment had highly refined procedures for determining who were "visible saints" and, therefore, which settlers were eligible for church membership (and the right to vote). Williams disagreed. Nobody, he said, could be sure of anyone's election but his own. To underscore his point, he said that he prayed with his wife but he did not know for certain if she was truly saved. Only she and God knew that.

Williams concluded that religion and government—church and state—should be entirely separate. If no one could know who was truly saved and who not, there must be no religious test, such as in Massachusetts, to determine the right to participate in civil affairs.

Because church members were a minority in Massachusetts, this teaching threatened the Winthrop group's control of the commonwealth, the very reason they had come to America. If the damned majority were to make laws to suit their unregenerate selves, the Lord's covenant would soon lay in tatters, and God would "surely break out in wrath" against the colony.

Rhode Island: "The Sewer of New England"

Williams also offended Massachusetts authorities by challenging the validity of the royal charter on which Puritan control of Massachusetts was legally based. The land had been occupied when the English arrived, Williams pointed out, and the Indians' right to it was as good as anyone's anywhere. The king of England could not give it away; it was not his to give. Only by purchasing land from the natives could settlers justly take possession of it. The charter was "a solemn public lie."

In fact, the Puritans usually paid the Indians for the land they settled, although their bargaining practices were not always saintly. Nevertheless, when Williams assailed the charter on which the Puritans based their control of Massachusetts, he touched the same tender nerve he had bruised in calling for the separation of church and state. By 1635, Winthrop and his party had had enough. Williams was ordered to return to England. Instead, he escaped into the forest, wintered with the Narragansett Indians, and in 1636, established a farm and township, Providence, on land purchased from that tribe.

If Roger Williams knew in his heart that the king of England had no right to give away Indian land, he was also a realist who knew how to play the political game. In 1644, he sailed to London where he secured a charter for his colony, Rhode Island. The Puritans of Massachusetts, staking so much on the sanctity of their own royal charter, would not dare violate Rhode Island's. Moreover, with Williams and his blasphemous followers dwelling outside the boundaries of Massachusetts, the worst Puritan fears were allayed: The Massachusetts Bay colony would not suffer for the doctrines Williams preached. In an ironic way, Rhode Island was indispensable to Massachusetts. It was a place to which they could banish the dissenters they found obnoxious. They called the colony the "sewer of New England."

Anne Hutchinson

In 1638, another dissenter was banished to the shores of Narragansett Bay. Like Williams, Anne Hutchinson was devout and a member of the elite. (She was John Winthrop's close neighbor.) Taking seriously the admonition that saints should study the word of God, she invited people into her home after Sunday services to discuss the sermon they had just heard. Hutchinson's own observations were often critical and sometimes acidic. When her informal meetings grew in popularity, they raised the hackles of preachers who were wounded by her sharp intelligence and formidable wit.

They shook their heads that a woman should dabble in subtle theology. "You have stept out of your place," Winthrop told Hutchinson. "You have rather bine a Husband than a Wife and a preacher than a Hearer." Her behavior was not "fitting" for her sex. In fact, the governor believed that women jeopardized their mental balance by pondering theological questions.

Still, had Hutchinson's offense been no greater than crowing, she might have gotten off with a scolding. She had influential supporters. But Hutchinson also taught that the Holy Spirit directly inspired some persons, such as herself, to speak out. This tenet, like Williams's, challenged Puritan control of Massachusetts. If the Holy Spirit spoke personally to some people, what they said was not "subject to controll of the rule of the Word or of the State." The doctrine was unacceptable. Puritans shuddered to contemplate—and they could imagine it—a society like our own in which anyone may say just about anything he or she wanted.

© Bettmann/Corbis

▲ *This representation of Anne Hutchinson being questioned in Boston by Governor Winthrop nicely captures the occasion. Records of the confrontation reveal that Hutchinson was confident, unyielding, and witty too. She several times bested Winthrop; but the governor had the power, and Hutchinson was banished.*

Known as antinomianism, Hutchinson's teaching pointed logically, like Williams's, to the separation of church and state. To make sure she was convicted, she was charged with 80 heresies and banished to Rhode Island. She later moved to New York, where, in 1643, she was killed by Indians.

New Hampshire and Connecticut

New Hampshire had been the proprietorship of one Sir Fernando Gorges, but he did nothing with it. The colony was populated beyond coastal Portsmouth only when disciples of Hutchinson, led by her brother-in-law, John Wheelwright, left Massachusetts in 1638. New Hampshire did not, however, have Rhode Island's reputation for eccentricity. Most of its settlers were conventional Puritans looking for land.

The richness of the bottomlands of the Connecticut River valley was the major draw of Connecticut. However, personality conflicts and religious bickering in Massachusetts also played a part. Fed up with Winthrop, Reverend Thomas Hooker and his followers moved there in 1636 and founded Hartford.

The migration so far inland caused a conflict with the Pequot Indians, the most powerful tribe of lower New England. In May 1637, after a Pequot raid on the Connecticut village of Wethersfield, the Massachusetts and Plymouth colonies sent a combined force that, by night, surrounded and set fire to the largest of the tribe's villages. As the Pequot fled the flames, the New Englanders shot and killed more than 400 of them, women and children as well as warriors. After a few smaller actions, the Pequot were for all practical purposes exterminated.

During the Pequot War, Theophilus Eaton and John Davenport, ministers concerned that Massachusetts was too soft on moral offenders, settled at New Haven on Long Island Sound. New Haven was the strictest of the Puritan commonwealths, and its strictures influenced Connecticut, into which New Haven was incorporated in 1662.

ROYAL AND PROPRIETARY COLONIES

Except for New Hampshire, the New England colonies were *corporate* colonies. Their constitutions, patterned on commercial charters of incorporation, provided for broad powers of self-government. Corporate colonies acknowledged the sovereignty of the king, but even this was little more than a symbolic gesture. In practice, the New England colonies were self-governing commonwealths responsible to those having the right to vote.

Virginia was such a corporate colony until 1624, when James I took it over. Then, as a *royal* colony, Virginia was ruled directly by the king through an appointed governor. Royal colonies had elected assemblies with extensive powers over the treasury, but the royal governor could veto any law these assemblies enacted. By the time of the American Revolution in 1776, 9 of the 13 colonies, including New Hampshire from its inception, were royal colonies.

Feudal Lords

Proprietary colonies had yet another structure of government. Ironically for a system that worked quite well in the New World, the principle underlying the proprietary system was antiquated, dating to the Middle Ages. Proprietors of colonies—wealthy gentlemen and nobles who won the king's favor—were, in effect, feudal lords of the American land granted to them. Their rights and privileges were defined as those held by the bishop of Durham in the Middle Ages. The bishop had been the king's vassal in the far north of England and was allowed greater independence than most nobles because he commanded the first line of defense against the Scots.

Moneymaking

Even the proprietors' method of making money was feudal, although, once again, it worked. Like the London Company and later the king in the royal colonies, proprietors encouraged people to settle on their lands by granting headrights: so many acres per head (the amount varied from colony to colony) to each person who came and for each person whose transportation a settler paid.

In return, landowners were required to pay the proprietor an annual "quitrent." This was not rent in our sense of the word. The settlers owned the land; they were not tenants. The quitrent principle dated from the time when the feudal system was breaking up in England (around 1300) and landowners commuted, or changed, their tenants' obligations to work for them into an annual cash payment. People who held land in "free and common socage" were "quit" of (released from) their old obligations, such as serving their lord as a soldier, shearing his sheep, repairing the castle moat, or whatever the lord of the land required.

Colonial quitrents were usually small: the idea was to get people to come to America, not to bleed them for doing so. For example, in Maryland for each acre owned in freehold (that is, owned outright), settlers paid an annual quitrent of two pence' worth of tobacco. The quitrent for 100 acres in New York was a bushel of wheat a year. In Georgia, the quitrent was two shillings per 50 acres.

Not much, but for the proprietor of a vast domain, thousands of such pittances added up to a handsome income, whereas the quitrents the proprietors owed the king were purely symbolic: two Indian arrowheads a year for Maryland, two beaver pelts a year for Pennsylvania.

Maryland: A Catholic Refuge—Briefly

Making money was a major motive of every proprietor, but the two grandest of the breed had other agendas as well. Maryland, chartered in 1631 and formally settled in 1634, was intended by its proprietors, George Calvert and his son Cecilius, the first and second Lords Baltimore, to be a refuge for English Catholics like themselves. The Calverts favored Catholics in making land grants, and they invited priests to the colony.

Catholics took the Calverts up on their offer, but they were a minority in Maryland from the start. By 1689, Catholics were just a quarter of the population. Because they were often the richest planters, Catholics were the targets of social

Courtesy of Enoch Pratt Free Library, Baltimore

▲ *Cecilius Calvert, second Lord Baltimore, was the actual founder of Maryland, although the idea of a refuge for English Roman Catholics like the Calverts originated with his father, George Calvert. Originally, the Calverts planned to found their sanctuary in Newfoundland, but two visits there persuaded them to look farther south.*

resentment as well as religious distaste. In 1649, Cecilius Calvert feared for their future and approved the Act of Toleration. It provided that "noe person or persons whatsoever within [Maryland] . . . professing to believe in Jesus Christ, shall from henceforth bee any waies troubled, Molested or discountenanced for or in respect of his or her religion."

It was not complete toleration: Jews were not welcome, as they were in Rhode Island and in the Dutch colony of New Amsterdam. Nevertheless, protecting Catholics as it did, the act was too much for Maryland's Protestant majority. They revolted in 1654 and repealed it, inflicting double taxation and other disabilities on Roman Catholics. In 1689, John Coode led a successful rebellion of Protestants, who, three years later, forbade Catholics to worship publicly. (Oddly, three of Coode's four closest associates were married to Catholics.)

Maryland's Catholics were too well established to be chased out. The colony remained a center of American Catholicism, and in 1808, the first Catholic bishop in the United States was seated in Baltimore.

Politically Correct Maryland

The contemporary university is not unique in forbidding the use of words that might offend someone. Lord Calvert's Act of Toleration called for whipping "Persons reproaching any other within the Province by the Name or Denomination of Heretic, Schismatic, Idolater, Puritan, Independent, Presbyterian, Popish Priest, Jesuit, Jesuited Papist, Lutheran, Calvinist, Anabaptist, Brownist, Antinomian, Barrowist, Round-Head, Separatist, or any other Name or Term, in a reproachful Manner, relating to matters of Religion."

New Netherland and New Sweden

In 1624, a Dutch trading company established New Netherland between the two English settlements of Virginia and Plymouth. The town of New Amsterdam, at the tip of Manhattan Island, defended what the Dutch hoped would be a prosperous farming and fur-trading colony strung along the Hudson River.

Curiously, because the Dutch were a progressive people at home, they tried to populate the Hudson valley by means of a bizarrely archaic plan. The company granted huge "patroonships," vast tracts of land with 18 miles of Hudson River frontage, to any worthy who settled 50 families—people to be beholden to their patroon—on their land. Only one patroonship succeeded, 700,000-acre Van Rensselaerwyck, south of Fort Orange (present-day Albany, New York).

As buyers of furs and deer hides from the Indians, the Dutch were successful, exporting more than 60,000 pelts during New Netherland's first year. Annually, hundreds of Dutch ships tied up at New Amsterdam or anchored in the best harbor (New York harbor) on the Atlantic seaboard. There were problems. Governor Willem Kieft, as incompetent an official who ever breathed American air, slaughtered peaceful Indians who had taken refuge with the Dutch. Several Algonkian tribes retaliated, with results as devastating as the Jamestown Massacre, reducing the population of the colony to 700.

The new governor, Peter Stuyvesant, peg-legged and cantankerous ("his head is troubled," people said, "he has a screw loose") brought the colony back to prosperity, increasing the European and African population to 6,000. Stuyvesant also expanded Dutch holdings. In 1655, ships from New Amsterdam sailed south to the Delaware River, where they took over New Sweden, a string of tiny riverfront settlements of Swedes and Finns. New Sweden had been founded in 1638 by Peter Minuit, a Dutchman who had also been the first director-general of New Netherland. It was Minuit who purchased Manhattan Island from the Manhattan Indians for the equivalent of $24.

New York: An English Conquest

Fair for the Dutch was fair for the English, and easy too, when, after 17 years, Stuyvesant had offended just about everyone in New Amsterdam. In 1664, a British fleet commanded by the Duke of York (the king's brother) threatened to bombard the city but also offered, if there was no resistance, to protect the Dutch language, Dutch religion, and Dutch inheritance laws, which differed significantly from England's. Stuyvesant wanted to fight; no one else did. Without a shot being fired, New Netherland became New York, and New Amsterdam became the city of New York.

New York was a proprietary colony until, in 1685, the Duke of York was crowned King James II, whereupon it was royalized. Unpopular at home because he was a Roman Catholic, the duke was well liked in his colony. Dutch men and women continued to come. Stuyvesant himself stayed and prospered. Tolerance and cosmopolitanism characterized life. There were blacks in the city from the beginning and a small Jewish community. A French Jesuit priest, Isaac Jogues, heard 18 languages on the streets. A Virginian observed that the inhabitants "seem not concerned what religion their neighbor is, or whether hee hath any or none."

The Quakers

In 1681, Charles II gave a large tract of land, including the present states of Pennsylvania and Delaware, and parts of New Jersey, to William Penn, the son of an admiral to whom the king owed £16,000. Unlike other proprietors, Penn was no conventional courtier. He was a member of a fringe religious sect, the Society of Friends, or, as they were called because they trembled with emotion at their religious services, "Quakers."

The Quakers were figures of scorn, amusement, and some anxiety. They worried authorities because they preached Christian pacifism. Friends were forbidden to take up arms, even in self-defense. Seventeenth-century armies were not made up of draftees, but pacifism was still a challenging doctrine in an age when war was unapologetically considered a normal state of affairs.

The Quakers also disturbed the establishment because they taught that every individual had the light of God within, a teaching similar to Anne Hutchinson's. They said that Christians had no need of priests, ministers, or bishops. Some Quakers challenged the legitimacy of civil authority and social class. When they were haled before magistrates, Quakers refused to remove their hats and to take oaths. Telling the truth was the individual's responsibility to God, they said, and none of the civil authority's business.

The Quakers dramatized their belief in the equality of all people before God by addressing everyone, including nobles and the king himself, in the familiar *thee, thy,* and *thou* forms of the second-person pronoun. This seems quaint today, and it amused Charles II. (He removed his hat when Penn appeared before him because, he said, when the king is present, it was customary that only one man wear a hat.) Nevertheless, for those with less humor than Charles, it was insulting to be called *thee* by a social inferior or even a stranger.

Sunday in Massachusetts

Early Sunday morning, before sunrise in winter, Puritan families bundled up and walked to the meetinghouse. Few skipped services, even during a blizzard. Absence was fined, and, if winter weather could be withering, the distance to be traveled was short. Most New Englanders lived in villages, their homes clustered together near the meetinghouse.

They went to a *meetinghouse,* not to a *church.* To call the simple, unpainted clapboard structure a church would have been "popish"; the Puritans shunned every emblem hinting of the Church of Rome. There were no statues or other decorations such as adorned Catholic and Anglican churches. The meetinghouse was a place of preaching and worship—period. A weathercock rather than a cross crowned the steeple. It reminded the congregation that St. Peter denied to the Romans that he knew Christ before the cock crowed three times. Sinfulness was a theme on which the Puritans constantly harped.

In winter, the meetinghouse was scarcely warmer than the snowy fields surrounding the village. There may have been a fireplace, but the heat had little effect on those sitting more than 10 feet from it. The congregation bundled in fur envelopes—*not* sleeping bags; there was a fine for nodding off! People rested their feet on brass or iron foot warmers that contained coals brought from home. In towns that prohibited the use of foot warmers (they were a fire hazard), worshipers brought a large, well-trained dog to lie on their feet.

In some meetinghouses, women sat on the left side with their daughters. Men sat on the right, but boys, apt to be mischievous, were placed around the pulpit, where a churchwarden could lash out at fidgety ones with a switch. He probably often had his work cut out for him, since the service went on and on, sermons running an hour and a half and sometimes three hours. And, lest anyone wonder how long the sermon was lasting, an hourglass sat conspicuously on the preacher's pulpit; when the sand ran down, the hourglass was turned by the man who kept watch over the boys.

Although the Puritans had no instrumental music in their meetinghouses, they sang psalms, using the *Bay Psalm Book.* It was written with accuracy of translation rather than poetry in mind. Psalms exquisitely beautiful in the King James Version of the Bible (which the Puritans shunned) were awkward and strained. For example, in the Puritan translation, the magnificent and touching Psalm 100 is barely comprehensible:

> The rivers on of Babylon, there when we did sit downe;
> Yes even then we mourned, when we remembered Sion.
> Our harp we did hang it amid upon the willow tree,
> Because there they thus away led in captivitie,
> Required of us a song, thus asks mirth; us waste who laid
> Sing us among a Sion's song unto us then they said.

Services ended about noon. Families returned home for a meal that had been prepared before sundown the previous day. Like observant Jews on the Sabbath, the Puritans took the Lord's Day seriously: no cooking, no work, and certainly no play. Even conversation was spare on Sunday. It was no more proper to talk about workaday tasks than to perform them. At most, a pious family discussed the morning's sermon and other religious subjects. In the afternoon, the family returned to the meetinghouse to hear secular announcements and another sermon and to sing a few more psalms.

Finally, believing that all were equal before God, Quaker women actively preached and testified. This affronted the popular feeling that women should play no role in public life, least of all in religious matters. It is not difficult to imagine Anne Hutchinson, had she survived, becoming a Quaker. In fact, one of her followers, Mary Dyer, was condemned to the gallows in Massachusetts for preaching Quaker doctrine.

Penn's "Holy Experiment"

William Penn was the Quakers' savior. Whereas most Quakers were lower class, he was an educated and wealthy gentleman. Penn used his prestige to moderate some of the Quakers' more extravagant practices, and he gave them a refuge. Like other colonial proprietors, he saw Pennsylvania

(which means "Penn's woods") as a way to make money (to which the Friends could think of no objection). But he also envisioned Pennsylvania as a "holy experiment" in toleration. All people who believed in "One Almighty and Eternal God" were welcome.

Pennsylvania thrived from the start. Pietists from the German Rhineland and from Switzerland, whose ideas resembled those of the Quakers, settled there in some numbers. They developed the fertile rolling land of southeastern Pennsylvania into model farms. Their descendants survive as the Pennsylvania Dutch, observing seventeenth-century customs.

Along with Charleston, South Carolina, Philadelphia was a planned city. The streets of the "greene countrie towne" were laid out on a gridiron, making possible a tidiness that even the well-ordered Puritans had been unable to command of Boston. Philadelphia became the largest and most prosperous city in English North America, at least in part because of Quaker liberality. By the mid-1700s, it was "the second city of the British empire," smaller only than London in the English-speaking world.

New Jersey and Delaware developed separately as proprietary colonies. However, they too were heavily populated by Quakers and practiced many of the same policies as Pennsylvania.

The Carolinas: A Feudal Experiment

The proprietor of the Carolina Grant of 1663 (named after King Charles II, *Carolus* in Latin) was a consortium of eight gentlemen and nobles. In 1669, they attempted to enforce on their grant a social structure more fantastic than the patroonship plan for New Netherland. The scheme was outlined in The Fundamental Constitutions of Carolina, the brainchild of Anthony Ashley Cooper, one of the most active of the proprietors. Its 120 detailed articles were written by his secretary, the political philosopher John Locke, whose primary place in history is as a defender of principles of political liberty. In the Fundamental Constitutions, curiously, Locke created a rigidly structured social blueprint.

Carolina was divided into square counties, in each of which the proprietors ("seigneurs") owned 96,000 acres. Other contrived ranks of nobility called "caciques" (an Indian title) and "landgraves" (European) would have smaller but still large tracts. The work would be done by humble "leetmen" and even humbler African slaves, over whom their owners were guaranteed "absolute power and authority."

Some historians think that this fantastic system was simply a promotional device designed to excite English land buyers with the promise of puffed-up titles. Certainly it was unworkable. A city might be laid out in squares, but not a country shaped by rivers, creeks, hills, swamps, and mountains. The mere abundance of land meant that development would be free and open, not a subject of strict regulation. Although the Fundamental Constitutions technically survived for decades, they did not much affect the actual development of the Carolinas.

Two Carolinas

Geography shaped the colony. Differing environments in the northern and southern parts of Carolina determined that settlements there would develop in significantly different ways.

In the north, most settlers were small farmers who drifted down from Virginia and planted tobacco, as they had done at home. Centered on Albemarle Sound, northern Carolina was poor, rather democratic in mood, and independent. It was quite isolated even from Virginia by the Great Dismal Swamp. In 1677, a Virginian named John Culpeper led a rebellion in northern Carolina that briefly defied all outside authority.

In the southern part of the grant, settlers from Barbados (an English sugar-growing island) founded Charleston where the Ashley and Cooper Rivers flowed into the Atlantic. At first, southern Carolina was a trading colony, tapping the interior as far inland as present-day Alabama for furs and hides, and converting the surrounding pine forests into timber and naval stores. By 1700, however, the outline of a plantation system had taken shape.

Probably from African slaves, the planters learned how to grow rice, a lucrative export crop. The easily flooded lowlands along the rivers were ideally suited to its cultivation. Long-staple cotton, used in manufacturing fine textiles, found favorable conditions on the sandy sea islands that fringed the coast. Indigo, a plant that produced a coveted blue dye, was later added to the list of Carolina products that were sold profitably abroad. Indigo was invaluable because it was cultivated and harvested when rice was not in season, thus keeping laborers busy year-round.

All of southern Carolina's crops lent themselves to being worked on large plantations by gangs. By 1700, half of the 5,000 people in the colony were slaves. This was by far the highest proportion of Africans in the population of any mainland colony.

The slaves' owners dominated southern Carolina society to an extent that even the tobacco grandees of Virginia might have envied. The low country that produced their wealth was unhealthy, "in the spring a paradise, in the summer a hell, and in the autumn a hospital." It was actually more like a morgue, thanks to mosquito-borne diseases (malaria, yellow fever) and plague levels of other killers, particularly dysentery. The small elite took to keeping town houses in Charleston, which was open to sea breezes. There they spent at least the summer and fall and, increasingly with the years, the better part of the year.

The result was, at the top, an urban and cosmopolitan society obnoxious to the small farmers of northern Carolina. In 1712, in a recognition of differing social bases rare in the eighteenth century, the proprietors granted the two Carolinas separate assemblies and governors. When they sold their holdings to the king in 1729, he confirmed them as distinct royal colonies: North Carolina and South Carolina.

Georgia: A Philanthropic Experiment

Georgia was the last of the 13 colonies to be founded. It was chartered in 1732, with Savannah established the next year. The Crown wanted a military buffer state protecting valuable South Carolina from the Spanish in Florida. Although Spain had recognized England's right to its colonies in 1676, 10 years later, an armed force destroyed a small English settlement on the Florida side of the boundary. During an English–Spanish war between 1702 and 1713, Charleston was threatened.

In Colonel James Oglethorpe, Parliament found the perfect man to develop a fortress colony. Oglethorpe was an experienced soldier. He was also a philanthropist who was troubled by the misery of the English poor, particularly jailed debtors. At the time (and for a century in America too), a person could be imprisoned for debt and not released until his obligation was paid. Oglethorpe conceived of Georgia (named for the king) as a place to which such unfortunates might go to begin anew.

He and his associates received the colony as a "trust." That is, they were not to profit from the colony, as proprietors did. Landholdings were to be small, only 50 acres, both to discourage speculators and to encourage the formation of a compact, easily mobilized defense force. Slavery was forbidden. Oglethorpe did not want to see the emergence of a slave-owning elite such as dominated South Carolina. He also prohibited alcohol, believing drunkenness to be a major cause of crime and poverty.

As a buffer state, Georgia was successful. In 1742, a Spanish flotilla of 36 ships transported 2,000 soldiers from Cuba to capture Savannah. Oglethorpe could raise only 900 men. But they defeated the Spanish in several skirmishes on St. Simons Island, and the Spanish withdrew. Oglethorpe then destroyed a fortified Spanish town north of St. Augustine.

As a philanthropic enterprise, Georgia was a failure. The trustees sent about 1,800 debtors and paupers to Georgia. Another 1,000 came on their own. Among them were South Carolinians who brought slaves with them. Although Oglethorpe was inclined to be a tyrant, he was unable to enforce the ban on slavery (or on rum). He returned to England disgusted. In 1752, the trustees returned control of the colony to the king, one year earlier than their charter required.

Other English Colonies

With the founding of Georgia, the 13 colonies that were to become the United States were marked on the maps of North America and recorded in the books of the Board of Trade, the agency that administered the colonies for the Crown. It should be noted, however, that England was active elsewhere in the Western Hemisphere. In fact, several English possessions still tied to Great Britain are older than most of the colonies that became part of the United States.

Belize, in Central America, dates from the early 1600s, although, as a haven of pirates, it was hardly an official colony. Bermuda, east of Georgia, was settled in 1609 when a ship bound for Virginia was wrecked there (the inspiration of William Shakespeare's play *The Tempest*). Tobago, a tiny island off the coast of Venezuela, was seized by English adventurers in 1616, four years before Plymouth was founded. Nearby Barbados, where many early South Carolinians originated and through which many of the ancestors of African Americans passed, dates from 1627. Local tradition insists that English settlement in Barbados dates from 1605, two years before Jamestown.

In 1621, Sir William Alexander received a charter to found English colonies in Acadia, present-day Nova Scotia. However, the French controlled most of that rugged land until 1713. In 1655, an English fleet under Admiral William Penn, the father of the founder of Pennsylvania, seized Jamaica from Spain. Several continuously occupied trading posts on Hudson Bay, which was claimed for England by a Dutch navigator, Henry Hudson, were planted in the 1670s. The Bahamas, where Columbus first saw the New World, have been British since about the late seventeenth century.

Tropical islands where sugar cane grew were the most lucrative colonies from the Crown's point of view. To ordinary folk interested in actually settling in the New World, the 13 mainland colonies beckoned more seductively. There, society was remarkably free, and those colonies offered the greatest economic opportunities in the world.

for FURTHER READING

See the appropriate chapters of Charles M. Andrews, *The Colonial Period of American History*, 1934–1938; Curtis E. Nettels, *The Roots of American Civilization*, 1938; Daniel Boorstin, *The Americans: The Colonial Experience*, 1958; Clarence Ver Steeg, *The Formative Years*, 1964; John E. Pomfret with Floyd Shumway, *Founding the American Colonies*, 1970; and Jack P. Greene and J. R. Pole, eds., *Colonial British America*, 1984.

Plymouth colony is one of those rare subjects about which the first book to read is the first that was written: Governor William Bradford's *History of Plimmoth Plantation* (numerous editions). Also see George Langdon, *Pilgrim Colony: A History of New Plymouth, 1620–1691*, 1966.

On Massachusetts Bay, the classic, highly critical of the Puritans, is James Truslow Adams, *The Founding of New England*, 1930. Subsequent appreciation of the Puritans owes largely to the work of two historians, Perry Miller and Edmund S. Morgan. See the following by Perry Miller: *The New England Mind*, 1939, 1953; and *Errand into the Wilderness*, 1964. See these books by Edmund S. Morgan: *Visible Saints*, 1963; *The Puritan Dilemma: The Story of John Winthrop*, 1958; and *The Puritan Family*, 1966. Also see Roger Williams, *The Church and the State*, 1967.

On Anne Hutchinson, see Emery Battis, *Saints and Sectarians: Anne Hutchinson and the Antinomian Controversy in Massachusetts*, 1962. On Rhode Island, see Sydney V. James, *Colonial Rhode Island: A History*, 1975.

In the 1970s, special studies of Puritan society and culture were numerous, and many are of the highest quality. The following are a brief sampling: Sacvan Bercovitch, *The American Jeremiad*, 1978; Andrew Delbanco, *The Puritan Ordeal*, 1989; John Demos, *A Little Commonwealth: Family Life in Plymouth Colony*, 1970; Philip Greven Jr., *Four Generations: Population, Land, and Family in Colonial Andover*, 1970; Kenneth Lockridge, *A New England Town*, 1971; Samuel Powell, *Puritan Village*, 1963; David Stannard, *The Puritan Way of Death*, 1977; Michael Walzer, *The Revolution of the Saints*, 1965; and Larzer Ziff, *Puritanism in Old and New England*, 1973.

For Pennsylvania, see Edwin B. Bronner, *William Penn's "Holy Experiment,"* 1962; Gary Nash, *Quakers and Politics: Pennsylvania, 1681–1726*, 1971; and James T. Lemon, *The Best Poor Man's Country: A Geographical Study of Early Southeastern Pennsylvania*, 1972. On New Netherland/New York, see Michael Kammen, *Colonial New York*, 1975; Robert C. Ritchie, *The Duke's Province*, 1977; and the appropriate chapters of the superb book by Edwin G. Burrows and Mike Wallace, *Gotham: A History of New York City to 1898*, 1999. On New Jersey, see J. E. Pomfret, *The Province of East and West New Jersey*, 1956.

For the later southern colonies, see William S. Powell, *Colonial North Carolina*, 1973; Eugene Sirmans, *Colonial South Carolina*, 1966; and Phinizy Spalding, *Oglethorpe in America*, 1977.

Visit the source collections at http://ajaccess.wadsworth.com and http://infotrac.thomsonlearning.com, and use the Search function with the following key terms to explore documents, images, audio and video clips, articles, and commentary related to the material in this chapter:

Anne Bradstreet
Anne Hutchinson
John Locke
Massachusetts Bay colony
Plymouth colony
Puritans
William Penn

Additional resources, exercises, and Internet links related to this chapter are available on *The American Past* Web site:
http://history.wadsworth.com/americanpast7e.

HISTORY ONLINE

Religion in Colonial America
http://lcweb.loc.gov/exhibits/religion/rel01.html
Broad sampling of information about the place of religion in the colonies.

Colonial Slavery
http://cghas.dade.K12.A.us/slavery/british_america/default.htm
Aspects of slavery unique to colonial America.

ENGLISH LEGACIES, AMERICAN FACTS OF LIFE

Colonial Society in the 1600s

Reproduced from the Collections of the Library of Congress

And those that came were resolved to be Englishmen,
Gone to the world's end but English every one,
And they ate the white corn kernels parched in the sun
And they knew it not but they'd not be English again.

Stephen Vincent Benét

THE BRITISH LIKED to say that they created their empire in a fit of absentmindedness. There is a bit of truth in that. The Crown's approval, in the form of a charter, was essential if a colony was to be legal. However, neither king nor Parliament took an active part in establishing a single American dominion. Every colony was financed and promoted in what we would call the "private sector," while the Crown generally failed to notice what was going on.

The colonial entrepreneurs were investors or courtiers hoping to make money, religious dissenters seeking sanctuary, and visionaries with images of a better society dancing in their heads. So casual was the Crown concerning its American real estate—in the law, it all began as royal property—that many colonial boundaries were vague and overlapping, breezy strokes of a goose-quill pen on maps in London that caused endless bickering on the actual ground.

Absentmindedly or not, the empire grew. By 1702, when Queen Anne was crowned, 300,000 of her subjects made their homes in English—soon to be British—North America, which stretched, however thinly in many spots, a thousand miles north to south, from above Portsmouth, New Hampshire, to Charleston, South Carolina.

TRADE LAWS

Parliament first tried to frame a coherent colonial policy during the 1650s, when there was no king. Parliament had beheaded Charles I and now (along with a military dictator, Oliver Cromwell) ruled England. When monarchy returned with Charles II in 1660, the colonial policy Parliament had established, the Navigation Acts, was confirmed, and the Crown created a committee (later known as the Board of Trade) to advise the king on colonial affairs. As the board's name indicates, colonial commerce was what interested the English. Charles II said it in 1668: "The thing that is nearest the heart of the nation is trade."

▲ *Ships carrying goods to the colonies and returning with colonial exports tied up at wharves like this one in London, or in other English ports such as Bristol and Plymouth.*

Mercantilism

The economic philosophy that underlay England's trade policy is known as mercantilism. Its principles were first systematized in 1630 in Thomas Mun's *England's Treasure by Foreign Trade,* although the English, French, Dutch, and even the Spanish unsuccessfully had acted in mercantilistic ways for a century.

The object of mercantilism was to increase a nation's wealth in gold and silver—the wealth of all the realm's subjects, not just the royal treasury. The key to doing this was a favorable balance of trade. That is, the people of the nation must sell goods and services abroad that were more costly than the goods and services that they imported from other countries.

Thus the word *mercantilism,* because overseas merchants (*mercator* is Latin for "merchant") were of special value in this philosophy. If a ship out of Bristol carried a cargo of Dutch cloth to the Spanish colony of Cuba and Cuban sugar back to France, the coin he charged the shippers for his services enriched England at the expense of three rival nations. Mercantilist policy was, therefore, to encourage England's merchants in their business in every way possible.

Manufacturing was also dear to the mercantilist heart. Long before 1600, the English learned that it was economic lunacy to send raw wool to Flanders and the Netherlands, as they did, and then to buy it back in the form of cloth. The manufactured cloth cost considerably more than the wool from which it was spun and woven. The difference was coin

drained out of England. The Crown, therefore, forbade the export of raw wool and, through subsidies and other favors, encouraged the carders, spinners, dyers, and weavers whose skills and labor added value to the sheep's fleece. Mercantilists urged the Crown to favor all manufacturers with such protections and inducements.

The Colonial Connection

In the best of all possible mercantilistic worlds, England would be totally self-sufficient. The nation would produce everything its people needed and buy nothing abroad. Gold and silver earned from exports and the carrying trade would roll in; none would depart.

In the real world, self-sufficiency was out of the question. An island nation in a northerly latitude, England imported any number of tropical products. The English people produced little wine but drank a good deal of it: Wine was imported from France, Portugal, and the Rhineland. England consumed large quantities of furs for the manufacture of clothing and felt. These came from Muscovy, as Russia was known. As a maritime nation, England needed timber and naval stores (tar, pitch, fiber for rope) in quantities far beyond the productive capacity of the country's depleted forests. Forest products had to be imported from Scandinavia.

In practice, then, the object of mercantilism was to minimize imports, which cost money, and maximize exports and trade, which brought money in. It was at this point that mercantilists became promoters of colonies.

Colonies reduced England's dependence on foreign countries. The forests of North America, seemingly limitless and teeming with beaver, mink, and other fur-bearing animals, meant that England could reduce the flow of gold and silver to Scandinavia and Russia. By occupying islands in the West Indies, the English produced their own sugar and stopped paying Spaniards for it. And by settling dutiful subjects overseas, the Crown created exclusive and dependable markets for English manufacturers. The colonists themselves had to scare up the coin with which to purchase these goods as best they could.

The Navigation Acts

The Navigation Acts of 1660–1663 wrote mercantilism into law. They minced no words in defining the purpose of the American colonies as the enrichment of the mother country. The prosperity of the colonies was a consideration and received attention. However, when the economic interests of colonials clashed with those of the mother country, the latter were what counted. Colonies were tributaries, not partners.

So the Navigation Acts stipulated that all colonial trade be carried in vessels built and owned by English or colonial merchants. These ships were to be manned by crews in which at least three seamen in four were English or colonials. Not even niggardly seamen's wages were to be paid to foreigners, who might take their earnings home with them.

Next, the Navigation Acts required that European goods intended for sale in the colonies be carried first to certain English ports called "entrepôts" (places from which goods are distributed). There they were to be monitored and only then shipped to America. The purpose of this law was to ensure a precise record of colonial trade, to collect taxes on it, and to see to it that English merchants and port laborers benefited from every colonial transaction.

Important and lucrative trade goods fell under this provision. Wealthy colonists had a taste for French claret and the sweet, fortified wines of Spain and Portugal. But they could not import them directly from the source. First, the bottles and casks had to pass through one of the entrepôts in England. Of course, this raised the cost of drinking, but that was the idea. The premium colonials paid for their wines went into English purses.

The Navigation Acts also designated some colonial exports as "enumerated articles." These could be shipped only to English ports, even if they were destined for sale on the continent of Europe. Once again, the object was to guarantee that part of the profit in colonial trade went to English merchants. Moreover, taxes on the enumerated articles were an important source of government revenue. Charles II collected £100,000 a year from the tax on tobacco alone.

The enumerated articles included most colonial products that were readily sold on the world market: molasses, furs and hides, naval stores, rice, cotton, and tobacco. Foodstuffs (grain, livestock, salted fish), and lumber not suited to shipbuilding, were less profitable and not enumerated. Colonials could ship them directly to foreign ports.

MERCANTILISM IN THE SOUTH

The Navigation Acts applied to all colonies. However, the diverse topographies, climates, and social structures of England's far-flung provinces meant that they affected colonials in sharply differing ways.

Well before 1700, the English and American colonials thought in terms of the New England colonies, the Middle Colonies, and the South. New England was New Hampshire, Massachusetts, Rhode Island, and Connecticut. (Maine was a part of Massachusetts; Vermont was Indian territory.) To the south and west lay the Middle Colonies: New York, New Jersey, Pennsylvania, and Delaware. The South included Maryland, Virginia, North Carolina, South Carolina, and, after 1732, Georgia. (Florida was Spanish territory.)

With good reason, English merchants smiled when they thought of the southern colonies. The southern colonies produced tobacco—the most profitable of all the enumerated articles except the sugar that came from the islands of the West Indies. Like the West Indies, the southern colonies were home to a large, bonded labor force of white servants and black slaves for whom cheap clothing, shoes, and tools had to be purchased in England. By 1700, an increasingly rich and extravagant master class, living off the labor of these workers,

The Tobacco God
When Edward Seymour was asked to support the creation of a college in Virginia because the ministers trained there would save souls, he replied, "Souls! Damn your souls! Make tobacco!"

had emerged—an upper class that coveted every luxury any merchant ever thought to load on a sailing ship.

Tobacco: Blessing and Curse

The colonies had a monopoly on tobacco production in the empire. English farmers were forbidden to grow it, a rare instance of a colonial economic privilege. By the 1660s, however, Maryland's and Virginia's advantage was not enough to ensure prosperity. The wholesale price of a pound of tobacco (the price at which the planters sold) collapsed from two pence and a halfpenny to a halfpenny. So much land had been planted in tobacco that the markets for it no longer absorbed production.

To planters, the solution to the problem of falling prices was obvious. The Dutch reached markets the English did not; but because the Navigation Acts forbade the sale of an "enumerated article" to England's chief commercial rival, Dutch buyers were banned from the colonies. Planters complained: "If the Hollanders must not trade to Virginia, how shall the planters dispose of their tobacco? . . . The tobacco will not vend in England, the Hollanders will not fetch it from England. What must become thereof?"

One thing that became thereof was evasion of the Navigation Acts. Smuggling was common and not at all unrespectable. Dutch traders arriving at wharves in Virginia and Maryland did not have to listen to many lectures about English trade law. They had little difficulty persuading planters to sell them tobacco. Such defiance of the Navigation Acts was not difficult, thanks to the topography of the Chesapeake region.

The Tidewater

The Chesapeake is a huge estuary fed by innumerable smaller ones. Along with countless briny creeks and inlets, the rivers that empty into the great bay—the Potomac, the Rappahannock, the James, the Choptank—are broad, slow-moving streams. They were deep enough for the small seagoing vessels of the seventeenth and eighteenth centuries to sail as many miles inland as high tide pushed salt water. The ships—legal and illegal—might careen in river mire when the tide ebbed, but twice a day, the sea dependably returned to float them and their cargoes back to Europe.

The land washed by this salt water, a series of peninsulas called "necks," was known as the Tidewater. It was the first part of the tobacco colonies to be settled, and it became home to an elite that dominated Virginia and Maryland society.

▲ *A tobacco factor (buyer) and planter negotiating the sale of a tobacco crop at the planter's wharf. Tobacco was packed in hogsheads, huge barrels, as most goods transported by ship were. Barrels could be easily rolled, they were watertight, and, properly stacked on their sides, they did not shift in rough seas.*

Although their descendants did not like to admit it, few Tidewater aristocrats were aristocratic when they settled in America. English men and women of high station did not emigrate to a land where the life expectancy was 40 years. Nor, however, were most Tidewater aristocrats descended from the dregs of English society: convicts, beggars, destitute farm laborers. Most of the men and women of the "first families of Virginia" were from the artisan, petty merchant, or yeoman class—the middling sort. They brought enough capital with them to develop plantations, but social pretensions were possible only because of the tobacco boom.

Depression at the End of the World

The chances of going from rags to riches in the tobacco colonies dwindled in the later 1600s. Indeed, making a decent living became a struggle for all but the planters with vast acreage. The collapse in the price of tobacco bankrupted hundreds of small farmers so that larger planters who, like the rich in all times and places, were less vulnerable to the downturn, picked up small holdings in the Tidewater and enhanced their dominance.

After 1660, even ambitious immigrants to Virginia were forced to trek to build an estate. There in the Piedmont, or foothills of the Appalachians, they found hundreds of hardscrabble frontiersmen. Some had been dispossessed in the Tidewater. Others were freed servants without land: unmarried, boisterous young men who got along by hunting, trapping, doing casual work for wages, and less savory things.

In 1676, differences between these Piedmonters and the Tidewater planters erupted in a miniature civil war, ragtag and improvised, but plenty nasty.

East-West Conflict

The royal governor of Virginia in 1676 was Sir William Berkeley. In the colony for more than 30 years—a long time for an English gentleman—he had done quite well for himself. Berkeley was a major landowner, the doyen of Jamestown society, and the political leader of the Tidewater planters.

Berkeley and his friends supplemented their income from tobacco by carrying on a prosperous trade with the Indians. In return for furs and buckskins, they provided manufactured goods, especially woven blankets, iron products ranging from pots to traps and guns, and rum, the cheapest alcohol available. When the bottom dropped out of tobacco prices in the 1660s, this business loomed larger in their accounts. It also provided the Berkeley group with a reason to cultivate a good working relationship with the tribes that supplied the hides and furs.

Settlers in the Piedmont, by contrast, looked on Indians as enemies. As the whites expanded their fields, they encroached on the hunting grounds of the Susquehannock and other peoples, including tribes that had already been forced off their ancestral lands in the Tidewater. Inevitably, there were clashes. The Indians complained to Berkeley of white interlopers. The settlers of the Piedmont complained of hit-and-run raids on their farms. Berkeley and his associates,

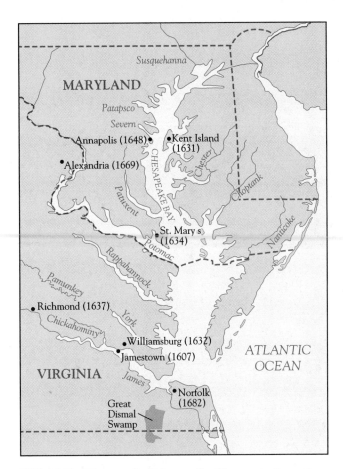

MAP 4:1 The Chesapeake Estuary The Chesapeake Bay region is a land of water. Even seagoing ships could penetrate far up its innumerable tidal rivers and creeks. When Virginians and Marylanders traveled locally, they went by boat. Most important, with the entire early plantation area accessible to ships, there was no need for towns, let alone cities, that were commercial centers.

with the white Virginians against the Susquehannock, who raided them too! No matter—they were Indians. Bacon crushed them and then turned his "army" toward the colonial capital of Jamestown.

Angry words led the governor to arrest Bacon as a rebel, but he was forced to release him when Bacon's supporters made it clear they were quite capable of laying the little town waste. After a spell of uneasy stalemate between the Tidewater and the Piedmont, Bacon returned to Jamestown and blustered that he would hang the governor. Berkeley took him seriously; he fled across the Chesapeake. For several months, Nathaniel Bacon and his frontiersmen governed the colony nearly as extensively as the royal governor and his council had.

We do not know how the Crown would have dealt with the touchy situation. In October 1676, at age 29, Nathaniel Bacon fell ill and died. He must have been a compelling man. With him gone, the rebels lost heart and scattered into the forests. Berkeley returned, rounded up several dozen of the rebels, and hanged them. But the governor was finished too. Charles II was disgusted by Berkeley's vindictiveness, remarking, "The old fool has hanged more men in that naked country than I have done for the murder of my father." Berkeley was recalled to England, where he died within a few months.

The suspicion and ill feeling between the Tidewater and the Piedmont did not die. The Tidewater aristocracy continued to dominate Virginia's economy, government, and culture, and the people of the backcountry continued to resent them.

A Land Without Cities

The great planters' domination of Virginia and Maryland was so thoroughgoing because, in politics, there was no other social group able to compete with them. There was no urban middle class of merchants, bankers, and manufacturers in Virginia and Maryland because there were no centers of commerce, no real cities.

One Marylander attributed this curiosity to the appetite for tobacco lands. "Tobacco," he wrote, "requires us to abhor communities or townships. . . . A planter cannot carry on his affairs without considerable elbow room." Moreover, because the Potomac, James, York, Nanticoke, and Choptank Rivers were navigable so far inland, ships tied up at the private wharves of the great Tidewater plantations. They did not need a central port, a Philadelphia or New York, in which to drop anchor. The planters sold their crop and received the goods that they had ordered the previous year, in their own backyards. Small farmers whose lands did not front on water depended on the great planters' facilities for their trading.

They were exhilarating days in the naked land when the merchantmen arrived. Servants and slaves rolled hogsheads (large barrels) of tobacco to the dock, enjoying the hospitality of the master, which was expansive. Farmers, backcountry planters and their families, and Indians gathered to dance, drink, race on foot and horseback, and shoot targets. For women, who lived a more isolated life than the menfolk, the arrival of a tobacco factor (agent) was a rare opportunity to enjoy company.

their trading and political interests caught in the middle, tried to resolve the conflict by building a system of defensive stockades along the line of white settlement.

The plan did not win over the Piedmont whites. The forts were so far apart that Indian marauders, especially the aggressive Susquehannock, easily slipped between them, wreaked havoc, and retreated. More important, like frontier settlers for two centuries to come, Virginia's backcountry pioneers did not think in terms of holding a line against the Indians. Ever increasing in numbers, they were expansive. They meant to clear the land of the natives, not to share it with them.

Bacon's Rebellion

When the death toll of backcountry whites climbed to more than a hundred, and kidnappings of women and children increased, the Piedmont planters took matters into their own hands. Nathaniel Bacon, a recent immigrant of some means, set himself up as the commander of a force that decimated the Oconeechee tribe. The Oconeechee had not attacked whites; indeed, they had expressed interest in an alliance

▲ *The artist's sympathies in depicting the confrontation between Nathaniel Bacon and Virginia governor Berkeley are not disguised. Bacon is a forthright, handsome cavalier. A pathetic Berkeley is intimidated and cowering. By no means was this opinion of Bacon's Rebellion universal.*

Everyone discussed the news that the shipmasters brought with them about European battles and the machinations of the kings they had left behind. Some received letters from old-country family, friends, and associates. The sailors enlivened the carnival with their giddiness at being ashore after weeks at sea, spending their wages on games and drink and the favors of women.

A People Who Lived on Imports

Central to the headiness of the occasion was the arrival of the manufactured goods on which the colonists depended in order to live in something resembling European style. A single ship might be loaded with spades, shovels, axes, and saws; household items such as kettles, pots, pans, sieves, funnels, pewter tankards, and tableware; odds and ends such as buttons, needles, thread, pins, and ribbons. There were textiles for both the planter families' fine clothing and rough wraps for servants and slaves; shoes and boots; bricks, nails, and paint; goods to trade with the Indians (all of the above plus trinkets, mirrors, and the like); and firearms, shot, and gunpowder. For the very wealthy few, there were luxuries: silver candlesticks, chests and other fine furniture, wine, brandy, spices, books, and even violins and harpsichords with which to grace a parlor and cheer an evening.

Business that was carried out in cities elsewhere in the world, including the northern colonies and Charleston, was transacted at the great plantations of Maryland and Virginia for a few weeks each year. When the ships departed for London, Plymouth, or Bristol, not only did they bring tobacco; they also became Virginia's and Maryland's banks and factory outlets. The commercial middle class of the tobacco colonies lived across the Atlantic. Virginia's and Maryland's shops were afloat.

Even the capitals of the tobacco colonies, Jamestown (Williamsburg after 1699) and Annapolis, were ghost towns when the assemblies were not in session. County seats were mere clusters of buildings at the crossings of trails, nothing more, and nothing at all when court was not in session and there was not an election. Small farmers lived isolated by forest from one another. Churches were few and scattered; public houses—inns and taverns—fewer. Travelers depended on an invitation to a private home, humble or grand, for dinner and shelter from the night.

A Life of Some Elegance

By the end of the seventeenth century, the great planters of Virginia and Maryland were creating a gracious style of life patterned after that of the English country gentry. They copied as best they were able the manners, fashions, and quirks of English squires and their ladies. When tobacco was returning a good price, they built fine houses in the style of English manors and filled them with good furniture. They stocked their cellars with port and Madeira, hock from the Rhineland, and claret from France, which they generously poured for one another at dinners, parties, balls, and simple visits that marked the origins of the famous "southern hospitality."

Finding the Way

Sailors in the African or Asian trade often found their way by the ancient expedient of keeping the coastline in sight. They sailed like the pilot of a small airplane flies, by following landmarks. Deepwater seamen—transatlantic sailors—depended on the compass, the prototype of which Europeans had received from the East in ancient times, and on the astrolabe.

By the seventeenth century, the ship's compass was a brass bowl marked with 32 directions, in the center of which a magnetized needle was delicately balanced. It was positioned within sight of the helmsman and mounted on pivots so that it remained level when the vessel pitched and rolled.

The compass, invented in China, was made into a navigational instrument in medieval Italy. The astrolabe, perfected in Portugal in the 1400s, enabled navigators to measure the angle between the horizon and the sun by day and between the North Star (or below the equator, the Southern Cross) by night. With this information, shipmasters could determine their latitude, that is, the distance of their position from the equator. With an astrolabe, a sailor knew on which east-west line his ship was sailing.

So an English captain seeking to make a landfall at Cape Cod, which he knew was located at about 42 degrees north latitude, sailed in a southerly direction out of England until his ship arrived at 42 degrees. Then, using his compass, he sailed due west. It was simple to the extent winds and currents were cooperative.

What sailors could not determine with any accuracy was longitude—their position on the imaginary arcs that run north-south from pole to pole. On an east-west voyage such as across the Atlantic between the colonies and the mother country, navigators had only an approximate idea of how far they had sailed from their port of departure and, therefore, how far they were from their destination.

There were rude instruments for determining speed, which is what longitude is on an east-west voyage. The log line was a rope knotted every 48 feet with a wood float tied to the end. It was thrown overboard and, measuring minutes with a sandglass, the captain counted the number of knots that passed over the stern in a given period of time. Since the log was not blown as the ship was, the speed of the wind could be roughly ascertained. However, the log line did not take account of the action of ocean currents, which could radically increase or decrease a ship's progress—the log was in the grip of the current just as the ship was.

Not until the mid–eighteenth century was the problem of determining longitude systematically attacked. In 1752, a German astronomer, Tobias Mayer, devised a set of tables and a mathematical formula for determining longitude from the position of the moon, but the method was not practical. Even a skilled mathematician needed four hours to complete the calculation required. In 1767, the Royal Observatory at Greenwich, England (which was to become zero degrees longitude worldwide), issued the *Mariner's Almanac,* a volume of tables that somewhat abbreviated the calculations.

But not until Larcum Kendall invented the chronometer, a highly accurate clock, was longitude mastered. Set to Greenwich mean time at the beginning of a voyage, the chronometer enabled a navigator to know what time it was in Greenwich wherever he was in the world, to compare that with the time aboard his ship (determined from the position of the sun), and thus to establish his position on the globe.

Some Tidewater families educated their sons at Oxford, Cambridge, or the Inns of Court (the law schools of England). Or if they feared the effects of English miasmas on innocent American bodies (smallpox, a deadly scourge in Europe, did not spread so easily in rural America), they schooled their heirs at the College of William and Mary, founded at Williamsburg in 1693.

The grandeur of the great planters' social and cultural life must not be overblown. William Byrd of Westover (one of the richest of them—he owned 179,000 acres when he died in 1744) was well educated and cultured: He preferred living in London. When his first wife, Lucy Park, died, Byrd sailed to England to find the daughter of a wealthy nobleman to replace her. When he found her and proposed, the bride he chose had an annual income equal to Byrd's entire fortune. The lady's father, quite naturally, rejected Byrd as too poor for her. William Byrd looks like a duke in a portrait he commissioned in London. The fact was, even the richest of tobacco planters was a poor relation among the English upper classes.

A Habit of Debt

Like many poor relations with pretensions, the planters were constantly in debt. When the profits from tobacco dropped, Virginians and Marylanders found it difficult to break the pleasant habits of consumption. They continued to order luxuries from England. To pay for them, they mortgaged future crops—at a discount, of course—to the merchants who were to deliver their goods. It was not unusual that, by the time the tobacco went into the ground in spring, the imports it was to pay for had already been purchased and, in the case of wine, consumed.

Planter debt gratified mercantilists. It meant yet more money in the form of interest and discounts flowing from colony to mother country. In time, chronic indebtedness would make anti-British rebels of practically the entire Tidewater aristocracy.

South Carolina

The social structure of South Carolina—with its small, wealthy elite, a struggling class of small farmers, and masses of bonded laborers—was similar to that of Virginia and Maryland. The rhythms of life in South Carolina were, however, quite different. The cash crops there were rice and, by the mid-1700s, indigo, a plant that yielded a precious blue pigment for dying cloth. Indigo was developed as a crop by Eliza Lucas Pinckney on her father's Wappoo plantation.

▲ *Charleston, South Carolina, the only true city south of Philadelphia, was built between the Ashley and Cooper Rivers, which provided this superb harbor. Open to sea breezes, Charleston was home to planters whose wealth was based on crops produced by slave labor in unhealthy, marshy land.*

Rice and indigo nicely complemented one another. They required intensive labor at different seasons, so South Carolina's servants and slaves produced wealth for their masters 12 months a year. However, because the marshy rice lands were breeding grounds for mosquitoes and mosquito-borne diseases—malaria and the dreaded yellow fever—the slaves and hired white overseers were left to be bitten, ail, and die, while South Carolina's planters lived in airy Charleston.

By congregating in a genuine city, South Carolina's elite was all the more conscious of its privileged position, all the more united in its determination to preserve it. No colony (or state) was dominated by so small an aristocracy as ran South Carolina for more than 200 years.

NEW ENGLAND

New England was peopled by immigrants similar in background to the English men and women who went south.

However, the Puritan heritage shaped New England society long after the generation of Winthrop and Cotton died off and their zeal was a memory. Just as important in explaining New England's way of life was geography. The land and the climate decreed an economy and society for Connecticut, Rhode Island, Massachusetts, and New Hampshire quite different from those in the Chesapeake colonies and Carolina.

Geography and Society

The preeminent geographical facts of life in New England were the cold, long winters, short growing season, and the rocky character of the soil.

Winter and summer temperatures in New England were 10 to 30 degrees cooler than in Virginia. The subtropical diseases of the South were unknown. Consequently, New Englanders lived, on average, 10 years longer than southerners. Twice as many children survived infancy in Massachusetts than in Virginia. The result was a large number of

▲ *Clearing land for crops in New England was many times more difficult than elsewhere in the colonies. Not only did the forest have to be cleared—rocks and boulders had to be removed from the soil as well. Felled trees were burned. Stumps were gone in a few years. Removing rocks and boulders went on and on. There was no destroying them; they were piled into stone fences.*

large extended families. In fact, colonial New England was the world's first society in which it was commonplace to have known one's grandparents personally.

In its soil, New England was less fortunate. Geologically, New England is a glacial moraine. It was there that the continental glaciers of the Ice Age halted their advance. When they receded, they deposited the boulders and gravel they had scooped from the earth on their trip from the Arctic.

Before the farmers of New England could plow effectively, they had to clear rocks by the thousands from every acre, breaking up the boulders and piling the lot in the endless stone fences of the region that are so picturesque to those of us who did not have to build them. This backbreaking toil went on for generations, for each winter's freeze heaved more rocks to the surface.

The intensive labor required to clear and plant the land reinforced the Puritans' ideological commitment to a society of small family farms. The demanding New England countryside produced a variety of foods for a fairly dense population. But there were no plantations, no big commercial farms. Families grew their own sustenance and a small surplus for sale in towns and cities.

How Do You Deal with a Ten-Ton Boulder?

Clearing New England's earth of rocks did not mean just the diverting task of hauling 150-pound stones to the fence line. Boulders of granite heaved to the surface could weigh 500 pounds, a ton, multiple tons. Farmers let the very largest outcroppings go, to become highlights of today's suburban landscape. Others, smaller and definitely in the way, had to be broken up. Sledgehammers were of limited value. There was no dynamite, and gunpowder was too expensive to be used in the quantities needed. The solution was water. Cracks and holes in boulders or outcroppings, natural and created, were filled with water in winter. Falling temperatures froze the water into ice, which is greater in volume than water. The ice split the rocks—preferably into fragments that could be hauled or, at least, hammered with a maul. It was not a one winter's job.

The Need for Coin

Few of New England's products could be sold in Old England. The crops New Englanders produced in no plenitude were much the same as those that flourished in the mother country: grain, squash, beans, orchard nuts, apples, livestock. So English mercantilists looked less approvingly at New England than at the South and the West Indies.

Indeed, England's shipbuilders, merchants, and fishermen found competitors in New England. Boston was sending ships down the ways before 1640. The shipwright's craft flourished in every town with a harbor. Whaling, a calling New Englanders would come to dominate, began as early as 1649. Nantucket and New Bedford, Massachusetts, became synonymous with whalers. New England fishermen sailed out of Portsmouth, Marblehead, New London, and other ports to harvest more than their fair share of the codfish of the North Atlantic. As for commerce, the nickname "Yankee trader" everywhere conjured up a shrewd businessman not quite to be trusted. Newport, Rhode Island, was a center of the African slave trade, another pursuit the English would have preferred to reserve for themselves.

New Englanders had no choice but to compete. It took money—gold and silver coin—to purchase English manufactured goods. With no cash crop, whaling, fishing, and trade were the only solutions to the colonies' balance-of-payments problem.

Yankee Traders

Some New England traders plied routes of three legs. A ship might call in West Africa, purchase captives, and transport them to the West Indies, Barbados, or Jamaica, where they were exchanged for molasses made from sugar cane. The molasses was sailed to New England, where it was distilled into rum. The rum went to West Africa to be exchanged, along with other goods, for slaves. Not only did shippers in this "triangular trade" profit from each exchange of cargoes, but the colonies improved their balance of payments by distilling cheap molasses into higher-priced rum.

There were other so-called triangles. New Englanders carried provisions from the Middle Colonies to the West Indies; sugar and molasses to England; and English manufactured goods back home. Others transported tobacco from Maryland and Virginia to England; manufactured goods to the West Indies; molasses back home or slaves to the southern colonies. (In the 1600s, very few enslaved blacks came to the North American colonies directly from Africa; in fact, almost all were imported from the tiny island of Barbados.)

Not many ships were systematically involved in triangular trading. Most plied a leg or two of these streams of trade when opportunity offered or necessity required. In fact, a majority of New England's merchant vessels were "coasters," small sloops transporting whatever needed to be moved from one colonial port to another: Boston, Newport, New York, Philadelphia, Charleston, and dozens of smaller

MAP 4:2 A Triangular Flow of Trade   Very few British and colonial individual ships routinely plied these three-legged routes. Ships' captains were opportunists, taking aboard what was available and taking it where the cargo could be sold. But these triangular routes illustrate the general flow of trade involving seventeenth-century English America.

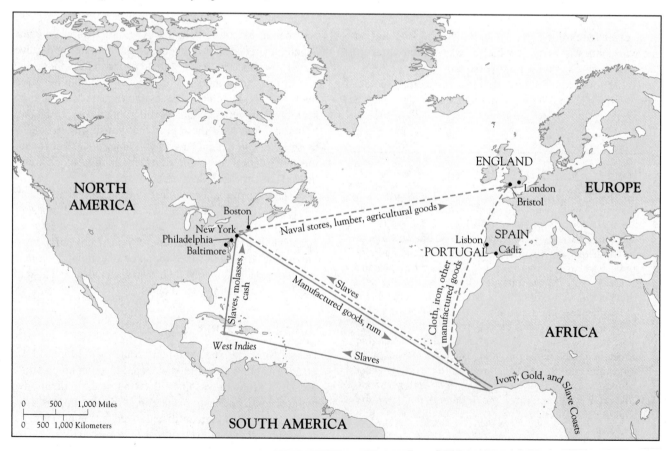

towns. Transatlantic ships did not sail those waters—coastal merchants did; thus the large number of shipwrecks off places like Cape Hatteras and Cape Fear in North Carolina.

An Independent Spirit

To English mercantilists, the Yankees of New England were no better than common smugglers. Indeed, pious Puritan and Quaker shipmasters saw no sin in dodging British trade laws. Because their charters gave them such extensive powers of self-government, the corporate colonies of Massachusetts, Rhode Island, and Connecticut functioned like independent commonwealths. Their leaders—some of them—drank toasts to the king. Some of the grandchildren of the Puritans still entertained the fiction that they were members of the Church of England. But these were little more than the pleasantries of a century when two English kings were dethroned, one of them decapitated, and when it took at least a month, and often two, for a ship to cross the Atlantic connecting the mother country with its colonies.

During the years when Oliver Cromwell ruled England (1649–1658), the New England colonies disregarded almost every directive he and Parliament issued. In 1652, Massachusetts minted its own money, the "pine tree shilling," assuming a right reserved to sovereign rulers since antiquity. Massachusetts did not retreat when Charles II became king in 1660. The colony continued to strike the shilling, to evade royal edicts, and to protect smugglers and even pirates. Charles was forced to sue to have the Massachusetts charter revoked. In 1684, he won his case.

The Dominion of New England

The next year, the new king, James II, combined all the New England colonies into a single unit—the Dominion of New England. (New York and New Jersey were later added.) He abolished local assemblies and endowed his governor, Sir Edmund Andros, with a viceroy's powers. Andros never had a prayer. He was detested in New England from the day he disembarked, and James II's reign proved to be short. In 1688, the king was forced to flee England in the Glorious

---

And the Award for Incompetence in Colonial Government Goes To . . .

By far the stupidest innovation of the Dominion of New England was a law invalidating all titles to land held under the abrogated Massachusetts charter. *Every* land title in the colony dated earlier than 1685 had been granted under the charter!

James II and Sir Edmund Andros did not intend to evict every Massachusetts family from its land. The idea was to enrich the treasury by collecting fees for the paperwork of revalidating the titles (and to provide opportunities for graft among Sir Edmund's cronies, who, for a consideration, would and could expedite the process).

Revolution. This news was the signal for popular uprisings in several colonies. In Maryland, John Coode seized power from the Catholic proprietors who he assumed had fled with the Catholic James II. In New York, a German named Jacob Leisler gained control, claiming that, in the name of the new sovereigns, William and Mary, he was ridding New York of "Popish Doggs & Divells." In New England, the merchant elite, so briefly out of power, simply resumed acting as it always had—independently. Andros prudently put to sea.

However, the Calverts of Maryland had waffled; they had not committed to James II. When the dust settled, they regained their proprietary rights. In New York, an overconfident Leisler ordered a volley fired at arriving troops, who really did act for William and Mary. He and an aide were sentenced to be "hanged by the Neck and being Alive their bodys be Cutt Downe to the Earth that their Bowells be taken out." On second thought, the judge decided that plain hanging would suffice.

As for New England, William and Mary knew better than to revive the hated Dominion, but they had no intention of allowing Massachusetts to return to its quasi-independent ways. They restored the charters of Connecticut and Rhode Island (there had been little tumult there), but they made Massachusetts, with Plymouth incorporated into it, a royal colony. After 1691, the governor of the Massachusetts Bay colony was no longer elected. He, like the governors of Virginia and the others, was appointed by the Crown.

This was no easy pill for vestigial Puritans to swallow. Their forebears had regarded their mission in America as divinely mandated. That God should allow the Crown to take control of the "citty on a hill" was bitter medicine.

Bully Boy Hysteria

It has been suggested that the loss of the charter and New England's suffering in King Philip's War (see Chapter 5) help to explain the strange hysteria that convulsed Massachusetts in 1692—the Salem witchcraft scare. That is, Puritans believed that God punished the community that tolerated sin within it. The loss of the charter and the devastation wreaked by the Indians led by King Philip could have looked like such punishments. And only the most terrible of sins could account for God's anger at Massachusetts. In 1692, some troubled New Englanders believed they knew what that sin was.

Two pubescent girls of Salem, a village north of Boston, were seized by fits of screaming and crawling about while making odd throaty sounds. Their physician found no earthly affliction. He reckoned that the girls had been bewitched by Satan's servants—witches.

Few were shocked and fewer laughed at the suggestion of witchcraft. A majority of Europeans and Americans of the era believed that individuals struck bargains with Satan. Witchcraft was a capital offense; the Bible said, "Thou shalt not suffer a witch to live." Since the Reformation, thousands had been executed for devil worship, practicing black magic, or for having sexual intercourse with imps called "incubi"

▲ *The woman (or girl) at the left, face covered, accuses a young woman of witchcraft. She has a male defender and lives in a substantial house. In reality, most of the witches hanged at Salem were poor and friendless or nearly so.*

and "succubi." Only a year before the hysteria erupted in Salem, a witch had been hanged in Boston.

The girls who started it all had been agitated by the spooky tales of a West Indian slave in the home of Reverend Samuel Parish named Tituba. Finding themselves the center of attention, the girls began to accuse villagers of bewitching them. Their targets could not have been better chosen for vul-

---

"Put on More Weight"

The Salem witches were not burned at the stake, as was the fate of many convicted witches in Europe. All were hanged except one man who was "pressed" to death. He was laid prostrate on the ground under a heavy plank. Stones not needed urgently for fence construction were heaped on the plank one by one until he expired, probably of suffocation before his skeleton crumbled.

Why his special treatment? He refused to plead either innocent or guilty when he was accused of being a witch. His reason was mercenary, although not to his own benefit. To plead not guilty and then to be convicted, which he knew was in the cards, meant that he and therefore his heirs would forfeit the property he owned. After each stone was laid on the plank, the magistrates begged him to plead. Even a guilty plea would end the torture.

He refused. His final words were, "Put on more weight."

---

nerability by a committee of sociologists: Most were women (as were almost all the accusers); some were eccentrics or people unpopular in the community for good reason and bad; several were loners with no friends to defend them; most of the women had no adult sons to speak up on their behalf. Tituba was a slave, easy pickings. Another Salem witch was an impoverished hag who may have been senile; yet another was deaf and probably did not understand the charges against her. There was an 88-year-old man notorious as a crank and, in his younger years, an unabashed open adulterer.

Accusers and accusations multiplied. In time, better-established people were named, most of whom had been on the wrong side of a local squabble involving Reverend Parish. Before it was over—accusation of the wife of the governor was going too far—130 people were accused of witchcraft, 114 were charged, and 19 were hanged. Only one of the 19 was a male of respectable social station.

THE MIDDLE COLONIES

Not everyone believed in witchcraft. At the height of the Salem hysteria, William Penn was asked if there might not also be witches in Pennsylvania. He replied that people were quite free to fly about on broomsticks within the boundaries of his colony. The liberality of the Middle Colonies, particularly policies of religious toleration and easy access to land, ensured that New York, Pennsylvania, New Jersey, and Delaware were generally prosperous and placid.

Balanced Economies

There were great estates in the Middle Colonies, but they were uncommon. As in New England, the agricultural pattern was a patchwork of small family farms (though larger than New England's) tilled by the landowners themselves with some servants and slaves. The climate of the Middle Colonies provided a long growing season, and the soils in the alluvial valleys of the Hudson, Delaware, Schuylkill, and Susquehanna Rivers were deep and rich.

Unlike New England, the Middle Colonies produced a large surplus of grain and livestock. Pennsylvania earned the nickname "breadbasket of the colonies." Because foodstuffs (except rice and molasses) were not enumerated, the products of the Middle Colonies could be sold wherever sellers could find a market. A canny merchant class in Philadelphia and New York soon found an insatiable one. They shipped grain and meat animals on the hoof to the sugar islands of the West Indies, where a small master class forced huge gangs of black slaves to grow cane and little else. The Middle Colonies found a comfortable niche for themselves within the imperial system. They were neither overdependent on the mother country nor sharply in competition with British shippers.

The merchants of Philadelphia and New York governed those cities as though they were personal property. However, because landowning farmers (and therefore voters) were numerous in the Middle Colonies, the merchants never dominated the elected assemblies as planters dominated them in the South; and because their businesses were diverse, they were far more likely than southerners to disagree politically among themselves.

Liberal Institutions

New Jersey and Delaware practiced religious toleration on the same Quaker grounds as Pennsylvania. In New York, the Church of England was established, but laws proscribing other forms of worship were largely ignored. A Roman Catholic, Thomas Dongan, was governor of New York, and a Jewish synagogue established under Dutch rule in 1654 continued to function unmolested under the English.

Indeed, once the Puritan grip on Massachusetts was broken, tacitly accepted religious toleration was the rule in all the colonies. America was a young country in need of people. Whatever the law said, there were few serious attempts to discourage immigration on the basis of religion.

Until 1700, most colonists either had been born in England or had English-born parents or grandparents. There was some ethnic diversity: about 25,000 colonials of African origin, almost all slaves; a handful of Jews in Rhode Island, New York, and South Carolina; a contingent of French Protestants in South Carolina, who had fled persecution at home; and the beginnings of what would become a flood of German emigration in Pennsylvania.

for FURTHER READING

Once again, see the pertinent chapters of Charles M. Andrews, *The Colonial Period of American History,* 1934–1938; Curtis E. Nettels, *The Roots of American Civilization,* 1938; Daniel Boorstin, *The Americans: The Colonial Experience,* 1958; Clarence Ver Steeg, *The Formative Years,* 1964; John E. Pomfret with Floyd Shumway, *Founding the American Colonies,* 1970; and Jack P. Greene and J. R. Pole, eds., *Colonial British America,* 1984. See also Louis B. Wright, *Cultural Life of the American Colonies, 1607–1763,* 1957; and Lewis C. Gray, *History of Agriculture in the United States to 1860,* 1933.

On the southern colonies, see Thomas J. Wertenbaker, *The Planters of Colonial Virginia,* 1927; Louis B. Wright, *The First Gentleman of Virginia,* 1940; and Carl Bridenbaugh, *Myths and Realities: Societies of the Colonial South,* 1963. The standard work on Bacon's Rebellion is Wilcomb E. Washburn, *The Governor and the Rebel,* 1957.

For New England, Bernard Bailyn, *The New England Merchants in the Seventeenth Century,* 1955, is just about old enough to qualify as a classic. See also Stephen Foster, *The Long Argument: English Puritanism and New England Culture, 1570–1700,* 1991; Philip J. Greven Jr., *Four Generations: Population, Land, and Family in Colonial Andover, Massachusetts,* 1970; and Howard S. Russell, *A Long, Deep Furrow: Three Centuries of Farming in New England,* 1976.

Witchcraft in Salem cannot help but be a popular subject. Once the standard explanation, and still provocative, is Marion G. Starkey, *The Devil in Massachusetts,* 1969. Books adding new dimensions to the topic include Paul Boyer and Stephen Nissenbaum, *Salem Possessed,* 1974; John Demos, *Entertaining Satan: Witchcraft and the Culture of Early New England,* 1982; and Carol Karlsen, *The Devil in the Shape of a Woman,* 1987.

 AMERICAN JOURNEY ONLINE AND INFOTRAC COLLEGE EDITION

Visit the source collections at http://ajaccess.wadsworth.com and http://infotrac.thomsonlearning.com, and use the Search function with the following key terms to explore documents, images, audio and video clips, articles, and commentary related to the material in this chapter:

Bacon's Rebellion
Glorious Revolution
Salem witch trials

HISTORY ONLINE

An American Time Capsule

http://memory.loc.gov/ammem/rbpehtml/pehome.html

A Library of Congress collection of "broadsides"—single sheet handouts designed to arouse public opinion—from the seventeenth century to the present.

Witchcraft in Salem

http://etext.virginia.edu/salem/witchcraft

Documents, resources, and maps of Salem and Salem Village important in understanding the politics of the witch trials.

OTHER AMERICANS

The Indians, French, and Africans of Colonial North America

From the Collections of the Library of Congress

Why will you take by force what you may obtain by love? Why will you destroy us who supply you with food? What can you get by war?

Chief Powhatan

This country has twice the population of New France, but the people there are astonishingly cowardly, completely undisciplined, and without any experience in war. . . . It is not at all like that in Canada. The Canadians are brave, much inured to war, and untiring in travel. Two thousand of them will at all times and in all places thrash the people of New England.

Officer, Troupes de la Marine

Is it not enough that we are torn from our country and friends to toil for your luxury and lust of gain? Must every tender feeling be likewise sacrificed to your avarice?

Olaudah Equiano

MOST OF THE English men and women who emigrated to the colonies thought of America as a place where they could improve their lives. Other peoples had other perspectives. To Africans living around the Gulf of Guinea, America was a dread place to which human beings were carried in chains, never to return. To the French, longtime rivals of the English, the colonies were a threat to France's own overseas empire. And then there were those for whom North America was not over any sea, but home, their native land.

THE INDIANS OF NORTH AMERICA

The most striking characteristic of the Native Americans was diversity. Indeed, the story of the Indians is a lesson in just how rapidly and radically cultures diversify when the population is thin and the land is vast, when people of differing beliefs, morals, and ways of doing things are not in constant, intimate contact with one another. Although all North American Indians were descended from culturally similar bands of Asian hunters, they divided and divided again into a patchwork quilt of linguistic and cultural groups, and even distinct physical types.

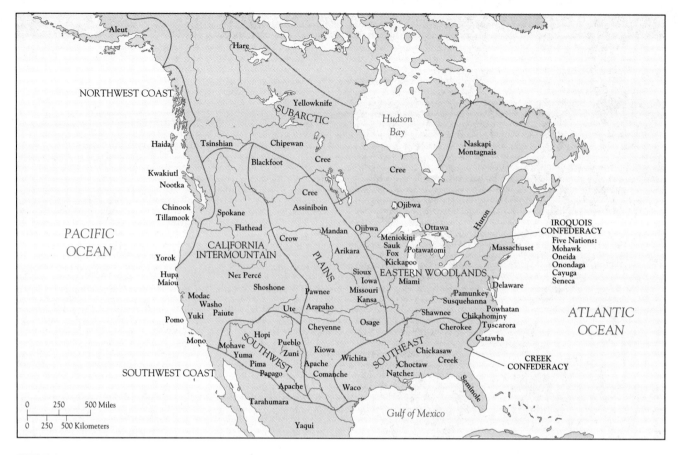

MAP 5:1 The Native American Tribes, 1650–1750 As many Native American peoples as appear on this map, there were many more tribes and autonomous divisions of tribes. By 1700, the English colonies had made contact with most of the Eastern Woodlands and southwestern peoples. The Spanish in Texas and New Mexico were familiar with the Indians of the Southwest and Southern Plains. The French out of Canada had at least confronted the tribes of the Mississippi drainage.

Cultural Diversity

Native American political systems ran the gamut from sophisticated legislative assemblies (such as those of the Iroquois) to the absence of the idea of government among some peoples of the Great Basin. Socially, there were caste systems so complicated that tribes (such as the Natchez) supported genealogists as the only means to keep track of who was who, and there were egalitarian and democratic tribes (such as many of California's dozens of tribes).

There were tribes in which authoritarian men ignored the existence of every woman but their wives and others in which women, among themselves, spoke a language significantly different from that of the men. Yet other tribes were matrilineal, tracing an individual's descent through the female line, endowing almost all property to women, and looking to councils of women to make important tribal decisions. The variety of social relationships among the Indians at the time of European incursion was broader than the social structure was in Europe.

Manners and morals varied too. The Cherokee considered it rude to address another person directly. The Yahi each gave themselves names that they never revealed to another person. Unmarried Natchez girls sold sexual services in order to build up a dowry. The Plains Indians guarded the virginity of their girls as closely as Montagues and Capulets. In the Northeast, rape was the only crime punishable by death, and the warriors of some tribes of that region were bound to strict sexual continence when they were on the

What's in a Name?

The name most Indian tribes gave themselves translated into English as "the people" or "the human beings." Tribes referred to other Indians in terms that were usually unflattering, like "the other things."

In some cases, like *Kiowa,* we have adopted the name tribal members gave themselves. In others, when whites were introduced to a tribe by a neighboring people, they adopted that people's negative designation, and it stuck. Thus, *Mohawk* is Narragansett for "blood sucker," *Sioux* is Chippewa for "snake," and *Apache* is Zuñi for "enemy."

Then there are names given to tribes by Europeans from their own languages: *Pueblo,* from the Spanish for "village"; *Nez Percé,* from the French for "pierced nose," after a cosmetic practice of that tribe; *Delaware,* from the English for the homeland of the Leni-Lenape, which the English had named after an English investor, Baron De La Warr.

warpath. The incest taboo was so strict in some areas that one had to marry outside one's clan, whereas the Tlingit of the Pacific Northwest prized marriages of first cousins. Some tribes of the Great Plains allowed homosexuals special privileges. Others found homosexual practice as abominable as any Puritan did.

Some Indians were warlike and aggressive, renowned for their cruelty toward enemies. There is the site of a village near Crow Creek, South Dakota, where, in the fourteenth century, some 500 men, women, and children were massacred. Every tribe in the Northeast came to fear the Iroquois, a name that meant "terrifying man" in the Algonkian languages. The Pueblo Indians fought only in defense, never taking the initiative against other peoples. Yet other Indians were gentle folk, principled pacifists who survived only by finding secluded nooks of the continent in which to dwell.

Many eastern Indians were functional monotheists who worshiped a single manitou, or Great Spirit. Others were fetishists. They concerned themselves with supernatural powers in stones, trees, bugs, and birds, and consulted magicians to cope with otherworldly powers.

Economy, Ecology, and Language

Indians shaped the environment to the degree their technology allowed. For instance, there was intense irrigated cultivation and a quasi-urban way of life among the Pueblo of New Mexico and Arizona, whereas the Indians of southern New England methodically burned the underbrush in their hunting grounds, creating park-like forests in which grasses and herbaceous plants thrived, luring moose, deer, rabbits, and other game into a created habitat.

In California, by contrast, whole peoples subsisted on little but acorns, roots and berries, and the odd small animal they snared. In the Pacific Northwest, food was so abundant and nutritious (salmon) that some tribes expressed a disdain for material goods, a phenomenon we associate with rich and wasteful economies. Periodically, families that had accumulated great stores of food and other possessions gave them away at festivals called "potlatches," even destroying valuable goods and impoverishing themselves to demonstrate how unimpressed they were with possessions.

There was greater linguistic difference among the Indians than there was among the nationalities of Europe. In one corner of North Carolina, several small tribes living within 10 miles of one another for at least a century could not communicate except by sign language. Some peoples dwelling in comparable proximity were so distinctive physically their ethnicity could be identified from half a mile's distance.

About the only generalization that can confidently be made about the Indians of North America is that, in the end, they were all to be subordinated by the Europeans, whose arrival dated from Ponce de León's search for the Fountain of Youth.

From the Collections of the Library of Congress

▲ *This watercolor of the village of Secotan in North Carolina was painted by John White about 1585. It shows an orderly society and the fact that the inhabitants planted at least two crops of corn each year in order to extend their food supply.*

PEOPLE OF THE EASTERN WOODLANDS

People speaking Algonkian languages occupied New England and the eastern parts of the Middle Colonies down to North Carolina. Tribes in this language group included Mohegan (or Mohican), Narragansett, Abenaki, Leni-Lenape (Delaware), Pequot, Ojibwa (Chippewa), and, of course, the Powhatan. Algonkians were the first Native Americans with whom English settlers made contact. They were also the first to be victimized by the English, who eventually made enemies of most of them by taking the Algonkians' lands. The colonists adopted quite a few Algonkian words (and more numerous Algonkian place names) that are now an integral part of American English. A few are *hickory, hominy, moccasin, succotash, tomahawk, totem, wigwam, Massachusetts, Connecticut, Susquehanna,* and *Chesapeake.*

The second major language group of the Eastern Woodlands was Iroquoian. This language group extended over a large wedge-shaped territory running from the eastern Great Lakes through New York and into Pennsylvania. The Conestoga and Erie spoke an Iroquoian language, as did the Tuscarora of inland Virginia and North Carolina and the Huron of New France (what is now Canada). But the most important Iroquois as far as the English were concerned were five large tribes that had joined together in a confederation under the legendary figure Hiawatha in about 1570. The Five Nations of the Iroquois Confederacy were the Cayuga, Mohawk, Oneida, Onondaga, and Seneca.

The earliest southern colonials had less contact with the third major linguistic group of the Eastern Woodlands, the Muskogean. The tribes in this language group included the Apalachee, Chickasaw, Choctaw, Creek, Natchez, and Seminole. These socially sophisticated tribes lived in what is now Georgia, Alabama, Mississippi, and Tennessee. Few English settlers penetrated this country until late in the seventeenth century, when South Carolinians developed a slave, fur, and deerskin trade there. In Florida, however, Spanish incursions and the spread of European diseases were already decimating small Muskogean tribes that would, in time, disappear: the Timucuan, Calusa, and Jaega.

Hunters Who Farmed

The economies of the three Eastern Woodlands groups were similar. Agriculture was based on the "three sisters": maize (corn), beans, and squash. They were planted together in small hills heaped up by means of a spade roughed out of stone or wood. (Woodlands Indians had no metallurgy.)

Maize was the easily preserved staple and provided the stalks on which bean vines climbed. Pumpkins and other squash covered the roots of both plants with their foliage, preserving moisture as well as providing food. Here and there, peas, cabbages, melons, and, of course, tobacco were cultivated.

Farmland was cleared by the slash-and-burn method, which was undemanding and therefore suited the Eastern Woodlands Indians, who were primarily hunters and gatherers. Well adapted to an environment in which land was abundant and labor scarce, the slash-and-burn method was adopted by the white pioneers in the densely forested eastern third of the country.

A ring of bark was stripped from around the trunks of the mostly deciduous trees, thus killing them. When the last foliage fell, admitting sunlight to the forest floor, the Indian women (who were the chief farmers in the east) burned the underbrush. In these ghost forests, they planted their crops. There were no plows or beasts of burden among the eastern tribes. Dogs and turkeys were the only domesticated animals.

So casual a mode of cultivation did not itself provide sufficient food. Every tribe looked as much to forest as to field for its survival, depending on hunting, fishing, trapping, and gathering edible plants, fruits, and nuts. Thus each tribe competed with its neighbors for range.

The Eastern Woodlands Indians valued their weapons, tools, and household goods. They thought of them as exclusive personal property, much as Europeans did. But hunting and gathering do not require constant occupation or exclusive control of a specific tract of land. Consequently, the European concept of real estate—private, exclusive ownership of land—was alien to the Indians. Land was God's. People used it and competed to use it, sometimes violently. But no one "owned" it. When a New Englander commented that the Indians "do but run over the grass, as do also the foxes and wild beasts," an Indian might well have shrugged, "Yes. So what?"

Outside of Eden, foraging for food makes for a precarious livelihood. So the Eastern Woodlands Indians' communities were inclined to be small and scattered so that no individual tribe put too much of a strain on the hunting and gathering grounds in the vicinity. The Powhatan, whom the first Virginians encountered, gathered in villages of 500 people during the summer. In winter, however, they split up into smaller groups. European-style agriculture made larger concentrations of population possible. But the Indians benefited from the newcomers' productivity for only a short time.

CONFRONTATION

To the Eastern Woodlands Indians, the world was land, lake, and stream. The Atlantic Ocean was an abyss, the end of the earth. None of them were seafarers. The Indians saw the pale-skinned people as members of a new tribe. Incursion by strangers was not new to them, and the white tribe was soon more numerous than any other they had known. Nonetheless, for many decades, the Indians viewed the English as just another people with whom to fight, to trade, and to compete for the necessities of life. Except as a novelty, skin color meant nothing to Native Americans.

Two Different Worlds

The experience of the Indians who confronted the English was rather different from that of Native Americans who lived in lands the Spanish invaded. First of all, there were not as many of them. Probably about 150,000 Indians lived

Fate Worse Than Death

Colonial women who were captured by Indians, adopted into a tribe, and not rescued within a year or so often decided to remain Indians when they were given the choice of returning. They had formed personal attachments and, if they had borne children, knew that their children would live as equals among the Indians but be outcast half-breeds among whites.

Appalling as such decisions were to colonials, Esther Wheelwright's choices were worse. In 1704, she was kidnapped in Maine by Abenaki and taken to Quebec. There she converted to Roman Catholicism, became a nun, and, in time, mother superior of the Ursuline order. She was the highest-ranking churchwoman in North America.

in the parts of North America the English penetrated during the 1600s. More Aztecs lived in Tenochtitlán alone when Cortés first entered the city.

And yet, the English had a more difficult time dominating the Native Americans than the Spanish had in Mexico and Peru. In large part, this was due to the fact that the English did not wish to conquer the locals, live among them, and govern them, which was precisely the Spanish goal.

The English enslaved captured Indians (which the Spanish were forbidden to do). In 1708, Indian slaves in South Carolina numbered 1,400, accounting for 14 percent of the colony's population. But Indians escaped too easily in a land that was, after all, their home. Imported white servants and black slaves were more dependable. Already by 1708, there were 4,100 black slaves in South Carolina.

The sexual balance of the English colonial population served to keep Indians and Europeans in different spheres. Unlike New Spain, which was conquered by soldiers—all males—New England was settled by families. Even in the plantation South, by the time of Queen Anne, the English population was approaching sexual parity. Only a few colonial men looked to the Indians for wives. One scholar has identified only three Indian-white marriages in Virginia during the colony's first century, including John Rolfe and Pocahontas. With marriage within the race relatively available, it was feasible in English America to define intermarriage as disreputable, the practice of low-life whites. There was plenty of miscegenation, of course, but the colonials consigned "half-breeds" to the Indians, thus creating the first American color line.

In fact, most whites who consorted with Indians eagerly chose to live with their spouse's people, where loyalty to the tribe was what counted, not skin color. So did many of the women and children who were kidnapped by Indians specifically for the purpose of replacing tribal members who had died. A New Yorker commented incredulously in 1699 that he could not "persuade the People that had been taken Prisoners by the French Indians, to leave the Indian Manner of

The "Walking Purchase"
Pennsylvania's "Walking Purchase" of 1683 was once a staple of history textbooks. The story was that canny Quakers agreed with Indians to pay a sum for land as far as a man could walk in a day. The Indians, who knew quite well about how far that was, found they were hornswoggled when, to prepare for the walk, the purchasers cut a path through the forest and stationed young men along it to run in relays as far as they could.

The trouble is, there is no record of such a transaction; it was not William Penn's style; and when the story was first published in 1737, none of the oldest living inhabitants of Pennsylvania had heard of it.

living." White male captives were more likely to view rescue as a liberation.

Land Hunger

The goal of English colonization was to replicate the way of life the settlers knew back home. Indians had no place in this vision. The object was to acquire the Indians' land by purchase or force, pushing the dispossessed survivors outside the pale of white settlement, which almost always meant to the west.

Conscientious colonials devised moral and legal justifications for taking Indian land. The Pilgrims approved their occupation of Plymouth on the grounds that no one was living there when they arrived. Roger Williams, the Pennsylvania Quakers, and, usually, the Dutch in New Netherland bought the land they wanted. Their view of the transactions, however, differed sharply from that of the Indians. To Europeans, purchase meant acquiring exclusive use of the land, as intensive agriculture required. The earliest Indian sellers believed they were agreeing to share the land with the newcomers. Thus Staten Island could be "sold" to the Dutch three times over. To the Dutch, their multiple purchase proved the Indians were dishonest connivers. From the Indian point of view, three different tribes were accepting the Hollanders' presence on Staten Island.

Many Indians must have been bewildered by European real estate deals. Jasper Danckhaerts wrote of a transaction in New York in 1679, "The Indians hate the precipitancy of comprehension and judgement [of the whites], the excited chatterings, . . . the haste and rashness to do something, whereby a mess is often made of one's good intentions."

Many colonials lacked good intentions. They shot, took, and shrugged. Possession by right of conquest was not a universally approved principle in the seventeenth century, but it had a long pedigree and compelling recommendations to the party with the military edge.

Bringers of Baubles

Few Eastern Woodlands Indians were flabbergasted by the appearance of whites as the Arawak and Mexicans had been.

English Legalism
New Englanders were as legalistic as the Spaniards in justifying the taking of land from Indians. The Puritans based the legality of their seizures on the Bible. In 1630, John Cotton spelled out the three ways in which "God makes room for a people." First, in a just war, which God blessed (Psalms 44:2–"Thou didst drive out the heathen before them"), the victors had the right to the land they conquered. Second, newcomers could purchase land or accept land as a gift "as Abraham did obtaine the field of Machpelah" or as the pharaoh gave the land of Goshen "unto the sons of Jacob." Third—and this was major-league legal loophole making–"When Hee [God] makes a Countrey though not altogether void of inhabitants, yet voyd in that place where they [the newcomers] reside . . . there is liberty for the sonne of Adam or Noah to come and inhabite, though they neither buy it, nor aske their leaves."

explorers and fishermen camped on Atlantic
[sh]or[es for] decades before the founding of Jamestown and
[Plymouth.] Gossip among tribes had informed most eastern
[people] of the existence of the white tribe before they con[fronted a]n Englishman face to face.

[The e]arliest English settlements posed little threat, however, and the colonists offered trade goods that were highly
desirable to a Neolithic people. There were the famous
baubles, of course: glass beads, ribbons, trinkets, mirrors.
New to Indians, they were accorded the high status and price
of any novelty. It was with the equivalent of $24 worth of
such goods that Peter Minuit purchased Manhattan Island in
1626. A European introduction brimming with tragedy, but
coveted nonetheless, was liquor, usually rum (or cheap
brandy in New France). Some eastern tribes had made a
weak beer from corn but nothing as potent as distilled spirits. From the first, the Indians took with tragic zest to "firewater." It devastated many tribes both physically and morally.

More important to a people who smelted no metals were
the European commodities that improved their standard of
living: brass and iron vessels; tools (spades, hatchets); woven
blankets (which were warmer than hides) and other textiles;
and firearms, which allowed the Indians to hunt more efficiently and get a military leg up on old tribal enemies.

In return, the Indians provided foodstuffs to the earliest settlers. When the English became agriculturally self-sufficient, they supplied furs and hides in exchange for
goods that had become necessities in a native economy that
was no longer self-sufficient.

The Fur and Hide Trade

In the decline of the Eastern Woodlands tribes, furs and
hides played a more fundamental role than liquor and the
military superiority of the English. The English (and Dutch
and French) appetite for animal skins resulted in the destruction of the ecology of which the eastern Indians had comfortably been a part.

Before the whites arrived, the Woodlands tribes killed
only the moose, deer, beaver, and other animals that they
needed for food and clothing. Why kill more? Because the
Indians were few, their needs had minimal impact on the animal population. Indeed, their harvests of game may have
had a healthy effect on wildlife by preventing overpopulation and disease.

But Europeans could not get too many skins and pelts.
The upper classes back home coveted the lush furs of the
beaver, otter, marten, and weasel. Both furs and deerskin
were made into felt, which was pressed into hats and dozens
of other salable goods. In order to increase production and
buy more of what the Europeans offered, the tribes rapidly
extirpated the valuable creatures in hunting grounds that had
been adequate for centuries.

It does not take long to effectively destroy a species
when hunting is relentless and systematic. In only a couple
of generations, nineteenth-century Americans would annihilate a population of passenger pigeons that previously

Scalping

In the 1870s, a crusader for Indian causes, Susette
LaFlesche, told audiences that whites taught scalping to
Indians. Native Americans knew nothing of the practice,
she said, until the advent of the English and French.

Her contention, based on the fact that the British army
and colonial governments paid Indian allies bounties for
the scalps of hostile tribespeople, was revived in the later
decades of the twentieth century.

In fact, there is no record of Europeans scalping one another or even a word for the practice in the English,
French, and Spanish languages until after 1535, when
Jacques Cartier described scalping among some Indians
he confronted. It appears that scalping was the peculiar
custom of the Mohawk, which only after time was
adopted by other tribes of the Northeast and Canada.
There seems little doubt, however, that it was white exploration and expansion across the continent that made
the gory mutilation the practice of tribes living as distant
from the Mohawk as the Dakota and Apache.

darkened the skies. The nearly total destruction of the North
American bison after the construction of the transcontinental railroad took only 10 years! Thus it happened in the Eastern Woodlands, as Indians and the odd white hunter and
trapper set out greedily after deer and beaver.

Unlike the case of the passenger pigeon, but very much
like the case of the bison, the destruction of the animals of
the eastern forests meant the destruction of a way of life.

A New Kind of Warfare

The demands of the fur traders introduced a new kind of warfare to the world of the Indians. War was not new to them. Violent conflict with other tribes was an integral part of Iroquois
and Algonkian culture. But traditional Indian warfare was
largely a ritualistic demonstration of individual bravery. A
young man gained as much glory among his people in "counting coups," giving an enemy a sound knock on the head, as in
taking his life. Women and children were not typically killed
in Indian warfare—where was the glory in that?—although
they were kidnapped to be enslaved, married, or adopted.

Once they became suppliers to an intercontinental economy, however, the Indians embraced a different concept of
warfare. No longer was the object glory, live captives, and
thievery; it became the exploitation of other tribes' hunting
grounds and, if necessary, the elimination of the competition. Revenge and retribution had always been a part of
Indian culture, but on nothing like the scale the Iroquois
practiced once they gained access to English firearms.

In 1649, the Iroquois virtually exterminated their neighbors, the Erie. There were probably 30,000 Huron living
north of the Iroquois when the French settled in Huron territory. By 1640, European diseases had reduced the Huron to
12,000. In 10 more years, the Iroquois killed all but several
hundred of the survivors. Then, in the quest for furs, they

A HURON—TYPE.

▲ *A Huron warrior. The Huron were the first Indians to befriend the French, a decision that doomed them. They were nearly exterminated during the 1600s by repeated epidemics of diseases contracted from French settlers in Canada and relentless attacks by the mortal enemy of the French, the Iroquois Confederacy.*

drove other tribes out of the Ohio Valley, which did not return until the mid-1700s, when the Iroquois were neutral in the Anglo-French wars.

The colonials—French and English—encouraged intertribal genocide by paying bounties for scalps from enemy tribes. In 1721, Pennsylvania paid the equivalent of $140 for an Algonkian warrior's scalp and $50 for a squaw's. To make the purpose of the bounty unmistakable, a live prisoner was worth a paltry $30.

King Philip's War

Indians battled whites too, of course. In the mid-1640s, having finished off the Huron, the Iroquois Confederacy came very close to driving the French out of North America. In 1675, in King Philip's War, an alliance of New England tribes harbored hopes of at least stemming the advance of the English, if not driving them into the sea.

The war began when Plymouth hanged three Wampanoag for murdering Sassamon, a Christian member of their tribe. The Wampanoag chief, Metacomet, whom New Englanders derisively called "King Philip," was already seething with hatred for the colonials over a personal insult and the obvious dissipation of his tribe's culture.

Metacomet persuaded two other powerful chiefs, Pomham of the Nipmuck and Canonchet of the Narragansett, to join him in a coordinated attack on outlying colonial towns. Through most of 1675, their warriors were unstoppable. Fifty-two of 90 New England towns were attacked;

12 were wiped off the map. A tenth of the New England males of military age were killed or captured.

The next year, the tide turned. Metacomet's armies ran short of provisions and were troubled by internal dissension. Most of the "praying Indians" of New England—Christians, who were about a fourth of the Native American population—allied themselves with the whites. Several tribes of "wild Indians," including the Pequot and Mohican, either joined with the New Englanders or declared neutrality. In an attack on the Narragansett, 2,000 of 3,000 enemy Indians were killed. Metacomet was killed, his head mounted on a stake in best seventeenth-century fashion. Canonchet's head was impaled in Hartford, Connecticut.

Contempt and Respect

The colonials both respected the Indians and held them in contempt. The native peoples were "different." Practices ranging from the trivial (the Indians' toilet habits) to the significant (cruel treatment of some captives) appalled settlers who had less than an anthropologist's appreciation of cultural diversity. The Indians were "savages." Colonials frequently compared them to the Irish, who were despised in the old country for their perceived lack of civilization.

By contrast, some colonials admired and envied aspects of Indian culture. Even Benjamin Franklin, the Pennsylvanian who sanctified hard work and squirreling away money, betrayed a certain wistfulness when he wrote of the Indians: "Having few artificial wants, they have abundance of leisure for improvement by conversation. Our laborious manner of life, compared with theirs, they esteem slavish and base."

Indians regarded the whites with a mix of awe and disdain. Few Native Americans turned their backs on the trade goods the colonials offered. However, as Franklin observed, the nonmaterial benefits of European civilization were lost on them. In 1744, Virginia invited the Iroquois to send six of their boys to the College of William and Mary. The confederacy replied that it had had bad luck with Indian lads educated at New England colleges: "When they came back to us, they were bad runners, ignorant of every means of living in the woods, unable to bear either cold or hunger, knew neither how to build a cabin, take a deer, or kill an enemy; they were totally good for nothing."

However, the Iroquois understood that the whites meant well: "If the gentlemen of Virginia will send us a dozen of their sons, we will take great care of their education, instruct them in all we know, and make men of them."

Tribal Peoples

The concept of "Indian-ness," the idea that all Native Americans had an essence in common with one another that pit them against all whites, is a political conceit of our own times. American Indians, during the colonial period and long thereafter, were tribal to the core. It was tribal identification that gave individuals identity and community and distinguished them from outsiders. Race, racial solidarity, and racism—all meaningful among colonial whites, and a nearly universal obsession today—had little meaning for Indians of the colonial period.

Tribes readily adopted members of other tribes and whites too, a practice rare among English colonials. Inter-tribal conflicts involving only Indians were common, but conflicts in which one side was entirely white and the other entirely Indian were rare after the very first skirmishes in Virginia and Massachusetts. The Narragansett and Mohican joined the white New Englanders in the massacre of the Pequot in 1634. Almost as many Indians fought against Metacomet as fought for him. The English colonials and Indians, chiefly the Iroquois, made war off and on for more than a century against French colonials (and the Indian allies of the French) in Canada. To the French and English, alliances with Indians were expedient. To the Indians, both sides were alliances of tribes; that two of the inimical tribes were pale of skin was incidental. Indeed, it confirmed the absence of racial categorization among the Indians.

THE FRENCH IN NORTH AMERICA

New France was founded at Quebec and Port Royal, Nova Scotia, in 1608, just a year after Jamestown, by Samuel de Champlain. As in English America, the colony was governed by a commercial company, the Company of the Indies, to be taken over by the French crown in 1663.

Grand Empire, Few People

With the same motives as the English crown, the Bourbon kings of France were determined to keep pace with their national rival in North America. But they were disappointed by the reluctance of French men and women to emigrate across the Atlantic. For farmers, which most of the French were, the disincentive was the climate and soil of New France. The earth was rockier than New England's, and the winters were worse. A high proportion of the immigrants in Canada were people who had been urban laborers in the old country, and about two-thirds of those returned to France to feed the anti-Canadian prejudice with their horror stories.

France might have populated New France with religious dissenters as England populated New England. The Huguenots, Protestants much like Puritans, were a nuisance at home. Many would gladly have emigrated to escape the disabilities, persecution, and uncertainty they knew at home, while remaining French, which was as important to them as remaining English was to Pilgrims and Puritans. But Louis XIV, who reigned more than 70 years, forbade all but Catholics in Canada.

Louis could not, however, with a variety of inducements, build a Catholic population in Canada to rival the numbers in the English colonies. French indentured servants were bound to serve only three years, as opposed to as many as seven years in the English colonies, and the French indentured servants were granted land when their term of service was up. It did little good. The French crown forced emigration on people deemed expendable at home. Entire villages of poor and rugged Brittany were uprooted against their will and shipped to Quebec. Soldiers stationed in North American forts were ordered to remain in Canada when their service was complete. Prostitutes (*filles du roi,* or "the king's daughters") were rounded up and dispatched to be wives of settlers—as were orphan girls and the daughters of peasants who got into trouble with the tax collector.

But New France just would not grow. By 1713, after a century of settlement, the French population in North America was 25,000, about the same number of people as lived in the single English colony of Pennsylvania, which was but 30 years old.

French Expansion

The boldness of the French Canadians almost compensated for the poverty of their numbers. French traders, trappers, and priests fanned out in the north woods surrounding the Great Lakes, whereas the English huddled within a few miles of ocean breakers. Like few English colonials, these coureurs de bois (literally, "runners of the woods") were willing—indeed eager—to adapt more than halfway to the way of life by which the Indians flourished in the wilderness.

Brown Brothers

▲ *In 1673, a French Jesuit missionary stationed in what is now Michigan, Father Jacques Marquette, accompanied a fur trapper, Louis Joliet, on a voyage by canoe down the Mississippi to the mouth of the Arkansas River. The French penetrated the heart of the continent before the English settled the Carolinas and Pennsylvania.*

Champlain encouraged amalgamation with the natives: "Our sons shall wed your daughters and we shall be but one people"—a sentiment unimaginable in the English colonies. In doing so, and in adopting Indian dress with a few of their own affectations added, the coureurs de bois won the friendship and respect of most of the tribes they confronted. When a governor of Virginia reached the crest of the Appalachians, he celebrated by covering a table with pressed linen and setting it with fine china, silver, and crystal. When a Frenchman broke new ground hundreds of miles deeper in the interior, he roasted a slab of venison and ate it with his hands while hunkering in the dust.

Intrepid French explorers charted what is now the central third of the United States. In 1673, Louis Joliet and Father Jacques Marquette, a Jesuit priest, navigated the Mississippi to the mouth of the Arkansas River. They turned back only because Indians told them of other whites to the south, whom Marquette and Joliet correctly reckoned to be Spaniards, hostile to the French.

In 1682, when Pennsylvania was getting started on the hospitable banks of the Delaware, René-Robert Cavelier, Sieur de La Salle, reached the mouth of the Mississippi. In 1699, a generation before the founding of Georgia, Pierre Le Moyne Iberville planted settlements at New Orleans and on the Gulf of Mexico at Mobile. New Orleans became the hub of the second French province in North America, Louisiana.

French America was a flimsy empire by English standards, a string of lonely log forts and trading posts: Kaskaskia and Cahokia in the Illinois country; St. Louis where the Missouri flows into the Mississippi; dots on a map connected by lakes, rivers, creeks, and *portages* (a word that Americans learned from the Canadians, meaning a place canoes had to be *carried* from one waterway to another).

Contrasting Ways of Life

The French had their conflicts with the Indians, most notably with the Iroquois Confederacy, but also, after 1700, with the Fox in Wisconsin and the Natchez of Tennessee, who, in 1729, killed every Frenchman in their territory. Generally, however, the French had better relations with Indians than the English did. There were several reasons for this, none more important than their small numbers. In remaining so few, the French did not threaten the natives with inundation as the ever growing English colonies did.

Second in importance, the English colonial way of life clashed head-on with Indian culture, whereas French interests only benefited the tribes (or so it seemed). Both European peoples offered desirable trade goods in return for furs and hides. However, New France was not much more than a string of trading posts; the English colonies were primarily agricultural. The French waited in their forts for Indians to come to them, or glided through the forests with them. The English insatiably occupied more and more land and chopped the forests down. Each acre of land put to the plow was an acre less where deer could be shot and berries gathered.

▲ *No Protestant denomination in the English colonies was nearly as devoted and industrious in attempting to convert and educate Indians as the Jesuit priests in New France were. They were immensely successful—eventually even among the Iroquois, who martyred six of them in the 1640s and mutilated others.*

Religion

Functional differences between the Roman Catholicism of the French and the Protestant religions of the English, particularly Puritanism, affected Indian-white relations. Both the English and French gave lip service to the goal of winning Indians' souls to Christianity. The establishment of missions was mentioned in every colonial charter. Some pious Englishmen, like Roger Williams and John Eliot, the "Apostle of the Indians," took the task of converting Indians seriously. Dartmouth College in New Hampshire originated as a school for Indians. Virginia's College of William and Mary provided for Indian education. Many Indians in English America accepted baptism.

It was not difficult, however, for English colonials to lose interest in saving savage souls. The Church of England was nationalistic; Puritanism was highly ethnocentric. The religion of the English settlers was intimately wrapped up with their English customs, prejudices, language, manners, and even the cut of the clothes they wore.

The Puritans, moreover, looked upon salvation as a gift of God bestowed on very few of their own kind. They regarded Spanish and French Catholics as near-satanic and saw other Europeans' modestly different customs and manners as evidence of their inferiority. How could such people view Indians—half-naked, with ways of doing things far more exotic to them than the ways of Spaniards and Frenchmen—as "visible saints"? It could be done, but it was not easy to do it.

The French had their own bag of cultural prejudices. (*Huron,* the name they gave their first Indian allies, meant "lout" or "ruffian.") However, it was a basic tenet of their Roman Catholicism that God meant every human being to belong to the church. (*Catholic* means "universal.") So the Roman Catholic Church had been shaped by a history of accommodating a galaxy of different cultures within it. Accepting baptism in the "one true church" was what mattered, not the clothing one wore or the foods one preferred. When French Jesuits preached to Indians, they emphasized the similarities between Indian tradition and Catholic practice. English Protestant preachers seemed always to be talking about the old ways the Indians had to give up.

The priests of New France also had an advantage over Protestant missionaries in the ornate and mystical Roman Catholic ritual. The mystery of the Mass, the welter of ceremonies, and the vividly decorated statues appealed to the Indians' aesthetic sense. The Puritans, by contrast, were a people of the word. Individual study of the Bible and long sermons rooted in European learning and European logic were the foundations of their worship. Indians did not read. European learning was not Indian learning.

The Five Nations

Nonetheless, the English had very valuable Indian allies in the Iroquois, who had long warred with Algonkian tribes and the Huron, who turned to the French. When the Canadians outfitted their allies with firearms, the Iroquois suffered. The hardships and fears their defeats engendered ensured that when they found European contacts—first the Dutch in Fort Orange, then the English, who replaced them in what they called Albany—they embraced the newcomers. They would have embraced devils who brought guns. They had a generation's worth of scores to settle.

Settle them they did. The Iroquois took the offensive against the Algonkians, the Huron, and the French with a terrifying vengeance. Their cruelties shocked both English and French, people who, practicing disembowelment of live convicts, might have been more understanding. The Iroquois slowly burned and chewed the fingers and toes from their captives. They dined on husbands before the eyes of their wives and mothers in front of their children. Canada's coureurs de bois so feared the Iroquois that, in order to avoid them, they detoured as many as a thousand miles when they trekked to the trapping grounds in the Illinois country. Better months of circuitous, laborious travel than crossing the path of Iroquois warriors.

AMERICANS FROM AFRICA

To the English who came to the colonies to farm, the Indians were impediments, like the massive oaks and maples of the forests. They thought in terms of clearing the land of people as well as trees. Colonists came to view America's third great people, however, as essential to economic development. These were people of the black race, mostly from around the Gulf of Guinea in West Africa, who were imported to America against their will in order to solve the commercial farmer's problem of getting things done in a country where land was limitless but backs to bend over it were few.

Slavery and the English

Enslaved Africans and their children had been the backbone of the labor force in the West Indies, in the Spanish mainland colonies, and in Portuguese Brazil long before the founding of Jamestown. So the English, particularly those in the tobacco colonies who needed cheap, dependable labor, had an example to which to look.

The colonists did not, however, turn to Africa or to slavery to bring their crops in—at least not right away. The English lacked a tradition of owning human beings as property. Slavery, even serfdom, had vanished from England centuries before the age of colonies. As for Africa, the English, unlike the Spanish and Portuguese, had little experience of trade and war with its darker-skinned peoples. By the latter 1500s, some English seafarers, notably John Hawkins and Francis Drake, were buying and selling black slaves in the Caribbean. As late as 1618, however, when an African merchant on the Senegal River offered slaves to Richard Jobson in payment for English trade goods, Jobson replied indignantly, "we were a people who did not deal in any such commodities, neither did wee buy or sell one another, or any that had our owne shapes." The African was astonished, saying that other white men who came to his country wanted nothing but slaves. The English captain answered, "They were another kinde of people different from us."

Had this goodly man's principles prevailed, North America would have been spared a great historical wrong, the enslavement of Africans and their descendants. However, just months after the curious incident on the Senegal—and a year before the *Mayflower* anchored at Plymouth, Massachusetts—the history of African Americans began at Jamestown with their enslavement for life.

New Uses for an Old Institution

During the first century of colonization, the English settlers solved their labor problem by adapting to America an institution by which, back home, skills involving long training and practice were passed from generation to generation and by which communities provided for the raising of orphans and illegitimate children.

In England, boys were trained to be blacksmiths, coopers (barrel makers), bakers, and other types of tradesmen by binding them as apprentices to a master of the craft. For a

Enslavement

Unless they were convicts or warriors captured in battle, West Africans taken into slavery were usually seized at night. Whether their captors were Europeans or Africans, darkness provided them with an edge. The clamor of nocturnal raid heightened the terror of the victims and made them more manageable, a fact that twentieth-century secret police forces also understood. Mostly, the traders took men, but teenage girls—healthy and young enough to have a long life of childbearing ahead of them—were also desirable merchandise. The elderly, who could not work or withstand the rigors of the "middle passage," were clubbed to death or, if lucky, left behind.

Captives were marched quickly toward the sea in "coffles"—they were tied or chained together—to discourage the defiant and desperate from making a break for the bush. The practice

North Wind Picture Archives

was adopted by slave traders in America, not to mention prison guards. If the raiders feared a retaliatory attack, there was no delay on behalf of the ill, injured, or exhausted. They were cut out of the coffles and often killed on the spot.

At the mouths of the Niger, Volta, and other rivers, captives were confined in a stockade called a "factory." There they might languish for weeks, fed on yams and millet. If there had not been whites in the capture party, the victims soon made their acquaintance. Well-guarded, white buyers walked through the stockades, kneading muscles and examining teeth as if they were buying horses. They paid (in 1700) about £5 per slave in iron bars, cloth, rum, guns, kettles, and axes. Who can know what thoughts tortured the captives' minds? They had likely heard of others who had been kidnapped but had little idea what happened to them.

The ship on which slaves were transported across the Atlantic was possibly, by the eighteenth century, specially constructed for the trade. In these "slavers," captives were packed side by side on their backs, on shelflike decks, one deck 2 feet above the other. They were chained, wrist to wrist and ankle to ankle. Most vessels in the slave trade, however, were ordinary merchant ships, "multipurpose," on which conditions might be better, or maybe worse.

Scurvy or dysentery commonly swept through the hold. Every morning, the crew's first task was to look for dead, cut

any out, and dump the bodies overboard. If the weather was bad or the captain nervous about mutiny, the Africans would not be allowed a break on deck. The stench and filth in the hold—from sweat, vomit, urine, feces, and death—can hardly be imagined. Some people simply cracked, killing themselves or others in fits of insanity.

Young girls were vulnerable to sexual abuse. It depended largely on the character of the captain. He might be so hardened by the trade that he allowed his men full rein. However—rather more difficult to understand—many slave traders were pious, morally strict Calvinists or Quakers. The business of treating humans like livestock did not challenge their scruples, but they punished rape with whipping.

Comparatively few Africans were taken directly to the continental colonies. Most went first to the West Indies, usually Barbados or Jamaica, both because it shortened the voyage and for "seasoning"—in effect, teaching men and women just what they were: slaves. Arrival in Virginia or South Carolina (or New York or Massachusetts) was practically a deliverance for the captives. There were horrors yet to be undergone—the sale at market, the emotionally devastating experience of settling into a new, altogether foreign way of life, and the lifetime of hard forced labor for which they had been seized and sold. But anything must have seemed for the better after the nightmarish middle passage and seasoning.

period of years—commonly seven—the master was entitled to the apprentice's complete obedience and to the use of the boy's labor, in return for housing, board, clothing, and teaching the lad the mysteries of his trade. Ideally, master, apprentice, and society benefited.

Similarly, communities provided for orphans, girls as well as boys, by binding them to householders as servants. In return for the child's labor, the family that took an orphan in assumed the community's financial responsibility to care for him or her until adulthood.

Apprentices and servants were not free. As delineated in the Elizabethan Statute of Artificers of 1562, masters exercised the same broad authority over them that parents exercised over their children, including the legal right to administer corporal punishment that was often nasty. The brutalized servant is a stock character in literature and folklore.

At the same time, apprentices and servants were not slaves. They were not the property of their masters. They retained certain individual rights their masters were legally bound to respect, and the term of their servitude was specified

Before the *Mayflower*

Most indentured servants were British: English, Scots, Welsh, and Irish. As early as 1619, however, a Dutch vessel sailed up the Chesapeake and displayed to the Jamestowners about 20 black Africans whom the Dutch had captured from a slave trader bound for the Spanish West Indies. The Virginians bought them and continued to buy blacks throughout the 1600s.

First- and second-generation African Americans were servants, not slaves. One of the black men who arrived in Jamestown in 1619 took the name Anthony Johnson and became a prosperous farmer with several white servants bound to him. As early as 1650, there was a small, free black population in the Chesapeake colonies. The only plausible origin of this community is the fact that, like white servants, the first blacks in Virginia and Maryland were freed after a specified term of service.

Also by 1650, however, the assemblies of Virginia and Maryland were enacting laws stating that black servants would, in the future, serve *durante vita* ("for life"). This significant turn in law and cruel twist in the fate of African Americans was due to changing economic and social circum-

in a legal document. The day came when the apprentice and the maidservant walked off as free as anyone of their class.

Indentured Servants

Colonial planters and farmers who needed labor, adapted this familiar institution as indentured servitude. For an outlay of £6 to £30 to pay the cost of transatlantic passage and the fee of the contractor who signed up servants in England, a colonist secured the services of a worker bound as a servant for between four and seven years. The price and the length of time served depended upon just how badly American masters needed field hands and how many English men and women were willing to sign an "indenture," as the document was called.

The system worked. Well into the 1700s, indentured servants brought in the bulk of America's cash crops in every colony but South Carolina. The proportion of servants in the population was highest in Virginia and Maryland. Eighty percent were men; by custom, English women were less likely to work in the fields, and that was where a bound laborer was profitable.

A large majority of servants signed their indentures voluntarily. They were more than willing to trade several years of their wretched lives for the chance of a fresh start afterward. However, the practice of filling the hold of a servant ship by kidnapping boys or careless young men in English seaports was common enough. It was unwise to drink too heavily in a tavern near the harbor on the night a servant ship was scheduled to weigh anchor. In addition, English courts sentenced criminals—guilty of petty or vicious crimes—to "transportation" to the colonies, where they joined the ranks of indentured servants.

stances, to problems inherent in the institution of indentured servitude, and to the peculiar vulnerability of an identifiable minority in a society in which the vast majority was white.

Declining Death Rate, Collapsing Prices

A black slave serving *durante vita* cost considerably more than a white servant bound to labor for his master for a few years. The difference in price could amount to several tons of tobacco. Transportation costs from Africa were higher than for servants brought from Britain. And, unlike the agents who signed up white servants at no cost to themselves, slave traders in West Africa had to pay for their human cargoes.

Despite the higher cost, the African slave would seem, on the face of it, to have been a better deal than the white servant. His master could work him for a lifetime; there was no need to replace him after five or seven years. But in fact, the cheaper white servant was the better buy during most of the 1600s. Thanks to malaria, typhoid fever, yellow fever, and other contagious diseases ranging from smallpox to influenza, everyone coming to the Chesapeake colonies faced poor prospects of living a long life. Life expectancy for male immigrants to Maryland was 43. Governor Berkeley of Virginia estimated that, during the 1660s, four out of five indentured servants in that colony died within a few years of arriving.

So it did not matter much that the law gave planters possession of Africans for life. African slave and Irish servant alike were apt to be dead within a few years of purchase. The best buy in such circumstances was the laborer whose purchase price was lower. Term of service was little more than an abstraction. As long as tobacco prices were high, the best business decision was to get your workers as cheaply as you could and squeeze as much tobacco out of them as you could before you wrapped them in a shroud.

In the 1660s, however, the price of tobacco began its decline. By the end of the century, the death rate had noticeably declined too. After 1700, planters were presented with an incentive to save on the *annual* cost of their laborers rather than on the initial outlay. If all Virginians and Marylanders, black and white, were living longer, it made sense to buy workers who served longer. Moreover, blacks seemed more resistant to some of the diseases that toppled whites in the South's semitropical climate, and, as Bacon's Rebellion

illustrated so dramatically, white servants and former servants could be troublesome people—more trouble, planters thought, than black slaves. Finally, by 1700, the law in every colony held that the children of slave parents (or just a slave mother) were also slaves, the property of the master. The children of white servants were free, but still an expense to their mother's master during their infancy.

The Trouble with Servants

Colonial courts were crowded with masters complaining about servants' insolence, negligence, and laziness, about stolen food and drink, rowdy parties, and pregnancy, which exempted women from work for as long as a year. (Servants took their masters to court for mistreatment too, but rarely, and even more rarely did they win their case.)

Then there were runaways. Throughout the colonies, even in the most populated parts of the Tidewater, America was mostly woods. Farms and plantations were gaps in the forest. In Virginia and Maryland, the grandest plantations were separated from one another by belts of virgin hardwood or second-growth "pineys," old fields gone to scrub. In the South, towns were few. Roads were often just tracks, some of them so narrow two horsemen could not pass without jostling.

Determined servants found it a challenge, but far from impossible, to run away, hide, and elude capture. Planters' letters were flecked with annoyance about lost workers and lost investments. The recapture and return of runaways was a major activity of sheriffs, the only law enforcement officers in rural areas, and the source of much of their income. Officials in cities like Baltimore and Philadelphia were flooded with descriptions of runaways. Punishment was harsh—a whipping and extra time in service. Nevertheless, the opportunities of freedom and the odds of success tempted many.

The Badge of Race

The sympathy of many colonials for fugitive servants and the ease with which a white runaway could blend into an urban crowd were two more reasons planters slowly turned from a workforce of white indentured servants to black slaves.

Runaways found help or, at least, passive commiseration. The most famous colonial runaway, Benjamin Franklin, walked out on his master in Boston (his brother) in 1723 and traveled to Philadelphia by sea and land. Any number of people guessed he was a fugitive servant, but no one turned him in.

If a runaway reached a city, Philadelphia, New York, even still little Baltimore, he or she had a good chance of invisibility in the swarms of strangers, newly arrived immigrants, who were always present. An African American's color, however, was a badge, a "red flag." An escaped slave could not lose himself so easily in the throngs. If authorities assumed that blacks were slaves unless they could prove otherwise (free blacks carefully preserved precious documents

> **An Unusual Verdict**
> In New York City in 1728, Margaret Anderson, a servant, sued her master for her freedom for "very often Immoderately Correcting her"—beating her badly, in other words. She won her case. Her victory was not unique, but it was unusual. Only a clearly sadistic master could lose such a suit.

establishing their status), black strangers were detained and possible owners informed. Constables and sheriffs collected fees, and for planters, the workforce was that much more controllable.

In 1625, after the Jamestown Massacre, there were 25 black servants in Virginia, 2 percent of the population. In 1660, there were 9,000 blacks in Virginia, less than 4 percent of the population. (It is not clear how many were free or would know freedom.) In 1670, there were 20,000 blacks in Virginia, a majority of them slaves under a law enacted that year. After 1700, the colony's slave population grew rapidly until, by the time of the Revolution, it approached 200,000.

South Carolina was the one colony where, before 1700, slaves formed the bulk of the workforce; African Americans were almost a fifth of the colony's population in 1680. By 1720, 67 percent of South Carolinians were black, all but a few in bondage. A British officer observed, "They sell the servants here as they do their horses, and advertise them as they do their beef and oatmeal."

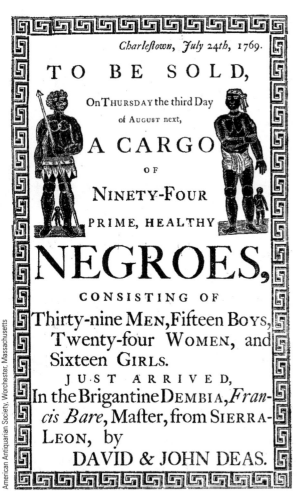

▲ *A typical advertisement of a slave auction. This one in Charleston in 1769 was unusual in that the people to be sold had been brought directly from Africa. Most African slaves in the colonies made a stop in the West Indies, where they were "seasoned."*

THE SLAVE TRADE

This demand for slave labor transformed attitudes toward trading in African slaves. Ships from England and New England, most famously Newport, Rhode Island, sailed annually to Africa to capture or purchase slaves. The acquisition of slaves in the West Indies, especially Cuba and Jamaica, was an even bigger business.

Collaboration in Atrocity

Some whites ventured up the rivers of West Africa and themselves seized, or "panyared," villagers. A trader of 1787 explained, "In the night we broke into the villages and, rushing into the huts of the inhabitants, seized men, women, and children promiscuously."

Primarily, however, the slave trade was a collaboration between African and white merchants. At first, African kings and lesser chiefs sold their own criminals, unsuccessful rivals, or garden variety troublemakers to the white-skinned strangers. As the demand for slaves grew and profits soared, some aggressive tribes launched raids inland in search of fresh sources of supply among other peoples. The economy of the great Ashanti Confederation of West Africa depended more than casually on the commerce in slaves. By 1750, King Tegbesu of Dahomey was pocketing £250,000 annually by selling slaves to the Americas.

Whites anchored their ships off the coast or fortified themselves in stockades on defensible islands like Gorée off Dakar or at the mouths of rivers. They offered iron bars, steel knives, brass, glass bottles, kettles, bells, cloth, guns, powder, liquor, and tobacco in return for human merchandise. It was not race versus race; it was business. A Dahomeyan felt no more kinship with an Oyo than with a Portuguese or a Quaker.

The vilest part of the slave trade was the sea crossing, called the "middle passage" because it was preceded and followed by overland marches. Rather than providing the most healthful circumstances possible for their valuable, vulnerable cargo and keeping mortality low, the traders crammed the slaves in "like herrings in a barrel."

If only one in 20 captives died, the voyage was considered an extraordinary success. If one in five died, which was by no means unusual, the profits were still considerable. A slave who cost £5 to £10 in Africa in 1700 sold in the New World for a minimum of £25. Only as the eighteenth century progressed did mortality on the middle passage decline. By the late 1700s, shipmasters reported that proportionally more slaves survived than crewmen—of whom, in the Guinea trade, one in five sailors failed to complete a voyage. (Deaths at sea on the North Atlantic routes were one in every 100.)

West African Roots

Most Africans fated to be North Americans were from lands bordering the Gulf of Guinea, the present-day nations of Gambia, Senegal, Guinea, Liberia, Sierra Leone, Ivory

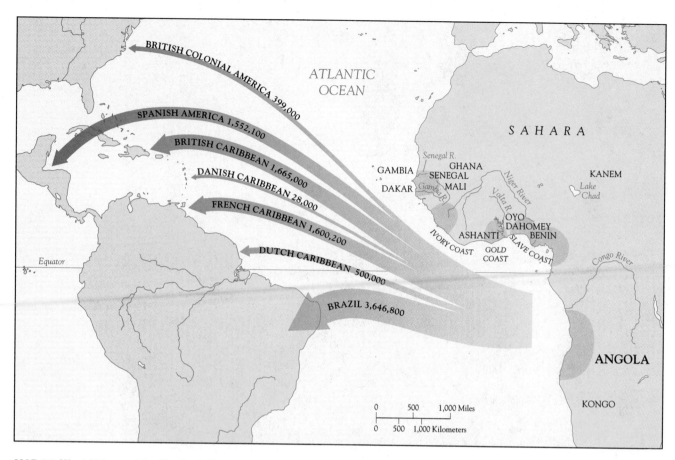

MAP 5:2 West Africa and the Roots of Slavery, 1500–1810 Extensive research indicates that enslaved Africans transported to English North America were a tiny fraction of the massive depopulation of West Africa. Most African Americans are descended from ancestors who were taken first to the West Indies, especially Cuba, and only later—a year or two, or a generation or two later—sold in what became the United States.

Coast, Ghana, Togo, Benin, and Nigeria. In ethnic origin, the majority were probably Wolof, Malinke, Oyo, Mandingo, Ashanti, Yoruba, Hausa, and Ibo.

Much of the coastline of West Africa was mangrove swamp, but approximately 100 miles inland the country pitches upward. It provided a living that was rich enough to support a large population and sophisticated cultures. Religiously, most West Africans were polytheists who worshiped a complicated hierarchy of gods and spirits. Many tribes venerated the spirits of dead ancestors, and sacrifice was central to most religions. Islam and Christianity were making headway as Arab slave traders came from the north and Christians from the sea.

West Africa was no Eden. The people who lived there had to be skilled, hardworking agriculturists. Ironically, their range and skills increased as slave traders introduced new crops: maize, cassava, peanuts, and sweet potatoes. The fact that intensive farming was a bulwark of West African culture helps to explain why West Africans were more appealing to American planters than Indians were. In addition to rice cultivation, which Africans probably introduced to the Carolinas, they utilized the heavy hoe, which was the mainstay of chopping weeds in the fertile southern soil.

The Vulnerability of a Disunited People

There was no such person as a typical captive. Male slaves might have been princes, priests, farmers, or murderers. Most commonly, however, they were ordinary people who had the bad luck to catch the eye of raiders. Most female slaves also came from the ordinary classes. Their condition as women in Africa depended on the tribe to which they belonged. In most, women did a major part of the heavy labor. In other tribes, such as the Ashanti, descent was traced in the maternal line, and women were accorded high status, although hardly equality.

Once in the colonies, these diverse peoples adopted English because it was the only feasible means of communication among themselves. In time, they also found in their masters' Protestantism, albeit with a great deal of emphasis on the stories of the ancient Hebrews' captivities and deliverance, a solace in their misery. For the most part, however, they were shut out of the mainstream of American development for more than three centuries after the first African stepped nervously from the gangplank of the Dutch ship anchored at Jamestown in 1619.

▲ *The slaves' cabins at South Carolina's Mulberry Plantation were far more substantial than the descriptions of most slave housing of the early 1700s. Mulberry was an outlying development. The handsome "big house" was designed as a fortress in which slaves and neighbors could shelter in case of an Indian attack.*

for FURTHER READING

On Indians, see Alvin M. Josephy, *The Indian Heritage of America*, 1968; Harold E. Driver, *Indians of North America*, 1970; Wilcomb E. Washburn, *The Indian in America*, 1975, and *Cambridge History of the Natives of the World*, vol. 3: *North America*, 1993; and Robert F. Spencer et al., *The Native Americans: Ethnology and Background of the North American Indians*, 1977.

James Axtell is the leading historian of Native Americans in the colonial period. See Axtell's *The European and the Indian*, 1981; and *The Invasion Within: The Contest of Cultures in Colonial America*, 1985. Also see Gary Nash, *Red, White, and Black*, 1982; and Neal Salisbury, *Manitou and Providence: Indians, Europeans, and the Making of New England*, 1982.

A series of books by nineteenth-century literary historian Francis Parkman remain fine reading about the French in North America: *French North America: The Pioneers of France in the New World*, 1865; *The Jesuits in North America*, 1867; *The Old Regime in Canada*, 1874; *Count Frontenac and New France*, 1877; and *LaSalle and the Discovery of the Great West*, 1879. A fine single-volume history of the subject is William J. Eccles, *France in America*, 1972. Also see Eccles's *The Canadian Frontier, 1534–1760*, 1969.

On indentured servitude and the evolution of African slavery in English America, see David W. Galenson, *White Servitude in Colonial America*, 1981; and Edmund S. Morgan, *American Slavery, American Freedom*, 1975. Philip D. Curtin, *The Atlantic Slave Trade*, 1969, is still the definitive work on that subject. An invaluable overview is David B. Davis, *The Problem of Slavery in Western Culture*, 1966. The beginning portion of Kenneth Stampp, *The Peculiar Institution*, 1956, provides important information on early slavery.

AMERICAN JOURNEY ONLINE AND INFOTRAC COLLEGE EDITION

Visit the source collections at http://ajaccess.wadsworth.com and http://infotrac.thomsonlearning.com, and use the Search function with the following key terms to explore documents, images, audio and video clips, articles, and commentary related to the material in this chapter:

Algonquian
Atlantic slave trade
Five Nations
Iroquois
King Philip's War (or Metacom's War)

Additional resources, exercises, and Internet links related to this chapter are available on *The American Past* Web site: http://history.wadsworth.com/americanpast7e.

HISTORY ONLINE

The Iroquois

www.tolatsga.org/iro.html

Quick, thoroughgoing essay on the history of the Iroquois, the indispensable Indian allies of the English colonists.

Virtual Museum of New France

www.civilization.ca/vmnf/vmnfe.asp

Comprehensive Canadian site: Text and illustrations on the early years and chief personalities in the development of New France.

African Americans

www.pbs.org/wgbh/aia/home.html

A Public Broadcasting System Web site on African American history beginning in the 1600s.

CHAPTER

6

A MATURING SOCIETY

Society, Culture, and War in the 1700s

North Wind Picture Archives

God hath sifted a nation that he might send choice grain into this wilderness.

William Stoughton

Sir, they are a race of convicts, and ought to be thankful for anything we allow them short of hanging.

Samuel Johnson

IN 1706, A BOY was born into the household of a Boston tallow maker, an artisan who made candles and soap from animal fats. There would have been little fuss made over the arrival of Benjamin Franklin; he was the tenth child in the family.

Large families were common in the colonies. Typically, a woman married in her early 20s, several years younger than women in Britain. She bore 6 to 8 children, a majority of whom, in the 1700s, survived to be adults, a higher proportion than in Great Britain. Children were economic assets then, not the costly creatures they are today. Children consumed little but food, which was cheap in the colonies. There was productive work for them by the time they reached 5 or 6: feeding chickens, gathering eggs, fetching water and firewood. Teenagers (neither the word nor the concept of adolescence as a distinct stage of life was known) put in a full day's work, thus contributing more to a household's economy than they took from it. Many families willingly took in teenagers not their own for this reason.

Benjamin Franklin went to work in his father's workshop at the age of 10. At 12, he was apprenticed to his half brother, a printer. They did not get along, and, at 17, Ben ran away to Philadelphia. But he had learned the trade, which, in the eighteenth century, involved writing as well as setting the words of others in type. Franklin was good, imitating the elegant style of the fashionable English essayists Joseph Addison and Richard Steele.

No one faulted him for imitation. Colonials did not say, as Noah Webster and Ralph Waldo Emerson would say a century later, that Americans should write distinctively American literature in a distinctively American language. Bostonians (and New Yorkers, Philadelphians, and country folk) were pleased to be colonials. They were proud to be the overseas subjects of a realm they believed the most beneficent on earth, "a mighty empire in numbers little inferior to the greatest in Europe, and in felicity to none." They gladly took their customs and culture, as well as their laws and the manufactured goods they needed, from the mother country (after 1707, no longer "England" but "Great Britain").

During Franklin's long life (he lived until 1790), British America flowered, then fruited, outgrowing the colonial mentality. Franklin did not miss a turn on the road. He grew rich and became the best-known American of his time, respected at home, lionized in Europe. Founding libraries, learned societies, the first American hospital, and the first trained fire department, he was devoted to social improvement. He was an inventor (the lightning rod, bifocals, and an efficient stove for heat were among his inventions), a scientist, and, as he grew wealthy and famous, a celebrity. He devised a scheme to unite the colonies in 1754, the Albany Plan of Union. (It was rejected.) He signed the Declaration of Independence and the Constitution. Slavery, which during his lifetime quietly evolved from a minor colonial institution into a matter of grave concern, did not escape Franklin's notice. His final public statement called for its abolition.

SOCIETY AND ECONOMY

Between 1700 and 1776, the population of the colonies increased tenfold, from about 250,000 people to 2.5 million. Natural increase accounted for much of this astonishing growth. Both family size and life expectancy were greater in North America than anywhere else in the world. In New England (with the exception of infants, whose first years were dangerous, and women dying in first childbirth), life expectancy was nearly as high as it is today with all of our precautions and medicine. New Englanders were the first people in history to have personally known their grandparents as a matter of routine.

Their grandfathers, anyway—unlike today, when women outlive men by half a dozen years, men were longer-lived in the eighteenth century. The reason was, of course, childbirth, which cut short the lives of young wives. However, a New England male of 20 was apt to die nearer 70 years of age than 60; an inhabitant of the Middle Colonies, more than 60. Life expectancy was less in the South: 45 in Virginia and Maryland, 42 in the Carolinas and Georgia. (Life expectancy for a white person of 20 in the British West Indies was 40; West Indian slaves died in such chilling numbers that there was virtually no natural increase of the black population during the 1700s.)

Large, healthy families were only part of the growth of the colonies. The colonies were also flooded by immigrants, as many as 800,000 between 1700 and the War for Independence. By no means were they all English.

North Wind Picture Archives

▲ *Benjamin Franklin (1706–1790). Until the War for Independence made George Washington famous, Franklin was the only American widely known in Europe. Rich, an inventor, the founder of numerous institutions in Philadelphia, a lobbyist in London for Pennsylvania and Massachusetts, he was to be a successful diplomat during the Revolution.*

Immigration from Germany

Germans and German-speaking Austrians responded enthusiastically to William Penn's invitation to take up farms in Pennsylvania. By the 1750s, they were so numerous in Philadelphia, Lancaster, and York counties that Benjamin Franklin, who called them "the most stupid of their nation," was alarmed. They will "Germanize us instead of us Anglifying them," he wrote, "and will never adopt our Language or Customs." Germans were a third of Pennsylvania's population in 1776; it was seriously proposed that German, not English, be the official language of the then independent state.

Many German immigrants were members of the plain-living Moravian, Amish, Mennonite, and Hutterite sects. Like the Quakers, they were pacifists and reflexively supported the Quaker party in elections. No doubt, their bloc voting annoyed Franklin, a leader of Pennsylvania's anti-Quaker political faction, as much as the sounds of the German language on Philadelphia's streets.

The Scotch-Irish

More numerous than the Germans (and more widely disliked) were the Scotch-Irish. They were descendants of Protestant Scots whom, a century earlier, James I settled in northern Ireland to displace the rebellious Catholic Irish there. By the 1700s, however, they had lost favor with the Crown and were suffering from steep increases in rent and parliamentary acts undercutting the weaving industry, on which many depended for their livelihood. About 4,000 Scotch-Irish a year gave up on the Emerald Isle and emigrated to the colonies, "huddled together like brutes without regard to age or sex or sense of decency."

They were a combative people in Ireland, ever ready with cudgels to battle Catholics, and they did not mellow in American air. James Logan, the agent of the Penn family in Philadelphia, wrote in consternation, "I must own, from my experience in the land office, that the settlement of five families from Ireland gives me more trouble than fifty of any other people."

The Scotch-Irish wanted land. To get it after 1700, they had to move to the hilly backcountry of western Pennsylvania, Virginia, and the Carolinas. There, with muskets and rifles rather than cudgels, they confronted Indians with whom Quakers like Logan tried to have amicable relations.

The Scotch-Irish frontiersmen made their own Indian policy. Far from the capital of Philadelphia, they attacked their Native American neighbors for good reason and bad. Franklin's anti-Quaker party generally supported them in the colonial assembly and, when Britain and France went to war, so did the Crown, for most of the Indians of the region were at least casual allies of the French in Canada.

The pacifist Quakers were realists during the Anglo-French wars. They accommodated the Crown by such contrivances as voting money "for the king's use," laying on royal shoulders the sin of spending it on guns and soldiers, or for "grain," not specifying whether the grains be of wheat or gunpowder. During periods of peace between Britain and France, however, homegrown Scotch-Irish aggressiveness presented the Quaker establishment with a stickier moral problem. If they stood by their commitment to popular government, they became parties to frontier carnage, a mockery of their pacifism. If they insisted on peace and fair dealings with the Indians, they would defy the demands of the majority of Pennsylvanians, a mockery of their democratic inclinations.

By the end of the 1750s, many Quaker officials gave up, retiring from public life. Thus they preserved their personal

(No. II.)

Philadelphische ZEITUNG.

SONNABEND, den 24 Jun. 1732.

WIEwohl ich geglaubet hätte, dass
sich unter denen teutschen Ein-
wohnern dieses Landes mehr Lieb-
haber solten gefunden haben, die
dieses zumahl vor junge Persohnen
so nützliche werck, die ausgabe der Zeitungen
nehmlich, befördern, und dazu mit anstehen
würden; so erstrecket sich doch die anzahl de-
rer die sich dazu unterschrieben haben vor jetzo
nicht über 50. Nichts desto weniger habe auf
meiner seiten nicht ermangeln wollen damit einen anfang zu machen, der hoffnung lebende,
dass sich noch mehrere einfinden werden selbi-
ges zu befördern, sonsten ich mich genöthiget
sehen würde, bald wieder damit auf zu hören.
Ich hatte zwar in meiner ersten Zeitung ver-
sprochen dieselbe alle 8 tage zu publiciren, doch
die meisten stimmen haben erwählet dieselbe lieber vor 5. Schillinge das gantze Jahr alle 14.
tage einmahl zu haben; weilen alsdann függli-
cher zwey und zwey eine zeitung halten, und
jede person gemächlicher die helffte bezahlen
könte; Welches ich mir dann auch gefallen las-
se, und selbige von nun an alle 14. tage einmal
heraus geben will. Die Ansprache des Königes
von England, welche ich in meinem vorigen ver-
sprochen, weil sie allzulang, und ich einen andern vorrath von Neuigkeiten bekommen, habe
lieber wollen auslassen, wie ich auch um der ur-
sachen willen meine erklährungen, die wohl ü-
ber einige sachen nöthig gewesen wären, lieber
auf eine andere gelegenheit verspahre, und nur
die brieffe von wort zu wort jetzo mittheile.

Constantinopel Decemb. 15.

HIer ist ein Courier angekommen, mit der
Copey eines Friedens-Tractats, welchen
der König von Persien dem Bassa in Babilonien
zugesandt; nachdem selbige von dem Gross-Vi-
zier denen andern Ministern in dem Seraglio ist
communiciret worden, hat man sie in einem general Divan, welcher am 12. dieses monaths zu
dem ende expres ist gehalten worden, gelesen,
und nur wenige veränderungen darin gemacht.
Man sagt dass vermöge dieses Tractats der grosse Sultan verpflichtet sey, alle die von Persien
eroberte Provintzien wiederum zu geben, ausge-
nommen Georgia und die alte Provintz von Babilonien: Degestan solle dem Printzen wieder
eingeräumet werden, der dessen Souverainer
Herr eigentlich ist, und welcher alhier schon an-
derthalb Jahr um diese restitution angehalten:
Dass die zwey durch diesen Frieden vereinigte
Machten ihre kräffte zusammen spannen sollen,
die Moscowiter zu zwingen alles was sie von Persien genommen haben, auch wieder zu geben;
doch dass sie diesfals zu keiner thätlichkeit kom-
men sollen, biss sie vorhero alle mittel der un-
terhandlung versuchet haben; im fall die Cza-
rin aber solches weigern solte, sie ihre waffen
nicht niederlegen wollen, biss alle die Länder
wieder erobert seyn. Was eine jede von diesen
zweyen Machten währenden diesem Kriege er-
obern werde, solle derselben verbleiben.
Weiters wird versichert, dass der Gross Vizier
gewissen fremden Ministern ein Memorial hat
lassen einhandigen, worinnen er trachtet die noth-
wendigkeit zu behaupten, dass man sich der all-
zu grossen Anwachsung der Moscowitischen
macht entgegen setze; und von was grossem ge-
wicht es vor das Ottomannische Reich sey, die-
selben von der Caspischen See zu vertreiben.
Es werden verschiedene Kriegs-Schiffe vom ersten und zweyten rang gebauet, und grosse Ma-
gazinen von geschütz und mund provision auf-
gerich-

▲ *One of several German-language newspapers published in colonial Philadelphia. Franklin and others worried that their city might become more German than English.*

scruples (and prospered mightily in trade) while the back-country settlers, Franklin's party, and the Crown had free rein to pursue their Indian wars.

Family, Politics, Property

Whatever the ethnicity or religion of colonials, the family had a standing in law, custom, and sentiment that can be difficult to comprehend today. The family, with broad authority vested in patriarch and matriarch (ultimately in the husband), was the basic social and economic institution, much more than the amorphous, sentimental association it is today. Early Puritan laws requiring all people, including bachelors, spinsters (unmarried women), infants, and the elderly to live within a household were long gone, but the practice survived: The "loner" was looked upon with suspicion.

The family, not the individual, was the political unit. Only the male heads of property-owning families voted. (Women could be heads of household but not voters.) There might be several adult males in a household—grown children, servants, and employees—but they did not vote. Just how much property was required for participation in elections varied from colony to colony, but it was not very much. Whereas about one British male in three could vote, almost three-fourths qualified in the colonies. Actual participation was something else: Less than a quarter of male Bostonians actually cast votes; as many as 40 percent of Pennsylvanians and New Yorkers; about half the adult males in Connecticut.

Property laws, adapted from Britain's, were designed to protect the proprietor class and to maintain its families' status in society. For example, Virginia, Maryland, and South Carolina enacted laws of primogeniture and entail. Primogeniture required that a landed estate be bequeathed as a whole to the eldest son of the deceased head of household, or, if there was no male heir, to his first daughter. Entail meant that a property could not be subdivided for sale. To transfer ownership of an estate in any way, one was required to keep it intact.

The purpose of such laws was to preserve the economic power and social privileges of the propertied, particularly the wealthy. If a tobacco planter with a thousand acres and 30 slaves, enough to support his family in grand style, were legally free to divide his estate among four or five children, the result would be four or five households of middling means. If these properties were subdivided by inheritance, the result, from grandparents to grandchildren, would be a gaggle of struggling subsistence farmers where once there had been a grandee. Entail prevented an individual with an opportunity to make a killing in real estate from ripping the social fabric with his greed. Primogeniture kept paternal sentimentality in check.

The colonial rich, especially in the cities, grew richer during the eighteenth century. In 1700, the richest tenth of Philadelphia's population owned about 40 percent of the city's wealth. By 1774, the richest tenth owned 55 percent.

Social Mobility

People of property were not, of course, insensitive to the fate of their daughters and younger sons. They could and did bequeath them money (*personal* as opposed to *real* property) and gave them land not part of an entailed estate. As in Britain, second sons might be educated for a profession: the

Dutch Women in New York

Married women in New Netherland (New York plus enclaves in New Jersey and Delaware) had significantly different property rights than married women in the English colonies. They owned family property *jointly* with their husbands, not in *coverture.* When one spouse died, the survivor inherited the whole. If the survivor was a woman and she remarried, her property from her previous marriage remained hers independently of her second husband. When she died, the property from her first marriage was divided equally among the sons *and daughters* from the first marriage.

The English guaranteed these property laws when they accepted the surrender of New Netherland in 1664. In time, English law displaced Dutch. However, ethnically Dutch women in New York stubbornly clung to another Dutch practice at odds with English custom. As late as the nineteenth century, many continued to use their maiden names throughout life, rather than their husbands' surnames. Annetje Krygier, married to Jans van Arsdale, remained Annetje Krygier throughout life.

ministry, medicine, law, or the military. A profession maintained their social standing and the possibility of making an advantageous marriage without breaking up the family lands.

George Washington provides a good example. His older brother, Lawrence, inherited the extensive Washington lands. He helped George train as a surveyor (which meant land speculator in the colonies) in the hope George would himself "found a family," that is, acquire property. Washington was also an officer in the Virginia militia, and he kept an eye open toward that other avenue leading to property ownership—an heiress or wealthy widow to court and marry, which he found in Martha Custis.

Daughters of the propertied classes were provided with dowries of money or unentailed land, sometimes quite grand dowries, in order to attract husbands of means or, at least, of the same social class. The woman who came into property as a daughter without brothers, or as a widow, was not surprised to have suitors not many days after she buried her husband. The woman who wished to control her property, which only an unmarried woman could do, required a strong will to resist such pressure to remarry.

In fact, there was a great deal to be said on behalf of marriage for the heiress and younger widow. Few women had the training to supervise an estate or business, and heading a propertied household was, for women, awkward at best. Moreover, a woman could ensure, even enhance, her children's wealth and social position by a shrewd marriage. Mary Horsmanden had two husbands and was far more the founder of several prominent Virginia families, including the Carters and Byrds, than either of the husbands she survived. Frances Culpeper successively married three governors of Virginia, continuing to enjoy a social station she obviously relished.

Woman's Place

The woman of property who married did not, as is often said, lose ownership of it. Her husband had the *use* of it. That is, he managed it and decided how to spend the income it provided; in fact, he could make all decisions regarding his wife's property except the decision to sell it. The legal principle of coverture held that "husband and wife are one, and that one, the husband." However, the property a woman brought to a marriage reverted to her if the marriage was dissolved, which meant, in practice, her husband's death. (Divorce was extremely rare.) And it was hers to bequeath to whom she liked; it was not entailed with her husband's property.

If the colonial woman's status and legal standing were inferior to that of the menfolk, she enjoyed a more favorable situation than women in Europe. In most colonies, husbands were forbidden to beat their wives, which sounds like little but, comparatively, was a great deal. At least one man in Massachusetts was fined because he publicly referred to his wife as "a servant"; that is, he demeaned her. Visitors from Europe unfailingly commented on the deference colonial men paid women and the protections women were provided by custom. In the former Puritan colonies, a woman could sue

The Bright Side of Coverture
In legally submerging the wife into the husband, coverture had its bright side for women too. If her husband controlled her property, he alone took the fall for a criminal act they performed as a couple *if* the wife could plausibly plead she was submitting to her husband in the doing of the dirty deed: "If through constraint of his will, she carries out her duty of obedience to the excess of doing unlawful acts, she shall not suffer for them criminally." In a few recorded cases, women went scot-free, although they appear to have acted more like Lady Macbeth than like Melanie Wilkes.

for divorce on the grounds of adultery, bigamy, desertion, impotence, incest, or absence for a period of seven years.

The Lower Orders

Laws pertaining to property were of no meaning to people of the lower classes. In the countryside, free workers and poor farmers were, along with servants and sometimes slaves, often at odds with the propertied classes. In the seaports—the only true cities in the colonies—unskilled workers, journeymen, and apprentices, along with a marginal class of servants, ex-servants, slaves, poor free blacks, sailors on leave, roustabouts, and the omnipresent derelicts, found enough work to be done to keep them alive, but not enough compensation to generate a sense of belonging to the community or to have much respect for conventional morals.

Every port, even small ones, had a disreputable quarter where drunkenness and brawling were endemic and the makings of a mob ever ready to combust. The patterns of underclass crime were much as they are today. In New York City, 95 percent of crimes of violence were committed by men, as were 74 percent of thefts. Rape must have been common but was rarely charged among the lower classes and even more rarely prosecuted because convictions were difficult. The victim was unlikely to be a woman of virtue, and her personal morality was of compelling importance to judges and juries. Statutory rape cases were virtually unknown. The traditional English age of consent was 10! Colonial assemblies upped this, but only to 12 and 14. What colonials called statutory rape we call child molestation.

With witchcraft prosecutions disreputable after the Salem hysteria, the only major crime associated with women was infanticide. With high infant mortality a fact of life, it, like rape, was a difficult crime to prove in court. In New York between 1730 and 1780, 20 women were charged with killing their newborns, but only one was convicted. Illegitimate births were common. A third of all colonial births—and not just among the lower classes—occurred outside marriage or in significantly less than nine months after the wedding.

The colonial urban poor were racially mixed, thereby earning the further contempt of their betters. "The crowd" they formed was kept under control by strict laws and erratic but no-nonsense enforcement. Nevertheless, the crowd made its presence and wishes known in occasional "bread riots," and the lower classes were to play a major part in the tumult that preceded the American Revolution. As with submerged classes of people before and since, riot was the most accessible means of political expression.

Slave Rebellions

The lowliest of the lowly were the slaves. Except in New York, they were not numerous north of the Mason-Dixon line, the boundary between Pennsylvania and Maryland—between North and South—surveyed in 1769. Slaves were only 8 percent of the population in Pennsylvania and 3 percent in Massachusetts.

In the southern colonies, by contrast, slavery grew in importance during the eighteenth century. The number of blacks in Virginia, most of whom were slaves, rose to about 40,000 in 1700 to more than 200,000 at the time of the American Revolution. In a few Virginia counties and over much of South Carolina, blacks outnumbered whites.

Now and then, slaves rebelled. In 1712, slaves in New York City staged an uprising, and, in 1741, a series of arsons there was blamed on slaves and poor whites led by a Catholic priest. Eighteen blacks and four whites were hanged; 13 African American slaves were burned alive; 70 slaves were sold to the West Indies.

In 1739, about 20 blacks from the Stono plantation near Charleston seized guns, killed several planter families, and came within an ace of capturing the lieutenant governor. They put out a call for an uprising, and about 150 other slaves joined them. "With Colours displayed, and two Drums beating," they began to march toward Florida, where, they had learned through a remarkable African American grapevine, the governor of the Spanish colony would grant them freedom.

Most were captured within a week, but some managed to reach St. Augustine and settled to the north of the town in the fortified village of Santa Teresa de Mose. They swore to "shed their last drop of blood in defense of the Great Crown of Spain, and to be the most cruel enemies of the English." The threat—or at least the attraction that Santa Teresa held out to other slaves—was great enough that, the next year, General Oglethorpe of Georgia attacked the village.

THE COLONIES AT WAR

The fabulous growth of the 13 mainland colonies during the eighteenth century, coupled with their physical isolation from the mother country, ensured that the expansive and ever more confident Americans could not remain the tail on the British imperial lion. This is not to say that American independence was inevitable. However, some independence of interests and actions surely was. This was evidenced between 1689 and 1763, when the mother country was involved in a series of wars with France. Colonials participated, or withheld participation, according to what they perceived to be their interests, as opposed to the interests of Great Britain.

Another Kind of War

The European wars of 1689–1763 were fought worldwide, for Britain and France both possessed far-flung empires. Battle raged not only in Europe and North America but also in the Caribbean, in South America, in India, and wherever ships flying belligerent flags met on the high seas.

Broad in scope, the wars were not, however, broad in the extent to which they involved ordinary people. In the late seventeenth and the eighteenth centuries, war was considered an extension of diplomacy, the concern of rulers. They fought frankly to win or to defend territory or trade from rivals, or, like medieval barons, to avenge what one prince took as the insult of another. There was no clash of ideologies, no claims that one social, economic, or political system was engaged in a mortal struggle with another.

Armies were made up of professional soldiers, rough men for whom fighting was a means of making a living. Soldiers did not imagine they were defending a nation or furthering an abstract ideal, such as freedom. If they were attached to anything, it was to their fellow soldiers, who were their community, and sometimes to their commander, who saw to it that they were fed, housed, and paid.

Piracy's Golden Age

There have been pirates as long as ships have carried cargoes worth stealing. Between about 1660 and 1725, the crime became a major problem for merchants in the colonial trade.

A pirate is a seafaring armed robber and usually a murderer, at least as an accomplice. Pirates were rapists infrequently only because they preyed on merchant ships—where the goods were—and a woman was rare aboard such vessels.

Pirates in American waters were called "buccaneers" because the first of them were

From the Collections of the Library of Congress

riffraff from Hispaniola (present-day Haiti and the Dominican Republic) who lived by hunting before they turned to the sea, cooking their meat by slow-smoking it (*boucaner* in French). The commercial wars of the era contributed to the growth of the profession when, to save money in their naval budgets, France, Holland, Spain, and England commissioned privateers, well-armed privately owned ships, to seize (at a percentage of the take) the ships of the countries they were fighting. Privateering could be lucrative. In 1668, Henry Morgan took a break from seizing Spanish ships, captured Portobelo in Panama, and collected a ransom of 250,000 pesos from Spain.

When peace treaties were signed, some privateers found it difficult to give up the business. They continued to raid ports and steal from ships at sea without regard to the flag their victims were flying. In 1701, Captain William Kidd, a New Yorker, was hanged by the British. Just a few years earlier, they had issued him the privateer's Letters of Marque and Reprisal.

Who were the buccaneers? In the early 1720s, 98 percent of those who were captured had started life as "honest seamen," mostly on the merchant ships upon which they came to prey. A large number said that liquor led them to opt for their life of crime. Indeed, according to the records, life on a pirate vessel can seem to have been one long drunken revel so that, on a given day, a large proportion of the crew was incapacitated.

There were other reasons young men (almost all pirates were in their 20s or younger) became pirates. The honest seaman's life was dull, brutalized, poorly paid, laborious, and likely to terminate in an early death. Piracy was exciting, eternally an attraction to young men vexed by frantic hormones. Pirates might risk their lives during their robberies, and the gallows was their fate if they were caught. But each job filled their purses, and, whether or not they were drunk nonstop between hits, they did not work very much. A merchant sloop (a small vessel with one mast) of 100 tons was sailed by a crew of about a dozen; the same vessel under the black flag of piracy had 80 men aboard to handle the same tasks. Even then, with so little to do, pirates who captured slaves put them to work while they looked for buyers. Captain Kidd spoke of stealing 12 slaves whom his crew "intended to make good use of to do the drudgery of [their] ship."

What did ordinary farmers, artisans, and shopkeepers have to do with such a business? As little as they could. At best, war meant heavier taxation. At worst, people were unlucky enough to make their homes where armies fought or marched. Then they suffered, no matter what flag the fighting men were waving.

Otherwise, ordinary people went on as in peacetime. Because princes neither expected nor sought popular support for their wars, it was not a matter of treason in the modern sense of the word when, as in the world wars of 1689 to 1763, many Americans simply sat out the conflict or even traded with the French enemy.

"Little War"

The wars began when William of Orange, a Dutchman, became king of England in 1689. William's life had been dedicated to preventing the expansion of France, and he meant to throw the resources of the British Isles into the struggle.

In 1689, when Louis XIV of France announced his right to take possession of a minor principality on the Rhine River, William strapped on his sword. Few Americans cared who ruled what in the Rhineland. Unconsciously, but with a certain elegance, they proclaimed their disinterest by calling the War of the League of Augsburg, its official name, "King William's War."

Algonkian allies of the French struck in the winter of 1689–1690 with a series of raids on frontier settlements in New York, New Hampshire, and Maine (then part of Massachusetts). These were hardly great battles in the European pattern. Although often led by French officers, they were Indian-style attacks in which warriors hit without warning at isolated farms, killing or capturing the settlers and burning houses and fields. The French called it *petite guerre* ("little war") and viewed the raids as statements that frontier colonials were trespassing on French lands.

Petite guerre worked. Each successful raid moved the unmarked boundary between New France and New England

Pirate crews were so large because their numbers were one key to their success. They were robbers. They did not want to destroy the ships they attacked with their cannon (which they carried for defense). They wanted to board their victims' vessel with the loot undamaged and take what was worth taking. The captain of a merchant ship with 12 seamen who were not fighting men was a fool to resist when faced with 80 vicious pirates armed with cutlasses, knives, and pistols. Few did. Merchant captains knew that those who gave up without a fight were usually spared the hideous cruelties of which the pirates were capable. The principle was the same as the advice given today to the unlucky soul confronted on a dark street by a thug with a knife: Give him the wallet.

Another key to success in piracy was speed. Pirates needed to catch target vessels in order to exhibit the size of the force they had aboard. So while a few famous pirates like Bartholomew "Black Bart" Roberts and Edward "Blackbeard" Teach had large 40-gun ships, most pirates sailed sloops, large enough to accommodate a hundred drunken cutthroats but fast.

Of course, treasure, such as "pieces of eight" (Spanish currency), was the most desirable booty. Slaves were probably the second favorite; they could be readily sold. When pirates tortured captives who had given up without resisting, it was usually to learn where any money aboard was hidden. Mostly, however, pirates took the food and drink they wanted for their own use and whatever cargo was aboard, even hogsheads of tobacco. Selling the contraband could be a problem. Unlike licensed privateers, pirates could not sail into a port and advertise for buyers. There were a few wide-open pirate towns in the Bahamas and Belize, and in Port Royal in Jamaica, where the governor liked having armed pirate ships in the harbor to discourage Spanish attack. Blackbeard was looking for a site for a new development on Ocracoke Inlet in North Carolina when he was trapped and killed in 1718. But none of the sanctuaries lasted very long. The wildest of them, Port Royal, was destroyed by an earthquake in 1692, to the satisfaction of moralists.

Curiously, pirate vessels were more democratic than New England town meetings. Where to hunt prey, from Newfoundland to the West Indies, was determined by majority vote, as was the decision whether or not to attack a vessel the pirates spotted. The captain (who was elected and could be voted out) claimed a far smaller proportion of booty than the masters of merchant vessels or whalers received, and his allowance of food and drink was equal to that of other crewmen. Only when "fighting, chasing, or being chased" did he have the absolute authority of the commander of a naval vessel.

Pirates in American waters were of a dozen nationalities, although, during the "golden age," most were British or colonials, including blacks. In his last stand, Blackbeard was backed by 13 whites and 6 blacks. In 1722, Black Bart's force of 268 men was captured; 77 of them were African Americans. Observing that the pirate community was entirely male, a few historians have claimed that it was a gay society, but the evidence indicates homosexuality was uncommon among pirates.

The golden age of buccaneering came abruptly to an end during the Long Peace, when the colonial powers could direct their warships against the pirates. In 1720, between 1,500 and 2,000 pirates in about 25 vessels worked the Caribbean and the North American coast. By 1723, their numbers were down to 1,000; by 1726, to 200. There were 50 attacks on merchant vessels in American waters in 1718 but just 6 in 1726. Relentless pursuit of pirates, followed inevitably by hanging, ended the threat. Moreover, men were lured out of the profession by announcements of pardons. Many pirates had, they claimed, been forced into the life when, as "honest seamen," they were captured. The large number of pirates who applied for pardons implies they were telling the truth.

deeper into country the colonials considered their own. More aggravating to the New England commercial elite, quite secure from Indians in Boston, were assaults on their merchant and fishing vessels by French ships out of Port Royal in Acadia (Nova Scotia). In 1690, an expedition from Massachusetts captured Port Royal but in vain. At peace negotiations in 1697, the fortress was returned to France. King William had not fared well in Europe; he gave Port Royal back in order to limit concessions to France in the Rhineland. New Englanders were reminded that their interests were subordinate to England's interests in Europe as interpreted, in this case, by a Dutchman.

Queen Anne's War, 1702–1713

Militarily, the French took North America more seriously. Even before the brief peace of 1697–1702, they constructed a series of forts stretching from the Gulf of Mexico to Canada, sketching the new colony of Louisiana on the map.

Then, in 1700, Europe again went to war to decide who would sit on the throne of Spain. This time around, southern colonials, who had ignored King William's War, were in the thick of things. South Carolinians, who competed with both the Spanish and French in the fur and hide trade with the southern Indians, did not care to see their two rivals ruled by the same family. South Carolina's network of Indian contacts extended beyond the Mississippi River, but they also had formidable Indian enemies in what are now Georgia, Alabama, and Mississippi. Slave-catching expeditions among the Creek and Cherokee peoples kept the southwestern frontier in a state of chronic *petite guerre*.

In the north, the French and their Indian allies were more audacious than before, wiping out the substantial town of Deerfield, Massachusetts, in 1704. Once again, New Englanders and the Royal Navy captured Port Royal, and this time, Great Britain kept it and the whole of Acadia. Little, however, changed as far as colonial merchants were concerned. The French retired to Cape Breton Island and built a

▲ *Deerfield, Massachusetts, was no mere cluster of frontier cabins when Indians and French soldiers burned it to the ground in 1704. It was a substantial, comfortable town founded 35 years earlier. The utter destruction of so apparently secure a place set all New England on edge.*

new Atlantic fortress and shelter for commerce raiders, Louisbourg.

In the south, the treaty resolved few difficulties for the simple reason that the European nations did not hold the ultimate power there. The Creek and Cherokee were numerous and confident, less dependent on Europeans than were the Indians of the north. They had buttressed their strength by selectively adopting the ways of the whites, including agricultural techniques and the exploitation of black slave labor, which made them more than self-sufficient in food. The 30 to 40 Cherokee villages began to coordinate their decisions, which was to lead to full confederation in the 1750s.

The Middle Colonies played no notable role in the war, except to profit from it by trading with both sides. "War is declared in England," a New York businessman wrote in his diary, "universal joy among the merchants." The colony of New York actually issued a formal declaration of neutrality.

THE LONG PEACE, 1713–1739

For a quarter of a century, France and Britain were at peace. Tobacco never again sold at bonanza prices, but it returned a handsome enough profit on the Chesapeake. Rice, naval stores, and hides and furs continued to be lucrative, although harder to get. Colonials began to export ginseng (or "sang" as it was called on the frontier), most of which found its way in British ships to China. The colonial merchant marine grew in size so that there was almost as much tonnage in American ports as in British. In troubled times to come, Americans with a memory would look back on the Long Peace of 1713–1739 as a golden age.

Salutary Neglect

They identified the good times with the policies of the first British prime minister, Robert Walpole. Avuncular and easygoing, fancying his daily outsized bottle of port, Walpole believed that the best way to govern was to govern as little as possible. As far as the colonies were concerned, if they were bustling, prosperous, and content, thus enriching British merchants, then why in the world should Britain do anything to disturb them? Walpole's policy was known as "salutary neglect." Inaction was healthful—salutary—even if it meant ignoring colonial violations of the Navigation Acts, which were common

Alas for history's Walpoles, there are always people who demand government action on behalf of their interests or whims. In 1732, London hatmakers complained that the growth of that industry in the northern colonies was hurting their sales in North America. The prime minister quieted them by forbidding colonials to sell hats outside the boundaries of their own colony and to train African Americans in the craft. London's hatters were mollified. American hatmakers ignored the law. Colonial officials enforced it now and then, but not too often. Walpole dined with friends.

The Molasses Act

The Molasses Act of 1733 was enacted in response to complaints by sugar planters in the British West Indies that Americans were buying molasses from French islands, where it was cheaper. They argued that mercantilism entitled them to a monopoly on the huge molasses market in New England. (Rum, distilled from blackstrap, was the common man's liquor in the colonies and also valuable in the slave trade.) Did not the tobacco growers of Virginia and Maryland have a monopoly on the sale of their product in Great Britain?

What to do? In the Molasses Act, Walpole levied a duty of 6 pence per gallon on French molasses, placating British sugar planters, and then made little effort to collect it, pleasing colonials buying from the French. The colonists either smuggled bootleg French molasses into New England ports or presented customs officers with fraudulent invoices stating that their cargo came from Jamaica or Barbados, British islands. The officials were not often fooled by the phony documents. But they could be bribed, and if a gift of a few pence per barrel pleased them too, that was the idea of salutary neglect. Walpole was not offended by the far grander bribery in which his best friends were involved.

Another law that was ignored in the interests of prosperity and calm was passed in 1750 at the behest of English iron makers, who wanted a monopoly on the colonial market. The act forbade colonists to engage in most forms of iron manufacture. Not only did colonial forges continue to operate with impunity; several colonial governments actually subsidized the iron industry within their borders. Salutary neglect was a wonderful way to run an empire—as long as times were good.

Assemblies and Governors

One consequence of Walpole's easygoing colonial policy was the steady erosion of the mother country's political control of her American daughters. In part, the piecemeal acquisition of governors' powers by colonial assemblies merely reflected what was going on in England at the time. During the eighteenth century, Parliament assumed governmental functions formerly exercised by kings and queens. In the colonies, elected assemblies took powers from the governors, who were appointed by the monarch or, in Maryland and Pennsylvania, proprietors.

Collection of The New York Historical Society

▲ *This portrait is believed to be of Lord Cornbury dressed as a woman. Some historians doubt its authenticity. It resembles Lord Cornbury but did not surface until several decades after his death in 1723. If it is the viscount, it may well have been painted as a smear rather than with the governor sitting for the artist.*

The key to this shift in the structure of government was the British political principle that the people, through their elected representatives, must consent to all tax laws. In Great Britain, Parliament held the power of the purse; all money bills had to be approved by the House of Commons. In the colonies, the elected assemblies—whether called the "House of Burgesses," the "House of Delegates," or whatever—possessed this important prerogative.

Theoretically, the governor of a colony could veto a budget bill that he disliked. But to do so was risky. An assembly determined to have its way could retaliate by denying the governor the funds he needed in order to operate his office and even to maintain his personal household, that is, "starve him into compliance" as a hungry royal governor of New York phrased it.

The power of the purse was a formidable weapon. Few who served as governors in America were excessively wealthy before they took their jobs. Englishmen and Scots rich enough to maintain themselves opulently in London or Edinburgh did not choose to rough it in Portsmouth, Williamsburg, or Charleston. Most royal and proprietary governors were men on the make; that was why they sought positions overseas. To make money in the colonies, however, they had to get along with powerful colonials, the men who sat in their councils or were elected to seats in the assemblies.

Of course, it was possible to get along too well with influential Americans, to yield too much to them. That could excite the displeasure of Crown or proprietor. But during the era of salutary neglect, it came easily for governors to be cooperative: As long as the quitrents flowed back to Great Britain, a governor was doing the important part of his job.

That Old-Time Religion

Even religious developments seemed to reflect British neglect. Although toleration had been the rule in the colonies after the collapse of Puritan power in New England, official religious regimentation almost evaporated in the eighteenth century.

Except in Rhode Island and Pennsylvania, colonials were required to contribute, through a tax, to support the established church, the Congregational Church in Massachusetts and Connecticut, the Church of England elsewhere. In some colonies, members of other denominations were not allowed to vote, serve on juries, or exercise other civil rights. For example, Catholics were penalized in Maryland.

But rarely did authorities interfere with worship. In this atmosphere, one of the peculiarities of American society to this day took root: the bewildering multiplicity of religious denominations. The governor of New York wrote that "of all

sorts" of religious opinions "there are some, and the most part none at all." By midcentury, it was not uncommon for modest villages to support two or even three meetinghouses close enough to one another that the congregations might have harmonized their hymns. During the 1740s, religions divided along yet finer lines, and another distinctly American institution, the revival, was born.

The Great Awakening

The first American revival, the Great Awakening, broke out almost simultaneously in several colonies, inspired by numerous preachers. Reverend Jonathan Edwards of Northampton, Massachusetts, was a towering figure. At the age of 17, he was stunned by an emotional conversion experience, "a direct intuitive apprehension of God in all his glory," and it became the theme of his career. In 1734, Edwards began to preach sermons emphasizing the sinfulness of humanity, the torment all deserved to suffer in hell, and the salvation that could be had only through divine grace. Edwards did not honey his message. "The God who holds you over the pit of hell," he said in his most famous sermon, "much as one holds a spider or some loathsome insect over the fire, abhors you, and is dreadfully provoked."

This was good Calvinism, but Edwards might have been suspect in early Massachusetts. In John Winthrop's time, Puritan ministers closely scrutinized the claims of men and

▲ *George Whitefield rarely preached to so small a congregation. His emotional sermons were so popular that news the tireless traveler would speak attracted thousands of colonials.*

women who said they had been saved. Jonathan Edwards was inclined to admit to the fold everyone who displayed the physical, highly emotional signs of being visited by the Holy Spirit.

Revivals were designed to stimulate the trauma of salvation. People broke down weeping, fainting, frothing at the mouth, shrieking, and rolling around on the floors. Many had to be restrained lest they injure themselves. Edwards himself took care not to inspire false conversions with theatrical arm waving and flouncing around. It was said that during all the hysteria, he stared at the bellpull at the entrance to his church.

Other revivalists had fewer scruples. Demagogic preachers tore their clothes and rolled their eyes like lunatics. They pranced and danced around pulpit and platform; they whooped and hollered. They devised a large bag of psychological tricks to arouse their audiences to a state of high excitement.

A Groping for Equality

The Great Awakening affected all social classes, but revivalism appealed most to ordinary people, especially the poorest. Just between 1740 and 1742 (when the population of New England was 300,000), 50,000 people joined a church for the first time in their lives.

The possibility of genuine religious redemption aside, the intense emotion of the revival offered a break from the stress and struggle of surviving on the margins of society. The assurance of happiness in the hereafter compensated for deprivation in the here and now. The emphasis on the equality of all men and women before God rendered society's disdain for the unsuccessful more bearable.

Equality was the message of the farthest ranging of the Great Awakening's ministers, English-born George Whitefield. Traveling tirelessly throughout the colonies—he made seven trips to America—Whitefield often preached 60 hours in a week. During one 78-day period, he delivered more than a hundred *lengthy* sermons. His voice was "an excellent piece of music," Benjamin Franklin said. Far more than those of Edwards, Whitefield's presentations reeked of hell's sulfur.

Many revivalist preachers were without license from a church and even without much education. Their credentials were their claims that the Holy Spirit was in them. In this, they echoed what Anne Hutchinson had claimed a hundred years earlier, but with oratorical and theatrical fireworks that would have disturbed her. The college education of traditional ministers counted for nothing with these "New Lights." What counted was the hand of God on their shoulders. Civil authority had been quick to clamp down on Hutchinson; the freer atmosphere of the eighteenth century permitted the Great Awakening to burn over the colonies.

Curiously, given the anti-intellectual bias of revivalism, the Great Awakening led to the foundation of a number of New Light colleges. In 1747, on the grounds that established institutions of learning like Harvard and Yale were dominated by "dry husks," or passionless intellectuals (in 1722,

the entire faculty of Yale, except Jonathan Edwards, converted to the staid Church of England), the College of New Jersey (Princeton) was founded; Jonathan Edwards was its third president. Other new colleges, such as Brown in Rhode Island, King's College (Columbia) in New York, and Queen's College (Rutgers) in New Jersey, were founded by the "Old Lights" to defend against the new preaching, which they regarded as ignorant and a threat to order.

The Age of Enlightenment

The Old Lights and people of no particular religious inclination, like Benjamin Franklin, embraced to varying degrees the worldview of the European Enlightenment. According to Enlightenment philosophy, human reason by itself, without revelation from the heavens, could unlock the secrets of the universe and guide the improvement, even the perfection, of humanity and society.

The origins of eighteenth-century rationalism lay in the writings of the English scientist Sir Isaac Newton, especially the *Principia Mathematica* (1687) and *Opticks* (1704). In these difficult books, Newton showed that forces as mysterious as those that determined the paths of the planets and the properties of light and color worked according to laws that could be reduced to mathematical equations.

Although Newton was a physicist and mathematician (and his personal religion was rather mystical), the impact of his discoveries was felt in practically every field of human knowledge and art. The order and symmetry that Newton found in the universe were translated into architecture by strict laws of proportion and in literature into inflexible classical rules of style and structure. Baroque music explored the multitudinous variations that could be played on simple combinations of notes.

Enlightenment philosophers likened the universe to a clock—intricate, but understandable when it is dismantled and its parts are examined rationally. According to "deism," as the rationalists called their religious belief, God did not intervene in the natural world. Rather, like a clock maker, he had set nature in motion according to laws that human beings could discover and understand, then he retired to allow his creatures to follow natural law and understand it by means of their precious reason. The educated members of the final generation of colonial Americans were to some degree exponents of this worldview.

THE END OF FRENCH AMERICA

In 1739, Great Britain went to war with Spain in the War of Jenkins' Ear. (Parliament was supposedly enraged when a ship's captain, Robert Jenkins, arrived in London with his ear in a box. It had, he said, been separated from his head by savage Spanish customs officials.) Georgia, South Carolina, and Virginia were involved from the start, not out of sympathy for the disfigured Jenkins but because they were chronically at odds with the Spanish in Florida. It was at this time that Oglethorpe beat back the Spanish assault on Savannah

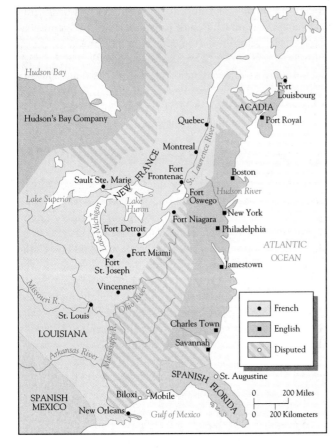

MAP 6:1 **French and British Empires in North America** France claimed much more American acreage than Britain. However, beyond narrow strips of fairly dense settlement on the St. Lawrence River and Gulf Coast, French America was largely wilderness, far more under Indian control than French.

and himself attacked the African American fortress town of Santa Teresa de Mose.

King George's War, 1740–1748

In 1740, France joined the war on the side of Spain. The eight-year conflict that began that year is known in world history as the War of the Austrian Succession; in the colonies, it was known as King George's War.

Petite guerre flickered once more on the frontiers of New England, this time extending into New York, but there was nothing on the scale of the Deerfield disaster. Much better prepared than previously, a force of 4,000, mostly from Massachusetts, besieged the French fortress at Louisbourg. On June 17, 1745, the French commander surrendered.

This was a significant victory. Louisbourg was considered impregnable, "the Gibraltar of North America." As the base from which French privateers operated, the fortress was a cloud looming over New England merchants and fishermen. But the American celebration was short-lived. Under the terms of the Treaty of Aix-la-Chapelle, Louisbourg was returned to the French.

Parliament reimbursed Massachusetts for the expense of the campaign, but this did not make up for the 500 men who had lost their lives on Cape Breton Island or for the fact that the French commerce raiders were restored to their sanctuary. The protest was mild. The colonists were loyal British subjects. But the nullification of the greatest military victory Americans had ever won rankled in many breasts.

Struggle for a Continent

The world war that broke out in 1756 differed in several ways from those that preceded it. Most important to Americans, the British regarded North America as a theater at least as important as the battlefields of Europe. This time, Britain would not return North American fortresses in exchange for territory on the Rhine or in India. From the beginning, a large party in Parliament made it clear that their major object was to drive France out of North America.

Despite their usual success at *petite guerre,* the French were in a perilous situation. There were only about 50,000 whites in all of French-claimed territory and fewer than 20,000 Spaniards north of Mexico, compared with 1.2 million white colonists in the 13 English colonies plus Nova Scotia. The French still claimed the goodwill of most Indians in the region, but others were neutral.

For the first time in the Anglo-French wars, the largest colony, Virginia, took a serious interest in the fighting. The Virginians were looking beyond the Appalachian Mountains to the Ohio River valley for lands that were firmly under Indian control. This country was particularly attractive to the wealthy tobacco planters of the Old Dominion because a combination of exhausted soil and a new glut in the international tobacco market was undercutting their income. They saw speculation in Ohio Valley real estate as the likeliest means of maintaining their fortunes.

Humiliations in the Woods

With the heart of New France populated thinly, the French had little hope of effectively occupying the Ohio Valley. But the country was of vital interest to French trappers; French policy was to help the local Indians, friendly to France, retain control of the region. As early as 1753, at Indian urging, the French began to lay out a string of small forts in what is now western Pennsylvania.

Governor Robert Dinwiddie of Virginia responded by sending 22-year-old George Washington to inform the French that they were trespassing on Virginia soil. Accompanied by 150 men, Washington was to construct a fort where the Allegheny and Monongahela Rivers join to form the Ohio (the site of present-day Pittsburgh).

Washington never got that far. Attacked by Indians and French, he built Fort Necessity, little more than a log palisade, and was handily defeated in a battle that he prudently kept almost bloodless. The French occupied the conjunction of rivers and built Fort Duquesne. Washington returned to Virginia, where he accepted a commission under British general Edward Braddock. Again, things went worse than poorly. Braddock, a stubborn, unimaginative soldier, was soundly defeated in 1755 in the Pennsylvania forests; 977 British and colonials were killed, including General Braddock, but only 39 French and Indians. The rout left the frontier vulnerable to raiding fiercer than any since the destruction of Deerfield. The French were also winning the war in Europe and India. For the British Empire, it was a dismal hour.

Germ Warfare and Refugees

Both Braddock and, later, the overall commander of British forces in North America, Sir Jeffrey Amherst, employed a primitive form of germ warfare against the Indians. They saw to it that blankets used by smallpox victims fell into the natives' hands.

In Nova Scotia, the British feared that the French farmers and fishermen who were the majority in the province would rebel, even capture Halifax, a vital naval base. To forestall such a revolt, they launched a mass deportation. Thousands of Acadians—*Acadie* was the French name for Nova Scotia—were forced aboard ship and dispersed throughout the other English colonies from Massachusetts to Georgia and the West Indies. A few managed to make their way back home overland. Others found a haven in the French territory of Louisiana, where their descendants still form a distinct ethnic and cultural group in the state of Louisiana, the Cajuns. (The word *Cajun* is a corruption of the French *Acadien*.)

Pitt and Wolfe

Then, two men appeared on the scene to change the course of North American history. William Pitt became prime minister of Great Britain in 1757. He selected the young General James Wolfe to join Amherst's army in North America. Pitt turned the war around by generously paying Prussia to fight the French and Austrians in Europe while he concentrated British power across the Atlantic. Wolfe engineered one of the most daring attacks on a city in military history.

A nervous, frail-looking young man, brittle in his intensity, perhaps quite insane, Wolfe looked at French Canada as a woodsman eyed a tree. Quebec was the root structure that supported the whole. The St. Lawrence, Ohio, and Mississippi Rivers were but trunks and branches. It was all very well to snip and hack at leaves here and there, as Wolfe saw even the capture of Louisbourg. The secret to a conclusive victory over French Canada was to strike at the source of its life.

The theory was easier than its practical application. Quebec stood atop a steep, rocky cliff. On September 12, 1759, after leading several futile frontal attacks on this natural fortress (which lulled the French commander, Louis de Montcalm, into overconfidence), Wolfe quietly led 4,000 troops up a steep, narrow trail under cover of night. When the sun rose over the Plains of Abraham, a prairie on the minimally defended landward side of Quebec, Montcalm saw a scarlet-coated army in full battle formation.

▲ *General James Wolfe died defeating the French outside their fortress at Quebec. A difficult man in life—some thought him mad—the dead Wolfe was immediately immortalized as a national hero. The pensive Indian is a member of the Iroquois, the Native American allies indispensable to British success.*

North Wind Picture Archives

The Glorious Victory

Wolfe's gambit was risky. He had no supply line or avenue of retreat. If the battle did not end in total triumph (and few military victories were total in the eighteenth century), Wolfe's entire army would have been captured. Montcalm, however, was so unnerved by Wolfe's gamble that, despite his superior position and artillery, he joined battle with little preparation. After a single close-range exchange of musket fire, Montcalm lost his life and with it the French empire in America. Wolfe did not live to savor his triumph. He too died on the battlefield, only 32 years of age.

Bickering over the terms of peace dragged on, but, as far as the colonials were concerned, the war was over when British colors flew over Quebec. Finally, in the Peace of Paris in 1763, the map of North America was officially redrawn. Great Britain took Florida from Spain as well as Canada from France. To compensate Spain for the loss of Florida, France handed over Louisiana (the central third of what is now the United States) to the Spanish. In the Western Hemisphere, France was down to its possessions in the West Indies and two tiny, rocky islands in the North Atlantic. French fishermen could call there, but the islands were useless militarily.

By contrast, the British Empire was in glorious bloom. The mercantile British had elected to make their future not in Europe but as a vast empire overseas, and they had succeeded on every front. Or so it seemed.

for FURTHER READING

Basic works on relations with the mother country include Daniel Boorstin, *The Americans: The Colonial Experience,* 1958; Ian R. Christie, *Crisis of Empire,* 1966; Richard Hofstadter, *America at 1750,* 1971; Leonard W. Labaree, *Royal Government in America,* 1930; James Henretta, *Salutary Neglect,* 1972; and Stephen Webb, *The Governors-General,* 1979. Absolutely essential is Bernard Bailyn, *The Origins of American Politics,* 1968. Also consult the early pages of John C. Miller, *Origins of the American Revolution,* 1957; and Edmund S. Morgan, *The Birth of the Republic,* 1956.

On the Anglo-French wars, the great Francis Parkman is again the classic historian. See Parkman's *A Half Century of Conflict,* 1892, and his *Montcalm and Wolfe,* 1884. See also Howard H. Peckham, *The Colonial Wars, 1689–1762,* 1964; Douglas E. Leach, *Arms for Empire: A Military History of the British Colonies in North America,* 1973; and Fred Anderson, *A People's Army: Massachusetts Soldiers and Society in the Seven Years' War,* 1984. On the Indian role in the conflicts, see two works by Francis Jennings: *Empire of Fortune,* 1990; and *The Ambiguous Iroquois Empire,* 1984. On the same subject, see also James Merrell, *Beyond the Covenant Chain: The Iroquois and Their Neighbors,* 1987.

On cultural developments, see Louis B. Wright, *Cultural Life of the American Colonies,* 1957; Alan Heimert and Perry Miller, eds., *The Great Awakening,* 1967; Perry Miller, *Jonathan Edwards,* 1958; Edwin S. Gaustad, *The Great Awakening in New England,* 1957; and Henry F. May, *The Enlightenment in America,* 1976.

Benjamin Franklin's autobiography, in various editions, will never cease to be a good read. Also see Carl Van Doren, *Benjamin Franklin,* 1938.

American Journey Online and InfoTrac *College Edition*

Visit the source collections at http://ajaccess.wadsworth.com and http://infotrac.thomsonlearning.com, and use the Search function with the following key terms to explore documents, images, audio and video clips, articles, and commentary related to the material in this chapter:

Benjamin Franklin	Molasses Act
French and Indian War	Seven Years' War
Great Awakening	Smallpox

Additional resources, exercises, and Internet links related to this chapter are available on *The American Past* Web site: http://history.wadsworth.com/americanpast7e.

HISTORY ONLINE

Primary Sources—Colonial Period
http://personnal.pitnet.net/primarysources/
A broad selection of documents of the colonial period.

Religion in America
http://lcweb.loc.gov/exhibits/religion/rel02
Religion in eighteenth-century America.

7

YEARS OF TUMULT

The Quarrel with Great Britain 1763–1770

Harcourt Picture Collection

Westward the course of empire takes its way;
*   The first four acts already past,*
A fifth shall close the drama with the day:
*   Time's noblest offspring is the last.*

George Berkeley

An idea, strange as it is visionary, has entered into the minds of the generality of mankind, that empire is traveling westward; and every one is looking forward with eager and impatient expectation to that destined moment, when America is to give law to the rest of the world. But if ever an idea was illusory and fallacious, I will venture to predict, that this will be so.

Andrew Burnaby

I N 1763, CHURCH BELLS pealed throughout the 13 colonies to celebrate Britain's triumph in the Seven Years' War. In 1775, a dozen years later, these same colonies took up arms against the mother country; after another year, they declared their independence of her. Observing this rush of events, Oliver Wolcott of Connecticut wondered what had gone wrong. "So strong had been the Attachment" of Americans to Great Britain in 1763, he wrote, that "the Abilities of a Child might have governed this Country."

Wolcott blamed the bust-up on British folly, incompetence, and tyranny. He had a point about folly and incompetence. Blunder after stupidity upon miscalculation tells the story of British colonial policy between 1763 and 1776. But it would be a mistake, given the education in tyranny that the twentieth century has provided us, to entertain Wolcott's third explanation of the American Revolution. Far from oppressed by tyrants, colonial Americans may have been the world's freest people.

What made men like Wolcott into rebels was a mismanaged shift in British imperial administration from salutary neglect, with which colonials were happy, to a genuine, although far from oppressive, supervision. What made it possible for colonials to translate their apprehensions into anger, and then into rebellion, was the self-confidence born of the colonies' extraordinary growth.

THE PROBLEMS OF EMPIRE

Wolfe's capture of Quebec put Canada in British hands. Before the peace negotiators gathered in Paris in 1763, however, there was some question as to whether or not the British would retain the vast colony. Influential Britons, like the Duke of Bedford, suggested that it would be wiser to return Canada to France, as Port Royal and Louisbourg had been returned. Better, the duke said, to take as the fruits of victory the French West Indian islands of Martinique and Guadeloupe.

One Side of the Story

A land of endless forest and tundra, mostly unexplored, was not so glorious a trophy, the argument went. What use was Russia's subarctic empire to her? Moreover, the Indians of Canada and the Ohio Valley—former French allies—were numerous, powerful, and suspicious of the British. What could the 50,000 *habitants*—the French Canadian farmers, merchants, trappers, and tradesmen living along the St. Lawrence River—be as British subjects except trouble? Britain had recently deported a much smaller number of French men and women from Nova Scotia for fear they would rebel. The Irish had been periodically rising against English authority for two centuries and showed no sign of calming down. What sense did it make to create yet more unwilling and culturally alien subjects?

The sugar islands, by contrast, were tiny. They could be managed by small military garrisons. The handful of French planters who lived on Guadeloupe and Martinique, exploiting masses of cruelly used black slaves, cared less about the design of the flag flying over their harbors than about the presence of soldiers to keep their laborers in check and about the price for which they sold their crop.

There was yet another consideration. By 1763, the 13 Atlantic colonies, taken together, constituted a substantial country. Was it not possible—even likely—that the colonials had remained loyal to Great Britain only because of their fear of the French and Indian alliance? Remove that threat from their backyard, as the acquisition of Canada would do, and the Americans would have no need of British naval and military protection, and certainly would not be grateful for it. They might well unite, in the words of a Swedish observer, Peter Kalm, and "shake off the yoke of the English monarchy."

All That Red on the Map!

These arguments did not carry the day. British taxpayers were weary of war. They had paid monstrously large sums to fight France. If Canada and Louisiana remained French, another North American conflict was inevitable. Influential colonials like Governor William Shirley of Massachusetts and Benjamin Franklin, who was then in England as agent of Pennsylvania and Massachusetts, warbled lyrically of the potential of the Canadian landmass.

The lobbyists found allies in the sugar planters of the British West Indies. These few but rich and well-connected men—sugar was the British Empire's most valuable product ("white gold")—feared that raising the Union Jack over Martinique and Guadeloupe would glut the imperial sugar mar-

White Gold

By the eighteenth century, sugar had displaced tobacco as the most profitable product of the British colonial empire. Per capita consumption in Britain doubled in just a few decades as the population became addicted to sweet coffee, tea, chocolate, candies, and cakes. Even the poorest British smeared molasses on their bread.

Sugar cane was grown not in the mainland colonies but in the West Indies. French, Dutch, and Spanish islands produced it, but the British dominated the world market from the sugar islands of Barbados, Tobago, Trinidad, Jamaica, and a dozen specks on the map now best known as vacation wonderlands. Thanks to the Navigation Acts, colonial ships hauled almost as much of the "white gold" and molasses (partially processed sugar) as British ships did. Molasses was a vital part of the New England economy because, when distilled into rum, it could be sold anywhere in the world. Rum was also the chief liquor of America below the highest social classes. There was no cheaper drink.

The sugar islands were dominated by an oligarchy of rich planters even smaller than the rice and indigo aristocracy of South Carolina. They were protected by detachments of soldiers such as not even South Carolinians would have tolerated. They needed protection. Sugar required three times as much labor as tobacco, and West Indian slaves were treated with an inhumanity that would have sickened the hardest bitten slave owner on the mainland. Between 1700 and 1775, 1.2 million chained Africans were transported to the West Indies. The black population of the islands was a fraction of that in 1775 because sugar slaves typically died within five years of arriving. Because of their physical condition, slave women were unable to bear children. Infanticide was widespread among slaves; mothers preferred smothering their newborns to raising them to the miseries of the life they knew. Slaves on the mainland, by contrast, worked less arduously, lived longer lives in better health, and increased in numbers naturally at the same rate as free blacks and white colonials.

ket, driving down the price of their commodity just as overproduction of tobacco had shattered the price of that crop.

In the end, the French peacemakers preferred handing over Canada and keeping the sugar islands, and most of Parliament was unreflectively confident of American loyalty. In 1763, it was far more than smug to assume that anyone who had a choice would not choose to be anything but British.

Les Habitants

The Canadians could imagine otherwise. For one thing, they were Roman Catholic, pious communicants of a faith that was disliked and discriminated against in eighteenth-century Britain. Catholics were generally unmolested in the 13 colonies. But there too they were distrusted, and there was a big difference between tolerating a small, quiet, and largely genteel Catholic minority in Maryland and the odd Romanist

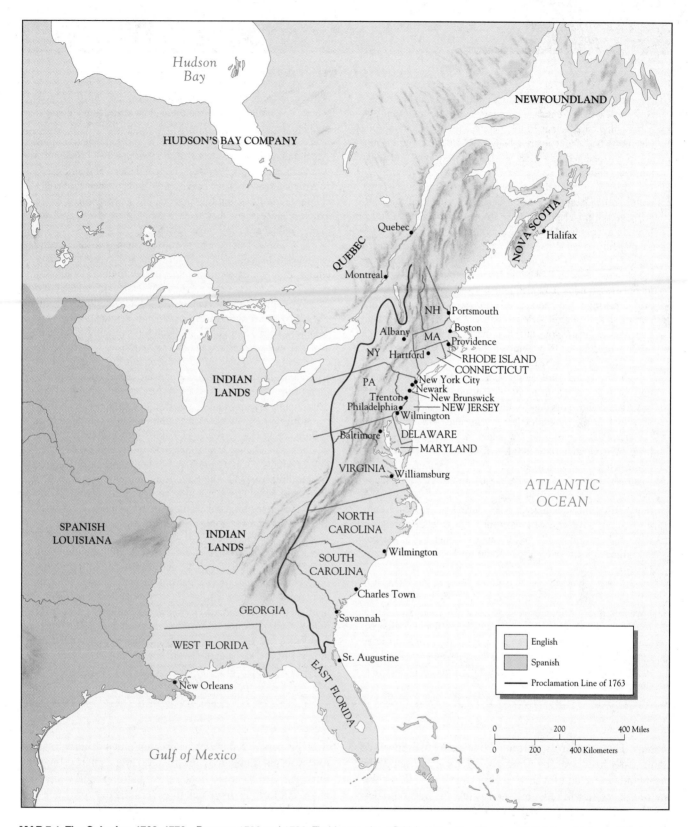

MAP 7:1 The Colonies, 1763–1776 Between 1763 and 1783, Florida was also a British possession. However, Florida was thinly populated, and almost every European there was a Spaniard; Americans did not think of it as a fourteenth colony.

church in Philadelphia and New York and coming to terms with a sprawling province in which almost everyone, Indians included, was Catholic.

The precedent of Englishmen governing foreign Catholics was not encouraging. For two centuries, Catholic Ireland had been a province; in effect, it was England's first

The Matriarchal Iroquois

By the mid–eighteenth century, the Iroquois Confederacy—the Cayuga, Seneca, Onondaga, Oneida, and Mohawk tribes—numbered about 15,000 people and securely controlled much of what is now upstate New York. Iroquois hunters and war parties ranged much farther, to the Mississippi and as far north as Hudson Bay.

Iroquois men, being hunters and warriors, and carrying out the delicate diplomatic negotiations that kept the confederacy together, traveled constantly. Iroquois women stayed home in more or less fixed towns of longhouses in which, semiprivately, families belonging to the same clan lived. Women raised the corn that was the staple of the Iroquois diet. They cared for the children, educating them in Iroquois values. They kept the longhouses in repair and maintained order, governing by social pressure—reputation and social approval were extremely important to the Iroquois—rather than by coercion. Finally, with their husbands and sons absent much of the time, the women effectively decided by whom they would have children or, at least, with whom they would lie.

Descent, therefore, could be reliably traced only through the maternal line. Clans of 50 or 60 people (their animal symbols carved above the door of their longhouse) included the eldest female member and her sisters and daughters, male children, and the sons-in-law when they happened to be in town. When a man married (always outside the clan—the Iroquois had a broad incest taboo), he left the clan into which he was born and joined his wife's, moving into her longhouse. With marital relationships fragile and transitory, many Iroquois men drifted through several clans during their lives. At any given time, however, an Iroquois male was solemnly obligated to defend the honor of his wife's clan. If a member of her clan was killed, injured, or insulted and the matriarch insisted on retaliation, a warrior was obligated to do what was asked, even if the offender belonged to the clan into which he had been born.

In addition to their authority to declare vendettas (they were infrequent, often resolved by discussion, and governed by intricate rules when negotiation failed), the female elders selected the 49 male delegates who met regularly to keep peace among the five tribes of the confederacy. Women participated in these meetings, but quietly, behind the scenes. The men handled the oratory.

The system worked quite well. The Iroquois heartland was secure, peaceful, well governed, and ably defended by the most dreaded warriors in the Northeast. A Quaker wrote of the Seneca, "[They] appear to be naturally as well calculated for social and rational enjoyment, as any people. They frequently visit each other in their houses, and spend much of their time in friendly intercourse. They are also mild and hospitable, not only among themselves, but to strangers, and good-natured in the extreme, except when their natures are perverted by the inflammatory influence of spirituous liquors."

Alcohol was, however, a serious problem. The sale of pelts and hides to the colonials inevitably launched an orgy of drunkenness among men, women, and children that would shock a pirate crew. Nor was drinking the only element introduced into Iroquois culture by their contact with whites, into its fifth generation by the middle of the eighteenth century. Trade with colonials also meant guns and metal tools ranging from scissors, knives, awls, kettles, and other household goods, to hatchets and axes. The latter influenced Iroquois building methods: By the mid-1700s longhouses were made less often in the traditional way—sheets of elm bark lashed to bent saplings—and increasingly of heavy logs and even milled siding.

Indeed, by the time of the colonials' quarrel with Great Britain, many Iroquois were abandoning residence by clan in longhouses and clustering in single-family cabins. The adoption of whites' farming methods made for a more productive agriculture; by 1750, the Seneca alone produced a million bushels of corn. There was little choice in this matter. Game was scarce in the Iroquois heartland after a century of overtrapping. Moreover, both neighboring and distant tribes that the Iroquois had routinely savaged during the 1600s had secured European firearms of their own and were holding the line.

Iroquois appearance changed. European calico shirts, linen loincloths, and woolen blankets characterized the Iroquois eighteenth-century Americans knew. Nevertheless, the Iroquois continued to shun Christian missionaries. Some had converted, to both Catholicism and Protestant denominations. But others "made obscene gestures" when anyone suggested that the colonial way of life was superior to their own.

---

colony. The conquerors of Ireland (including men involved in the early history of the American colonies) had seized the best lands in Ireland for their estates and been guilty of numerous atrocities in reducing the Irish to submission. Their descendants, the Anglo-Irish gentry, looked on the Catholic Irish masses as lazy, superstitious, and barbaric.

As in Ireland, however, the British held the military trump card in Canada. The *habitants* had no experience with representative government (New France had been governed by the military) and no inclination to bombard the Crown with protests and supplications such as the assemblies of the 13 colonies did. To the French Canadians, taking orders from officers in red uniforms was not much different in day-to-day terms from being governed by Frenchmen in blue and buff. The British could hope for a breathing spell while they devised a formula by which to govern the new province.

Pontiac's Conspiracy

The Indians, former allies of the French, presented a more difficult and more urgent problem. Unlike the French army, the warriors of the Ohio River valley had not been decisively defeated in battle. The Treaty of Paris might proclaim them subjects of King George III. In reality, they were securely in possession of the forests west of the Appalachians and comfortable in a culture that was nearly intact and even strengthened by what they had borrowed from their European neighbors.

Almost immediately, the British blundered in dealing with them. General Sir Jeffrey Amherst, entrusted with this task, looked on Indians as "wretched people" whose proper condition was subjection. He informed the western tribes that they would no longer receive the regular "gifts" of blankets, iron and brass tools and vessels, firearms, and liquor that they were accustomed to getting from the French.

Neolin, a religious leader of the Delaware, a tribe that had been driven west by colonials, preached that "if you suffer the English among you, you are dead men." An Ottawa chieftain, Pontiac, attacked the British fort at Detroit and was soon joined by 18 tribes on a thousand-mile front. Detroit and Fort Pitt (Pittsburgh) held out; but 10 western forts were overrun, and 2,000 people were killed in Virginia and Pennsylvania—more than were lost in any battle of the French and Indian War. Amherst tried germ warfare again. He urged his men to "try to inoculate the Indians by means of Blankets, as well as to try Every other Method that can serve to Extirpate this Execrable Race." The British forces regrouped and defeated Pontiac at Bushy Run near Pittsburgh. But they had only stung the Indians, not "extirpated" them.

The Proclamation of 1763

Amherst restored the gifts and informed the Crown of the problem. In October 1763, in order to let tempers cool, London drew an imaginary line on the Appalachian divide, the crest between the sources of rivers that emptied into the Atlantic and those that flowed into the Ohio–Mississippi River system. The Crown proclaimed, "We do strictly forbid, on pain of our displeasure, all our loving subjects from making any purchases or settlements whatever" west of the line. The frontiersmen who had already settled in the no-go zone were forced to return east; impatient emigrants were urged to head for northern New England, Upper Canada (Ontario), Georgia, and Florida, which was also now British. Land sales west of the Appalachians were frozen.

Colonials considered the Proclamation Line to be what one land speculator, George Washington, called "a temporary expedient to quiet the minds of the Indians." Too many influential colonials dreamed of riches in Ohio Valley real estate to consider the line permanent. Indeed, superintendents of Indian affairs, royal officials, began to purchase western territory from Indians before news of the settlement reached their more remote tribes. In the south, the line of 1763 was redrawn—farther west—within a few months. Regularly over the next decade, trans-Appalachian lands were opened to speculation and settlement.

Nevertheless, by interfering temporarily, even on paper, with the colonials' lust for land, British policy touched a tender nerve. Americans would remember the proclamation of 1763 as an early example of King George III's campaign to throttle their "liberties."

The Redcoats

In the wake of Pontiac's Rebellion, General Amherst asked Parliament for a permanent American garrison of 5,000 to 6,000 troops. The soldiers would be stationed in Canada and in the frontier forts. Parliament responded by voting Amherst 10,000 soldiers, more than double the contingent in North America during the years of the French menace.

Within a few years, when some of these soldiers were billeted in coastal cities in order to police riotous colonial crowds, they became the hated "redcoats" or "lobsters." When they first began to arrive, however, the Americans' biggest concern was the expense of maintaining them—£200,000 a year. The Quartering Act of 1765 charged the cost of the troops' shelter, food, and drink to the colony in which they were posted. Indeed, one of Parliament's motives in doubling Amherst's request for men was to pension off veterans of the French and Indian War at colonial expense. The men had some reward coming to them, but the British traditionally shied away from keeping a large standing army at home. Soldiers looked on duty in America as easy: not much to do, and in a society where the people were friends, not conquered foreigners.

But the "friendly" colonials disliked standing armies too. Soldiers out in the woods watching Indians were one thing; soldiers marching around Boston and New York, quite another.

Reorganization of the Empire

The flurry of changes in the wake of the Seven Years' War signaled that the men who governed Great Britain were taking a new, keener interest in colonial affairs. Some sort of change was in order and easily justified. Counting Canada, the West Indies, and British Honduras, 20 colonies in the Western Hemisphere now flew the British flag. If each were to go merrily its own way, pretty much governing itself as the 13 "ancient provinces" of North America were accustomed to doing, the result would be chaos. Even during the French and Indian War, "the king in Parliament" made it clear that salutary neglect was history. The postwar British Empire was to be supervised more closely from London and integrated into a more rational—more regular—imperial regime.

Money, Money, Money

Before the war, Parliament had been content that the colonies profited British land speculators, manufacturers, and merchants. Since Robert Walpole, ministries had been little concerned that the administration of the colonies was a net cost to the exchequer (the British treasury). The government expected to subsidize mercantilism; administrative costs seemed a most worthwhile expenditure. Before the French and Indian War, governing the colonies cost the Crown, on average, £70,000 a year, whereas colonial trade pumped as much as £2 million a year into the British economy. Who could complain? Who could be bothered?

▲ *Parliament consisted of two houses, the House of Lords, in which seats were inherited or held by appointed bishops of the Church of England, and the House of Commons, pictured here. The Commons was elected by men who owned property. Members were gentlemen from the highest social class below the "lords," as members of the nobility were called.*

By 1764, however, the cost of colonial government had soared to £350,000 a year, and Parliament faced new and serious financial difficulties. Prime Minister William Pitt had levied heavy taxes on the British in order to fight the war. And he had borrowed every penny anyone would lend him. A national debt of £130 million (twice what it had been before the war) had Britain teetering on the edge of bankruptcy. Half of each year's revenues was going to paying interest.

Cost cutting is always an alternative in financially trying times, if never attractive to politicians for whom those costs are personal bread and butter. The British government in the 1760s was top heavy, with officials who slopped at the public trough without doing anything in particular. At every level, it was shot through with graft: padded government contracts, bribes, kickbacks, and pensions were as much a part of the system as they are in the United States today.

Some budgets were slashed. The Royal Navy received £7 million in 1762 (during the last years of the war), £2.8 million in 1766, and £1.5 million in 1769. However, Parliament preferred to look for more revenue rather than inflict similar cuts across the board.

Heavier taxes at home were out of the question. Each year, British landowners paid 20 percent of their income into the exchequer, a crushing burden in an agricultural society. Other taxes were also high. When Parliament tried to increase a small tax on cider, the daily drink of southwestern England, there were riots approaching rebellion.

£/s/d

The British monetary unit was (and is) the pound sterling, designated by a stylized capital *L* (from the Latin word for "pound," *libra*) with one or two slashes: £. Since 1970, British money has been decimalized, 100 new pence ("p") to the pound. Before 1970—in the eighteenth century—the system was more complex. The pound was divided into 20 shillings ("s"). The shilling was divided into 12 pence ("d," from the Latin word for "penny," *denarius*).

So money was expressed in pounds, shillings, and pence, £/s/d. The very smallest British coin was the farthing: four farthings to the penny.

Grenville: The First Villain

The thankless job of reorganizing government finance fell to George Grenville, who became first lord of the treasury in 1763. Grenville was a talented man, an expert in fiscal matters who thought in terms broader than accounting. If the reforms he introduced had succeeded, history might well have recorded him as the architect of a rationalized British Empire. Instead, he is a walk-on in British history and, to Americans, a villain.

Along with his abilities, Grenville brought a fatal limitation to his task. Like most British politicians of the time, he knew little about Americans and saw no sense in learning more. He had a vision of worldwide British power, but he contemplated it through the half-closed eyes of the complacent British upper crust. To Grenville, Americans were half-civilized louts whose opinions were not worthy of consideration. He would have smiled at Samuel Johnson's famous quip, "I am willing to love all mankind, except an American."

Grenville knew that Americans paid few taxes. He calculated that the average English taxpayer paid an annual tax of 26 shillings, whereas a British subject living in Massachusetts paid one shilling a year, and the average Virginian, only five pence. (One shilling equaled 12 pence.) And yet, the virtually untaxed colonials had gained the most from the French and Indian War, the cause of the national debt that threatened to bankrupt Great Britain. The colonials, therefore, should do more to pay off the debt and, in the future, to shoulder the expenses of governing their colonies.

It is difficult, from a distance, to fault Grenville's reasoning. Indeed, few Americans openly denied that they had a moral obligation to do more financially than they had in the past. Unfortunately, even if the 13 colonial assemblies had been willing to vote Grenville enough money to meet his needs, they did not get the chance to do so. Instead of requesting grants from the colonies, as his predecessors had done, Grenville treated his money problems as part and parcel of his plan to reform imperial administration.

The Sugar Act of 1764

Grenville's first move was to overhaul the ineffective Molasses Act of 1733. Its six-pence-per-gallon tax on molasses

▲ *First Lord of the Treasury George Grenville looked like what he was, a British aristocrat who had climbed to the top of the political heap. His failure to make good on his promise to raise revenue in the colonies contributed to his fall from high office after only two years.*

imported into the colonies from non-British sources was so high that American merchants did not hesitate to evade it. Instead of paying the duty, they bribed customs collectors a penny or so per gallon. If they were arrested as smugglers, they could count on juries of their neighbors to acquit them regardless of the evidence—and then join them at the nearest inn for a drink of rum, the principal by-product of molasses.

The Sugar Act of 1764 struck at both the revenue problem and the problem of law enforcement in the colonies. It enlarged the customs service and transferred the task of enforcing the import duty from local courts to a new system of vice admiralty courts that would try violators without juries. To sweeten the pot, Grenville cut the molasses tax to three pence per gallon. He calculated that American importers would pay the lower rate (not much more than the customary bribe) rather than run the risk of conviction in courts over which they had no control. Also in 1764, Grenville levied duties on imported wines, silks, tropical foods, and other luxury goods. They were modest. Grenville wanted money; he did not want to discourage imports.

The First Protest

In New England, where molasses was a major item of trade, protest was loud and fierce. The Boston town meeting de-

clared that the city would import no British goods of any kind until Parliament repealed the obnoxious tax. Other cities, including New York, followed suit. Even "the young Gentlemen of Yale College" announced that they would not "make use of any foreign spirituous liquors" until Grenville backed down from his importunity. This sacrifice, heroic for students, was eased by the fact that limitless quantities of domestic beer and cider were available for after-hours revels.

Grenville was unmoved. He assumed that the Americans simply did not want to pay any taxes, that they wished to enjoy the benefits of being a part of the British Empire at no personal cost. No doubt he was the better part of right. Importers of molasses, sippers of Madeira, and wearers of silk wanted the best bargains they could get. To this extent, the Sugar Act protest was sheer self-pity.

The Rights of British Subjects

And yet, there were principles at stake too. Politically (in the larger sense of that word), colonials were heirs of the British "country party," as opposed to the "court party." They were Whigs, adherents to a political philosophy that considered Parliament to be the foundation of British liberties. In a century, Parliament had beheaded one "tyrannical" king (Charles I); deposed another (James II), creating its own monarch in his place (William III); and, in 1714, chosen as king a German who never learned English (George I) over 40 princes with a better claim to the throne. In other words, Parliament had established its supremacy over the monarchy. The most important of the rights of British subjects that Parliament asserted was the principle that, through Parliament, British subjects consented to the taxes they paid.

Parliament had enacted the Sugar Act, but that parliament sat in Westminster, colonials said. It was not their parliament. They did not elect members to it. Their parliaments were the 13 colonial assemblies, which alone had the right to raise money from the colonies through taxation. On this foundation was built a decade of debate about the nature of representation in government—sometimes hairsplitting, self-serving, and precocious, but at its core, a debate of great seriousness.

Daniel Dulany of Maryland responded to the Sugar Act of 1764 by comparing it to the Molasses Act of 1733, which the colonials had (more or less) accepted. As a tax designed to reduce the importation of French molasses into the empire, Dulany said, the Molasses Act had regulated trade. This was perfectly legitimate. Parliament had the right to regulate the empire's trade. But the Sugar Act of 1764 was not designed to keep foreign molasses out. Indeed, as far as Grenville was concerned, the more foreign molasses the colonies imported legally, the better. His goal was to collect the three pence per gallon. The official title of the Sugar Act was the American Revenue Act.

It was Grenville's goal—revenue—that raised the ticklish constitutional question of the "sacred right" of British subjects to consent to taxes levied on them. The Sugar Act was a tax. The colonials had not consented to it. It was that simple.

Trial by Jury

There was another issue: the right of a British subject accused of a crime to be tried before a jury of his peers. This right, with origins dating to the Magna Carta of 1215, colonials (and British Whigs) believed, set them apart from—made them superior to—the French, Spanish, Poles, Chinese, Hottentots, Shawnee, and everyone else in the world. By denying colonials this ancient right, as the jury-less vice admiralty courts did, George Grenville was tampering with the essence of British liberty.

It is impossible to say what would have happened if Grenville's program had ended with the Sugar Act. The Americans were noisy; some of their language was inflammatory. But there was no violence. The Sugar Act protest began with high-level debate and ended with a legal boycott of imports. To the extent that colonial opposition to the tax on molasses was a manifestation of greed, the protest might well have petered out. The duties of 1764 seriously affected only wealthy consumers and a small number of shippers and distillers, and them not gravely. When, in 1766, the molasses duty was reduced to a penny (the level of the traditional bribe), protest and boycott evaporated, although "the principle of the thing" remained quite intact.

But Grenville did not stop with the Sugar Act. In 1765, he announced a new bill to raise money in America by means of a tax that could not be ducked or stymied by a boycott because those who did not pay it suffered from the very act of noncompliance.

THE STAMP ACT CRISIS

English people had been paying a stamp tax since 1694. In order to be legal, documents such as wills, bills of sale, licenses, deeds, insurance policies, and other contracts had to be inscribed on paper that was embossed with a government stamp. Purchase of the paper, therefore, constituted payment of a tax. Evasion was not feasible. A proof of marriage not inscribed on the stamped paper was not accepted in court when there was a dispute between spouses over property. The transfer of a farm written on ordinary paper was not enforceable.

The Stamp Act of 1765

Grenville's Stamp Act of 1765 went further than the English law. It required that (in addition to colonial legal documents) newspapers, pamphlets, handbills, and even playing cards were to be printed on the embossed government paper. The tax varied from a halfpenny on a handbill announcing the sale of taffeta to one pound for a tavern's license to sell liquor. The sum was significant in both cases.

Enforcement of the law was entrusted to the unpopular vice admiralty courts. However, Grenville tried to gain colonial favor by providing that all money raised under the Stamp Act would be used solely in "defending, protecting, and securing the colonies." Not a farthing would go back to England to retire the debt or for any other purpose.

Stamps

What we call a postage "stamp" is, by eighteenth-century standards, a misnomer. The adhesive-backed evidence that postage has been paid on a letter was invented only in 1834 (the perforations in 1854). When it was, the speakers of no other European language chose *stamp* to name the ingenious device. To them, and to colonial Americans, a stamp was something impressed on or stamped into paper, not something stuck on it. Eighteenth-century stamping was what we call "embossing."

Thus, the stamp that caused all the excitement in 1765 was an embossment, pressed into the paper to be used for licenses, newspapers, and so on. Few Americans ever saw Stamp Act stamps anyway. Except for a few sales in Georgia, none of the embossed paper was ever used.

American sensibilities were not soothed. On the contrary, the stipulation that revenues from the Stamp Act were to be raised and spent entirely within the colonies led a Quaker grandee of Pennsylvania and Delaware, John Dickinson, to devise a detailed constitutional distinction between legitimate *external taxes,* duties on trade between the colonies and other places, and unacceptable *internal taxes,* duties collected within the colonies and spent there.

The Stamp Act was plainly internal, Dickinson said, a direct tax on the people by a body in which they were not represented, Parliament. Only a colonial assembly could enact such a tax within its boundaries. (Massachusetts had, in fact, experimented with a stamp tax in 1755.)

Grenville had no ear for Dickinson's argument. In his administrative scheme, Parliament was the supreme governing authority for the entire empire. Most members of Parliament agreed with him. A dull debate addressed few of the issues that were to explode in the colonies. The House of Commons voted 204 to 49 to enact the Stamp Act. Many prominent Americans also failed to see a problem in the new tax. Richard Henry Lee of Virginia, the man who would introduce the resolution for independence in 1776, applied for a job as a stamp tax collector in 1765.

A Stupid Law

Constitutional niceties aside, the Stamp Act was politically stupid. Its burden fell most heavily on just those colonials who were best able to stir up a fuss. Newspaper editors, with their influence on public opinion, were hard hit. Advertisements, a newspaper's bread and butter, were taxed two shillings, and every edition had to be printed on stamped paper. Printers, who profited by putting out broadsides (posters used for announcing goods for sale and public meetings—including protest meetings), saw their business taxed at every turn of the press.

Lawyers, then as now the single largest group in colonial public office, and persuaders by profession, had to pay a tax on every document with which they dealt. Keepers of taverns, saddled with more expensive licenses by the new

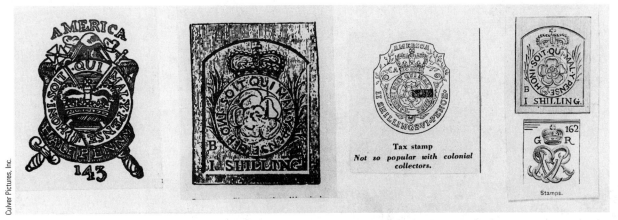

▲ *These stamps, what we call "embossments," pressed into paper, were the cause of the Stamp Act crisis of 1765. Few colonials ever saw them. Except for a few in Georgia, none were sold.*

law, were key figures in every town and neighborhood. Their establishments were the gathering places where, over rum, brandy, coffee, and tea, locals gathered to read newspapers and discuss affairs, such as taxes.

What was worse, most of these groups were concentrated in cities, where they could easily meet with one another, cooperate, organize, and have an impact out of proportion to their numbers. It was one thing to upset such groups one at a time, as the Sugar Act had riled shippers and distillers. The Stamp Act hit all of these key elements of the population at once, and, possibly to everyone's surprise, the protesters won the support of large numbers of working people and even the tumultuous underclass.

Riot

Parliament approved the Stamp Act in February 1765, scheduling it to go into effect in November. As soon as the news reached the colonies, they erupted in anger. Local organizations called Sons of Liberty (a phrase used to describe Americans by one of their parliamentary friends, Isaac Barré) condemned the law and called for a boycott of British goods.

Some of the Sons of Liberty turned to violence. When the stamped paper was delivered to warehouses in port cities, mobs broke in and made bonfires of it. Men appointed stamp masters were shunned if they were lucky, hanged in effigy, or roughed up. A brutal method of punishing stamp tax collectors was to daub them, sometimes naked, with hot tar, roll them in chicken feathers, and carry them, straddling a fence rail, around town.

One official in Maryland was forced to flee for his life to New York. That was a mistake, because the New York Sons of Liberty were the most volatile of all. They located the Marylander and forced him to write a letter of resignation. Led by Isaac Sears, the captain of a merchant vessel, the New Yorkers frightened their own lieutenant governor (a future revolutionary named Cadwallader Colden) so that he went into hiding. When they could not find Colden, they

burned his carriages. In Boston, the crowd looted and burned the homes of several British officials.

Rowdies are seldom popular, but the Stamp Act rioters were. When one governor was asked why he did not call out the militia to restore order, he pointed out that it would mean arming the very people who were wreaking havoc in the streets. The British had expected protests. Isaac Barré had warned of resistance. But everyone was taken by surprise by what seemed to be the whole American people on a rampage.

The Stamp Act Congress

Among those surprised were prominent wealthy colonials who opposed the Stamp Act but shuddered at the sounds of mobs. Mobs are beasts that take on a life of their own, independent of the personalities of those who constitute them. They move easily from one target to another, for the action itself takes the place of a mob's initial goal. The colonial elite knew this and knew that the colonial crowd had as many grievances against them as against Parliament. In October 1765, in an attempt to control the protest, 37 delegates from nine colonies assembled in New York City in the Stamp Act Congress.

Although the congress was the brainchild of one of the most volatile agitators, James Otis of Massachusetts, the 14 resolutions and the "Declaration of Rights and Grievances" that the delegates adopted were largely the work of more cautious and conservative men, like John Dickinson. The Stamp Act Congress criticized the Stamp Act, Sugar Act, and other parliamentary policies while the delegates prominently made it clear they acknowledged "all due subordination" to the Crown.

THE BRITISH CONSTITUTION

What did "all due subordination" mean? Loyalty to the king? Unquestionably. Just about everyone in the eighteenth

▲ *A New Hampshire man who had applied to be a seller of Stamp Act paper is tortured in effigy, probably just outside his home. He was a lucky one. Mobs like this—riffraff but substantial working men too—beat and tortured other men who had taken the same job.*

century agreed on the importance of the monarch as the symbol that unified the people of a nation or an empire. Lèse-majesté ("injuring the king") was the gravest of political crimes, punishable by hanging, often followed by disembowelment and quartering (harnessing a horse to each of the traitor's four limbs and cracking the whip).

On other basic questions of governance, however, Britons and colonials disagreed. Fundamental disagreement was possible because, whereas the British constitution included a few hallowed written documents, like the Magna Carta of 1215 and the Bill of Rights of 1689, it was largely unwritten. Most of the principles and practices of British governance had won acceptance over the centuries through tradition and usage.

The Question of Representation: The Colonial Case

Colonial protesters said that Parliament had no right to tax them because they were not represented in Parliament; colonials did not elect members of Parliament—it was that simple. Their own assemblies, which they did elect, were their little parliaments. These assemblies alone were empowered to tax them.

The colonial case is easy for us to understand, for it is the governing principle of representation in the United States today. In order for an individual to be represented in government, he or she must be entitled to vote for a city council member, county supervisor, state legislator, representative, or senator. The senators from Kentucky are not held to represent Iowa farmers. Only those senators for whom those farmers vote represent them. Reforms of voting laws throughout United States history—extending the

vote to men who did not own property, to African American men, and to women—have been based on the concept that one must be able to vote in order to be represented.

James Otis spoke for this way of thinking at the Stamp Act Congress when he proposed that Parliament end the dispute by allowing colonials to elect members to Parliament. However, Otis's colleagues virtually ignored him. They did not want to send representatives to Parliament. They wanted Parliament to recognize the authority of their own assemblies.

Grenville missed a grand opportunity. He could have confounded and splintered the colonial protest by acting favorably on Otis's proposal. If they voted as a bloc, which was unlikely, given the 13 colonies' disparate interests, colonial members of Parliament would constitute but a tiny party, able to influence policy only when the rest of Parliament was evenly divided, which, in matters of taxing the colonies, it was not. Grenville did not consider this alternative because he and other members of Parliament, including those who sympathized with the colonials, believed that the Americans were already represented in Parliament.

Virtual Representation: The British Case

By the lights of the eighteenth century, Grenville and the members of Parliament were correct. The British concept of representation differed (and differs) from our own. For example, it was not (and is not) necessary that a member of the British parliament reside in the electoral district that sends him or her to the House of Commons. While it is unlikely to happen in our own time, a member of Parliament may never set foot in the district from which he or she is elected. British electoral districts are for the sake of convenience in balloting, but each member of Parliament is regarded as *virtually* representing the entire nation. Edmund Burke, a friend of the Americans, put it this way to his constituents in the city of Bristol during the dispute with the colonies: "You choose a member . . . but when you have chosen him, he is not a member of Bristol, but he is a member of Parliament."

Colonials practiced virtual representation in their own elections. George Washington and other Virginians were elected to the House of Burgesses from counties in which they did not reside. Would-be burgesses stood for seats in more than one county at a time so that they were covered in the event they were defeated in one. Few objected to this practice. It was assumed that those who were elected would act with the interests of all Virginians in mind.

The colonists also practiced virtual representation in their restriction of the suffrage to free, white, adult male heads of household who owned property. The number of actual voters in colonial elections amounted to a small proportion of the inhabitants in every colony. Nevertheless, the colonists considered penniless white men, all women and children, and even, in a strange way, African American slaves, to be virtually represented in their elected assemblies. The assumption was that assemblymen acted on behalf of all, not just on behalf of the freeholders who voted for them.

This was precisely the position Parliament took when the colonials complained that they were not represented in Parliament: The colonists were virtually represented.

BRITISH POLICIES AND POLICY MAKERS

The Stamp Act crisis was not resolved by adding up debaters' points. If the protesters' constitutional argument was flimsy, they formed a powerful and articulate group in every colony with support among all social classes. None of them spoke of independence or, after the riots, of rebellion. But they were adamant that Americans were not represented by Parliament.

Poor Leadership

Some members of Parliament appreciated the colonial position. William Pitt, now earl of Chatham, rejoiced that America had resisted. "Three millions of people so dead to all the feelings of liberty," he said, "so voluntarily to submit to be slaves, would have been fit instruments to make slaves of the rest." Americans returned the compliment. They idolized Pitt.

Edmund Burke, the father of traditional conservatism, saw the colonists as defenders of British tradition and the Grenville group as dangerous innovators. The radical John Wilkes egged on the colonial protesters because he saw them as natural allies in his agitations on behalf of a free press and in opposition to George III. Charles Fox, a future cabinet minister, part opportunist and part man of principle, spoke on behalf of the Americans, as did Isaac Barré.

Unfortunately for the future of the empire, except for a brief interlude in 1766 and 1767, these men were in the opposition. The makers of colonial policy were men unable to see beyond constitutional fine points and their disdain for colonials. This narrow-mindedness was a consequence of the way English politics functioned during the reign of King George III.

Although members of Parliament used the party names "Whig" and "Tory," there was no two-party system resembling the party systems in the United States and Great Britain today. Parliament was a collection of half a dozen—or more—shifting factions. Some, such as Burke's Old Whigs, ever on the watch for violations of traditional liberties, were drawn together by agreement on a principle. So were, ironically, the "High Tories," reflexive supporters of the king because he was a king. Most parliamentary factions, however, were alliances of expediency, cliques of men who cooperated with one another because they were relations by blood or marriage or because, by working together, they could serve their individual, sometimes tawdry, interests.

Colonial Williamsburg Foundation

▲ *When George III was crowned in 1760, he was immensely popular, both at home and in the colonies. Truly an Englishman, unlike his truculently German predecessors, George I and George II, he was personally likable, had the common touch, and was sympathetic to the colonies. Times and opinions change.*

King George III

A new wrinkle was added after 1760, when George III was crowned king at the age of 22. His predecessors, the first two Georges, had used royal favors to reward military heroes, to support musicians and artists, or simply to keep congenial companions hanging around the palace. The first two Georges were German. George I never learned English. George II spoke it but preferred to communicate in French. Coming from the middling German state of Hanover, the Georges were delighted merely to have the large royal income of Britain at their disposal. Neither took much interest in domestic matters, a situation much to the liking of the Whigs.

George III, by contrast, was raised English. His mother had urged him, "Be a king, George"—that is, govern your realm. The days when an English monarch could do much of anything by royal decree were long gone. But George could and did use the patronage he controlled to create a parliamentary faction beholden to him. His party was known as the "King's Friends."

The King's Friends were no more venal than the men of other parliamentary factions. Nor was George III evil, as the Americans would come to paint him. Far from it. He accepted the British constitution; he was conscientious, with a strong sense of duty; he wrote his own letters and speeches. He ate and drank moderately (he feared the obesity that ran in the family). He was a likable person, far more at ease in the company of ordinary folk than any British monarch since. George III could not have been a tyrant had he wished to be. Indeed, several times during his first 10 years as king, he used his influence to support conciliation with the colonies and won American favor for his efforts. There would be plenty of statues of George III to be toppled when American opinion of the king changed.

▲ *An interesting artifact: a "souvenir teapot" celebrating the repeal of the Stamp Act. It was made in Great Britain. The potteries of Staffordshire were multiproduct, mass-production operations. They manufactured everything from cheap everyday tableware to items like this teapot, exploiting a specialty market, much as the people who silk-screen slogans on T-shirts do today. After the Revolution, the potteries shipped statuettes of George Washington to their American outlets.*

Unfortunately, this well-meaning king was stupid, vain, and stubborn. He was uneasy with politicians whose abilities exceeded his own and peevish with those who refused to flatter him. By excluding such men from office, and promoting mediocre men and sycophants to positions of influence, he denied power to those who best understood the American situation. And the king was erratic, dismissing even supporters on slight pretexts. Much later in life, he lost his sanity. It is possible he periodically suffered mild previews of his progressive disease during the quarrel with the colonials.

Mixed Victory

Thus, George III dismissed the able Grenville in July 1765 over a matter unrelated to colonial taxation. Early the next year, during the short ministry of Lord Rockingham, Lord Chatham (William Pitt) moved to repeal the Stamp Act, and it was done. The colonial celebrations were so noisy that few paid attention to the fact that king and Parliament had not yielded on principle. Parliament also passed the Declaratory Act, which stated that Parliament "had, hath, and of right ought to have, full power and authority to make laws and statutes of sufficient force and validity to bind the colonies and people of America, subjects of the Crown of Great Britain, in all cases whatsoever."

Not only did the Declaratory Act deny the Americans' claims for their own assemblies, but the wording was lifted from a law of 1719 that made Ireland completely subject to Great Britain. That should have given colonial protesters pause, for the status of the despised Irish was precisely, and understandably, what they were determined to avoid. But few seemed to notice. Chatham succeeded Rockingham as prime minister and ignored the Declaratory Act with the slickness of Robert Walpole. Chatham also eliminated another aggravation when he reduced the duty on molasses from three pence to a penny per gallon. The colonial protesters were Georgian politicians too. What did a piece of paper matter when a good friend held the reins?

Then, in one of those historical accidents that have grave consequences, Chatham fell seriously ill and ceased to play an active part in government. From the perspective of the colonists, the man who stepped into the vacuum was as bad a stroke of luck as George Grenville had been.

"Champagne Charley" and the Townshend Duties

Charles Townshend was, in fact, no more wicked a fellow than Grenville or King George. He was rather too convivial and charming; he won the nickname "Champagne Charley" because of his habit of arriving at the House of Commons giggling and unsteady on his feet. (In fairness to Townshend, Parliament met in the evening, and, on a given night, any number of members were at less than their best.)

Townshend was chancellor of the exchequer, a post equivalent to our secretary of the treasury, and he hoped to

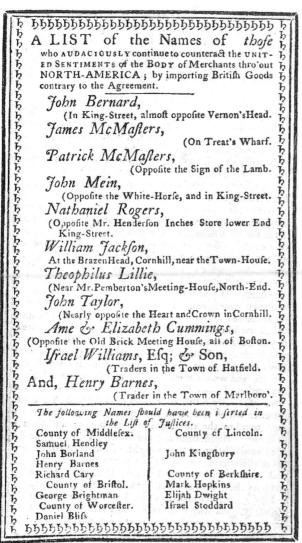

A LIST of the Names of *thofe* who AUDACIOUSLY continue to counteract the UNIT-ED SENTIMENTS of the BODY of Merchants thro'out NORTH-AMERICA ; by importing Britifh Goods contrary to the Agreement.

John Bernard,
(In King-Street, almoft oppofite Vernon's Head.

James McMaflers,
(On Treat's Wharf.

Patrick McMaflers,
(Oppofite the Sign of the Lamb.

John Mein,
(Oppofite the White-Horfe, and in King-Street.

Nathaniel Rogers,
(Oppofite Mr. Henderfon Inches Store lower End King-Street.

William Jackfon,
At the Brazen Head, Cornhill, near the Town-Houfe.

Theophilus Lillie,
(Near Mr. Pemberton's Meeting-Houfe, North-End.

John Taylor,
(Nearly oppofite the Heart and Crown in Cornhill.

Ame & Elizabeth Cummings,
(Oppofite the Old Brick Meeting Houfe, all of Bofton.

Ifrael Williams, Efq; *& Son,*
(Traders in the Town of Hatfield.

And, *Henry Barnes,*
(Trader in the Town of Marlboro'.

The following Names fhould have been inferted in the Lift of Juftices.

County of Middlefex.	County of Lincoln.
Samuel Hendley	
John Borland	John Kingfbury
Henry Barnes	
Richard Cary	County of Berkfhire.
County of Briftol.	Mark Hopkins
George Brightman	Elijah Dwight
County of Worcefter.	Ifrael Stoddard
Daniel Blifs	

▲ *By 1770, when protesters called for a boycott of these merchants because they sold goods imported from Britain, the furor over the Townshend Duties was already abating (as, perhaps, the shopkeepers listed here understood).*

be prime minister. To earn that prize, Townshend planned to cut taxes at home and to make up the loss of revenues in the colonies. He studied the Americans' distinctions between external taxes for regulating trade and internal taxes for raising money. He thought them nonsense but nonetheless designed a series of duties that were undeniably external. The Townshend Duties were imposed on paper, paint, lead, glass, and tea—all goods little made in the colonies and, therefore, imported from Britain.

It was an odd combination of goods. If none of them were produced in the colonies in any quantity, all except tea could be manufactured there. Townshend invited a boycott, and he got it. Trade between Britain and America fell off by 25 percent and then by 50 percent. Townshend had predicted that his duties would bring in £40,000 annually. The actual take was £13,000 in 1768 and less than £3,000 in 1769, hardly enough to operate a few frontier forts.

There was little violence. The boycott was organized by well-to-do merchants who were still nervous about the Stamp Act riots. But it worked. English merchants felt the pinch and petitioned Parliament for repeal. They pointed out that if Townshend had answered the colonial distinction between internal and external taxes, he had also penalized goods that English manufacturers and merchants shipped to America. In 1770, with the exception of a three-pence-per-pound tax on tea, Parliament repealed the Townshend Duties. The tea tax was kept in the spirit of the Declaratory Act. It was Parliament's statement that it retained the right to tax the colonies.

for FURTHER READING

Among the general histories of the events leading to the American Revolution (and differing radically in their explanations) are J. R. Alden, *A History of the American Revolution,* 1969; Bernard Bailyn, *The Ideological Origins of the American Revolution,* 1967, and *British Politics and the American Revolution,* 1965; Lawrence H. Gipson, *The Coming of the Revolution,* 1954; Jack P. Greene, *The Reinterpretation of the American Revolution,* 1968; Merrill Jensen, *The Founding of a Nation,* 1968; Robert Middlekauff, *The Glorious Cause: The American Revolution, 1763–1789,* 1982; Edmund S. Morgan, *The Birth of the Republic,* 1956; Don Higginbotham, *The War of American Independence, 1763–1789,* 1971;

Alfred T. Young, *The American Revolution: A Radical Interpretation,* 1976; and Pauline Maier, *From Resistance to Revolution, 1765–1776,* 1972.

Special studies include John Brook, *King George III,* 1972; Edmund S. Morgan and Helen Morgan, *Prologue to Revolution: The Stamp Act Crisis,* 1953; and Arthur M. Schlesinger Jr., *The Colonial Merchants and the American Revolution, 1763–1776,* 1951. On Pontiac's uprising, see Howard H. Peckham, *Pontiac and the Indian Uprising,* 1947; and Wilbur R. Jacobs, *Wilderness Politics and Indian Gifts,* 1966.

Visit the source collections at http://ajaccess.wadsworth.com and http://infotrac.thomsonlearning.com, and use the Search function with the following key terms to explore documents, images, audio and video clips, articles, and commentary related to the material in this chapter:

George Grenville   Stamp Act
Pontiac   William Pitt
Proclamation of 1763

Additional resources, exercises, and Internet links related to this chapter are available on *The American Past* Web site:
http://history.wadsworth.com/americanpast7e.

HISTORY ONLINE

The American Revolution and Its Era
http://memory.loc.gov/ammem/gmdhtml/armhome.html
Period maps of the colonies and the early United States.

Stamps Required by the Stamp Act
www2.gasou.edu/special_collections/artifacts/stamps.html
Examples of Stamp Act embossments in both Great Britain and the colonies; background information.

FROM RIOT TO REBELLION

The Road to Independence 1770–1776

> He has dissolved Representative Houses. . . . He has obstructed the Administration of Justice. . . . He has kept among us, in times of peace, Standing Armies. . . . He has plundered our seas, ravaged our Coasts, burnt our towns, and destroyed the lives of our people.
>
> The Declaration of Independence

> I can have no other Object but to protect the true Interests of all My Subjects. No People ever enjoyed more Happiness, or lived under a milder Government, than those now revolted Provinces. . . . My Desire is to restore to them the Blessings of Law and Liberty . . . which they have fatally and desperately exchanged for the Calamities of War, and the arbitrary Tyranny of their Chiefs.
>
> King George III

THE ISSUE OF Parliament's right to tax the colonies was not resolved by the repeal of the Townshend Duties. Neither Parliament nor colonial protesters yielded an inch. Nevertheless, almost everyone involved in the long dispute was relieved to see an end to confrontation and boycott. For three years after 1770, Parliament avoided provocations. In America, anti-British protests were few and muted. In fact, tensions may have been easing before mid-1770, when news of the repeal reached the colonies. A door-to-door survey of New Yorkers revealed that a majority were willing to buy all the Townshend items except tea, which could be had more cheaply from Dutch smugglers. Imports into New England, the most obstreperous colonies, began a steady rise from a low of £330,000 to £1.2 million, more than ever before. As perhaps most people always do, Americans wanted calm—business as usual—a resumption of daily life unaggravated by the folderol of politics.

STORMS WITHIN THE LULL

Nevertheless, several incidents between 1770 and 1773 indicated that not all was harmonious in British North America. On the streets of Boston, a bloody brawl between workingmen and British soldiers dramatized a simmering hostility toward the redcoats stationed in the colonies. In North Carolina, frontier settlers took up arms against the elite of the eastern counties who governed the colony. And in Rhode Island, farmers protected smugglers who burned a British patrol boat.

▲ *This engraving of the Boston Massacre, by silversmith and Son of Liberty Paul Revere, was propaganda, not an attempt to portray the incident accurately. The redcoats were actually backed against a wall in genuine danger; the Boston mob was more numerous than the victims here and crowded all around. Revere himself drew an accurate map of the incident for the trial of the soldiers.*

The Boston Massacre

On March 5, 1770, the weather in Boston was frigid. The streets were icy; heaps of gritty snow blocked the gutters. No doubt aggravated by the severity of the winter, which brought unemployment as well as discomfort, some men and boys exchanged words with British soldiers who were patrolling the streets. A handful of hecklers became a crowd cursing and throwing snowballs at the redcoats. A few dared the soldiers to use their muskets.

When the mob pressed close on King Street, backing the redcoats against a wall, they fired. Five, including a boy and an African American named Crispus Attucks, fell dead. Boston, with scarcely more than 15,000 people, was shocked. A few men who had been active in the Stamp Act protest tried to revive anti-British feelings. A silversmith, Paul Revere, engraved a picture of soldiers aggressively attacking innocent people. Samuel Adams, a former brewer, circulated prints of the "Boston Massacre" and tried to rouse tempers. Joseph Warren, a physician, embroidered passionately on the theme. "Take heed, ye orphan babes," he told a public meeting, "lest, whilst your streaming eyes are fixed upon the ghastly corpse, your feet slide on the stones bespattered with your father's brains."

But the agitation failed to bear fruit. Most people seemed to blame the incident on the mob. John Adams, cousin of Samuel and a friend of Warren, represented the soldiers in court. Adams was nobody's stooge, least of all for the British. He was strong-headed to the point of self-righteousness and a critic of British policies. In arguing the redcoats' case, Adams roundly criticized the practice of stationing professional soldiers in cities like Boston. "Soldiers quartered in a populous town will always occasion two mobs where they prevent one," he said. "They are wretched conservators of the peace." Nevertheless, Adams blamed an unsavory mob, not the indicted redcoats, for the tragedy. The jury agreed, acquitting all of the defendants but two and sentencing them only to branding on the thumb, a slap on the wrist by eighteenth-century standards.

The Hated Redcoats

The significance of the Boston Massacre and the Battle of Golden Hill (a soldier-civilian riot in New York in January) was that the vast majority of colonials let them pass. Still, they dramatized a sore spot in colonial city life: Americans did not much like the scarlet-uniformed soldiers in their midst. Property owners resented paying for their keep. Ordinary working people disliked rubbing shoulders with men who commanded little respect. Colonials of the same social class as the soldiers were hostile simply because the redcoats were outsiders.

The eighteenth-century soldier was not the boy next door in uniform, defending the nation and its ideals. He was a rough and lusty young man sieved from the dregs of a rigidly stratified society. Some soldiers were convicted criminals who were in the army because it was offered to them as an alternative to prison. Others, guilty of no crime, were pressed into service simply because they were unable to support themselves.

At best, civilians were wary of them; many despised them. To their officers, *scum* was the word that leapt first to mind when they described soldiers. Redcoats were regularly and brutally punished. If not slaves, they were in bondage, apt to be hanged if they deserted. There was no feeling among them of service to king and country or of commitment to an ideal. In America, they were further alienated by the fact that few colonials enlisted. The "lobsters" were almost all from Great Britain.

A Dangerous Relationship

As long as the soldiers lived in frontier forts or in isolated bases such as Castle Island in Boston Harbor, there was little conflict. However, after the Stamp Act riots, the Crown stationed large detachments within cities and towns. Some 4,000 redcoats were camped on Boston Common at the time of the massacre. Others, under the terms of the Quartering Act of 1765, were billeted in whatever vacant buildings and taverns quartermasters could locate.

This brought the tightly knit redcoats into intimate daily contact with working-class colonials. They were young men, and some found girlfriends—which, naturally, stirred up resentment among colonial men. Others coarsely accosted young women. When off duty, redcoats competed with local men and boys for casual work. There was a fistfight over jobs at a rope factory in Boston just a few days before the Boston Massacre. Redcoats also passed idle hours in the taverns where colonials gathered.

▲ *Most redcoats were rough, crude, even dangerous men. Their intrusion into taverns, the social centers of colonial cities, had more to do with making rebels of ordinary city folk than arguments about taxation and representation.*

Inns and taverns were not just hostels where travelers supped and bedded down. They were a focal point of urban social life—neighborhood meeting places, like contemporary English pubs. Local workingmen popped in throughout the day for a cup of tea or coffee and, in the evening, for a shot of rum, a mug of mulled cider, a pipe of tobacco, and a chat with friends about work and politics. Those with time on their hands, such as the unemployed and seamen between voyages, spent even more time at the "ordinaries," as taverns were called, if only to stand in front of the fire for a bit. The intrusion of uniformed foreigners, laughing loudly and carrying on by themselves, caused resentment even when, as between 1770 and 1773, relations with Great Britain seemed to be good.

Street People

The redcoats had more to do with the anti-British feelings of lower-class colonials than parliamentary taxation did. Poor people worried about the next day's meal, not about the fine points of the British constitution. Such people were central to the protest that boiled over into riot in 1765 and rebellion after 1773. Workingmen, the unemployed, boisterous street boys and apprentices, and the disreputable fringe elements of colonial society did the dirty work in the Stamp Act crisis. They were the ones who taunted soldiers in the streets and who were killed in the Boston Massacre.

They had little to lose as a consequence of rash action. Many of the street people were themselves social outcasts by virtue of their class, their occupation (or lack of one), or their race. Seamen, suspect because they came and went, belonging to no community, were prominent in colonial crowds. (Crispus Attucks was a seaman out of work.) John Adams described the mob on King Street as "Negroes and mulattoes, Irish teagues and outlandish jack-tars." And yet, the revolution he was to join with enthusiasm owed much to the boldness of this motley bunch.

Demon Rum

It is worth noting the curious role of alcohol in the agitation. Soldiers liked their drink. It was standard military practice to pass around rum before battle, and the royal governor of New York dissolved the colonial assembly in 1766 when its members refused to provide the redcoats with their accustomed ration of five pints of beer or four ounces of rum a day.

Colonials were hard-drinking folk too—they drank much more per capita than Americans today—and people at the bottom of the social scale, with more to forget, were the thirstiest of all. Many signal episodes on the road to independence seem to have been carried out by men in their cups. "The minds of the freeholders were inflamed," wrote an observer of the Stamp Act protest in South Carolina, "by many a hearty damn . . . over bottles, bowls, and glasses." The crowd that precipitated the Boston Massacre had come out of the taverns. The Sons of Liberty, who ignited the last phase of the revolutionary movement with the Boston Tea Party of 1773, assembled over a barrel of rum.

▲ *Some inns resembled the Blue Anchor in Philadelphia, catering to elegantly well-mannered gentlemen. Workingmen's taverns and ordinaries, however—those into which redcoats were likely to intrude—were ruder, crowded, and far less decorous, even on the slowest days.*

Upper-crust protest leaders had mixed feelings about this kind of agitation. They were more than willing to exploit angry, and perhaps inebriated, crowds by stirring up resentment of the British, then winking at the mobs' mockeries of the law. John Adams, so scornful of the Boston Massacre mob in 1770, called the men at the Boston Tea Party of 1773 "so bold, so daring, so intrepid." But many thoughtful upper-class colonials, and not just those who remained loyal to Great Britain, worried about the "rabble." They knew that mobs do not always fade graciously away after having played their historic role.

The Regulators

Conflict between colonial classes was, as it had been during the seventeenth century, clearer in the countryside. In the backcountry of South Carolina, between 1767 and 1769, frontiersmen rebelled against the refusal of the colonial assembly, which was dominated by Charleston planters, to set up county governments in the west. They created their own counties to which they paid taxes that were legally to go to Charleston. The rebels called themselves "Regulators" because they said they would regulate their own affairs.

In North Carolina, a similar dispute led to actual battle. A band of westerners rode east to demonstrate their resentment of the colony's penny-pinching policies. In May 1771, they were met and defeated by a smaller but better-trained militia at the Battle of Alamance. Only nine men were killed (six were later hanged), but the modesty of the clash did not

sweeten the bitterness in the backcountry. When the Revolution began in 1775, poor, backcountry Carolinians with memories were, more than any other lower-class white colonials, likely to be pro-British.

The *Gaspée*

In June 1772, a British schooner patrolling Narragansett Bay in Rhode Island, the *Gaspée,* spied a vessel suspected of smuggling and sailed after it toward Providence. About seven miles from the port, the *Gaspée* ran aground. That night, men from eight boats boarded the schooner, roughly set the crew ashore, and burned the *Gaspée* to the waterline.

Because the *Gaspée* was a royal vessel, this was an act of rebellion. The authorities were pretty sure the ringleader of the gang was a merchant named John Brown, who had had several run-ins with customs collectors. However, neither a £500 reward nor the fact that Rhode Island's elected governor took part in the investigation persuaded anyone to provide evidence. The commission of inquiry finally disbanded angrily only in June 1773. By that time, the three-year lull in British–American relations was drawing to a close.

THE MARCH TOWARD WAR

The quiet years ended in the spring of 1773, when Parliament once again enacted a law that angered Americans. This time, however, instead of spontaneous protests under the control of

▲ *Rhode Islanders burning the grounded British customs schooner* Gaspée *in Narragansett Bay in 1772.*

no one in particular, resistance to British policy was aroused and organized by a number of able, deliberate men.

They may be described as professional agitators. Some were orators; some, propagandists of the pen. Others were organizers, people willing to devote their time to shaping anger into rebellion. There can be no revolutions without such revolutionaries. Men like James Otis and Samuel Adams of Massachusetts and Patrick Henry of Virginia made the difference between spontaneous incidents like the Boston Massacre and calculated provocations like the Boston Tea Party.

The Troublemakers

James Otis was a Boston attorney, once an effective prosecutor before the unpopular vice admiralty courts. Like celebrated criminal attorneys today, he was a showman, always excitable, an exponent of anything-to-win-a-case litigation, and often vituperative. He described one group of legal adversaries as a "dirty, drinking, drabbing, contaminated knot of thieves," and, what's more, "Turks, Jews, and other infidels, with a few renegade Christians and Catholics." This kind of rhetoric always has its enthusiasts. Otis could fire up the passions of a jury or a town meeting as few of his contemporaries could.

In 1761, Otis led Boston's fight against "writs of assistance." These were broad search warrants empowering customs agents to enter warehouses and homes to search for any evidence of smuggling. Arguing against the writs, Otis

made them an issue of the sacred, basic rights of British subjects, apparently coining the phrase soon to be the slogan of a revolution: "Taxation without representation is tyranny." John Adams would later say of Otis that "then and there the child Independence was born."

For inflammatory rhetoric, Patrick Henry of Virginia was Otis's equal. No deep thinker, Henry was a sharp-tongued, Scotch-Irish shopkeeper who educated himself to become one of the colony's most successful trial lawyers and a member of the House of Burgesses, a station to which few of his class rose. He won notice far beyond Williamsburg when he denounced George III as a tyrant because the king reversed a law passed by the burgesses, something monarchs had been doing since 1624.

During the Stamp Act excitement, Henry caused an even more widespread furor when he was quoted as saying, "Caesar had his Brutus, Charles I his Cromwell, and George III may profit by their example." Naming the king in series with two historical rulers who had died by the knife was pretty heady stuff. Henry was shouted down with cries of "treason." Legend soon had him replying, "If this be treason, make the most of it." Henry would be prominent in the final drive toward independence. He called for the establishment of a colonial army in May 1775 with more words for the quotations books: "Give me liberty or give me death."

Less excitable than Otis and Henry, and no orator (he was nervous at a podium, trembling and stumbling over his words), Samuel Adams of Massachusetts was the most substantial of the three. A brewer as a young man (and a tax collector between 1756 and 1764!), Adams devoted himself to moral censorship and anti-British agitation. Indeed, personal morality and civic virtue were fundamental to his dislike of British rule. He was obsessed by the concept of republican virtue that the educated people of the era attributed to the ancient Greeks and Romans. Adams said that Boston should reconstitute itself as a "Christian Sparta." Humorless, cheerless, bored by socializing, he believed that political power was legitimate only when in the hands of men who lived austerely and were ever vigilant to preserve liberty.

Adams was in the middle of every major protest in Boston: against the Sugar Act, the Stamp Act, the Townshend Duties, the Boston Massacre. He was indispensable, a sober organizer among oratorical prima donnas. He was the man who handled the humdrum but essential tasks that transform protest into politics. He also served as the go-between for the Boston elite (men like the rich merchant John Hancock) and the Sons of Liberty, men of Adams's own artisan class, and through them, the crowd.

Fatal Turn: The Tea Act

Samuel Adams may have daydreamed of the colonies independent of Great Britain by the mid-1760s. If he did, he shared his musings with few other colonials, for they would have seen him as a fantasist. John Adams's opinion aside, the child Independence was born not when James Otis challenged the writs of assistance nor when Patrick Henry threatened George III with executioners. The baby was delivered—that is, responsible colonials began to consider independence as a genuine possibility, in numbers growing steadily like an infant, a child soon to be on its feet—on May 10, 1773, when Parliament's Tea Act became law. After the Tea Act, the colonies' quarrel with the mother country did not, as before, burn out and die. By progressive steps, it intensified into an explosion.

The Tea Act was not designed to tax the colonies. Its purpose was to bail out the East India Company, a corporation invaluable to the Crown. In return for a monopoly on trade with India, the company governed Britain's holdings in India, maintaining an army to defend and expand them: It was empire on the cheap. In 1773, the company was on the edge of bankruptcy. In just a few months, East India shares plummeted in value from £280 to £160 (and many members of Parliament owned shares). Some 17 million pounds of company tea sat in warehouses, and there were no buyers.

To prevent disaster, the company proposed that it be allowed to sell its tea directly in the colonies rather than auction it to middlemen. Because the tea was being dumped—any price was preferable to none—East India tea would be significantly cheaper than the smuggled Dutch tea that had become fashionable in America. To sweeten the cup further, the company asked Parliament to repeal the Townshend tax on tea that had been left in place.

Parliament met the company nine-tenths of the way. The prime minister, Frederick, Lord North, supported by George III, saw a chance to succeed where Grenville and Townshend had failed. Even with the tax, Tea Act tea was a bargain. It would cost colonials money to uphold the cause of no taxation without representation. Like many others, Lord North and the king believed that colonial protest was about greed.

The Tea Parties

They were wrong. When a dozen East India Company ships carrying 1,700 chests of tea sailed into American ports, they were greeted by the angriest defiance of British authority since 1765. The Americans would not be bought. Under the Tea Act, tea may have been cheap, but buying it set the precedent of allowing Parliament to grant monopolies on goods colonials had to import.

The tea was landed in Charleston; it was hastily locked up in a warehouse, where an angry crowd could not get to it. The governors of New York and Pennsylvania ordered the ships to return to England for fear of riots. In Annapolis, Maryland, a tea ship was burned. But it was a milder action in Boston that triggered the crisis.

The American-born governor of Massachusetts, Thomas Hutchinson, would not permit the tea ships to depart Boston. Instead, while sparks flew at public meetings, he hatched a plan to get the cargo under royal (this is, his) control and not that of a private company: He planned to seize the tea for failure to pay port taxes and work from there.

It was a clever idea, but Samuel Adams was cleverer and quicker. On December 16, 1773, the day before Hutchinson could gain custody of the tea, Adams presided over a protest meeting attended by a third of the population of Boston. Some 60 Sons of Liberty slipped out of the meetinghouse, had a few drinks, dressed up as Mohawk Indians, and boarded the East India Company ships. To the cheers of a huge crowd, they dumped 342 chests worth £10,000 into Boston Harbor.

The Indian costumes had a touch of political genius to them. They disguised the perpetrators but also lent the air of a prank to the affair—thus the name "Boston Tea Party." Adams and his colleagues knew that Britain could not let the incident pass; they guessed that Parliament would overreact. Parliament did, grotesquely and foolishly. Instead of

---

The Morning After

If the men of Boston who dumped the tea into Boston Harbor had been drinking, not all suffered hangovers. One participant remembered what he did the morning after the Boston Tea Party:

The next morning . . . it was discovered that very considerable quantities of [tea] were floating upon the surface of the water, and to prevent the possibility of any of its being saved for use, a number of small boats were manned by sailors and citizens, who rowed them into those parts of the harbor wherever the tea was visible, and by beating it with oars and paddles so thoroughly drenched it as to render its entire destruction inevitable.

---

flushing out the individuals involved in the party and trying them as garden-variety vandals (the dumped tea had not been under government control), Lord North decided to punish the city of Boston and the colony of Massachusetts.

The Intolerable Acts

A few politicians, like reliable Lord Chatham, feverishly warned that the Coercive Acts of 1774—Americans called them the "Intolerable Acts"—were ill advised, but they sailed through Parliament. First, the port of Boston was to be closed to all trade until the city (not the individual culprits) paid for the spoiled tea. Second, the new governor (a military man, General Thomas Gage) was empowered to transfer out of the colony the trials of soldiers or other British officials accused of killing protesters. It was not unreasonable to see this as an invitation to the redcoats to shoot on the slightest pretext. Third, the structure of the government of Massachusetts was overhauled, with elected bodies losing powers to the king's appointed officials. Fourth, a new Quartering Act further aggravated civilian–soldier relations—this time, to the breaking point. It authorized the army to house redcoats in occupied private homes!

Lord North hoped that by coming down hard on Massachusetts, he would isolate the colony, which had never been popular elsewhere in North America, and thereby issue a warning to protesters elsewhere. Instead, the Coercive Acts proved to be intolerable everywhere. Several cities shipped food to paralyzed Boston. More ominous than charity, when Massachusetts called for a continental congress to meet in Philadelphia to discuss a united response to the Intolerable Acts, every colony except Georgia sent delegates.

Salt in the Wound: The Quebec Act

The Quebec Act of 1774 was not designed as one of the Coercive Acts, but it also agitated many colonials by officially recognizing the French language and giving official status to the Catholic religion in the province of Quebec. Anti-Catholicism was not as rabid in Britain and the colonies as it had been a hundred years earlier, but it was far from dead. (In the Gordon Riots in London in 1780, mobs burned the churches and homes of Catholics for three days.) In 1774, New Englanders shuddered that the Crown was protecting, even promoting, Catholicism in a colony that bordered their own.

Colonials having no particular hostility toward Roman Catholics were agitated by the Quebec Act's second provision, which expanded Quebec's boundary into the Ohio Valley. Had not the French and Indian War been fought to win these lands for the colonies? Speculators with claims to land in the Ohio Valley and farmers eyeing the possibility of moving there were alarmed.

Finally, the Quebec Act did not provide for an elective assembly in the colony. It was true enough that French Canadians had never had an elected assembly. But Canada was British now. Again, the deadly serious issue of the rights of British subjects came to the fore.

THE BEGINNING OF A REVOLUTION

If the Tea Act marks the beginning of a progressive march toward revolution, the Intolerable Acts and the Quebec Act mark the beginning of a coordinated colonial resistance. Before 1774, only the informal "committees of correspondence," groups exchanging news and views among the colonies via the mails, connected one colony's protesters to those of others. Now, while the delegates to the Continental Congress who trickled into Philadelphia during the summer continued to think of themselves as New Hampshiremen and New Yorkers and Carolinians, they were acting in concert—continentally—and with something like formal authority.

The Delegates

The 56 delegates to the Continental Congress began their discussions on September 5. Some of them, such as hometowner Benjamin Franklin, were already famous. Others, like Samuel Adams and Patrick Henry, had recently become notorious. Most, however, were men of only local renown, and, since each of the colonies had closer relations with Britain than with any other American province, few of the delegates had met one another.

They differed in temperament, in their sentiments toward Great Britain, and in their opinions as to what should be done, could be done, and ought not be done. But they got along remarkably well. The heritage they were soon to rebel against gave them much in common. They were all gentlemen in the English mold: merchants, planters, and professionals, particularly lawyers. They prized education and civility. They knew how to keep debates decorous and impersonal. In the evening, they recessed to a round of festive dinners and parties with Philadelphia high society. George Washington of Virginia rarely dined in his own chambers. John Adams gushed in letters to his wife, Abigail, about the lavishness of the meals he was served. Only Samuel Adams, nurturing his ideals of Roman republican frugality, shunned the social whirl and won the reputation of being a killjoy.

The Issues

None of the delegates had an "ideology"; few had an agenda. Most were troubled and uncertain about what to do.

Planter Politicians

William Byrd was born in Virginia in 1674. His father was quite wealthy, so it was Byrd's good fortune to come into his maturity when the Tidewater plantation aristocracy was entering its golden age—no longer struggling to build fortunes, but able to devote its comfortable leisure to sport, "society," scholarship, and politics.

Byrd enjoyed the great planters' unending rounds of entertaining one another at feasts and balls; he loved the chummy men's club atmosphere of Williamsburg, the colonial capital; and he was a social butterfly during two extended periods of residence in London. He seems to have cared less than most planters for hunting with the hounds, one of the planters' many imitations of the British aristocracy, which they admired. Byrd loved books more than most of his peers. Educated in Europe, he began each day reading for several hours in Hebrew, Greek, Latin, French, and Dutch.

What Byrd and the vast majority of eighteenth-century planters had most in common was politics. They regarded holding public office as a social, even sacred, duty and as the responsibility of men whom wealth and breeding provided with leisure, education, and—they liked to say—a selfless disinterestedness. Indeed, the planters were born "governing." As the owners of numerous slaves, they grew up managing the affairs of communities, which large plantations were.

They inherited or bought their slaves. But they had to win election to public offices, the most coveted of which was a seat in Virginia's assembly, the House of Burgesses. (Appointment to the royal governor's council was a step up from that, but open only to the cream of the class, like Byrd.)

Few Virginians who were not planters were eligible for election to the House of Burgesses (or had the time for the job). The property qualification was substantially higher than it was for the right to vote. Middling farmers, including those who owned no slaves, voted but never thought of being a burgess.

These were the "yeomen" whom Thomas Jefferson, born the year before William Byrd died, idealized as the "bone and sinew" of a healthy society and the people whose support the planter had to win in order to be elected to office.

Politics was highly personal. In his own county, the planter candidate knew by name almost every voter who assembled at the courthouse on election day; if he was a candidate in another county (quite legal if he owned property there), the voters knew a lot about him because of his wealth. Elections were intimate. Weather permitting, they were held outdoors. Candidates set out spreads of food and drink, and politely but formally greeted all. There was no gushing; the candidate did not try to act like the same "ordinary fellow" the voters were. Such obvious patronizing would have been a ticket to rejection. The point was this: The candidate was a member of a social class a notch up, the governing class.

Balloting was public. Each voter approached the pollers, who sat at a table, and announced his choice. His candidate stepped forward to thank him, again quite formally. Debate in the House of Burgesses at Williamsburg was equally decorous. There were disturbing moments, as when Patrick Henry savaged the king and was shouted down as a traitor. Mostly, however, since the burgesses were of the same social class, sharing its well-defined code of conduct, and since many were related by blood or marriage, the tiny House of Burgesses was a deliberative assembly with an integrity not always found in state legislatures today.

The leaders of the Revolution from Virginia were educated in this superb political school. Washington, Jefferson, Peyton Randolph (the president of the First Continental Congress), and all of the Virginians who signed the Declaration of Independence were alumni of the House of Burgesses. So was Patrick Henry, although he was no planter, a fact surely remarked upon after his bad behavior at Williamsburg.

They were angry, even those who would later remain loyal to Britain, and they were determined to settle the squabble with Parliament. The congress adopted a defiant set of declarations called the Suffolk Resolves, which were rushed to Philadelphia from Boston (Suffolk County), by the rebellious silversmith who publicized the Boston Massacre, Paul Revere. The resolutions stated that the Intolerable Acts were invalid, and called for a boycott of trade with Britain if the obnoxious laws were not repealed.

But there was no king-bashing in the style of Patrick Henry (although he was present). The delegates toasted themselves tipsy, raising glasses to King George. They agreed to British regulation of colonial trade, and they almost adopted a conciliatory plan designed by Joseph Galloway of Pennsylvania just a few days before they voted for the hard-line Suffolk resolutions. The very notion of rebellion was repugnant.

Unhappily, George III did not share their mood. He was determined to stand firm and, having the military might, more than willing to win the argument with force. "Blows must decide whether they are to be subject to the country or independent," George told Lord North at a time when no colonial leader had publicly mentioned the possibility of independence. Learning of the king's intransigence, the delegates had no alternative but to respond in kind. One of their last actions before adjourning was to call on Americans to organize and train local military units.

Colonial Soldiers

Little encouragement was needed. In the Massachusetts countryside, tempers were already aflame. A British spy, sent out from Boston to get a feel for the people's mood, asked an ancient farmer why, at his age, he was cleaning his gun. The old man replied that "there was a flock of redcoats in Boston, which he expected would be here soon; he meant to try and hit some of them." Did his neighbors feel the same way? Yes, most of them. "There was one Tory house in sight," the old man said, "and he wished it was in flames."

Young men also oiled their guns and collected on village greens to elect officers and drill, as well as they knew how. Practically every adult male in rural America was armed, for guns were tools. Many farm families still hunted for some of their food, and the days when they had to be on guard against Indian raids were not long in the past.

Americans were excellent marksmen, even with smoothbore flintlock muskets, which were not reliable at any distance. Some had adopted the *Jaeger,* the rifle introduced into the colonies by German immigrants. Americans extended the length of its barrel for even greater accuracy at a distance. A British officer observed, "Provided an American rifleman were to get a perfect aim at 300 yards at me, standing still, he most undoubtedly would hit me unless it was a very windy day."

As soldiers, however, colonials had a bad name. Astonishingly few responded to British attempts to recruit them. Militia training was close to a joke. During the French and Indian War, the camps of American militiamen were notoriously filthy; often, the colonials did not dig latrines but made do in the woods. Many more of them died from disease—contaminated water—than did the disciplined redcoats who marched with them. The Americans had been unreliable in battle so often that General John Forbes said, "There is no faith or trust to be put in them." General Wolfe had called his American militia "the dirtiest, most contemptible cowardly dogs you can conceive." Considering the lineaments of eighteenth-century warfare, however, this was almost a compliment.

The Way Battles Were Fought

Eighteenth-century warfare was highly structured. In battle, two armies in close formation maneuvered to face one another in open country from the better position, which usually meant higher ground. After an exchange of artillery, soon to be the key to battle but not yet fully appreciated, the attacking army closed the gap to the oddly cheerful music of fife and drum (or bagpipes if the soldiers were Scots). The armies exchanged musket fire in volleys. The men pointed, rather than aimed, their weapons—muskets were not accurate. The side that stood its ground amidst the horror of smoke, noise, and companions next to them dropping to the sod—in other words, the army that continued to be an army—defeated the one that panicked, broke ranks, and fled the field.

The key to winning battles was long, hard, and tedious training according to manuals written mostly by French and Prussian tacticians. These drills (and a dram of rum or gin before battle) were designed to make a machine of thousands of individual human beings. Marksmanship counted for little. Individual initiative was a curse, to be exorcised by brutal discipline. The goal was nothing less than unnatural behavior on a mass scale: not fleeing from a terrifying experience.

Lexington and Concord

And so, when General Gage decided to seize rebel supplies at Concord, 21 miles from Boston, he did not worry about the "minutemen," farmers pledged to be ready to fight the British at a minute's notice. How could play-soldiers stand up to one of Europe's finest armies? On April 19, 1775, he sent 700 troops to capture the munitions and, if possible, to arrest Samuel Adams and John Hancock, who were thought to be hiding in the area.

The Americans were warned by the midnight ride of Paul Revere (and by William Dawes and Samuel Prescott, who actually got farther than Revere), bringing the news to

John Carter Brown Library

▲ *This depiction of the Battle of Lexington shows the minutemen inflicting casualties on the redcoats in the background. It is patriotic but not accurate. The British sustained no casualties, and their volley scattered the colonials, who may have begun to disperse (accounts of the incident differ) before the redcoats fired.*

crossroads and village commons: "The British are coming!" When Major John Pitcairn arrived at Lexington, a few miles shy of Concord, he found 70 nervous minutemen drawn up in a semblance of battle formation. Their fate seemed to confirm British contempt for American warriors.

In fact, the Americans were sensibly frightened and confused at the sight of the solid ranks of tough, grim men who outnumbered them ten to one. They stood around uncertainly, murmuring among themselves for a few minutes. Pitcairn twice ordered them to disperse. Then a shot was fired.

No one knew who fired it—a colonial hothead determined to force the issue or a British soldier mishandling his musket. Nor did it matter. In London, on the same day as the Battle of Lexington, Parliament was passing another Intolerable Act, which banned Massachusetts fishermen from the Grand Banks of Newfoundland. When Americans heard of that law, which was designed to finish off the already crippled New England economy, it would surely have set off armed rebellion in New England.

Pitcairn's men cleared Lexington Green in minutes and marched on to Concord, where a larger group of Americans met them at a bridge. Surprised by the size of the resistance and the Americans' effectiveness from their superior position, Pitcairn ordered a retreat to Boston. All the way back, minutemen sniped at the British soldiers from behind trees and stone fences; they were in their element, fighting the redcoats as they fought Indians. They inflicted serious casualties. When the British troops reached the city, more than 250 were dead or wounded. The minutemen, elated by their victory, set up camp outside Boston, where others joined them daily.

Bunker Hill

Soon, 16,000 rebels surrounded the city. In London, Edmund Burke pleaded with Parliament to evacuate Boston and allow tempers to cool. As usual, the most thoughtful politician of the age was heard for his eloquence, then ignored. Lord North dispatched another 1,000 troops to Boston, along with three more generals—Henry Clinton, John "Gentleman Johnny" Burgoyne, and William Howe. Curiously, all three, as well as Gage, were personally sympathetic to Americans.

Howe talked Gage into allowing him to occupy high ground on a peninsula across the Charles River. The day before he moved, however, the Americans took the peninsula, including Bunker Hill and, nearer to Boston, Breed's Hill. When Howe's men took to their boats, 1,600 armed colonials were dug in on the summit of Breed's Hill.

Howe sent 2,000 crack troops up the slopes. Puzzlingly, no one returned their fire. Then, when the Americans could "see the whites of their eyes" (in other words, when they could aim rather than volley), they let loose. The redcoats staggered and retreated. They regrouped and again advanced, and again they were thrown back. Now, however, Howe correctly calculated that the Americans were short of powder and shot. Reinforcing his badly mauled front line with fresh men, Howe took Breed's Hill with bayonets.

The British had won. Or had they? Hearing that 200 men had been killed and 1,000 wounded, General Clinton remarked that too many such "victories" would destroy the British ability to fight. Ninety-two officers were lost (one-sixth of the British officers who would be lost over the next six years). Clinton was right. The misnamed Battle of Bunker Hill was an American triumph. Casualties were 370, most of them killed or wounded during the flight from the hilltop. The British gained nothing, for the colonial militias maintained their circle around Boston, while revolutionaries secured their control of the New England countryside.

Ticonderoga

Rebel morale had another boost in the spring of 1775. Soon after Lexington and Concord, the Massachusetts Committee of Safety instructed Benedict Arnold, scion of a wealthy Connecticut family and a proven soldier, to raise an army and attack Fort Ticonderoga on Lake Champlain. Before he started, Arnold learned that backwoodsmen from what is now Vermont, a kind of guerrilla group calling themselves the "Green Mountain Boys," were preparing to march on the same fort, led by an eccentric land speculator named Ethan Allen.

Arnold caught up with the Green Mountain Boys, but he was unable to get the headstrong Allen to recognize his authority. Quarreling all the way to the fort, the two shut up just long enough to capture Ticonderoga on May 10. When the British commander, who had heard nothing of Lexington and Concord, asked in whose name he was being asked to surrender, Allen allegedly replied, "in the name of the great Jehovah and the Continental Congress." Striking and memorable as the words are, Allen was unlikely to have spoken them just that way, since he was an aggressive atheist.

The Arnold–Allen group captured several other British forts. There were no big battles, hardly battles at all. The British garrisons, languishing in the forests, were caught entirely by surprise. But along with Bunker Hill, these actions established that a war had begun, forcing Americans to take sides. Nowhere was the psychological impact greater than in Philadelphia, where the *Second* Continental Congress was already in session.

The Second Continental Congress

The delegates to the Second Continental Congress were less restrained than those of the first congress. Some conservatives, such as Joseph Galloway, were not present. Their places were taken by militants like Thomas Jefferson, a 32-year-old Virginian who had written several scorching anti-British polemics.

The situation had changed radically in a year. Armed rebellion was now a reality: Lexington, Concord, Ticonderoga, Bunker Hill, and an unsuccessful attack by Benedict Arnold on Quebec. Without bloodshed, royal authority was disintegrating everywhere as governors fled to the safety of British warships and self-appointed rebel committees took over the functions of government. If the Continental Con-

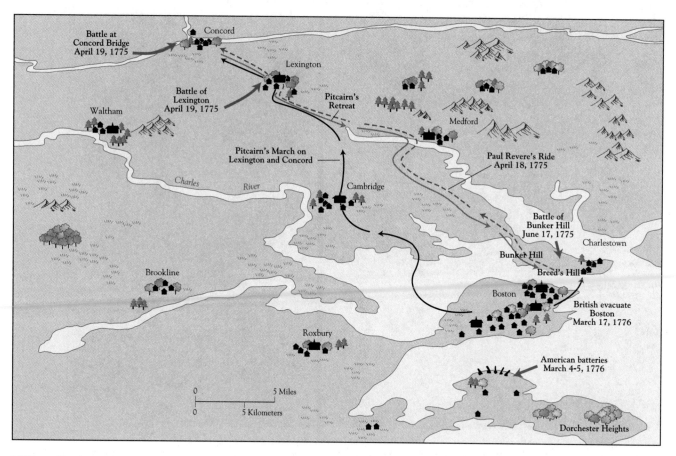

MAP 8:1 The First Battles of the Revolution, 1775–1776   The redcoats' march to the villages of Lexington and Concord, which are now suburbs, and their retreat to Boston, was through farmland in 1775. Note that the Battle of Bunker Hill was actually fought on the slopes of Breed's Hill.

gress were to retain the authority ostensibly bestowed upon it by Ethan Allen, the delegates had some catching up to do. They did. They sent George Washington of Virginia, silently voicing his aspirations in the military uniform he wore, to take command of the troops around Boston.

Delegates were discussing independence now, but not officially. In its "Declaration of the Cause and Necessity of Taking Up Arms" in July 1775, the Continental Congress insisted that the rebels sought only their rights as British subjects. But the inconsistency of shooting at George III's soldiers while swearing love for the king was preying on the minds of all. With Lord North refusing to propose any kind of compromise, the Continental Congress held back because of a thread of sentiment—the commitment of virtually all of Western civilization to the necessity of monarchy and a lingering affection for the person of George III, who had once been so popular.

The Final Breakaway

The man who snipped the thread of sentiment was not an American but an Englishman, 38 years of age in 1775, and only recently arrived in the colonies: Thomas Paine. Benjamin Franklin sponsored Paine's emigration. Perhaps because both

men were of the artisan class—Paine was a corset maker—Franklin saw beyond Paine's history of failures in business, his "loathesome" personal appearance, and his vainglorious opinion of himself.

Common Sense

Paine's egotism and contentiousness were difficult to take. But his talents as a rouser of protest were formidable. In January 1776, he published a pamphlet that ranks with Luther's 95 Theses and the *Communist Manifesto* as a work of few words that shaped the course of history. In his pamphlet, *Common Sense,* Paine argued that it was foolish for Americans to risk everything for the purpose of British approval. He shredded the Americans' sentimental attachment to King George III, whom he called a "Royal Brute." Indeed, Paine attacked the very idea of hereditary monarchy. Kingship was "an office any child or idiot may fill" that required "only the animal figure of a man."

With a genius for propaganda that would produce many stirring calls on behalf of democracy and liberty over the next 20 years, Paine made converts by the thousands. Within a year, a population of 2.5 million bought 150,000 copies of *Common Sense;* within a decade, 500,000 copies. Every

▲ *This engraving of John Trumbull's classic painting of the signing of the Declaration of Independence depicts an assembly that never existed. By the time the document was ready for signing, most of the delegates had left for home. They signed without ceremony, singly or in twos and threes, later on in the summer or fall of 1776. However, Trumbull went to great lengths to find likenesses of every signer.*

American who could read must have at least skimmed it. Paine boasted that it was "the greatest sale that any performance ever had since the use of letters."

Paine's depiction of the king seemed to come to life with every dispatch from London. George III refused even to listen to American suggestions for peace, and he backed Lord North's proposal to hire German mercenaries to crush the rebels. As the spring of 1776 wore on, colony after colony formally nullified the king's authority within its boundaries. Some instructed their delegates in Philadelphia to vote for independence.

Independence

On June 7, Richard Henry Lee of Virginia introduced a resolution stating that "these United Colonies are, and of right ought to be, free and independent states." For three weeks, the delegates debated the issue. New England and the southern colonies were solidly for independence. The Middle Colonies were divided. New York never did vote for independence, but Pennsylvania, the large, prosperous, strategically located "keystone" of the colonies, gave in when the pacifistic Quaker John Dickinson and the cautious financier Robert Morris agreed to absent themselves so that the deadlock in the delegation could be broken in favor of the resolution. (Both men later supported the patriot cause.)

Delaware, also divided, swung to the side of independence when Caesar Rodney galloped full tilt from Dover to Philadelphia, casting the majority vote in his delegation. On July 2, the maneuvers concluded, and the Continental Congress broke America's legal ties with England. "The second day of July 1776," an excited John Adams wrote to Abigail, "will be the most memorable epoch in the history of Amer-

The Funny S

In documents of the revolutionary era, including the Declaration of Independence, the letter *s* is often written *f*. This is not a lowercase *f*. The character was written with only half a crossbar (and sometimes not that).

The funny *s* originated in German handwriting and was adopted by printers in the old German printed alphabet known as Gothic. It made its way to England because the movable type used by early English printers was imported from Germany, where printing originated.

Use of *f* was governed by strict rules. It was a lowercase letter, never a capital at the beginning of a proper noun or sentence; the familiar *S* served that purpose then as now. The *f* appeared only at the beginning or in the middle of a word in lowercase, never at the end. Thus, *business* was *bufinefs*, and *sassiness* was *faffinefs*. This form of the letter died out during the early nineteenth century.

ica." He was two days off. The "Glorious Fourth" became the national holiday when, on that day, the congress gathered to adopt its official statement to Americans and to the world of why it chose to dissolve the political bands that tied America to Great Britain.

The Declaration of Independence

Officially, the Declaration of Independence was the work of a committee consisting of Thomas Jefferson, Roger Sherman of Connecticut, John Adams, Benjamin Franklin, and Robert Livingston of New York. In fact, appreciating better than we do that a committee cannot write coherently, the work of composition was assigned to Jefferson because of his "peculiar felicity of style." The lanky Virginian, sometimes as careless of his personal appearance as Tom Paine, holed up in his rooms and emerged with a masterpiece.

Franklin and Adams changed a few words, and the congress made some alterations, the most important of which was to eliminate Jefferson's sly, backhanded attack on the institution of slavery. King George, Jefferson had written, "has waged cruel war against human nature itself, violating its most sacred right of life and liberty in the persons of a distant people who never offended him, captivating them into slavery in another hemisphere." Whatever and whomever were to be blamed for slavery, George III was not a culprit. Jefferson knew it, as did fellow southerners in the congress, especially South Carolinians, who were wedded to the institution and who insisted the section be deleted.

King George bore the brunt of all Jefferson's indictments. He was blamed for practically everything that was wrong in the colonies but the weather and worms in apple barrels. The personalization of the attack was nonsense in that the king was beholden to Parliament for every colonial policy. He needed parliamentary support to raise an army. As propaganda, however, Jefferson's device was brilliant. The Declaration of Independence focused anger on a visible and vulnerable scapegoat.

Universal Human Rights

The Declaration of Independence is not remembered for its catalog of George III's high crimes and misdemeanors. It is one of history's great political documents because, in his introductory sentences, Jefferson penned a stirring statement of human rights. For Jefferson did not write solely of the rights of American colonials. He put their case for independence in terms of the rights of all human beings: "We hold these truths to be self-evident, that all men are created equal, that they are endowed by their Creator with certain unalienable Rights, that among these are Life, Liberty and the pursuit of Happiness." And he tersely codified the principles that government drew its authority only from the consent of the people governed and that when the people withdrew that consent, they had the right to rebel.

Wording from the Declaration of Independence would, over the next two centuries, be borrowed by many peoples asserting their right to freedom, from the republics of Central and South America early in the 1800s to the Vietnamese on September 2, 1945. In the United States, groups making demands on society—from African Americans and feminists to labor unions and organizations lobbying against smoking tobacco in bars—have based their demands on their inalienable rights. In the summer of 1776, however, Americans were not thinking of the future of the Declaration of Independence. The rub was to confirm it on the battlefield.

for FURTHER READING

See J. R. Alden, *A History of the American Revolution,* 1969; Bernard Bailyn, *The Ideological Origins of the American Revolution,* 1967; Lawrence H. Gipson, *The Coming of the Revolution,* 1954; Jack P. Greene, *The Reinterpretation of the American Revolution,* 1968; Robert Middlekauf, *The Glorious Cause: The American Revolution, 1763–1789,* 1982; Edmund S. Morgan, *The Birth of the Republic,* 1956; Don Higginbotham, *The War of American Independence, 1763–1789,* 1971; Alfred T. Young, *The American Revolution: A Radical Interpretation,* 1976; and Pauline Maier, *From Resistance to Revolution, 1765–1776,* 1972.

Carl Becker, *The Declaration of Independence,* 1922, is as readable and enlightening today as when it was published. Also see Garry Wills, *Inventing America: Jefferson's Declaration of Independence,* 1978. Special studies include Robert A. Gross, *The Minutemen and Their World,* 1976; Benjamin W. Labaree, *The Boston Tea Party,* 1964; John Shy, *Toward Lexington: The Role of the British Army on the Coming of the Revolution,* 1965; and Hiller B. Zobel, *The Boston Massacre,* 1970.

Relevant biographies include Bernard Bailyn, *The Ordeal of Thomas Hutchinson,* 1974; Richard R. Beeman, *Patrick Henry: A Biography,* 1974; Eric Foner, *Tom Paine and Revolutionary America,* 1976; Noel B. Gerson, *The Grand Incendiary: A Biography of Samuel Adams,* 1973; and Pauline Maier, *The Old Revolutionaries: Political Lives in the Age of Samuel Adams,* 1980.

AMERICAN JOURNEY ONLINE AND INFOTRAC COLLEGE EDITION

Visit the source collections at http://ajaccess.wadsworth.com and http://infotrac.thomsonlearning.com, and use the Search function with the following key terms to explore documents, images, audio and video clips, articles, and commentary related to the material in this chapter:

Battle of Concord	Declaration of Independence
Battle of Lexington	First Continental Congress
Boston Massacre	Paul Revere
Boston Tea Party	Second Continental Congress
Crispus Attucks	

Additional resources, exercises, and Internet links related to this chapter are available on *The American Past* Web site: http://history.wadsworth.com/americanpast7e.

HISTORY ONLINE

The Boston Massacre Trial
www.aw.umkc.edu/faculty/projects/ftrials/bostonmassacre/bostonmassacre.html
Documents of the trial of the British soldiers defended by future patriot, John Adams.

Battle of Bunker Hill
http://masshist.org/bh
A comprehensive look at the Battle of Bunker Hill by the Massachusetts Historical Society.

9

THE WAR FOR INDEPENDENCE

Winning the Revolution 1776–1781

North Wind Picture Archives

The history of our Revolution will be one continual lie from one end to the other. The essence of the whole will be that Dr. Franklin's electrical rod smote the earth and out sprang George Washington. That Franklin electrified him with his rod—and thenceforward these two constructed all the policy, negotiations, legislatures, and war.

John Adams

*By the rude bridge that arched the flood,
Their flag to April's breeze unfurled,
Here once the embattled farmers stood,
And fired the shot heard round the world*

Ralph Waldo Emerson

THE SIGNERS OF the Declaration of Independence pledged their lives, their fortunes, and their sacred honor to the cause of independence. This was no empty vow. Had George III won the quick victory he expected, the men of the Second Continental Congress would have been punished severely, many probably hanged. The noose had been the fate of Irish rebels and would be again. The Americans called themselves patriots. In the king's eyes, they were traitors, pure and simple.

THE IMBALANCE OF POWER

To an objective observer of 1776, the patriots' chances of success were not bright. Despite the military and moral victories of 1775, the patriots had challenged Europe's premier naval power and one of its finest armies. And they did not even have a majority of Americans behind them.

The Numbers

After the fighting around Boston in 1775, Lord North's military adviser, Lord George Germain, assembled 400 ships and dispatched 32,000 soldiers in them to join the redcoats already in America. It was largest military operation in British history. In addition to British regulars, Germain contracted with several petty German princes, who rented out trained soldiers as their source of revenue, for the services of 18,000 (later 30,000) troops at £7 a head (double the money if the man was killed). Although these mercenaries came from six different principalities, Americans called them "Hessians"—men from Hesse. During much of the war, Britain had 50,000 troops ready for battle.

▲ *George III had been popular in the colonies. Statues of him were erected in several cities. In the giddy days of 1776, they were pulled down by excited patriots and melted for casting into cannons.*

Culver Pictures, Inc.

In 1776, the Americans could field only hastily mobilized militia made up of farm boys, apprentices, and city laborers. George Washington thought no more highly of them than British officers did. He observed in the minutemen he took command of around Boston "an unaccountable kind of stupidity." Of other militias he said, "To place any dependence on them is assuredly resting on a broken staff." Terms of enlistment were short, geared to the demands of agriculture. At harvest time every year, whole armies evaporated. Nevertheless, militiamen played a key role in the Revolution. Some, like South Carolina's, fought splendidly and successfully, albeit not according to conventional methods. The shakiest militias asserted patriot authority in areas the British did not occupy.

The Continental Congress created its own force, the Continental Army, but Washington himself was never to command more than 18,500 of these better-trained soldiers at one time. On several occasions, his command dwindled to 5,000. Still, the continental soldiers impressed foreign observers with their commitment to the cause of independence and their willingness to endure setbacks and sometimes terrible hardship. Some 4,400 patriot soldiers were killed in battle, perhaps 20,000 more died of illness. It would have been far worse had Washington not had his troops inoculated against smallpox. A smallpox epidemic raged throughout North America during the war, laying 130,000 people in their graves.

The patriot navy was a joke. Washington had to pay personally for the first American warship, the *Hannah,* a schooner with only four guns. Some merchant vessels carried more. The Continental Congress eventually appropriated funds to build 13 frigates, one for each state, but they fared poorly against the finest navy in the world. Of the eleven frigates actually completed, one was destroyed in battle, seven were captured, two were scuttled in order to avoid capture, and one was accidentally set afire by its own crew. Nor were American seamen much praised: "tinkers, shoe-makers, and horse jockeys," one officer lamented. A high proportion of Continental sailors were pressed into service—drafted.

The Loyalists

The patriots could not always rely on the civilian population. John Adams overshot the mark when he estimated that a third of the white population was Tory, loyal to the king; one-sixth is closer to the mark. Nevertheless, in March 1776, when General Howe evacuated Boston, a city of 15,000 people and notoriously anti-British, a thousand Americans went with him. When Howe established his headquarters in New York in September, he was welcomed more as a liberator than as a conqueror. Some 19,000 Americans joined the British army. At the end of the war, between 60,000 and 100,000 Americans (1 in 30) left their native land for England, the West Indies, or Canada, particularly

Anne S. K. Brown Military Collections, Brown University, Providence, RI

▲ *A watercolor, painted in the field, intended to illustrate different uniforms worn by American soldiers. One of them, an African American, is a reminder that most northern blacks—freemen— supported the patriot cause and enlisted in large numbers. With slavery dying in the North, they looked forward to improved lives with independence. In the South, where most African Americans were slaves, blacks inclined to be pro-British, for the British promised freedom in return for military service.*

Nova Scotia. In 1812, 80 percent of the population of Upper Canada (Ontario) was American-born.

A majority of northern Anglicans were Loyalists. So were some rich merchants with close commercial ties to Britain and, in the South, many farmers from the backcountry Regulator counties. Imperial officials supported the Crown, of course, as did some rich South Carolina and Georgia planters who feared that the social disruptions that accompany war would lead to slave uprisings.

In fact, the British actively sought and won support among southern slaves by offering freedom in return for military service. Some 50,000 African Americans ran away from their masters during the war, many of the men enlisting with the British. After the war, Britain evacuated about 20,000 blacks to Nova Scotia, England, Jamaica, and Sierra Leone in West Africa.

Alexander Hamilton, Washington's aide-de-camp, urged southern patriots to free their slaves if they agreed to take up arms on the American side. "I have no doubt," he wrote, "that the Negroes will make excellent soldiers." He got nowhere. Not even Washington, sacrificing a great deal for the cause, freed any of his slaves for military service. Free northern blacks inclined to be patriots. About 5,000 African Americans donned American uniforms.

Indians were also divided in their choice of sides. After first declaring neutrality, the Iroquois Confederacy split wide open. The Oneida and Tuscarora were patriots. The Seneca, Cayuga, and Mohawk were led to the British side by a high-ranking brother and sister, Joseph Brant and Mary Brant, who believed Iroquois lands would be more secure under British than under American rule.

Patriot Chances

If the odds were unpromising, the patriot cause was far from doomed. The Americans were fighting a defensive war in their homeland, a kind of conflict that bestows a number of advantages on the rebels. Militarily, the patriots did not have to destroy the British army. Rebels on their own ground need only to hold on and hold out until weariness, demoralization, dissent, and a telling defeat here and there take their toll on the enemy.

An army attempting to suppress a rebellion, by contrast, must wipe out the enemy force and then occupy and pacify the entire country. The patriots' loyal friend in Parliament, Edmund Burke, pointed out the immensity of this challenge as early as 1775. "The use of force alone is but temporary," he said. "It may subdue for a moment; but it does not remove the necessity of subduing again; and a nation is not governed which is perpetually to be conquered."

The British never were able to crush the patriot military; they came close only once. Redcoats occupied most port cities through most of the war. As late as 1780, they captured Charleston. But only one American in twenty lived in the seaports. The countryside remained largely under patriot control, a sanctuary for rebel armies. The huge British garrison had to be provisioned from abroad. Even grain for horses was carried by ship from England and Ireland. At one point, British commanders believed they would have to import hay!

The patriots had British friends. Influential politicians like Burke, Charles Fox, John Wilkes, and the Marquis of Rockingham sniped at Lord North's ministry throughout the war. They believed that the Americans were more right than wrong. Even Lord North had his doubts, grave ones; but he was fiercely loyal to the king, who had none.

The patriots also had reason to hope for foreign help. Since 1763, the major powers of Europe had been uneasy with Great Britain's preeminence. In Spanish Louisiana, Governor Bernardo de Gálvez provided arms to the Americans from the start. France, so recently humiliated by the British in North America, India, and Europe, was even more helpful. In May 1776, the French government began to funnel money and arms to the rebels through a not-so-secret agent, Pierre de Beaumarchais, who also provided money to the Americans from his own purse. During the first two years of the war, 80 percent of the patriots' gunpowder came from France.

Business and Pleasure in Paris

In September 1776, the Continental Congress sent Benjamin Franklin, 70 years old but just slightly creaky, to Paris to lobby for a French alliance. Franklin was a social sensation. The French aristocracy was enamored of him. Wigged and powdered ladies and lords were in the throes of a "noble savage" craze. The gist of the fad, based on the writings of Jean-Jacques Rousseau, was that primitives like peasants and the rustic Americans led happy, wholesome lives because of their simplicity and closeness to nature.

Queen Marie Antoinette had a model peasant village built at Versailles, a kind of private theme park. She and her ladies-in-waiting dressed like shepherdesses, milked well-scrubbed cows, and giggled along behind flocks of perfumed geese. Well aware of this nonsense, Franklin (who preferred the high life) made a point of appearing at court and balls wearing homespun wool clothing, no wig on his bald head, and the rimless bifocal spectacles he had invented.

French high society loved it, but the foreign minister, Charles, comte de Vergennes, had his reservations. Quasi-secret arms shipments were one thing. Before Vergennes would commit the French army and navy to open war with Britain, he wanted evidence that the patriots were more than rioters. He insisted on seeing an American victory in a major battle. Through 1776 and most of 1777, the Americans provided little but defeats.

The Times That Try Men's Souls

General Howe, who took command of all British forces despite his comeuppance at Bunker Hill, had learned to be more cautious. He meant to move only when sure of the consequences. Early in 1776, caution dictated that he should evacuate Boston. (Edmund Burke, no soldier, had said the same thing a year earlier.) The citizens of Boston were overwhelmingly anti-British, and, when Massachusetts general Henry Knox arrived outside Boston with 43 cannons and 16 big mortars from Fort Ticonderoga, Washington positioned them on Dorchester Heights, high ground south of the city. If there was a bombardment, Howe's army would be devastated. Washington agreed to allow the redcoats to board ships without firing; after resting in Nova Scotia, Howe decided to relocate his headquarters to New York, where Loyalists were more numerous. Washington would have to fight on ground more favorable to the British.

The Battle for New York

On July 2, 1776, the same day the Continental Congress voted for independence, Howe landed 10,000 men on Staten Island, just south of Manhattan. In New York harbor, he had another 20,000 troops on 400 transport vessels, two men-of-war, and 25 frigates, with 1,200 cannons and 13,000 seamen under the command of his brother, Lord Richard Howe. After a few weeks, Howe invaded Long Island, where Washington's much smaller force had dug in. The American position was untenable, as Washington knew. Control of New York City depended on controlling the waters that surround it. Against Admiral Howe's armada, Washington could call on only a few hundred fishermen from Massachusetts to ferry his soldiers about.

Vision of the Future
Circumstances, John Adams believed, made him a politician and a revolutionary. But he envisioned another kind of future for his country:

I must study politics and war, that my sons may have liberty to study mathematics and philosophy, geography, natural history and naval architecture, navigation, commerce, and agriculture, in order to give their children a right to study painting, poetry, music, architecture, statuary, tapestry and porcelain.

Military Music
Drum, fife, and trumpet were an essential part of armies. Boys of 12 and 13 beat snare drums to set the cadence for soldiers on the march. With his men stepping off 96 paces of 30 inches each in a minute, a commander knew that the army covered 3 miles in 50 minutes, allowing 10 minutes per hour for a breather and a drink.

Fifers played both to entertain the men and to communicate orders: "Pioneers' March" was the signal for road-clearing crews to get started ahead of the infantry. "Roast Beef" meant it was time to eat. Fife and drum were also vital in battle. The men could hear them above the roar of firearms when they might not hear an officer's shouts.

Cavalry also used music for communication, but kettle drums instead of snare drums so as not to be confused with infantry. Cavalry used valveless trumpets (bugles) instead of fifes because, requiring only one hand, bugles could be played on horseback.

On August 27, the Howes almost surrounded Washington at the Battle of Long Island, but the Americans slipped away to fortifications on Brooklyn Heights, just across the East River from Manhattan. Again the redcoats and Hessians punished the 5,000 patriots, but, in a brilliantly executed overnight maneuver, Washington's fishermen managed to spirit the bulk of the army to Manhattan. Howe pursued him, capturing 3,000 at Fort Washington and forcing General Nathaniel Greene to abandon Fort Lee, across the Hudson River in New Jersey. Once again, Washington and his bedraggled troops escaped within hours of capture, north to White Plains and then across the Hudson into New Jersey.

MAP 9:1 Years of Defeat and Discouragement, 1776–1777 The year 1776 was a bad one for the patriot military. General Washington was chased out of Long Island, Brooklyn, and Manhattan Island, and fled across New Jersey. He avoided disintegration only when he captured Trenton and Princeton at the end of the year. The next year was no better for Washington. He was repeatedly driven back from Philadelphia.

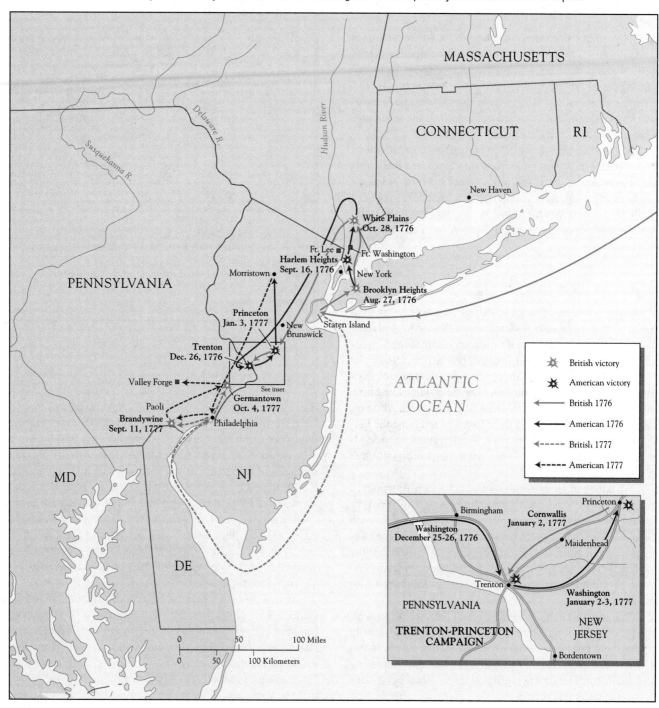

The Fox and the Hounds

General Howe was having a good time. The campaign reminded his officers of the gentry's favorite sport, the fox hunt. When the Americans were on the run north of New York, the British infuriated Washington, always supersensitive about his dignity, by sounding the traditional bugle call of the chase.

In truth, Washington's army was as desperate as a fox dodging hounds. Washington had to retreat rapidly across New Jersey to avoid another fight. When he crossed the Delaware River into Pennsylvania, his men were demoralized and ready to desert en masse. In Philadelphia, one day's march to the south, the Continental Congress panicked and fled to Baltimore.

"These are the times that try men's souls," Thomas Paine wrote. "The summer soldier and the sunshine patriot will, in this crisis, shrink from the service of his country." Thousands of captured patriot soldiers in New York and New Jersey took an oath of allegiance to the Crown. The Revolution was close to being snuffed out before all the signatures were affixed to the Declaration of Independence.

But William Howe soldiered by the book, and the book said that an army went into winter quarters when the leaves fell. Howe settled into New York, where his mistress and a lively round of dinners and parties beckoned. He recalled the hounds from Washington's hocks, leaving only small garrisons of Hessians to guard Trenton and Princeton, the front line.

The Crossing of the Delaware

Washington was no more an innovator than Howe was. Had his army not been near disintegration, he too would have followed the book into winter quarters. Instead, on Christmas night, the fishermen rowed the army across the Delaware River into New Jersey, the boats dodging ice floes and, in a thick fog, one another. The troops marched nine miles to Trenton, the most isolated British outpost. At dawn, they caught the Hessians in their bedrolls and none the better for their holiday celebrations. Washington captured almost the entire garrison of 900, while sustaining only five American casualties.

An annoyed Howe sent two forces to stop Washington before the Americans could press close enough to New York to ruin the holidays. Washington wisely avoided a fight with General Charles Cornwallis, but, on January 3, 1777, he defeated a small garrison at Princeton. Cornwallis held the line at New Brunswick, within range of reinforcement from New York. Washington set up winter quarters at Morristown on the Delaware.

Trenton and Princeton were small battles, but in winning them, Washington saved the patriot cause. His sally across the Delaware provided a boost indispensable to patriot morale. Still, Howe's position in New York was snug and dominant. The strategy he hatched with his subordinates between parties was promising.

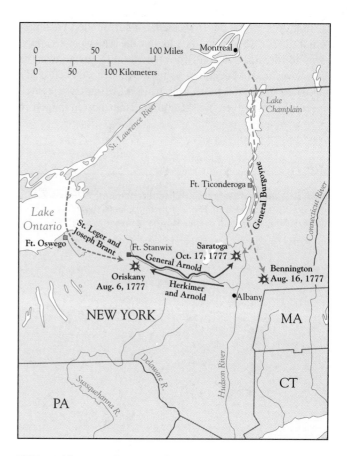

MAP 9:2 **Victory at Saratoga, October 17, 1777** While Washington's army sat outside Philadelphia defeated and demoralized, the British and Hessians suffered a series of defeats in New York at Fort Stanwix, Bennington, and, most important, at Saratoga, where a British army surrendered. Saratoga heartened the French to join the Americans as allies.

The Hudson River Strategy

Howe's plan to win the war in 1777, conveyed by letter to Lord Germain, was to march north up the Hudson, joining forces with Iroquois warriors led east on the Mohawk River by Barry St. Leger and with a larger British army moving south out of Montreal. This pincers movement would isolate New England from the rest of the colonies. With the Royal Navy blockading New England's ports, the British army could easily subdue Massachusetts, Connecticut, and Rhode Island. Thinly populated New Hampshire would fall into line. If the loss of New England was not enough to persuade Washington to ask for terms, the British would move against his army at their leisure.

It was an excellent plan. Germain was persuaded by General John Burgoyne, who had returned to Boston from England and was betting his career on it. A playwright and charming bon vivant popular in London society, Burgoyne would command the army of 8,000 strong, with more than 100 cannons, in Montreal—visions of military glory! Howe, in New York, saw Burgoyne's visions too; Burgoyne was setting things up so that he, not Howe, would get credit for the campaign. Resentment made Howe receptive to the pleas of a prominent Loyalist then in New York, Joseph Galloway of Pennsylvania, to march south rather than north to join Burgoyne. Galloway argued that taking Philadelphia, the colonies' largest city and the de facto capital of the rebellion, would knock the Middle Colonies out of the war and demoralize the rest of the country.

The Watershed Campaign of 1777

In the summer of 1777, leaving just 3,000 men in New York under General Henry Clinton, Howe moved by sea to Pennsylvania. Washington followed overland and, yet again, on September 11, was defeated at Brandywine Creek, southwest of Philadelphia. On September 26, after another victory at Paoli, Howe occupied Philadelphia. On October 4, Washington attacked at the suburb of Germantown. Although he came close to victory this time, he was repulsed again. His army had to fall back to winter quarters at Valley Forge, not even a town like Morristown but rolling farmland. Howe was again ensconced in a comfortable city.

Alas for glory, the success of Howe's campaign was tarnished by news from the forests of New York. In June, Burgoyne had left Montreal, heading south; in August, Loyalists and Iroquois commanded by St. Leger and Mohawk chief Joseph Brant advanced from the west. Their army disintegrated after a series of battles with Nicholas Herkimer and Benedict Arnold around Fort Stanwix, not halfway across the state. Burgoyne's march went well at first. The ancient Indian trail from Montreal to Lake Champlain was now a road. The lake itself provided an even better highway for 125 miles. Fort Ticonderoga, at the foot of Lake Champlain, fell without a fight.

Then the isolation of his position began to take a toll. Burgoyne's artillery and the provisions required by 8,000

troops (and 2,000 camp followers) could be moved only slowly on a trail. Burgoyne's personal baggage was immense, filling 30 carts with a living and dining suite fit for the toast of London. There were heavy beds and tables, linens, china, crystal, silverware, wine, and brandy. Patriots felled trees across the road, creating a far more difficult job of chopping for British axmen. During one three-week spell, Burgoyne's army advanced less than a mile a day.

Bad news fell on Gentleman Johnny like summer rain. He learned there would be no reinforcements under St. Leger and Brant. Hessians Burgoyne sent east on the apparently easy task of seizing supplies in Bennington, Vermont, were wiped out by militia. In a series of skirmishes around Saratoga, another fort, Burgoyne lost more men. By this time, Burgoyne knew that Howe was en route to Philadelphia.

He should have backtracked to Canada. The planned occupation of New England was out of the question. The best Burgoyne could hope for was to save his army. But there was plenty of claret and brandy left. Burgoyne dug in and hoped for help from General Clinton in New York. American General Horatio Gates jumped on Burgoyne's blunder and surrounded him. On October 17, Gates accepted the surrender of 5,700 soldiers. The Battle of Saratoga was the most important event of the year, perhaps of the war. All New England remained under patriot control until, much later, the British took Newport, Rhode Island, from the sea, which, even then, they could hold only by tying down a sizable fleet.

A TURNING POINT

Saratoga was precisely the news for which Franklin and his colleagues were waiting in Paris. The victory allayed Vergennes's doubts about the patriots' chances. The rout of an army of 8,000 crack redcoats and German mercenaries was no skirmish. When Lord North heard of the defeat, he wrote to Franklin that King George would end the war on the terms demanded by Americans up to July 1776. The Intolerable Acts and other obnoxious laws enacted between 1763 and 1775 would be repealed. Great Britain would cede to the colonies control of their internal affairs in return for swearing loyalty to the king. In effect, Lord North proposed to organize the empire as a commonwealth of autonomous dominions, the status Britain was to accord Canada, Australia, and New Zealand in the nineteenth century.

But victory is a tonic, and American blood was up. By the end of 1777, American animosity toward the mother country had intensified. Patriot propagandists made hay of the murder and scalping of Jane McCrea (a Loyalist, ironically) by Indians under Burgoyne's command, who went unpunished. In New Jersey, British troops had brutally bullied farmers, raping women and girls. The old rallying cry "the rights of British subjects" had lost its magic. The French offered a military alliance that was more attractive than returning, however victoriously, to the British Empire.

War Crimes

Soldiers and Native Americans on both sides were guilty of atrocities. Colonel Henry Hamilton, the British commander of the fort at Detroit, was called the "Hair Buyer" because he paid Indians for patriot scalps, including those from the heads of women and children. In 1776, Cherokee devastated the Virginia and Carolina frontiers, massacring everyone they found. In July 1778, Loyalists and Indians scourged Pennsylvania's Wyoming Valley, and, in November, a similar force swept through Cherry Valley in New York. Two hundred patriots were murdered in Pennsylvania, 40 in Cherry Valley.

At King's Mountain in 1780, American troops fired on redcoats who had surrendered. Virginia and North Carolina militia burned 1,000 Cherokee villages and destroyed 50,000 bushels of corn, not bothering to count the fatalities. In March 1782, Pennsylvania militia murdered 96 Delaware Indians who had tried to stay out of the conflict.

▲ *Burgoyne's march from Montreal to Saratoga was vexed by frustration and defeat at every turn. When he surrendered to General Horatio Gates in October 1777, the news was enough to bring France into the war as a patriot ally. Americans disappointed in Washington, who was being repeatedly defeated outside of Philadelphia, plotted to replace him as overall commander with Gates. They failed, fortunately. Gates was nowhere near Washington's equal and, later in the war, was a rather disappointing general.*

Foreign Friends

In December 1777, Vergennes formally recognized the United States. In February 1778, he signed a treaty of alliance, to go into effect if France and Britain went to war (which they did in June). The agreement provided for close commercial ties between France and the United States and stated that France would assert no claims to Canada after the war. France's reward at the peace table would be in the West Indies.

The war could not have been won without the French alliance. Not only did "America's oldest friend" pour money and men into the conflict; France provided a fleet, which the Americans lacked and could not hope to create. Individual patriot seamen like John Paul Jones (who said, "I have not yet begun to fight") and John Barry (no particularly memorable sayings) won naval victories. But the superiority of the Royal Navy enabled the British to hold Philadelphia and New York for most of the war, and even to capture Savannah and Newport near the end. Without the French navy, the entire coastline might have been blockaded.

In fact, patriot merchant ships had little difficulty moving goods in and out of the many small ports on the Atlantic. Until 1781, when the British occupied the island, Dutch St. Eustatius in the West Indies was, along with French Martinique, the major destination of American merchants. Holland was neutral, but well disposed to the Americans. Ships of all nations brought cargoes destined for America to St. Eu-

statius, where American ships collected them for delivery to the continent. When the British fleet finally seized St. Eustatius with a surprise attack, they found 50 American merchant ships in the harbor, and 2,000 American seamen in the port.

Spain had no love for anticolonial rebels but, in her own interests, sent Bernardo de Gálvez into British Florida, where he soon occupied every fort. Vergennes averted a war brewing between Prussia and Austria that would have tied down French troops in Europe, a traditional British objective. He persuaded both countries, as well as Russia, to declare their neutrality. Vergennes denied Britain the allies she sorely needed.

Mercenaries for Liberty

Peace in Europe meant that many military professionals were unhappily unemployed. Aristocratic officers, hungry for commissions with salaries attached, flocked to the United States. There was plenty of deadwood in the bunch; but others were able soldiers, and some were motivated by more than money.

Commodore John Barry was an Irishman; John Paul Jones, a Scot. Marie-Joseph, marquis de Lafayette was a 19-year-old noble (the British called him "the boy") who proved to be an excellent field commander. Also an idealist was Casimir Pulaski, a Pole who had fought Russia for his country's independence. Recruited in Paris by Benjamin Franklin, Pulaski was a romantic figure, a cavalry commander in gaudy uniform and waxed mustache. He was killed

Possibly more valuable than combat officers were specialists like Thaddeus Kosciuszko, a Polish engineer who was an expert in building fortifications, a military field in which few Americans were trained. Friedrich Wilhelm von Steuben, a Prussian who styled himself "Baron" (he was a captain, and there was no *Burke's Peerage* for German baronies), was an expert in drill. He supervised the training at Valley Forge in the winter of 1777–1778 that transformed Washington's continentals into a disciplined army. By 1781, fully one patriot officer in five was a foreigner.

The Continuing War

Steuben in particular arrived in the nick of time. Washington lost 2,500 men to disease and exposure during the winter at Valley Forge, and, by the spring of 1778, it was obvious that the war would go on for years. The Americans did not dare to force the issue in an all-or-nothing battle. Their strategy was to hold on, fighting only under auspicious conditions. Lord Germain and General Clinton (who took over from Howe in May 1778) could hope only to throttle the American economy with a naval blockade and concentrate land operations in the South.

Beginning with the occupation of Savannah, Georgia, in December 1778, the redcoats won a series of victories in the South, but they could not break the stalemate. For each British victory, the Americans won another, or, in losing ground, they cost the British so heavily that the redcoats had to return to the coast, within reach of supply ships.

The war wore heavily on the American side too. Prices of necessities soared. Imports were available only at exorbitant costs. When the Continental Congress failed to pay and provision troops in 1780 and 1781, mutinies erupted on the Connecticut, Pennsylvania, and New Jersey lines. In September 1780, Washington learned that Benedict Arnold, commanding the important fortress at West Point in New York, sold it and his services to the British for £20,000.

The campaign of 1781 opened with American spirits lower than they had been since before Trenton. Washington was idle outside New York. The most active British army, led by Lord Charles Cornwallis, lost a battle at Cowpens,

▲ *Benjamin Franklin, assigned to win an alliance with France, loved Paris and Versailles, and the French aristocracy adored him, titillated by his American simplicity, which Franklin encouraged. John Adams, also in Paris, thought Franklin spent much time partying (and lecherously courting a scandalous widow), but the old reprobate got the job done.*

leading a charge at the Battle of Savannah late in the war. Johann Kalb, a Bavarian who affected the title baron de Kalb, also lost his life during the war, at the Battle of Camden.

Jean-Baptiste, comte de Rochambeau, arrived in Newport, Rhode Island, in 1780 and played a key role in the decisive American victory at Yorktown, Virginia, the next year.

Despair at Valley Forge
The winter of 1777–1778 was extremely difficult for American soldiers. Inadequately fed, clothed, and sheltered at Valley Forge, many fell into deep despair. Albigence Waldo, a surgeon with Connecticut troops, wrote in his journal on December 14, 1777:

Poor food–hard lodging–cold weather–fatigue–nasty cloathes–nasty cookery–vomit half my time–smoked out of my senses–the Devil's in't–I can't endure it–Why are we sent here to starve and freeze?–What sweet felicities have I left at home: A charming wife–pretty children–good beds–good food–good cookery–all agreeable–all harmonious! Here all confusion–smoke and cold–hunger and filthyness–a pox on my bad luck!

▲ *Washington and "the boy," the French general Lafayette, at Valley Forge during the dismal winter (for the patriots) of 1777–1778. Lafayette was 25 years younger than Washington, but they became close friends almost from their first meeting and remained so until Washington's death. Lafayette regarded Washington as the giant of the age.*

South Carolina, but then repeatedly pummeled Nathaniel Greene the breadth of North Carolina. Cornwallis then joined with other commanders (including Benedict Arnold) to amass 7,500 men in Virginia.

An Opportunity for Washington

But Cornwallis had problems. Anywhere away from navigable waters was dangerous ground. On August 1, 1781, he set up what he regarded as a routine encampment at Yorktown, Virginia, on the same neck of land where the first permanent English settlement in America was planted. Cornwallis requested supplies and orders from General Clinton in New York. In mid-August, with Clinton dawdling, Washington learned that a French admiral, Count François de Grasse, was sailing from the West Indies to the Chesapeake Bay with 3,000 French troops aboard 25 warships.

Yorktown was George Washington's backyard. He knew the terrain intimately and realized that, if de Grasse could cut Cornwallis off, Washington had him trapped. He scrapped detailed, almost finalized plans for an assault on New York, maneuvered around the city so that a confused Clinton would sit tight, and raced his best units, from Rhode Island, New Jersey, and New York, across New Jersey. In September, his troops joined with others under Lafayette, Rochambeau, Steuben, and de Grasse. The combined army of 17,000 outnumbered Cornwallis's 8,000, almost the first time in the war that the patriots enjoyed numerical superiority.

Yorktown

Cornwallis did not panic. His men were well dug in, and he expected to move them out by sea, resuming the war of attrition elsewhere. But between September 5 and 10, de Grasse sent the British evacuation fleet sailing off empty to New York. Further defense was futile. On October 17, Cornwallis asked for terms, and on October 19, he surrendered.

Lord Cornwallis was no America basher. He had been only one of four lords in Parliament to oppose the Declaratory Act. But he found his defeat at Yorktown humiliating. Claiming sickness, he sent an aide to the field to surrender his sword. The aide tried to hand it to Rochambeau, but the French general gestured him to Washington. Rather than accept the symbol of capitulation from an inferior officer, Washington delegated the honors to General Benjamin Lincoln, whom the British had similarly humiliated at Charleston. During the ceremonies, the British army band played the hymn "The World Turn'd Upside Down."

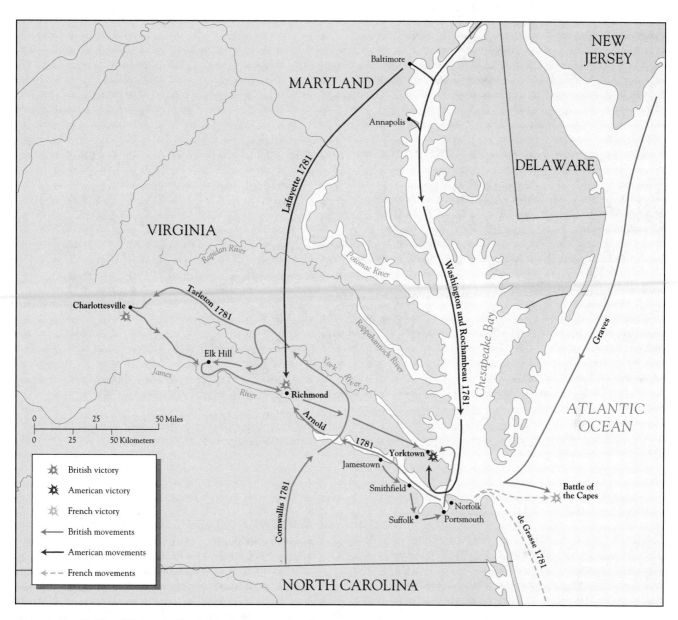

MAP 9:3 **The Battle of Yorktown, May–October 1781** After wandering around South Carolina, harassed by American militia under Francis Marion, General Cornwallis moved into Virginia, setting up headquarters at Yorktown. There, he assumed, he could be resupplied or evacuated by sea. The coordinated arrival of a large American army and the French fleet resulted in the British defeat that ended the war.

The Treaty of Paris

The British could have fought on. They still had 44,000 troops in North America, far more than the patriots and the French. But eighteenth-century wars were fought with limited, practical objectives, balancing the values of the goals with the costs of reaching them. Rulers did not burrow into bunkers and tell their subjects to fight nobly on until the last of them was dead. In February 1782, the House of Commons voted to end the war. Lord North resigned and was succeeded by the marquis of Rockingham, the Whig who had arranged the repeal of the Stamp Act in 1766.

It took two years to put the Treaty of Paris together. In part, the delay was due to growing suspicions between the Americans and the French. And with good reason: The American delegation in Paris came to terms with the British without French knowledge. The treaty, signed in September 1783, recognized the independence of the United States with the Mississippi River the western boundary. Americans were to have fishing rights off British Newfoundland and Nova Scotia (which New Englander John Adams made his personal project), and the United States promised not to molest Loyalists and to urge the states to compensate them for property that had already been seized.

▲ *There are dozens of artists' depictions of the British surrender of Yorktown, each with its unique focus. This one makes a point more important than the contest of ceremonial one-upmanship between Cornwallis and Washington, emphasizing the critical part played by sea power—de Grasse's French fleet's control of the Chesapeake, which prevented British escape by ship.*

The "Father of His Country"

George Washington, heaped with adulation in Europe as well as America, was, in some ways, an unlikely "father of his country." In most of the particulars by which greatness is measured, Washington comes up short. He lacked originality and boldness. He was no thinker; he seems to have read little and contributed nothing to the literature of colonial protest. Personally, he was reserved, listening far more than speaking. As a field commander, his failures outnumbered his successes. During most of the war, his army was in retreat and more than once on the verge of disintegration.

And yet, it would be difficult to overstate Washington's role in the establishment of the American republic. It was in successful retreat that his military contribution to independence was invaluable. He kept an army in the field in the face of repeated defeats, superior British forces, inadequate provisions, disease, poor shelter, poor support from the Continental Congress, and even a cabal, after the campaign around Philadelphia, to replace him as commander of the army.

In order to explain Washington's achievement, it is necessary to fall back on the intangibles that transfixed his contemporaries. Radicals like Samuel Adams, conservatives like Alexander Hamilton, intellectuals like Thomas Jefferson, warriors like Israel Putnam, and cultivated European aristocrats like Lafayette and Rochambeau all deferred to the Virginian. Washington's deportment, integrity, personal dignity, and disdain for petty squabbles set him head and shoulders above the best of his contemporaries, just as his height of 6 feet 2 inches made him a very tall man in the eighteenth century. He held the Revolution together with that not quite definable quality known as "character." If such a notion rings a little sappy in our time, the dishonor is not to the era of the American Revolution.

Between Yorktown and the Treaty

Between 1781 and 1783, when the Treaty of Paris was signed, British troops remained in and around New York City, so the Continental Congress could not very well send the men of the Continental Army home. They set up quarters in Newburgh, New York. The congress, as always, was negligent in providing for them, and the soldiers were restive. Washington, who sorely wanted to get back to his Virginia plantation, remained with the troops. He lobbied the Continental Congress for pensions and bounties, and, by his own example, discouraged a full-blown mutiny. (A smaller camp of veterans in Lancaster, Pennsylvania, did march on Philadelphia, causing the members of the Continental Congress to flee.)

British soldiers left New York City once the treaty was signed. For decades, New Yorkers celebrated Evacuation Day, November 25, with more gusto than they observed July 4. Independence Day was comparatively decorous; Evacuation Day was party time.

Ignoring the Revolution

John Adams estimated that a third of Americans were patriots, a third were Loyalists, and a third were not particularly interested in who won or lost the war. Francis Hopkinson, a patriot and poet from New Jersey, called the patriots "birds" and the Tories "beasts"; the others were "bats," cozying up to whichever species, haired or winged, seemed to be on top at the moment.

This is unfair; Adams's less acerbic characterization of the "neutrals" is better. However great the issue, whatever the historical era, and whoever the people involved, a large proportion of every population sees no compelling reason to take an interest, let alone to take sides. They "mind their own business."

Such Americans were to be found in every section, but particularly west of the Appalachians. There was combat there, but battles were small and isolated, with mostly Indians involved. The most famous westerner (and Indian fighter) of the era, Daniel Boone, although a major in the Virginia militia, avoided involvement in the great cause, continuing to mind his businesses of hunting, trail blazing, road building, and land speculation. His reputation suffered. He was accused of collaborating with the Shawnee Indians and, through them, with their British allies. Had this been true, and proved, he could have been shot as a traitor.

Born near Reading, Pennsylvania, in 1734, Boone emigrated to western North Carolina. In 1755, driving a wagon, he was part of the disastrous Braddock campaign in western Pennsylvania, but, given his lowly job, did not make the acquaintance of Braddock's young aide, George Washington.

Like Washington, however, Boone survived, spending most of the 1760s and 1770s in the forests of what is now Kentucky. The land there appealed to him as a commodity on which he could get rich by developing and selling, particularly since Kentucky's Native American population was sparse. Both the Cherokee from the south and the Shawnee from the north

hunted in Kentucky—Boone had his run-ins with both tribes—but neither lived there in great numbers.

In 1775, when the fighting began back east and the Second Continental Congress assembled, Boone was supervising 30 axmen building the "Wilderness Road" through the Cumberland Gap into Kentucky and connecting it with the Warrior's Path. Just when news of the Declaration of Independence and the full-scale war with the British reached him is not clear, but his only military service was a scouting mission for the Virginia militia, when he was captured by Shawnee and taken to be questioned by British officers north of the Ohio River. Because Boone was gone for a year and returned both unharmed and with nothing to say, he was accused of being a Tory.

Boone denied it and refused to elaborate. He returned to developing Boonesboro and other frontier settlements in Kentucky. His fame as a woodsman and pioneer—Boone engineered a spectacular and well-publicized rescue of his daughter, who had been kidnapped by Indians—made him Kentucky's most effective promoter, but as a land speculator, he was a failure. In part, he was too possessed of a sense of personal honor to succeed in a business in which ethics were a prohibitive burden. He sold thousands of acres to compensate associates for losses in which he shared and felt responsible. He spent thousands on lawyers but had no stomach for going to court himself, whence he lost other huge tracts of Old Kentuck'.

In 1799, Kentucky's most famous resident left the state for Missouri and never returned, despite numerous invitations. He was bitter and broke. When, in 1815, a creditor traveled to Missouri hoping to get Boone to pay him, Boone's son told him, "You have come a great distance to suck a bull and, I reckon, you will have to go home dry." Boone died in 1820, a national hero with a shadow hanging over his patriotism.

for FURTHER READING

See J. R. Alden, *A History of the American Revolution,* 1969; Robert Middlekauff, *The Glorious Cause: The American Revolution, 1763–1789,* 1982; Howard Peckham, *The War for Independence,* 1952; and Christopher Ward, *The War of the Revolution,* 1952.

Focused on special aspects of the war years are Samuel F. Bemis, *The Diplomacy of the American Revolution,* 1935; Don Higginbotham, *The War of American Independence: Military Attitudes, Policies, and Practice,* 1971; J. Franklin Jameson, *The American Revolution Considered as a Social Movement,* 1926; Robert M. Calhoon, *The Loyalists in Revolutionary America,* 1973;

Richard B. Morris, *The Peacemakers,* 1965; Mary Beth Norton, *Liberty's Daughters,* 1980; Charles Royster, *A Revolutionary People at War,* 1979; John Shy, *A People Numerous and Armed,* 1976; and Paul H. Smith, *Loyalists and Redcoats,* 1964. Barbara W. Tuchman, *The First Salute: A View of the American Revolution,* 1988, emphasizes the important role of the French fleet in the war and the role of the Dutch island of St. Eustatius.

Two classic biographies of George Washington are James T. Flexner, *George Washington in the American Revolution,* 1968, and Douglas S. Freeman, *George Washington,* 1948, 1957.

Visit the source collections at http://ajaccess.wadsworth.com and http://infotrac.thomsonlearning.com, and use the Search function with the following key terms to explore documents, images, audio and video clips, articles, and commentary related to the material in this chapter:

Daniel Boone
General William Howe
George Washington

Saratoga
Yorktown

Additional resources, exercises, and Internet links related to this chapter are available on *The American Past* Web site: http://history.wadsworth.com/americanpast7e.

HISTORY ONLINE

The American Revolution

www.multied.com/wars.html

Maps and descriptions of important battles.

Espionage in the Revolution

www.si.umich.edu/spies/index-main2.html

Techniques of spying, accounts of espionage, and the people involved.

10

INVENTING A COUNTRY

American Constitutions 1781–1789

The National Archives

Without some alteration in our political creed, the superstructure we have been seven years raising at the expense of so much blood and treasure, must fall. We are fast verging to anarchy and confusion.

George Washington

I am uneasy and apprehensive, more so than during the war. . . . We are going and doing wrong, and therefore I look forward to evils and calamities.

John Jay

AMERICANS WERE NOT the first people to fight for independence. The history of empires is the history of uprisings to be free of imperial control. The American Revolution was, however, singular in the fact that rebels had to invent a country and a sense of common nationality. They were not already "a people" as the Dutch were when they fought to be independent of Spain. Nor had they been subdued by foreigners, as were the periodically rebellious Irish. Most Americans were British by descent; those who were not had emigrated into a British society—all but the Africans, gladly. Moreover, the 13 colonies—states now—had no political links with one another before the Revolution. Their only links were with the mother country.

The political superstructure the patriots forged, the Articles of Confederation, was just a little more than an alliance of independent states with a common foe. Only in 1787, a decade after the Declaration of Independence and six years after Yorktown, in the Constitution that remains the basic law of the land today, did "we the people of the United States" venture to ordain "a more perfect union."

THE REVOLUTION ON PAPER

The constitutions of 11 of the 13 states were drawn up during the Revolutionary War and reflected the patriots' hostility to most things British. (Connecticut and Rhode Island, quite democratic as colonies, merely rephrased their charters.) The simple fact that they were written and comprehensive, covering every contingency of which the men who drafted them could think, was itself a break with British practice. The largely unwritten British constitution had served Britain well and still does. But the debate over the extent of Parliament's powers was central to the grievances that led to the Revolution. The patriots believed that Parliament had violated the unwritten constitution in trying to tax the colonies, but they could not win the point without resorting to force of arms. Written constitutions could be violated too, of course. However, as Thomas Jefferson wrote, "They furnish a text to which those who are watchful may again rally and recall the people."

Limitation of Power, Elimination of Privilege

In Great Britain, Parliament is the government. There is no appeal of what it does, neither to courts nor, by the eighteenth century, to king or queen. The Americans' state constitutions, however, were written not by their little parliaments, the state assemblies, but by conventions elected specifically for the purpose of constitution making. The conventions' work was then ratified by a popular election and could be altered only by a similar procedure, *not* by the legislature. The principle that sovereignty (ultimate government power) rested with the people was thereby institutionalized.

Because the patriots resented the colonial office-holding elite, they guarded against creating their own by requiring that most officials stand for election annually. Many state constitutions (and the Articles of Confederation) limited to a few years the term a person elected to office might serve.

The authors of the first American constitutions feared executive power most of all; the royal governors had been George III's executive officers, agents doing his (and Parliament's) bidding. In order to preclude the emergence of similar centers of power independent of elected assemblies, the new state governors were little more than administrators and ceremonial heads of state. In Pennsylvania, which had the most radical state constitution, there was no governor. Nor was there a chief executive in the government created by the Articles of Confederation.

Other old resentments surfaced in the movement to separate church and state. Except in New England, the Church of England had been the established church, supported by taxes. (The Anglican clergy had been largely Loyalist.) Patriots in the former royal colonies disestablished the Anglican Church—abolished its privileged position and financial support—transforming it into the Protestant Episcopal Church, a private denomination on a par with the Presbyterian and Baptist Churches and, in most states, even the Catholic Church.

And They're Off . . .
Reaction against things British in the wake of the Revolution found form in more than constitution writing. The adoption of the dollar, which was Spanish, rather than the British pound as the American unit of currency was, in part, a patriotic gesture. It was also just after the Revolution that American horse races were run counterclockwise around tracks rather than clockwise, as they were in Britain and had been in the colonies.

Democratic Drift

There were limits to denominational neutrality. In New Hampshire, Connecticut, and Massachusetts, where the pro-patriot Congregationalist Church was established, it remained tax-supported for 40 to 50 years after independence. Eight more state constitutions expressed some preference for Protestant Christianity. Roman Catholics were not permitted to vote in North Carolina until 1835. A Jew or nonbeliever could vote in Pennsylvania but could not hold public office.

Nevertheless, in every new state, the right to vote was extended to more people than had enjoyed it under the Crown. In Georgia, Pennsylvania, and Vermont (a state in fact if not in name), every adult male taxpayer could vote. In most of the others, the property qualification was lowered so that only a few free white males were excluded. Women could vote in New Jersey. In New Jersey, North Carolina, and Massachusetts, free blacks who met other tests were enfranchised. In 1777, New York joined Rhode Island in granting full citizenship to Jews.

Eight states specified rights that were guaranteed to every citizen, beginning with Virginia's constitution in 1776. After the vice admiralty courts, the quartering acts, and arbitrary actions by the British army, the patriots were determined that there would be no vagueness on the subject of government's power over an individual. The rights later listed in the first 10 amendments to the United States Constitution, the Bill of Rights, were found in one or another of the state constitutions written during the Revolution.

Liberty's Limits: Sex and Race

In 1777, when the air was thick with talk of liberties, Abigail Adams wrote to her husband, John, who was engaged in writing the Articles of Confederation, to plead for the rights of "the ladies." But neither Mr. Adams nor many other Americans, male or female, seriously entertained the notion that there was anything amiss in the inferior civil status of women. Only in 1792 would Mary Wollstonecraft publish *Vindication of the Rights of Woman,* and decades passed before noticeable numbers of men and women absorbed her

---

Gradual Emancipation in Pennsylvania
A Pennsylvania law of 1780 proclaimed that no more slaves could be brought into the state and that all children born to slaves in Pennsylvania would be free at age 28. The act was more than obliging to slave owners in the state. Although their claim that they had compensation coming for supporting the children of their slaves when they were children had merit, compensating a slave owner for a child's sustenance with the fruits of his labor until age 28 was clearly excessive. In fact, many Pennsylvania slave owners manumitted their slaves in the decades after the Revolution. Others, however, found a loophole in the gradual emancipation law, selling slaves under age 28 out of state.

North Wind Picture Archives

▲ *Women (and free blacks) who were heads of household could vote in New Jersey between 1776 and 1807. They were disenfranchised the latter year because, apparently, too many were exercising their right.*

Petition for Freedom

On November 12, 1779, 19 of New Hampshire's African Americans petitioned the state assembly to free slaves on the basis of the ideals of liberty that patriots were asserting. The petition concluded:

Your humble slaves most devoutly pray for the sake of injured liberty, for the sake of justice, humanity and the rights of mankind, for the honor of religion and by all that is dear, that your honors would graciously interpose in our behalf, and enact such laws and regulations, as you in your wisdom think proper, whereby we may regain our liberty and be ranked in the class of free agents, and that the name of slave may not more be heard in a land gloriously contending for the sweets of freedom.

feminist views. New Jersey, still writing "he or she" in reference to voters in 1790, rescinded female enfranchisement (and the enfranchisement of African Americans) in 1807.

In the northern states, slavery was dying out with or without the Revolution. Quasi-independent Vermont abolished the institution in 1777. In Massachusetts in 1780, Elizabeth Freeman (her slave name was "Mumber") sued for her freedom on the grounds that the state constitution stated "all men are born free and equal." The courts agreed, thus ending slavery in the Bay State by court order. New Hampshire followed suit in 1784. Pennsylvania, Connecticut, and Rhode Island adopted formulas that eliminated slavery gradually,

dooming the institution while not financially injuring slave owners. In all, 11 states abolished the slave trade, outlawed the buying and selling of slaves, or prohibitively taxed such transactions, a halfway measure clearly intended as a prelude to further antislavery action.

These 11 states, of course, included most southern states. Southern patriots could hardly ignore the fact that they were fighting for liberty—*they* would not be slaves!—while they held African Americans in bondage. Delaware, Maryland, and Virginia made manumission (freeing individual slaves) easier. By 1810, a fifth of Maryland's slaves were manumitted.

In 1784, Patrick Henry hoped to extend Virginia's liberties to Native Americans when he proposed that the state pay a bounty of £10 to every free white person who married an Indian and £5 for each child born of such unions. Another Virginian, John Marshall, later commented that the bill "would have been advantageous to this country" had it been enacted. He added, "Our prejudices, however, opposed themselves to our interests, and operated too powerfully for them."

AMERICA UNDER THE ARTICLES OF CONFEDERATION

The constitution written to coordinate the affairs of all 13 states—the Articles of Confederation—reflected the same ideals as the state constitutions. Drafted during the heady years 1776 and 1777, the Articles of Confederation created no president or other independent executive. Congress alone was the government. Members were elected annually and could serve only three years out of every six. That is, a man elected to Congress three years in a row was ineligible to serve again until he sat out three years.

Divided Authority

Under the Articles of Confederation, the United States of America was explicitly *not* a nation. It was "a firm league of friendship." Georgia, North Carolina, and the rest retained their "sovereignty, freedom, and independence," each state the equal of every other. Members of Congress, for example, voted not as individuals but as members of their state's delegation. If two of three delegates voted "nay," their state cast a single negative vote.

Congress was authorized to wage war and make peace, to maintain an army and navy, and to supervise diplomatic relations with foreign countries and the Indian nations. Congress was entrusted with maintaining a post office and empowered to establish a system of uniform weights and measures. Congress could mint coins, issue paper money, and borrow money.

Having granted these powers to Congress, however, the Articles of Confederation also permitted the states to issue money and to ignore Congress's standards of measurement. The states could individually negotiate commercial treaties with other countries. A state could even, "with the consent of Congress," declare war as a state on a foreign power. It would be quite "constitutional," in other words, if Delaware went to war with Holland while neighboring New Jersey agreed by treaty to sell gunpowder to the Dutch.

The weakness of the ties binding the states was not the consequence of idiocy, incompetence, or even awkward compromise. Weakness was deliberately written into the Articles of Confederation because of the revolutionary generation's aversion to a powerful central government. Nor was the Confederation government a disaster. On the contrary, it was under the Articles of Confederation that Americans defeated Europe's premier military power. The Confederation Congress created a bureaucracy that adequately administered the day-to-day business of the government. States did contribute, albeit reluctantly sometimes, to the Confederation treasury. And Congress solved a problem that might easily have torn apart a far more powerful government.

The Western Lands

The issue was the land beyond the Appalachians that Great Britain had closed to settlement in 1763 and ceded to the United States in the Treaty of Paris. The question was, who owned it? Colonial charters were responsible for the problem. They had been drafted at different times by different British officials with little knowledge of North American geography and little concern about lands that were then wilderness firmly under the control of Indian tribes.

So the boundaries of the former colonies overlapped in a snarl of conflicting claims. Virginia's colonial charter gave the state boundaries that flared both north and south at the crest of the mountains, encompassing the entire trans-Appalachian region. Connecticut conceded that New York's and Pennsylvania's charters, drafted later than Connecticut's, removed the lands of New York and Pennsylvania from what had been Connecticut's jurisdiction, but the state claimed a "western reserve" beyond those states in what is now Ohio. Massachusetts, New York, North Carolina, South Carolina, and Georgia also had claims in the west.

The snarl was complicated by the fears of six states with no chartered claims to western lands: New Hampshire, Rhode Island, New Jersey, Pennsylvania, Delaware, and Maryland. Reasonably enough, leaders of those states worried that the states with western lands would be able to finance themselves indefinitely by selling trans-Appalachian land, whereas the states without western lands would drive their citizens out because they had to tax them more heavily. On these grounds, Maryland refused to sign the Articles of Confederation until 1781.

There was an obvious solution, suggested by John Dickinson as early as 1776. However, because it called on human beings to give up potential wealth in the interests of an ideal, it was not a solution that promised to be easy. Dickinson proposed that the landed states cede their western territories to the Confederation so that all states shared in the benefits of owning them. Amazingly, cession turned out to be rather easy. Virginia—with the greatest and best western claims—had good reasons to turn its western lands over to Congress. Virginians played prominent roles in the Confederation government, and they did not want to see it fall apart. Moreover, many Virginians believed that free republican institutions could not survive in large states. For the sake of hard-won freedoms, they preferred to see new states, approximately the size of the original states, carved out of the west rather than bickering endlessly in a fight to retain an unmanageable "Great Virginia."

The Northwest Ordinances

In January 1781, Virginia ceded the northern part of its western lands to the Confederation. Within a few years, all the

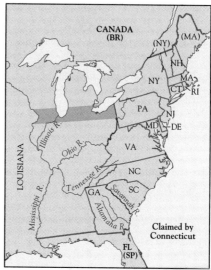

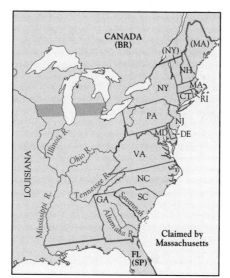

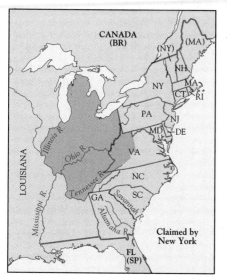

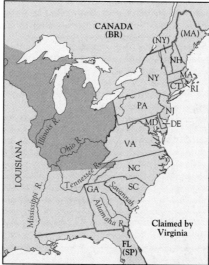

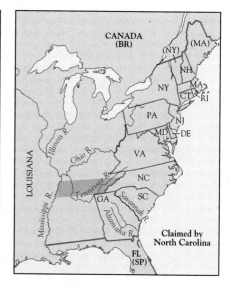

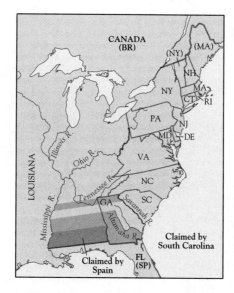

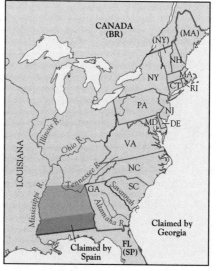

MAP 10:1 The States' Western Claims   British carelessness in drawing colonial boundaries in the west resulted in a tangle of conflicting claims. The crisis did not lead to interstate wars because all the states with western claims ceded those claims (some reluctantly) to the Confederation Congress.

states with western claims except Georgia followed suit. In 1792, Virginia added its southern claims to what was by then a *national* domain. (Georgia held out long after it was realistic to do so, until 1802.)

This remarkable act—European nations went to war over far lesser tracts of real estate—was followed by two congressional acts that were equally novel: the Northwest Ordinances of 1784 and 1787. These ordinances provided a procedure for the creation in the Northwest Territory, the region north of the Ohio River and east of the Mississippi, of five states that would be the equals of the original states. (The five that emerged were Ohio, Indiana, Michigan, Illinois, and Wisconsin.)

The Northwest Ordinances stated that the United States would hold no colonies subordinate to it, as the 13 colonies had been Britain's provinces. As soon as the population in a "territory" in the northwest equaled the population of the smallest state in the Confederation (Delaware in 1787) and met some other reasonable requirements, that territory would be recognized as the equal of the existing states.

Thomas Jefferson was the chief architect of the Northwest Ordinances, and he included an antislavery provision. The act of 1787 forbade slavery in the Northwest Territory. The west would be reserved for the independent yeoman family farmers Jefferson idealized, protecting them by law from an economic competition with slave owners such as had resulted in the aristocracy that dominated much of the South.

The Rectangular Survey

In 1785, Congress adopted a system of survey to prepare the Northwest Territory for public sale. Townships 6 miles square were divided into 36 "sections" of 1 square mile (640 acres) each. Initially, a section was the smallest tract that could be purchased, at a dollar an acre. A square mile was a lot of land, absurdly more than a family needed or could use. It was assumed that well-to-do developers—land speculators—would buy the land from the government and subdivide it for further sale, freeing the government from the massive job of retail sales.

The size and price of the tracts were debated for decades. However, the thinking that underlay the rectangular survey of the west was clearly wise and fruitful from the start. Had purchasers been able to enter public lands and map their own property, they would have carved out oddly shaped parcels of prime agricultural land, making the most of their dollar per acre. Hills, marshes, and rocky ground would remain government property. However, although no one would pay taxes on these scattered plots, settlers would surely exploit them by grazing livestock, cutting wood, digging gravel and stone, and extracting minerals. How, in so vast a domain, could the government monitor such trespassing? The rectangular survey forced buyers to take the poor land with the good. When, in 1791, Alexander Hamilton tried to slip a repeal of rectangular survey through the post-Confederation Congress, he was promptly foiled.

DIFFICULTIES AND FAILURES

Despite the Confederation's achievements, every year that passed convinced more and more prominent Americans—particularly those who thought of themselves as Americans and not as New Yorkers, Pennsylvanians, or Virginians—

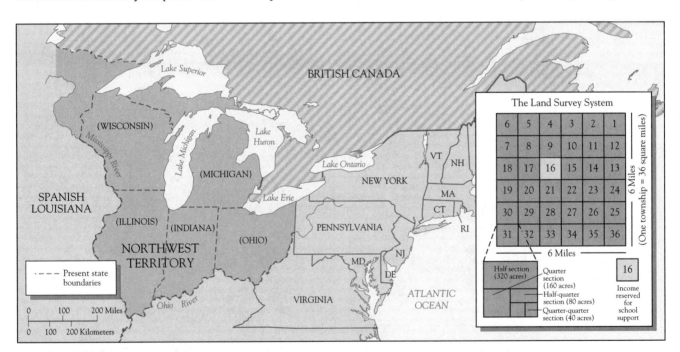

MAP 10:2 The Northwest Territory and the Rectangular Survey The rectangular survey, an American innovation, avoided chaos and conflict when the Northwest Territory (and lands farther west, later added to the United States) was populated.

▲ *Confederation era money. The "dollar" was borrowed from Spain. However, the Spanish divided their dollar into eighths. The division into sixths illustrated here was a remnant of British practice. Decimalization—100 cents to the dollar—came only in 1791.*

that the government was too weak, that a disaster lay around the corner.

Money Problems

Government finance was a tenacious problem. Even during the war, delegates in Congress bickered and connived, denying or delaying the funds needed to fight. Congress was capable of dithering for hours about whether a man who claimed a mere $222.60 for ferrying troops should be paid. The difficulty was that all 13 states had to approve financial measures. In 1781, of the 13 states, Rhode Island alone refused to approve a tariff of 5 percent on imports. On another occasion, New York alone killed a tax bill.

Because, in effect, Congress could not levy taxes, it resorted to a risky alternative, printing increasingly larger amounts of paper money popularly called "Continentals," which no one would exchange at face value for "hard money"—gold and silver coin. From $6 million in paper money in 1775, Congress printed $63 million in 1778 and $90 million in 1779. By 1781, it required almost 150 paper dollars to purchase what one silver Spanish dollar would buy. "Not worth a Continental" was a catchphrase that long survived the Articles of Confederation.

The states also printed paper money. The assembly of Rhode Island, controlled by farmers in debt, issued it in absurd quantities. Rhode Island's notes were worthless outside the state—no one would accept them—but legal tender within the state, at face value, for payment of debts. Tales were told of creditors fleeing Rhode Island in order to avoid repayment of loans with the wretched paper and of debtors gleefully waving handfuls of the stuff in hot pursuit. Men of property everywhere shuddered to hear such stories. Merchants especially needed a sound paper currency valid in every state and accepted abroad. Such a currency needed a strong central government backing it.

Diplomatic Vulnerability

Squabbles among the states made it difficult for American diplomats to negotiate with other nations and encouraged foreign meddling. In 1784, a Spanish diplomat, Diego de Gardoqui, played on the commercial interests of the northern states in an attempt to split the United States in two. He offered to Congress to open Spanish trade to American ships (which meant northern ships) if Congress gave up the treaty right of Americans to ship goods down the Mississippi River.

New Englanders and New Yorkers cared little about trade on the Mississippi. Their delegations tried to ram de Gardoqui's treaty through Congress. Had they succeeded, the southern states would have been under great pressure to go their own way. The Ohio–Mississippi River system was vital to the tens of thousands who had moved to what are now Kentucky and Tennessee but were then still claimed by Virginia, North Carolina, and Georgia.

Britain schemed to detach Vermont from the United States. Traditionally a part of New York but also claimed by New Hampshire, the isolated Green Mountain country functioned as an independent commonwealth during the 1780s, dominated by Ethan and Levi Allen, two eccentric and cranky Revolutionary War veterans who trusted no one but one another. The Allens actively attempted to make a treaty with the British that would have tied Vermont more closely to Canada than to the Confederation. Congress was powerless to stop them, even militarily; the Continental Army had shrunk to 700 men. Only because the British failed to act quickly did the project fall through.

Wounded Pride

Great Britain also refused to turn over a string of Great Lakes forts that were American under the terms of the Treaty of Paris. Nor did the British send a minister (ambassador) to America. A British diplomat poked fun at American diplomatic impotence, joking that it would be too expensive to outfit 13 men with homes and the other accoutrements of office. In London, the American minister to Great Britain, John Adams, was snubbed and mocked when he acted with the dignity of a national delegate.

There were insults elsewhere. A world-traveling American sea captain said that the United States was regarded "in the same light, by foreign nations, as a well-behaved negro is

Forest to Farm

The Northwest Ordinances looked to the future. During the Confederation era, the Northwest Territory was, in fact, firmly under the control of Indian tribes. During the 1780s, western Pennsylvania, a hilly land of hardwood and conifer forests from which Indians had largely been pushed, was the region that beckoned to young men and women looking to develop frontier farms.

Settlers tried to arrive in April. Winter's snows had melted, but the overarching trees were just beginning to leaf. The pioneers' first tasks were to kill the trees and build a cabin so as to be sheltered by mid-May, when a crop of corn, beans, and squash had to be planted. Pines, spruce, and firs–softwoods with long, straight trunks–were felled for the logs of which cabins and barns were built. The gigantic oaks and maples were girdled, the bark chopped through a couple of feet from the ground. What leaves there were withered and fell, admitting sun to the earth. The "fields" were far from pretty, but the soil was rich, producing even the first year 40 to 50 bushels of corn, wheat, or rye per acre.

Building a log cabin, rude, sometimes windowless, sometimes just a three-sided shelter from the rain, required just one tool, an ax, and little skill—just the muscle power to move the logs into position. If the pioneer had an adze, a squaring tool, he hewed the logs on two sides for a tighter fit when they were stacked. The ends of each log were notched so that, by locking logs perpendicularly, it was possible to construct walls without uprights. The only task of cabin building requiring more than a single man's and woman's labor was raising the roof beam, itself a log. For this task, neighbors were summoned,

Smithsonian Institution

and entertained as thanks for their help. Even the author of an article in the *Columbian* magazine in 1786, who described the Pennsylvania pioneers as the dregs of society, admired the fact that roofs were raised "without any other pay than the pleasures which usually attend a country frolic."

Not only did a log cabin go up quickly; it was a tight, strong house. Its walls, chinked with moss and mud, provided better insulation from cold than sawed clapboards did. The walls were thick and almost invulnerable to arrowheads, musket balls, and fire. To burn a log cabin, it was necessary to set fire to the roof, which was made of shingles or thatched straw.

A pioneer might keep oxen (the chief beasts of burden), a few horses, and perhaps a milk cow, which were fenced or, just as often, hobbled—that is, their forelegs were bound with a rope or rawhide thong, loosely enough that they could walk but not run. For meat, settlers depended on hogs. They were cheap and, more than a match for any predator, ran loose. They were hunted rather than rounded up for the slaughter, after the October harvest; the settlers salted the meat and packed it into barrels. With deer (still abundant) to supplement the salt pork, meat shortage was less of a problem than keeping animals out of the fields and garden.

For this, pioneers built zigzag fences. Logs split into rails—again, only an ax and wooden wedges were needed—were stacked alternately, at angles a little more than 90 degrees, zigzag. No postholes needed to be dug. They were not very good fences. Deer could leap them while yawning, and the largest hogs could push them over. But they were a first line of defense.

According to the *Columbian* article, "the first settler in the woods" rarely stayed put more than a year or two. He was "generally a man who [had] outlived his credit of fortune in the cultivated parts of the State." Not a very good citizen, he was an anarchic, irreligious, and hard-drinking individual who could not "bear to surrender up a single natural right for all the benefits of government." Soon restless, he sold out to a newcomer who improved the farm, felling and burning the dead hardwoods and adding to the cabin. The people of the second wave were themselves in the business of turning a profit rather than putting down roots. They soon sold to the "the *third* and last species of settler," a solid citizen whose habits were a relief to the article's author. This third settler was, thank goodness, "commonly a man of property and good character."

in a gentleman's family," that is, as an inferior scarcely to be noticed. Even the venal Barbary States of northern Africa looked down on Americans. These little principalities lived

by piracy, collecting tribute (in the name of treaty rights) from nations whose ships traded in the Mediterranean. When Americans lost the protection the British annually purchased for vessels flying the Union Jack, American ships were sunk or captured. The bey (governor) of Algiers sold several American crews into slavery. Congress was unable either to ransom them (money again!) or to launch a punitive expedition. It was a sorry state of affairs for the young men of the Revolution who had dreamed of national greatness.

Calls for Change

A trivial conflict in domestic waters triggered the movement to overhaul the government. In March 1785, a small group of Marylanders and Virginians gathered at Mount Vernon, George Washington's home on the Potomac, to discuss the conflicting claims of Maryland's and Virginia's fishermen in the Chesapeake Bay. They were unable to come up with a boundary acceptable to the two states' fisheries. They did, however, conclude that the problem was only one in a morass of disputes between states and between the states and the Confederation government. They invited all 13 states to send delegates to a meeting the next year in Annapolis, Maryland, to discuss what might be done.

Only five states responded. Decisive action was out of the question. Undiscouraged, Washington's former aide-de-

camp, Alexander Hamilton of New York, persuaded the disappointed few delegates to try again in more centrally located Philadelphia. They should prepare, Hamilton said, to discuss all the "defects in the System of the Federal Government."

Hamilton and others, like James Madison of Virginia, had more than talking in mind. They intended a bloodless coup d'état, peacefully replacing the Articles of Confederation with a completely new frame of government. Rumors of their intentions spread quickly and met less than resounding

▲ *Shays' Rebellion began as bullying and beating up Massachusetts state officials but soon evolved into a genuine, if short-lived, armed insurrection.*

approval. Virginia governor Patrick Henry, Madison's rival in the state's politics, said that he "smelled a rat" and refused to endorse the proposal. Rhode Island officially declared the state would not participate. Hamilton's Philadelphia convention might have fizzled like the Annapolis meeting had it not been for a wave of protests in western Massachusetts that turned into armed rebellion.

Shays' Rebellion

Farmers in western Massachusetts resented the fact that the state's tax laws favored trade at the expense of agriculture. In 1786, hundreds of them held meetings at which they demanded that their property taxes be reduced. To make up for the loss of revenue, they called for the abolition of "aristocratic" public offices in the state government in Boston.

In several towns, angry crowds surrounded courthouses, harassed lawyers and judges, whom they considered parasites, and forcibly prevented the collection of debts. In September, a Revolutionary War veteran, Daniel Shays, led 2,000 armed men against the state arsenal in Springfield.

Shays and his followers did not regard themselves as destructive or dangerous, not even as revolutionaries. They believed they were carrying on the spirit and struggle of the War for Independence against a privileged elite. Then minister in France, Thomas Jefferson agreed with them. "A little rebellion now and then is a good thing," he wrote to a friend.

"The tree of liberty must be refreshed from time to time with the blood of patriots and tyrants." (When he was not on the scene, Jefferson was often titillated by social disorder.)

Shays' Rebellion collapsed in December. But the men who were preparing to gather in Philadelphia the next summer, and some who were considering it, determined not to face another such crisis. To them, it was not Jefferson's pine tree of liberty that needed attention; it was the ailing oak of social stability and order. Washington, Hamilton, and conservatives like them believed that disorders like the uprising in Massachusetts were the inevitable consequence of weak government.

THE CONSTITUTION

The American Constitution has been hailed with a reverence that can be called religious. Politicians, moralists, and historians—Americans and foreigners alike—have bowed before a legal document that could survive for two centuries during which technology, ideology, revolution, imperialism, and war turned the world upside down and then downside up. William E. Gladstone, prime minister of Great Britain in the midst of this tumultuous era, was neither alone nor excessive when he called the American Constitution "the most wonderful work ever struck off at a given time by the brain and purpose of man."

The National Archives

▲ *The "Founding Fathers." George Washington is presiding. Seated second from the left is an idealized Benjamin Franklin. The oldest delegate at 81, Franklin was not as lively as he is shown to be here. He died within three years.*

"Demigods"

The men who struck it off in the summer of 1787—the "Founding Fathers"—have been heaped with praise, as wise, selfless individuals who peered into their nation's future and designed for it a timeless gift. The Constitution was "intended to endure for ages to come," Chief Justice John Marshall proclaimed in 1819. On the floor of the Senate in 1850, a critical year for the union of states the Constitution created, Marshall was echoed by Henry Clay of Kentucky. "The Constitution of the United States," Clay said, "was not made merely for the generation that then existed but for posterity—unlimited, undefined, and endless, perpetual posterity."

The Constitution has in fact been a remarkably successful frame of government, and the generation of political leaders who wrote and debated it was as rich in talent and wisdom as any generation before or since. But the Founding Fathers were not demigods, as Thomas Jefferson feared Americans would make them out to be. They were decidedly human, with prosaic faults and, along with their ideals, very immediate purposes to serve.

The Constitutional Convention

The convention in Philadelphia began on May 25, 1787. The 55 delegates almost immediately agreed that the Articles of Confederation could not, realistically, be revised. Ironically, it was easier to effect a coup d'état, to create a government from scratch, than to amend the Articles of Confederation. Amendment required that all 13 states concur. Rhode Island had already made it quite clear, by sending no delegates to Philadelphia, that it opposed any change of government. The convention was quite willing to form a new union of 12 states in place of the confederation of 13.

The Constitutional Convention met in secret from beginning to end. For four months, the delegates bolted the doors and sealed the windows of the Pennsylvania statehouse (Independence Hall), a demigod-like sacrifice in the hot and humid Philadelphia summer. Every delegate swore not to discuss the proceedings with others. George Washington, who presided, was furious when one misplaced a page of his notes.

The secrecy was not sinister. The goal of the convention—a new frame of government—was common knowledge. The delegates sequestered themselves because they wanted to proceed with caution. As James Wilson of Pennsylvania said, "America now presents the first instance of a people assembled to weigh deliberately and calmly, and to decide leisurely and peaceably, upon the form of government by which they will bind themselves, and their posterity." That was no small matter—never before had a nation been invented. There was an immediate and practical reason for secrecy too: The delegates were politicians; they wanted to voice their frankest opinions without fear that what they said would affect their careers back home.

Moreover, they knew there would be opposition to their new constitution. Wilson said that "the people" were assembled in Independence Hall. The Constitution begins with the words "We the People of the United States." In fact, most of the Founding Fathers represented just one of several American political tendencies. They wanted their platform complete before they had to debate its merits with their critics.

The Delegates

They finished in September 1787. After a bibulous celebration, the delegates scattered north and south to lobby for their states' approval. They were a formidable lot, all of them influential at home by virtue of their wealth, education, and political prominence. Of the 55, only two, Roger Sherman of Connecticut, who had been a cobbler as a young man, and Alexander Hamilton, the bastard son of a merchant in the West Indies, could be said to have been born with anything less glittering in their mouth than a silver spoon.

Lifetimes devoted to justifying independence and creating state governments made many of the delegates keen students of political philosophy. During the years just preceding the convention, James Madison augmented his library with 200 books on the subject. Just as important was the delegates' practical experience: 7 had been state governors; 39 had sat in the Continental Congress.

The Founding Fathers were young. Only nine signers of the Declaration of Independence were among them (and three of them refused to sign the Constitution). Only Benjamin Franklin, at 81, was truly antique. The other Founding Fathers averaged 40 years of age, and the two leading spirits of the movement were only 36 (Madison) and 32 (Hamilton). Ten delegates were less than 35 years of age, and one was 26. Such men had been just old enough in 1776 to play minor roles in the war. They had been children during the Stamp Act crisis. They were heirs of the Revolution, not makers of it.

The youth of the Founding Fathers is of some importance in understanding the nature of the Constitution they wrote. Most of the delegates had never thought of themselves as

---

Social Butterfly

George Washington was, of course, the "star" of the Constitutional Convention. In 128 days in Philadelphia, he rode every morning at five o'clock, dined out 110 times, attended 69 afternoon teas, went out in the evening on 20 occasions to attend lectures, concerts, and plays, had his portrait painted four times, and went fishing at least once.

And a Partridge in a Pear Tree

Two days before the Founding Fathers signed the Constitution, most of them gathered at the City Tavern for a party in honor of George Washington. They consumed 7 bowls of punch, 8 bottles of cider, 8 bottles of whiskey, 12 bottles of beer, 22 bottles of port wine, 54 bottles of Madeira, and 60 bottles of claret.

colonials. By 1787, most wanted to think of themselves not as New Hampshiremen or South Carolinians, but as Americans. Unlike their more provincial forebears, they had moved freely and often from one state to another. In the Continental Army (a third of the delegates had been soldiers, mostly junior officers) and in the Confederation Congress, they met and formed relationships with men from other states. They thought in terms of a continent rather than of coastal enclaves looking back to a mother country for an identity.

A Conservative Movement

Youth does not, as we are often told to think, equate with radicalism. The men who drew up the Constitution were conservatives in the classic (not the contemporary) meaning of the word. They did not believe with Jefferson (then in France) that human nature was essentially good and eternally malleable, that people and society were perfectible if left free. Most of the Founding Fathers feared the darker side of human nature. They believed that, without strong institutional restraints, selfish individuals were quick to trample on the rights of others. To such conservatives, democracy and liberty did not go hand in hand. On the contrary, if "the people" were untrammeled in their power, they would destroy liberty and a good deal more.

The most pessimistic of the lot was Alexander Hamilton. Sent by friends who recognized his genius to King's College in New York (now Columbia University), Hamilton never returned to the West Indies. He left college to serve Washington as aide-de-camp during the war, impressing the general with his intelligence and, no doubt, with his conservatism, for Washington too viewed democratic ideals with distaste. A few years after the adoption of the Constitution, Hamilton would listen to Thomas Jefferson expound on the wisdom and virtue inherent in "the people" and snap, "Your people, sir, are a great beast."

Had Hamilton been an Englishman, he would have defended those institutions that British conservatives believed helped to control the passions of the masses: the monarchy, the privileged aristocracy, the established church, and the centuries-old accretion of law and custom that is the British constitution. In fact, Hamilton was an admirer of English culture and government. Like Edmund Burke, he thought of the American Revolution as a conservative movement. In rebelling, the Americans had defended tradition against a reckless, innovative Parliament.

© Copyright Yale University Art Gallery, Alexander Hamilton by John Trumbull

▲ *Alexander Hamilton was one of the youngest Founding Fathers. He thought the Constitution allowed the states too much power and the president too little. But he accepted it as a great improvement on the Articles of Confederation.*

In the Constitution, Hamilton wanted to recapture as much of tradition as practicable. He suggested that president and senators be elected for life, thus creating a kind of monarch and aristocracy. Hamilton also wanted governmental power centralized to such a degree that the states became little more than administrative districts.

He was unable to sway his fellow delegates on either count. As much as many of them may have shared Hamilton's apprehensions, they understood better than he that Americans valued their states and would not tolerate backsliding toward hereditary privilege. What the majority of delegates did approve, and Hamilton accepted as preferable to "anarchy and convulsion," was a system of government that had room for democratic yearnings but placed effective checks on them. The government they created was, in the words of John Adams (who, like Jefferson, was not present—he was serving as minister in Britain), a "mixed government": a balance of the "democratical" principle (power in the hands of the many), the "aristocratical" (power in the hands of a few), and the "monocratical" (power in the hands of one).

Checks, Limits, Balances

The House of Representatives was "democratical." Representatives were elected frequently (every two years) by a broad electorate—most free, white, adult males. The Senate and the Supreme Court reflected Adams's "aristocratical" principle.

Hamilton on Democracy

"All communities divide themselves into the few and the many. The first are the rich and the wellborn, the other the mass of the people. . . . The people are turbulent and changing; they seldom judge or determine right. Give therefore to the first class a distinct, permanent share in the government. They will check the unsteadiness of the second, and as they cannot receive any advantage by change, they therefore will ever maintain good government."

Senators were elected infrequently (every six years) and by state legislatures, not by popular vote. They were thus somewhat insulated from the fickleness of the crowd.

The Supreme Court was almost totally insulated from popular opinion. Justices were appointed by the president, but, once confirmed by the Senate, they were immune to his or the Senate's or the people's influence. Justices served for life. They could be removed from the bench only by a difficult impeachment process.

The "monocratical" principle was established in the presidency and was, therefore, the most dramatic break with the Confederation. The president alone represented the whole nation, but he owed his power neither directly to the people nor to Congress. He was put into office by an electoral college that played no other role than selecting the president.

An intricate web of checks and balances tied together the three branches of government. Only Congress could enact a law, and both democratic House and aristocratic Senate had to agree to its last syllable. The president could veto an act of Congress if he judged it adverse to the national interest. However, Congress could override his veto by a two-thirds majority of both houses.

Judging specific cases according to these laws was the job of the judiciary, with the Supreme Court the final court of appeal. In time (it was not written into the Constitution), the Supreme Court claimed a quasi-legislative role of its own in the principle of judicial review; that is, in judging according to the law, the Supreme Court also interpreted the law. Implicit in this process was the power to declare a law unconstitutional and, therefore, void.

Finally, the Constitution can be amended, although the process for doing so was deliberately made difficult. An amendment may be proposed in one of two ways. Two-thirds of the states' legislatures can petition Congress to summon a national constitutional convention for the purpose. Or Congress can submit proposals to the states (this is the only method by which the Constitution has ever been amended). If three-fourths of the states ratify a proposed amendment, it becomes part of the Constitution.

The Federal Relationship

Another network of checks and balances defined the relationship between the central government and the states. Under the Articles of Confederation, the United States was a confederation of independent states, each of which retained virtually all the powers possessed by sovereign nations. Under the Constitution, the balance shifted, with preponderant and decisive powers going to the federal government. The states were not reduced to administrative districts, as Hamilton would have liked. Nationalistic sentiments may have been high in 1787, but local interests and jealousies were far from dead. If the Constitution were to win popular support, the states had to be accommodated.

Small states, like Delaware, New Jersey, and Connecticut (not to mention Rhode Island), were particularly sensitive in this matter. Delegates from the small states insisted

that if their states were not to be bullied and even absorbed by larger, wealthier neighbors, they must be accorded fundamental protections. These they received in the decision that states rather than population would be represented in the Senate. That is, each state elected two senators, no matter what its population. Virginia, the largest, was ten times as populous as Delaware but had the same number of senators. Without this "great compromise," which was accomplished only after intense debate in July 1787, the Constitution would not have been completed.

The Constitution and Slavery

The different status of America's 700,000 slaves in the North and the South was reflected in another compromise. By 1787, the institution of slavery was clearly dying in all the states north of Maryland and Delaware. Northern delegates were inclined to hope it would disappear everywhere. Indeed, with the exception of the delegates from South Carolina, few of the southern Founding Fathers looked favorably on slavery. Tellingly, the word "slave" does not appear in the Constitution, as if the framers were embarrassed that such persons existed in a country consecrated to liberty.

Rather, in a provision that prohibited Congress from abolishing the African slave trade for 20 years (Article 1, Section 9), slaves are referred to obliquely as "such Persons as any of the States now existing find proper to admit," a euphemism worthy of a university president. Elsewhere in the document, slaves are designated "all other persons." This expression was also used in the "three-fifths compromise" by which slaves and indentured servants were counted as three-fifths of a person for purposes of both taxation and representation in the House of Representatives.

But that was that. If many white southerners of 1787 hoped that slavery would die out, they did not know how to help the process along. Slaves were a fact of southern life, and "convenient" (embarrassed slave owner Patrick Henry's word) to those who owned them. Few whites could imagine freeing African Americans where they were numerous—in the South—without social turmoil that would make Shays' Rebellion look like minor mischief. Another embarrassed slave owner, Thomas Jefferson, said that living with the institution was holding "a wolf by the ears": One wished to be rid of it but could not let go.

Moreover, the Founding Fathers' first priority was getting the Constitution ratified. Significant action on the matter of slavery would surely have complicated that task, if not doomed it. They dodged the issue.

RATIFICATION OF THE CONSTITUTION

The Constitution provided that it would go into effect when nine states ratified it. Three did so immediately, Delaware and Connecticut almost unanimously, thanks to the "great compromise." Pennsylvania's ratification came quickly, but in a manner that dramatized the widespread opposition to the new government and the determination of the supporters of the Constitution to have their way, by hook and crook if necessary.

Federalist Shenanigans

Those who favored the Constitution called themselves "federalists." This was something of a misnomer, since they proposed to replace a genuinely federated government with a more centralized one. In Pennsylvania, the federalists secured ratification only by physically forcing two anti-federalist members of the state convention to remain in their seats when they tried to leave the hall. This rather irregular maneuver guaranteed a quorum so that the federalist majority could cast a legal pro-Constitution vote.

It was only the first of a series of manipulations that has led some historians to speculate that a majority of Americans probably preferred the Articles of Confederation to the Constitution. In Massachusetts, anti-federalists claimed that scheduling the election of delegates to the ratification convention in midwinter prevented many anti-federalist farmers from getting to the polls because they were snowbound. Even then, ratification was approved by the narrow margin of 187 to 168, and only because several delegates who had pledged to vote against the Constitution voted for it.

In June 1788, Edmund Randolph of Virginia, an announced anti-federalist, changed his vote and took a coterie of followers with him; the federalist victory in Virginia was by a vote of only 89 to 79. A switch of six votes would have reversed the verdict in the largest state, and that, in turn, would have kept New York in the anti-federalist camp.

In New York, a large anti-federalist majority was elected to the ratifying convention. After voting to reject the Constitution, they reversed their decision when news of Virginia's approval reached the state. Still, the vote was closer than in Massachusetts and Virginia, a razor-thin 30 to 27. Moreover, the New Yorkers saddled ratification with the proviso that a convention be called to amend the Constitution in several particulars. It never was. Technically, New York's vote was "nay."

The Anti-Federalists

North Carolina was decisively anti-federalist. Only in November 1789, eight months after the new government began to function, did the state reluctantly vote to ratify. Rhode Island held out longer, until May 1790. Rhode Island became the thirteenth state only when Congress threatened to pass a tariff that would have shut its products out of the other 12 states.

Today, now that the Constitution has worked successfully for 200 years, it can be easy to shrug off the anti-federalists of 1787 and 1788 as cranks. In fact, their reasons for favoring the Articles of Confederation were firmly within the tradition of the Revolution.

Among the anti-federalists were fiery old patriots who feared that centralized power was an invitation to tyranny. Samuel Adams, still padding around Boston shaking his

Unpredictable Critic

Mercy Otis Warren, sister of hell-raiser James Otis and wife of a prominent patriot, would be of a familiar type were she alive today. At the forefront of many radical causes, her blood was the bluest Massachusetts produced, and she knew it. She politely condescended even to those just a notch below her in social status, like John and Abigail Adams, to whom she was a lifelong friend. Her condescension was subtle because her pen was among the deftest of her era, often as precise and eloquent as Jefferson's. She authored several anti-Loyalist plays and a history of the Revolution.

Although a vociferous patriot, Mercy Warren was never, like other rebels, happy with the Articles of Confederation. She called Confederation America a "restless, vigorous youth, prematurely emancipated from the authority of a parent, but without the experience necessary to direct him to act with dignity or discretion."

That sounds like a federalist in the making, but Mercy Warren was no federalist. She regarded the Constitution as a plot, sinister in ways she never quite defined in writing, which was rare for her. Mercy Warren fit into no "type" in the 1780s. There was no other prominent American so critical of both the Articles of Confederation and the Constitution.

head at moral decadence, opposed the Constitution until Massachusetts federalists, needing the old lion's support, agreed to press for a national bill of rights. In Virginia, Patrick Henry battled James Madison around the state. Some of Henry's arguments against the Constitution were rather bizarre. At one point, he concluded that the Constitution was an invitation to the pope to set up court in the United States. Henry had his eccentricities.

But Henry and other anti-federalists also argued that free republican institutions could survive only in small countries such as Switzerland, the city-states of ancient Greece, and, of course, states like a sovereign Virginia. They had the weight of historical evidence on their side. Their favorite example was the Roman republic, which, when it grew into an empire, became despotic. Would the same thing happen to a large, centrally governed United States? Many anti-federalists believed so.

Answering such objections was the federalists' most difficult task. Madison, Hamilton, and John Jay of New York took it upon themselves to do so in 85 essays, the *Federalist Papers,* still a basic textbook of political philosophy. They argued that a powerful United States would guarantee liberty. These ingenious essays, however, were less important to the triumph of the federalists than their agreement, quite unhappy in Hamilton's case, to add a bill of rights to the Constitution.

The Bill of Rights

The Constitutional Convention paid little attention to the rights of citizens. The Founding Fathers were by no means hostile to individual rights, but their preoccupation was strengthening government. Moreover, they assumed that rights were protected in the state constitutions.

Because the Constitution created a national government superior to the states, however, anti-federalists like Samuel Adams and Edmund Randolph agreed to scrap their opposition to ratification only when the rights that had been adopted by the states since 1776 were guaranteed on the federal level. The Bill of Rights, the first 10 amendments to the Constitution, was ratified in 1791, but tacitly agreed upon during the ratification process. The First Amendment guaranteed freedom of religion, speech, the press, and peaceable assembly. The Second Amendment guaranteed the right to bear arms. The Third and Fourth Amendments guaranteed security against the quartering of troops in private homes (then still a sore point with older Americans) and against unreasonable search and seizure.

The famous Fifth Amendment is a guarantee against being tried twice for the same crime and, in effect, against torture. It is the basis of a citizen's right to refuse to testify in a trial in which he or she is a defendant. (British practice did not allow a defendant to testify.) The Sixth Amendment also pertains to criminal trials. It ensures the right to a speedy trial and the right to face accusers: no secret witnesses. The Seventh and Eighth Amendments likewise protect the rights of a person who is accused of committing a crime.

The Ninth and Tenth Amendments are catchalls. They state that the omission of a right from the Constitution does not mean that the right does not exist and that any powers not explicitly granted to the federal government are reserved to the states.

for FURTHER READING

The Confederation era and the Constitutional Convention have been fields of tumultuous controversy for almost a century. The origin of the dispute was Charles A. Beard, *An Economic Interpretation of the Constitution of the United States,* 1913. Beard broke with the general patriotic assumption that the Constitution was the work of selfless demigods striving to save the country from the chaos of the Articles of Confederation (a view best presented in John Fiske, *The Critical Period of American History, 1783–1789,* 1883). Beard instead contended that the Constitution reflected the Founding Fathers' quite immediate political and economic interests. Much of Beard's evidence and analysis have been discredited, but his book remains a "must-read" for students interested in the historians' debate.

Merrill Jensen, *The Articles of Confederation,* 1940, and *The New Nation,* 1950, are "Beardian" histories of the Confederation period. Other milestones in the debate are Jackson T. Main, *The Antifederalists,* 1961, and *Political Parties Before the Constitution,* 1973; Frederick W. Marks, *Independence on Trial,* 1973; Forrest MacDonald, *We the People: Economic Origins of the Constitution,* 1958; Andrew C. McLaughlin, *The Confederation and the Constitution,* 1962; Gordon S. Wood, *The Creation of the American Republic,* 1969; Garry Wills, *Interpreting America: The Federalist,* 1978; and Richard Beeman, Stephen Botein, and Edward C. Carter, *Beyond Confederation: Origins of the Constitution and American National Identity,* 1987.

See also David P. Szatmary, *Shays' Rebellion,* 1980; Lance Banning, *The Sacred Fire of Liberty: James Madison and the Founding of the Federal Republic,* 1995; and Arthur Zilversmit, *The First Emancipation: The Abolition of Slavery in the North,* 1967.

  ## AMERICAN JOURNEY ONLINE AND INFOTRAC COLLEGE EDITION

Visit the source collections at http://ajaccess.wadsworth.com and http://infotrac.thomsonlearning.com, and use the Search function with the following key terms to explore documents, images, audio and video clips, articles, and commentary related to the material in this chapter:

Abigail Adams
Alexander Hamilton
Bill of Rights
Constitutional Convention
First Amendment

James Madison
Northwest Ordinance
Patrick Henry
Shays' Rebellion

Additional resources, exercises, and Internet links related to this chapter are available on *The American Past* Web site: http://history.wadsworth.com/americanpast7e.

HISTORY ONLINE

Religious Facets of the Confederation Period
http://lcweb.loc.gov/exhibits/religion/rel06.html
Insightful multi-format presentation of the role of religion in the events of the 1770s.

Documents of the Continental Congress
http://memory.loc.gov/ammem/bdsds/bdsdhome.html
A multi-format survey of the Confederation period.

11

WE THE PEOPLE

Putting the Constitution to Work 1789–1800

The father of his country.

Francis Bailey

First in war, first in peace, first in the hearts of his countrymen.

Henry Lee

America has furnished to the world the character of Washington. And if our American institutions had done nothing else, that alone would have entitled them to the respect of mankind.

Daniel Webster

DURING THE DEBATE over the Constitution, one question never arose: Who would be the first president? In few monarchies has one figure towered over all others as George Washington towered above the United States. The first electoral college voted unanimously to install Washington in what was, at the time, an office unique in the world. He took the presidential oath in New York City on April 30, 1789.

THE FIRST PRESIDENCY

Washington possessed qualities indispensable to the launching of a government designed from scratch. He was committed to the republican ideal. His sense of duty was the foundation of his personality. He knew he had become one of his era's major historical figures. He knew that he would set a precedent with every presidential act, from signing a bill into law to the manner in which he greeted a guest at dinner.

Precedents Set

It is fortunate that Washington was a republican. Lionized as he was in 1789, he could likely have been crowned a king. Some members of the Order of Cincinnatus, a society of Revolutionary War officers, wanted to do just that. It was suggested that Washington be addressed as "Your Elective Majesty," but he settled for "Mr. President."

Not that the president was just one of the boys. Washington toyed with "His High Mightiness" as a possible title, and he was fussy about other trappings of his office. He lived surrounded by servants in livery and powdered wigs, and he drove around New York in a splendid carriage drawn by matched cream-colored horses. He looked and acted like the

Washington was hurrahed and feted all the way from Mount Vernon to his inauguration in New York City, then the nation's capital. He crossed the Hudson in a splendidly decorated barge and took the presidential oath on a balcony, cheered by thousands in the street below.

▲ Military men wear medals. The old soldiers in the Order of Cincinnatus wore this one to identify themselves. The inscription reads, "All sacrificed to serve the republic."

prince of a small European state, not quite regal but decidedly unique in his surroundings. On a bet that he would not dare do so, New Yorker Gouverneur Morris slapped Washington on the back at a public function. The president stared him down with such iciness that Morris retreated from the room, stammering. They were never quite cordial again. Morris said it was the costliest bet he had ever won.

In being as much a monument as a man, Washington won respect abroad. No European statesmen feared the United States, but neither did any of them mistake George Washington for a head-scratching bumpkin who had had a bit of luck on a battlefield.

The Cabinet

Washington was accustomed to wielding authority as a planter and soldier. A rarer quality among men raised high was his awareness of his personal limitations and need of advice. Far from resenting brighter people (as, for instance, George III did), Washington sought them out and listened to them. Those he saw regularly were five heads of executive departments entrusted with the workaday operations of the government, three of them titled "secretaries." They were soon collectively dubbed the president's "cabinet."

In making his appointments, Washington tried to balance political tendencies and sectional sensitivities. From

The Cincinnati

Lucius Quinctius Cincinnatus was a Roman who was twice made dictator when enemies threatened the republic. Both times, Cincinnatus was quickly victorious; but, instead of using the months remaining of his legal dictatorship to enrich himself and rule as a tyrant, he immediately resigned and retired to his farm. Educated Americans of the revolutionary era, steeped in classical history, thought of George Washington as their Cincinnatus.

In 1784, officers of the Continental Army formed the Order of the Cincinnati. It was controversial from the start. The society's proceedings were secret and membership was hereditary, passed down by charter members to their firstborn sons. In other words, the Cincinnati preserved the aristocratic principle of primogeniture that revolutionary era state governments had abolished in property law.

During the troubled Confederation period, members discussed the possibility of selecting something like a dictator. They were delighted to have Washington as president, but rumors of a military coup by the Cincinnati to increase his power disturbed the followers of Thomas Jefferson, who called the society "a nascent nobility."

Washington discouraged Cincinnati mutterings, and the membership grew long in the tooth without biting. The society abandoned the principle of primogeniture so that all male descendants of Revolutionary War officers might belong, and it evolved into an organization "devoted to the principles of the Revolution, the preservation of history and the diffusion of historical knowledge." As such it exists today.

▲ *The first cabinet, left to right: the president, Secretary of War Henry Knox (depicted at less than his 300 pounds), Attorney General Edmund Randolph, Secretary of State Thomas Jefferson, and Jefferson's rival (and soon to be enemy), Secretary of the Treasury Alexander Hamilton. There is a precedent here: no Vice President John Adams. Adams called his office "useless."*

Virginia came Attorney General Edmund Randolph and Secretary of State Thomas Jefferson. By naming Randolph, an opponent of the Constitution until the last moment, Washington extended a hand of reconciliation to the anti-federalists. Jefferson, by virtue of his agrarian book of 1785, *Notes on the State of Virginia,* was recognized as a spokesman for farmers who were suspicious of the nondemocratic features of the new government.

To balance the southerners, Washington named General Henry Knox of Massachusetts as secretary of war. Knox was a wartime crony of the president, but, more important, as the chief military official under the Confederation, he represented continuity from old government to new. Samuel Osgood of Massachusetts, the postmaster general, was a former anti-federalist like Randolph.

Dynamic Alexander Hamilton of New York was Washington's secretary of the treasury. Partly because his conservative instincts were in tune with the president's, partly because the most urgent challenges facing the new government were financial, Hamilton's power was second only to Washington's.

The First Debate: Funding

To pay the government's operating expenses, Hamilton asked Congress to enact a 5 percent tariff on imports. The duty was low, not enough to impede sales of foreign goods in the United States. Moreover, Hamilton had a penchant for making political statements. Rhode Island's veto of a 5 percent tariff under the Articles of Confederation had been a signal indication of the old government's helplessness in levying taxes.

Revenue from the tariff, Hamilton knew, would be woefully inadequate in a crisis—a war, for example. In fact, the tariff did not usually bring in enough to balance the government's books. The government, like all governments, would have to borrow money. Hamilton, therefore, set out to establish that its credit was sound.

This was no easy chore: The Confederation Congress had been grievously remiss in paying its debts. When it collapsed, it owed $12 million to foreign banks and governments and $44 million to American citizens. Many lenders were wary. Did a new government mean a repudiation of the old

Birthing

A woman who married during the Federalist period could expect to be pregnant about seven times during her life—if she did not die young. One in four women between 15 and 44 gave birth each year. Mothers nursed their infants for about a year. The rich and the very weak hired wet nurses, women already lactating from a recent birth.

There were no maternity hospitals. Children were delivered at home by midwives (*midwife* originally meant "with a woman"), possibly in the company of the mother-to-be's own mother, sisters, neighbors, and older daughters. Childbirth was an exclusively female event except during the early stages of labor, when the husband might be called in to pray with or comfort his wife.

Midwives served an apprenticeship or fell into the profession accidentally after getting "catched" in a number of childbirths and developing a reputation as someone who knew what to do. It brought in some extra money—the sole support of many midwives—and ensured the respect of the community. One Boston woman's tombstone attests that "by the Blessing of God" she had "brought into this world above 3,000 Children."

The presence of several women at a birth was practical. They heated water and washed linens. If the labor was prolonged, they prepared food. Few women gave birth lying on their backs; instead, they squatted or half-stood, supported by their attendants. Moreover, it was common for a new mother to remain in bed for several weeks after childbirth. Her friends and relatives performed her household duties during this final phase of her "confinement."

The attendants also served cultural, social, and psychological purposes. Their presence (and the exclusion of men) emphasized the uniquely feminine character of the suffering childbirth meant. (Liquor was the only anesthetic.) The pains of bearing children were still generally regarded as God's punishment for the sin of Eve. By their presence—because they too had undergone childbirth or expected to do so—the attendants shared in the travail. They also cheered the mother-to-be by distracting her with gossip, comparing her labor with more difficult labors they had suffered, and even making her laugh by telling bawdy jokes.

By 1800, male physicians were taking over the supervision of childbirth. The trend began in Britain during the 1740s when Dr. William Smellie was appalled by the incompetence of many midwives. "We ought to be ashamed of ourselves," he told physicians, "for the little improvement we have made in so many centuries." Smellie invented the forceps used for assisting difficult births.

The development of obstetrics as a branch of medicine also reflected the drift of educated people away from traditional religion. In 1804, Peter Miller of the medical school of the University of Pennsylvania wrote that the dangers of pregnancy and the death of so many newborns were sorrow enough for women. It was absurd to burden them with the message that they were doing penance. Dr. William Dewees, a pioneer of medical obstetrics in the United States, asked, "Why should the female alone incur the penalty of God?"

Among the urban upper and middle classes, male physicians supplanted midwives in a surprisingly short period of time. In Boston and Philadelphia during the Federalist period, physicians were called into childbirth cases only when there were serious difficulties. By the 1820s, doctors virtually monopolized the delivery of children in cities except among the poor.

The survival rate of both mothers and newborns improved, although not dramatically until later in the nineteenth century, when it was discovered that "childbirth fever" (puerperal fever) was caused by the failure of most physicians even to wash their hands before delivery. The triumph of medical obstetrics had other complications. The nineteenth century's demands for sexual modesty obligated doctors to ask questions "of a delicate nature"—just about all questions regarding childbirth—through a woman. It was an unwieldy procedure, to say the least, and in emergencies, dangerous. Moreover, the birth had to be carried out under covers, with the physician working entirely by touch. Even so awkward a procedure offended some. In *Letters to Ladies, Detailing Important Information Concerning Themselves and Infants,* published in 1817, Dr. Thomas Ewell told of a husband who "very solemnly . . . declared to the doctor, he would demolish him if he touched or looked at his wife."

---

government's obligations? Hamilton reassured them by funding the entire Confederation-era debt at face value. That is, by trading new federal bonds for old Confederation bonds—"restructuring the debt," we would say—the Constitutional government would immediately assert its fiscal reliability.

Few in Congress objected to repaying foreign creditors in full. The United States was cash poor. Big loans could only be had abroad. However, Hamilton's proposal to pay American creditors at par led to a serious debate.

The issue was speculation. Most of the domestic debt dated to the war years, when, moved as much by patriotism as by mercenary motives, thousands of Americans bought government bonds. As the years passed and the Confederation Congress failed to redeem these debts, many lenders lost hope. They sold their bonds to speculators at big discounts; better something than nothing. By 1789, most public bonds were in the strongboxes of financial adventurers.

Nor had they been so very adventurous. As James Madison explained in opposing the funding bill, some speculators, informed in advance of what Hamilton would propose, had scoured rural villages and towns, buying up all the Confederation bonds they could find at as little as a few cents on the dollar. In our parlance, they had traded on "insider information."

Madison said that Congress should not reward such profiteering. Instead, he proposed to pay the face value of the debts plus 4 percent annual interest to original lenders who still held the old bonds. Speculators who bought the bonds at bargain rates, however, were to receive half of the face value.

Madison's argument was morally appealing. It rewarded those who had stepped forward during "the times that tried men's souls." Hamilton replied that morality was beside the point. The issue was the new government's credit. By rewarding capitalists, including the connivers, his funding bill would encourage them to be lenders in the future. Hamilton believed that the moneyed classes were the key to the stability of the new government. He meant to wed them to it.

Hamilton's realism was compelling. And it did not hurt that several dozen members of Congress stood to profit personally from the funding bill. It was enacted.

Assumption and a New Capital

Hamilton next proposed that the federal government assume responsibility for debts contracted by the state governments since independence. By repaying loans that the states had not, the federal government would further strengthen its credit rating. In addition, assumption would enhance the prestige of the federal government vis-à-vis that of the states, an important goal of nationalists like Hamilton.

Money: The Dollar

The word *dollar* derives from the German *Taler,* a silver coin first minted in 1484. The Spanish called the coin *dolar.*

Why, in 1785, did the United States adopt a Spanish monetary unit rather than the British pound that had been the colonial standard? In part, it was another patriotic slap at the former mother country. More important than patriotic symbolism, there were far more Spanish dollars than British pounds circulating in America. The dollar was, as Jefferson said, "a known coin" and "the most familiar of all to the mind of the people."

In practice, Americans continued to trade in any and all gold and silver coins for half a century. Merchants had conversion tables or knew by heart what foreign coins were worth in dollars. As late as the California Gold Rush of 1849, businesses in San Francisco quoted their prices in British pounds, shillings, and pence.

Money: Bucks and Quarters

The word *buck,* slang for dollar, dates to the eighteenth century, when a deer hide, or "buckskin," was commonly used as money (by law in New York). In 1785, when Congress adopted the dollar, a buckskin sold for a Spanish dollar.

Although the American dollar was officially divided into 100 cents in 1793, Americans also divided it into quarters. This custom also reflected the abundance of Spanish coins in the young United States. Spanish dollars were divided into eight reales (the famous "pieces of eight"), which originated in the practice of actually sawing Spanish dollars into eight pieces, as a pie is sliced, to make change. Thus, the now moribund custom of calling a quarter "two bits" and half a dollar "four bits."

Again, James Madison led the opposition. He pointed out that some states, notably his own Virginia, had retired most of their debt. Other states, northern, had let their obligations ride, accruing interest for as many as 15 years. If the federal government now assumed responsibility for the debts of all states, the citizens of some—Virginians!—would, in effect, pay twice. They had dutifully retired their state's debt by paying state taxes. Now, they would pay federal taxes to help pay the debts run up and neglected by others—sometimes, apparently, out of irresponsibility. Was this fair? Just enough congressmen thought not. The assumption bill was defeated in the House of Representatives, 31 to 29.

Assumption was a vital part of Hamilton's financial program, his "primary object" to which "all subordinate points . . . must be sacrificed." He was not going to be foiled by a razor-thin defeat. And Hamilton had a card to play: An emotional issue before Congress was where to locate the permanent capital of the United States. Philadelphia had the best claim to the honor. Home of the Declaration of Independence and the Constitution, it was by far the largest city in the United States, abounding in public buildings and living quarters for government officials, and centrally located. In fact, during the debate over funding, Hamilton had offered to deliver the votes to Philadelphia in return for Pennsylvania's votes for that bill.

The deal proved unnecessary and fell through. In the meantime, some 40 towns and would-be towns had put in bids to be the capital. Virginians, who voted against assumption the first time around, wanted the capital in the South. Hamilton worked out a deal with Jefferson, Madison's political ally. If Jefferson influenced enough southern congressmen to vote for assumption that it was enacted, Hamilton would deliver the votes of enough New Yorkers and New Englanders to locate the capital on the banks of the Potomac. Thus, by means of a masterful political horse trade, Hamilton got assumption. And thus was selected the site of Federal City, later renamed Washington, D.C., in the woods and worn-out tobacco fields of the Tidewater.

Interpretation of the Constitution

The third pillar of Hamilton's fiscal program was the Bank of the United States (BUS), a central financial institution in which all government moneys would be deposited. With such vast resources at its disposal, the BUS would exercise immense power over other banks and the nation's finances in general. Hamilton's BUS was not, however, a government agency. Although the president would appoint 5 of the bank's 25 directors, the remaining 20 were to be elected by private shareholders—Hamilton's men of capital again.

Hamilton had nothing to swap with Jefferson in return for his support, and the secretary of state had had his fill of the marriage between government and capital. When the bank bill passed Congress, Jefferson urged Washington to veto it. He argued that Congress had overstepped its constitutional powers. Nothing in the document gave the government the authority to create such an institution.

▲ *The First Bank of the United States in Philadelphia. Imposing in size, its classical design, borrowed from ancient Greece, was novel and deliberate. While its size conveyed power and stolidity, the classical facade hearkened to the republics of antiquity, with which Americans liked to identify.*

Washington was impressed by Jefferson's reasoning. But Hamilton won the day by arguing that nothing in the Constitution specifically *prohibited* Congress from chartering a national bank. Therefore, the BUS was justified under Article 1, Section 8, which authorized Congress to "make all laws which shall be necessary and proper for" (among other things) regulating commerce, which the BUS would certainly do, and to "provide for . . . the general welfare," which, to Hamilton's way of thinking, the bank would also accomplish. Washington signed the bill.

In the debate over the BUS, Jefferson and Hamilton formulated fundamentally different theories of constitutional interpretation that survive to this day in some disagreements on the Supreme Court. Jefferson's "strict construction" held that if the Constitution did not spell out and properly punctuate a governmental power in black and white, that power did not exist. Hamilton's "broad construction" held that Article 1, Section 8, permitted Congress to exercise any legislative powers that were *not specifically denied* to Congress elsewhere in the Constitution.

Hamilton Rebuffed

Establishing the BUS was Hamilton's last hurrah. Congress rejected the fourth pillar of his financial edifice, a call for a protective tariff, outlined in his "Report on Manufactures" of December 1791. In that report, Hamilton argued, cogently as usual, that the United States already had a solid agricultural and commercial base. He proposed to promote manufacturing by protecting investors in factories from foreign competition. By placing high import duties on, for example, British cloth and shoes, Congress would price them out of the American market. This would encourage American investors to build textile mills and shoe factories in the United States, creating jobs and new founts of wealth.

Farmers were inclined to oppose the protective tariff, particularly southern planters with numerous slaves to clothe and shod. They were consumers of manufactured goods. Hamilton's tariff meant higher prices for them. Agriculturalists also feared that Britain and other European nations stung by high American tariffs on goods they exported would retaliate by enacting high tariffs on American agricultural produce. Some great merchants, otherwise staunch Hamiltonians, opposed the protective tariff. Their business was transporting freight. British mercantilism now excluded them or sharply limited their business in British ports. They did not want their own government shutting down other routes. Hamilton's high tariff was killed. Import duties remained low, providing revenue but not protecting American manufacturers from foreign competition.

Clouds on the Horizon

Washington was reelected without opposition in 1792. He continued to carry out most of his policies and to establish sensible precedents. Most important, he presided over the establishment of a stable government for 4 million people and 900,000 square miles of territory. The United States, so recently a gaggle of ex-colonies, was a going concern of 16 states: Vermont, Kentucky, and Tennessee were admitted to the Union under Washington.

Washington's success story was not unblemished. In effect, the four ongoing and related problems he described in his farewell address of September 1796 were a summation of problems he had been unable to resolve.

First, Washington urged his countrymen not to align themselves in political parties. Washington regarded parties as combinations of selfish men willing to sacrifice the common good in order to benefit their own narrow interests. He saw no good in parties.

Second, he admonished Americans to "discountenance irregular opposition" to the government. That is, they should voice opposition to policies they disliked peacefully through constitutional channels, not by resistance and rebellion.

Third, Washington regretfully identified signs of sectionalism in the United States. He feared that too many Americans pledged allegiance more to the North or to the South than to the federal union. Division along geographical lines was far more dangerous than division on party lines, for it was far more likely to lead to civil war.

Finally, Washington warned against "the insidious wiles of foreign influence"—attempts by European diplomats to entangle the United States in their chronic wars. Honor alliances already in effect, Washington said, but make no new permanent commitments to other countries. Enjoy the Atlantic Ocean as a moat insulating the United States from a corrupt Europe.

TROUBLES ABROAD

The Washington administration's most troubling problems were in the area of foreign policy. This should not be surprising.

As colonials, Americans had entrusted diplomacy to the mother country. In no other arena of statecraft were the Founding Fathers so poorly educated. Moreover, the 1790s were a decade when the cleverest of European diplomats were repeatedly confounded. The old order—old ways of understanding—had been turned upside down.

The French Revolution

They were turned upside down by the revolution in France in 1789. At first a violent rebellion against the extravagance and excesses of the monarchy, the French Revolution soon pushed far beyond what Americans had done in their rebellion.

In 1789, the year of Washington's inauguration, Americans rejoiced at the upheaval in France. Had not the Declaration of Independence spoken of the inalienable rights of all people? Now their ally in the war against Britain was joining them as another land of liberty. It became fashionable for Americans to festoon their hats with cockades of red, white, and blue ribbon—the badge of the French revolutionaries. Lafayette gave Washington the key to the Bastille, the gloomy fortress jail that had symbolized the oppression of the French kings; the president proudly displayed it to guests.

Soon, however, the French Revolution moved beyond liberty to the ideals of equality and fraternity. Conservatives like Washington and Hamilton were not comfortable with palaver of wiping out social distinctions and of the equality of ignorant laborers with men, like themselves, of education and social standing. As for *fraternity*, it meant a national brotherhood, which was inoffensive, but it also smacked of a universal coziness of human affections that was, to conservatives, as fantastic as sea monsters. Even Thomas Jefferson, no conservative and usually keen on everything French, worried privately that the French revolutionaries were moving too far too fast. He doubted that a people accustomed to a powerful monarchy could create overnight a free republic like the United States.

Terror and Reason

Found a republic the French did, and in January 1793, as Washington's first term was ending, King Louis XVI was beheaded. His queen, Marie Antoinette, mounted the scaffold within the year. The Reign of Terror followed—French radicals known as Jacobins guillotined or drowned thousands of nobles and political rivals. The blood that flowed in France was quite as unnerving to Europeans (and many Americans) as the Holocaust was to be in the mid–twentieth century.

Maximilien Robespierre became the virtual dictator of France for a year. In an attempt to wipe out religion, Robespierre converted Paris's Cathedral of Notre Dame into a "temple of reason" where paunchy politicians and perfumed actresses performed rituals that struck many as ridiculous, others as blasphemous.

Few Americans thought warmly of the Catholic Church. However, Robespierre attacked all religion. American preachers shuddered when they heard Americans admiring him. William Cobbett, an Englishman living in the United States, observed with distaste that crowds of city people guillotined dummies of Louis XVI "twenty or thirty times every day during one whole winter and part of the summer." He also reported fistfights between gangs of pro-English "Anglomen" and pro-French "cutthroats."

American Neutrality

Cobbett was observing a point of conflict that contributed to the birth of the political parties that Washington warned against. Americans who supported the French inclined to favor an expanded democracy and the curtailment of social distinctions at home. Working people in the cities, small and middling farmers, and some wealthy southern planters who resented the favors that Hamilton's financial program lavished on northern merchants and capitalists looked increasingly to Thomas Jefferson as their spokesman. They called themselves "Jefferson Republicans." Jefferson (who left Washington's cabinet in 1793) quietly—behind the scenes, really, from his home at Monticello—accepted leadership of the coalescing movement. James Madison was his public spokesman.

Conservatives like Washington, Hamilton, and Vice President John Adams began to call themselves "Federalists." They were neither enamored of democracy, which they equated with mob rule, nor hostile to clear social distinctions, which they regarded as buttresses of stability. Until 1793, they were content to attack the principles of the French Revolution on a philosophical level. Then, Great Britain declared war on France. Under the terms of the treaty of 1778, it appeared that the United States was obligated to join France as an ally.

Washington wanted nothing of it. The Royal Navy was more powerful than ever. The French navy had declined, and the United States had no navy worth noticing. Alexander Hamilton, who was frankly pro-British, found the legal loophole that kept the United States out of the conflict. He argued that the treaty of 1778 was not binding on two counts: It had been contracted with the French monarchy, which no longer existed; and it provided that the United States must help France only if Great Britain was the aggressor, which, with some justification, the British denied.

Washington announced that the United States would be neutral, "impartial toward the belligerent powers." Then, in April 1793, the French minister to the United States, Edmond-Charles Genet, styling himself "Citizen Genet" in the best revolutionary vocabulary, arrived in Charleston.

Citizen Genet

Genet was young and as subtle as flags and fireworks. Soon after stepping ashore, he began to commission American shipmasters as privateers, armed raiders under contract to France to seize British ships. Within a short time, a dozen of these raiders brought 80 British "prizes"—captured merchant vessels—into American ports where Genet presided over trials at which he awarded the loot to the captors. Everything was within the rules of war *except* the fact that Genet was performing a French governmental action on American soil. He spoke to sympathetic audiences as if he were the governor of a French province.

By the time Genet presented his credentials to the president, Washington was livid. Genet's privateers promised to drag the United States into a war with Britain that the president had determined to sit out. Washington received the minister coldly and ordered him to cease bringing captured British vessels into American ports and to subdue his politicking. Genet bowed, retired, and continued to appear at dinners and demonstrations, adding jibes at Washington to his speeches. When he commissioned a captured British vessel, the *Little Sarah,* as a privateer, Washington ordered him to return to France.

This was bad news. Genet's political party back home had been ousted and the Reign of Terror was in full swing. To return to France meant a rendezvous with the guillotine. Suddenly abject, Genet asked Washington for asylum, and the president granted it. Remarkably, Genet actually did quiet down. He married into the wealthy Clinton family of New York and lived a long, contented life as a gentleman farmer.

British Threats

Genet or no Genet, the British kept the threat of war boiling by proclaiming they would fight the war at sea under the Rule of 1756. This British policy asserted that the ships of neutral countries could not trade in ports from which they had been excluded before the war began.

The targets of this proclamation were American merchants who were carrying grain and livestock to the French West Indies—Martinique, Guadeloupe, and Saint-Domingue (present-day Haiti). These ports had previously been closed to Americans, who were now reaping bonanza profits on the sugar and molasses they brought back from the French West

Indies. Shipowners who had recently struggled with hard times were suddenly wealthy, moving their families from apartments in their warehouses on the waterfront, where they had lived amid dirt, clamor, and marginal dockworkers, to elegant "federal period" town houses in neighborhoods somewhat insulated from the lower classes. The elite of New England and Philadelphia, with social lives as elegant as those of southern planters, little resembled their Puritan and Quaker forebears. (New York's great merchants had never been saddled with a gospel of austerity.) The fleets of Philadelphia, New York, and Boston grew until their combined tonnage rivaled that of Great Britain.

The British did not want war with the United States, but they were concerned about the explosive growth of the American merchant marine. Would Britain defeat the French only to discover that their overseas trade had been swiped by upstart Yankees? Enforcing the Rule of 1756 was more an attempt to retard the growth of American maritime commerce than it was retaliation for actions that hindered the British war effort. In any case, it made the news. In 1793 and 1794, British warships and privateers seized 600 American vessels, half of them in West Indian waters, a few within sight of American shores.

American shipowners griped, but not much more. Overseas trade was a high-risk enterprise in the best of times. The wartime business with the West Indies was so lucrative that merchants, great and aspiring, could absorb losses of ships and still end the year in the black. Moreover, the merchant class was generally more sympathetic to Britain than to France. Better to wink at British depredations at sea than to have French atheists victorious.

Impressment

The pro-French party, on the other hand, was hot for a fight with Britain. While Jefferson himself laid low (an unattractive facet of his character), his propagandists, especially the vituperative newspaper editor Philip Freneau, railed against the British seizures of American ships as an affront to national honor. Seamen and their families had a more personal grievance: the Royal Navy's application of the ancient practice of impressment.

Britain (and other seafaring nations) empowered the commanders of warships to replace seamen who died or deserted by means of an impromptu draft. If a ship was in port, press gangs roamed the streets forcing likely young men into service. At sea, warships ordered merchant vessels flying their own flag to heave to—the proverbial shot across the bow—whereupon press gangs boarded them and took their pick. Impressment was unpopular with everyone. Seamen on a signaled merchant vessel feigned crippled legs or idiocy. Serving in the Royal Navy had its advantages over sailing on the merchant ship (there was less heavy labor); but in wartime, naval discipline was brutal, and death in combat was no remote risk.

If British merchant seamen hated impressment, Americans were infuriated when warships flying the Union Jack took crewmen from American ships. Britain claimed the legal right to impress only British subjects, and there were plenty of them on American ships, where conditions and pay were better than in the British merchant marine. But American citizens were also impressed. Whereas the United States naturalized (bestowed citizenship on) British immigrants who applied for it, Great Britain maintained that anyone born British remained British lifelong. Hundreds of seamen were caught in the middle. Impressment aggravated American touchiness about the issue of national independence.

Jay's Treaty: Peace at a Price

In April 1794, faced with a growing clamor for war, Washington sent the chief justice of the Supreme Court, John Jay of New York, to Britain to appeal for peace. This alone was enough to raise the hackles of the knee-jerk anglophobes, especially when the news trickled back that Jay was hobnobbing in London society and had kissed the hand of the queen. But that fuss was nothing compared with the reception given to the treaty Jay brought home. The British made a few concessions. They agreed to evacuate the western forts they should have evacuated in 1783, to compensate American shipowners for vessels seized in the West Indies, and to allow some trade with British possessions. In return, the Americans pledged not to discriminate against British shipping and to pay debts owed to British subjects from before the Revolution.

Nothing was said about impressment, however, the issue most charged with emotion. Like Hamilton's fiscal policy, Jay's Treaty could be interpreted as benefiting only wealthy merchants.

Protest swept the country. When Washington submitted Jay's Treaty to the Senate for ratification, he was attacked personally for the first time, and not gently. Jay resigned from the Supreme Court and joked uneasily that he could travel the length of the country by the light of the effigies of him that were burned by furious Jefferson Republicans. Crowds shouted, "Damn John Jay! Damn everyone that won't put lights in his windows and sit up all night damning John Jay!"

It was, to say the least, an eruption of party spirit, for Washington, Adams, Hamilton, and their supporters did not damn John Jay. However disappointing the terms with which Jay returned, they believed he had done the country a service by preserving peace. They did not yet call themselves a party. With Washington in power, the Federalists dared not organize a formal party apparatus. But the lines between two political parties, already penciled in, were drawn a bit more clearly.

Pinckney's Treaty

The détente between Britain and the United States worried the Spanish too. Spain also had been warring with revolutionary France but, by the end of 1794, wanted out of the conflict. The French were willing to come to terms, but the

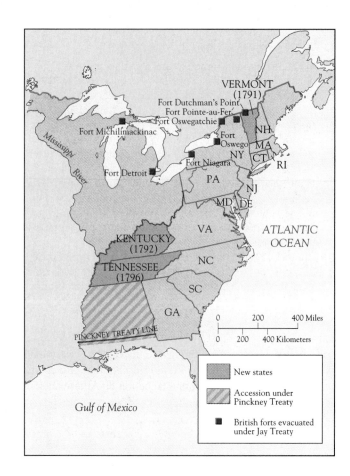

MAP 11:1 The Federalist Treaties Britain's agreement, in Jay's Treaty, to turn over seven frontier forts to the United States was a diplomatic victory but not perceived as such because the British had violated the Treaty of Paris in continuing to occupy them. In giving up, in Pinckney's Treaty, what are now the states of Mississippi and Alabama (except the Gulf Coast), Spain eliminated a dispute that would likely have led to war with the United States.

Spanish worried that, if they ended hostilities, the reconciled British and Americans might make common cause and invade Spanish Louisiana. The fear was not far-fetched!

To head off the possibility, Spanish ministers met with diplomat Thomas Pinckney and acquiesced to practically every demand that the Americans had made on Spain since 1783. In Pinckney's Treaty (officially the Treaty of San Lorenzo), Spain agreed to recognize the American version of the boundary between the United States and Louisiana, to open the Mississippi River to American navigation (the Spanish owned the western bank), and to grant Americans the "right of deposit" in New Orleans. The right of deposit allowed Americans to store their exports (mostly foodstuffs and timber) in New Orleans and to carry on the commercial transactions needed to dispose of them.

These concessions, which somewhat muted the resentment of Jay's Treaty, were invaluable to the more than 100,000 people who, by 1795, had settled in Kentucky, Tennessee, and the Northwest Territory.

THE TUMULTUOUS NORTHWEST

Life west of the Appalachians contrasted sharply with life on the Atlantic coast, settled now for up to seven generations. The killing labor of wrenching a farm out of a forest combined with disease to generate a death rate in the west as high as it had been in seventeenth-century Virginia and Maryland. The mountain barrier to transportation meant that manufactured goods, whether American or European, were expensive—when they were available. Western folkways reflected the hardships. Easterners saw frontier settlers as dangerously violent, "still more depraved than in Virginia," which, apparently, was saying something. "Like dogs and bears," it was said, "they use their teeth and feet, with the most savage ferocity, upon one another." And they used their firearms upon the numerous Indians who lived between the Appalachians and the Mississippi.

We the Marauding People

The federal government sincerely meant to keep the treaties it negotiated with the western tribes. It may have been delusory, but it was not cant when Congress wrote in the Northwest Ordinance of 1787 that "the utmost good faith shall always be observed towards the Indians; their lands and property shall never be taken from them without their Consent; and in their property, rights and liberty they shall never be invaded or disturbed."

Officials did not violate Indian treaties—the people did. New settlers, individually and in groups, crossed treaty lines and skirmished with Indians to whom the lands had been guaranteed. Nothing but "a Chinese Wall or a line of troops" could stop white "encroachment," an exasperated Washington exclaimed.

Nevertheless, when Indians responded violently to white incursions, the government came to the settlers' rescue.

MAP 11:2 Indian Wars in the Northwest Territory By abandoning their claims to southern and eastern Ohio in the Treaty of Greenville, the tribes of the Northwest Territory merely delayed further war with the expansive United States (as dissident Indian leaders protested). American settlers were soon moving north and west of the treaty line.

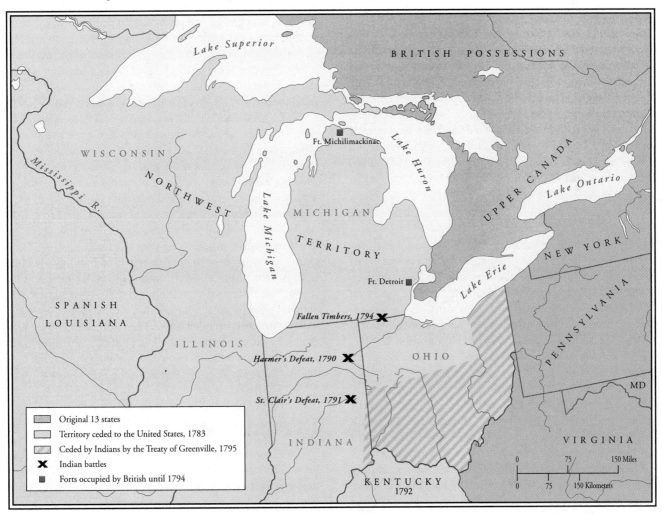

Dark and Bloody Ground

The most familiar image of Indian wars is set on the Great Plains in the latter nineteenth century. Here were the dramatic battles of pulp novel and film, the Seventh Cavalry in dusty blue battling mounted warriors of Sioux and Comanche in the wide-open spaces. In fact, the confrontations of the late eighteenth century between Americans and the tribes of the Northwest Territory—Miami, Shawnee, Ottawa, Ojibwa (Chippewa), Sauk, Fox—were fiercer and bloodier than the wars on the plains.

For one thing, the tribes of the Eastern Woodlands were more numerous than the Plains Indians. In the 1790s, supplied with firearms by the British in Fort Detroit, they were capable of fighting massive pitched battles. George A. Custer's column at the endlessly celebrated battle of Little Big Horn in 1876 numbered 265 men. In Ohio in 1794, General Anthony Wayne commanded an army 10 times that number. In Kentucky, casualties were so high that both Indians and whites called it "the dark and bloody ground."

In 1790, in retaliation for several Indian attacks on settlers, President Washington sent Josiah Harmer to subdue the Miami and Shawnee under the effective war chieftain Little Turtle. Poorly supplied, wracked by dysentery and malaria, and handicapped by unfamiliarity with the country, Harmer and his men were decimated near the site of present-day Fort Wayne, Indiana. The next year, a better-prepared expedition under Arthur St. Clair met the same fate; 600 soldiers were killed. Washington blamed both defeats on the fact that the soldiers were militiamen, for whom he never had a good word. In 1794, he sent General Anthony Wayne ("Mad Anthony") into Ohio with regular troops who defeated the Miami and Shawnee at the Battle of Fallen Timbers near Toledo. (The trees on the battlefield had been leveled by a tornado.) In the Treaty of Greenville, which followed, the tribes ceded the southern half of Ohio and a sliver of Indiana to the United States. The settlers had their way.

Of Pioneers and Whiskey

The men and women of the frontier were heavy drinkers. They launched their days with an "eye-opener" or "flem-cutter" of whiskey. A jug sat on shop counters; general stores doubled as saloons. Men and women swigged whiskey like wine with their meals and like water with their work. Preachers refreshed themselves with it during sermons. Virginian William Henry Harrison said that he "saw more drunk men in forty-eight hours succeeding my arrival in Cincinnati than I had in my previous life."

Disease played a part in the drinking. Frontier settlers suffered chronically from the alternating chills and fevers of malaria (they called it the "ague"). The medicine for which they reached was alcohol. Isolation contributed. Travelers in the Ohio Valley invariably described conversations with men, and especially women, who commented mournfully on the lack of company. Whiskey was a companion.

Finally, whiskey was cheap. The corn, wheat, and rye from which it was first made were easy to grow. The tech-nology was simple and required little labor: Ferment the mash of grain and water; boil it; condense the steam. Fuel was less than free—the wood from endless land clearing that had to be burned anyway. Many family farmers kept a small still percolating day and night. A market back east for the raw, white whiskey encouraged commercial distillers to set up large operations.

Of Whiskey and Rebellion

Whiskey became a cash crop because, before Pinckney's Treaty, westerners could not ship their grain down the Mississippi River. The cost of transporting such a low-value bulk commodity over the Appalachians was prohibitive. A pack horse could carry a burden of about 200 pounds: 4 bushels of corn, rye, or wheat. Four bushels of grain, in the food-rich United States, sold for pennies.

However, a horse could carry the equivalent of 24 bushels if the grain was converted into liquor. A gallon of whiskey sold for 25 cents or more, which provided just enough profit to make the trek plausible. Hamilton's excise tax of 1791 (7 cents per gallon) wiped the profit out. Like Daniel Shays' followers in Massachusetts, farmers in western Pennsylvania roughed federal tax collectors and rioted in river towns.

The parallels between Shays' Rebellion and the Whiskey Rebellion were not lost on Washington and Hamilton. They recognized an opportunity to demonstrate the contrast between the weakness of the old Confederation and the authority of the Constitutional government. The president himself set out at the head of 15,000 troops to suppress the rebels. He left the column when news reached him that the rebels had scattered. But Hamilton, who had a yen for military glory, pushed on and arrested a few Pennsylvanians who were convicted of treason and sentenced to death. Washington pardoned them, calling them mental defectives. Perhaps they were; perhaps it was just Washington's way of showing his contempt for the rebels and demonstrating that, among his other virtues, he did not thirst for blood.

In one sense, the suppression of the Whiskey Rebellion was a farce. An army as large as the one that had defeated the British—and much larger than the force at Fallen Timbers—was organized to crush a rebellion it could not even find. But the political significance of the episode was profound. The Federalist Hamilton was delighted to assert the national government's right to enforce order within one state with troops raised in other states. The resentment of the westerners, however, ensured that when political parties emerged full blown, they would not vote for Hamilton's party.

Federalists Versus Republicans

By the summer of 1796, when Washington announced that he would retire, warning Americans against political parties, two parties existed in everything but name. On every controversy that arose during Washington's presidency, Americans divided along the same lines.

▲ *The Whiskey Rebellion began with Pennsylvania frontiersmen assaulting federal tax collectors like this man, stripped, tarred, and feathered. Washington and Hamilton regarded the participants in the Whiskey Rebellion as what we would call "lowlifes," a judgment with which the artist agrees.*

Party Lines

The Federalists supported Hamilton's financial policy, abhorred the French Revolution as a fount of atheism and social disorder, were well disposed toward Great Britain, accepted Jay's Treaty, and believed that the federal government should act decisively and powerfully to maintain internal order. Vice President John Adams and Alexander Hamilton were the Federalists' chief spokesmen (although personally suspicious of one another). The party also included John Jay, the Pinckneys of South Carolina, conservatives like Gouverneur Morris of Pennsylvania, and, whether he liked it or not, George Washington himself. In New England, where money was made in trade and speculation, the urban rich were almost unanimously Federalist. In every state, Federalists were suspicious of "the people." "The many do not think," Massachusetts senator George Cabot put it.

The Jefferson Republicans opposed Hamilton's financial policies. Farmers (and some great planters) believed that they paid the taxes that financed funding and assumption while benefiting little from them. Republicans were friendly to the ideals of the French Revolution, although many of them cautiously. Republicans were generally suspicious of Britain as the former oppressor (Jefferson's anglophobia was lifelong) and as the ally and provisioner of the Indians in the west. Recent exiles from France and, after a rebellion was suppressed in 1797, from Ireland, were vociferously Republican. The Irish were, according to Connecticut senator Uriah Tracy, "the most God-provoking democrats this side of hell." Republicans despised Jay's Treaty. Inclining to democratic values that the Federalists spurned, the Republicans worried about a powerful national government quick to use soldiers against protesters such as those involved in the Whiskey Rebellion.

Washington the Villain

Washington was not universally adored. The invective heaped on him by editor Benjamin Bache (Benjamin Franklin's nephew) rivals anything found in newspapers today. In 1796, Bache wrote, "If ever a nation was debauched by a man, the American nation has been debauched by Washington." When Washington turned over the presidency to John Adams in March 1797, Bache exulted, "If ever there were a period for rejoicing, it is this moment. Every heart, in unison with the freedom and happiness of the people, ought to beat high in exultation, that the name of Washington ceases from this day to give a currency to political iniquity and to legalize corruption."

Election of 1796

Thomas Jefferson was the Republican candidate for president in 1796. Officially, Vice President John Adams of Massachusetts was the Federalists' man, and diplomat Thomas Pinckney of South Carolina, the Federalist vice presidential candidate. They were confident of victory. However, Hamilton, who could not resist a scheme, tried to manipulate the electoral college and put Pinckney in Adams's place. Pinckney dependably did Hamilton's bidding; Adams did not.

Hamilton's plot was possible because, before 1804, presidential electors did not vote separately for president and vice president. Each elector wrote two names on a ballot. The candidate with the most votes (it had to be a majority) became president, the runner-up, vice president. Because, in 1796, electors from nine states were selected by their legislatures—popular elections were held in just six states—Hamilton was able to persuade some Federalist politicians in the South to cast one of their two votes for Pinckney but the other, which should have gone to Adams, to somebody with no chance of winning. The hope was that enough southern Republicans would vote for Pinckney because he was a southerner that Pinckney would finish higher than Adams.

It might have worked. Hamilton's conspiracies were usually well thought out. But Adams's Federalist supporters in New England caught wind of the plot and retaliated by withholding votes from Pinckney. The result was anticipated by no one. Adams won but Pinckney did not finish second. Jefferson did. The president was the titular leader of one political party; the vice president was the actual leader of the other. The vice presidency was not a powerful office. But if the 61-year-old John Adams had died, his political rival, instead of a member of his own party, would have taken his place.

"His Rotundity"

After 200 years, it is easy to admire John Adams. When he was dispassionate, he was a moderate man who acted according to admirable principles. He could be humorous. When scandalmongers said that he had sent Pinckney to London to procure four loose women for his and Adams's use, he responded, "I do declare upon my honor, General Pinckney has cheated me out of my two." His relationship with his wife, Abigail, had a modern ring to it. He sought her advice on everything and often took it. "The President would not dare to make a nomination without her approbation," an opponent said. Adams was "always honest and often great," in Benjamin Franklin's words.

However, it is easier to admire Adams at a distance. He was also, as Franklin added, "sometimes mad." Neurotically insecure, he was vain and peevish. A raging temper often incinerated his judgment, and Adams could be laughably pompous. When wits sniggered at his short, dumpy physique ("His Rotundity," they whispered) and gossiped about his wife, Adams cut himself off, almost becoming a hermit. He spent astonishingly little time in the national capital, Philadelphia, until the last year of his presidency. During his four years as president, he spent one day out of every four at his home in Quincy, Massachusetts. By comparison, Washington was absent from his post fewer than one day in eight. The flaws in Adams's personality and the fact that he kept Washington's cabinet, almost all of them Hamilton's flunkeys, made the second president a president with only half a party behind him.

Another War Scare

Like Washington, Adams was preoccupied with the threat of war, this time with France as the enemy. Angered by Jay's Treaty, the French government ordered its navy and privateers to treat American ships as fair game. By the time Adams was inaugurated in March 1797, the French had seized 300 American vessels. Moreover, the French defined American sailors captured off British ships (many of whom had been pressed involuntarily into service) as pirates, who could legally be hanged. The American minister in Paris,

▲ *President John Adams, "His Rotundity," was able and principled but also "sometimes mad." He kept the United States out of a war with France despite extreme provocation and strident demands for war from his fellow Federalists.*

Charles Cotesworth Pinckney, was threatened with arrest. The French minister in the United States, Pierre Adet, railed against Adams almost as intemperately as Genet had assailed Washington.

Hamilton's supporters, the "High Federalists" who had reacted calmly to British seizures of American ships and sailors, demanded war with France. Determined to keep the peace, Adams dispatched two ministers, John Marshall and Elbridge Gerry, to join Pinckney in Paris, asking for negotiations.

The XYZ Affair

Marshall and Gerry were shunned for weeks, unable to get near the French foreign minister, the charming, devious, and corrupt Charles-Maurice de Talleyrand. Then, Talleyrand sent word through three henchmen—identified in code as "X," "Y," and "Z"—that he would speak with the Americans if they agreed in advance to a loan to France of $12 million and a personal gift to Talleyrand of $250,000.

Bribes were routine in diplomacy; but the sum Talleyrand demanded was excessive, and the tempers of the Americans were worn thin from waiting and humiliation. "Not a sixpence," Pinckney snapped. Back in the United States, Pinckney's reply was dressed up (and changed into the new American currency) as "millions for defense but not one cent for tribute."

The High Federalists were delighted by Talleyrand's insult. Hamilton pressured Adams to mobilize an army of 10,000 men. Washington agreed to become its titular commander on the condition that Hamilton be second in command. Not only did this mean Hamilton would jump rank over a large number of Revolutionary War officers, but it also humiliated Adams and put him in fear of a military coup.

Adams was more comfortable with the navy. He came from a maritime state, and sea power posed no threat to domestic order. (A country cannot be subdued from a ship.) Moreover, although it was difficult to say where France and America might fight on land, an undeclared war already raged on the seas. Adams authorized the construction of 40 frigates and lesser warships, a huge jump from the 3 naval vessels he inherited from Washington's administration.

The Alien and Sedition Acts

Jefferson's Republicans, still pro-French, trumpeted loudly against all preparations for war. The Federalists responded to the protest with a series of laws called the Alien and Sedition Acts of 1798.

The first extended the period of residence required for American citizenship from 5 to 14 years. This was a tacit admission that most newcomers to the United States were Republicans. Another Alien Act allowed the president to deport any foreigner whom he deemed "dangerous to the peace and safety of the United States." To leave no doubt of their political purpose, the Alien Acts would expire shortly after Adams's term ended in 1801.

The Sedition Act provided stiff fines and prison sentences for persons who published statements that held the United States government in "contempt or disrepute." Twenty-five cases were brought to trial; 10 people were convicted. Two Jeffersonians in Newark, New Jersey, were imprisoned because, when Adams was saluted by a volley of gunfire while visiting the city, one said, "There goes the president and they are shooting at his ass." The other responded, "I don't care if they fire through his ass." George Washington's nephew, Judge Bushrod Washington, ruled that these were seditious words exciting resistance to lawful government.

Other prosecutions were not so comical. In an effort to crush the opposition, Federalists convicted four important Republican newspaper editors of sedition.

The Virginia and Kentucky Resolutions

Jefferson and his protégé, James Madison, believed the Alien and Sedition Acts were unconstitutional, a violation of the Bill of Rights. But who was to declare when Congress enacted, and the president signed, a law violating the Constitution? The Constitution did not say. The answer Jefferson and

A Death in the Family

George Washington, 67 years of age, took to his bed in December 1799 with a sore throat and fever. Modern physicians have convincingly diagnosed a bacterial infection, strep throat. The existence of bacteria was unknown in 1799, but Washington's doctors could only have hastened his death. The gargles (tea and vinegar) and syrups (molasses, vinegar, and butter) to ease the pain in his throat could not have hurt, and the emetics (tartar and calomel) might have helped reduce his fever. But the bloodletting—bleeding patients by applying leeches to their skin—a therapy that doctors seem to have prescribed whenever they were confused, surely weakened the old man. The doctors took 82 ounces of blood in about a week: 5 pints! Blood donors today rest briefly after being relieved of a single pint.

Madison gave was to haunt American history for half a century and contribute to the Civil War of 1861 to 1865.

In the Virginia and Kentucky Resolutions, adopted in the legislatures of those states in 1798 and 1799, Madison and Jefferson wrote that the federal government was a voluntary compact of sovereign states. Congress, therefore, was the creation of the states. When Congress enacted a law that a state deemed to be unconstitutional, that state had the right to nullify the law within its boundaries. Acting on this principle, the Virginia and Kentucky legislatures declared that the Alien and Sedition Acts could not be enforced in those states.

The logic of the Virginia and Kentucky Resolutions had its merits, but their implications were ominous. They marked a return to the supremacy of states, which, under the Articles of Confederation, no one had denied. In doing so, they challenged the supremacy of the federal government, which, Federalists maintained, the Constitution was written to establish. Nothing came of the challenge in 1799. No other state embraced the resolutions. The death of George Washington in December 1799 briefly calmed political tempers, and, as the election of 1800 drew nearer, it became increasingly obvious that instead of helping the Federalists, the Alien and Sedition Acts were so unpopular that they improved the chances of a Republican victory.

The Bizarre Election of 1800

As it happened, Jefferson's electoral victory over Adams in 1800 was nearly as tight as Adams's victory over Jefferson in 1796, and it was marked by a far more calamitous confusion in the electoral college. Jefferson won 73 electoral votes to Adams's 65. The only significant change in the political alignment of the states was the switch of New York from the Federalist to the Republican column; with 19 electoral votes, New York was the third biggest prize in presidential elections. This neat trick was the handiwork of a man who was Hamilton's rival for control of the state and his equal in political scheming.

Aaron Burr, 44 years old, brilliant and creative, was the Republican vice presidential candidate who swung New York for the Republicans. However, because none of the 73 Republican electors dropped Burr's name from his ballot so that he would finish in second place, the official count had the New Yorker tied with Jefferson.

The Constitution provided (and still provides) that when no candidate wins an absolute majority in the electoral college, the House of Representatives, voting by states, not by individuals, chooses the president. In 1800, this gave the Federalists the balance of power. The votes of nine states were required for election. The Republicans, who dutifully voted for Jefferson, controlled only eight state delegations in the House.

A Vote for Stability

When the first ballot was taken, Jefferson received eight votes to Burr's six; two states were evenly divided. Most Federalists voted for Burr, some because they believed that Jefferson was a dangerous radical, others because they hoped to throw the Republicans into disarray. Burr did not actively lobby Congress on his own behalf. At the same time, he said nothing to help elect Jefferson. He went into seclusion and hoped.

After 35 deadlocked ballots, a Delaware Federalist, James A. Bayard, fearing that the crisis would destroy the national government, announced he would change his vote to Jefferson on the next ballot. In the end, he did not have to do so. Hamilton's agents had contacted Jefferson and extracted vague commitments that he would continue Federalist foreign policy and maintain the Hamiltonian financial apparatus. Just as important, Hamilton loathed Aaron Burr. If Burr became president, Hamilton said, he would form an administration of "the rogues of all parties to overrule the good men." He conceded that Jefferson had at least a "pretension to character."

It was not much of a compliment, but it was enough. Hamilton pressured a few Federalist congressmen from key states to abstain on the thirty-sixth ballot. Jefferson was elected on February 17, 1801, two weeks before inauguration day.

Recognition of Political Parties

The original method of selecting the president was based on the premise that electors dedicated to the health of the republic would select the best man to be president and the second best to be vice president. It worked only as long as George Washington was on the scene. The election of 1796 showed that party politicians were willing to manipulate the electoral process to serve factional ends. The election of 1800 demonstrated that parties were fixtures of the American political process.

The original procedure of electing the president was no longer workable. It promised manipulations ignoring popular elections every four years. In 1804, the Twelfth Amendment provided that, from then on, electors would vote separately for president and vice president—the system that survives today. The amendment tacitly recognized political parties, which made nominations, as part of the constitutional process.

FOR FURTHER READING

A solid survey of the period is John C. Miller, *The Federalist Era,* 1960. The person of George Washington loomed over the era, so Douglas S. Freeman, *George Washington,* 1948, 1957, remains basic. See also Marcus Cunliffe, *Man and Monument,* 1958; James T. Flexner, *George Washington: Anguish and Farewell,* 1972; Forrest MacDonald, *The Presidency of George Washington,* 1974; Edmund S. Morgan, *The Genius of George Washington,* 1980; and Garry Wills, *Cincinnatus: George Washington and the Enlightenment,* 1984.

On the Adams presidency, see Stephen G. Kurtz, *The Presidency of John Adams,* 1957; and Ralph Brown Adams, *The Presidency of John Adams,* 1975. David McCullough, the finest living American biographer, recently turned his attention to Adams with excellent results. See McCullough's *John Adams,* 2001. John Adams cannot be fully appreciated without reference to his thoughtful wife, whose advice he valued above that of any other person. See Lynne Withey, *Dearest Friend: A Life of Abigail Adams,* 1981.

The emergence of political parties in America is treated (with differing interpretations) in William D. Chambers, *Political Parties in a New Nation,* 1962; Joseph Charles, *The Origins of the American Party System,* 1956; and Richard Hofstadter, *The Idea of a Party System,* 1969. Also see Daniel Boorstin, *The Lost World of Thomas Jefferson,* 1948; and Merrill Peterson, *Thomas Jefferson and the New Nation,* 1970. On Jefferson's great rival, see Jacob E. Cook, *Alexander Hamilton,* 1982.

Sources for episodes of the 1790s include Harry Ammon, *The Genêt Mission,* 1973; Leland D. Baldwin, *Whiskey Rebels: The Story of a Frontier Uprising,* 1939; Gerald A. Combs, *The Jay Treaty,* 1970; Samuel F. Bemis, *Pinckney's Treaty,* 1926; Leonard W. Levy, *Legacy of Suppression: Freedom of Speech in Early America,* 1960; and James M. Smith, *Freedom's Fetters: The Alien and Sedition Laws and American Civil Liberties,* 1956.

  AMERICAN JOURNEY ONLINE AND INFOTRAC COLLEGE EDITION

Visit the source collections at http://ajaccess.wadsworth.com and http://infotrac.thomsonlearning.com, and use the Search function with the following key terms to explore documents, images, audio and video clips, articles, and commentary related to the material in this chapter:

Aaron Burr
Abigail Adams
Alexander Hamilton
George Washington

James Madison
John Adams
Whiskey Rebellion
XYZ Affair

Additional resources, exercises, and Internet links related to this chapter are available on *The American Past* Web site: http://history.wadsworth.com/americanpast7e.

HISTORY ONLINE

The Avalon Project
www.yale.edu/lawweb/avalon/debates/debcont.htm
A superb guide to the debates at the Constitutional Convention prepared by Yale Law School; includes a "Search" function.

White House
www.whitehouse.gov/history/presidents/index.html
An official government resource for presidents from George Washington to the present.

JEFFERSONIAN AMERICA

Expansion and Frustration 1800–1815

Smithsonian Institute, Bureau of American Ethnology

The immortality of Thomas Jefferson does not lie in any one of his achievements, or in the series of his achievements, but in his attitude toward mankind.

Woodrow Wilson

Since the days when Jefferson expounded his code of political philosophy, the whole world has become his pupil.

Michael MacWhite

IN 1962, PRESIDENT John F. Kennedy invited American winners of the Nobel Prize to the White House. He greeted them by saying, "This is the most extraordinary collection of talent, of human knowledge, that has been gathered at the White House, with the possible exception of when Thomas Jefferson dined here alone."

Kennedy was cleverer than he was precise. Nobelists are honored for profound contributions to knowledge. Jefferson's intellect was not deep; he was not an original thinker. But his intellect ranged more broadly than the combined intellect of a dozen research scientists. Few men and women—certainly no other American president—had so oceanic a breadth of interests and serious studies as the tall, slightly stooped man with graying red hair who took the presidential oath of office in March 1801.

THE SAGE OF MONTICELLO

After writing the nation's birth certificate, the Declaration of Independence, Jefferson was wartime governor of Virginia, then the Confederation's minister to France. He was the first secretary of state, and, from his home at Monticello in Virginia, a political strategist who, in dozens of letters a day, organized the party that elected him president in 1801.

Jack of All Trades

Jefferson was a scholar, constantly in a book, of which there were more than 6,000 in his personal library. He read and spoke several European languages and studied Native American tongues. He wrote better than any other president. His English was precise in vocabulary and mellifluous in its rhythms. He published only one short book, *Notes on Virginia,* but it was superb. His shorter works and letters (18,000 survive) fill bookshelves.

▲ *Monticello, Jefferson's home in Charlottesville, Virginia. He designed the home and supervised the large plantation and the great number of slaves who supported him. Here, for most of his life, he studied and carried on a correspondence that occupied many hours daily.*

Jefferson founded, and designed the buildings of, the University of Virginia. He designed Monticello and anonymously entered the competition of architects to design the president's mansion—the White House. He invented the dumbwaiter and the swivel chair. He was a gourmet who may have introduced pasta to America. He was a spendthrift. Shopping—frantic, expensive shopping—was a high priority when he lived in Paris and visited London. He spent as much as $2,800 a year on wines and $50 in a day on groceries when a turkey cost 75 cents. He employed French chefs at home and in Washington.

Mixed Reviews

Jefferson was no demigod. His vision of America's future was shallow next to Hamilton's. He could be as peevish as John Adams and more vindictive (perhaps only because he held power longer). He was no orator, partly out of shyness, partly because he was self-conscious of a lisp.

Nor was Jefferson universally admired—not by a long shot. Adams rarely missed an opportunity to snipe at him (although they were reconciled as old men). Hamilton thought him softheaded and frivolous. Other Federalists believed that he was a voluptuary and a dangerous radical. During the presidential campaign of 1800, the *Connecticut Courant* warned that Mad Tom's election would mean "your dwellings in flames, hoary hairs bathed in blood, female chastity violated, children writhing on the pike and the halberd." Not yet exhausted, the editor continued, "Murder, rape, adultery, and incest will be openly taught and practiced" in a

Wine Snob

Jefferson loved his wine and subjected many a guest at dinner to perhaps lengthier discourses on the nuances of the beverage they were sipping than they appreciated. It was a long-standing interest. As early as 1773, Jefferson gave Filippo Mazzei of Florence 200 acres adjoining his own plantation so that he could plant a vineyard from Italian cuttings. Unfortunately, just as it was beginning to produce, Mazzei enlisted to fight the British and never returned.

Jefferson believed that "we could in the United States, make as great a variety of wines as are made in Europe, not exactly of the same kinds, but doubtless as good." He planted several vineyards at Monticello (mostly Italian grapes) but never succeeded in pleasing his palate.

Jeffersonian America. Phlegmatic anti-Jeffersonians contented themselves with the gossip that one of Jefferson's slaves, Sally Hemmings, was his concubine.

JEFFERSON AS PRESIDENT

Jefferson knew he owed his election to Federalists in the House of Representatives. In his inaugural address, he attempted to woo those Federalists who were not "devoted to monarchy" by saying that "every difference of opinion is not a difference in principle. We have called by different names brethren of the same principle. We are all republicans, we are all federalists." Privately, he wrote of "honest and well-intentioned" Federalists.

Continuities

To a degree, the new president acted on his hint of transpartisanship. He quietly abandoned some prepresidential positions and adopted Federalist policies that he had condemned. Nothing more was heard from him or his secretary of state, James Madison, about the doctrine of nullification they had put forward in the Kentucky and Virginia Resolutions. Jefferson allowed Hamilton's financial program to work for him, including the Bank of the United States, which he had called unconstitutional. He appointed as secretary of the treasury the Swiss-born Albert Gallatin of Pennsylvania, who proved to be as responsible a money manager as his Federalist predecessors, without their coziness with northeastern speculators.

Republican Simplicity

Jefferson brought a new style to the presidency. He disliked the pomp and protocol that had been important to Washington and Adams. Instead of exchanging bows, he shook hands. He abolished presidential levees (regularly scheduled, highly formal receptions). Much to the annoyance of some officials and diplomats, he paid scant heed to protocol, the rules that assigned a rank of precedence—a chair at the dinner table, a position in a procession—to every senator, representative, judge, cabinet member, and minister from abroad. Even at state dinners, guests scrambled for the places they believed suited to their dignity. Indeed, Jefferson preferred small dinner parties at which he wore bedroom slippers and served the meal himself.

Jefferson's "republican simplicity" was made easier by the move of the capital, the summer before his inauguration, from sophisticated Philadelphia to Washington. It was no city at all in 1800, but a bizarre hodgepodge of partly completed public buildings and ramshackle boarding houses, isolated from one another by woods and marshes in which strangers often got lost. There were precious few private homes; for years, there would be no place in Washington for congressmen's families. Social life was masculine and on the raw side: smoky card games, heavy drinking, brawls, even the odd gunfight.

Changes

Not all Jefferson's innovations were stylistic. He pardoned the people imprisoned under the Sedition Act, all of whom were his supporters, of course. He restored the five-year residency for citizenship and replaced Federalist officeholders with Republicans. (There were not many jobs to bestow. In 1800, the government employed 3,000 mostly part-time post office workers, 700 clerks, and just 316 people appointed by the president.)

Jefferson and Gallatin slashed government expenditures, reducing the army's budget from $4 million to $2 million and the navy's from $3.5 million to $1 million. Their army consisted of only 3,000 troops; the navy, of just seven ships. Gallatin devised a plan to retire the national debt by 1817.

But these actions hardly constituted the "Revolution of 1800" that Jefferson called his election. The only fundamental innovation in the government during the Age of Jefferson was effected by Jefferson's enemy (although his cousin), the Federalist chief justice of the Supreme Court, John Marshall.

Marbury v. Madison

Shortly before Adams turned the White House over to Jefferson, he appointed 42 Federalists to the bench. Federal judges served for life, so Adams was securing long-term employment for loyal supporters. He also wanted to ensure that the judiciary, which was independent of both presidency and Congress would remain a bastion of Federalist principles.

Adams was setting a precedent. The appointment of "midnight judges" (and issuing last-minute pardons) would become standard operating procedure for outgoing presidents whose party had been defeated at the polls. Like incoming presidents who would follow him, Jefferson could only sit and steam to contemplate the salaries that were lost to his own Republicans.

The case of William Marbury was an exception. Thanks to the inefficiency and oversight that would also become a feature of American government, the document that entitled Marbury to a judgeship was not delivered before March 4, when Jefferson took office. On the face of it, Adams's dereliction was immaterial. According to the Judiciary Act of 1789, the secretary of state—James Madison as of March 4, 1801—was obligated to deliver Marbury's commission. When Madison refused to do so, Marbury sued for a writ of mandamus—a court order that compels a government official to perform his duty (*mandamus* is Latin for "we compel").

By 1803, the case was before the Supreme Court, dominated for three decades by Chief Justice Marshall. The force of his personality was so great, his willingness to do the lion's share of the Court's work so eager, and his legal mind so acute, that Marshall almost always had his way with the other justices. In the case *Marbury v. Madison,* Marshall scolded Madison for unseemly behavior. However, instead of mandating him to deliver Marbury's commission, Marshall ruled that the section of the law under which Marbury had sued was unconstitutional. Congress, Marshall said, had no constitutional right to give the federal courts the powers that the Judiciary Act of 1789 accorded them.

The Doctrine of Judicial Review

Marbury v. Madison was a masterstroke. By sacrificing the paycheck of one Federalist politico and canceling part of one Federalist law, Marshall asserted the Supreme Court's right to decide which acts of Congress were constitutional and which were unconstitutional and therefore void. The Supreme Court not only judged cases *according to* the law; the Court judged the validity of the law itself.

Nothing in the Constitution vested the Court with this substantial power. Jefferson and Madison had claimed it for the state legislatures. And Marshall did not decisively confirm the power for the Supreme Court. Only usage—very cautious usage—established judicial review as unquestioned. (The next time the Supreme Court declared an act of Congress unconstitutional was in 1857.)

Jefferson could not fight Marshall on high ground. Instead, he approved a campaign of machinations against the Federalist judiciary. First, he tried to get rid of Federalist judges by abolishing their jobs. Then, the Republicans impeached and removed from office a Federalist judge in New Hampshire, John Pickering. That was easy; Pickering was given to drunken tirades in court and was probably insane. Jefferson's supporters then inched closer to Marshall by impeaching Supreme Court justice Samuel Chase.

Chase was an inferior jurist, grossly prejudiced, overtly political, sometimes asinine. But the Senate refused to find him guilty of the "high crimes and misdemeanors" that the Constitution sets as grounds for impeachment. Like other presidents unhappy with the Supreme Court, Jefferson had no choice but to wait until seats fell vacant. He was able to name three justices, but they too were captivated by Marshall's mind and will.

THE LOUISIANA PURCHASE

If John Marshall tweaked the Constitution, Jefferson gave it a mighty wrench in the most significant act of his presidency, the purchase of Louisiana from France for $15 million. The Louisiana of 1803 was not the present-day state of that name. As a French (later Spanish) colony, Louisiana included the better part of the 13 states that, today, lie between the Mississippi River and the Rocky Mountains, 828,000 square miles. The United States paid less than three cents an acre, the greatest real estate bargain of all time.

Sugar and Food

Such a deal was possible only because the French emperor, Napoleon Bonaparte, abandoned the notion of creating a new French American empire, an idea he had toyed with. His plan was based on the fact that France's possessions in the West Indies—the islands of Martinique, Guadeloupe, and Saint-Domingue (present-day Haiti)—were valuable producers of sugar and coffee but also vulnerable because their large slave populations depended on food imported from Spanish Louisiana and the United States to survive.

Napoleon's plan was to force Spain, a client state, to return Louisiana to France, after which the West Indian islands would no longer be dependent on American foodstuffs. There were only about 50,000 people of European descent in Louisiana, but the endless lands bordering the Mississippi River invited agricultural development. In 1801, Napoleon regained Louisiana (supposedly in secret, but France's reacquisition of the territory was well known).

A Vital Interest

At Napoleon's request, the Spanish revoked the right of deposit that Pinckney's Treaty had guaranteed—the right of Americans to store and trade their products in New Orleans. The response among the 400,000 Americans who lived in Kentucky, Tennessee, and the Northwest Territory was near panic. They annually shipped 20,000 tons of provisions down the Mississippi to New Orleans on log rafts, which they broke apart and sold in the city for lumber. To westerners, in James Madison's words, the Mississippi was "the Hudson, the Delaware, the Potomac, and all the navigable rivers of the Atlantic formed into one stream." Jefferson added, "There is on the globe one single spot, the possessor of which is our natural and habitual enemy. It is New Orleans."

War with France seemed inevitable. Congress voted funds to call up 80,000 state militiamen. But any attack on New Orleans would require a naval blockade of the port as well as an overland assault, and Jefferson was in the process of eviscerating the American navy. The British, sworn enemies of Napoleon, would be glad to lend a hand, but such an alliance was repugnant to a president who had written the Declaration of Independence.

An Offer Not to Be Refused

Jefferson gambled that there was an alternative to war arm-in-arm with the British. He instructed his minister in France, Robert R. Livingston, to offer Napoleon $2 million (voted him by Congress) for a tract of undeveloped land on the lower Mississippi, where the Americans might build their own port. In January 1803, impatient that no news had arrived from France, Jefferson gambled: He sent James Monroe to Paris to offer up to $10 million (a sum that had appeared in no congressional appropriation) for New Orleans and West Florida—what is now the Mississippi and Alabama coast.

When Monroe arrived, he was stunned to learn that, a few days earlier, the French foreign minister, Talleyrand again, had offered Livingston all of Louisiana for $15 million.

This remarkable turnabout had nothing to do with American wants and needs. Louisiana had become worthless to Napoleon. Black rebels in Haiti, France's most valuable West Indian colony, both slaves and free men, had battered a crack French army. Some 30,000 French troops were killed in battle or incapacitated by tropical fevers. "Damn sugar," Napoleon said on hearing of the debacle. "Damn coffee. Damn colonies! Damn niggers!"

He might have damned Britain too, for he was planning for war with the old enemy, and he knew that the Royal Navy would promptly and easily seize New Orleans and Louisiana.

Constitutional Niceties

The Louisiana Purchase was sealed despite the fact that it was without congressional or even constitutional sanction. The Founding Fathers had made no provision for acquiring territory or, as required by the terms of the sale, conferring United States citizenship on the residents of Louisiana. But it was far too great an opportunity to be rejected.

Some Federalists called Jefferson a hypocrite for abandoning, with a vengeance, his strict constructionist theory of the Constitution. Jefferson—one hopes sheepishly—wrote that "what is practicable must often control what is pure theory." He instructed Republicans in Congress that "the less we say about constitutional difficulties respecting Louisiana the better." Even members of Jefferson's party far more zealous in their legalism than he, like John Randolph and John Taylor of Virginia, held their tongues. What is beneficial and practicable must indeed control what is pure theory.

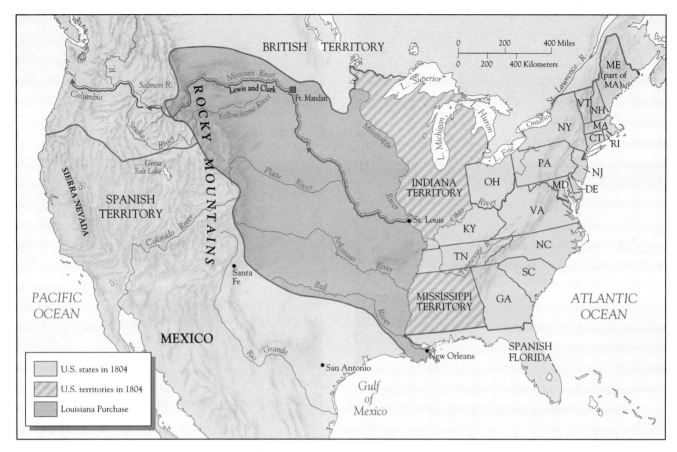

MAP 12:1 **The Louisiana Purchase and the Lewis and Clark Expedition, 1804–1805**   The Louisiana Purchase virtually doubled the size of the United States. Little was known about the new land and its peoples, however, until a series of explorations that began with the great journey of the Lewis and Clark expedition up the Missouri River and down the Columbia.

The Northwest Passage

The first explorers of North America were looking for a "northwest passage"—a sea route to East Asia through or around the top of the continent. In 1592, Juan de Fuca claimed to have found it from the Pacific and that it was an easy 20-day trip through a land rich in gold. Others looked vainly for de Fuca's "Strait of Anian." Despite their failure, belief in the strait's existence did not completely die until the time of the American Revolution, when explorers James Cook and George Vancouver conjectured, surely correctly, that de Fuca had sailed around Vancouver Island from the north and, reaching open sea, figured it was the Atlantic, then returned the way he had come.

When Jefferson sent Lewis and Clark across the continent, all hoped they would find a workable passage to the Pacific, that is, a *mostly* water route. They found the Rocky Mountains.

Throughout the nineteenth century, intrepid adventurers attempted to sail ships between North America and the Arctic ice cap, no longer in hopes of a trade route but so as to be treated to dinner at the Explorer's Club. A few survived, although their ships were crushed by the ice. Finally, success was attained. In 1958, the first nuclear submarine, *Nautilus,* circled North America by cruising under the ice cap.

The Magnificent Journey

Louisiana aroused Jefferson's lifelong interests in natural science and the still mysterious interior of the continent. He persuaded Congress to appropriate $2,500 to finance an expedition across the continent for the purposes of looking for a feasible overland trade route and to gather scientific data.

African American Explorer

In the informality demanded by wilderness, William Clark's slave, York, participated in the great expedition as an equal. Meriwether Lewis recorded that when many Indians first saw York, they believed he was a white man wearing paint. Only after trying to rub his color from him did they accept York's explanation of himself. Lewis noted that "instead of inspiring any prejudice, his color served to procure him additional advantages from the Indians," a decorous way of saying he had a way with the Indian ladies who wanted a black child. Clark freed York after the expedition, but not gracefully. Despite what he and his human property had accomplished together, Clark wanted to keep York in bondage. York and Clark's friends wore him down only after considerable effort.

▲ *York was one of the most valuable members of the Lewis and Clark expedition, a party of men and one Indian girl who were selected so carefully as to be a perfect complement. He was William Clark's slave and, despite his services, Clark had to be pressured to reward him with his freedom by friends disturbed by Clark's reluctance to do so.*

Jefferson entrusted the mission to a Virginian neighbor, Meriwether Lewis, and William Clark, Lewis's friend and former commanding officer. He must have yearned to go himself, for he attended to the most picayune details of preparation, listing in his own hand the provisions the explorers would need.

The trek exceeded anything ventured by conquistadores or voyagers. Lewis, Clark, and a crew of 40 rowed, poled, and pulled their skiffs up the Missouri to the river's spectacular falls (present-day Great Falls, Montana). After portaging 16 miles, they enlisted the help of the Mandan, Shoshone, Nez Percé, and other tribes of the region to find a tributary of the Columbia River. Following it, they reached the Pacific on November 15, 1805. There they lived four and a half months and returned to St. Louis in September 1806.

Lewis and Clark were among the last Americans to confront Indians untouched by Western civilization. Their experience is instructive. Although there were a few uneasy moments with the Sioux and Shoshone on the trip west, the explorers engaged in nothing resembling a fight with the dozens of tribes they confronted. (They did kill two Blackfoot on their return trip.) Almost all the native peoples of the interior were hospitable. When Lewis needed to show he was not a member of a hated tribe, he exposed his arm to show his skin was white. York, Clark's slave (freed at the end of the expedition), was a source of endless fascination among the Indians because of his color.

The Shoshone, with whom the expedition could communicate through Sacagawea (a Shoshone teenager who joined the expedition), gave key advice on finding the Pacific, which the Shoshone themselves had never seen. The tribes of the Pacific Coast, however, had traded with American and European seamen, whalers, and fur traders. One woman had the name "Jonathan Bowman" tattooed on her leg. The coastal Indians had adopted as their own the words "misquit, powder, shot, nife, file, damned rascal, son of a bitch."

Jefferson believed that the country Lewis and Clark traversed would provide land for Americans for a thousand generations. His estimate was off by 999. By the 1820s, Americans were trudging through Louisiana to settle in Mexican Texas. There was no frontier line anywhere in the purchase by 1890.

The Further Adventures of Aaron Burr

Louisiana also figured in the bizarre career of Aaron Burr. His fortunes tumbled downhill immediately after his election as vice president in 1801, when Jefferson snubbed him

▲ *Aaron Burr as a young man, painted by Gilbert Stuart. He was a handsome, charming, intelligent, and persuasive man. He was also a rogue grounded in few principles and ruined his political career with his schemes and passions.*

because of Burr's behavior in the election controversy. And Burr, like Adams and Jefferson, found that the vice presidency provided him with little to do.

When men like Burr are bored, they scheme; when Burr schemed, he schemed big. With a few embittered New England Federalists (called the "Essex Junto"), he plotted, apparently, to detach New York and New England from the United States. The plan depended on Burr winning election as governor of New York, but he was defeated, in part because of campaign propaganda authored by Alexander Hamilton. Burr challenged Hamilton to a duel.

Hamilton disapproved of dueling. His son had only recently been killed in a duel. But the feud was beyond shrugging off, and, on July 11, 1804, the two men and their seconds rowed across the Hudson with 0.54 caliber pistols to Weehawken, high on the New Jersey Palisades. They fired at one another from 20 paces. Hamilton's bullet went astray; some said he deliberately shot high, as reluctant duelists often did. Burr aimed; his bullet pierced Hamilton's liver and lodged in his spine. Hamilton died the next day.

The first secretary of the treasury was never beloved, but the death of so eminent a man in a duel shocked the nation. Burr was indicted for murder in New York and New Jersey. He fled to the South while friends ironed out his legal difficulties. Not yet 50 years of age and full of energy, his political career was finished. What next?

The Burr Conspiracy

Like thousands of his contemporaries, Burr went west. He linked up with one Harman Blennerhasset, an Irish exile who lived opulently, on wealth never explained, on an island in the Ohio River. Blennerhasset constructed 13 flatboats, including a barge for Burr outfitted with glass windows, a fireplace, a promenade deck, and a wine cellar. With 60 men, the flotilla meandered down the Ohio and the Mississippi.

Burr met secretly with Andrew Jackson, a prominent politician and soldier in Tennessee, and, in New Orleans, with the head of the Ursuline convent, Louisiana's most powerful woman. He had a number of discussions with James Wilkinson, the territorial governor of Louisiana and a character so devious as to make Burr look like a bumpkin.

What was up? Burr was accused variously of planning to invade Spanish Mexico and of organizing a secession of the western states and Louisiana Territory from the United States. Jefferson was of a mind to believe the worst. When Wilkinson, possibly in a panic over what he had considered, accused Burr of plotting treason, Jefferson had the New Yorker arrested and returned to Richmond, where he was tried before Chief Justice John Marshall.

Marshall was apt to snipe at anything dear to Jefferson, even if it was to the benefit of the likes of Aaron Burr. He insisted on defining treason strictly, as requiring an overt act. No matter: The prosecution's case was sloppy, few accusations were corroborated, and the unsavory Wilkinson was a weak reed on which to support an allegation. Nothing of substance was proved against Burr, and he was acquitted.

Burr moved abroad for a few years, then returned to New York, where one more scandal put him back in the newspapers. His second wife, Eliza Bowen Jumel, formerly a prostitute, claimed to be the only woman in the world to have slept with both George Washington and Napoleon Bonaparte.

FOREIGN WOES

Like Washington and Adams, Jefferson found foreign affairs a frustration. In fact, Jefferson helped to set himself up for trouble by allowing Adams's navy to dwindle to a few ships. He soon learned that a country with vital interests in international trade had to be able to protect its merchant ships.

The Barbary Pirates

One trouble spot was the Mediterranean, where the economy of the Barbary ("Berber") States—Morocco, Algiers, Tunis, and Tripoli—was based on piracy. The Berbers seized

Tribute to the Pasha
The annual payment to the pasha of Tripoli, which Jefferson attempted to cancel in 1801, consisted of $40,000 in gold and silver, $12,000 in Spanish money, and an odd assortment of diamond rings, watches, and fine cloth and brocade. The rulers of the Barbary States thought of these as gifts from friends rather than as extortion. For example, in 1806 the bey of Tunis, who also received tribute, sent Jefferson a gift of four Arabian horses.

▲ *Stephen Decatur led several punitive expeditions to the Barbary States. Here he is shown bombarding Tripoli (in present-day Libya). His assaults were effective and popular at home, but it was only when France began to establish imperial control of North Africa that the menace of the pirates was put to rest.*

the vessels of seafaring nations that did not pay annual tribute to their beys and pashas. France, Britain, Spain, Holland, and Venice found paying "protection money" cheaper than maintaining warships to protect their thousands of Mediterranean merchant ships. During the 1790s, the United States paid too, about $2 million.

The indignity of it rankled on Jefferson, who ignored the demands of the pasha of Tripoli for another installment. Tripolitan pirates promptly seized the crew of an American ship and demanded ransom. Jefferson ordered a punitive expedition. After four years of intermittent bombardment and a daring amphibious attack by marines led by Stephen Decatur (commemorated in "to the shores of Tripoli" in the Marine Corps hymn), Jefferson gave up, paying Tripoli $60,000 for the release of captive Americans, a transaction not immortalized in song. Barbary Coast piracy, kidnapping, and slave trading continued for another decade until Decatur returned to North Africa, and France began to establish imperial control over North Africa.

America in the Middle Again

A more serious threat was the war between France and England that began shortly after the purchase of Louisiana. Jefferson declared neutrality, and, at first, American shipowners were delighted to reap profits trading with both sides. Especially lucrative was the reexport trade—West Indian products brought to the United States and then shipped to Europe under the neutral American flag. In two years, this business more than quadrupled in value, from $13 million to $60 million.

Then, in 1805, the Anglo-French conflict reached an impasse with the Royal Navy supreme at sea and Napoleon unchallengeable on the European continent. Both sides dug in for a protracted economic war, each aiming to ruin the other by crippling its trade. The British issued the Orders in Council, forbidding neutrals to trade in Europe unless their ships first called at a British port to purchase a license. New England merchants, who inclined to be pro-British, did not find the Orders in Council intolerable. However, Napoleon retaliated with the Berlin and Milan decrees of 1806 and 1807, enacting what he called the "Continental System": Any neutral vessels that observed the Orders in Council would be seized by the French.

American merchants were caught in the middle. Within a year, the British seized 1,000 American ships, and the French, about 500. Even then, the profits from successful voyages more than compensated for the losses. One Massachusetts senator calculated that if a shipowner sent three vessels out and two were dead losses, the profits from the third made him a richer man than he had been. Statistics bear him out. In 1807, at the height of the seizures, Massachusetts merchants earned $15 million in freight charges alone.

A British press gang boards an American merchant ship and takes a resisting seaman for service in the Royal Navy. If he lived and later proved he was American-born and had never served in the British Navy, he would be released (thousands were)—but not compensated for his impressment.

The patriotic uproar was deafening. The *Chesapeake* was no merchant ship taking a chance on a commercial expedition but a naval vessel cruising American waters. Jefferson had to act. He chose what he called "peaceable coercion."

The Embargo

Under the Embargo Act of 1807, American ships in port were forbidden to leave. Foreign vessels were sent to sea in ballast (carrying boulders or other worthless bulk in their hulls). All imports and exports were prohibited. The embargo was total economic war, designed to force the British, who also benefited from American trade, to respect American claims.

For Jefferson, who had seen economic boycott bring Parliament around during his youth, the embargo looked like a sure thing. In 1807, however, the British were at odds not with their own colonies but with a national rival sworn to reduce Great Britain to a dependency. The British wanted American trade, but not at any price.

Americans suffered more from the embargo than Great Britain did. Staple farmers lost their foreign markets, the livelihood of many of them. Seaports suffered across the

Impressment Again

Richly paid humiliation is a situation with which a great many human beings have lived and always will. However, the issue in the wars of the 1800s involved more than the balances in American ledgers. Britain's massive naval effort also meant a renewal of the impressment problem of the 1790s. Chronically short of sailors, British captains once again began to board American merchant vessels and draft crewmen who, they insisted, were British subjects. There were plenty of such men on American vessels. Conditions under the American flag were much better than on British ships, the pay sometimes three times as much. As many as a quarter of the 42,000 seamen on American ships were born in Britain.

The trouble was, many of them had become American citizens, a transfer of allegiance British captains did not recognize. Yet others impressed into the Royal Navy were American by birth. About 10,000 bona fide citizens of the United States (by American standards) were forced to serve in the Royal Navy during the Napoleonic Wars. Some 4,000 were released as soon as they reached a British port, but, at sea, arrogant or merely desperate naval officers were grabbing more.

The impressment crisis came to a head in June 1807, when, within swimming distance of the Virginia shore, the HMS *Leopard,* with 50 guns, ordered the lesser American frigate *Chesapeake* to stand by for boarding. The American captain refused, and the *Leopard* fired three broadsides, killing several sailors. A British press gang then boarded the *Chesapeake* and removed four men, including two American-born black men who had once served in the Royal Navy.

The Two-Term Tradition

When Washington rejected a third term as president, he made no point of principle about it. He was old and tired, he said. In 1805, beginning his own second term, Jefferson consciously founded the two-term tradition. He wrote of Washington's example, "I shall follow it, and a few more precedents will oppose the obstacle of habit to anyone after a while who shall endeavor to extend his term. Perhaps it may beget a disposition to establish it by an amendment to the Constitution."

Madison, Monroe, and Andrew Jackson all retired after two terms. So did Ulysses S. Grant in 1877; however, in 1880, broke and not yet old, he tried (unsuccessfully) to run again. Theodore Roosevelt retired after nearly eight years in office, although, having been elected only once, he could have run again without violating the tradition. Like Grant, Theodore Roosevelt also tried to return to the White House four years after leaving it. Woodrow Wilson and Calvin Coolidge would both have liked to have a third term but dared not say it, so powerful had the tradition become. Only in 1940, with Europe at war, did Franklin D. Roosevelt seek and win a third term (and four years later, a fourth).

Franklin D. Roosevelt's defiance of the tradition—not the precedents for which Jefferson hoped and got—resulted in the constitutional amendment Jefferson imagined. In 1947, Republicans who had simmered during Roosevelt's long presidency, took a posthumous slap at him by proposing the Twenty-Second Amendment to the Constitution. It forbids a president to serve more than two terms. Ironically, the two presidents since who could probably have won a third term were popular Republicans, Dwight D. Eisenhower and Ronald Reagan.

board. Ships rode at anchor, rotting; tens of thousands of seamen and shore laborers had no work; businesses dependent on their wages struggled if they did not close their doors. The Federalist party, badly maimed when Jefferson was reelected in 1804, began to make a comeback in maritime New England and New York.

By early 1809, the embargo had cost the American economy three times the estimated price of a war. The protests were so loud and widespread that Congress, though overwhelmingly Jeffersonian, was forced to abandon it. Joylessly, Jefferson signed the bill. In just three days, his handpicked successor, the ever dependable James Madison, would be sworn in as president. Jefferson would not burden him with his debacle.

JEMMY APPLEJOHN AND THE WAR OF 1812

James Madison was a profound student of political philosophy. He is still widely read not out of curiosity but for his wisdom. But Madison was not cut out to be head of a government. He was the butt of gossipy sarcasm, even ridicule, in the highest circles. Short and slight, he encouraged perceptions of him as weak with interminable complaints of aches, pains, and ailments. (Madison's constitution was sound enough—he lived on, sniffling, moaning, and groaning, until he was 85.) His face was pinched by furrows, inspiring the writer Washington Irving to quip that "Little Jemmy" looked like a "withered applejohn," that is, an apple that had been dried so as to be stored. He was "too timid" in the words of a critic, Fisher Ames, and "wholly unfit for the Storms of War" according to his supporter, Henry Clay.

The Non-Intercourse Act and Macon's Bill No. 2

The embargo expired on March 15, 1809, and was superceded by the Non-Intercourse Act. The act reopened trade with all nations *except* England and France and provided that the United States would resume trading with whichever of those two belligerents agreed to respect the rights of neutral American shipping. But all Jefferson and Madison had done (Jefferson signed the Non-Intercourse Act before Madison's

---

The Emperor of America

President Madison was content to be addressed as "Mr. President." But, in one communiqué, the bey of Algiers called him "His Majesty, the Emperor of America, its adjacent and dependent provinces and coasts and wherever his government may extend, our noble friend, the support of the Kings of the nation of Jesus, the most glorious amongst the princes, elected among many lords and nobles, the happy, the great, the amiable, James Madison, Emperor of America."

---

inauguration), like chess players of limited skill, was to open the board for a gambit by cleverer players.

The British moved. David Erskine, the British minister to Washington, agreed to American terms, and Madison opened trade with Britain. Then, back in London, the British Foreign Office repudiated Erskine's treaty. Madison was humiliated.

A year later, in May 1810, the Jefferson Republicans replaced the Non-Intercourse Act with Macon's Bill No. 2. It *opened* commerce with both Britain and France, with the proviso that if either of the two ceased to molest American shipping, the United States would cut off trade with the other. In other words, the United States would take its licks at sea for the present but collaborate with the belligerent power that stopped harassing American ships. If the object was to stay out of all-out war, Macon's Bill No. 2 was the worst of the three Jeffersonian trade laws. It effectively proclaimed America's willingness to become an ally of either France or Britain in their economic war.

This time, Napoleon advanced a pawn. With no intention of depriving French privateers of the pleasure of taking American prizes, he revoked the Continental System. Madison, as Macon's Bill No. 2 required, terminated trade with Great Britain. Economically, Americans were allies of France. The British were alarmed. On June 16, 1812, so as to reopen trade with the United States, they canceled the Orders in Council.

It was too late. Only two days later, with the news still aboard a ship just catching the winds out of Britain, Madison bowed to war fever at home and asked Congress for a formal declaration of war against Great Britain. It had been a series of miscalculations, stupidities, and blunders—the history of humanity compressed into five years.

The War Hawks

Madison said that the War of 1812 was fought to defend American shipping and the security of American seamen. However, the mercantile states did not want "Mr. Madison's War." New England, New York, and New Jersey voted 34 to 14 against it. Not a single Federalist congressman voted for war (and the antiwar Federalists increased their contingent in Congress, mostly in the mercantile states, from a low of 24 in 1808 to 68 in 1814).

Who wanted the War of 1812? Jefferson Republicans, almost all of them representing agricultural regions, where, if salt water was needed, people had to dump salt into a cistern. Pennsylvania, the South, and the western states voted 65 to 15 in favor of war.

The prowar party was led by an exuberant claque of congressmen known as the "War Hawks." The Hawks were young—none as old as 40—with the cocky belligerence of youth, and no personal experience of being colonials. To them, the War for Independence was history taught by superpatriotic teachers, authors, and relatives. They were learned anglophobes, the most strident kind. They were ultranationalists who dreamed of conquering Canada and annexing it to the United States.

Socializing on the Frontier

When Europeans traveled through newly opened parts of the United States, they invariably complained about the food of the frontier—greasy fried salt pork and cornmeal mush or fire-roasted corn bread. Many were shocked by the westerners' heavy drinking. But most of all, they shuddered at the isolation of the people building a life in a new country. The Europeans who wrote books about their American experiences were sophisticated and literate; they were accustomed to a full social life. Outside of a few cities, there was nothing like that beyond the Appalachian ridge.

Frances Trollope, an English woman who wrote a celebrated book, *The Domestic Manners of the Americans,* blamed the emotional excesses of western religion on the absence of recreation and of release from daily toil and tedium, even in the large river port of Cincinnati. "It is thus," she wrote, in the shrieking, howling, and rolling around the floor that she witnessed at churches, "that the ladies of Cincinnati amuse themselves; to attend the theatre is forbidden; to play cards is unlawful; but they work hard in their families and must have some relaxation."

Just a few miles outside of Cincinnati, Trollope met a hard-bitten frontier woman who showed off her farm and boasted that it produced everything the household consumed except tea, sugar, and whiskey. When Trollope prepared to depart, her hostess sighed and said, "'Tis strange for us to see company; I expect the sun may rise and set a hundred times before I shall see another *human* that does not belong to the family."

Frontier life was lonely, but it was not without social occasions. In the 1820s, William Cooper Howells, a printer who saw northern Ohio develop from wild forest into a populous industrial center, looked back on the parties of his youth with fond nostalgia. Ohio pioneers, Howells wrote, combined amusement with work.

The raising of a cabin or barn was done collectively by neighbors. The host had cut all the logs he needed. They were brought to the building site by means of a community "logroll." The men who best handled an ax notched the logs at each end; others raised them into place. "The men understood handling timber," Howells wrote, "and accidents seldom happened, unless the logs were icy or wet or the whisky had gone around too often." Howells himself, still quite a young man in Ohio's early years, took pride in taking on the job of "cornerman." While others built the walls, he "dressed up" the corners with an ax. "It was a post of honor," he wrote. The job was less laborious

North Wind Picture Archives

than that of raising the walls, but it took a head that "was steady when high up from the ground."

When a gathering of men for such a purpose took place there was commonly some sort of mutual job laid out for women, such as quilting, sewing, or spinning up a lot of thread for some poor neighbor. This would bring together a mixed party, and it was usually arranged that after supper there should be a dance or at least plays which would occupy a good part of the night and wind up with the young fellows seeing the girls home in the short hours or, if they went home early, sitting with them by the fire in that kind of interesting chat known as sparking.

In addition to logrolling and barn raisings, the tedious task of processing flax (for linen and oil) was done in combination with a community party. Other tasks—splitting logs into rails for fences, for example—were spiced up by holding a competition. Abraham Lincoln first ran for political office on his reputation as a virtuoso rail splitter. But by far the most enjoyable kind of work party, remembered wistfully in practically every reminiscence of the frontier, was the husking bee. Not only was the job of husking Indian corn less laborious than other jobs that took place in the autumn, when the harvest was done and the weather was cool. It was also the season when good food was most abundant and spirits were highest.

The ears of corn to be husked were divided into two piles. Two captains chose up sides, selecting their teams alternately from among the young men, boys, young women, and girls. The two teams started husking, standing with the heap in front of them. They threw the husked corn to a clear space over the heap and tossed the husks (for animal fodder) behind them. From the time they began until the corn was all husked, there was no pause except to take a pull at the jug of inspiration (whiskey) that passed along the line.

When one team had finished husking, it let out a great shout (which was the signal to lay a community dinner on the table), briefly exchanged taunts for the excuses of the losers, and then helped the losers finish their husking. Another rule of the game that increased interest was the provision that a boy who husked a red ear could claim a kiss from one of the girls at the party. But Howells concluded, "I never knew it necessary to produce a red ear to secure a kiss when there was a disposition to give or take one."

In 1812, the notion of conquering Canada was not far-fetched. Many Americans, and not just Loyalists, had settled in Upper Canada, the prime lands north of Lake Ontario.

Some were open about their desire to be Americans again. A few Canadians with no American connections preferred the American political system to their colonial status. Militarily, the prospect never looked better. Great Britain, obsessed with defeating Napoleon in Europe, had reduced the professional army in Canada to just 2,200 soldiers. Canadian militias had no better a reputation than American state militias.

The only discouraging factor was the power and effectiveness of the Indians of the Northwest Territory and western New York. They were well supplied by the British, were staunch British allies, and had been reinvigorated by a remarkable religious revival. Then, in November 1811, that formidable impediment to American aggression seemed to crumble.

The Prophet's Revival

For two decades, Canada's defense had depended on the Delaware, Pottawottamie, Miami, some Iroquois, Shawnee, and other peoples living south of the Great Lakes. Defeated and demoralized in 1794, about 10 years later, ever increasing numbers of these tribes were converted to the gospel of a reformed Shawnee drunk, Tenskwatawa, whom the whites called the "Prophet."

Tenskwatawa's religious message was one that would be heard again in Native American history: In order to stop the relentless advance of white settlers—in order, indeed, to rid the Indians' world of them—Indians must forget ancient tribal hostilities and join together. They must abandon the ways of the whites they had embraced—living in American-style houses, wearing clothing made of purchased cloth, using the white man's tools. The Prophet preached that Indians must extinguish their fires, for they had been ignited using the whites' flint and steel, and start new ones by Indian methods. Most important of all, they must give up alcohol, so obvious to all as a major reason for Indian dissipation.

There were other purification ceremonies. Like other founders of new religions, once Tenskwatawa got started, he found it difficult to stop. Despite the gospel of pan-Indian

Smithsonian Institute, Bureau of American Ethnology

▲ *Tecumseh, a Shawnee chief born about 1768 and killed in battle in 1813, was the most thoughtful and effective of the many Indian leaders who tried to unite formerly hostile tribes in order to stop the advancement of white settlers into their homeland. The blunders of others, rather than his own mistakes, doomed him.*

cooperation, his followers killed shamans who opposed the Prophet and drove out Indians who remained Christian.

"Panther Lying in Wait"

The religious revival did not concern white settlers until, after 1808, Tenskwatawa's followers began to concentrate their numbers in Tippecanoe (Prophetstown) in western Indiana and the Prophet's brother, Tecumseh ("Panther Lying in Wait"), made himself, by force of intelligence and personality, chief of a confederation of virtually all the tribes of the Northwest Territory.

Where Tenskwatawa was a cockeyed mystic and no warrior (he was morbidly obese), Tecumseh had both feet on the ground and a reputation for bravery in battle dating back to the victory over St. Clair in 1791, when Tecumseh was only a young brave. Tecumseh understood the whites' culture better than his brother, for he had lived within it for 10 years. In 1798, he formed a friendship with an Ohioan, James Galloway. He studied Galloway's library of 300 books and, in 1808, proposed marriage to his daughter, Rebecca. She consented, but on the condition that Tecumseh abandon Indian ways and live like an American.

Instead, Tecumseh joined his brother at Tippecanoe, becoming the political and military leader of his followers. Tecumseh saw to it that firearms were removed from the

American Hero
Aside from low-life western Indian haters, the kind William Henry Harrison said considered "the murder of the Indians in the highest degree meritorious," Americans admired and respected Tecumseh as much as they feared him. Richard M. Johnson of Kentucky, who claimed to have killed him at the Battle of the Thames, built his political career (he rose to be vice president) on little else. In Lancaster, Ohio, in 1820, where memories of the live Tecumseh were still vivid, a boy was born and named for the great chief. There may have been many others. We know of this one because he was William Tecumseh Sherman, one of the key generals in the winning of the Civil War.

Tecumseh was depicted as a heroic figure in John Dorival's *Battle of the Thames,* painted in 1833, and as godlike in Frederick Pettrick's *The Dying Tecumseh,* begun in 1837. More books have been written about Tecumseh than about William Henry Harrison and Richard Johnson combined.

Prophet's list of taboos and ended persecution of Indians who did not unquestioningly embrace the Prophet's every teaching. He embarked on long journeys to enlist more tribes in his pan-Indian confederation and rarely failed, as western whites soberly noted. Tecumseh was the greatest leader Native Americans ever had. None of his contemporaries sold him short. The British in Canada regarded him as their most important ally. William Henry Harrison, territorial governor of Indiana, called him "one of those uncommon geniuses who spring up occasionally to produce revolutions and overturn the established order of things."

In 1811, Tecumseh embarked on the most important of his journeys, deep into the South, to enlist the powerful Cherokee, Creek, Choctaw, and Chickasaw in his confederacy. Had he succeeded and launched a coordinated attack on the frontier from Lake Michigan to the Gulf of Mexico, the white westerners would have suffered a devastating defeat.

It was not to be. Tecumseh had ordered the Prophet to keep the peace until he returned. However, in November 1811, William Henry Harrison arrived at Tippecanoe, camping about a mile away with 1,000 men. Harrison had come to fight but was alarmed by the size of the Indian force, possibly 3,000 braves. He was considering withdrawing when the Prophet, knowing his superior numbers, ordered an attack. The Indians came within an ace of overrunning the Americans, but the Americans held, won the day, totally leveled Tippecanoe, and made Harrison a hero.

No longer did the War Hawks in Washington have to pause when they were reminded of Tecumseh's confederacy.

Bunglers in Battle

The assault on Canada was, nonetheless, a fiasco. New York militia refused to cross the Niagara River. They delayed their mass desertion only long enough to watch a duel between two American officers (which Canadians across the river also enjoyed). Surprised at American ineffectiveness, the British, Canadians, and Indians counterattacked and captured Detroit. An Indian force destroyed the stockade at Chicago, then called Fort Dearborn.

A Canadian-Indian offense (in five of the seven land battles of the war, Indians formed the bulk of the enemy forces) was stalled when, in September 1813, Captain Oliver Hazard Perry, although outgunned by a Canadian-British flotilla, secured control of Lake Erie for the Americans. Receiving Perry's famous message, "We have met the enemy and they are ours," William Henry Harrison then led 4,500 men toward York (now Toronto), the capital of Upper Canada.

There, the British and Canadians proved as inept as the Americans and, according to Tecumseh, who had returned from the south, cowards. He told the commanding British general, "We must compare our father's conduct to a fat dog that carries its tail upon its back, but when afrightened drops it between its legs and runs off." Harrison defeated the combined British, Canadian, and Indian force at the Battle of the Thames and burned the public buildings in the city. Tecumseh was killed.

In the meantime, the British invaded New York via Burgoyne's route and were stopped at Lake Champlain, again by the navy commanded by Captain Thomas Macdonough. Ironically, although the Americans won few victories on land, American naval forces on both the lakes and the ocean won most of their encounters.

The British revenged the burning of York in August 1814 when they launched a daring amphibious raid on Washington, D.C. The troops burned the Capitol and the White House. British officers claimed that they ate a dinner, still warm, that had been set for James and Dolley Madison. In fact, the president narrowly escaped capture when he drove out to view a battle and the American army fled without fighting.

New Orleans

The British had not wanted war, but, when Napoleon abdicated in the spring of 1814, freeing troops for American service, the British combined the beginning of peace talks at Ghent in Belgium with a plan to seize lower Louisiana from the United States. An army of 8,000 excellent soldiers was dispatched under General Sir Edward Pakenham to attack New Orleans. What augured to be a disaster for the Americans turned out to be an amazing victory and the making of a national hero, Andrew Jackson of Tennessee.

A self-taught lawyer, slave-owning planter, land speculator, Indian fighter, and duelist, Andrew Jackson cobbled together a force of 2,000 Kentucky and Tennessee volunteers, New Orleans businessmen, two battalions of free blacks, some Choctaw Indians, and artillerymen employed by a pirate-businessman, Jean Laffite. Jackson threw up

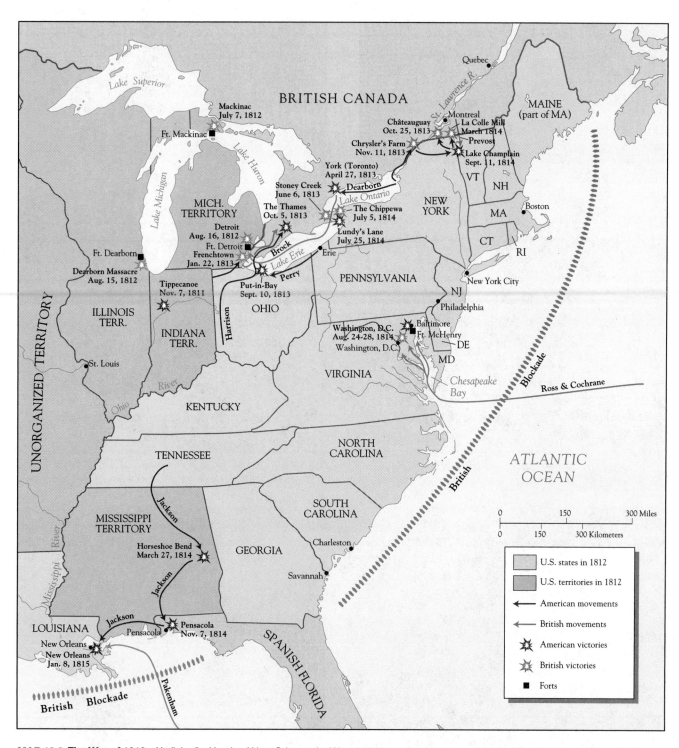

MAP 12:2 The War of 1812 Until the final battle of New Orleans, the War of 1812 was fought at sea and on the Canadian-American border. The war is unique in that the capitals of both combatants were burned by the enemy, York (now Toronto) in April 1813, Washington, D.C., in August 1814.

earthworks 5 miles south of New Orleans, the Mississippi River on his right, an impenetrable swamp on his left. He had created a wide-open battlefield with his army entrenched, textbook perfect.

Disdainful of his motley enemy, Pakenham sent his soldiers through the morning fog on a frontal assault. Laffite's cannoneers raked them with grapeshot, and, when the redcoats were 200 yards from the earthworks, the riflemen opened up with "a leaden torrent no man on earth could face." More than 2,000 redcoats fell dead—1 in 4 on the expedition! Miraculously, only seven Americans were killed, four of them when they mindlessly pursued the fleeing British. (After the battle, Jackson hanged as many American soldiers for desertion as were killed during it.)

▲ *In August 1814, British raiders burned the public buildings of the nation's capital in retaliation for the burning of York (Toronto), the capital of Upper Canada.*

▲ *The Battle of New Orleans. Like many patriotic paintings, this splendid one was more concerned with arousing national pride (and celebrating Andrew Jackson) than with accuracy. The British troops never got closer than a hundred yards from the American position. General Jackson did not direct the battle from a vantage where he could be easily killed by the enemy.*

The Treaty of Ghent, which restored British-American relations to what they had been before the war, was actually signed before the Battle of New Orleans was fought. Nevertheless, the news of the astonishing victory had an electrifying effect on the country. So glorious a conclusion to an ill-advised, unnecessary, and calamitous war seemed a reaffir-mation of the nation's destiny. When, within three years, Jackson crushed the powerful Creek tribe in the southeast and Stephen Decatur returned to the Barbary Coast to sting the Algerians, Americans could imagine they had won respect in a world where armed might was a measure of greatness.

for FURTHER READING

A nineteenth-century classic provides an excellent overview of this period: Henry Adams, *History of the United States During the Administration of Thomas Jefferson and James Madison,* 1889–1891. The most thoroughgoing biography of Jefferson is Dumas Malone, *Jefferson and His Time,* 6 vols., 1948–1981; of Madison, Irving Brant, *James Madison,* 6 vols., 1941–1961. See also Marshall Smelser, *The Democratic Republic, 1801–1815,* 1968; Noble Cunningham, *The Jeffersonian Republicans in Power,* 1973; Merrill Peterson, *Thomas Jefferson and the New Nation,* 1970; and Robert A. Rutland, *The Presidency of James Madison,* 1990. Controversial from the day it was published, but an enjoyable read, is Fawn Brodie, *Thomas Jefferson: An Intimate Biography,* 1974.

Alexander Deconde, *This Affair of Louisiana,* 1976, treats the great purchase in detail. The reigning standard on the Lewis and Clark expedition is Stephen Ambrose, *Undaunted Courage: Meriwether Lewis, Thomas Jefferson, and the Opening of the American West,* 1996. But students should also go to the horses' mouths: Bernard DeVoto, ed., *The Journals of Lewis and Clark,* 1953. Jefferson's problems with John Marshall are treated in Richard Ellis, *The Jeffersonians and the Judiciary,* 1971. On Marshall himself, see Leonard Baker, *John Marshall: A Life in Law,* 1974. For "Mad Tom's" other great nemesis, see Nathan Schachner, *Aaron Burr,* 1984.

On the brief renaissance of the Ohio Valley Indians, see R. David Edmunds, *Tecumseh and the Quest for Indian Leadership,* 1984. On the War of 1812, see Reginald Horsman, *Causes of the War of 1812,* 1962, and *The War of 1812,* 1969; and Donald R. Hickey, *The War of 1812: A Forgotten Conflict,* 1989.

  AMERICAN JOURNEY ONLINE AND INFOTRAC COLLEGE EDITION

Visit the source collections at http://ajaccess.wadsworth.com and http://infotrac.thomsonlearning.com, and use the Search function with the following key terms to explore documents, images, audio and video clips, articles, and commentary related to the material in this chapter:

Aaron Burr
James Madison
Lewis and Clark
Louisiana Purchase
Marbury v. Madison

Sally Hemmings
Tecumseh
Tenskwatawa
Thomas Jefferson

Additional resources, exercises, and Internet links related to this chapter are available on *The American Past* Web site: http://history.wadsworth.com/americanpast7e.

HISTORY ONLINE

Historical Maps of the United States
www.lib.utexas.edu/Libs/PCL/Map_collection/histus.html
Reproductions of period maps tracing the territorial growth of the United States.

The War of 1812
www.multied.com/wars.html
A collection of text, pictures, and maps dealing with the War of 1812.

BEYOND THE APPALACHIANS

The West in the Early Nineteenth Century

When I reflect that all this grand portion of our Union, instead of being in a state of nature, is now more or less covered with villages, farms and towns . . . that hundreds of steamboats are gliding to and fro over the whole length of the majestic river . . . When I remember that these extraordinary changes have all taken place in the short period of twenty years, I pause, wonder, and although I know it all to be fact, can scarcely believe its reality.

John J. Audubon

THE APPALACHIANS ARE not high as mountains go, and there were narrow passes—gaps—through which people, livestock, and, with a little clearing and excavation, vehicles could cross. Western Pennsylvania, the banks of the Ohio River, and much of Kentucky and Tennessee were populated by subsistence farmers, with ambitions to amount to more, before 1800. "Development," however, the creation of a society approximating the society of the original states, with a diversified economy and rich people as well as poor, awaited the new century. Then it was "development" at a rate that exceeded anything that had ever been seen, even in colonial America. The runaway growth of the West, in itself, seemed to justify America's independence of Great Britain.

THE FIRST AMERICAN WEST

By 1830, a quarter of the American population dwelled west of the Appalachians. A majority had been born "back East." The westerners, or their parents, had cut their ties, packed up what they could cart, and struck off to where land was cheap and, therefore, the future lay. Land was synonymous with opportunity in the ordinary American's mind.

The West, which was to loom large in the American imagination for a century, was as much an idea as a place. By 1830, the word *frontier* was defined in the United States rather differently than it was in Europe. In Europe, a frontier was a boundary between principalities. In America, it came to mean exclusively the belt of territory where white civilization phased into wilderness and the domain of the Indians. No one spoke of the Canadian "frontier": That was a *border*. It was the Kentucky "frontier." European frontiers were moved in fits and starts, most commonly after wars. The American frontier was a place of constant motion and chronic conflict.

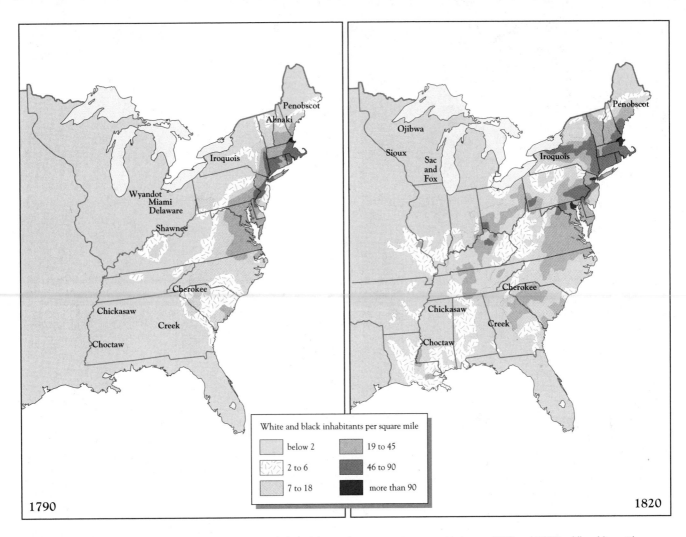

MAP 13:1 Population Density, 1790–1820 The population of the northeastern states soared between 1790 and 1820, while white settlers (and, in the South, their slaves) displaced Indian tribes throughout the trans-Appalachian West.

White and black inhabitants per square mile

- below 2
- 2 to 6
- 7 to 18
- 19 to 45
- 46 to 90
- more than 90

1790

1820

Population Explosion

Between 1800 and 1820, the population of present-day Mississippi grew from 8,000 to 75,000. Alabama, with about 1,000 whites and blacks in 1800, was home to 128,000 in 1820.

The states north of the Ohio River grew even more dramatically. In 1800, there were 45,000 white people in Ohio and a very few blacks, all free because of the Northwest Ordinance. Ten years later, the state's population was 230,000. By 1820, Ohio was the fifth largest state in the Union! By 1840, with 1.5 million people, it was fourth. Only New York,

Pennsylvania, and Virginia had larger populations. Ohio, little more than a generation old, was home to more people than Finland, Norway, or Denmark.

Between 1800 and 1840, the white population of Indiana grew from next to nil to 685,856; Illinois, from a few hundred to 476,183. In 1800, American Michigan consisted of one wretched lakefront fort inherited from the French and British. In the 1830s, New Englanders flocked as thickly as passenger pigeons to Michigan's "oak openings," small fertile prairies amidst hardwood forests. Already by that time, the Mississippi itself had ceased to be the frontier. Missouri, on the west bank of the river, had been a state for 10 years.

Ohio, the Forty-Eighth State

Congress could be casual about the proprieties in 1803. On March 1, it seated Ohio's first representatives while neglecting to vote to admit Ohio as a state. The oversight was rectified only 150 years later when Congress voted to admit the forty-eighth state on August 7, 1953.

People on the Move

The abundance of land is not enough to explain this extraordinary influx of people. Russia was blessed with even more land to the east and had a larger and poorer population in its heartland. However, Siberia attracted few Russians until the government dragooned people into moving there. Americans

▲ *The Conestoga wagon was the vehicle of choice for easterners emigrating to the trans-Appalachian West. Dogs were a must—to keep other dogs away from the oxen—but the artist was mistaken to show the driver whipping the oxen. They were prodded and kept moving by constant repetition of voice commands. You could hear an ox team coming.*

as a people seemed inherently restless, as agitated as the "painters" (panthers) they chased deeper into the woods and swamps. To Europeans, and sometimes to themselves, Americans seemed incapable of putting down roots.

The young couple saying their marriage vows and promptly clambering aboard a wagon to head west was as familiar a scene in New England as stone fences between cornfields. During the first decades of the century, white Virginians, some with slaves, headed across the mountains as rapidly as a high birthrate could replace them. In central and western Pennsylvania, the site of a major wagon road west, the economy was closely tied to emigration. Inns and the stables of horse traders dotted the highways. The Conestoga Valley gave its name to the wagon its inhabitants manufactured, a high-slung, heavy-wheeled vehicle designed for travel where there were no roads.

"In the United States," marveled Alexis de Tocqueville, the most observant of foreign tourists, "a man builds a house in which to spend his old age, and he sells it before the roof is on." An Englishman looking over lands in the Ohio Valley reported that if, to be polite, he admired the improvements a settler had made, the man was likely to propose selling everything on the spot so that he could begin again farther west. There was a joke that, in the spring, American chickens crossed their legs so they could be tied up for the next push.

PATTERNS OF SETTLEMENT

Some of these pilgrims were simply antisocial, the "eye gougers" and "frontier scum" of legend and lore. Others were as respectable as the King James Bible and wanted as much company as they could persuade to join them. They meant to re-create the way of life they knew back East, only better, with title to much more land between their house and their neighbor's.

Yet others were developers—a profession still with us and sometimes still honored—dreamers, schemers, and promoters of new Edens, Romes, and Lexingtons. Indeed, the men who, like Abraham Lincoln's father, Tom, made a business of clearing a few acres and building a cabin to sell to a newcomer were developers of a small sort. Rather more important were those who purchased large tracts of land, trumpeted its glories, and sold subdivisions at a profit.

Town boosters named streets before a tree was felled in imagined intersections. Some were merchants or even manufacturers who planned to stay and prosper as the country grew. Others were professional boomers who made their bundle and moved on, as rootless as hunters and trappers, never to invest another thought in the communities they created.

Cities

The military was the cutting edge on some frontiers. Soldiers posted in the West to keep an eye on Indians had to be fed, clothed, and entertained. Shopkeepers, saloon keepers, and log-cabin prostitutes clustered around lonely military installations. The security of the fort encouraged trappers, hunters, and others who tramped the woods to congregate there in winter and during times of Indian trouble. Indians hooked by American goods, alcohol all too often, gathered there. Their wants stimulated the growth of a mercantile economy before there was much tillage in the neighborhood. Vincennes, Detroit, and other towns that were originally French forts developed in this way.

In other areas, cities came first. Only after a fairly advanced (if not refined) urban life had evolved did the hinterland fill in with farmers to provision the town. Cincinnati, Louisville, Lexington, and Nashville were true, if small, cities before agriculture was well developed in the surrounding country. Occupying good locations at which river travelers could tie up their keelboats, canoes, and rafts, they also served as jumping-off points for emigrants. When the cotton lands of the lower Mississippi Valley began to boom, sending out calls for provisions for their slaves, the citizens of the river ports responded with shipments of grain and livestock. Cincinnati, "the Queen City of the West," became famous for its slaughterhouses and packing plants when, not many miles away, the great hardwood forests blocked the sun from the earth and lonely men and women battled malaria.

There were other kinds of manufacturing in the woods. In 1815, when there were no more than 15 steam engines in the whole of France, a nation of 20 million people, half-tamed Kentucky boasted six steam mills that turned out cloth and even paper. Before the War of 1812, St. Louis had a steam mill that was six stories high. Like medieval cities determined to outdo the cathedral of the next nearest city, Cincinnati built a mill nine stories high.

By 1828, in fact, Cincinnati boasted nine factories building steam engines, nine cotton mills, 12 newspapers, 40 schools, two colleges, and a medical school. A metropolis, but unmistakably western: Only one street was paved, and pigs were everywhere.

Speculation as a Way of Life

Such rapid development encouraged heated financial speculation. Many people went to Ohio or Michigan or Alabama neither to farm, run a shop, nor pack pork. They were speculators, men with some capital and plenty of big ideas about growing rich by the timeless, if risky, game of buying land cheap and selling it dear. Some were sharpers by anyone's definition, out to line their pockets and let the buyers beware.

Others were responsible—"builders"—who supervised an orderly development which was, indeed, preferable to the semisavage disorder of the squatter frontier. In a country where growth was the essence of life, just about everyone who could spare (or borrow) a few dollars was attracted, on at least a small scale, to buying land to sell to others.

Daniel Boone is remembered as a hunter, a trailblazer, and an Indian fighter. He thought more about acquiring land in the hope of selling it. He was not very good at speculation; Boone was repeatedly ensnarled in lawsuits he usually lost because he was too disgusted to show up in court. A speculator, shady or ethical, had to spend a lot of time in the company of lawyers and judges. Tom Lincoln had his failures too. When he sold his Indiana farm in 1830, with improvements made over 14 years, he was paid less than the cost of the forest he had purchased. John Crockett, the father of fabled

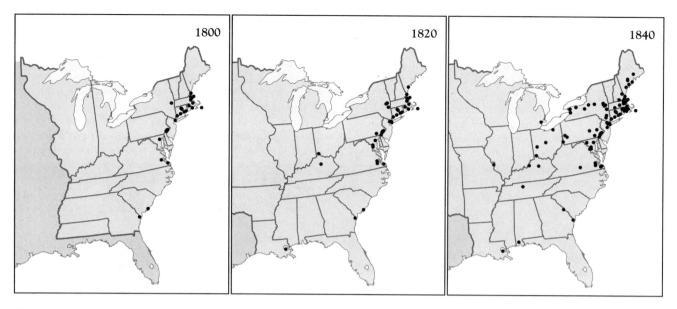

MAP 13:2 Cities of At Least 5,000 Inhabitants, 1800–1840 Eastern cities grew rapidly between 1800 and 1840, but most striking, as shown in these maps, was the emergence of cities in the West where there had been virtually no whites or blacks before the new century.

Davy, managed to move from clearing forest to owning a gristmill and inn, but he was never far from bankruptcy.

Land Policy

The speculative mentality made the price at which the government disposed of its land a matter of considerable interest. (All western land, except for old French grants in the Louisiana Purchase, was government land.) During the 1790s, the federal government offered tracts of 640 acres of western lands at a minimum price of $1 an acre—cash. Settlers protested that 640 acres were more than a family could work, and $640 more than ordinary folks could raise. From the Federalist point of view, the complaint was irrelevant. The land would be developed by the inevitable demand for it by a growing population. Administrative efficiency and the Federalist inclination to favor men of capital dictated that the government be a wholesaler, disposing of the land in large chunks and leaving the retailing of small farms to the private sector.

Jefferson's Republicans, in power after 1800, believed in disposing of land in such a way as to favor the people who actually settled on it with plow and oxen. Jefferson's idealization of the independent, small family farmer mandated a liberal land policy: "The price of land is the thermometer of liberty—men are freest where lands are cheapest." In 1804, a Jeffersonian Congress authorized the sale of tracts as small as 160 acres. The minimum price was $2 an acre, but a buyer needed a down payment of only $80 and could pay the balance of $240 over four years.

The Land Act of 1804 made the government a retailer and a very obliging one. However, it neither shut out sharpers nor satisfied settlers. Sales on credit actually benefited speculators because, unlike conservative emigrants uneasy about debt, speculators had no compunctions about borrowing heavily and making down payments on as much land as possible. The idea—or at least the hope—was that they would sell at a profit before the second installment came due.

"Wildcat banks," often irresponsible, sprang up all over the West to encourage and—again, it was hoped—to profit from credit speculators. On printing presses carted over the mountains, they churned out paper money with which borrowers made their down payments to the government land office. For a while after the War of 1812, the wildcat banks did quite well. Land sales soared. In 1815, the government sold about 1 million acres; in 1819, more than 5 million.

Much of it went for a higher price than the government minimum: Before land was let go at $2 an acre, it was offered at auction. Auctions also favored speculators. Settlers with families had budgets. They were often unable to bid on the most attractive land against pathological optimists who cared little how much borrowed money they handed across the counter. Some government lands in the cotton belt sold for more than $100 an acre—on paper.

Booms and Busts

The speculative boom in western lands depended, as does all speculation, on greed and the human species' marvelous capacity for self-delusion. Speculation—in land, gold, dot-com stocks, or, as in seventeenth-century Holland, tulip bulbs—is built on the principle of "the greater fool." One person pays an irrationally high price for a commodity on the assumption that there is a greater fool just around the corner chafing to pay him even more. A great deal of money

▲ *Chicago, in 1834, was a collection of rude buildings on a muddy flat on Lake Michigan. Its explosive growth came only later, when it became the northern terminus of the Illinois Central Railroad, the western terminus of several eastern lines, and the eastern end of several transcontinental railroads.*

has been made in speculation. When easy money and greed couple, they beget a great many fools.

A great deal of money has been lost in speculation too. If foolishness is infinite, the supply of potential buyers is not. When it runs dry, and speculators conclude that prices have peaked and it is time to get out and run, the result is a bust, a crash. When big players liquidate their supply of tulip bulbs or land at a modest loss, others follow at a moderate loss, and prices plummet, with the last in line losing everything. When speculators dealt in borrowed money, as the western land speculators of the 1810s did, a significant drop in values was enough to cause a panic to sell so that at least some loans might be repaid. Indeed, if the lenders—the bankers—decide that values are declining, they can trigger a panic by calling in their loans, forcing speculators to sell at whatever prices they can get.

The Panic of 1819

This is what happened in 1819. The directors of the Bank of the United States (BUS), cautious and conservative eastern gentlemen, began to worry about the freewheeling practices of the western banks. They called in the money those banks owed the BUS.

Having loaned their resources to speculators (many times over—the paper money they issued far exceeded what the BUS had loaned them), the wildcat banks called in their loans. When speculators were unable to repay because they could not sell the land on which they had made down payments, the whole paper structure came tumbling down (to use an expression coined the previous century, "the bubble burst"). Speculators as rich in acres as Charlemagne could not meet their obligations to either the banks or the Land Office. Wildcat banks folded by dozens, leaving those thrifty souls who had deposited money in them broke. Worthless banknotes went to the outhouse, the land reverted to government ownership, and the BUS lost money and grew more conservative.

In 1820, chastened by the disaster, Congress abolished credit purchases and tried to dispose of the lands that had reverted to the government by reducing the minimum tract for sale to 80 acres and the minimum price per acre to $1.25. With financial recovery, the speculators were back. In the meantime, western settlers had devised several ways of dealing with speculators and other problems of living beyond the mountains.

PROBLEMS AND PROGRAMS

The word *squatter* has a disagreeable ring to it today, but in the context of the West in the early nineteenth century, it should not. Squatters were settlers who, out of innocence, ignorance, or orneriness, began to develop farms on the public domain before they purchased the land on which their cabins and barns stood. Such improved property was particularly attractive to speculators; buildings and a cleared field substantially increased the land's value. When government surveyors and the Land Office arrived, many squatters saw their claims "jumped." The home they had built on government land was purchased at auction by a newly arrived slicker with a wad of borrowed banknotes in his purse.

In some areas, squatters combated these speculators by vigilante action. Banded together in "land clubs," they promised physical reprisals against anyone who bid on a member's land. Not infrequently, they made good on their threats. But speculators could respond by hiring thugs and cutthroats, never in shortage on the frontier, and more than a match for ordinary farmers. And the law was on the speculators' side.

"Old Bullion" Benton

So it was to the lawmakers that the squatters and other ordinary westerners turned. Their hero was Thomas Hart Benton, called "Old Bullion" because he despised paper money; gold bullion was the only money for him. Born in North Carolina, Benton was among the earliest American settlers in Missouri. Although well read in the classics and supremely eloquent, Benton knew how to turn on the boisterous bluff that appealed to rough-hewn westerners. "I never quarrel, sir," he told an opponent in a debate. "But sometimes I fight, sir; and when I fight, sir, a funeral follows, sir."

Elected senator from Missouri shortly after the Panic of 1819, Benton inveighed at every turn against bankers, paper money, and land speculators. He fought consistently throughout his long career for a land policy that would shut all three out of the West.

Benton's pet project was preemption, or, as it was popularly known, "squatter's rights." Preemption provided that the man who actually settled on and improved land before

---

Western Rhetoric

The following statement was made before a land auction in Missouri by Simeon Cragin, who was not, it would seem, a settler, but himself a speculator:

I own fourteen claims, and if any man jump one of them, I will shoot him down at once, sir. I am a gentleman, sir, and a scholar. I was educated at Bangor, have been in the United States Army, and served my country faithfully. I am the discoverer of the Wopsey, can ride a grizzly bear, or whip any human that ever crossed the Mississippi, and if you dare to jump one of my claims, die you must.

Frontier Violence

The Mississippi Valley frontier's reputation for violence may have been overstated. John J. Audubon, who wandered the region for 25 years, collecting and painting specimens of birds and animals, thought so. He was personally threatened only once, in 1812. As an Indian had warned him, frontier thugs planned to rob and kill him at the cabin where he was lodging. Fortuitously, two more travelers arrived before bedtime, and nothing happened.

"Indeed," Audubon wrote, perhaps in an overstatement of his own, "so little risk do travelers run in the United States that no one born there dreams of any [violence] to be encountered on the road."

---

the government officially offered it for sale would be permitted to purchase it at the minimum price. He would not be required to bid at an auction.

Another Benton program was "graduation." Land that remained unsold after auction would be offered at one-half the government minimum, and after a passage of time, at one-quarter. In a word, the price of the land was graduated downward in order to increase the number of people able to afford it. Eventually, Benton hoped, land that went unsold would be given away to people willing to settle it.

Benton's sentiments were soundly Jeffersonian. He favored those who tilled the soil, "the bone and sinew of the republic" in Jefferson's phrase, over financial interests associated with Alexander Hamilton and, in Benton's era, the Whig party.

Sectional Tensions

Opposition to liberal land policy was strongest in the East. People who lived on the oldest streets of Plymouth and on the James neck of Virginia had no interest in purchasing land in Missouri or Michigan. But they had a stake in how and for how much the federal government sold it. To them, the western lands were a national resource—their wealth as well as that of westerners—a fount from which the government's expenses should be paid. They feared that if the national domain was sold off as quickly and as cheaply as Benton and his allies wished, the old states would lose population. The state and local taxes easterners paid, principally property taxes, would have to increase to make up for the loss.

Northern factory owners feared that, if land was dirt cheap and too inviting, their pool of laborers would shrink. The workers who remained, being in short supply, would demand higher wages.

Well-to-do southern planters, dependent on slave labor, feared that disposing of western lands too cheaply would force the federal government to depend more heavily on the tariff—import duties—to finance its operations. As major consumers of cheap British cloth, shoes, tools, and other products that would be larded with the new duties, they preferred to finance the government through land sales that actually made money.

Land policy, whether it was to generate income or favor western settlers, threatened to set section against section.

Handsome Henry Clay

The man who stepped forward with a plan to avert such a cleavage was himself a westerner, Henry Clay. Perhaps because his home was Kentucky, a state a generation older than Benton's Missouri, Clay was more concerned with welding the West to the old states than with populating it. He wanted to see land in the hands of actual settlers. But he also wanted to see the public domain used in such a way as to integrate the economies of North, South, and West. Clay was a nationalist, with a vision of a future beyond the next election.

Born in Virginia in 1777, Henry Clay trained as a lawyer and settled in Lexington at 21 years of age. He prospered as a planter, a land speculator, and especially in politics. Elected to the House of Representatives in 1810, Clay won notoriety as one of the most bellicose of the War Hawks, who pushed President Madison into war in 1812. When the fighting bogged down in stalemate, Madison named Clay to represent the War Hawk element at the peace talks in Ghent.

In Kentucky, in Europe, and in Washington, Clay had a taste for the high life. Keenly intelligent, famously handsome, graciously mannered, witty, ever sociable, he charmed women and won the friendship and loyalty of men. He was equally comfortable sipping claret with an interested lady and playing faro with the boys until the whiskey was gone. Although he was a poor shot and killed no one, Clay fought several duels, almost a prerequisite of success in western politics at the time.

But Clay's prominence—he hovered near the center of power in the United States for four decades—owed itself only incidentally to his style. Like Benton, he worked to build up the West. Transcending Benton and other westerners, Clay had a vision of a great and united nation that owed much to Alexander Hamilton. Clay, however, lacked Hamilton's contempt for ordinary folk.

The Open Road

Henry Clay's special cause as a young politician was internal improvements, particularly the building of better roads to tie the far-flung sections of the United States together— the costs of construction to be underwritten by the federal government. This was decidedly a western cause. Although the roads and highways of the eastern seaboard were wretched by the standards of western Europe, more than a century of population and development had resulted in a network of sorts. Beginning about 1790, the states and counties of the Northeast had graded and graveled old trails. The Old Post Road between Boston and New York allowed year-round long-distance travel on that important route, albeit an uncomfortable trip.

The Old Post Road was maintained by public moneys. Other eastern highways were privately constructed toll roads known as "turnpikes" because entrances were blocked with

North Wind Picture Archives

▲ *Henry Clay of Kentucky as a young congressman. Handsome, charming, and "one of the boys," his political career was to span four decades. He was beloved by his supporters and disdained by his enemies as devious and obsessed with being president.*

a pole resembling a pike that was turned to allow access when the toll was paid. One of the most successful, the Lancaster Pike, connected the rich farm town of Lancaster, Pennsylvania, to Philadelphia, some 60 miles away.

By 1820, there were 4,000 miles of such toll roads in the United States. Some were surfaced with crushed rock, or macadam, a British import that was the forerunner of blacktop paving. A cheaper surfacing, more likely in the West, was made of planks, or even logs, laid across the roadbed. The latter were called "corduroy roads." The ride they provided was bumpy and shattered many hubs and axles, but they kept narrow wagon wheels out of the mud.

Federal Finance

Few entrepreneurs were willing to invest in roads in the sparsely populated West. There were not enough toll payers. Nor could the young western states afford to do much about the problem. They were caught in the vicious circle of needing good roads in order to attract population and move their products out, while lacking the population and, therefore, the tax base necessary to finance the roads.

Digging the Erie Canal

Thomas Jefferson inscribed his opinions on so many subjects that he may be excused for a gaffe now and then. When he heard of the plan to connect the Hudson River to the Great Lakes by digging a canal, he wrote that "it is little short of madness."

The Erie Canal opened in November 1825, months before Jefferson died. The fabulous excavation climbed (and descended) 500 feet just west of Troy. The hills were scaled by means of 83 locks—fantastic, but not mad. The unnatural waterway cut travel time from Albany to Buffalo from 20 days to 8, and later to 6. The cost of moving a ton of freight across the state was slashed from $100 to $10, and later to $5. The $7 million cost of digging the ditch was repaid with interest in just 12 years.

Then again, Jefferson might not have revised his opinion of the adventure. He had written in *Notes on Virginia,* "Let our workshops remain in Europe." Jefferson believed that "mobs" of workers who do not till the soil "add just so much to the support of pure government, as sores do to the strength of the human body." The 3,000 Irishmen who were lured to upstate New York to do the dirty work and joined by thousands of Americans to expand, maintain, and "navigate" the canal, constituted one of Jefferson's "great cities," albeit one stretched thinly for many miles, like a contemporary "strip city."

They were a rough lot, the "canal boys," fresh off the wretched little potato patches from which the English landlords allowed them to feed themselves. Only a sense of history rare among peasants, a rich oral tradition, and their deep Roman Catholic piety raised them above barbarism. The cash wages they were paid to shovel and heave the dirt of upstate New York threatened to return them to it.

Brothels, gambling dens, and prototypes of the American saloon followed the work crews. The drunken, eye-gouging, ear-biting "ructions" of the canal workers were prodigious. As portions of the canal were opened and work camps became towns and cities built around locks, depots for horses and mules, and junctures for feeder canals, the atmosphere hardly changed. It just moved from tents to clapboard and brick buildings. Canal boats moved around the clock. The canal towns roared around the clock.

The fact that the boisterous, brawling boatmen worked an economic miracle did not often enter into the reflections of the proper New Englanders who traveled the canal. Many authors of accounts of travel on the Erie seem to have trembled for their personal safety when they passed through locks aboard one of the "queer-looking Noah's Ark boats."

Ironically, they were not only quite secure, but they were enjoying a trip that was definitely more bearable than any alternative. Travel on the Erie was rather comfortable for some and elegant for those who could pay the fare on a first-class boat.

The most expensive way to travel on the canal was on the packets. At least 80 feet long and 15 feet wide, they kept to a schedule, whereas other boats moved when they were loaded. The packets were towed around the clock by three trotting horses, which, of course, were changed often. Because the passengers' quarters on a packet were quite comfortable, horses that were resting were not brought aboard, as was done on second- and third-class boats. The companies that ran packets—the Pilot, Telegraph, Merchant's, Washington, Citizen's, and Commercial—maintained large stables at intervals of 10 to 12 miles.

For five cents a mile, a first-class passenger moved at between 4 and 6 miles per hour. The packets overtook slower boats by means of a procedure that was routine but, nonetheless, the occasion of some altercations. The slower boat slackened its tow line and the line of the quicker packet was passed over it. It required even more dexterity when the towpath changed sides: The horses cleared a bridge and galloped up and over it. The best of the canal men took pride in negotiating this maneuver without so much as a tug on boat or horse collar.

On a packet, men and women sat on stuffed sofas in the "saloon," which ran the length of the boat. Meals were served there. Allowing for the era's disinterest in gourmet food, complaints about the cooking on the first-class boats were rare. At locks and stables, or when heavy traffic slowed the pace, passengers could stretch their legs on the towpath ahead of the vessel.

At night, the saloon was divided into separate quarters for men and women. The sofas became beds. Upper bunks folded from the cabin walls. They were not roomy, scarcely more than 5 feet long with just enough room to roll over without unduly disturbing the passenger above.

The solution, in the view of westerners such as Henry Clay, was the federal government. As citizens of states that had been created by the Union, rather than states that were creators of it, westerners were more apt to look to Washington for aid than easterners were. Moreover, the construction of a highway system in the vast West was a massive project. As men like Clay saw it, only the federal government, with its vast resources, could bear the expense.

Clay worked tirelessly on behalf of the first federal construction project in the West—the national road that connected Cumberland, Maryland, on the Potomac River, with Wheeling on the Ohio River. It cost $13,000 per mile to build—an astronomical sum. The terrain was rugged, but the road was completed in 1818. Delighted by what this access to oceangoing commerce meant for Kentucky, Clay worked to have the national road extended to Vandalia, Illinois.

Clay was uncommonly successful as a highway lobbyist, but he had formidable opponents. Many southerners, nationally minded before the War of 1812, began to worry about the cost of internal improvements—and the taxation needed to pay for laying crushed rock and dredging rivers. Some westerners, such as General Andrew Jackson, Clay's archrival for leadership of the section, believed that federal finance of improvements was unconstitutional. Moreover, while Clay was personally blameless, many manipulators made fortunes on unnecessary or wasteful projects, generating opposition to Clay's free spending.

Before the 1820s, congressmen from the New England states inclined to oppose spending federal money on internal improvements. Their own road system was adequate; little federal money would be spent in their backyards. However, the densely populated Northeast would pick up the biggest part of the bill in taxes. Moreover, until the embargo and the War of 1812 disrupted the shipping business, New England's elite thought in terms of the Atlantic as the fount of their economic life. Factory owners feared that an improved West would attract their own people.

The American System

To counter such sectional thinking, Clay revived Alexander Hamilton's gospel of "continentalism." He urged Americans to seek their future, first of all, on the North American continent. He called his program the "American System."

First, Clay argued that northeastern industrialists had no reason to fear the consequences of internal improvements in the West. A populous West, connected to the Northeast by good roads, would provide a massive domestic market for the manufactured goods of New England and the Middle Atlantic states. He confronted the problem of taxes by compromising the Jeffersonian principle that western lands were to be disposed of as cheaply as possible. Although not advocating extremely high prices—Clay supported graduation, for example—he proposed that revenues from land sales pay the greater part of the costs of internal improvements. He also appealed to manufacturing interests by advocating a high tariff that would protect northeastern factories from foreign competition.

To westerners, largely farmers who might otherwise oppose a high tariff, Clay pointed out that a flourishing industry would lead to large urban populations of workers who would buy western food products. Higher prices for manufactured goods—the consequence of the high tariff—were a small price to pay for such a bonanza. To complete the circular flow of products among the regions, the South would supply the mills of New England with cotton.

The capstone of Clay's nationalistic program was the second Bank of the United States. Chartered in 1816, its role in the American System was to regulate the money supply needed to fuel the integrated economy.

The weak link in Clay's program was the South, to which it did not offer very much. Southerners needed no help in finding profitable markets for their cotton and needed to make no concessions to sell it. The mills of Manchester, Leeds, and Bradford in England gobbled up all the fiber that southern planters could grow. With the exception of a few special-interest groups like Louisiana sugar planters, who wanted tariff protection against West Indian competitors, southerners inclined to oppose Clay's program. To them, the

American System meant bigger price tags on the manufactured goods that they, as agriculturists, had to buy.

THE TRANSPORTATION REVOLUTION

In the end, Clay had to be content with levering bits and pieces of his comprehensive program through Congress, not at all what he had in mind. Moreover, many of his victories were temporary. His bills were repealed when his enemies captured Congress and the White House. The American economy was to be integrated less by vision and legislation than by a revolution in transportation that conquered seasons, leveled mountains, and diverted the course of rivers.

The Erie Canal

The state of New York led the way in a revolution in transportation. In 1817, after years of promotion by Governor De Witt Clinton, the legislature voted funds to dig a canal from the Hudson River to Lake Erie, from Albany on the Hudson to Buffalo on the lake. The idea was to funnel the produce of the Great Lakes basin through New York City and to make New York "the great depot and warehouse of the western world."

With picks and shovels and little more, for wages of $10 a month, gangs of rough, muscular laborers, many of them immigrants from Ireland, excavated a ditch 4 feet deep, 40 feet wide, and, when it was completed in 1825, 364 miles long. (The canal was later enlarged to 7 feet deep and 70 feet wide.) The Erie Canal was expensive—$7 million, or almost $20,000 per mile. Skeptics waited for the state of New York to buckle under its financial burden. But even before the ditch was finished, the canal was turning a profit.

Travel on the Erie Canal was slow. Mules on towpaths dragged the long, flat-bottomed canal boats carrying up to 50 tons at a lazy 4 miles an hour. Passenger boats accommodated up to 40 people. For a cent a mile, canal travel was none too comfortable, but for five cents a mile, a pilgrim could travel the Erie Canal first class. Far more important, it cost only $8 a ton to move factory goods west or western crops east. That was a 90 percent cut in the cost of overland transport!

The Canal Craze

When the Erie Canal was begun, there were about 100 miles of canal in the United States. They served only small regions; the longest ran only 28 miles. Now, those who had laughed at the Erie Canal's prospects went berserk in their rush to imitate it.

The most ambitious was the Mainline Canal in Pennsylvania. Smarting under the loss of commercial preeminence to New York, Philadelphia merchants pressured the state legislature into pumping millions into the venture. The Mainline was shorter than the Erie. However, whereas the New

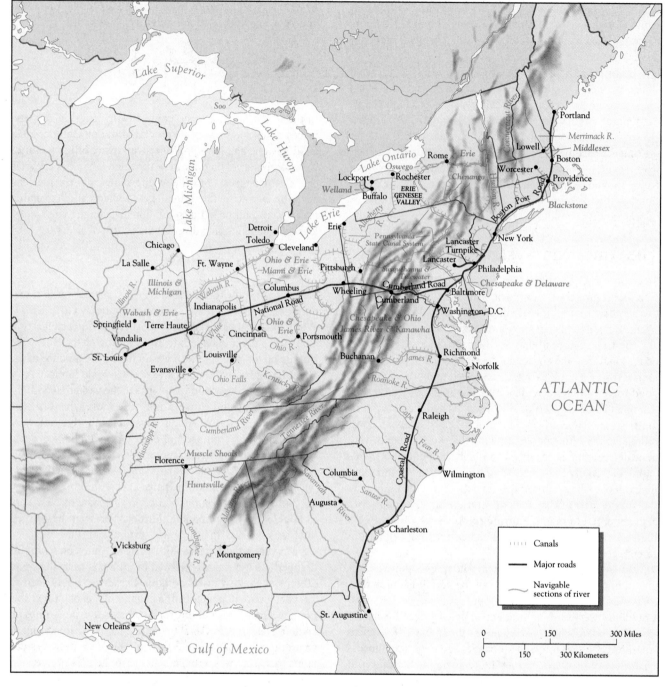

MAP 13:3 Rivers, Roads, and Canals, 1825–1860 During the first half of the nineteenth century, the United States boasted two of the world's longest continuous highways, the routes of today's U.S. 1/I-95 and U.S. 40/I-70. American canals, now almost all gone, were even more extensive.

York route rose only 650 feet above sea level at its highest point and required 83 locks to control its water, the Mainline Canal rose 2,200 feet and needed 174 locks. At the Allegheny ridge, the highest in the Pennsylvania Appalachians, boats were hauled out of the canal and over the mountain on fantastic inclined planes. Miraculously, the Mainline Canal was completed—Pennsylvania operated 608 miles of canal—but it was never the gold mine that the Erie was. There were too many bottlenecks crowded with swearing boatmen in the mountains—where no boatman belonged.

All in all, some 4,000 miles of canal were dug in imitation of the Erie. Another 7,000 miles were on the drawing boards when the bubble burst. Although many of the canals were of inestimable local value, only a few made enough money to cover the money invested in them. So many states drained their treasuries to fund poorly advised projects that many politicians, including westerners, swore never again to finance internal improvements. As late as 1848, the constitution of the new state of Wisconsin forbade the expenditure of tax money on such ventures.

▲ *Two locks on the Erie Canal. Long stretches were idyllic, as this artist's depiction shows. Some canal towns were rough-and-tumble places, however, as wild during the construction of the canal as a cow town or mining camp.*

Railroads

The canal craze was also brought to an end by the appearance of a more flexible means of overland transportation, the railroad. As the Mainline Canal showed, canals were plausible only where the terrain was easily passable and the supply of water plentiful and constant. Even the Erie was out of commission during the winter months, when it froze. Railroads never provided transportation as cheaply as canal boats. But railroads could run almost anywhere faster and, except during catastrophic blizzards, every day of the year.

The New York and Erie Railroad

In order to offset the economic advantages that the Erie Canal had brought to the northern counties of New York State, the southern counties proposed to build a railroad between the Hudson River and Lake Erie. Chartered on April 24, 1832, the New York and Erie Railroad (later the Erie) spanned 446 miles between Piermont on the Hudson (26 miles from New York City) and Dunkirk on Lake Erie.

In 1851, trains carried President Millard Fillmore and his cabinet on what was then the longest continuous railroad in the world. Secretary of State Daniel Webster had, it was reported, "on a flat car, at his own request, a big easy rocking-chair provided for him to sit on. He chose this manner of riding so that he could get a better view and enjoy the fine country through which the railroad passed."

The first two railroads in the United States were constructed in 1827, just two years after the first railroad in England proved workable. One line connected the granite quarries of Quincy, Massachusetts, with the Neponset River. The other carried coal from Carbondale, Pennsylvania, to the Lehigh River. Both were only a few miles long and served single business enterprises, supplementing existing routes and means of transportation. In 1833, the Charleston and Hamburg railroad was the longest in the world—at just 136 miles.

The potential of the railroad lay in using it, like the Erie Canal, as the trunk of a transportation system independent of traditional, regional routes. The first entrepreneurs to recognize this were Baltimoreans hoping to put their city back in the race with New York for trade with the West. In 1828, work began on America's first trunk line, the Baltimore and Ohio (B&O).

Construction of the B&O was repeatedly stalled by financial difficulties, but in 1853, the line was finally completed to Wheeling on the Ohio River. In the meantime, dozens of less ambitious railroads were constructed. By 1848, there were more than 6,000 miles of railroad track in the United States. Fewer than 3,000 miles of track existed in the rest of the world.

The railroad conquered time and, eventually, the isolation of the West. At the end of the War of 1812, it took more than seven weeks to ship a cargo from Cincinnati to New York by keelboat, wagon, and riverboat. In 1852, when the two cities were connected by rail, it took six to eight days.

▲ *It cost more to ship by railroad than by canal, but canals could not be dug over mountains. This locomotive was one of the first to cross the Appalachians. The celebrants posing on the "cowcatcher" are probably company officials and their wives. Unless the engine had been scoured for the occasion, they were dirty when they climbed down.*

The cost of constructing a railroad was immense. In addition to securing right of way and hiring armies of laborers, a railroad company had to buy its own rolling stock, freight cars. (Canals and turnpikes collected tolls from users with their own boats and vehicles.) As a result, despite the total mileage of American railroads, few individual lines went very far. Indeed, competitive jealousies among the companies worked against true systems connecting distant points. Railway entrepreneurs deliberately built their lines in different gauges (distances between the tracks) so that the cars of competing lines could not be used on them.

The major canals and the B&O linked the West to the Northeast. However, the West's great natural north-south artery, the Mississippi River, was not neglected during the revolution in transportation.

"Old Man River"

It could not have been otherwise. With its two great tributaries, the Ohio and the Missouri, and dozens of smaller but navigable feeders, the Mississippi (the "Father of Waters") tapped the central third of the continent.

Westerners who lived on the Mississippi system could easily ship their corn or livestock to New Orleans on large log

rafts that, broken up and sawed into lumber, were themselves a source of income. The problem was in bringing goods back upstream. Sailing ships could not do the job. The Mississippi is broad; but its current is mighty, and its channels are narrow and shifting, the playthings of capricious sandbars. High riverbanks periodically stole the wind from sails. Oceangoing vessels could not penetrate much beyond New Orleans, and small sailboats carried too little to be worthwhile.

Some cargo was rowed upriver, some by poling small skiffs. Both methods were arduous and expensive. Savage keelboat men, like the Ohio River's legendary Mike Fink, literally pulled their vessels upstream. The keelboater lashed a heavy line to a tree on the riverbank and, from the deck of the craft, heaved in the ropes, repeating the process with another tree farther on.

It was no job for the languid, nor was it an efficient way to move anything but expensive goods. It took about six weeks for a huge raft to float pleasantly downstream from Pittsburgh, where the Ohio River begins, to New Orleans. It took four to five months to bring a much smaller tonnage back on a keelboat, with even more men drawing wages. It was far more expensive to ship a cargo of English cloth or furniture from New Orleans to Illinois than to sail it from England to New Orleans.

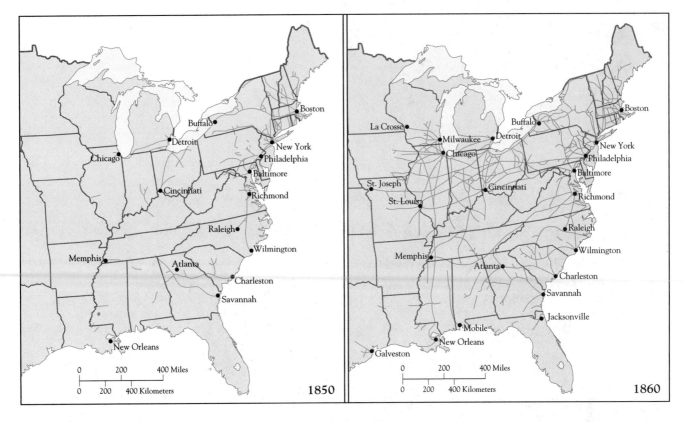

MAP 13:4 Railroads, 1850–1860 In 1850, American railroads were short and fragmented, serving only regions. By 1860, there were more miles of railroad in the United States than in the rest of the world, including several routes running continuously from the Northeast to the West for a thousand miles.

Steamboat A-Coming

The marvel that resolved this dilemma was the flat-bottomed steamboat, which was a long time coming. James Watt, the Scot who first harnessed the power of steam pressure to pump water out of mines, regarded ships as the second most important application of his discovery. However, it was not until 1787 that a Connecticut Yankee named John Fitch ran a 45-foot steamer down *and up* the Delaware River. Several delegates to the Constitutional Convention in Philadelphia witnessed the spectacle.

The "Lord High Admiral of the Delaware," as Fitch commissioned himself, solved most of the problems and briefly provided regular service between Philadelphia and Burlington, New Jersey (not much of a trip). But Fitch was a star-crossed man, obstreperous and obnoxious with his most generous backers. Nor was his humor improved by the indifference of eastern capitalists who still thought in terms of the sea. They could not imagine how a vessel in which a good portion of the hold was committed to carrying fuel could compete with a sleek sailing ship drawing its energy from God's good winds.

In fact, the age of sail was far from over. For more than a century after the perfection of the steamship, clipper ships

and great steel-hulled windjammers dominated many world trade routes, particularly the long ones around Cape Horn. Worldwide, the tonnage carried in steamships exceeded that carried in sailing ships only in 1893.

But steamboats conquered the rivers. In 1807, Robert Fulton's *Clermont* wheezed and chugged up the Hudson River from New York City to Albany at five miles per hour. The *Clermont* was three times as long as John Fitch's boat, but the dimension that thoughtful people noticed was that it drew only seven feet of water. The boat was able to clear obstacles that would have upended a sailing ship with less capacity.

Queens of the Mississippi

The steamboat paid its way on eastern rivers like the Hudson. (Fulton's success helped to inspire the campaign to dig the Erie Canal.) But it was in the West that the great vessels found their natural home. In 1817, only 10 years after the *Clermont*'s maiden voyage, there were 17 steamboats on the Mississippi. By 1830, there were 187, with new ones being constructed more quickly than the old ones blew up.

Boiler explosions were no small problem. In order to minimize the weight of the boats, boilers were constructed more flimsily than good sense prescribed. Nevertheless,

▲ *The ingeniously-designed flat bottoms of the river steamboats meant that they could tie up on river banks far from docks. Here a steamboat is taking cotton aboard. More commonly, the boats tied up in remote locations to buy firewood cut by locals, sometimes by slaves working on their own time.*

after the *Tecumseh* set a record of eight days and two hours from New Orleans to Louisville in 1827, Mississippi riverboat captains found it difficult to resist the challenge or just a race. As on the railroad, speed sold tickets and attracted shippers. So, despite the opulence of some riverboats, a trip on one was a bit of a gamble. At the peak of the steamboat age, 500 people died in accidents each year. In the explosion of the *Moselle* in 1838, 150 people were lost.

Designers competed just as frantically to adapt boats to the western rivers. The greatest natural obstacles were the shifting sandbars of the Mississippi and Missouri, and snags—fallen trees that were to the river what icebergs were to the North Atlantic, quiet predators capable of tearing a gaping hole in a wooden hull.

In 1841, the *Orphan Boy* was completed and eased onto the water. It could carry 40 tons of freight plus passengers. Even when fully loaded, however, it skimmed atop water only two feet deep! The *Orphan Boy* was the ultimate, but a good many paddle wheelers needed only three or four feet. Not only was this quality necessary to navigate the Father of Waters and the even trickier Missouri River, but it enabled

the boats to tie up at almost any bank in order to take on the cordwood that steamboats burned in prodigious quantities.

Symbols of a New Era

The locomotive and the steamboat knit the far-flung reaches of the United States together. In the words of a Cincinnati booster, they brought "to the remotest villages of our streams, and to the very doors of our cabins, a little Paris, a section of Broadway, or a slice of Philadelphia to ferment in the minds of our young people." The moving machines belching acrid smoke symbolized a sense of nationality as surely as the person of George Washington had symbolized the common cause of independence and constitutional union.

When the steamboat was still in its infancy, however, and the first railroad a decade in the future, Americans were already drawing together in their hearts, or so it seemed. In the wake of the War of 1812, a sense of American nationhood seized on the imaginations of the people of West, North, and even—ever so briefly—the South.

for FURTHER READING

On the first American West, see Ray A. Billington, *America's Frontier Heritage,* 1967; R. S. Philbrick, *The Rise of the West, 1754–1830,* 1965; Dale Van Every, *The Final Challenge: The American Frontier, 1804–1845,* 1964; and Malcolm J. Rohrbough, *The Trans-Appalachian Frontier,* 1978. Every inquiry into the American West should look to the "founding father" of western history, Frederick Jackson Turner, in *The Frontier in American History,* 1920.

Important studies dealing with topics treated in this chapter include Richard D. Brown, *Modernization: The Transformation of American Life, 1600–1865,* 1976; W. Elliott Brownlee, *Dynamics of Ascent: A History of the American Economy,* 1979; Thomas C. Cochran, *Frontiers of Change: Early Industrialists in America,* 1981; Eugene S. Ferguson, *The Americanness of American Technology,* 1975; F. W. Gates, *The Farmer's Age: American Agriculture, 1815–1860,* 1960; Walter Havighurst, *Voices on the River: The Story of the Mississippi Waterways,* 1964; L. C. Hunter, *Steamboats on the Western Rivers,* 1949; Philip D. Jordan, *The National Road,* 1948; Douglas C. North, *The Economic Growth of the United States, 1790–1860,* 1951; R. M. Robbins, *Our Landed Heritage: The Public Domain,* 1942; Ronald E. Shaw, *Erie Water West: A History of the Erie Canal, 1792–1854,* 1966; George R. Taylor, *The Transportation Revolution, 1815–1860,* 1951; Richard C. Wade, *The Urban Frontier,* 1964; and Sam B. Warner Jr., *The Urban Wilderness,* 1972.

Pertinent biographies are William Chambers, *Old Bullion Benton: Senator from the New West,* 1970; and Glyndon D. Van Deusen, *The Life of Henry Clay,* 1937.

  ## AMERICAN JOURNEY ONLINE AND INFOTRAC COLLEGE EDITION

Visit the source collections at http://ajaccess.wadsworth.com and http://infotrac.thomsonlearning.com, and use the Search function with the following key terms to explore documents, images, audio and video clips, articles, and commentary related to the material in this chapter:

Erie Canal
Henry Clay
James Monroe

Additional resources, exercises, and Internet links related to this chapter are available on *The American Past* Web site:
http://history.wadsworth.com/americanpast7e.

HISTORY ONLINE

The First American West
http://memory.loc.gov/ammem/award99/icuhtm/fawhome.html
Excellent multi-format look at the Ohio River valley frontier.

The Conestoga: A Brief History
www.dvhi.net/wagonworks/history.html
Information and excellent pictures of the wagon on which emigrants headed across the Appalachians (and later across the continent) traveled.

14

NATION AWAKENING

Political and Economic Development 1815–1824

© Bettmann/Corbis

Our country! In her intercourse with foreign nations, may she always be in the right; but our country, right or wrong.

Stephen Decatur

I can never join with my voice in the toast which I see in the papers attributed to one of our gallant naval heroes. I cannot ask of heaven success, even for my country, in a cause where she should be in the wrong. Let justice be done though the heavens fall. My toast would be, may our country be always successful, but whether successful or otherwise, always right.

John Quincy Adams

HENRY CLAY'S VISION of an integrated national economy, transcending state and sectional loyalties, did not spring full blown from his ruminations. The idea of an "American System" was hatched during an era when a nationalistic spirit permeated American society and culture. The era had its beginnings in 1815 with Andrew Jackson's victory at New Orleans and Stephen Decatur's punishment of insolent Algerians. The news of both events was greeted with the discharging of muskets and pistols, flag waving, sounding church bells, shouting and singing, and patriotic oratory.

THE ERA OF GOOD FEELINGS

In the decade after the divisive War of 1812, Americans in every section of the country embraced an image of themselves as a new chosen people—unique and blessed on the face of the earth, unsullied by the corruption of Europe, nurtured by their comparative closeness to nature, committed in the marrow of their bones to liberty, democracy, and progress.

It was during this period that the Fourth of July became a day of raucous popular celebration. Formerly observed with religious services and decorous promenades of the social elite in city squares, the Glorious Fourth burst into prominence as a day when everyone paid homage to the nation with games, feasting, overdrinking, and boisterous gaiety.

Patriotic Culture

It was an era of patriotism in popular art. Woodcarvers and decorators trimmed canal boats, sailing ships, stagecoaches, and private homes with patriotic motifs: screaming eagles clutching braces of arrows; the idealized, vigilant female

pious as Numa; just as Aristides; temperate as Epictetus; patriotic as Regulus; impartial as Severus," and on and on.

Another influential author of the time was Noah Webster, whose *American Spelling Book,* first published in 1783, sold more than 60 million copies in perhaps 300 editions. Webster did not, however, get rich; in 1808, he sold the rights to the book for $2,365. From the "blue-backed speller," schoolchildren learned that the American tongue was superior to British English because Webster had stripped it of Old World affectations. Many of the differences in spelling between American English and British English today (*labor, theater, curb,* and *jail,* as opposed to *labour, theatre, kerb,* and *gaol*) owe to Webster's linguistic tinkering.

Webster was also the father of that great event of the American elementary school, the spelling bee, for Webster believed in uniform spelling. He observed unhappily that even so great a patriotic hero as William Clark, in his journals of the great expedition across the continent, spelled *mosquito* 19 different ways. His *American Dictionary of the English Language,* published in 1828, also distinguished American English by including hundreds of words adopted from Indian tongues.

James Monroe

The gentleman who presided over this outpouring of national pride was, like three of the four presidents who preceded him, a Virginian—James Monroe of Westmoreland County. His is a blurred figure in the history books, a personality with few hard edges.

figure that represented liberty; and the flag, the only national ensign in the world that had progress sewn into it. Between 1816 and 1820, six new stars were added to Old Glory as six new states entered the Union.

The needlepoint samplers that girls made to display their skills began to depict patriotic themes as often as religious themes: the Stars and Stripes or the saying of some national hero, like Nathan Hale's "I regret that I have but one life to give for my country" or Decatur's "Our country right or wrong." Newspapers published exuberant verses that touted the glories of the United States. Songwriters churned out lyrics that celebrated American grandeur.

In 1817, William Wirt wrote a biography of Patrick Henry in which he implied that Virginians led the movement for independence and fought the war more or less single-handedly. Piqued patriots from other states looked for and dependably found patriotic demigods of their own: Paul Revere of Massachusetts, Nathaniel Greene of Rhode Island, Francis Marion of South Carolina, and so on.

Less controversial because of its singular subject was Mason Locke Weems's *The Life and Memorable Actions of George Washington.* Although originally published in 1800, Weems's unblushing study in hero worship peaked in popularity during the 1810s and 1820s, running through 59 editions. It was Weems who originated the story of the boy Washington chopping down the cherry tree and of an older Washington throwing a silver dollar across the Rappahannock River. So noble was the father of his country that he could not fib; so far was he above other nations' leaders that even in physical strength he was a superman. Weems wrote of Washington, "It is hardly an exaggeration to say that he was as

▲ *The Fourth of July 1818. Twenty years earlier, it was a holiday to which only the genteel paid much attention, promenading in their best clothing. After the War of 1812, Independence Day became somewhat raucous, often lubricated by free-flowing liquor.*

Monroe's achievements can be listed. He was one of Jefferson's most loyal disciples (and the most radical who was close to Jefferson). He was a successful diplomat, a good administrator, and utterly incorruptible. "Turn his soul wrong side outwards," Jefferson said, "and there is not a speck on it." It can be noted that his wife was thought one of the most beautiful women in the country. Portraits of Monroe reveal that his dress was eccentric; he wore the old-fashioned, skintight knee breeches of the revolutionary era while his contemporaries were pulling on the utilitarian trousers of the nineteenth century.

But a two-dimensional oil painting is what James Monroe remains. Perhaps it is because he was so successful as president, faced with problems far less serious than those that vexed his predecessors, calmly dispatching those that did arise, and telling the country what it wanted to hear in pious generalities.

History, like the audience at a play, thrives on conflict. It grows torpid in times of stability. James Monroe had the political good luck, and the historical misfortune, of being president during an interlude of calm between two times of crisis. He could declare in his second inaugural address, and probably believe it, that the United States would "soon attain the highest degree of perfection of which human institutions are capable."

Political Stability

The Founding Fathers' hopes for a government without political parties briefly came to pass under Monroe. The Federalists, revived during the War of 1812, collapsed when the shooting concluded. After Jackson's victory at New Orleans, their opposition to the war seemed more like disloyalty than good sense.

The number of congressmen styling themselves Federalists declined from 68 during the war to 42 in 1817 and 25 in 1821 (compared with 158 Jeffersonian Republicans). By 1821, there were only 4 Federalists in a Senate of 48 members. Old John Adams, in retirement in Quincy, Massachusetts, took scant interest in the evaporation of the party he had helped to found. His son, John Quincy Adams, joined the party of Thomas Jefferson and became Monroe's secretary of state.

During the 1810s, Republican congressmen and senators chose their presidential candidate (and therefore, in effect, the president) in a caucus. Monroe, the choice in 1816, handily defeated Federalist Rufus King. King won only the electoral votes of Delaware, Connecticut, and Massachusetts. The next year, when President Monroe visited Boston, where Jefferson was loathed and Madison despised, he was received as a hero. A Boston newspaper congratulated him for inaugurating an "era of good feelings."

In 1820, Monroe was unopposed in the presidential election. (One member of the electoral college cast his vote for John Quincy Adams so that no president but Washington would have the distinction of being his country's unanimous choice.) With only one political party, the United States had, in effect, no parties at all.

Smooth Sailing

Indeed, voters and even politicians were almost indifferent toward presidential politics. In 1816, William Crawford of

Georgia might have won the Republican presidential nomination over Monroe if he had thought the prize worth a fight. He did not. His supporters did not bother to attend the caucus at which the candidate was named.

Nor was there much popular interest in national elections. In 1816, only 6 of 19 states chose presidential electors by statewide popular vote; in 1820, only 7 of 24 states did. In most of the others, the state legislatures made the choice, and they treated the task as though it were routine, like confirming the governor's proclamation of a Thanksgiving holiday or voting a pension to a retiring doorkeeper. In 1820, the returns from Richmond, Virginia, a city of 12,000 people, revealed that only 17 men had bothered to vote.

There is nothing intrinsically wrong in a subdued presidency and popular indifference to politics, particularly according to the tenets of the Jeffersonian faith. Jefferson said that the government that governed least governed best. The absence of deeply divisive issues during Monroe's presidency reflected the relative prosperity of the times and the American people's concern with westward expansion and economic growth. Moreover, if Monroe was neither mover nor shaker, movers and shakers often do a good deal of mischief. Monroe did none. He was a conscientious, competent, and hardworking executive. His administration was efficient, and, without a popular clamor to distract them, he and his nationalistic secretary of state, John Quincy Adams, had an unbroken string of diplomatic successes.

Reconciliation with the Mother Country

In the Rush-Bagot Agreement of 1817, the United States and Britain agreed to limit the number of armed vessels on the Great Lakes. It was the first major concession that the former mother country made to the Americans since the Revolution. More important, the partial disarmament set the pattern for future policies that established the world's longest unfortified international boundary.

In 1818, Britain and the United States also established the southern boundary of British Canada at 49 degrees north latitude, a line that now runs west from Lake Superior to Puget Sound. Although American claims in the Pacific Northwest were flimsy and American interests there were next to nil, the British conceded Americans equal rights in what was called the "Oregon Country": present-day Oregon, Washington, the Idaho panhandle, and British Columbia.

Florida Secured

With Spain, Monroe-Adams diplomacy reaped even greater rewards. By 1819, the Spanish Empire was quaking. There were rebellions in practically every province, and rebel armies were winning most of the battles. The leaders of the independence movement—Simón Bolívar, José de San Martín, and Bernardo O'Higgins—paid flattering homage to the example set for them by the United States. Their praises of the United States as the beacon of their own freedom provided more fodder for the Americans' bumptious national pride.

The disintegration of the Spanish Empire also gave Florida to the United States. The peninsula never was very valuable. Thinly populated by Europeans and mostly controlled by Indians, Florida was held by the British for 20 years after 1763. In 1818, in pursuit of Indian warriors, Andrew Jackson brazenly crossed the border, ignored Spanish authority, and (on foreign soil) executed two British subjects for treason against the United States!

When the Spanish minister in Washington protested, Secretary of State Adams responded by offering to buy Florida. For $5 million, Spain agreed; it was obvious the Americans were going to take Florida one way or another. Adams had only to confirm Spain's version of the disputed boundary between American Louisiana and Spanish Texas, which was no concession at all. The United States had never seriously contested the Mexican boundary. In the Adams-Oñis Treaty, the United States was guaranteed every acre to which the country had a reasonable claim.

The Monroe Doctrine

John Quincy Adams was also the chief author of the American policy that, almost alone, has earned Monroe's name an entry in the history books. In December 1823, the president wrote in a message to Congress (and to Europe) that the United States was no longer to be considered an appendage of the Old World. With an "essentially different" destiny, the United States pledged not to dabble or intervene in European affairs. In return, Europe was to consider the Western Hemisphere closed to further colonization. Monroe said that any European attempts to establish or reestablish American colonies would be defined in Washington as "an unfriendly disposition." In carefully muted words, he threatened war.

The proclamation of the Monroe Doctrine (a name given it only years later) was prompted by two developments that disturbed the sensitive Quincy Adams. The first was expanded Russian exploration and fur trapping south of Alaska, which had been Russian by right of discovery since 1741. The Russians built an outpost, Fort Ross, provocatively close to Spanish San Francisco, and in February 1821, the czar ordered foreign ships to keep at least a hundred miles clear of Russian America's shores.

Fort Ross was thousands of miles and three mountain ranges from Missouri. Adams was more troubled by rumblings in Austria and France, which had threatened to send troops to the Western Hemisphere to help Spain regain control of its lost colonies.

Assertion of American Identity

Neither worry amounted to anything. The Russians were interested not in settlements but in the plush pelts of the California sea otter. By the early 1820s, trappers had just about wiped out the animals in California's coves. In 1824, the Russians abandoned Fort Ross and withdrew to Alaska. The French and Austrians had other problems more pressing than the fall of the Spanish Empire, and the project, never more than talk, was stillborn. In fact, the United States had no army to send anywhere. If the Adams-Monroe closure of the New World to colonization had any force, it was because the British, now supreme on the Atlantic, wanted Hispanic America to be independent.

In fact, the British foreign minister, George Canning, had proposed that Great Britain and the United States jointly proclaim the Americas closed to further colonization. Previously restricted in the extent of their trade in the rich markets of the old Spanish Empire, the British were the chief beneficiaries of Spanish American independence.

Adams decided to act alone in asserting the different destiny of the Western Hemisphere so that the United States would not look like "a cock-boat in the wake of the British man-of-war." To nationalistic American sensibilities, British friendship was as threatening as British antagonism.

Nationalism in the Courtroom

While Adams and Monroe proclaimed the national dignity of the American republic, Chief Justice John Marshall buttressed the constitutional primacy of the national government in a series of decisions that are still basic American law. Marshall's court never again invalidated a law of Congress, as it had done in *Marbury v. Madison.* But the Court repeatedly asserted its powers in other theaters.

While cultivating a personal reputation for physical laziness and a squalid appearance, Marshall dominated his fellow Supreme Court justices until 1835. In chambers by day and at the boardinghouse (where several justices lived together) by night, over law books and tumblers brimming with whiskey, Marshall whittled away at the power of the states. In *Fletcher v. Peck* (1810), the Marshall court declared a state law unconstitutional, thus establishing the right of the Supreme Court to act in matters that concerned one state alone. In *Martin v. Hunter's Lessee* (1816), Marshall established the Court's authority to reverse the decision of a state court. In *McCulloch v. Maryland* (1819), Marshall forbade the state of Maryland (and all states) from taxing the nationally chartered Bank of the United States. "The power to tax is the power to destroy," the Court declared. No state had the right to interfere with the national government's obligation to legislate on behalf of the common good.

In *McCulloch,* Marshall also propounded his view on the extent of governmental power. If the goal was legitimate and the law did not run counter to the Constitution, Congress and the president had the power to enact whatever legislation they chose to enact. It did not matter that the government in Washington was not specifically authorized by the Constitution to take a certain action, such as the establishment of a national bank—the issue that caused the first split between Hamilton and Jefferson. Now with Hamilton and his party both dead, John Marshall made "broad construction" of the Constitution the prevailing law of the land.

John Marshall served as chief justice during the administrations of six presidents, three of whom served two full terms while he lived. It would be difficult to argue that any of them contributed more to the shaping of American government than Marshall. In 1833, the only Supreme Court justice of the Marshall era whose legal mind rivaled his own, Joseph Story, published *Commentaries on the Constitution of the United States.* Essentially, it was a commentary on fundamental law as John Marshall perceived it.

THE INDUSTRIAL REVOLUTION IN AMERICA

Another of Hamilton's dreams for the United States—and one of Jefferson's nightmares—also headed for fulfillment during the second and third decades of the nineteenth century. To some extent in the West, but particularly in New England and the Middle Atlantic states, manufacturing came to rival agriculture in economic importance, and population began a significant shift from farms and villages to the towns and cities where factories were centered. In this process, the people of the northeastern states were early participants in the Industrial Revolution.

The Implications of Industrialization

Machine technology, the factory system for making goods, and the rapid growth of industrial cities were not revolutionary in the sense that people's lives were changed overnight. But the consequences of machines that made goods quickly and cheaply changed the terms of human existence far more profoundly than any battle or the beheading of any king or queen.

For example, in the United States today, less than 8 percent of the population works in agriculture and no farmers produce more than a tiny fraction of the food they consume and the goods they use. They buy the commodities of life

CEO

Women industrialists were rare, but not unknown. Rebecca Pennock Lukens owned and managed the Lukens Steel Company for a quarter of a century. Her father had turned the company over to her husband, Charles Lukens. When Lukens died in 1825, Rebecca was 30, with three children, but she took the factory over and won respect as an iron manufacturer. She retired in 1849, handing the prosperous company over to the husband of one of her daughters.

with money received for performing very specialized jobs. Even the typical farm family raises only one or two crops for market, and purchases the same mass-produced necessities and luxuries that city dwellers buy.

Before industrialization, in colonial and early national America, the situation was reversed. Roughly 90 percent of the population (the proportion was constantly declining) lived on farms or in agricultural villages. They personally produced a sizable proportion of the food they ate and the goods they used. For most people, very little was purchased: shoes; some clothing; tools, such as axes and guns; pottery and tin or pewter wares; some services, such as milling flour, shoeing horses, and so on. As for other necessities, ordinary people improvised them from materials on hand.

The preindustrial farmer or shopkeeper had to be handy. A man with a door to hang made the hinges himself. A woman who kept a tidy house made the broom with which she swept it. In all but the half dozen largest cities, townspeople of some means kept gardens of an acre or so, often a dairy cow, commonly a brood sow. The Industrial Revolution changed that kind of unspecialized, largely self-sufficient life into the specialized, interdependent economy we know today.

Cloth: Where It All Began

The first industrial machines were devised for the manufacture of textiles. This should not be surprising. Cloth is a universal necessity, but making it by hand is tedious, difficult, and time consuming.

In North America, as in much of the Western world, cloth making was largely woman's work, and the process took up much of the spare time of that half of the population. On poor and even middling American farms, cloth was made at home from scratch. Natural fiber from animals (wool) or plants (cotton, and flax for linen) was gathered, cleaned, carded (untangled and combed), spun into thread or yarn, dyed, and then woven or knitted by hand into a fabric that

▲ *A commercially printed fabric of the 1810s. It was probably intended for a wall covering or for drapes in a middle-class home.*

Making Mittens

In the manufacture of goods that resisted mass production in factories, the "putting out" system continued to flourish and still does, in a small way, today. In fact, Abby Condon of Penobscot, Maine, became a cottage-industry industrialist at just about the same time John D. Rockefeller went into the oil business.

In 1864—wartime, with an attractive government contract in hand—Mrs. Condon collected 25 cents for each pair of soldier's mittens she knitted. After the war, the price collapsed to 6 cents a pair. Instead of quitting, Mrs. Condon became a jobber, recruiting at least 250 knitters—every girl and woman knew how to knit—to make mittens for her, which she resold to civilian retailers. By 1882, knitting machines were replacing nimble fingers. Mrs. Condon purchased 4 of the devices and built a small factory to house them. When she died in 1906, she owned 150 knitting machines. Her business consumed 6 tons of woolen yarn a year, producing 96,000 pairs of mittens.

could warm a body, cover a bed, protect a wagonload, or propel a ship.

Because the process took so much time and required hard-learned skills at every turn, fabric was expensive. The poor dressed in hand-me-downs scarcely better than rags. People of modest means made do with one set of clothing for work and another for attending church on Sunday.

Cottage Industry

Well-to-do people dressed rather more handsomely, of course, and they did not pick, shear, card, spin, and weave. Cloth also had to be made in quantity for plantation slaves, soldiers, and sailors. Before industrialization, the needs of such groups were met by cottage industry, or what was sometimes called the "putting-out system."

It worked like this: Farm wives and daughters contracted with a cloth dealer, sometimes called a "factor," to receive fiber from him and spin it into yarn or thread in their homes. Working in odd, snatched moments, they were paid not by the hour but by the piece. They were, in our terms, independent contractors. The women and children (and sometimes men) in another family might weave cloth under the same arrangements, most of them, again, in their spare time.

This system of production did not significantly disturb traditional social structure and values. Households involved in cottage industry were able to participate in the money economy to the extent of what their women earned. Socially, however, these women remained farmers' wives or daughters, or spinsters (unmarried women in a household). They were not textile workers. Their values and the rhythm of their lives were essentially the same as those of their neighbors who were not part of "putting out."

In England in the middle of the eighteenth century, this system began to change. English inventors devised water-powered machines that spun thread and wove cloth at many

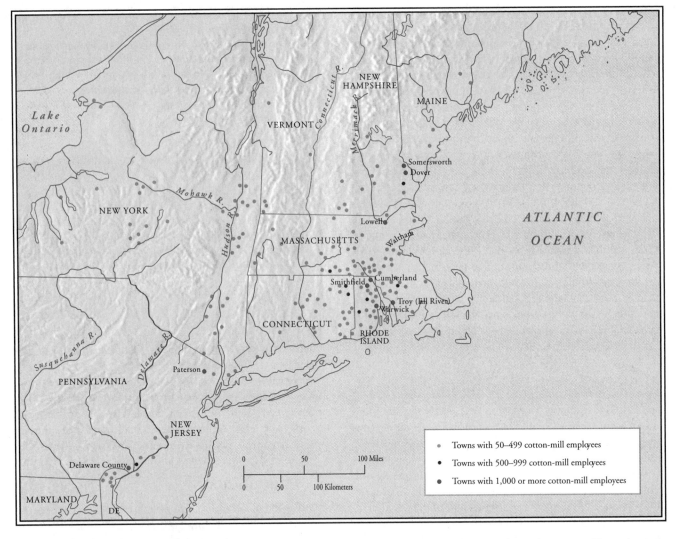

MAP 14:1 Cotton Mills, 1820 Although the mill towns appear to be scattered, they had, in fact, one significant feature in common: All were located next to waterfalls or river rapids where the stream descended many feet within a short span. The mills captured the power of the falling water by running it through a mill race—a ditch—where it turned a waterwheel. Lowell, Massachusetts, was built at the 32-foot falls of the Merrimack River. Paterson, New Jersey, was built where the Passaic River, wandering willy-nilly to the Hudson River, found its route by creating dramatic falls and, therefore, power.

times the speed that hand spinners and weavers could do it and, as a result, at a fraction of the cost. With a monopoly on this technology, Britain prospered, supplying the world with cheap fabric. Not only were most women from Canada to Calcutta delighted to be spared the tedium of spinning and weaving, but the machine-made cloth was cheap enough for almost all to buy, and it was generally of better quality than homemade cloth. England found a market for its cheap cloth everywhere in the world. Comparable machines were developed for other forms of manufacture.

Power

The key to exploiting the new machines was power—a fast-moving river or, somewhat later, the steam engine. A waterwheel or mighty, hissing piston could turn hundreds of machines much faster than any foot-driven spinning wheel. Power is where it is found or made, however. The process of

making cloth had to be centralized, brought under one roof; the machines had to be run for as long as there was light by which to see. Industrialization created the factory and a pace of labor governed by the clock, the tireless machines, and the capitalist's need to use his investment to the utmost.

Industrialization also created a class of workers who did nothing but tend machines. No longer was thread spun by a farmwife in odd, snatched moments. The industrial textile worker spent six days a week, from dawn to dusk, at the factory. Because she worked virtually all the daylight hours, she had to live close to the factory. The mill hand was a town dweller, no longer the farmer's daughter. A new social class emerged—the industrial working class.

Early Factories

The British protected their monopoly on industrial technology as a magician guards his bag of tricks. It was illegal to

▲ *The first cotton-spinning mill in America, built by Samuel Slater and Moses Brown at Pawtucket, Rhode Island. Note the falls of the river, which were the power that ran the machines. Also note that neither the scale of the mill nor its design was obtrusive to the small village in which it was constructed.*

export machinery or plans for it. Indeed, engineers and mechanics expert in building or repairing textile machines were forbidden to leave the country.

One such engineer was Samuel Slater, 23 years old in 1790, and quite clever enough to know that the knowledge that provided him a comfortable life in England would make him rich in America. Rather than risk being caught with plans for spinning machines, Slater committed to memory long and intricate lists of specifications. He slipped away from his home and shipped off to the United States, where he struck a bargain with a Rhode Island merchant, Moses Brown, who had tried without success to build spinning machines.

Brown and a partner put up the money; Slater contributed the expertise. In 1790, they opened a small water-powered spinning mill in Pawtucket, Rhode Island. The little factory housed only 72 spindles, a pip-squeak operation compared with what was to come. Still, they were the equivalent of 72 spinning wheels in 72 cottages, and each of the Slater devices turned many times faster and spun much longer than any farmwife could manage.

The capital investment was substantial but operating expenses small. The whole mill could be run by one supervisor and nine children between the ages of 7 and 12. Their labor cost Slater and Brown 33 to 60 cents per worker per week. Within a few years, both men were rich. Slater lived to be one of New England's leading industrialists, owning mills in three states.

There were other such acts of technological piracy. In 1793, two brothers from Yorkshire, John and Arthur Schofield, illegally emigrated to Byfield, Massachusetts, where they established the first American woolens mill.

American Ingenuity

The American fascination with gadgets and novel mechanical devices is almost as old as the republic. Foreign observers noted—some wryly, some aghast—that Americans leaped into tinkering without planning. As an engineer supposedly said, "Now, boys, we have got her done. Let's start her up and see why she doesn't work."

Between 1790 and 1800, Americans took out 306 patents. Between 1850 and 1860, the Patent Office cleared more than 28,000. Just a year earlier, in 1849, an Illinois lawyer named Abraham Lincoln patented a device that would float steamboats over shoals. Ostensibly, that is—Lincoln never learned if it worked, because he did not start it up.

Francis Cabot Lowell smuggled plans for a power loom out of England. Throughout the nineteenth century, Englishmen would bring valuable technological advances in their sea trunks or heads.

Costly Labor

Once aroused, Americans proved more than able to advance the Industrial Revolution on their own. Alexander Hamilton had observed "a peculiar aptitude for mechanical improvements" in the American people. In the 1820s, a foreign observer marveled that "everything new is quickly introduced here. There is no clinging to old ways; the moment an American hears the word 'invention' he pricks up his ears."

One reason for the American infatuation with the machine was the labor shortage that vexed employers since the earliest colonial days. Land was abundant and cheap in the United States. Opportunities for an independent life were so ample that skilled artisans demanded and generally won premium pay. In the early nineteenth century, an American carpenter made about three times as much in real income as his European counterpart. Even an unskilled worker in the United States lived considerably better than the day laborers of the Old World. What was sauce for the worker, however, was poison to the men who hired help. The machine, which did the job of many handworkers, was inevitably attractive to the hirers.

Inventors Galore

Thus, Oliver Evans of Philadelphia earned a national reputation when he contrived a continuously operating flour mill. One man was needed to dump grain into one end of an ingenious complex of machinery. Without further human attention, the grain was cleaned, ground, weighed, and packed in barrels. Only at this point was a second man required to pound a lid on the keg. Evans saved millers half their payroll.

In 1800, Eli Whitney devised a rotary cutting tool that quickly and cheaply milled small cast iron parts. Whitney's invention promised to make highly skilled gunsmiths and watchmakers obsolete, for, in making new guns and watches and in repairing broken ones, they had to construct each of many moving parts from scratch. Every musket was "custom made," the lock of each individually fashioned by hand; no two guns were the same. Whitney's milling device made it possible to mass-produce parts of muskets that were interchangeable.

He appeared before a congressional committee with 10 functional muskets he had constructed, took them apart, shuffled the components, and reassembled 10 working muskets. His dramatic little show won him a government contract to make 10,000 of the weapons.

Many cultures produce inventors, but the United States was unique in raising the inventor to the status of a hero, quite the equivalent of a conquering general or a great artist. Even bastions of tradition embraced practical science. In 1814, Harvard College instituted a course called "Elements of Technology." In 1825, Rensselaer Polytechnic Institute, a college devoted entirely to the new learning, was founded at Troy, New York. Others followed in quick succession, for Americans found nothing bizarre in teaching engineering side by side with Greek and Latin. Indeed, they were more likely to be suspicious of those who studied the classics.

A COUNTRY MADE FOR INDUSTRY

A cultural predilection to technology was only one of America's advantages in the Industrial Revolution. The United States was also blessed with the other prerequisites of an industrial society: resources (needed to feed the new machines), capital (surplus money to finance the building of factories), and labor (people to work in the factories).

Resources

For a providentially minded people, it was as if the Creator had shaped the northern states with water-driven mills in mind. From New England to New Jersey, the country was traversed with fast-running streams that, dammed and channeled, provided power for factories. When steam power proved superior to water power, there were dense forests and rich deposits of coal to stoke the boilers. America's forests and strong agricultural base produced the raw materials the new industry required, from lumber to leather to hemp for rope. At the same time the textile industry was growing in New England, cotton cultivation expanded throughout the South to provide enough of the snowy fiber for both England and America.

Capital

Money for investment in industry came from the merchants and shippers of the Northeast. Ironically, many of these capitalists were pressured to convert their wealth from ships into mills by the restrictions on trade that they thought would be the ruin of them. In 1800, at the beginning of the Napoleonic Wars, there were only seven mills in New England, with a total of 290 spindles. After Jefferson's embargo, Madison's restrictions on trade, and the War of 1812 had disrupted shipping for 15 years, there were 130,000 spindles in 213 factories in Massachusetts, Connecticut, and Rhode Island alone.

▲ *The Second Bank of the United States in Philadelphia, chartered by Congress in 1816. Alexander Hamilton's First Bank of the United States operated for 20 years, until an indifferent Jeffersonian Congress allowed its charter to expire. Within a few years, the mistake was recognized—the fast-growing country needed to control its currency—and the Second Bank of the United States was created.*

On the Road

The dictionary defines *road* as "an open way, generally public, for the passage of vehicles, persons, and animals." Roads were the first means of overland transportation, of course. But not until the automobile age would Americans invest the massive sums in them that were plunged into canals and railroads. The explanation is not obscure. Roads of any distance were expensive to build and a nuisance, financially and politically, to maintain. And no one could get rich doing either. Even in densely populated New England, with roads connecting each town to its neighbors, voters resisted taxes and labor levies required to keep them repaired. (Connecticut required "every teeme and person fitt for labour" living on a road to devote two days a year of his and his draft animals' labor to maintaining it.)

As long as most Americans lived near water that would float a boat, they preferred to travel, as well as move their goods, by water. From Portsmouth to Savannah, rivers and sheltered coastal inlets were filled with boats sailing or rowed to and fro. George Washington needed four days on horseback to get from Mount Vernon to Williamsburg. On the Chesapeake, he could get there in half the time and without aching muscles. Providence was connected to Hartford and New Haven by the Pequot Trail, early widened to accommodate wagons, but anyone living near Long Island Sound traveled on it. Philadelphia was only a hundred miles from New York, and there was a fairly good road between them by 1700. Nonetheless, better-off travelers rounded New Jersey by schooner or sloop.

Early American roads followed routes blazed centuries earlier by Indians. The Boston Post Road (present-day U.S. Route 1) followed the Pequot Trail. The road British general Braddock built to battle (and be killed by) the French and Indians followed Nemacolin's Path. Daniel Boone renamed the Shawnee and Cherokee Warriors Path through Kentucky the Wilderness Road.

The Granger Collection, New York

Boone did more than rename it. Indians walked, single file at that. Their paths were rarely wider than a foot, too narrow for a horse, let alone a vehicle. They curled and twisted around large trees and outcroppings of rock. Grade was of no interest to hikers traveling light. So, to build even an equestrian road, it was necessary to "underbrush out" the saplings and small trees and to find or build grades that would not injure a horse. To make a road wide and straight enough for wagons—at first, commonly a rod (sixteen and a half feet) wide—the larger trees had to be felled, leaving stumps no higher than 2 feet, so that the wagons could clear them. Even then, low-lying stretches collected water and were impassable mud pits much of the year; when they did dry out, they were rutted deeply enough to break horses' legs and cart wheels.

There was no money to be made in road building, so only government, with interests other than profit, could undertake such projects. Until independence and the adoption of the Constitution, American governments were incapable of financing any roads but post roads (roads over which letters were carried), and they needed to accommodate only horses.

The great breakthroughs in road surfacing and road finance came simultaneously in the wake of the Constitution. A Scot, John McAdam, discovered that it was not necessary to lay roadbeds of large stone blocks, as the Romans had done, to have a roadway that remained firm after heavy rains. His road base (named macadam after him), raised a foot or two above the terrain for drainage, was constructed of small, uniformly sized stones, either broken by hand or mined from gravel deposits. The traffic would continually compact the roadbed.

In 1794, having seen McAdam's success in Britain, Philadelphia capitalists won a charter from the Pennsylvania legislature to build a macadam road 65 miles from Philadelphia to the important farm town of Lancaster. Their reward would be tolls. Locals going a few miles and people going to church drove the Lancaster Turnpike free. Freighters paid tolls to use the road; it was a "limited-access" highway with tollhouses at each entrance and a pole resembling a pike, the obsolete weapon, blocking entrance until money changed hands. The Lancaster Turnpike (present-day U.S. Route 30) was so successful that hundreds of copycat turnpikes were built within 20 years.

The first great free, federally funded highway was the Cumberland Road, approved by Congress in 1811 and completed from Cumberland, Maryland, on the Potomac to the Ohio River in 1818. It was macadamized, 4 rods wide, ditched on both sides, and it crossed streams on sturdy stone bridges.

Canals and, later, railroads stimulated the construction of feeder roads. Not all had macadam beds. A much cheaper surface in forested areas was made by laying 8-foot logs of 6 to 8 inches in diameter across the roadway. (Eight feet of good old dirt road ran alongside so that vehicles could pass, although not always cordially.) Known as "corduroy roads" for obvious reasons, they were built in newly developed areas until late in the nineteenth century. The ride was bumpy and could be dangerous; but corduroy roads kept wagon wheels out of the mud, they were cheap, and they were easy to repair.

Aware of a good thing once they saw it work, industrialists continued to expand. By 1840, there were 2 million spindles in the United States.

Banks and Money

Banks made it easier to channel capital where it was needed, though not everyone was pleased at the multiplication of lending institutions from 30 in 1801 to 88 in 1811. A bank issued more money in paper certificates than it actually had on hand in gold and silver. In 1809, anticipating the obsession of Thomas Hart Benton, John Adams growled that "every dollar of a bank bill that is issued beyond the quantity of gold and silver in the vaults represents nothing and is therefore a cheat upon somebody."

However, as long as the people who built a mill, supplied it with fiber, and worked the machines accepted the paper dollars lent by a bank to the mill owner, and as long as their grocers, landlords, and business associates accepted the paper money from them, it did not matter that the bank owned only $100,000 in gold and issued $1 million in paper. As long as the people who traded in the bills believed that they could present the paper to the bank and receive gold, capital was increased tenfold. As long as confidence and optimism were in rich supply, banks were a source of energy more powerful than the 32-foot falls of the Merrimack River.

The Jeffersonians had allowed the First Bank of the United States to die when its charter expired in 1811. Within five years, they recognized their error and chartered a Second Bank of the United States with much the same powers as the first.

Industry and Politics

With the increasing importance of industrial interests in the Northeast, the section's political interests shifted. Traditionally, New England shipowners were suspicious of high tariffs on imported goods. If taxes on imports were high, fewer Americans bought them, and there was less business carrying manufactured goods across the ocean. Alexander Hamilton failed to get the tariff he wanted partly because New England merchants, Federalists on other issues, joined with farmers (who were consumers of manufactured goods and wanted the lowest prices possible) to defeat him.

As late as 1816, many New England congressmen voted against high tariffs. One of them was Daniel Webster, a 34-year-old representative from New Hampshire who numbered Portsmouth shipmasters among his legal clients. By 1823, when Webster returned to Congress, he had moved to Massachusetts and become counsel and confidant to several manufacturers. Now he was a strong and eloquent supporter of a high tariff. If infant industries were to grow, they had to be protected from competition with the cheaper goods that the older and better-developed British manufacturers could produce.

Labor

Industrialization eventually undercut and almost destroyed handicraft. Many people were needed to tend the machines in the new mills, and the United States lacked England's surplus of "sturdy beggars" roaming the countryside and overcrowding the cities. Few white Americans were desperately poor. Few men who could freely choose among farming profitably, moving west, or working in small independent shops were attracted to low-paying, highly disciplined factory work.

The difficulty of recruiting labor from among traditional groups was reflected in the failure of the "Fall River system." In Fall River, Massachusetts, the mill owners attempted to hire whole families to work in the mills. It was an honest mistake. The family was the unit of production on the traditional farm and in the artisan's shop. But the system did not work very well in factories. In Rhode Island, mill owners put the man of the house on a small farm and put his wife and children to work in the mills.

The Lowell Girls

Rather more successful than both, because it found a niche within the traditional social structure, was the system developed by Francis Cabot Lowell, who built several large mills in Waltham, Massachusetts, in 1813, and in a town he founded and named Lowell in 1826. Lowell dispatched recruiters to roam rural New England. They persuaded farmers to send their young daughters to work in the mills. For 70 hours a week at the machines, the girls and young women earned three dollars, paying half of that for room and board at company-supervised lodging houses. Most—frugal lasses—banked the rest.

The long workweek put off no one. It was a normal enough regimen for a farm girl. The money was attractive too. Farming the stony New England soil never made anyone rich, and Yankee farmers burdened with large families inevitably liked the idea of subtracting one diner from the table, especially if that diner was a daughter who, by going to Lowell for a few years, could save a dowry large enough to attract a suitable husband. The Lowell system was successful precisely because it drew on a body of people for whom there were few other opportunities.

The trick was to persuade straitlaced New Englanders to allow girls of 16 and 17 to leave home. Lowell worked it by providing a closely regulated life for his employees during off hours as well as working hours. The Lowell girls lived in company-run dormitories, attended church services, and were kept busy (as if 70 hours at work were not enough!) with a variety of educational and cultural programs.

Most of the first American industrial workers were women—and children. In 1820, about half the factory hands in Massachusetts mills were under 16 years of age. A society of farmers, in which everyone down to 6 years of age had assigned chores, did not find this inhumane. And the pace of

▲ *New England mill girls, not long off a New England farm. There was no shame in working at a mill. The experience, the new friends, and the cash income (modest though it was) must have been exhilarating to many.*

▲ *Workers at the Lowell Mills and most other factories lived closely supervised lives; attending church (a church of their choice) was a condition of employment. The factory provided after-hours programs of "cultural uplift." As if at college, the workers at Lowell published a literary magazine of their own, the* Lowell Offering. *Supervisors monitored "dating" closely, and there seem to have been few illegitimate pregnancies. But almost all the mill girls found husbands either in the mill towns or back home near the family farm.*

the early factory was far slower than that of a twenty-first-century assembly line. Operatives minding textile machines shut them down when they thought it necessary to do so. In some mills, girls were permitted to entertain visitors while they watched their spindles. English tourists commented that American factories were idyllic compared with England's "dark, satanic mills." Nevertheless, Lowell was no idyll. In 1834 and 1836, angry Lowell Girls shut down the mills until their demands for better compensation were met.

THE SOUTH AT THE CROSSROADS

While westerners tamed land and northeasterners built a society dominated by mills and swelling cities, southerners reaffirmed their agrarian heritage. There were those who would have had it otherwise. In 1816, when Daniel Webster was still speaking for the shipping interests of old New England, John C. Calhoun of South Carolina dreamed of cotton factories in his state.

But Calhoun's flirtation with industrialization, like his War Hawk supernationalism in 1812, was already doomed. His future lay in defending southern sectionalism, the plantation system, and the institution of slavery on which they rested. Ironically, this brilliant political theorist (and somewhat less able politician) was chained to such anachronistic institutions because of a machine that, if its technology was rudimentary, was profound in its dramatic consequences.

Slavery in Decline

When John C. Calhoun was born in 1782, African American slavery appeared to be dying out. The northern states abolished it before Calhoun was an adult. Slavery also declined in the South during the revolutionary era. The world price of tobacco, one of the few crops for which slave labor was profitable, collapsed. On top of that, many of the old Chesapeake and Carolina tobacco fields were exhausted. Other slave-raised crops, such as South Carolina's rice and indigo, lost some luster when British subsidies were lost following independence.

Southerners, as well as northerners, were moved by the ideals of the Declaration of Independence. Thomas Jefferson, its author, agonized throughout his life over the injustice of human bondage. In their wills, Jefferson, George Washington, and many other planters freed at least some of their slaves. Few spoke of slavery as anything better than a tragic social burden, a necessary evil. As late as 1808, only a few southerners objected when Congress (as the Constitution allowed) outlawed further importation of enslaved blacks from abroad. At the peace talks in Ghent in 1815, American and British commissioners discussed the possibility of cooperating in suppressing illegal traders. It is reasonable to suggest that the institution would have been phased out peacefully in the United States (as it was in the British Empire) had it not been for the "absurdly simple contrivance" invented by Eli Whitney.

The Cotton Gin

In 1793, seven years before his demonstration of interchangeable parts, Eli Whitney was living on a plantation near Savannah, Georgia. He saw his first cotton plant and learned that it flourished everywhere in the upland South, where there was plenty of rain and 210 frost-free days spring to fall. Cotton fiber was worth 30 to 40 cents a pound—a fabulous price for the by-product of a plant—but the upland cotton could not be exploited commercially because of the costs of separating the fiber from the plant's sticky green seeds. The job could be done only by hand, and the most nimble-fingered of people could process no more than a pound of fluff a day, hardly enough to justify hiring employees to do it, let alone setting an expensive slave to the job.

On the sandy sea islands off the coast of South Carolina and Georgia, cotton had been cultivated profitably since 1786. But the variety planted there was long-staple cotton with shiny, smooth black seeds that could be popped out of the fiber by running the raw cotton between two rollers. When this method was tried with the cotton of the uplands, the sticky green seeds were crushed, fouling the fiber with oil.

Whitney's device was so simple that a planter who had a decent collection of junk on the grounds could make a

▲ *A lithograph celebrates the revolution in the economy and society of the Deep South wrought by the invention of the cotton gin. The glee of the planters at the left makes sense; the joy of the slaves working the gin does not. The boom in cotton created by the cotton gin increased the demand for slave labor which had been in steady decline everywhere but in the rice growing regions of South Carolina.*

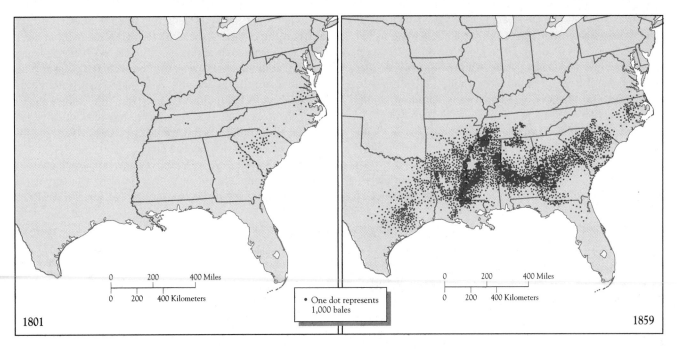

1801

1859

• One dot represents
1,000 bales

MAP 14:2 The Spread of Cotton Production Short-staple, green-seed cotton grew like a weed across the Deep South. The cotton gin made it possible to grow the fiber as a very lucrative crop.

workable version. In fact, the ease of constructing the cotton "gin" (short for *engine*) denied Whitney the fortune he deserved for inventing it. His patents were ignored, and he was ground down into exhaustion in the courts.

Essentially, Whitney dumped the bolls into a box at the bottom of which were slots too small for the seeds to pass through. A drum studded with wire hooks revolved so that the hooks caught the fibers and pulled them through the slots, leaving behind the seeds without crushing them. Another drum, revolving in the opposite direction, brushed the fiber from the wire hooks.

It was a magnificent device. A single slave cranking a small gin could clean 10 pounds of cotton a day—$3 to $4 worth of cotton at 1790 prices. A larger machine turned by a horse on a windlass could clean 50 pounds a day (worth $15 to $20!). Once steam-powered gins were introduced, the capacity for producing cotton was limited not by the processing problem but by the number of acres that a planter could cultivate.

The Revival of Slavery

Technology had come to the South, but industry had not. The effects of Eli Whitney's machine were the revival of the South's traditional one-crop economy, the domination of southern society by large planters, and the reinvigoration of slavery. Like tobacco, cotton was well adapted to gang cultivation. The crop required plenty of unskilled labor: plowing, planting, chopping (or weeding, an endless process in the hot, fertile South), ditch digging and maintenance, picking, ginning, pressing, baling, and shipping.

Moreover, the fertile belt of uplands that extends from South Carolina and Georgia through eastern Texas was nat-

ural cotton country. Seduced by the same charms of riches that turned western farmers into speculators and doughty New England merchants into industrial capitalists, southerners streamed into the "Old Southwest" (Alabama, Mississippi, and northern Louisiana) and eventually into Arkansas across the Mississippi River. In 1800, excluding Indians, there were about 1,000 people in what is now Alabama. In 1810, there were 9,000; in 1820, 128,000! The growth of Mississippi was less dramatic but not lethargic: in 1800, 8,000; in 1810, 31,000; in 1820, 75,000.

Nor was this an emigration of buckskin-clad frontiersmen with no more baggage than a long rifle and a frying pan. Wealthy planters from the old states made the trek, bringing their slaves with them. In 1800, there were 4,000 blacks in Alabama and Mississippi. In 1810, there were 17,000 blacks, virtually all of them slaves. In 1820, there were 75,000. Almost half the population of Mississippi was African American and in bondage.

The price of slaves soared, doubling between 1795 and 1804. Blacks who were becoming financial burdens in Maryland and Virginia became valuable commodities in the new cotton South. The most humane masters found it difficult to resist the temptation of the high prices offered for their prime field hands, males between 18 and 30 years of age. Slave owners from as far north as New Jersey liquidated their human holdings, selling them to cotton planters.

The Missouri Crisis

There were still a few slaves in the North to be sold in 1819. Most states had adopted a gradualist approach to emancipation, by which no person born or brought into the state after a certain date could be enslaved. (There were a handful of aged slaves in New Jersey as late as the Civil War.)

But there was also, by 1819, a clear-cut line between slave states and free states. North of the Mason-Dixon line (the Maryland-Pennsylvania border) and the Ohio River, slavery was forbidden or in the process of abolition. South of it, the institution remained a vital part of society and the economy. In 1819, quite in the middle of the "Era of Good Feelings," the sectional character of the institution briefly became an explosive issue.

It was ignited by the application of the Missouri Territory to be admitted to the Union as a state. Although west of the Mississippi River, all but a tiny fraction of Missouri lay north of the mouth of the Ohio River. Quite able to read a map and voicing moral objections to slavery, Congressman James Tallmadge of New York proposed that Missouri be admitted only after its proposed state constitution was amended to forbid the further importation of slaves and to free all slaves within the state when they reached 25 years of age. In a word, Missouri would eliminate slavery gradually, as the northern states had done.

Some northern representatives and senators leapt into the breach Tallmadge opened. One described slavery as "a sin which sits heavily on the soul of every one of us." On

MAP 14:3 Missouri Compromise, 1820   Note that Missouri, a state in 1820, was largely north of the line demarcating slave and free states. Henry Clay persuaded enough northern congressmen to accept this anomaly on the condition that slavery would be forbidden in all future states so far north. As of 1820, only Arkansas and Florida territories were open to slavery, and it was not guaranteed existence even there.

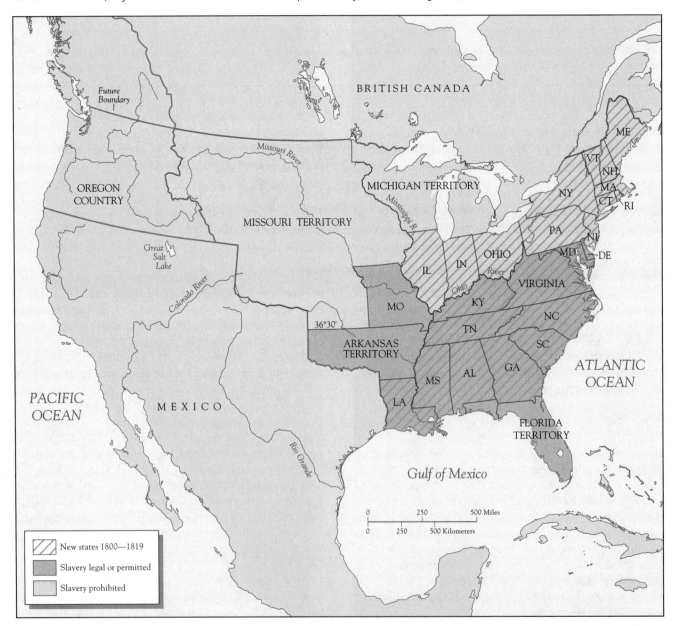

hearing such rhetoric, old Thomas Jefferson wrote from Monticello that he was startled as though he had heard "a firebell in the night." John Quincy Adams expressed concern. What worried both men was that once the morality of the discussants enters a debate, conflicts are not easily resolved by cutting a deal or trading tit for tat. Indeed, southern congressmen, particularly representatives of cotton states like Mississippi and Alabama, replied to their northern censors in fierce and furious language.

The Compromise

Ever unflappable, James Monroe was not unduly disturbed. A Virginian who was ambivalent to the future of slavery, he encouraged compromise in Congress. The deal was actually devised, however, by another southerner who wanted no part of moral imprecations in discussions of slavery, Henry Clay.

Earning the nickname the "Great Compromiser" for his scheme (known as the Missouri Compromise), Clay proposed that Missouri be admitted to the Union as those who wrote its constitution wished, as a slave state. This soothed southern feathers. In order to mollify northerners for whom slavery was an important issue, Clay proposed that the southern boundary of Missouri, 36 degrees, 30 minutes north latitude, be extended through the remainder of American territory—to the crest of the Rocky Mountains. North of that line, slavery was forever prohibited. In territories south of the line, which meant the Arkansas Territory and recently acquired Florida, the citizens living there could decide whether the state would be slave or free.

Passions cooled, tempers eased. Congressmen who had glared at one another shook hands and turned to other business. But Jefferson's "firebell" continued, however muted, to echo in the distance and with a new timbre to its peal. For Clay's compromise implied an equity, even a balance, between free states and slave states. There were 22 states in the Union in 1819, 11 free, 11 slave. When Missouri was admitted, Congress also detached "the Maine District" from Massachusetts and admitted it as a free state.

For 30 years to come, Congress would admit states virtually in pairs, preserving the balance. But because the Missouri Compromise forbade slavery in the major part of the Louisiana Purchase, it was inevitable that, sooner or later, a territory would seek admission to the Union as a free state with no slave state to balance it.

The population of the North was increasing much more quickly than the population of the South. Until 1810, the two sections grew at an uncannily similar rate. In 1820, however, despite the explosive growth of Mississippi and Alabama, there were nearly a million more people in the North than in the South: 5,219,000 versus 4,419,000. As the disparity increased—and all signs said that it would—the good feelings that made James Monroe's presidency such a happy one were bound to be among the casualties.

for FURTHER READING

Comprehensive histories of this era include the appropriate chapters of John R. Howe, *From the Revolution Through the Age of Jackson,* 1973; Robert Heilbroner, *The Economic Transformation of America,* 1977; W. Elliott Brownlee, *Dynamics of Ascent: A History of the American Economy,* 1974; and George Dangerfield, *The Era of Good Feelings,* 1952.

Research subsequent to Dangerfield's work has been incorporated into John Mayfield, *The New Nation, 1800–1845,* 1981. A superb social history, part of which covers these years, is Daniel Boorstin, *The Americans: The National Experience,* 1965.

The standard biography of the president of the Era of Good Feelings is William P. Cresson, *James Monroe,* 1971; the standard biography of Monroe's secretary of state is Samuel F. Bemis, *John Quincy Adams and the Foundation of American Foreign Policy,* 1949. See also Henry F. May, *The Making of the Monroe Doctrine,*

1975; and Dexter Perkins, *The Monroe Doctrine,* 1927. On the major political issue of the Monroe presidency, see Glover Moore, *The Missouri Controversy,* 1953; and Donald L. Robinson, *Slavery in the Structure of American Politics, 1765–1820,* 1979.

Early American industrialization has been a subject of lively inquiry in recent decades. Students should see Thomas Cochran, *Frontiers of Change: Early Industrialism in America,* 1981; Allan Dawley, *Class and Community in Lynn,* 1976; Thomas Dublin, *Women at Work: The Transformation of Work and Community in Lowell, Massachusetts, 1826–1860,* 1979; David J. Jeremy, *Transatlantic Industrial Revolution: The Diffusion of Textile Technologies Between Britain and America,* 1981; Bruce Laurie, *The Working People of Philadelphia, 1800–1850,* 1980; and Leo Marx, *The Machine in the Garden: Technology and the Pastoral Ideal in America,* 1964.

 AMERICAN JOURNEY ONLINE AND INFOTRAC COLLEGE EDITION

Visit the source collections at http://ajaccess.wadsworth.com and http://infotrac.thomsonlearning.com, and use the Search function with the following key terms to explore documents, images, audio and video clips, articles, and commentary related to the material in this chapter:

Eli Whitney   Missouri Compromise
John Quincy Adams   Monroe Doctrine

Additional resources, exercises, and Internet links related to this chapter are available on *The American Past* Web site: http://history.wadsworth.com/americanpast7e.

HISTORY ONLINE

Erie Canal Online
www.syracuse.com/features/eriecanal/
Brief history; links to other sites about the Erie Canal.

Mill Girls
www.nps.gov/low/loweweb/Lowell%20History/Millgirls.htm
Treasury of insights on early industrialization in Lowell, Massachusetts, with a focus on the workers, the mill girls.

HERO OF THE PEOPLE

Andrew Jackson and a New Era 1824–1830

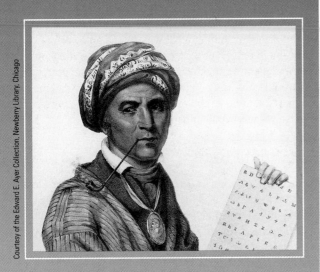

Courtesy of the Edward E. Ayer Collection, Newberry Library, Chicago

Thou great democratic God . . . who didst pick up
Andrew Jackson from the pebbles; who didst hurl him
upon a warhorse; who didst thunder him higher than a
throne! Thou who, in all Thy mighty, earthly marchings,
ever cullest Thy selected champions from the kingly
commons.

Herman Melville

Except an enormous fabric of executive power, the
President has built up nothing. . . . He goes for
destruction, universal destruction.

Henry Clay

THE SINGLE-PARTY system of the Monroe years had its
virtues. At the top, at least, administration was efficient,
and political culture was closer to noble than it would be
again until the 1930s. In Congress, debate was candid and
eloquent, almost always on a higher plane than in eras when
partisanship has reigned. At best, party loyalty is less edifying than loyalty to home, country, or principle. At worst, it
rewards tawdry, servile hacks. The Era of Good Feelings was
spared the worst that American politics can produce. The
era was not, however, spared ambitious men. A single party
could not accommodate the hunger of every politician who
wanted a better job. There were not enough nominations and
appointments to go around.

So, in 1824, as James Monroe packed up in the White
House, the Jefferson Republican party flew into pieces—
half a dozen pieces attached to men who wanted to be president. Four years later, most of these fragments coalesced
into two new parties, the Democratic Republicans (soon
simply "Democrats") and the National Republicans (later
renamed "Whigs").

THE SKEWED ELECTION OF 1824

During the quarter century the Jefferson Republicans dominated national politics, three traditions had grown up around
the presidency: "King Caucus," the "Virginia Dynasty," and
succession to the White House by the secretary of state, who
was appointed by his predecessor. In 1824, two of these institutions were toppled, and the third was discredited.

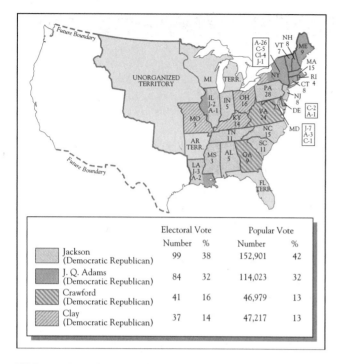

	Electoral Vote		Popular Vote	
	Number	%	Number	%
Jackson (Democratic Republican)	99	38	152,901	42
J. Q. Adams (Democratic Republican)	84	32	114,023	32
Crawford (Democratic Republican)	41	16	46,979	13
Clay (Democratic Republican)	37	14	47,217	13

MAP 15:1 Presidential Election of 1824 Andrew Jackson was the only one of the four presidential candidates who carried states in the North, the South, and the West.

Caucus, Dynasty, and Succession

The first to be dethroned was King Caucus. This was the name given (by those who did not much like it) to the method by which the Jeffersonians had nominated their presidential and vice presidential candidates. In election years, Jefferson Republican members of Congress met in caucus (that is, as members of the party) and named their nominee for the general election. Until 1824, unsuccessful candidates accepted the decision of King Caucus, as did the party's supporters.

Indeed, fights within the caucus were without much spirit. Monroe challenged Madison in 1808, lost, and three years later became his secretary of state. William Crawford of Georgia ran against Monroe in 1816, lost narrowly, and entered Monroe's cabinet. Partly by chance, but also because of the gentility with which caucus fights were fought, Madison and Monroe both stepped from the office of secretary of state into the White House. An orderly means of succession seemed to be established—presidents, like Roman emperors, "adopting" their heirs.

Americans spoke of a "Virginia Dynasty." All three of the Jefferson Republican presidents—Jefferson, Madison, and Monroe—were Virginians. Until 1824, it was all quite tidy and proper, especially to Virginians.

In 1824, however, the secretary of state was John Quincy Adams, so much a Massachusetts man that southern Jeffersonians regarded him as a Federalist in disguise. They were suspicious of Adams's strident nationalism and disliked his belief that the national government should exercise extensive

powers in shaping both the economy and society. Most southern politicians hoped to make the secretary of the treasury, William Crawford, the party's presidential nominee.

Crawford was from Georgia, but, having been born in Nelson County, Virginia, he could qualify as the Virginia Dynasty's legitimate heir. At odds with Adams, Crawford was an orthodox Jeffersonian who feared a powerful central government and favored strict construction of the Constitution. President Monroe and the party caucus supported him. The trouble was, only Crawford supporters attended the caucus in 1824. Others repaired to their own states, where state legislatures named other candidates.

Candidate Stew

For a while, it appeared that New York governor DeWitt Clinton, the builder of the Erie Canal, and South Carolina senator John C. Calhoun would enter their names in the contest. Clinton dropped out when he attracted little support outside his state. Calhoun found his chances slim and settled for second best, running as vice president with two other candidates.

One of them was John Quincy Adams. Adams's supporters rallied around the tradition that the secretary of state should succeed to the presidency. They also liked Adams because of his assertive and successful foreign policy, his support of a high tariff to protect infant industries, and his belief that the federal government should take an active role in promoting economic prosperity, including a federally financed program of internal improvements. Adams was nominated by the Massachusetts state legislature.

Henry Clay, nominated by the legislature of Kentucky, shared Adams's views. The two men differed in little but their personal aversion to one another's personal habits. When they were negotiators in Ghent, the high-living Clay mocked the hardworking Adams as dull and prudish. Adams, in turn, looked on Clay's drinking, gambling, and womanizing as dissolute. Now, in 1824, they divided the votes of those who favored their nationalistic economic program. Clay's hope was that he would win as the spokesman for the growing West.

Unfortunately, there was another westerner in the contest, General Andrew Jackson of Tennessee. So magical was his name as the conqueror of the British and half a dozen Indian tribes that it did not matter that Jackson's political principles were something of a mystery. Only on the questions of currency and banking was Jackson known to have taken a strong stand. Although rich—the wealthiest man in Tennessee, some said—Jackson detested banks and paper money. He had been ruined in a panic in the 1790s and, as all Americans were soon to learn, Andrew Jackson did not forget a grudge.

In 1824, Jackson's supporters did not allow voters to forget the Battle of New Orleans or the fact that Jackson was a man of action who crossed the Appalachians poor and by hook and crook and wiles and will—the American way—became a hero. "He has slain the Indians and flogged the British," a Jackson man put it, "and therefore is the wisest and greatest man in the nation."

Who Won?

This appeal to sentiment and the support of Calhoun, who was also Jackson's vice presidential candidate, was enough to win Jackson more popular and electoral votes than any of his opponents. He was also the only candidate of the four to win electoral votes in all three sections: Northeast, South, and West. But Jackson fell short of a majority in the electoral college. As in the election of 1800, the task of naming the president fell to the members of the House of Representatives, voting by states.

▲ *John Quincy Adams was one of the ablest individuals ever to be president. He may also have been the most inept politician to live in the White House.*

The Metropolitan Museum of Art, Gift of I. N. Phelps Stokes, Edward S. Hawes, Alice Mary Hawes, Marion Augusta Hawes, 1937.

Under the terms of the Twelfth Amendment, the House selected from among the top three finishers in the electoral college, which eliminated Clay. William Crawford also seemed to be out of the running. He had suffered a stroke that left him bedridden and unable to speak. Crawford's supporters insisted he would recover, and, in time, he did. But they were unable to arouse any enthusiasm outside the southern states.

Jackson's followers were confident of victory. As they saw it, the House of Representatives was morally bound to ratify the election of the man preferred by more voters than any other. It was a good argument—the democratic argument—but it did not carry the day. Instead, because of the political beliefs and personal ambitions of the influential Henry Clay, and perhaps the impulse of Stephen Van Rensselaer, an elderly congressman from New York, the second-place finisher in the election, John Quincy Adams, won the prize.

"Corrupt Bargain!"

Van Rensselaer, who cast the vote that threw the New York delegation and the election to John Quincy Adams, said that he was praying for guidance, glanced at the floor, and saw a piece of paper on which was written "Adams." He took it as a sign from on high. Long before this providential moment, however, Clay had decided to back Adams, and, as Speaker of the House, he was well placed to reward congressmen who were persuaded by his arguments. Clay favored Adams because, despite their personal distaste for one another, they agreed on most political issues. Jackson, on the other hand, was a sworn enemy of one of Clay's favorite projects, the Bank of the United States.

Moreover, Clay wanted to be president—if not in 1824, then later—and Jackson was surrounded by would-be successors: Calhoun of South Carolina (who easily won the vice presidency), John Eaton of Tennessee, and Richard M. Johnson from Clay's own Kentucky. There was no room in the Jackson crowd for Henry Clay. Adams, by contrast, was a cranky, solitary man with few close friends. Because he had spent much of his life abroad as a diplomat, Adams had no circle of political cronies and heirs apparent.

Clay and Adams did not sit down across a table and hammer out a tit-for-tat understanding. Clay was a man for such a deal—how else win the title "Great Compromiser"?—but Adams was too stubborn, proper, and self-righteous to "talk turkey." His distaste for the dirty work of politics would, soon enough, shatter his career as a national politician. Nevertheless, when Clay threw his influence in the House of Representatives behind Adams and Adams later appointed Clay secretary of state, the losers of 1824 were sure they had been cheated by two cynical schemers.

John Randolph of Roanoke, a Crawford supporter, sneered at the union of "the puritan and the blackleg," an insult that led Clay to challenge him to a duel. (No one was hit.) The Jacksonians settled for shouting "corrupt bargain," obstructing the Adams presidency, and planning for revenge.

A New Party

Between 1824 and 1828, Jackson's loose alliance of supporters coalesced into a new political party. It included Jackson's western following and southerners led by John C. Calhoun. Despite this formidable base, the Jacksonians still had to break the grip of the Adams-Clay forces in the populous Northeast. Toward this end, Martin Van Buren of New York called on Jackson at his Tennessee mansion, the Hermitage, and put his influence in his native state at the general's service.

The South, the West, and New York formed the consortium that allowed Jefferson and Aaron Burr to throw the first Adams out of office in 1800. Also, like the Jefferson Republicans of 1800, the Jacksonians appealed to the ordinary fellow—the "common man"—and depicted their opponents as the party of privilege.

This was mostly nonsense. The leaders of the Jackson party were of the same social class as the people close to Adams and Clay, and Andrew Jackson was no common man. He had warned against the "undisciplined rising of the masses." But the Jacksonian appeal to democracy versus a conniving elite came naturally after the "corrupt bargain" controversy. "Let the people rule!" the Jacksonians cried even before Adams was inaugurated. Let them have the president that most of them chose in 1824. Seizing on the theme, the Jacksonians called themselves "Democratic Republicans," soon shortened to "Democrats."

THE AGE OF THE COMMON MAN

Like his father, John Quincy Adams brought impressive credentials to the White House. On paper, no one—surely not the laconic General Jackson—was better qualified for the job. Although Jackson could claim to have been slashed in the face by a British officer at the age of 14, John Quincy Adams at that age was in government service, secretary to an American minister abroad (his father). He had himself been minister in several European countries, senator from Massachusetts, and a secretary of state whose successes still rank him among the most able ever to hold that post.

Another Unhappy Adams

Also like his father, Adams's qualifications ended with his achievements. In temperament, he was out of tune with his times, unable to provide what more and more Americans were demanding of their leaders. In an age of electrifying political personalities—Benton, Clay, Jackson, Calhoun—Quincy Adams excited no one. Among a people beginning to prize equality and easy informality, Adams was standoffish, stuffy, and self-conscious of his abilities, learning, ancestry, and achievements.

In an era when government was becoming more democratic at every level, Adams spoke contemptuously of being "palsied by the will of our constituents."

Worst of all, political horse trading, if far from new, was now open, frank, fast, and furious. Quincy Adams tried to stand above partisan politics. He allowed open enemies to hold office under him. To have removed them and filled their posts with his supporters, Adams felt, would have been to stoop to the level of shabby politics that—unjustly in his opinion—he was accused of in the "corrupt bargain" controversy.

Adams was also thin skinned and short tempered. He took criticism, and sometimes mere suggestions, as affronts to his office and his person. He cut himself off not only from a majority of voters but from allies who had honest, minor disagreements with him. By the end of his term, he had a smaller political base in Washington than any previous president, including his unhappy father.

A Democratic Upheaval

Quincy Adams's view of himself as a member of a "natural aristocracy" of wealth, education, manners, and talent was the view of the previous generation of American politicians, Thomas Jefferson included. During the 1820s, however, politics ceased to be primarily the concern of the leisured, educated classes and came to preoccupy much of the white male population. The foremost foreign commentator on American attitudes, Alexis de Tocqueville, wrote that "almost the

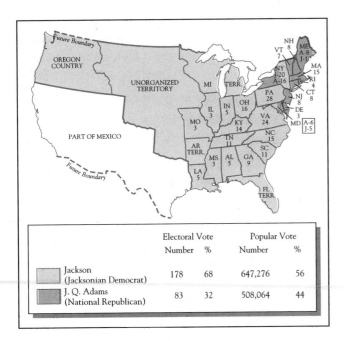

	Electoral Vote		Popular Vote	
	Number	%	Number	%
Jackson (Jacksonian Democrat)	178	68	647,276	56
J. Q. Adams (National Republican)	83	32	508,064	44

MAP 15:2 Presidential Election of 1828 Jackson swept the electoral college, even winning one electoral vote in New England.

only pleasure which an American knows is to take part in government." A less sympathetic visitor to the United States, Mrs. Frances Trollope, was appalled that American men would rather talk politics than mend their fences and tend their crops.

In part, this great democratic upheaval was the fruit of half a century of rhetoric that blatantly flirted with democracy. The Jeffersonians never ceased saying that the people should rule, and, like a slogan in a television commercial endlessly repeated, the idea caught on. The democratic upheaval of the 1820s and 1830s was also the consequence of the extraordinary growth and energy of the young republic. An increasingly prosperous people needed to struggle less in order to survive and had more time to think about public affairs. With issues like the tariff, land policy, and internal improvements bearing heavily on individual fortunes, ordinary folk had good reason to take an interest in politics.

Finally, the wave of democratic spirit that swept Andrew Jackson on its crest had a peculiarly western source. In order to attract population, the young western states extended the right to vote to all free, adult white males. All six states admitted to the Union between 1816 and 1821—Indiana, Mississippi, Illinois, Alabama, Maryland, and, back East, Maine—required no property ownership of voters. Western states enacted other laws designed to appeal to people of modest station. Kentucky abolished imprisonment for debt in 1821. No longer could a man or woman be jailed for financial misfortune.

Democratization spread south and east. Fearful of losing population to the West, most eastern states responded to liberal western voting laws by adopting universal male suffrage. In 1824, about half the states still insisted on some property qualifications in order to vote. By 1830, only North Carolina, Virginia, Rhode Island, and Louisiana did, and Rhode Island's conservatism in the matter was misleading. Still governed under the state's seventeenth-century colonial charter, which could not be easily amended, Rhode Island was rocked by a brief violent uprising in 1842, Dorr's Rebellion, which resulted in extending the vote to all adult white males.

In 1800, only 2 of 16 states named presidential electors by popular vote. In 1824, 18 of 24 states did. By 1832, only planter-dominated South Carolina clung to selecting electors in the legislature.

Given the right to vote, free adult white males did. In 1824, the first presidential election in which there was widespread participation, about one-quarter of the country's eligible voters cast ballots. In 1828, one-half of the eligible voters voted. In 1840, more than three-quarters of the electorate participated in the national election. If such a proportion of eligible voters voted today, it would be described as a political revolution.

The "Workies"

Some new voters built parties around social issues. During the 1820s, workingmen's parties sprang up in eastern cities. Casually called the "Workies" and supported largely by recently enfranchised "mechanics," as skilled artisans were known, they pushed in city and state elections for a variety of reforms to protect their class: abolition of imprisonment for debt, which hit independent artisans hard; mechanics' lien laws, which prevented creditors from seizing their tools; laws giving wage workers first crack at a bankrupt employer's assets; and free public education for all children. To the workingman of the Northeast, education was the equivalent of the westerner's free land, the key to moving up in the world.

The workingmen's parties had their local victories, especially in New York. But they dwindled when farther-seeing visionaries, most notably Scottish-born Frances "Fanny" Wright, tried to convert the Workies to broader reforms. Wright, for example, was a feminist before feminism's time and advocated "free love," the freedom of all, unmarried and married, to enjoy sexual partners who were not their spouses.

Mechanics had no more interest in modifying the legal status of women than mainstream politicians did, and they were quite as likely as their employers to regard traditional restrictions on sexual activity as right and proper. As inclined to dally as men and women of every social class, mechanics were also conscious of the fact that their social status was superior to that of the urban underclass in part because of the comparatively open promiscuity of the lower classes. When most of the Workies' bread-and-butter reforms were enacted, they drifted into the Democratic party.

The Anti-Masonic Party

The Anti-Masonic party was a curious expression of the democratic upheaval of the 1820s and 1830s. It was founded in upstate New York when a bricklayer named William Morgan

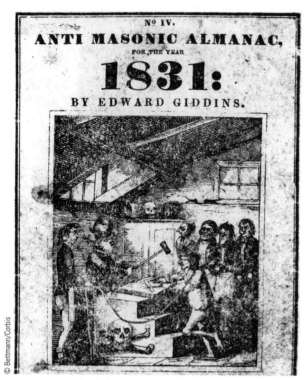

NO IV.
ANTI MASONIC ALMANAC,
FOR THE YEAR
1831:
BY EDWARD GIDDINS.

▲ *The Anti-Masons had such astonishing success at the polls because many believed the Society of Freemasons was a conspiracy of the well-to-do that secretly kept the common man down. However, as with many such movements, the Anti-Masonic movement focused on sinister and lurid Masonic rituals (many imagined) in their propaganda.*

published an exposé of the Society of Freemasons and, shortly thereafter, was murdered.

Originally, the Society of Freemasons was a secret association of freethinkers. Many of the Founding Fathers, including Franklin and Washington, had been members; the pyramid with an eye atop it on the back of our dollar bill is a Masonic symbol. After 1800, the Freemasons were largely a club of middling to upper-class gentlemen. Much of Morgan's book dealt with Masonic rituals behind closed doors (hocus-pocus ostensibly hearkening back to ancient Egypt) and the secret handshakes and passwords by which Masons identified themselves to one another in public. For example, Morgan quoted the initiation ceremony during which a new member swore "to keep all Masonic secrets under the penalty of having his throat cut, his tongue torn out, and his body buried in the ocean." When Morgan disappeared and a corpse apparently mutilated according to regulations was dragged out of the Niagara River, outrage swept the state.

Politicians pointed out that Morgan was a workingman whereas most Masons were prosperous farmers, merchants, bankers, and the like. The order, they said, was a conspiracy aimed at keeping Masons on top and the common man down. The handshakes and passwords, they pointed out, quoting from Morgan's book, were to identify fellow Masons so as to do business with them rather than with "any other person in the same circumstances."

Every governor of New York between 1804 and 1828 had been a Mason. What was going on? Secrecy, the Anti-

Masons said, had no place in a free society. Preferential treatment had no place in a free market. The Anti-Masons also benefited from traditional views about the sanctity of the family that Fanny Wright flaunted. By maintaining that some secrets must be shared only with fellow Masons, Anti-Masons pointed out, the order was insinuating itself between husband and wife. If a husband were required to keep secrets from his own spouse, he was violating the marriage contract as surely as a free lover did.

A brace of political leaders who would later play an important part in national politics first came to the fore as Anti-Masons: Thaddeus Stevens, Thurlow Weed, William H. Seward, and Millard Fillmore. In 1832, the party's candidate for president, William Wirt, won 33,000 votes and carried the state of Vermont. In the same year, the party elected 53 candidates to Congress.

President Andrew Jackson was himself an active Mason. Consequently, although democratic to the core, Anti-Masons inclined to join the anti-Jackson Whig party when their single-issue enthusiasm flagged.

In the meantime, the Anti-Masonic party made a lasting contribution to American politics. In Baltimore in 1831, the Anti-Masons were the first party to hold a national party convention. With the caucus system of making presidential nominations dead and nomination by state legislatures not firmly established, the major parties imitated the Anti-Masonic example. The first Democratic convention met in 1832, nominating Andrew Jackson. The Whigs followed suit a few years later.

THE REVOLUTION OF 1828

Thomas Jefferson had called the election of 1800 the "Revolution of 1800." But in 1800, there was not nearly as great a break with what had gone before as there was in Andrew Jackson's victory in the election of 1828. His election ended the era of sedate transfers of power from incumbent president to secretary of state. Jackson was the first chief executive to come from a western state. (He was the first president not from Virginia or Massachusetts.) And the campaign that led to his election was noisier, harder fought, and "dirtier" than any the United States had experienced to date.

Mudslinging

Personally, Jackson followed precedent by taking no part in the campaign of 1828. He sat in the Hermitage while his

---

Don't Vote for That Bastard

Among the campaign mud that found its way into print was this aspersion on Andrew Jackson's lineage:

General Jackson's mother was a COMMON PROSTITUTE, brought to this country by the British soldiers! She afterwards married a Mulatto Man, with whom she had several children, one of which number GENERAL JACKSON IS ONE!

supporters fired insulting salvos at President Adams. They depicted the incumbent as a usurper, an elitist, a man with decadent European tastes who squandered money filling the White House with elegant furniture and its cellar with European wines. The Democrats made a great fuss over Adams's purchase of a billiard table; billiards, by virtue of the high cost of the table, was a game of aristocrats. (In fact, Adams paid for his toy out of his own pocket.)

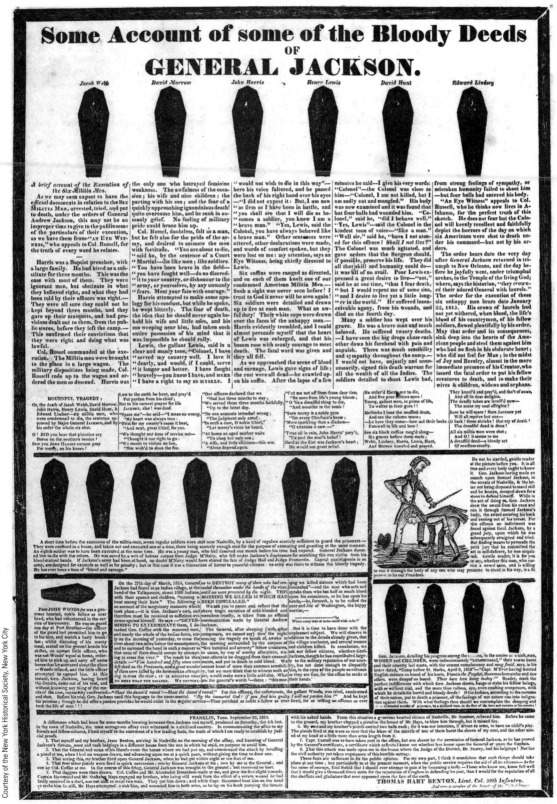

▲ The "coffin handbill," a widely distributed anti-Jackson advertisement describing in detail the men Jackson had "murdered." It was not needed in anti-Jackson New England; it had little effect anywhere else.

Dueling and Brawling the American Way

The duel—an arranged fight in cold blood between two men in front of witnesses, governed by strict rules—was not concerned with a person's guilt or innocence of a crime. The issue in dueling was a gentleman's honor. A man who believed that he or a woman under his protection was insulted challenged the offender to meet him on the "field of honor." It was not necessary that they fight to the death. Merely observing the intricate code that governed dueling established one's honor. In fact, a majority of duels ended when blood was drawn or, if by pistols, when each party discharged his weapon in the general direction of the other. The point was good manners. Only gentlemen dueled; the vulgar multitude brawled.

Although Edward Doty and Edward Leicester fought something like a duel in Virginia in 1621, the custom was almost unknown in colonial America. Scholars have found records of only a dozen before 1776. Then, during the Revolutionary War, French officers such as Lafayette, Rochambeau, and de Grasse introduced the *Code Duello* to their American friends. A decade later, when some French aristocrats fled the revolution in their country and settled in Louisiana, they made New Orleans the dueling capital of America. On one Sunday in 1839, 10 duels were fought in New Orleans. A woman wrote that the young men of her acquaintance kept score of their duels as young ladies kept count of marriage proposals.

Dueling spread rapidly, as sudden wealth created self-made men who were in a hurry to prove their gentility. Timothy Flint wrote of Mississippi, "Many people without education and character, who were not gentlemen in the circles where they used to move, get accommodated here from the tailor with something of the externals of a gentleman, and at once set up in this newly assumed character. The shortest road to settle their pretensions is to fight a duel." Librarian of Congress Daniel Boorstin has written that "of southern statesmen who rose to prominence after 1790, hardly one can be mentioned who was not involved in a duel."

Button Gwinnet of Georgia, a signer of the Declaration of Independence, was killed in a duel in 1777. James Madison fought a duel in 1797. Maryland-born Commodore Stephen Decatur fought one duel in 1801 and was killed in another in 1820. William H. Crawford, presidential candidate in 1824, fought a duel. John Randolph of Roanoke fought two, the second in 1826 with Henry Clay of Kentucky, who also dueled with other men. Senator Thomas Hart Benton of Missouri fought a number of duels and killed at least one of his opponents. Sam Houston of Texas fought a duel. A great many southerners later prominent in the Confederacy were involved in duels: William L. Yancey, Vice President Alexander H. Stephens, and General John C. Breckinridge. Confederate president Jefferson Davis was challenged to a duel by Judah P. Benjamin, who later became a fast friend and served in three cabinet positions. Romantic legend has it that duels were fought over ladies. In fact, as implied in this list, many were fought over politics.

The most famous American duelist was Andrew Jackson, who did fight over insults to his wife. His enemies said that Jackson was involved in a hundred duels. That is unlikely: Even Old Hickory was not so tough or so lucky as to survive that many tests of honor and marksmanship. In 1806, Jackson faced Charles Dickinson, a Nashville lawyer, in a duel, the written terms of which have survived:

> It is agreed that the distance shall be 24 feet, the parties to stand facing each other, with their pistols drawn perpendicularly. When they are ready, the single word fire to be given at which they are to fire as soon as they please. Should either fire before the word is given, we [the seconds of both parties] pledge ourselves to shoot him down instantly. The person to give the word to be determined by lot, as also the choice of position.

Neither Dickinson nor Jackson fired before the word was given, but Dickinson fired first, wounding but not felling Jackson. "Back to the mark, sir," Jackson said when Dickinson staggered in fear of what was to come. Then, according to Jackson's enemies, Jackson's pistol misfired, and in violation of the *Code Duello,* he pulled the hammer back and fired again. This breach of honor haunted Jackson for the rest of his life, for Dickinson died.

Perhaps it was because of this slur on his character that when a man whom Jackson considered no gentleman challenged him some years later, Jackson refused to duel. But he offered to shoot it out in some "sequestered grove" as long as both parties understood that it was not an affair between social equals.

According to *The Code of Honor,* written by a governor of South Carolina, a gentleman who was insulted by a social inferior was to cane him; that is, to flog the impudent lout on the head and shoulders with a walking stick. But Jackson's reaction points up the fact that dueling merged imperceptibly into plain brawling. Fanny Kemble told of a duel in Georgia in which one of the terms was that the winner could behead the loser and impale the loser's head on a stake on the boundary of the land the two were disputing. An Alabama law of 1837 that outlawed dueling also forbade the carrying of the decidedly ungentlemanly weapons "known as Bowie knives or Arkansas Tooth-picks."

Dueling was by no means an exclusively southern and western practice. Alexander Hamilton and Aaron Burr were not southerners. Benedict Arnold was from Connecticut, DeWitt Clinton was from New York, and Nathaniel Greene was from Rhode Island—and they all fought duels. Indeed, the practice was outlawed earlier in the South than in the North. Killing a person in a duel was defined as murder, punishable by death. South Carolina imposed a fine of $2,000 and a year in prison for seconds as well as duelists. Officeholders in Alabama were required to take an oath that they never had dueled or acted as seconds.

The laws were not rigorously enforced. None of the duelists listed here spent a night in jail for defending his honor.

Alarmed by the effectiveness of these tactics, Adams men replied that Jackson was a savage and a murderer. Calling themselves "National-Republicans," they reminded voters that Jackson had executed two British subjects in Spanish Florida in 1818 (conveniently forgetting that Adams had supported Jackson after the fact). They printed broadsides that listed the men whom Jackson had killed in duels and the soldiers whom he had ordered shot.

But the assault that stung Jackson was the claim that he and his beloved wife, Rachel, had lived in sin. "Ought a convicted adulteress and her paramour husband," wrote a Cincinnati editor, "be placed in the highest offices in this free and Christian land?" The circumstances surrounding the Jacksons' marriage were murky. At the least, Rachel's divorce from her first husband was not legally final when she wed Jackson, which required them to go through a mortifying second ceremony. Laxity in observing marriage customs was not rare on the frontier. (When Daniel Boone was absent from his home for two years, he returned to find a son just a few months old, fathered by Boone's brother; Boone shrugged.)

Nevertheless, whatever Rachel Jackson's inclinations as a young woman were, by 1828 she was a prim and proper lady, and she was tortured by the gossip. When she died shortly after the election, Jackson blamed Adams and his supporters for his deeply felt loss.

In the meantime, Jackson's party responded in kind, digging up a tale that, as minister to Russia, Adams had procured the sexual favors of a young American girl for the dissolute czar. Then there were whispers of bizarre perversions in the Adams White House. "Negative campaigning" had come to American politics with a vengeance. Everything was fair game for discussion except important issues.

The Symbol of His Age

It was not mudslinging that won the election of 1828 for Jackson. The Democratic party organization, cobbled together by Jackson, Vice President Calhoun, and Martin Van Buren, turned that trick. Jackson swept to victory with 56 percent of a total vote three times as large as the vote in 1824 and a 178 to 83 victory in the electoral college.

The upswing in popular participation carried over to inauguration day in March 1829, when 10,000 people crowded Washington. They shocked genteel society with their drinking, coarse shouting, and boisterous invasion of the White House. Invited there by the new president, the mob muddied

© Bettmann/Corbis

▲ *Inauguration day, March 1829. Washington, D.C., had never seen such a display. Thousands of Jackson's supporters, many of them common men indeed, poured raucously into the White House. Jackson himself was persuaded to flee for fear he would be injured.*

the carpets, broke crystal stemware, and stood on expensive upholstered sofas and chairs in order to catch a glimpse of their gaunt, white-haired hero.

The adoring mob was so unruly that Jackson's friends feared he might be injured. They spirited the president away through a window; he spent his first night as president in a hotel. Back at the executive mansion, servants lured the mob outside by setting up bowls of lemonade, whiskey punch, and tables heaped with food on the lawn.

The man whom these people worshiped was by no definition a "common man." Jackson's talents were exceptional, his will and integrity extraordinary. Nor was he the vicious desperado whom the Adams forces depicted. Jackson was "erect and dignified in his carriage" in the words of Fanny Kemble, an English woman who met him. He was a gracious gentleman whose manners were on the courtly side.

Jackson thought well enough of himself, but he also believed that his success—he was the first log cabin–born president—was due to the openness of American society. All people were not equally talented, but the good society provided every man the opportunity to exploit his abilities and

OK

OK, that curious American expression now heard in almost every language on earth, originated in the days of Andrew Jackson. Where did it come from? The theories are numerous. Some said it was borrowed from the Choctaw *okeh,* which had a similar meaning. Others said it was an abbreviation of *Old Kinderhook* (one of Martin Van Buren's nicknames), *Obadiah Kelly* (an obscure shipping agent), and even *Orrins-Kendall* (a brand of crackers).

A popular theory probably close to the mark was the contention that Jackson, the ignorant old general, marked state papers "o.k." for "oll korrect." In fact, Jackson was quite at home with the language. However, it is likely that anti-Jackson Whigs invented the term as a jibe at the president and it caught on. It first appears in print in a Boston Whig newspaper in 1839.

enjoy the fruits of his labor unimpeded by artificial social and economic obstacles. Government's task was to preserve this opportunity by striking down obstacles to it, such as laws that benefited some and, therefore, handicapped others.

Jackson's view of government was, therefore, essentially negative. He believed that government should, as much as possible, leave people, society, and the economy alone so that natural social and economic forces could operate freely. The common term for this point of view is *laissez-faire*, French for (roughly) "leave alone."

Attitudes of a Hero, Attitudes of a People

Jackson's vision of equal opportunity extended only to white males; but in this too, as in his attitudes toward women, children, blacks, and Indians, he embodied the opinion of his era.

Jackson believed that women lived in a different sphere than that of males. While menfolk struggled in a brutal

Thomas Sully, General Andrew Jackson, 1845, 97 × 61½, oil on canvas. In the Collections of the Corcoran Gallery of Art, Washington, D.C. Gift of William Wilson Corcoran.

▲ *A portrait of Andrew Jackson by Thomas Sully capturing the majesty in which his supporters saw him. No other individual, except perhaps Franklin D. Roosevelt, loomed over his age as Andrew Jackson did. And, like Roosevelt, he was despised by a minority of Americans.*

world, women guarded home and hearth. They were superior to men in religious and moral sensibility. Indeed, it was because of these feminine faculties that men had to shelter women from a public life that was hardening at best and often corrupting. Jackson and most Americans (women certainly included) agreed with the clergymen, increasingly dependent on female congregants, who preached the "gospel of pure womanhood." Woman's "chastity is her tower of strength, her modesty and gentleness are her charm, and her ability to meet the high claims of her family and dependents the noblest power she can exhibit to the world." The Reverend Edward Kirk of Albany, New York, preached that "the hopes of human society are to be found in the character, in the views, and in the conduct of mothers."

The reward due women for accepting their private and submissive role in society was the sacred right to be treated with deference. Jackson was famous for his chivalry. Rough as the old soldier's life had been, he was prim and prudish in mixed company. Even in the absence of the ladies, he habitually referred to them as "the fair." Adding the word *sex* would have violated his sense of delicacy.

Toward children, visitors were appalled to discover, the old soldier was a pussycat. The man who aroused armies to blood lust and slaughtered enemies without a wince, and the president who periodically exploded in rages that left him (and everyone else) trembling, beamed quietly as young children virtually destroyed rooms in the White House before his eyes. The British minister wrote that he could not hear the president's conversation because the two men were surrounded by caterwauling children. Jackson smiled absentmindedly and nodded all the while. At the table, the president fed children first, saying that they had the best appetites and the least patience.

Indulgence of children was not universal in the United States. Many New Englanders raised their families in the old Puritan manner. But Europeans commented in horror that American children generally had the manners of "wild Indians." Some also noticed that American children were more self-reliant than European children because of the freedom that was allowed them. It was this quality—"standing on your own two feet"—that Jackson and his countrymen valued in their heirs.

Democracy and Race

Toward Indians and blacks, Jackson also shared the prejudices of his age. Blacks were doomed to be subject to whites by the Bible or Mother Nature or both. Blacks *were* slaves, and American blacks were fortunate to have such enlightened masters. Jackson did not trouble himself with the implications of the doctrine of equal rights. Having lived with both the Declaration of Independence and human bondage for 50 years, a majority of Americans found them quite compatible.

As a westerner, Jackson had thought a great deal about Indians. He spent much of his life fighting Native Americans and seizing their land. More than any single person, he was responsible for crushing the military power of the great southeastern tribes—the Creek, Choctaw, Cherokee, and Chickasaw.

Although he was ruthless in these wars, Jackson was not the simple "Indian hater" portrayed by his enemies. He found much to admire in Native Americans (as he did not in black people). He admired their closeness to nature, a view promoted during the 1820s by the popular novelist James Fenimore Cooper, and their courage in resisting their conquerors. There was a tinge of tragic regret in Jackson's statement to Congress that the white and red races simply could not live side by side and, therefore, the Indians would simply die out. During the Quincy Adams administration, Commissioner of Indian Affairs Thomas L. McKenney commissioned portraits of Indian leaders who visited Washington, in part because he too believed the culture of a doomed people should be preserved for posterity.

Government by Party

Attitudes are not policies, but President Jackson lost no time in establishing the latter. As the first president to represent a political party frankly and without apologies, he made it clear that he would replace federal officeholders who had opposed his election with his own supporters.

There were about 20,000 federal jobs in 1829, and Jackson eventually dismissed about one-fifth of the people holding them. Even considering the fact that some federal officeholders supported him, that was by no means a clean sweep. John Quincy Adams, who never dismissed anyone, privately admitted that many of those Jackson fired were incompetent.

As for those who were able, when Jackson's critics claimed that the men who were best qualified by education and training should hold government jobs, Jackson answered with quite another theory. He said that every government job should be designed so that any intelligent, freeborn American citizen could perform it adequately. If that were so, it was perfectly legitimate to say, as New York Jacksonian William Marcy said, "To the victor belong the spoils."

Attacks on the spoils system were noisy but short-lived. When the anti-Jackson forces came to power in 1840, they carved up the spoils of office far more lustily than Jackson's men had done. The ruling party's patronage of its members became an established part of American politics.

ISSUES OF JACKSON'S FIRST TERM

When he became president, Jackson did not have particularly strong opinions on the questions of the tariff or internal improvements. In his first address to Congress, he called for a protective tariff, but he later drifted (again without passion) to the southern position of a tariff for revenue only.

Internal Improvements

As a westerner, Jackson understood the need for good roads and rivers free of snags. However, as an advocate of laissez-faire and of strict construction of the Constitution, he worried that it was not constitutional for the federal government to finance them. In 1830, when he vetoed a bill to construct a road between Maysville and Lexington, Kentucky, he told Congress that if the Constitution was amended to authorize such projects, he would approve them.

In the Maysville Road veto, Jackson seems to have been as interested in taking a slap at Henry Clay as in protecting constitutional niceties. The projected road would have been completely within Clay's home state of Kentucky, adding immeasurably to Clay's popularity there. Later, Jackson quietly approved other internal improvement bills when the expenditures promised to win votes for his own party.

On the rising constitutional issue of the day, the division of power between the federal government and the states, Jackson was again inconsistent according to how his personal sensibilities and party interests were involved. When the issue was Georgia's attempt to ignore the treaty rights of Indians, Jackson allowed the state to have its way. But when South Carolina attempted to defy his power as president, he moved quickly and decisively to crush the challenge—coming close to dusting off his old uniform, polishing his sword, and personally leading an army south.

Indian Removal

The rapid settlement of the West brought whites once again into close contact with large Indian tribes. Presidents Monroe and Adams both agreed that warfare was undesirable but living as neighbors impossible. To resolve the dilemma, they devised the policy of "removal," relocation of the tribes to an Indian Territory west of the Mississippi River that would be guaranteed to them "forever."

To implement removal meant scrapping old treaties that had also guaranteed the tribes the land on which they dwelled "as long as the water runs and the grass grows." Nevertheless, burdened by demoralization and faced with a combination of inducements and threats, many trans-Appalachian tribes agreed to "removal" farther west.

Others rebelled. The Sauk and the Fox of Illinois and Wisconsin rose up under Chief Black Hawk. The Seminole of Florida, their numbers augmented by runaway slaves, also fought back. Unlike the Sauk and Fox, the Seminole were never decisively defeated. They escaped into the swamps, from where, between 1835 and 1842, they fought an effective holding action against the army.

Sequoya

Still other tribes, such as the Choctaw, were defrauded. Federal agents bribed renegade chiefs to sign removal treaties that were then enforced on the entire people. Between 1830

▲ *Sequoya with the syllabary he created so that the Cherokee language could be written and printed. Sequoya was illiterate. His single-handed achievement, starting from scratch, was the equivalent of what other civilizations had accomplished over generations.*

and 1833, the Choctaw were forced to march west under army supervision. A fourth of them died on the way.

Like the Choctaw, the Creek, Chickasaw, and Cherokee were "Civilized Tribes." They had long since given up their traditional seminomadic ways, lived in American-style cabins and houses, and farmed intensively using Euro-American methods. They were part of the market economy, raising cotton for sale using African American slaves.

In 1821, an uneducated linguistic genius and silversmith named Sequoya recognized the power the white men drew from the markings on their books and papers. The Cherokee, he concluded, needed to be able to write and read. Had Sequoya been literate, he would have done what other Indians did—adapted the letters of the Latin alphabet to the tribe's language. But Sequoya could not read English, understanding only that the symbols on a page represented sounds.

He actually reinvented the wheel. Rejecting pictograms as unwieldy, Sequoya borrowed letters from an English spelling book and invented others. He created not a Cherokee alphabet (letters representing single sounds) but a *syllabary:* 86 symbols representing the 86 syllables (combinations consisting of a consonant sound and a vowel sound) that he counted in the Cherokee language. It was the same method that had produced writing in Minoan Crete 3,000 years earlier. Sequoya's syllabary was immediately adopted by the Cherokee, who printed newspapers and books and

Appeal of the Cherokee

In 1835, its legal rights ignored, the Cherokee nation appealed to Congress on the basis of the values Americans ostensibly prized, values the Indians had adopted as their own:

In truth, our cause is your own. It is the cause of liberty and of justice. It is based on your own principles, which we have learned from yourselves. . . . On your kindness, on your humanity, on your compassions, on your benevolence, we rest our hopes.

operated a school system, one of the best in the southern states.

The Cherokee in Court

The Cherokee also saw to it that some tribal members were educated in American professions, particularly law. According to their treaty with the United States government, the Cherokee were entitled to remain where they were. The tribe was recognized as a semisovereign nation within the United States. Therefore, they refused every attempt of the federal government to force them out and made friends in Congress, anti-Jacksonian northerners who agreed that the Cherokee cause was just.

Unlike Congress, Georgia was dominated by people who wanted the rich and developed Cherokee lands for themselves and who were willing to ignore federal treaties to get them. A Georgia court forced the issue by convicting a white missionary of a crime committed in Cherokee territory and, therefore, according to treaty, under tribal jurisdiction. The missionary and the Cherokee nation appealed the case, *Worcester v. Georgia,* to the Supreme Court.

Personally, Chief Justice John Marshall was no more sanguine about the prospect of whites and Indians living side by side than President Jackson was. But Marshall was a staunch defender of the sanctity of contracts, which the treaty with the Cherokee was. "The Cherokee nation is a distinct community," he ruled, "occupying its own territory, with boundaries accurately described . . . which the citizens of Georgia have no right to enter." Georgia could not force the Cherokee to give up their land.

The Trail of Tears

Marshall's decision seemed to settle the matter, and the Cherokee nation celebrated. But Georgia gambled. The state had voted for Jackson in 1828, and the president was a lifelong Indian fighter. Georgia defied the Supreme Court, held on to its prisoner, engineered some fraudulent agreements with Cherokee who could be bought, and began the forcible removal of the tribe.

Georgia won its bet. "John Marshall has made his decision," Jackson was quoted as saying. "Let him enforce it." Congress obliged, with the Indian Removal Act of 1830.

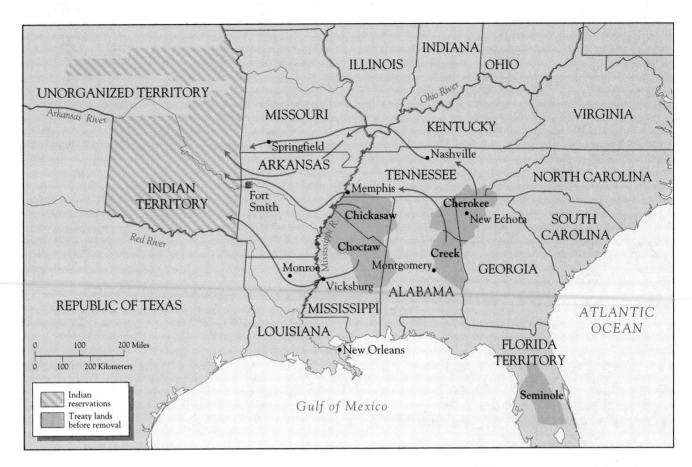

MAP 15:3 **Removal of the Southeastern Tribes, 1820–1840** The "Civilized Tribes" had created viable, even prosperous, societies and economies in lands promised them in various treaties. But the tribes were "removed," mostly to present-day Oklahoma, when white southerners coveted their lands. Most Seminole refused to go west but lost their treaty lands.

Thus began the several Trails of Tears, the 1,200-mile trek of the "Civilized Tribes" to what is now Oklahoma. General John E. Wool, sent to supervise one forced march, was disgusted by his assignment. "The whole scene since I have been in this country has been nothing but a heart-rending one," Wool lamented. Indians were forced from ancestral homes under the gaze of, in his words, "vultures ready to pounce on their prey and strip them of everything they have."

Two thousand people died in camps waiting for the migration to begin; another 2,000 died on the trail. About 15,000 Cherokee, and smaller numbers of Choctaw, Chickasaw, and Creek, made it to Oklahoma. It was all over by 1838.

Nullification

If Georgia succeeded in defying the Supreme Court, South Carolina had less luck with Congress and the president. The issue that brought Jackson into conflict with the Palmetto State and with his own vice president, John C. Calhoun, was the tariff.

In 1828, Congress enacted an extremely high protective tariff. Most southern planters hated this "Tariff of Abominations," but South Carolina's cotton planters were enraged.

They believed that their crop was paying the whole country's bills and underwriting industrial investment.

They had a point. Cotton accounted for fully half of the wealth that poured into the United States from abroad. Some of this income was effectively diverted to the North by the tariff that required everyone, including southern cotton planters, to pay higher prices for manufactured goods. Vice President John C. Calhoun, a South Carolinian, saw the problem as constitutional. In 1829, secretly, he wrote *The South Carolina Exposition and Protest,* an ingenious and mischievous interpretation of the relationship of states to the federal union.

The *Exposition* took up where the Virginia and Kentucky Resolutions left off. Calhoun stated that the Union had not been formed by the people of America (as John Marshall and other nationalists said) but by the people acting through the individual states of which they were citizens. This was not mere hairsplitting. It meant that the states were sovereign, not the federal government. That is, the states were the fundamental, indivisible units of government that formed a compact, the Union, for the benefit of the states.

When, Calhoun continued, the Union enacted a law to which a sovereign state objected, as South Carolina objected

▲ *This most famous painting of the Cherokee on the "Trail of Tears," from Georgia to Oklahoma, does not begin to capture the wretchedness of the trek. The accompanying army was not unsympathetic, but fully a fourth of those who set out on the trail died on it.*

to the Tariff of Abominations, that state had the right to nullify the law (prevent its enforcement) within its borders until such time as three-quarters of the other states overruled its decision. (Calhoun was here referring to the amendment process of the Constitution, which requires the ratification of three-fourths of the states.) In such an event, Calhoun concluded, the nullifying state could choose between capitulation to the decision of the other states or secession from the Union.

South Carolina's Declaration and Jackson's Response

Calhoun and his supporters hoped that the Tariff of Abominations would be repealed after Jackson was elected president, thus leaving the *Exposition* in the abstract. However, in 1832, Congress adopted another high protective tariff, and Jackson signed it into law. South Carolinians blew up, electing a convention that declared the Tariff of 1832 "null and void" within the borders of the sovereign state of South Carolina.

Jackson exploded in one of his trademarked rages. South Carolinians would rather rule in hell, he said, than be subordinate in heaven. They could write whatever they chose in expositions, but, Jackson threatened, if "a single drop of blood shall be shed there" in preventing the collection of the tariff, "I will hang the first man I can lay my hand on engaged in such treasonable conduct, upon the first tree I can find."

Congress backed him with a "force bill" authorizing military collection of the tax in South Carolina. Conflict was averted when no other state nullified the tariff, leaving South Carolina in isolation. Calhoun met quietly with Henry Clay to work out a compromise tariff just low enough that South Carolina could save face. In 1833, the state rescinded its nullification of the tariff but expressly did not repudiate the principle of nullification.

Jackson let it ride. It was all on paper, like Marshall's decision in the Cherokee case. He had had his way, and he had identified a new enemy—his own vice president.

FOR FURTHER READING

Andrew Jackson and what he meant for America have fascinated historians, and they have differed radically in their findings. For an overview of the era, see Glyndon G. Van Deusen, *The Jacksonian Era, 1828–1848,* 1959. Clashing interpretations can be found in Richard Hofstadter, *The American Political Tradition and the Men Who Made It,* 1948; Marvin Meyers, *The Jacksonian Persuasion,* 1957; Edward E. Pessen, *Jacksonian America,* 1978; Robert Remini, *Andrew Jackson,* 1966; Arthur M. Schlesinger Jr., *The Age of Jackson,* 1945; and John W. Ward, *Andrew Jackson: Symbol for an Age,* 1955.

Yet other explanations of the great upheaval of the 1820s can be found in books with a narrower focus, including Lee Benson, *The Concept of Jacksonian Democracy,* 1964; J. C. Curtis, *Andrew Jackson and the Search for Vindication,* 1976; William W. Freehling, *Prelude to Civil War: The Nullification Controversy in South Carolina, 1816–1836,* 1966; Walter E. Hugins, *Jacksonian Democracy and the Working Class,* 1960; Richard P. McCormick, *The Second American Party System: Party Formation in the Jacksonian Era,* 1966; Edward E. Pessen, *Most Uncommon Jacksonians: The Radical Leaders of the Early Labor Movement,* 1967; Robert Remini, *The Election of Andrew Jackson,* 1963; and M. P. Rogin, *Fathers and Children: Andrew Jackson and the Destruction of American Indians,* 1975.

On Indian removal, see John Ehle, *Trail of Tears,* 1988; Michael Green, *The Politics of Indian Removal,* 1982; and Ronald Satz, *American Indian Policy in the Jacksonian Era,* 1974.

  ## AMERICAN JOURNEY ONLINE AND INFOTRAC COLLEGE EDITION

Visit the source collections at http://ajaccess.wadsworth.com and http://infotrac.thomsonlearning.com, and use the Search function with the following key terms to explore documents, images, audio and video clips, articles, and commentary related to the material in this chapter:

Andrew Jackson	Sequoya
Indian Removal Act	Trail of Tears

Additional resources, exercises, and Internet links related to this chapter are available on *The American Past* Web site: http://history.wadsworth.com/americanpast7e.

HISTORY ONLINE

The History Buff
www.historybuff.com/library/index.html
A collection of newspapers such as became a staple of American political life during the Jacksonian era.

The Trail of Tears
http://ngeorgia.com/history/nghisttt.html
Details, illustrations, maps of the removal of the Cherokee from northern Georgia to Indian Territory.

IN THE SHADOW
OF OLD HICKORY

Personalities and Politics
1830–1842

Reproduced from the Collections of the Library of Congress

He prefers the specious to the solid, and the plausible to the true. . . . I don't like Henry Clay. He is a bad man, an impostor, a creator of wicked schemes. I wouldn't speak to him, but by God, I love him.

John C. Calhoun

[Calhoun is] a smart fellow, one of the first among second-rate men, but of lax political principles and a disordinate ambition not over-delicate in the means of satisfying itself.

Albert Gallatin

Such is human nature in the gigantic intellect, the envious temper, the ravenous ambition, and the rotten heart of Daniel Webster.

John Quincy Adams

Thank God. I—I also—am an American.

Daniel Webster

WHEN ANDREW JACKSON became president in 1829, many who knew him feared he would not live to finish his term. To his supporters around the country, Jackson was "Old Hickory"—a tough and timeless frontiersman as straight as a long rifle. In person, he was a frail, 62-year-old wisp of a man who often looked to be a day away from death.

More than six feet tall, Jackson weighed only 145 pounds. No other president was so frequently ill. He suffered from lead poisoning (he carried two bullets in his body), headaches, diarrhea, kidney disease, and edema, a painful swelling of the legs. He was beleaguered by coughing fits; as president, he suffered two serious hemorrhages of the lungs.

VAN BUREN VERSUS CALHOUN

Jackson's choice of a vice president, therefore, was a matter of some interest. In approving John C. Calhoun in 1828, Jackson was not simply pocketing South Carolina's electoral votes, he was naming his heir apparent as president and leader of the Democratic party.

John C. Calhoun

Like Jackson, Calhoun was of Scotch-Irish background, the descendant of those eighteenth-century emigrants invariably described as hot tempered and pugnacious. Calhoun was—

again like Jackson—a man of passion with a stubborn, steely will. Portrait painters captured a burning gaze just an eyelash short of rage, never the slightest hint of a smile, never a posture to indicate Calhoun knew even odd moments of peace of mind. Photographers, coming along later in his life, confirmed the painters' impressions. He was, in Harriet Martineau's words, "the cast-iron man, who looks as if he had never been born, and never could be extinguished."

By 1828, Calhoun was the captive of an obsession. He feared that the social institutions that were the backbone of his beloved South Carolina—African American slavery and the plantation aristocracy that owed its wealth and privilege to slave ownership—were mortally threatened by the rapid growth of population in the North, the increasing power of industrial capitalists, and what those developments meant for the policies of the national government in the future.

In this fear, Calhoun had broken sharply from the ideals of his youth. The young Calhoun was a nationalist and an proponent of industrialization. In 1815, he wanted to "bind the nation together with a perfect system of roads and canals."

In 1816, he introduced the bill that chartered the Second Bank of the United States (BUS), arguing the desirability of a powerful national financial center. Young man Calhoun urged South Carolinians to build steam-powered mills amid their cotton fields, monopolizing the profits from their coveted crop from seed to bolt of cloth.

But when the South did not industrialize and the North did, and the industrialists then demanded high protective tariffs that raised the prices of the manufactured goods southern agriculturalists bought from others, Calhoun changed his tune. He became a defender of agrarian society and the plantation system. He opposed protective tariffs, was critical of internal improvements because of the taxes required to make them, and even of the BUS he had helped to found. When voices were raised about the morality of slavery, he became a vociferous proponent of the virtues of the institution.

Jackson agreed with most of these sentiments, but the two men differed about the relationship between the federal and state governments. The president believed the national government should be supreme. In *The South Carolina Exposition and Protest,* Calhoun proclaimed the state governments sovereign.

So fundamental a clash was quite enough to sour Jackson on his vice president. However, philosophical differences were exacerbated by a tempest on the Washington social scene that created a rival to Calhoun as Jackson's heir.

Peggy O'Neill Eaton

The center of the storm was Peggy O'Neill, the once fetching daughter of a Washington hotel keeper. Peggy had been married to a sailor who was, as seamen are inclined to be,

▲ *President Jackson never asked Peggy O'Neill to cavort for his cabinet, as in this lampoon of the affair, but he discussed her with them at length. Martin Van Buren, the sole beneficiary of the hubbub, is at the right.*

rarely at home. In her husband's absence, she found solace and several children in the arms of her father's boarder, Tennessee congressman John Eaton, whom Jackson made secretary of war.

The affair was worth a whisper and a giggle, but not much more. Irregular conjunctions were not unheard of in the capital. Washington was no longer the largely male city it had been when Jefferson was president, but there was still a shortage of quarters suitable to families that lived well at home. Many congressmen continued to leave their wives behind and board at hotels. Inevitably, some found lady friends, and, as long as they exercised minimal discretion, little was made of it. Henry Clay was said to have been a roué, an alley cat, and Richard M. Johnson, vice president between 1837 and 1841, cohabited openly with a black woman who was also his slave.

Still, Clay's affairs were discreet, and Johnson left his mistress at home when he attended social functions. When Peggy O'Neill's husband died at sea and Eaton married her, he expected Washington society to receive her. Instead, there ensued a great hullabaloo. It was too much to expect women faithful to the gospel of true womanhood to sip tea with a fallen sister. Peggy O'Neill Eaton was roundly and brusquely snubbed.

The ringleader of the snubbers was Floride Calhoun, the moralistic wife of the vice president. The wives of cabinet members followed her example, and it aggravated Jackson. When his niece, his official hostess, refused to receive Peggy Eaton, Jackson told her to move out of the White House. Still mourning the death of his wife, which he blamed on scandalmongers, Jackson also happened to be charmed by the vivacious Peggy. He actually summoned a cabinet meeting to discuss the subject (as he rarely did on political and economic issues) and pronounced her "as chaste as a virgin." He told his advisers to command their wives to receive her socially.

This was too big an order, even for the "Gin'ral." If women were excluded from public life, morality and the rules of social life were squarely within their sphere. Peggy Eaton continued to find little chitchat at social functions. Only Secretary of State Martin Van Buren, who, as a widower, had no wife to oblige, dared to be seen admiring her gowns and fetching her refreshments.

The Rise of the Sly Fox

Charm and chitchat came naturally to Van Buren. His worst enemies conceded his grace and wit. His portraits, in contrast to Calhoun's, show a twinkle in the eye and a good-natured, intelligent smile.

But Martin Van Buren was much more than a jolly Dutchman. He was a devilishly clever politician, almost always several moves ahead of his rivals, particularly when they were impassioned true believers like Calhoun. Van Buren's wiles earned him the nickname "the Sly Fox of Kinderhook" (his hometown in New York).

He wrote no expositions, but he was the most successful political organizer of his time. He owed his high position in Jackson's cabinet to delivering most of New York's electoral votes in 1828. He understood that a political party, whatever its ideals, had first and foremost to be a vote-gathering machine; it had to win elections. Therefore, a political party must reward the activists who corralled the votes, by appointing them to government jobs.

Van Buren was ambitious for himself. His sensitivity to the feelings of Peggy Eaton may have been quite sincere, but his courtesy also won Jackson's favor. Then, Van Buren offered the impulsive president a way out of the Eaton mess when the affair threatened to paralyze the administration and shatter the leadership of the Democratic party.

Van Buren proposed to resign as secretary of state, and Eaton would resign as secretary of war. The other members of the cabinet, whose wives were causing the president so much anxiety, would have no choice but to follow their example. Jackson would be rid of the lot, but no particular wing of the Democratic party could claim to have been wronged. Jackson appreciated both the strategy and Van Buren's willingness to sacrifice his prestigious office. He rewarded Van Buren by naming him minister to England—then, as now, the plum of the diplomatic service.

Calhoun: His Own Worst Enemy

The Sly Fox of Kinderhook was lucky too. While he calculated each turning with an eye on a distant destination, Calhoun blundered and bumped into posts like a blind cart horse. While the Eaton business was still rankling Jackson, the

Courtesy Chicago Historical Society

▲ *Martin Van Buren—dapper, good humored, shrewd, and lucky until he became president during a serious depression.*

president discovered in some old cabinet reports that, 10 years earlier, Calhoun (then secretary of war) wanted to punish Jackson for his unauthorized invasion of Florida. Confronted with the evidence, Calhoun tried to explain his way out of his fix in a suspiciously long and convoluted monologue. The president cut him off by writing, "Understanding you now, no further communication with you on this subject is necessary."

Nor, it turned out, was there much further communication between Jackson and his vice president on any subject. In April 1830, Jackson and Calhoun attended a formal dinner during which more than 20 of Calhoun's cronies offered toasts to states' rights and even nullification. When it was the president's turn to lift a glass, he rose, stared at Calhoun, and toasted, "Our Union: It must be preserved." Calhoun got in the last word of the evening. He replied, "The Union, next to our liberty, the most dear." But Jackson took satisfaction from the fact that, as he told the story, Calhoun trembled as he spoke.

The old duelist delighted in such confrontations. Van Buren took pleasure in his enduring good luck, for he was in England during the nastiest squabbling between Jackson and Calhoun, when even the slyest of foxes might have chanced on into a hound.

Then Calhoun blundered again, ensuring that Van Buren would succeed Jackson. Seeking personal revenge, Calhoun cast the deciding vote in the Senate's refusal to confirm Van Buren's diplomatic appointment. This brought the New Yorker back to the United States, but hardly in disgrace. Jackson was yet more deeply obligated to him. Van Buren was named vice presidential candidate in the election of 1832, as he surely would not have been had Calhoun left him in London.

THE WAR WITH THE BANK

Jackson's bid for reelection in 1832 was fought over a serious issue—the future of the Second BUS. The Second BUS was chartered in 1816 for a term of 20 years. After a shaky start (the Panic of 1819), it fell under the control of Nicholas Biddle, a courtly Philadelphian who administered its affairs cautiously, conservatively, profitably, and, so it seemed, to the benefit of the federal government and the national economy. The BUS acted as the government's financial agent, providing vaults for its gold and silver, paying government bills out of its accounts, investing deposits, and selling bonds (borrowing money for the government when it was needed).

The Powers of the Bank

Every cent the government collected from excise taxes, tariffs, and land sales went into the BUS. It was a huge, fabulously rich institution. Its 29 branches controlled about a third of all bank deposits in the United States and did some $70 million in transactions each year.

With such resources, the BUS held immense power over the nation's money supply and, therefore, the economy. In a careless but revealing moment, Nicholas Biddle told congressmen that the BUS was capable of destroying any other bank in the country.

What he meant was that, at any moment, the BUS was likely to have in its possession more paper money issued by a state-chartered bank than the issuing bank had specie (gold and silver) in its vaults. If the BUS presented this paper to be exchanged for specie, the issuing bank would be bankrupt, and all investments in it would be wiped out.

On a day he was more tactful, Biddle said that his bank exercised "a mild and gentle but efficient control" over the economy. That is, simply because the state banks were aware of the sword the BUS held over them, they maintained larger reserves of gold and silver than they might otherwise have kept on hand. Rather than ruining banks, the BUS ensured that they operated more responsibly.

A Private Institution

Biddle was as proud of the public service he rendered as of the BUS's annual profits. Nevertheless, the fact remained that the BUS was powerful because of its control of the money supply—a matter of profound public interest—but was itself a private institution. BUS policies were made not by elected officials, nor by bureaucrats responsible to elected officials, but by a board of directors responsible to shareholders.

This was enough in itself to earn the animosity of a president who abhorred powerful special interests. Biddle therefore attempted to make a friend of the president by readily giving loans to key Jackson supporters. Biddle also designed a plan to retire the national debt—a goal dear to Jackson's heart—timing the final installments to coincide with the anniversary of the Battle of New Orleans. But Biddle's efforts were to no avail. Jackson shook his head and explained to Biddle that it was not a matter of disliking the BUS more than he disliked other banks; Jackson did not trust any of them. Like "Old Bullion" Benton, he was a hard-money man. Faced with a stone wall in the White House, Biddle turned to Congress for friends.

The Enemies of the Bank

Biddle needed friends because the BUS had plenty of enemies. Except for their fear or resentment of the bank, however, those hostile to the bank had little in common.

First, there was the growing financial community of New York City—the bankers and brokers who would soon be known collectively as "Wall Street." Grown wealthy from the Erie Canal and from New York's role as the nation's leading port, they were keen to challenge Philadelphia's last financial powerhouse, the BUS, and its control of the nation's money supply.

Second, the freewheeling bankers of the West disliked Biddle's restraints. Caught up in the optimism of the growing region, these bankers wanted a free hand to take advantage of land values, which were once again soaring. Oddly, the president, who hated all banks, had the support of a good

▲ *A satirical six-cent bill printed by one of Jackson's irresponsible "pet banks," the Humbug Glory. It is covered with Democratic party symbols: Jackson on the penny, a leaf from an old hickory tree, and, curiously, a donkey, which is usually thought to have become a Democratic symbol a generation later.*

many bankers in his hostility toward the BUS, and they were far from the most virtuous of their profession.

A third group that wanted to see the BUS declawed was even more conservative in money matters than Biddle was. Hard-money men (like Jackson and Benton) were opposed to the very idea of an institution that issued paper money in quantities greater than the gold and silver it had on hand. Most eastern workingmen supported the hard-money position. They had too often been paid in banknotes that, when presented to shopkeepers, were worth less than their face value because the banks that issued them were shaky.

BUS notes were "as good as gold." Nevertheless, the working-class wing of the Democratic party, called "Loco-focos" in New York, lumped Biddle with the rest and inveighed against his monopolistic powers.

The First Shot

Jackson did not start the fight that escalated into the "Bank War." Henry Clay fired the first shot when, in January 1832, he was nominated for the presidency by those who had supported John Quincy Adams four years earlier. (They still called themselves National Republicans.) Clay needed an issue. Although the BUS's charter did not expire until 1836, Clay persuaded Biddle to apply for a new charter immediately. A majority of both houses of Congress would support the bid, putting Jackson, as Clay saw it, on the spot.

That is, if Jackson gritted his teeth and signed the bank bill rather than bucking a congressional majority, all well and good. The BUS was one of the pillars of Clay's American System. If Jackson vetoed the bill, Clay would have the issue on which to wage his presidential campaign. Clay believed that, because the bank had proved its value to the economy, he would defeat Jackson by promising to rescue it.

Clay was not the last presidential nominee to believe that, presented with an issue, voters would decide on the basis of it rather than be dazzled by symbols. Congress rechartered the BUS. Jackson vetoed the bill. Clay ran on the issue and went down resoundingly in defeat. Jackson was still a hero, still the reed vibrating in harmony with the popular mood. He won 55 percent of the popular vote and 219 electoral votes to Clay's 49. (Anti-Masonic candidate William Wirt won 7 electoral votes, and South Carolina gave its 11 votes to John Floyd.)

Financial Chaos

In September 1833, six months after his second inauguration, Jackson took the offensive. He ceased to deposit government moneys in the bank, putting them instead into what were called his "pet banks," state-chartered institutions. The BUS, however, continued to pay the government's bills. Within three months, federal deposits in the BUS sank from $10 million to $4 million. Biddle had no choice but to reduce the scope of the bank's operations. He also chose, no doubt in part to sting Jackson, to call in debts owed the bank by other financial institutions. The result was a wave of bank failures that wiped out the savings of thousands of people, just what Jackson had feared BUS power might mean.

Presidential Vetoes

Jackson's veto of the bank bill was just another day's work. No previous president used the power of veto so often. In fact, the first six presidents, between them, vetoed a total of 10 acts of Congress. Jackson, the seventh president, vetoed 12.

Under pressure from the business community, Biddle relented and reversed his policy, increasing the national supply of money by making loans to other banks. This, alas, fed a new speculative boom. To Jackson's chagrin, many of the 89 pet banks to which he had entrusted federal money proved to be among the least responsible in lending money. They fed the speculation.

In 1836, Henry Clay made his contribution to what would be the most serious American depression since Jefferson's embargo. He convinced Congress to pass a distribution bill under the terms of which $37 million was distributed to the states for expenditure on internal improvements. Presented with such a windfall, the politicians reacted as politicians sitting on a bonanza usually do: They spent freely, crazily, backing the least worthy of projects and most questionable of promoters. Land values, both in the undeveloped West and in eastern cities, soared. Federal land sales rose to $25 million in 1836. Seeking to get a share of the freely circulating cash, new banks were chartered at a dizzying rate. There had been 330 state banks in 1830; there were almost 800 in 1837.

And there was no BUS to cool things down gradually, for its national charter had expired in 1836. Instead, the responsibility was Jackson's. In his last year as president, he did the only thing within his powers—he slammed a lid on the sale of federal land, the most volatile commodity in the boom. In July 1836, he issued the Specie Circular, which required that government lands be paid for in gold and silver coin; paper money was no longer acceptable.

Jackson's action stopped the runaway speculation, but with a heavy foot on the brake rather than the tug on the reins that the BUS might have used. In a repeat of 1819, speculators unable to pay what they owed the government for land went bankrupt. Banks that had fueled the speculators collapsed. Gold and silver were drained from the East, contributing to a depression there.

The Giant

Jackson's financial policy was a disaster built on ignorance, prejudice, and pigheadedness. It would have destroyed the career and reputation of a lesser man as, indeed, it destroyed Jackson's successor, Martin Van Buren. By the time the economy hit bottom, however, Jackson had retired to Tennessee. Seventy years old now, the man who many thought would be lucky to live through one term had cut and chopped his way through eight pivotal years in the history of the nation.

Though aching and coughing and refusing to mellow (he said his biggest regret was not shooting Henry Clay and hanging John C. Calhoun), Jackson would live for nine more years, observing from his mansion home an era that unfolded in his shadow. He was never a wise man. His intelligence was limited; his education, spotty; his prejudices, often ugly. He was easily ruled by his passions and confused them with the interests of his country. His vision of America was pocked with more flaws than that of many of his contemporaries, including his enemies.

▲ *Jackson in old age years after leaving the presidency. Until his death in 1845, American politics was played in his shadow.*

But for all that, Andrew Jackson was his era made flesh, the personification of a democratic upheaval that changed the character of American politics. He presided over a time of ferment in nearly every facet of American life. He set new patterns of presidential behavior by aggressively taking the initiative in making policy.

Jackson also impressed his personality on a political party and an era that would end only when African American slavery tore the country apart. Even the Whigs, the party his enemies formed during Jackson's second term, were held together, to a large extent, by hostility toward him and his memory. And the Whigs succeeded only when they imitated the style and methods of the Jacksonian Democrats.

THE SECOND AMERICAN PARTY SYSTEM

By 1834, the realignment of national politics was complete. In the congressional elections that year, the National Republicans joined with former Jacksonians who objected to one or another of Old Hickory's policies—his promiscuous use of the veto, his high-handed treatment of Indians, his blow against South Carolina, and his war against the BUS—and called themselves the Whigs.

Alma Mater

A university student today would have difficulty recognizing the colleges of the early nineteenth century. A student's life then more closely resembled college life in the Middle Ages than in the twenty-first century.

All but a few colleges were private institutions. As late as 1860, only 17 of the 246 colleges and universities in the United States were state funded. Most of the others were maintained by Protestant denominations to train ministers and to indoctrinate other young men in their creeds. This was particularly true of the colleges founded during the Jacksonian era, many of which were inspired by the evangelical commitment to reform society.

Colleges were male institutions. Higher education was regarded as the final polishing of a cultivated man, the foundation for public life and for the practice of the professions. Women, whose social role was domestic and private, had no need for higher learning.

This attitude was beginning to change. In 1833, Ohio's Oberlin College, a hotbed of reform, began to admit women students. A few colleges and universities followed suit, but the real expansion of educational opportunities for women came not with coeducation but with all-female institutions. The first of these were Georgia Female College in Macon (now Wesleyan College) and Mount Holyoke College in South Hadley, Massachusetts, founded by Mary Lyon in 1837.

College was not vocationally oriented, as it is today. That is, students were not taught the specifics involved in the career they planned to pursue. The young man who wanted to become an engineer, an architect, or a businessman apprenticed himself to someone in those callings, learning "on the job." Although some universities had established medical and law schools, apprenticeship was also the most common means of preparing for those professions.

College curriculum remained much as it had been for centuries, a strictly prescribed course of study in the liberal arts and sciences (*liberal* in this case meaning "suitable to a free man"). Students studied Latin, Greek, and sometimes Hebrew; literature; natural science; mathematics; and political and moral philosophy in accordance with the doctrines of the church that supported the institution. There were no electives. Every student took the same courses.

The colleges were small. Except at the very oldest, such as Harvard, William and Mary, and Yale, and some public institutions, such as the University of Virginia, the typical student body rarely numbered more than a few dozen, and the typical faculty, perhaps three or four professors and an equal number of tutors. Although faculty members and students came to know one another by sight and name, relations between them were far from chummy. On the contrary, professors erected a high wall of formality between themselves and those they taught, both because of the belief in the principle of hierarchy and out of the fear that too much friendliness would lead to a breakdown in discipline. The stiff-necked behavior by instructors often also owed to the fact that many of them were little older, and sometimes even younger, than their students. Joseph Caldwell became *president* of the University of North Carolina when he was 24 years old.

Student behavior was regulated by long lists of detailed rules. Students were expected to toe the line not only in class but also in their private lives. Attendance at religious services was mandatory at church institutions. Strict curfews determined when students living in dormitories turned out their lamps. Even impoliteness might be punished by a fine or suspension.

This was the theory, at any rate. In practice, college students were at least as rambunctious as students today. They defied their professors by day—the distinguished political philosopher Francis Lieber had to tackle students he meant to discipline—and taunted them by night. A favorite prank was stealing into the college chapel and ringing the college bell until dawn. They threw snowballs and rocks through their tutors' windows. They led the president's horse to the roof of three- and four-story buildings. Students at Dickinson College in Pennsylvania sent a note to authorities at Staunton, Virginia, where Dickinson's president was visiting, informing them that an escaped lunatic was headed that way, would claim to be a college president, and should be returned under guard.

There were rebellions. Professors were assaulted: stoned, horsewhipped, and fired on with shotguns. At the University of Virginia in 1840, Professor Nathaniel Davis was murdered. Writing to his own son at college in 1843, Princeton professor Samuel Miller warned against sympathizing with potential rebels. Miller lived in fear of student uprisings, perhaps because one rebellion at Princeton was so serious that the faculty had to call in club-wielding townspeople to put it down.

Why the discontent? One reason is that the rules of college life were written at a time when most college students were 14 to 18 years old, whereas, by the Age of Jackson, they were often in their mid-20s. Adults simply were not inclined to conform to behavior appropriate to adolescents, and in a society that took pride in individual freedom, they were quite capable of reacting violently.

Moreover, many college students lived not in dormitories but in private lodgings in town. They fraternized largely with other students and developed a defiant camaraderie directed against outsiders. Enjoying broad freedoms in their off-campus lives, they were unlikely to conform to strict rules of behavior when they were on the campus.

Finally, although the rules were strict, enforcement was inconsistent. "There were too many colleges," writes historian Joseph F. Kett, "and they needed students more than students needed them." Faculty members, ever nervous for their jobs, overlooked minor offenses until they led to greater ones, at which point, suddenly, they drew the line. Inconsistency, as ever, led to contempt for authority.

Colleges might suspend the entire student body for "great rebellion." However, financial pressures usually resulted in readmission of the students for the price of a written apology. Samuel Miller described student rebels as "unworthy, profligate, degraded, and miserable villains," but if they had the tuition, there was a place for them somewhere.

BORN TO COMMAND.

OF VETO MEMORY

HAD I BEEN CONSULTED.

KING ANDREW THE FIRST.

KING ANDREW
THE FIRST,
"Born to Command."

A KING who, possessing as much power as his Gracious Brother *William IV.*, makes a worse use of it.

A KING who has placed himself above the laws, as he has shown by his contempt of our judges.

A KING who would destroy our currency, and substitute *Old Rags*, payable by no one knows who, and no one knows where, instead of *good Silver Dollars.*

A KING born to command, as he has shown himself by appointing men to office contrary to the will of the People.

A KING who, while he was feeding his favourites out of the public money, denied a pittance to the *Old Soldiers* who fought and bled for our independence.

A KING whose *Prime Minister* and *Heir Apparent*, was thought unfit for the office of ambassador by the people:

Shall he reign over us,
Or shall the PEOPLE RULE?

▲ *The Whigs took their name from the British politicians who steadfastly opposed the monarchy's having any more than figurehead status. The Americans Whigs deftly depicted Jackson as a king and appealed to rule by the people, the slogan on which Jackson had ridden to power.*

Collection of The New York Historical Society

The Whigs

The name *Whig* was borrowed from Great Britain. There, the Whigs were the party inclined to reduce the powers of the monarchy and to enhance the sway of Parliament. In the republican United States, the American Whigs said, the monarch that needed reining in was "King Andrew I."

The Whigs were a disparate group, brought together by little more than their abhorrence of Jackson. In the North, the Whig party included most people of education, means, and pretension to social status. Four out of five merchants were Whigs, as were many skilled native-born artisans. There and in the West, supporters of the American System, who believed that the federal government should take the initiative in shaping economic development, were Whigs. Northeastern Whigs tended to support moral legislation: temperance laws, strict observance of the Sabbath, and a welter of moralistic reforms that would become bewildering.

In the South, high-tariff men, like Louisiana sugar planters and Charleston financiers, tended to be Whigs. The party was stronger in the plantation counties (competitive with the Democrats, in fact) than in counties where small farmers owning few or no slaves dominated. Some southern exponents of state supremacy, like John Tyler of Virginia and even the nullifier, John C. Calhoun, allied with the nationalistic Whig party, but that made no sense except as political opportunism.

During the 1830s, Anti-Masons drifted into the Whig party. Traditionalist New Englanders, suspicious of anything attractive to southerners, like Jackson's Democratic party, inclined to Whiggery. So did those few blacks who were permitted to vote, as well as the upper and middle classes of city and town who found the vulgarity of lower-class Democrats and the spoils system offensive. In 1834, this patchwork alliance was enough to win 98 seats in the House of Representatives and almost half the Senate, 25 seats to the Democrats' 27. Until the 1850s, while unlucky in presidential elections, the Whigs fought the Democrats on a basis of equality in the House, Senate, and states.

To the Whigs, "the party of hope," the Democratic party was "the party of fear"—fear of progress. On the state level, following Jackson's example, they hamstrung (and, in seven states, abolished) banks. They opposed government subsidy of railroad construction and took little interest in promoting industry.

The Godlike Daniel

Next to Henry Clay, the best-known Whig was Daniel Webster of Massachusetts. At the peak of his power in the 1830s, he was idolized in New England—a demigod. The adoration owed mostly to Webster's personal presence and his peerless oratorical powers. With a great face that glowered darkly when he spoke, his eyes burned like "anthracite furnaces."

A look from him, it was said, was enough to win most debates. Webster was described as "a steam engine in trousers" and "a small cathedral in himself." An admirer said he was "a living lie because no man on earth could be so great as he looked."

Webster was not a fraction as great as he looked. Although an able administrator and an effective diplomat, Webster possessed less than a shining character. Of humble origin, he took too zestfully to the high life available to the eminent. He dressed grandly, savored good food, and basked in the company of the wealthy. He was also an alcoholic and invested his money—he was never rich—as foolishly as he spent it. He was constantly in debt and periodically broke. This tied him yet more closely to the New England industrialists who regularly sent him money, no strings attached (none that were labeled, anyway). During the Bank War, Webster obliquely threatened to end his services as legal counsel to the BUS unless Biddle paid him off, which Biddle did.

Webster came to expect money in the mail after every speech on behalf of the tariff or even the ideal of the Union. As a result, although he remained popular in New England until the very end of his career, his not-so-secret vices provided an easy target for the Democrats and made him an object of suspicion among fellow Whigs who took personal integrity as seriously as they took public virtue.

Union and Liberty

And yet, it was this flawed man who gave glorious voice to the ideal that was to sustain the indisputably great Abraham Lincoln during the Civil War. In 1830, when Calhoun and Jackson were toasting the relative values of union versus liberty, Webster rose in the Senate to tell the nation that "Liberty and Union, now and for ever," were "one and inseparable."

He was replying to Robert Hayne of South Carolina, himself a fine orator who, when Calhoun was vice president, spoke Calhoun's lines on the floor of the Senate. Hayne identified the doctrine of nullification with American liberty. Webster declared that, on the contrary, the Constitution was the wellspring of liberty in the United States and the indissoluble union of the states was its greatest defense. "It is, Sir," Webster pronounced, "the people's Constitution, the people's government, made for the people, made by the people, and answerable to the people." The liberty and union speech transformed a political abstraction, the Union, into an object for which people were willing to die. (It also provided three generations of schoolchildren with something to memorize.)

1836: Whigs Versus a Democrat

The differences among the Whigs prevented the party convention of 1836 from drafting a platform. The delegates could not even agree on a compromise candidate to oppose Martin Van Buren, the Democratic nominee. Consequently, Whig leaders decided on the curious tactic—unique in American political history—of trying to throw the election into the House of Representatives, as had unintentionally happened in 1800 and 1824.

▲ *The Webster-Hayne debate of January 1830, still considered one of the greatest oratorical moments in the history of Congress. It was certainly Daniel Webster's finest hour. He is speaking for the second time. (The speech extended over two days.) Hayne is seated dead center. In an artistic masterstroke, the painter shows John C. Calhoun in shadows at the left. As vice president, Calhoun could not speak, but he was the coauthor of Hayne's defense of the South, sectionalism, and nullification.*

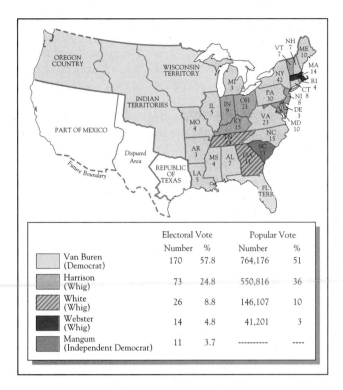

		Electoral Vote		Popular Vote	
		Number	%	Number	%
	Van Buren (Democrat)	170	57.8	764,176	51
	Harrison (Whig)	73	24.8	550,816	36
	White (Whig)	26	8.8	146,107	10
	Webster (Whig)	14	4.8	41,201	3
	Mangum (Independent Democrat)	11	3.7	----------	----

MAP 16:1 Van Buren's Victory in 1836 The Democrats and Whigs were both national parties. They carried states in the North, South, and West. A Whig carried Jackson's Tennessee, but, otherwise, Democrat Van Buren won on the combination of states he had helped Jackson engineer.

That is, the Whigs named three candidates to run against Van Buren, each in the section where he was most popular. Webster ran in lower New England. Hugh Lawson White of Tennessee was the candidate in the South. In the Northwest and upper New England, the Whigs' man was William Henry Harrison, the hero of the Battle of Tippecanoe. Although the battle was a quarter of a century in the past, the party hoped that the memory of it was still strong among a people ever hungry for new lands.

The strategy failed. Although all three Whigs (and cantankerous South Carolina's favorite-son candidate, Willie P. Mangum) won some electoral votes, Van Buren carried states in every section, with a comfortable 170 to 124 majority in the electoral college. The Whigs held their own in Congress, still a minority but, with South Carolina unpredictable, in a powerful position.

Depression

Election to the presidency was just about the last good thing that happened to Martin Van Buren. When his administration was just a few months old, the country reaped the whirlwind of Jackson's Specie Circular. Drained of their gold and silver, several big New York banks announced in May that they would no longer redeem their notes in specie. Speculators and honest workingmen alike found themselves holding paper money that even the institutions that issued it would not accept.

In 1838, the country sank into depression. In 1841 alone, 28,000 people declared bankruptcy. Factories closed because their products did not sell. Several cities were unsettled by riots of unemployed workers. Eight western state governments defaulted on their debts.

Van Buren tried to meet the fiscal part of the crisis. A good Jacksonian, he attempted to divorce the government from the banks, which he blamed for the disaster. He established the subtreasury system, by which, in effect, the government would keep its funds in its own vaults. The Clay and Webster Whigs replied that what was needed was an infusion of money into the economy, not burying it out of everyone's reach. But they could not carry the issue.

Van Buren also maintained the Jacksonian faith in laissez-faire by refusing to take any measures to alleviate popular suffering. The Founding Fathers, he said (in fact voicing Jackson's sentiments), had "wisely judged that the less government interfered with private pursuits the better for the general prosperity."

Whatever the virtues of Van Buren's position—and whatever the convictions of most Americans on the question of government intervention in the economy—it is difficult for any administration to survive a depression. The president, who reaps the credit for blessings that are none of his doing, gets the blame when things go badly, however nebulous his responsibility for the misfortune. By early 1840, the Whigs were sure that hard times would put their candidate into the White House.

Whig Dilemma

But who was to be the candidate? In that year of likely victory, Henry Clay believed that he deserved the nomination. For 25 years, he had offered a coherent national economic policy that, for the most part, was Whig gospel. For half that time, he led the fight against the Jacksonians. More than any other individual, he personified the Whig party.

Pop Art

In 1834, when the hero of the common man sat in the White House, Nathaniel Currier of New York democratized art in America. He began to sell prints depicting natural wonders, marvels of technology (such as locomotives), battles, prominent people, and scenes of everyday life, both sentimental and comical.

Currier and Ives (the partner arrived in 1852) sold their prints for as little as 25 cents for a small black and white to $4 for a hand-colored engraving 28 by 40 inches. They were cheap enough to be afforded by the poor yet just expensive enough to be acceptable as wall hangings in self-conscious middle-class households.

More than 7,000 different Currier and Ives prints were produced by a process that can only be called industrial. Some artists specialized in backgrounds; others, in machinery or faces; yet others, in crowd scenes. By the late nineteenth century, it was a rare American who could not have identified a "Currier & Ives."

But Clay's great career was also his weakness. In standing at the forefront for so long and being a deal maker by nature, Clay inevitably made mistakes and enemies, some of them bitter. Fellow Whig Edmund Quincy wrote (in purple ink) of "the ineffable meanness of the lion turned spaniel in his fawnings on the masters whose hands he was licking for the sake of the dirty puddings they might have to toss him."

Victory-hungry young Whigs, like Thurlow Weed of New York, argued against nominating Clay because of his baggage. Better, Weed said, to choose a candidate who had little or no political record but who, like Jackson, could be peddled as a symbol. In Weed's view, which echoed that of Martin Van Buren, the first and foremost objective of a political party was to win elections. Only then could it accomplish anything.

"Tippecanoe and Tyler Too"

By Weed's criteria, the ideal Whig candidate was William Henry Harrison. He was the scion of a distinguished Virginia family—his father had signed the Declaration of Independence—and, like Jackson, a victorious western warhorse, the victor of Tippecanoe. Harrison had done better than any other Whig in the peculiar election of 1836, and, best of all, he was associated with no controversial political position. Indeed, in 1836, his handlers admonished one another, "Let him say not one single word about his principles or his creed, let him say nothing, promise nothing. Let no [one] extract from him a single word about what he thinks. . . . Let use of pen and ink be wholly forbidden as if he were a mad poet in Bedlam."

Harrison was nominated in 1840 under pretty much the same conditions. To appeal to southerners, John Tyler of Virginia was nominated vice president—thus the party's slogan "Tippecanoe and Tyler Too!"

Harrison's Invented Image

At first, the Whigs planned to campaign simply by talking about Harrison's military record. Then, a Democratic newspaper editor made a slip that opened up a whole new world in American politics. Meaning to argue that Harrison was incompetent, the journalist sneered that the old man would be happy with an annual pension of $2,000, a jug of hard cider, and a bench on which to sit and doze at the door of his log cabin.

Such snobbery toward the humble life was ill suited to a party that had come to power as the champion of the common man. The Whigs, who suffered Democratic taunts that they were elitists, charged into the breach. They hauled out miniature log cabins at city rallies and country bonfires. They bought and tapped thousands of barrels of hard cider. They sang raucous songs like this little ditty:

> Farewell, dear Van,
> You're not our man,
> To guide our ship,
> We'll try old Tip.

Stealing another leaf from the Jacksonian campaign book of 1828, the Whigs depicted Van Buren as an effeminate fop who sipped champagne, ate fancy French food, perfumed his whiskers, and flounced about in silks and satins. Before he departed for Texas, death, and immortality at the Alamo, the colorful Whig politician Davy Crockett depicted Van Buren as "laced up in corsets such as women in a town wear, and if possible tighter than the best of them. It would be difficult to say from his personal appearance whether he was man or woman, but for his large red and gray whiskers."

It was all nonsense. Harrison lived in no log cabin but in a mansion. He was no simple country bumpkin but, rather, the opposite—a pedant given to tedious academic

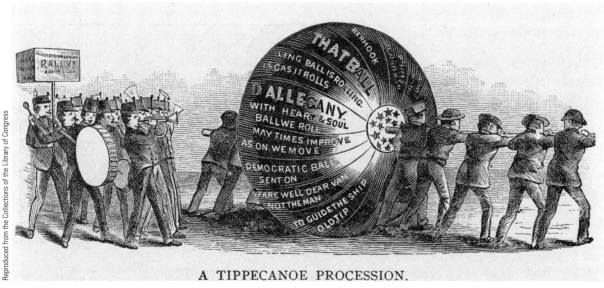

A TIPPECANOE PROCESSION.

▲ *The Whigs built mock log cabins for rallies on behalf of William Henry Harrison and also great balls covered with slogans and pushed from town to town on an axle. The phrase "keep the ball rolling," still common parlance, dates from that landmark campaign.*

discourse on subjects of little interest to ordinary, hardworking people. Van Buren, although quite the dandy, was of modest origins (his father had kept a tavern). He was naturally earthy, and he subscribed to much more democratic ideas than did old Tippecanoe.

But nonsense worked, as it often has since. Although Van Buren won 47 percent of the popular vote, he was trounced in the electoral college 60 to 234. Jacksonian chickens had come home to roost. From then on, rarely would a presidential election be contested without great fussing about symbols, images, and irrelevancies.

With their successful appeal to the prejudices of the common man, the Whigs of 1840 demonstrated that the democratic upheaval of the Age of Jackson was complete. Never again would there be political profit in appealing to the superior qualifications of "the better sort" in the egalitarian United States. Finally, what may be most notable about the election of 1840 is that a political candidate was marketed as a commodity—"packaged"—long before the techniques of modern advertising had been conceived.

Fate's Cruel Joke

Wherever William Henry Harrison stood on specific issues, he was fully in accord with one fundamental Whig principle—that Congress should make the laws and the president execute them. He was quite willing to defer to the party professionals, particularly Clay, in making policy. With large Whig majorities in both houses of Congress, the Great Compromiser had every reason to believe that, if not president in name, he would direct the nation's affairs. Old Tip dutifully named four of Clay's lieutenants to the cabinet.

Harrison would have done well to defer to Daniel Webster in his field of expertise—oratory. Webster wrote an inaugural address for Harrison, but the president politely turned it down, having prepared his own. It was the longest, dullest inaugural address in the archives, a turgid treatise on Roman history and its relevance to the United States of America circa March 1841. Not even historians could have enjoyed it, because it was delivered out of doors on a frigid, windy day. Harrison caught a cold that turned into pneumonia. For weeks, he suffered, half the time in bed, half the time receiving Whig office seekers as greedy for jobs as the Democrats of 1828. Then he ceased to rise and dress. On April 4, 1841, exactly one month after lecturing the country on republican virtue, he passed away.

John Tyler

At first, the Whigs did not miss a stride. Clay lectured "Tyler Too" that he was an "acting president," presiding over the formalities of government while a committee of Whigs chaired by Henry Clay made the decisions. John Quincy Adams, now a Whig representative from Massachusetts, concurred. Tyler would have none of it. A nondescript man who had little imagination and a provincial view of national problems, Tyler insisted that the Constitution authorized him

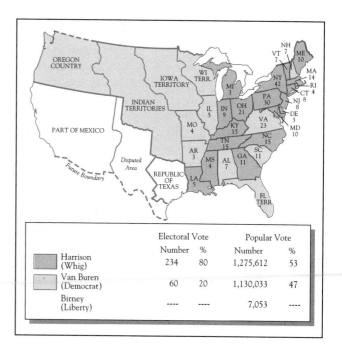

MAP 16:2 **The Whig Victory of 1840** Whig William Henry Harrison almost swept the Northeast in 1840 and won three southern states that voted Democratic in 1836.

to exercise the same presidential powers that he would exercise if he had been elected.

Tyler tried hard to get along with Clay. He went along with the abolition of the subtreasury system, and, although a low-tariff man, he agreed to an increase of rates in 1842 as long as the rise was tied to ending federal finance of internal improvements. Tyler also supported Clay's attempt to woo western voters from the Democrats with his Preemption Act of 1841. This law provided that a family who squatted on up to 160 acres of public land could purchase it at the minimum price of $1.25 per acre without having to bid against others.

A President Without a Party

But Tyler was no Whig. He had split with Jackson over "King Andrew's" arrogant use of presidential power. His views on other issues were closer to those of John C. Calhoun than to those of the nationalistic Whigs. Most notably, Tyler wanted no new BUS and warned Clay not to try to force one on him.

Clay tried anyway, and Tyler vetoed one bank bill after another. Furious, the majority Whigs expelled the president from the party, and Tyler's entire cabinet resigned (except Secretary of State Webster, who wanted to complete some touchy negotiations with Great Britain). Clay left the Senate in order to devote full time to winning the presidential election of 1844.

Tyler's new cabinet was made up of nominal southern Whigs who shared Tyler's views. The president's plan was to piece together a new party of states' rights Whigs and some Democrats. Toward this end, he named John C. Calhoun secretary of state. Whig party loyalty was too strong for Tyler's scheme to work. In effect, he was a president without a party.

British-American Friction

The major accomplishment of the Tyler administration was in the area of foreign affairs: solving a series of potentially dangerous disputes with Great Britain and paving the way for the annexation of the Republic of Texas.

The first was a Whiggish goal engineered by Daniel Webster. One of the problems was a boundary dispute between Maine and New Brunswick. According to the Treaty of 1783, the line ran between the watersheds of the Atlantic and the St. Lawrence River. Both sides had agreed to the boundary as drawn on a map in red ink by Benjamin Franklin.

The map had disappeared, however, and in 1838, Canadian lumberjacks began cutting timber in the Aroostook Valley, which the United States claimed. A brief "war" between the Maine and New Brunswick militias ended with no deaths, and Van Buren managed to cool things down. But he could not resolve the boundary dispute.

The Canadian-American line west of Lake Superior was also in question, and there were two more points of friction because of unofficial American assistance to Canadian rebels and the illegal slave trade in which some Americans were involved. The slavery issue waxed hot late in 1841, when blacks on the American brig *Creole* mutinied, killed the crew, and sailed to Nassau in the British Bahamas. The British hanged the leaders of the mutiny but freed the other slaves, enraging sensitive white southerners.

The Webster-Ashburton Treaty

Neither Britain nor the United States wanted war, but old rancor and the Canadians' determination to build a road through the disputed Aroostook country stalled a settlement. Fortuitously, Daniel Webster found a kindred spirit in the high-living British negotiator Lord Ashburton, and, over lots of brandy, they worked out a compromise. Webster made a big concession to the British, too big as far as Maine's loggers were concerned. Never above chicanery, Webster forged Franklin's map to show a red line that gave Maine less territory than he "won" from Ashburton. He warned that the United States had better take what it could get. (The real Franklin map surfaced some years later and showed that the United States was shorted.)

Ashburton was generous too. He ceded a strip of territory in northern New York and Vermont to which the United States had no claim and also about 6,500 square miles at the tip of Lake Superior. Although wilderness at the time, this area, later known as the Mesabi Range, was one of the world's richest iron ore deposits.

When the Senate ratified the Webster-Ashburton Treaty in 1842, every outstanding issue between the United States and Britain was settled except the two nations' joint occupation of the Oregon Country on the Pacific Coast. Webster had good reason to be pleased with himself, and he joined his fellow Whigs in leaving John Tyler's cabinet.

for FURTHER READING

For overviews, see Glyndon G. Van Deusen, *The Jacksonian Era, 1828–1848,* 1959; Edward E. Pessen, *Jacksonian America: Society, Personality, and Politics,* 1978; and Robert Remini, *The Revolutionary Age of Andrew Jackson,* 1985. To appreciate the political and cultural values that informed Jackson's era, see John W. Ward, *Andrew Jackson: Symbol for an Age,* 1955. The appropriate chapters of Richard Hofstadter, *The American Political Tradition and the Men Who Made It,* 1948, are still stimulating. Richard P. McCormick, *The Second American Party System Formation in the Jacksonian Era,* 1966, is essential.

Martin Van Buren, if almost forgotten in popular history, is the subject of three excellent biographical studies: D. B. Cole, *Martin Van Buren and the American Political System,* 1984; John Niven, *Martin Van Buren: The Romantic Age of American Politics,* 1983; and M. L. Wilson, *The Presidency of Martin Van Buren,* 1984. On his hapless nemesis, see Margaret Coit's now classic *John C. Calhoun: American Portrait,* 1950, and the more critical Richard N. Current, *John C. Calhoun,* 1966.

Dealing with the Bank War are Bray Hammond, *Bank and Politics in America from the Revolution to the Civil War,* 1957; Robert Remini, *Andrew Jackson and the Bank War,* 1967; and John McFaul, *The Politics of Jacksonian Finance,* 1972. Sympathetic to Biddle's position is Thomas P. Govan, *Nicholas Biddle: Nationalist and Public Banker,* 1959.

D. W. Howe, *The Political Culture of the American Whigs,* 1979, is a fine survey of a subject long neglected except in biographies. Among the best biographies of the Whigs are Glyndon G. Van Deusen, *The Life of Henry Clay,* 1937; Clement Eaton, *Henry Clay and the Art of American Politics,* 1957; Richard N. Current, *Daniel Webster and the Rise of National Conservatism,* 1955; Sydney Nathan, *Daniel Webster and Jacksonian Democracy,* 1973; and M. G. Baxter, *One and Inseparable: Daniel Webster and the Union,* 1984. On the election of 1840 and its aftermath, see R. G. Gunderson, *The Log Cabin Campaign,* 1957; and O. D. Lambert, *Presidential Politics in the United States, 1841–1844,* 1936.

 AMERICAN JOURNEY ONLINE AND INFOTRAC COLLEGE EDITION

Visit the source collections at http://ajaccess.wadsworth.com and http://infotrac.thomsonlearning.com, and use the Search function with the following key terms to explore documents, images, audio and video clips, articles, and commentary related to the material in this chapter:

Andrew Jackson	John Tyler
John C. Calhoun	Martin Van Buren

HISTORY ONLINE

Daniel Webster, Liberty and Union

www.nv.cc.va.us/home/nvsageh/Hist121/Part3/Webster.htm

Text of the speech of 1830 that immortalized Daniel Webster despite his obvious character flaws.

Tippecanoe and Tyler Too

www.multied.com/documents/Tippacanoe.html

Horace Greeley, a prominent Whig editor, writes of the Whig disappointment when William Henry Harrison died after one month in office.

17

ENTHUSIASM
Evangelicals, Utopians, Reformers

© Bettmann/Corbis

God has found it necessary to take advantage of the excitability there is in mankind, to produce powerful excitements among them, before he can lead them to obey. Men are so spiritually sluggish, there are so many things to lead their minds off from religion, and to oppose the influence of the Gospel, that it is necessary to raise an excitement among them, till the tide rises so high as to sweep away the opposing obstacles.

Charles G. Finney

B Y THE TIME of Andrew Jackson, the established churches of the colonial era were just two denominations among many. Anglicanism (now the Protestant Episcopal Church) was still the faith of the elites of the South, New York City, and, to a lesser extent, Philadelphia (where it was also respectable to be a Quaker). Preserving traditional rituals, valuing restrained preachers, and avoiding political controversy, the Episcopalians provided the comforts of church membership while requiring little more of parishioners than attendance on Sunday and financial support.

The Congregational Church lost its grip on upper-class New Englanders because, in a day where, it seemed, happiness was successfully pursued by individual human effort, the central doctrine of the Puritans, predestination, just did not fit in. New England's self-satisfied merchant elite and professionals quietly put Calvinism away as an old hat is tossed into the corner of the loft. They gravitated to the Anglicans or, more likely, the Unitarians, who coalesced as a denomination in the 1810s by replacing the disturbing doctrine of human depravity with a reassuring belief in human goodness. A newcomer to Boston during Jackson's presidency (a Presbyterian) observed that "all the literary men of Massachusetts were Unitarians; all the trustees and professors of Harvard College were Unitarians; all the elite of wealth and fashion crowded Unitarian churches."

The Congregationalists lost ground among ordinary New Englanders after 1800, when Thomas Jefferson came to power and blood did not run in the gutters of Boston and Hartford, as many Congregationalist ministers had warned. By the 1830s, Democrats could win elections in every New England state. Even Connecticut and Massachusetts abolished the privileges of the Congregationalists.

RELIGIOUS FERMENT

Old-time religion did not disappear. Denominations that had never enjoyed official favor—the Presbyterian Church of the

Scotch-Irish, the Baptists (for whom the separation of church and state was a basic tenet), the Methodists (an offshoot of the Anglicans), *and* hard-shell, old-line Congregationalists—preached the centrality of salvation by means of an emotional conversion experience that evidenced the visitation of the Holy Spirit. But their doctrine had one big, new, democratic, egalitarian difference: Salvation was available not only to a divinely elected few.

Like personal economic improvement, salvation was available to all men and (unlike economic opportunity) to all women. These churches were known as "evangelical" because unlike, for example, the sedate Episcopalians and Unitarians, they aggressively preached the gospel—that is, they "evangelized."

As a force shaping America in the first half of the nineteenth century, the evangelicals were as powerful as Jacksonian Democrats, who were decidedly not evangelicals. The evangelicals were the most durable and constructive part of a spirit of enthusiasm in the original Greek meaning of the word—being possessed by God and assured that God spoke directly to them (no matter how far-fetched the things he said).

Camp Meetings and Circuit Riders

The first signs of the new wave of religious enthusiasm were to be found on the trans-Appalachian frontier. Preachers styling themselves "revivalists" (because, they said, religion needed to be revived) began to organize "camp meetings" during the 1790s. These were multiday, or even weeklong, events held in openings in the forest, where thousands camped in wagons and tents. They listened, morning to midnight, to emotional sermons confirming what they knew all too well: that they were sinful creatures and that they were therefore damned to hell unless they prayed for and won God's grace.

The greatest of the camp meeting preachers was James McGready, who inveighed not only against the garden-variety sins of his listeners but against the greed of the southern elite. The culmination of McGready's career was the camp meeting at Cane Ridge, Kentucky, in 1801. As many as 20,000 people may have gathered there.

Such a concentration of humanity was itself exhilarating on the thinly populated frontier, and the atmosphere of the camp meeting was electrifying. Dozens of preachers—Presbyterians, Methodists, and Baptists—simultaneously harangued the crowd from well-constructed platforms, and freelancers preached from stumps.

Conversions were numerous and passionate. People fell to their hands and knees, weeping uncontrollably. Others scampered about on all fours, barking like dogs. A famous manifestation of God's presence was the "jerks," which caused people to lurch about, their limbs snapping and jerking wildly. At Cane Ridge, the rumor spread that a man who cursed God had been seized by the jerks and had broken his neck. When each day's final exhortations tailed off, the moans of excited people could be heard in every direction.

Plenty of people, especially young men, went to camp meetings for the company, the showmanship, and the chance to exploit the occasion with thieving, heckling, heavy drinking, and the sexual opportunities emotional excitement dependably provides. At first, the scoffers were welcome. Revivalism was, after all, about converting sinners. But violent assaults on preachers and oft-told tales of large numbers of girls conceiving persuaded some churches to abandon the camp meeting for the "circuit rider," a Methodist invention, to minister to scattered westerners. The circuit rider—intensely devoted, poorly paid, usually unmarried—visited, on an unending circuit, 10 or 20 little settlements that were too poor to support a church. They rode through thickets and forded swollen creeks in all weather, often carrying nothing but a Bible. They preached, performed marriages and baptisms, took their rest and meals in the cabins of the faithful, and rode on. For three decades, the most famous of them,

▲ *A camp meeting in the forest. The preacher has some of his listeners writhing in hysteria while others are impassive, there for the show.*

Finis Ewing and Peter Cartwright, were rarely off their horses for more than three days at a time.

The Second Great Awakening

Among the social sins the early evangelicals condemned was slavery. As early as the 1780s, Methodist circuit riders were ordered to free their slaves; all Methodists were pressured to do the same. The Baptist and Presbyterian Churches in the slave states of Kentucky and Tennessee called for the abolition of slavery there. Moral revulsion toward slavery went hand in hand with the "Second Great Awakening" in the eastern states too, as did many other reforms.

The frenzy of McGready-style revivalism was a phenomenon of marginal people. For that reason, it was disdained by the upper and middle classes of the Northeast, who prized propriety. The evangelical spirit was brought to them by a number of preachers who toned down the histrionics of revivalism while retaining the revivalist technique and the message that neither damnation nor social evils were divinely decreed.

The well-tuned revivalist sermon, whether delivered at Cane Ridge in 1801 or Rochester, New York, in 1835, had a form varying only in details. It began with a description, varying in emotion and images, of the capacity of human beings for sin. The second part of the sermon detailed the sufferings of hell, for which sinners were destined. Like good politicians, however, revivalists concluded on an optimistic note. Any person could be saved in the Christianity of equal opportunity if he or she repented and declared faith in Jesus Christ. Religion was voluntary and personal. Salvation was a matter not of God's will but of the individual man and woman. "Don't wait!" said Charles Grandison Finney, the greatest of the Awakening preachers. "Do it! Get saved!" He never failed to make the point that "God has made man a moral free agent."

Finney was a lawyer who, after an emotional personal conversion ("I wept aloud like a child. . . . I could feel the [Holy Spirit] like a wave of electricity going through and through me"), traversed the northeastern states during the Jackson years, preaching to largely middle-class gatherings. Finney emphasized the Christian's duty to fight social wrongs, not just because they were sins but because, by eliminating them, the arrival of the Christian Millennium, a thousand years when Christ would rule the earth, would be hastened. Finney lent support to all sorts of moral reformers, but, curiously, he balked for many years at supporting the greatest evangelical reform of the century, the movement to abolish slavery. It is curious that he should have embraced that cause only late in life because the Great Awakening profoundly influenced the religious beliefs of African Americans, particularly southern slaves, only a minority of whom had previously shown interest in Christianity.

▲ *William Miller's analysis of prophecies and his prediction of the end of the world were illustrated in this Adventist chart tracing the rise and fall of earthly kingdoms from Babylon through the "Mahometans." Like many Protestant groups and the Mormons, the Adventists dwelled on the popes of Rome as the most wicked of earthly rulers.*

The Adventists

The Second Coming of Christ was the core of the teachings of a Baptist, William Miller. About 1831, he began to preach that the world would end between March 21, 1843, and March 21, 1844. Miller convinced thousands in the northeastern states with a complex mathematical formula based on biblical prophecies.

At the beginning of the fateful year, a magnificent omen appeared in the sky, Halley's comet. Converts then flocked to join Miller's Adventists (*advent* means "coming" or "arrival"). Many sold their possessions, contributing the proceeds to the sect, which led critics to accuse Miller and his business manager, Joshua V. Himes, of fraud.

On March 21, 1844, so as to be first to greet the Lord, several thousand people throughout New York and New England climbed hills in "Ascension Robes" sold to them by Himes. When the sun set without incident—the "Great Disappointment"—Miller discovered an error in his computations and set the date of the end at no later than October 22, 1844. Again some towns frothed with anxiety and eager anticipation as the day approached. An even greater disappointment descended when, again, Christ did not appear. Miller

himself was bewildered, a broken man. But a disciple, Hiram Edson, reorganized the remnants of the Millerites around the more serviceable belief that the world would end *soon*. Because Edson observed the Jewish Sabbath, Saturday, rather than the Lord's Day, Sunday, the denomination became known as Seventh-Day Adventists.

The Mormons

Another new religion of the era that was certainly enthusiastic and committed to evangelizing for converts, but was otherwise unique, was the Church of Jesus Christ of Latter-Day Saints, the Mormons. Mormonism also originated in "the burned-over district" of New York State, so called because religious enthusiasts, from camp meetings to Adventism to Finney, had repeatedly scorched the land with their ardor.

The founder of the church was Joseph Smith, a daydreamer who preferred wandering the hills of the region, looking for legendary treasure, to the tedious chores of farm life. When he was 20, Smith told his family and neighbors that, on one of his rambles, an angel, Moroni, showed him gold plates bearing mysterious inscriptions that, using miraculous spectacles, Smith was able to read. He translated these inscriptions in *The Book of Mormon,* a Bible of the New World telling of the descendants of the Hebrews in America, the Nephites, whom Christ had visited.

To many, told from childhood that their country was a new Eden, it was not preposterous that Christ should have visited the New World as well as Judaea. To people unsettled by the frenzied pace of the Age of Jackson, it was not surprising that God should make his truth known in upstate New York. It was a time, as one of Smith's converts, Orson Pratt, wrote, when "wickedness [kept] pace with the hurried revolutions of the age." Poet John Greenleaf Whittier, who was no Mormon, wrote of the Latter-Day Saints, "They speak a language of hope and promise to weak, heavy hearts, tossed and troubled, who have wandered from sect to sect, seeking in vain for the primal manifestation of divine power."

Persecution

To a degree, Joseph Smith was his era's child. He extended the priesthood to all white males, thus appealing to the Jacksonian yearning for equality. And he went west, taking his ever increasing followers to Ohio, Missouri, and, in 1840, to Nauvoo, Illinois. The Mormons prospered. By 1844, Nauvoo was the largest city in the state!

The Mormons' prosperity as a group and their undisguised dislike of outsiders (whom they called the "gentiles") aroused envy and resentment locally. Nevertheless, because the Mormons of Nauvoo voted as a bloc, they were courted by both Whig and Democratic politicians. Joseph Smith could probably have been elected to high office in Illinois by trading Mormon votes for a major party nomination.

Instead, in 1844, he declared that he would be an independent candidate for the presidency. This news, added to fears of the well-armed Mormon militia of 2,000 men,

▲ *Joseph Smith reviews the Mormons' Nauvoo Legion at Nauvoo, Illinois. Although hardly the crack, spit-and-polish troops this painting portrays, and described by Smith as a defense force, the large private militia alarmed "gentiles" in western Illinois and contributed to the panic that resulted in Smith's arrest and murder.*

the Nauvoo Legion, led to Smith's arrest. On June 27, he and his brother were murdered in Carthage, Illinois.

Safe in the Desert

The Mormons might have foundered had not an even more remarkable (and politically wiser) Vermonter, Brigham Young, grappled his way to the top of the church hierarchy. Young also received revelations directly from God. The most important of these was the command that the Latter-Day Saints move beyond the boundaries of the sinful nation that oppressed them to lands that were legally Mexican but, in reality, were governed by no one.

The Mormon migration was organized to the finest detail. Advance parties planted crops that would be ready for harvesting when the multitudes arrived on the trail, and built almost a thousand log huts, where they could shelter during the winter. For his Zion, Young chose the most isolated and inhospitable region known to explorers, the basin of the Great Salt Lake.

"This is the place," he said, looking down from the Wasatch Mountains. There the Mormons laid out a tidy city with broad avenues and irrigation ditches fed by water from the surrounding peaks. Their desert bloomed. Within a few years, more than 10,000 people lived in the Salt Lake basin.

Alas, just as the Mormons were constructing their Zion, American victory in war with Mexico brought them back under the American flag. Young did not fight the troops that arrived in Salt Lake, but he made it clear that controlling Utah, which the Mormons called "Deseret," depended on cooperating with him. Prudently, the authorities named Young territorial governor.

Despite its large population, Utah was not admitted to the Union until 1896. About one in six Mormon men practiced polygamy. The others believed in multiple wives but could not afford them. Young, who could, had 27 wives and 56 children. Congress refused to grant statehood until Young's successor received a revelation that polygamy was to be abandoned.

UTOPIAN COMMUNITIES

The Mormons lived in regulated, authoritarian communities, as insulated from the "gentiles" as was possible. The individualism of the Jacksonians and the widespread American avarice for personal riches were subordinated to the good of the whole. Similar social experiments, without the authoritarian leader, appealed to other Americans distressed by the poverty and moral misery that were, along with material progress, the fruits of a wide-open competitive economy. Some of the communities they founded had religious foundations. Others were based on philosophical ruminations. Most were enthusiastic, broadly defined. There were dozens of such utopias. Most failed, and quickly. A few endured.

Failures

New Harmony, Indiana, was founded in 1825 by Robert Owen, a British manufacturer who believed that if property were held in common, life need not, as it did for most, consist of drudgery; life could instead be morally and intellectually fulfilling. Unfortunately for Owen, New Harmony attracted too many people passionately interested not only in the weekly philosophical discussions but also in the easy life Owen generously financed. They found other fulfilling things to do when it was time to work. Believing deeply in the goodness of human nature, Owen was incapable of throwing the freeloaders out. In 1827, disillusioned and poorer, he returned to Scotland.

Another star-crossed utopia was Fruitlands, Massachusetts, the brainstorm of Bronson Alcott. Alcott was a magnificent and lovable eccentric best remembered as the father of author Louisa May Alcott. Like many intellectuals, he was incapable of coping with workaday life. He could button his own shirt, but he inaugurated Fruitlands by planting several apple trees within two feet of the front door of the community house, dropping his shovel, and returning to his meditations and endless conversations.

It was crackpot heaven. One utopian refused to weed the garden because weeds had as much right to grow as vegetables did. Samuel Larned lived for one year on nothing but crackers (so he said) and the next year on nothing but apples. Another Fruitlander smashed dehumanizing, empty social conventions by greeting people, "Good morning, God damn you!" Everyone at Fruitlands agreed that, somehow, cows were loathsome in all ways, but this insight was not enough to sustain the community. Fruitlands lasted several years only because Mrs. Alcott, who did not take her husband seriously but did know what it took to set a table and raise children, did most of the work.

Success Stories

The Shakers, founded in England by Mother Ann Lee, were celibate. Believing (like the Millerites) that the end of the world was near, there was no need to perpetuate the human

race by the distasteful act by which children were had. Men and women lived separately in, by the 1830s, more than 20 tidy and comfortable Shaker communities. They shared equally the work, which, unlike at New Harmony, got done. Men and women came together for meals, conversation, and religious services.

The Shakers were never persecuted as the Mormons were. Sexual abstinence might strike people as peculiar, but it did not offend, as polygamy did. Moreover, unlike the Mormons, the Shakers were polite, hospitable, cooperative, open, and fair in their dealings with outsiders. Indeed, as a community that needed a constant influx of converts in order to survive, the Shakers, although never overweening, welcomed guests. Their communities served as orphan asylums that were free, always a plus for taxpayers. They took in and raised children unwanted by others, giving them the choice, when they reached adulthood, of remaining or returning to "the world." Shaker-style furniture is still an American standard. The evidence is strong that they invented the flat broom, the wooden clothes pin, the circular saw, and the apple parer. Very small Shaker communities of very old Shakers still exist.

John Humphrey Noyes was not troubled by sexual intercourse, but he disapproved of the institution of marriage. Wedlock, he said, was a form of property: Under American law and customs, the husband effectively "owned" his wife. Hence, Noyes said, both were miserable. Rejecting celibacy as an alternative, Noyes devised the concept of "complex marriage" as an adjunct to collective ownership or property.

▲ *The library at the Oneida Community. Like Robert Owen, Oneida's founder, John Humphrey Noyes believed that by owning property in common and by dividing labor equitably among all, there would be plenty of time for study and other fulfilling and ennobling activities. Owen was inundated by parasites; Oneida did not tolerate them, and it thrived.*

In his utopia at Oneida, New York, every man was married to every woman and vice versa. Couples who chose to have sexual relations for pleasure (the initiative was the lady's) could do so, but not for the purpose of procreation. Noyes was an proponent of what came to be called "eugenics": improving the quality of the human race by allowing only those superior in health, constitution, and intellect to reproduce. (The Oneida method of birth control was male continence.) After long and ardent prayer and study, Noyes concluded that he was an ideal male breeder.

Oneida's free love enraged the community's neighbors. Noyes fled to Canada to escape arrest. Oneida, nevertheless, enjoyed a long life. The community prospered from its manufacture of silverware, silks, and a superior trap for fur-bearing animals. Abandoning complex marriage in 1879, and communal ownership of property in 1881, the Oneidans reorganized as a commercial corporation.

TRANSCENDENTALISM

Noyes was a Perfectionist. That is, he believed that Christ's redemption of humanity was complete. Individuals had it within themselves to be perfect—that is, without sin—and therefore above rules that had been written for the imperfect. People had only to face up to their perfection, and it was so.

Perfectionism was evangelicalism triumphant—for those who were perfect. The evangelicals were determined to rid themselves and society of sin. Noyes had done it, albeit in just one community in upstate New York. Unfortunately, when Noyes put sinlessness into practice at Oneida by approving behaviors defined by his neighbors as quite sinful, he was run out of the country.

Ralph Waldo Emerson of Massachusetts, by contrast, became "America's philosopher" by calling Perfectionism by another name—transcendentalism—and by avoiding its implications in his pronouncements and certainly in the way he led his life.

Pantheism

Ralph Waldo Emerson's pantheism—the belief that nature is divinity—made for beautiful lyric poetry. In "The Rhodora," he reflected on the purple flower of that name that grows only in obscure nooks of the woods:

Rhodora! If the sages ask thee why
This charm is wasted on the earth and sky,
Tell them, dear, that if eyes were made for seeing,
Then beauty is its own excuse for being;
Why thou wert there, O rival of the rose!
I never thought to ask, I never knew:
But, in my simple ignorance, suppose
The self-same power that brought me here,
brought you.

▲ *Ralph Waldo Emerson was a superb writer and lecturer, able to live comfortably on his earnings as a philosopher. He might be considered America's second "celebrity" in our sense of the word. He was "famous for being famous," second in that role only to Benjamin Franklin.*

The Sage of Concord

Emerson was a Unitarian pastor in Boston whose assessment of human nature glowed with warmth. In 1832, he announced that he could no longer accept the Unitarian practice of celebrating the Lord's Supper; he resigned and moved to Concord, Massachusetts. "The profession is antiquated," Emerson said of preaching. But within a few years, he was preaching again, from a lectern rather than a pulpit. He shook his head sadly that people should cling to superstition, yet his own message was a welter of notions far more mystical than the Protestantism of sophisticated Boston.

Transcendentalism defied criticism. Based on feelings rather than reason, transcendentalism exalted a vague concept of nature's superiority to civilization, personal morality over laws, and the individual's capacity within himself to be happy, or sinless. When Emerson was faulted as fuzzy and contradictory, he responded that his critics were not capable of understanding that "consistency is the hobgoblin of little minds," that the enlightened human being could dispose "very easily of the most disagreeable facts."

Transcend means "to go beyond, to rise above." As used by Emerson and his disciples, it meant to go above reason and beyond the material world. God was not a being, but the oversoul, which was within all men and women because it was in nature. "Standing on the bare ground," Emerson wrote, "my head bathed by the blithe air and uplifted into infinite space—all mean egotism vanishes. I become a transparent eyeball; I am nothing; I see all; the currents of the Universal being circulate through me."

Writer Herman Melville, a contemporary, called Emerson's teachings "gibberish" and "self-conceit." But while Melville struggled to eke out a living, Emerson was lionized as the greatest mind of his time. While Melville scrutinized evil in the world, Emerson sniffed gifts of flowers.

Other Transcendentalists

Mostly, Emerson had fans. He supported himself in comfort by packing lecture halls throughout the Northeast and selling collections of his essays. But there were other transcendentalists famous in their own time. Emerson's neighbor in Concord, Henry David Thoreau, was the introspective son of a pencil manufacturer. Unlike the prim and proper Emerson (in Paris, Emerson was stunned into unprecedented speechlessness by the gaiety of Gallic free living), Thoreau flaunted his eccentricity. In 1845, he constructed a cabin in the woods near Walden Pond, just outside Concord. There he wrote *Walden* (1854), an account of his reflections while sitting by the pond.

Although *Walden* is the masterpiece of transcendentalism—possibly the best reflective writing of the century—it is marred by the same dilettantism that robs Emerson's works (also masterpieces of style) of lasting value. Thoreau wrote as if he had seceded from civilization and struck off into the wilderness: "I wanted to live deep and suck out all the marrow of life, to live so sturdily and spartan, like as to put to rout all that was not life, to cut a broad swath and shave close, to drive life into a corner, and reduce it to its lowest terms."

But Walden was no Rocky Mountain fastness. It was a short stroll to Concord, a walk that Thoreau took often when he had a yen for a well-cooked meal. Living deep and sucking the marrow out of life were rather like camping in the backyard.

PHILANTHROPISTS AND REFORMERS

Evangelicals soon moved from personal salvation to saving society by attacking and attempting to kill its sins, as they had done within themselves. They believed that it was their sacred obligation to bear witness against social evils and that it was their Christian duty not only to save the souls of their fellow creatures but also to improve their lives.

Gallaudet, Howe, and Dix

Some evangelicals were specialists. Thomas Gallaudet's concern was deafness and society's indifference to the deaf. Traditionally, Americans regarded deafness, blindness, and other disabilities as punishments for sin, as trials designed

How Others Saw Us

Literate Europeans thought of the United States as a cultural backwater, Americans of no more interest than the Indians whom they dispossessed and the Africans they enslaved. Sidney Smith, a famous British wit, wrote in 1820: "In the four quarters of the globe, who reads an American book? or goes to an American play? or looks at an American picture or statue? What does the world yet owe to American physicians or surgeons? What new substances have their chemists discovered? or what old ones have they analyzed? What new constellations have been discovered by the telescopes of Americans?—What have they done in the mathematics?" Few of Smith's readers would have disagreed, including those few Americans who imported his *Edinburgh Review.*

Times were changing, however. Just the next year, a New Yorker, Washington Irving, published two stories, "Rip Van Winkle" and "The Legend of Sleepy Hollow," that won the British intelligentsia's acclaim. James Fenimore Cooper, another New Yorker, was soon so gratifyingly lionized in England for his *Leatherstocking Tales,* novels about the clash of civilization and nature on the American frontier, that he stayed abroad for seven years.

It was the rise of Jacksonian Democracy, however, that piqued European interest in Americans as people, in their government and politics, and in the curious enthusiasms that seemed to thrive in the United States. Indeed, America became something of a mania among the intelligentsia. Before 1828, the year of Jackson's election, only some 40 books about America were published in Europe. In the decade that followed, hundreds were written in at least a dozen languages. Popular British authors such as Frederick Marryat, Anthony Trollope, Harriett Martineau, and Charles Dickens crossed the Atlantic specifically to describe the scenery, explain the political institutions, and wonder over the manners, morals, and quirks of Americans. The best of the books was *Democracy in America,* a two-volume treatise published in 1835 and 1840 by a French aristocrat, Alexis de Tocqueville, who came to the United States at the behest of the French government to study American innovations in penology.

Tocqueville found much to admire in the United States. Because he was himself a traditionalist, he was surprised to discover that democratic government worked. However, because Tocqueville believed that stability and continuity in human relationships were essential to a healthy society, he was concerned that Americans seemed always on the move. He was disturbed by the Americans' undiscriminating love of the new and disdain for the old and, most of all, by their relentless pursuit of money. He had no trouble liking Americans as individuals but also observed, as many of the literary tourists did, that Americans were chauvinistic and defensive about their country: "A stranger who injures American vanity, no matter how justly, must make up his mind to be a martyr."

Frances Trollope, whose *Domestic Manners of the Americans,* published in 1832, was much more popular than the "American book" of her writer son, Anthony, came to the United States not to write a book but to go into business in Cincinnati. And she did not like Americans a bit: "I do not like their principles. I do not like their manners. I do not like their opinions." With the eye of an eagle and a wit as sharp as talons, Mrs. Trollope swooped through American parlors, kitchens,

---

by God, or simply as an unhappy circumstance visited on some by the roll of life's dice. Whatever the case, handicaps were personal misfortunes. Care of the disabled was the province of the family. The individual who strove to overcome a disability was edifying, but the problem was personal, not society's concern.

Gallaudet believed that the Christian was his brother's keeper, and the unique social isolation of the deaf troubled him. In 1815, he went to England to study new techniques for teaching lipreading and sign language to the deaf. Good evangelical that he was, Gallaudet was disgusted to discover that they were trade secrets, articles of commerce guarded as closely by the people who profited from them as a textile manufacturer guarded the plans for his looms. With a Frenchman who shared his ideals, he returned to the United States and, in 1817, founded the American Asylum, a free school for the deaf in Hartford, Connecticut. Gallaudet taught his techniques to every interested party and encouraged others to establish similar institutions in other cities.

Samuel Gridley Howe organized the Perkins Institute for the Blind in Boston. He also publicized his techniques and toured the country with a young girl named Laura Bridgman, who was both deaf and blind. Howe had established communication with her, laying to rest the widespread assumption that such seriously disabled people were helpless. The most overwhelming impediments to human fulfillment, Howe said, could be overcome if men and women did their moral duty.

The insane aroused less sympathy than did those with physical disabilities. Traditionally, retarded people and harmless idiots were cared for by their families and otherwise ignored or mocked. Dangerous "lunatics" were locked up at home or by legal authorities. The line between violent insanity and criminality was blurred. Many a lunatic was hanged; others were recognized as not morally responsible for their actions but were, nonetheless, confined in prisons or asylums where treatment consisted of little more than restraint.

In 1841, Dorothea Dix, a teacher in Massachusetts, discovered in the Cambridge House of Correction that the insane were locked in an unheated room, even in winter. At 39, Dix had lived a genteel, sheltered personal life. She was pious and shy. Her discovery of evils in the treatment of the insane galvanized her, and she became one of the most effective reformers of the century.

In 1843, she scolded the Massachusetts state legislature because of the "state of insane persons confined within

cabins, steamboats, theaters, churches, and houses of business, finding something wrong with everything. Unlike Tocqueville, who wrote in generalities, many of which are eerily relevant today, Mrs. Trollope described the unpleasantness she found with pungent anecdotes. She too was disturbed by the runaway individualism, self-centered vanity, and materialism of Americans. On materialism, she cited an English resident of the United States who told her that "in following, in meeting, or in overtaking, in the street, on the road, or in the field, at the theatre, the coffee house, or at home, he had never overheard Americans conversing without the word DOLLAR being pronounced between them."

Mrs. Trollope observed that Americans rushed through hastily prepared meals. They jogged rather than walked. (Frederick Marryat wrote that a New York businessman "always walks as if he had a good dinner before him and a bailiff after him.") Americans fidgeted when detained by some obligation lest they miss something happening in another part of town. When they did sit down, they whittled, so incapable were they to be still. At least two foreign tourists remembered as the symbol of their American experience the spectacle of a team of horses pulling a house on rollers from one site to another. Nothing in the United States was rooted, neither homes nor the mighty oaks that were mowed like hay; neither customs nor social relationships nor religious beliefs that had served humanity well for centuries.

The great Charles Dickens came to the United States to persuade American publishers, who pirated his books, to pay him royalties. He failed, as Mrs. Trollope failed in business, and this no doubt colored his generally negative reflections in *American Notes* (1842). Fanny Kemble, an actress, came to America in 1832 and was a great success. However, she was swept off her feet, and off the stage, by Pierce Butler. She knew he was rich before they married in 1834 but, curiously, not that his family owned 700 slaves, making the Butlers one of the very largest slave owners in the nation. Fanny Kemble's first book about America, published in 1835, contradicted Mrs. Trollope in finding Americans courteous but agreed with her in other particulars—for example, the difficulty of finding solitude among a people who "take pleasure in droves, and travel by swarms," and the headaches of managing servants in a society in which all were equal. It was "a task quite enough to make a Quaker kick his grandmother."

Those were hired white servants, of course. The slaves who served her at her husband's Georgia plantation she found ignorant and dirty but hardly impudent. When she first arrived, she was mystified that the slaves kissed her dress, hugged her, and showered her with endearments. She later learned that she and her children represented a future less miserable. Her husband had been considering selling the plantation and slaves, which would have meant the breakup of the slaves' families. With Fanny in residence, there was hope.

But Fanny did not remain in residence for long. She left the plantation after less than a year, disgusted by the injustice and cruelties of slavery. She became an abolitionist, divorced her husband, and wrote an account of her life in Georgia that, unlike much antislavery propaganda, was firsthand, forthright, and unexaggerated. Published during the Civil War, Kemble's *Journal* was instrumental in dulling what popular sympathy for the South there was in Britain.

this Commonwealth in *cages, closets, cellars, stalls, pens! Chained, naked, beaten with rods, and lashed* into obedience." Dix's revelations did not square with New Englanders' image of themselves as the nation's most enlightened people. ("O New England," Noah Webster wrote, "how superior are thy inhabitants in morals, literature, civility, and industry!") The Massachusetts legislature promptly passed a bill to enlarge the state asylum and improve conditions elsewhere. Dix then carried her message throughout the nation and the world. She persuaded Congress to establish St. Elizabeth's Hospital for the Insane and 15 states to build humane asylums.

Crime and Punishment

Another institution that attracted the notice of reformers was the penitentiary. Large prisons for convicts serving long terms were new to the United States. Until the late eighteenth century, long prison terms were rare. The most serious crimes were punished by hanging: there were as many as 16 capital offenses in some states. Other felonies merited a flogging or physical mutilation. Thomas Jefferson advocated castration of rapists and homosexuals and boring a half-inch hole through the nose of lesbians. In Massachusetts, in 1805, counterfeiters, arsonists, wife beaters, and thieves were whipped, their ears cropped, or their cheeks branded with a hot iron. Petty offenses—being drunk and disorderly, disturbing the peace—were punished with fines or the humiliation of a dunking, the stocks, or the pillory.

During the 1790s, influenced by an Italian criminologist, Cesare Beccaria, most states reduced the number of capital offenses, abolished mutilation, and restricted the use of whipping. They turned to prison for the punishment of serious crime. The purposes were punishment and the protection of society; everywhere, the conditions of confinement were execrable. Connecticut used an abandoned mine shaft as its penitentiary.

Reformers pointed out that the security of society was not improved if prison transformed every convict into a resentful, hardened criminal. In confining burglars with rapists, penitentiaries acted as schools of the worst crimes. The evangelical alternative was the correctional institution, the prison as a place for moral and social rehabilitation. Theories as to how best to accomplish this worthy goal differed. The Pennsylvania system, for example, kept its convicts in solitary confinement. The idea was that inmates would meditate on their crimes and leave prison determined not to offend again.

▲ *A pillory (top) and the whipping post at New Castle, Delaware. Punishments, including executions, were public in the Age of Jackson. They were thought to deter crime, although many observers had long noted that most of the people who attended did so because they enjoyed the spectacle. Whipping (although not in public) as the penalty for wife beating was legal in Delaware into the 1950s.*

The flaws of the Pennsylvania system, obvious almost immediately, were twofold: individual cells were extremely expensive, and total isolation resulted in numerous cases of mental breakdown.

The Auburn system, named after the town in which New York's state prison was located, addressed the problem of isolation by marching prisoners each day to large workrooms and a common dining hall. Conversation was forbidden, both to prevent education in crime and to keep order. The Auburn system was adopted by other states, including Pennsylvania.

Another innovation of the period was the house of refuge, in which juveniles were kept isolated from adult criminals. By 1830, New York City, Philadelphia, and Boston maintained such facilities.

MORAL UPLIFT

Undesirable behavior among the masses also inspired reforms during the early nineteenth century. While Gallaudet, Howe, Dix, and the prison reformers attended to injustices suffered by a few, other evangelicals addressed social problems that afflicted the entire society.

Do-Gooders

The worthiness of a reform bears no relationship to the agreeableness of the enthusiasts who push it—in the Age of Jackson or in any other era when reform is in the air. The evangelicals whose zeal was essential to demands for change (both change that history has judged beneficial as well as reforms now seen as futile, bigoted, or ridiculous) were often tiresome, bothersome people. Orestes Brownson, who personally knew most of the New England utopians and reformers of the era, wrote:

Matters have come to such a pass, that a peaceable man can hardly venture to eat and drink, to go to bed or to get up, to correct his children or to kiss his wife, without obtaining the permission and the direction of some moral society.

Demon Rum

For example, Americans drank heavily. They always had, but consumption peaked in the 1820s, reaching the level of more than 7.5 gallons of alcohol for each American man, woman, and child! In part, this incredible bibulousness owed to the fact that grain was abundant and cheap. More was grown than was needed as food or could find markets abroad. English-style ales, cider, and rum were the everyday beverages of the East. In the West, the daily tonic was whiskey. Wine and brandy—most of it imported—were fixtures of middle- and upper-class life.

Except among the pathetic dregs of society, drunkenness was universally regarded as sinful and socially disruptive, or at least as disagreeable. Before 1800, Dr. Benjamin Rush of Philadelphia systematically described the physically destructive effects of excessive drinking. With the blossoming of the evangelical spirit during the 1830s, antialcohol reformers added two more arrows to the quiver.

First, they published statistics showing that a substantial number of crimes were committed by people who were drunk. Second, they drew a connection between poverty and drinking. A few said that the miseries of poverty led to drunkenness. Most, steeped in the evangelical sense of individual responsibility, believed that drunkenness was the cause of poverty.

A temperance movement spread rapidly. By 1835, there were 5,000 temperance societies in the United States with a membership of more than a million. In 1840, six reformed sots founded a national organization, the Washington Temperance Society. Two years later, a more militant association, the Sons of Temperance, began to promote sobriety as a basic religious duty.

One of the Sons' most effective lecturers was John B. Gough, an ex-drunk who rallied audiences with the lurid language of the camp meeting revivalist: "Crawl from the slimy ooze, ye drowned drunkards, and with suffocation's blue and livid lips speak out against the drink."

Prohibition

Temperance reformers quarreled and parted ways as promiscuously as drunks. One cleavage ran between the advocates of moderation in the use of alcohol and the complete abstainers. The former argued that drunkenness was the evil, not alcohol itself. They lodged no objection to the occasional sip of wine or the restorative shot. The abstainers, observing that alcohol was addictive, concluded that it was inherently dangerous and sinful. Moderation was asking for trouble. It was necessary to swear off drink "T-totally" (hence their name, teetotalers).

The teetotalers divided between moral suasionists, who regarded abstinence from drink as an individual responsibility, and legal suasionists, who considered the prohibition of the manufacture and sale of liquor as the means of destroying the evil. In 1838, Massachusetts experimented with a law designed to cut down alcohol consumption among the poor. The Fifteen Gallon Law prohibited the sale of whiskey or rum in quantities smaller than 15 gallons. However, the temper of the Age of Jackson ran against any device that provided privileges to the rich, who could afford to buy spirits in bulk. The Fifteen Gallon Law was repealed within two years.

In 1845, New York adopted a more democratic law, which authorized local governments to forbid the sale of alcohol within their jurisdictions. Within a few years, five-sixths of the state was "dry." In 1846, the state of Maine, led by Neal Dow, a Portland businessman, adopted the first statewide prohibition law. By 1860, 13 states had followed suit. But the custom of drinking was too much a part of the culture to be abolished by well-meaning ordinances. Prohibition laws were flagrantly violated; by 1868, they were repealed in every state but Maine.

Temperance and prohibition were largely Protestant movements supported by evangelical reformers and directed at native-born old-stock Americans. In the 1840s, however, the crusade against alcohol took on a new urgency because of the huge influx of immigrants who had (as far as reformers were concerned) an inordinate devotion to beer and whiskey.

The Stresses of Immigration

Only 8,400 Europeans came to the United States in 1820, hardly enough to excite notice. More than 23,000 arrived in 1830, however, and 84,000 in 1840. In 1850, 370,000 people stepped from immigrant ships onto wharves in the eastern seaports and New Orleans. Not only were the immigrants of midcentury numerous, but they were, in large part, adherents of religious faiths little known in the United States before 1840; and many spoke languages other than English.

Thirty-six hundred Irish came to the United States in 1820, most of them Protestant; 164,000 arrived in 1850, most of them Roman Catholic. Immigration authorities counted only 23 Scandinavian immigrants in 1820 and 1,600 in 1850, a number that would nearly triple within two years. In 1820, 968 Germans entered the United States; in 1850, 79,000 arrived.

Scandinavian and German immigrants inclined to cluster in large communities, retaining their languages and preserving Old World customs. Among these was the convivial beer garden, where families gathered to drink lager beer, which was first introduced to the United States in this era. To a teetotaler, the Irish were worse. They were notoriously given to gathering in saloons in cities and on construction sites, and they drank whiskey. Worse, they were Roman Catholic, as were about half of the Germans. Between 1830 and 1860, when the general population slightly more than doubled, the Roman Catholic population of the United States increased tenfold—from 300,000 to more than 3 million.

The "Whore of Babylon"

The growth of Catholicism was difficult for many Protestants to swallow. Since the days of the Puritans, they had been taught that the Church of Rome was not just another Christian denomination but the Bible's Whore of Babylon, a fount of evil.

▲ *In Philadelphia in 1844, militia try to subdue rioters, presumably Protestants because their faces are not in the stereotype used to iden-tify Irish immigrants at the time. Philadelphia did not have a professional police force until 1845; it was, in fact, the murderous riot that persuaded the city it needed one. Note the Catholic church in the background to identify the religious character of the rampage.*

This prejudice took on new life in the second quarter of the nineteenth century because the pope, the spiritual leader of the world's Catholics, was also the political head of a re-actionary and repressive principality. In the Papal States in central Italy, dissidents were jailed and, it was believed, tor-tured. The political principles of Catholicism—monarchy, aristocracy, deference to authority—were the antithesis of American traditions, particularly in the democratizing Age of Jackson. Because the Irish immigrants were intensely de-voted to their faith and deferred to the authority of their priests, many Protestants feared that they were the shock troops of political reaction. Many Whigs—and eastern evan-gelicals were Whigs in their politics—found it worrisome enough that the Irish flocked to the Democratic party.

Finally, the vast majority of the Irish immigrants were destitute. Landless in their native country, they were forced to emigrate because of extreme deprivation and, in the late 1840s, because of the failure of the country's potato crop. Once in the United States, they were willing to accept work at almost any rate of pay, prompting Protestant workingmen to regard them as a threat to the high standard of living that skilled artisans enjoyed. When economic unease combined with religious suspicion and the evangelical crusade against the new immigrants' drinking, the result was a social and political movement.

The famous painter and inventor of the telegraph, Samuel F. B. Morse, wanted to cut off the immigration of Catholics. Street wars between Protestant and Irish Catholic working-men regularly erupted in northeastern cities. In 1834, aroused by sermons that Catholic priests kept nuns for sexual pur-poses, murdering the infants born of such unions, a mob burned an Ursuline convent in Charlestown, Massachusetts. In Philadelphia in 1844, 20 people were killed and over a hun-dred injured in a riot pitting Protestants against Catholics.

Anti-Catholicism took political shape in the Order of the Star-Spangled Banner, a secret organization dedicated to shutting off further immigration. The order's members were called "Know-Nothings" because, when asked by outsiders about the organization, they replied, "I know nothing."

After 1850, the order came above ground as the Ameri-can party. Capitalizing on the disintegration of the Whigs and anxiety caused by the sectional hostility, the anti-Catholic, anti-immigrant movement swept to power in sev-eral states, including Massachusetts, where almost every elected official was a member. At its peak, the American party elected 75 congressmen.

Only a minority of Protestants believed in political ac-tion against Roman Catholics. The majority was indifferent to the faith of the newcomers or stood by the guarantees of religious freedom in the First Amendment. Many of these people, however, approved of attempts by various mission-ary societies to convert Catholics and other peoples to Protestant denominations.

The American Tract Society and the American Bible Society distributed literature among the Catholic popula-tion. By 1836, the Tract Society estimated that it had sold or given away more than 3 million publications explaining Protestant beliefs. Another group concentrated on converting the few Jews in the United States.

Blue Hawaii

Most missionary activity, however, was directed overseas. Nothing was more "evangelical" than taking the gospel to the heathen, of course. But the missionary movement received an additional boost because the numerous denominational colleges of the United States turned out many more ministers than there were pulpits to fill. Groups such as the American Board of Foreign Missions raised money to send zealous young men and women to the Indians of the distant West, to Africa, India, and China. No place in the world, however, attracted American missionaries more than the Sandwich Islands, Hawaii.

In 1819, a young Hawaiian Christian told the students of Andover Theological Seminary of the harm done to his homeland by sailors and whalers, Americans prominent among them. The islands' location in the central Pacific made Hawaii an inevitable landfall for whalers from New Bedford and Nantucket, who stopped in Hawaii to refit their vessels, replenish their provisions, and recover from scurvy on island fruits. The diseases they brought devastated the population. Between 1778 and 1804, the Hawaiian population was halved, from about 300,000 to 150,000. The goods the white men brought to trade with a people who had known a simple life irrevocably corrupted the culture of the survivors. Back in New England, evangelicals felt obligated to right these wrongs.

As early as 1820, young ministers and their wives, sisters, and mothers shipped out to Hawaii. Some Hawaiians resisted when the missionaries tried to force proper New England behavior on them. The most celebrated example of the missionaries' incapacity to distinguish religion from custom was their insistence that in the warm, humid climate of the islands, Christian girls and women dress in full-length calico and flannel "Mother Hubbard" dresses.

For the most part, however, the mission to Hawaii was an astonishing success. So disastrous to Hawaiian culture was contact with the West that traditional Hawaiian religious beliefs were discredited before the missionaries arrived; the missionaries brought the Bible into a void. By 1830, their schools enrolled 52,000 Hawaiians (40 percent of the population), teaching the indigenous language and evangelical religion in an alphabet the Americans introduced.

THE WOMEN'S MOVEMENT

Women were the backbone of the missionary movement, in part as a consequence of the migration to the West. Because young men were freer than young women to break old ties and strike off on their own, New England was left with a surplus of women for whom there were not enough spouses. Evangelical activity, being within the realm of morality, was considered an acceptable outlet for their energies. Indeed, preachers of the Great Awakening early recognized that the large majority of their converts were female. Single women were prominent in every reform movement of the era from temperance to abolitionism.

But there was more to the flowering of social activism among American women than demographics. In consecrating their lives to the deaf, the poor, the missions, and other good works, ostensibly privileged and comfortable middle-class women were able to protest, however obliquely, the private, domestic, and dependent status that American society assigned them. This discontent naturally found an outlet in the emergence of feminism as a social movement.

Feminism

In the summer of 1848, a group of women, mostly Quakers, called for a convention to be held at Seneca Falls, New York, to consider the "Declaration of Sentiments and Resolutions" they had drafted. The declaration was a deadly serious parody of the Declaration of Independence:

> When in the course of human events it becomes necessary for one portion of the family of man to assume among the people of the earth a position different from that which they have hitherto occupied, but one to which the laws of nature and nature's God entitle them, a decent respect to the opinions of mankind requires that they should declare the causes that impel them to such a course.

The injustices suffered by women included the denial of the right to vote even when it was extended to "the most ignorant and degraded men"; the forfeiture by a married woman of control over her own property; the nearly absolute power of the husband over a wife's behavior, which "made her, morally, an irresponsible being"—a state utterly reprehensible to an evangelical; and the exclusion of women from the professions and other gainful employment.

Only 68 women and 32 men signed the document, but the Seneca Falls declaration received national attention—sympathetic in reform newspapers, scornful and mocking in more conventional publications. Among the organizers of the conference were Lucretia Coffin Mott and Elizabeth Cady Stanton, who continued to play an important part in the feminist movement for a generation. Among the spectators was Amelia Jenks Bloomer, a temperance reformer who was soon to become famous as the advocate of a new style of dress that bore her name.

The high expectations of 1848—that equal rights for women was a demand whose time had come—were soon dashed to pieces. Americans, including most women, were not ready to think seriously about the civil equality of women. Even the vote, only one of the Seneca Falls demands, lay more than half a century in the future.

Evangelical reformers, although generally sympathetic to women's rights, urged the feminists to set their problems aside until a reform they considered far more important was achieved. This was the abolition of slavery, a cause that was entering its final phase when the Seneca Falls convention was called. "I do not see how anyone can pretend that there is the same urgency," the African American abolitionist (and feminist) Frederick Douglass said, "in giving the ballot to the woman as freedom to the Negro." Stanton and Mott, who were abolitionists before they became feminists, agreed, one of the rare moments in history when a reformer put anything above her or his own prized cause. The feminists never silenced their call for women's rights, but they stepped to the side in the belief that when the slaves were freed, women would have their day.

for FURTHER READING

For background and context, see Perry Miller, *The Life of the Mind in America from the Revolution to the Civil War,* 1966; I. H. Bartlett, *The American Mind in the Mid-Nineteenth Century,* 1967; Russell B. Nye, *Society and Culture in America, 1830–1860,* 1974; and Lewis Perry, *Intellectual Life in America,* 1984. Also valuable are S. E. Ahlstrom, *A Religious History of the American People,* 1972; and Martin E. Marty, *Righteous Empire: The Protestant Experience in America,* 1970, and *Pilgrims in Their Own Land: 500 Years of Religion in America,* 1984.

Basic general studies of nineteenth-century reform include C. S. Griffin, *Thy Brother's Keepers: Moral Stewardship in the United States, 1800–1865,* 1960, and *The Ferment of Reform,* 1967; Arthur M. Schlesinger Jr., *The American as Reformer,* 1960; and R. G. Walters, *American Reformers: 1815–1860,* 1978.

An old but delightful book with a jaundiced view of the American enthusiasms of the era is Gilbert Seldes, *The Stammering Century,* 1928. Also on revivalism, see Bernard R. Weisberger, *They Gathered at the River,* 1958; and C. A. Johnson, *The Frontier Camp Meeting,* 1955. Other titles dealing with religious and utopian sects in the nineteenth century include Leonard J. Arrington, *Great Basin Kingdom,* 1958; A. E. Bestor, *Backwoods Utopias,* 1950; Fawn M. Brodie, *No Man Knows My History: The Life of Joseph Smith,* 1945; Martin Cardin, *Oneida,* 1969; Whitney R. Cross and

Henri Destroche, *The American Shakers: From Neo-Christianity to Neo-Socialism,* 1971; and Robert O. Thomas, *The Man Who Would Be Perfect,* 1977.

On specific reforms, see Ray A. Billington, *The Protestant Crusade, 1800–1860,* 1938; F. L. Byme, *Prophet of Prohibition: Neal Dow and His Crusade,* 1961; M. E. Lender and J. K. Martin, *Drinking in America: A History,* 1982; H. E. Marshall, *Dorothea Dix: Forgotten Samaritan,* 1937; Blake McKelvey, *American Prisons: A Study in American Social History Prior to 1915,* 1936; W. G. Rorabaugh, *The Alcoholic Republic: An American Tradition,* 1979; David J. Rothman, *The Discovery of the Asylum,* 1970; and I. R. Tyrrel, *Sobering Up: From Temperance to Prohibition,* 1979.

On feminism, see Lois Banner, *Elizabeth Cady Stanton,* 1980; Carl M. Degler, *At Odds: Women and the Family in America from the Revolution to the Present,* 1980; Eleanor Flexner, *Century of Struggle: The Women's Rights Movement in the United States,* 1975; Aileen S. Kraditor, *Up from the Pedestal: Selected Writings in the History of American Feminism,* 1968; Gerda Lerner, *The Woman in American History,* 1970; Alma Lutz, *Susan B. Anthony,* 1979; William L. O'Neill, *Everyone Was Brave: The Rise and Fall of Feminism in America,* 1970; and Mary P. Ryan, *Womanhood in America,* 1975.

 AMERICAN JOURNEY ONLINE AND INFOTRAC COLLEGE EDITION

Visit the source collections at http://ajaccess.wadsworth.com and http://infotrac.thomsonlearning.com, and use the Search function with the following key terms to explore documents, images, audio and video clips, articles, and commentary related to the material in this chapter:

Elizabeth Cady Stanton	Mormons	Seneca Falls Convention	Temperance movement
Henry David Thoreau	Nathaniel Hawthorne	Suffrage	*The Book of Mormon*
Herman Melville	Ralph Waldo Emerson	Temperance	Transcendentalism

Additional resources, exercises, and Internet links related to this chapter are available on *The American Past* Web site: http://history.wadsworth.com/americanpast7e.

HISTORY ONLINE

Religion in America
http://lcweb/loc.gov/exhibits/religion/re101.htm
Documents and photographs about religion in the early nineteenth century.

Shakers and Shakerism
www.nypl.org/research/chss/grd/resguides/shaker.html
A research guide to the most successful of the nineteenth-century communitarians, prepared by the New York Public Library.

18

A DIFFERENT COUNTRY

The South

There must doubtless be an unhappy influence on the manners of our people produced by the existence of slavery among us. The whole commerce between master and slave is a perpetual exercise of the most boisterous passions, the most unremitting despotism on the one part, and degrading submissions on the other. Our children see this and learn to imitate it. . . . The parent storms, the child looks on, catches the lineaments of wrath, puts on the same airs in the circle of smaller slaves, gives loose to the worst of passions and thus nursed, educated, and daily exercised in tyranny, cannot but be stamped by it with odious peculiarities.

Thomas Jefferson

DOODLING AT HIS desk one day, Thomas Jefferson drew up a list of character traits in which, he suggested, northerners and southerners differed. Northerners were cool and sober, he wrote; southerners were fiery and "voluptuary." Northerners were hardworking, self-interested, and devious; southerners were lazy, generous, and candid. Northerners were "jealous of their own liberties, and just to those of others"; southerners were "zealous for their own liberties, but trampling on those of others."

He had a point. Jefferson usually did. And it could not have been easy for a man who called Virginia "my country" to tote up unattractive characteristics in his own people. Still, to fixate on differences between northerners and southerners would be to obscure the reality that they shared a common language and the same religious, cultural, and political heritage. By 1826, the year Jefferson died, they also shared 50 years of history, including the aspiration to relegate the institution of slavery to the dustbin of history.

SOUTHERN ANTISLAVERY

The northern states succeeded in doing so, although, because emancipation was gradual in most states, a few thousand northern blacks remained in bondage in 1826, most of them in New York and New Jersey. (There were legal slaves in New Jersey as late as 1860, all quite elderly.)

The southern states did not, although the same forces that ended slavery in the North made false starts there as well. Just about all southern Quakers freed their slaves by 1780. Wherever the Methodists spread their message, many of their converts freed the slaves they owned, most notably in Maryland and Delaware, where the Methodists converted many whites. (Southern African Americans, free and slave, expressed a preference for the Methodist Church.) Southern delegates to the Constitutional Convention supported the provision that forbade the importation from abroad of slaves after 1807. In fact, most southern states, including South Carolina, outlawed the African slave trade before it was terminated nationally.

Manumission and Race

Until the 1830s, very few of the most powerful southerners, those who owed their wealth, leisure, and status to the labor of their human property, aggressively defended slavery. Like northerners, they worried openly about the undesirable social, economic, and moral consequences of the institution. It was almost common for wealthy planters to manumit—to free—at least some of their slaves in their wills. Robert Carter, who owned more slaves than anyone else in Virginia, freed all of them at his death. George Washington was honored for freeing the 300 slaves he owned. George Wythe, who trained Jefferson, Marshall, and Clay in the law, freed most of his slaves in his will. Jefferson freed a few and has puzzled many of his admirers because he did not free more; Jefferson agonized over the injustice of slavery to the day of his death. In 1833, Virginian John Randolph freed the 400 black people he owned.

The possibility of total abolition arose periodically in the states of the upper South, but, in the end, not even Delaware, where there were only 3,300 slaves in 1830 (3 percent of the population) did so. The decisive factor was the assumption, almost universal among whites, that African Americans were innately inferior in intelligence, initiative, and even moral fiber, that they could not compete with white people in an increasingly competitive America and would, therefore, if free, be the cause of catastrophic social problems.

It was one thing, southerners said, for the northern states to abolish slavery. The black population was numerically insignificant almost everywhere in the North. In 1830, there were 125,000 African Americans in the Northeast in a total population of 5.54 million—African Americans were just 2 percent of the population. There were only 42,000 blacks among the 1.6 million people of the Old Northwest, about the same percentage. So tiny a minority could be ignored,

disdained, and pushed aside to root or die (as, indeed, northern blacks were) without worry of social disturbance.

But blacks were a substantial portion of the population of the South—2.16 million in 1830 alongside 3.54 million whites—and a majority in many areas. African Americans were an overwhelming majority in coastal South Carolina and Georgia and along the Mississippi River in the states of Mississippi and Louisiana. Moreover, they were the backbone of the workforce that brought in every important southern crop: cotton, rice, tobacco, and sugar. If exploiting them as slaves was unjust, immoral, and ultimately dependent on force, thus corrupting slave owners, the alternative of even gradual emancipation was, to most white southerners, hideous to contemplate. As for Delaware, Maryland, Missouri, and large parts of Kentucky, where slaves were a small fraction of the population, the whites who owned slaves dominated politics and, if they profited little from working them, could profit richly by selling them in the cotton states.

Frank confession of such mercenary self-interest is not, of course, one of humanity's strong points, and few slave owners ever confessed it. They did, however, say (many of them quite sincerely) that they were shouldering a burden strapped to them by history and protecting their slaves from the viciousness of poor southern whites, of whom the elite's opinion was not exalted.

Discoverer of Liberia
Paul Cuffee, an African American, was a master mariner who lived on the island of Martha's Vineyard in Massachusetts and was prosperous from coastal and overseas trade. During the 1810s, Cuffee visited Freetown, Sierra Leone, shortly after the British had confirmed their colonial authority there. He explored the coast (mostly mangrove swamp) south of the colony, hoping to locate a site where free American blacks disgusted with their plight in the United States might go. It is not clear if Cuffee pinpointed the future location of Monrovia in Liberia.

Jefferson's Bequest
Jefferson freed a few slaves in his will. Sally Hemmings, whom Jefferson's enemies claimed was his mistress, was not among them. She was bequeathed to Jefferson's daughter, Patsy. Does this prove the attacks on Jefferson were lies? Some historians think not. They point out that Virginia required manumitted slaves to leave the state. To have freed Sally Hemmings, who was well along in years in 1826, would have forced her to leave her friends and children.

Where Is Home?
In 1822, James Forten commented sarcastically on the proposal of the American Colonization Society to pay the way of people like him "back to Africa":

My great-grandfather was brought to this country a slave from Africa. My grandfather obtained his own freedom. My father never wore the yoke. He rendered valuable service to his country in the war of our Revolution; and I, though then a boy, was a drummer in that war. I have since lived and labored in a useful employment, have acquired property, and have paid taxes. . . . Yet some ingenious gentlemen have recently discovered that I am still an African; that a continent, three thousand miles away—and more—from the place where I was born is my native country.

▲ *Monrovia, the capital of Liberia, about the time the nation declared its independence of the American Colonization Society. The town was founded from scratch on empty land in 1822.*

The Colonization Movement

The American Colonization Society, founded in 1817, tried to resolve the dilemma of, on the one hand, an undesirable social institution and, on the other, social chaos. With the active support of distinguished southerners such as Madison, Monroe, John Marshall, and Henry Clay, the society proposed to raise money with which free blacks would be transported to West Africa. By providing a mechanism to eliminate from the South the unwanted population of free blacks, the colonizers hoped to encourage individual slave owners to free their slaves and even prompt state legislatures to adopt abolition laws.

In 1821, the society financed the emigration of a few former slaves to Sierra Leone, a British colony on what was then known as the Guinea Coast, which had been established as a refuge for slaves freed in the British West Indies. The next year, the society, partly with government funds, purchased a stretch of coastline south of Sierra Leone and established Liberia; in 1824, its capital was named Monrovia after President Monroe, who supported the project. About 11,000 African Americans went to Liberia, which functioned rather like an American territory (except that the American Colonization Society appointed the governor) until 1847, when Liberia declared its independence.

Colonization was obviously unrealistic. A few thousand from among a slave population of 1.5 million in 1820 was hardly reducing the black presence in the South, which, in fact, grew to 2 million by 1830—more than could live on a strip of African seacoast. Moreover, the American Colonization Society's antislavery side was something of a fraud, however unconsciously. Few slaves were manumitted so they could emigrate to Liberia. Those who went were blacks who were already free and persuaded, by one argument or another, to go. Indeed, 10,000 or 11,000 was only about 7 per-

cent of the South's free African Americans; there were 37,000 free blacks in Virginia alone in 1820. It is remarkable that so many people were interested in the colonization movement. Free African Americans' assessments of the degraded status in which they were kept may have ranged from misery, through bewilderment, to fury—but they were not Africans. Most were generations removed from their African roots and felt little more attraction to an unknown land than their African ancestors had felt toward America.

As for southern whites, who had been the mainstay of the colonization movement, the longer the price of cotton boomed on the world market, the less was heard about the antislavery side of colonization. When the Mississippi Colonization Society was founded in 1829, its pronounced purpose was to rid the state of all free blacks. Its officers disassociated themselves from the old goal of encouraging planters to free their slaves. Except for one last debate, by 1830, the southern antislavery movement was dead.

The Last Debate

In December 1831, Governor John Floyd of Virginia asked the legislature to consider a plan to phase out slavery gradually. Unlike in the northern states that had done so, slave owners were to be compensated for their losses. For the good of the state, taxpayers would accommodate those who lost property, just as if real estate were taken for the purposes of building a road. For three weeks in January 1832, the legislature discussed the proposal, for the most part moderately and intelligently.

Even the staunchest proslavery men were defensive. Typically, they introduced their speeches by regretting the fact that blacks were ever brought to Virginia and by saying that the state would be a better place if it were developed by free white labor. However, they also concluded that the past

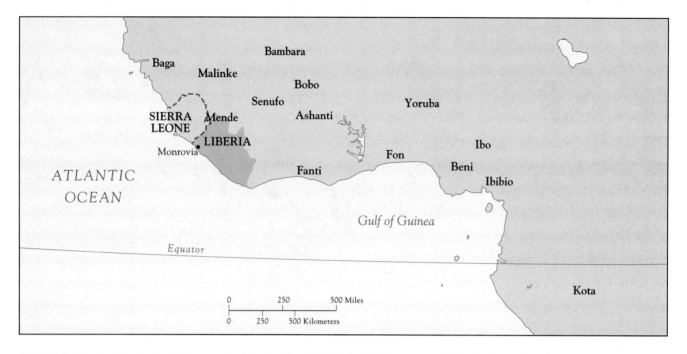

MAP 18:1 Liberia Liberia, legally the property of the American Colonization Society, was established in 1817. Monrovia was founded in 1822. Liberia declared its independence in 1847. West Africa was a tribal area. The Ashanti, centered east of Liberia, had been rich and powerful as one of the chief suppliers of slaves to European and American buyers, but the tribe had declined with the end of the African slave trade.

was history: Blacks constituted almost half of Virginia's population; so large a population of free blacks was out of the question; and the colonization movement was obviously a failure. However tragic it was for the Old Dominion, Virginia must continue to be a slave state.

The assumption that a biracial society would not work carried the day—but just barely. The legislature rejected Floyd's scheme by 73 to 58. A switch of only eight votes would have altered the course of American history, because the other states of the Upper South—Delaware, Maryland, and Kentucky—could not have ignored abolition in Virginia. Had those states also phased slavery out, the institution would not have split the Union across the middle. It would have been the peculiar institution of a few states in the Deep South, no more able to threaten the Union than the six states of New England. As it was, once Virginia's debate was concluded, no significant body of southern whites ever again considered the possibility of ridding themselves of their "burden."

THREATS TO THE SOUTHERN ORDER

Both Floyd's proposal and the Virginia legislature's rejection of it were profoundly influenced by two events that electrified the South in 1831: the emergence in the North of a new kind of antislavery agitator; and a bloody rebellion of slaves in southern Virginia, the third massive slave insurrection in 30 years and the first in which white people were murdered.

Early Abolitionists

Since the War for Independence, discussions and debates concerning slavery, in the North and South, had revolved around questions of political justice, economic wisdom, and social consequences. However, some voices, even before the evangelicals of the 1780s, spoke of the institution in moral and religious terms. Mostly, they were Quaker voices. French-born Anthony Benezet of Philadelphia, where he taught blacks, began to condemn slavery as immoral around 1750. About the same time, John Woolman of New Jersey, also a Quaker, began to wander the Middle Colonies and Upper South, admonishing Quakers who owned slaves and persuading many to free them. In *A Plea for the Poor,* published in 1763, he outlined the objection to slavery on Christian grounds.

Because Quakers were a small minority and concentrated in New Jersey, Delaware, and Pennsylvania, and because of the self-imposed gentleness of their methods of persuasion, neither Benezet nor Woolman had much impact. During the 1820s, Benjamin Lundy continued the tradition. Slavery was unchristian, he told southerners; but, recognizing economic realities and racial fears, he espoused gradual abolition and advocated colonization of African Americans in Liberia, the black republic of Haiti, Canada, and Texas (then a part of Mexico).

Educated blacks, most notably the mathematician, astronomer, and publisher of a popular almanac, Benjamin Banneker, published moral arguments against slavery. Like the Quakers, Banneker did not rage at slave owners. Indeed, he was as close to being a friend of Thomas Jefferson as Jefferson could imagine an African American as being. Jefferson persuaded Washington to name Banneker the surveyor of the District of Columbia.

The fraternal moral argument against slavery was summed up by the Boston Unitarian preacher William Ellery Channing, who told southerners, "We consider slavery your calamity and not your curse."

David Walker and William Lloyd Garrison

In 1829, language and mood took on new forms. In that year, a black dealer in cloth living in Boston, David Walker, published a pamphlet called *The Appeal*. After reviewing the traditional arguments about the immorality and injustice of slavery, Walker stated that unless whites abolished the institution, blacks had a moral duty to rise up in violent rebellion.

William Lloyd Garrison, a spare, intense young white man of 24, who had been an employee of Benjamin Lundy in Baltimore, did not believe in violent rebellion. Among the many evangelical reform movements he espoused was pacifism—opposition to all wars. However, when Garrison founded an antislavery newspaper in Boston in January 1831, *The Liberator,* his language was incendiary and aimed not only at the institution of slavery (the sin) but at the sinners—slave owners.

"I am aware," Garrison wrote in the first issue, "that many object to the severity of my language; but is there not cause for severity? I will be as harsh as truth, and as uncompromising as justice. On this subject I do not wish to think, or speak, or write, with moderation. No! No! Tell a man whose house is on fire to give a moderate alarm; tell him to moderately rescue his wife from the hands of the ravisher; tell the mother to gradually extricate her babe from the fire into which it has fallen;—but urge me not to use moderation in a cause like the present."

It was a declaration of war. To Garrison, the most extreme of evangelicals, the day of colloquy and persuasion was done. Slavery was evil, pure and simple; slave owners and those who accommodated them were doers of evil. Garrison described the slave owner's life as "one of unbridled lust, of filthy amalgamation, of swaggering braggadocio, of haughty domination, of cowardly ruffianism, of boundless dissipation, of matchless insolence, of infinite self-conceit, of unequaled oppression, of more than savage cruelty."

This sort of thing does not often go down well with those who are the subjects of it. In fact, Garrison was never popular in the North. Even in Boston, a center of evangelical reform and antislavery sentiment, Garrison was hooted and pelted with stones when he spoke in public. On one occasion, a mob threw a noose around his neck and dragged him through the streets. They might well have lynched him had not the aggressiveness of a group of abolitionist women momentarily stunned the mob; the women rescued him. (Garrison was also a supporter of women's rights.)

In the South, Garrison was a monster. Not merely because he was against slavery, at least not at first. Garrison and other extremist abolitionists were hated because they were believed to be inciting slave rebellion. In 1831, the fear of slave rebellion in the South was no abstraction.

The Fear of Rebellion

In 1798, slaves and free blacks in the French colony of Saint-Domingue (now Haiti) rose up in an immense rebellion, murdered hundreds of whites, defeated a crack French army, and forced most of the French who remained to flee the country. Many of them went to Louisiana, then under Spanish control; others, to South Carolina. The horrors they described were news nationally, but, emotionally, hit close to home among southern whites, especially in areas where slaves were numerous. South Carolina and Georgia forbade exiles from Haiti to bring slaves with them for fear they

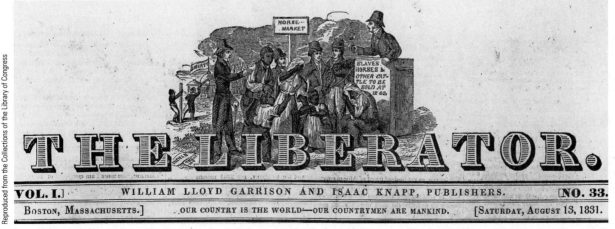

▲ *William Lloyd Garrison's* The Liberator, *a weekly, was the most extreme and intemperate of abolitionist newspapers but also one of the most popular and effective because of the controversy that swirled around it. Not every writer was as high-strung as Garrison. His newspaper contained many articles on slavery that were based on careful research and included well-reasoned commentary.*

Southern Anxieties

Both antislavery and proslavery southerners feared slave rebellion. The chief difference between them was in the tone in which they spoke of blacks.

Thomas Ritchie, an antislavery Virginian, said, "To attempt to excite discontent and revolt, or publish writings having this tendency, obstinately and perversely, among us, is outrageous—it ought not to be passed over with indifference. Our own safety—the good and happiness of our slaves, requires it."

By contrast, Edward D. Holland, a proslavery South Carolinian, wrote, "Let it never be forgotten that our NEGROES are truly the *Jacobins* of the country; that they are the *anarchists* and the *domestic enemy*, the *common enemy of civilized society,* and the barbarians who would, IF THEY COULD, become the DESTROYERS of our race."

would infect slaves in those states with the Haitian ideals of liberty and revolution.

In 1800, a near calamity in Richmond heightened white fears of slave rebellion. Gabriel (sometimes called Gabriel Prosser), a blacksmith slave, undoubtedly knew something about the events in Haiti. He was literate, and his daily associates were skilled tradesmen, whites and free blacks as well as slaves. Politics was a popular subject of discussion.

Just when Gabriel began to plan his own revolution is not clear, but the uprising was set for August 30, 1800. With a core of about 150, Gabriel expected hundreds more, who had heard the message, to join his army. Instructions were to kill only those who resisted, and to spare Quakers and Methodists, who were antislavery. The plan was to capture the governor (James Monroe) and key sites in the city, then to negotiate a settlement. Gabriel was neither racist nor apocalyptic. He believed poor whites would join his struggle against Virginia's aristocracy, and he was not deluded in thinking he had a chance to destroy Virginia society.

What might have happened? No one knows. Torrential rains on August 30 prevented the rebels from gathering. Individuals clearly up to no good were arrested and questioned, and Gabriel's plan was revealed. Twenty-seven of the leaders were hanged; others were sold outside of the state.

In 1822, a free black carpenter and Methodist preacher in Charleston, South Carolina, Denmark Vesey, hatched a plot to sack the city, seize ships in the harbor, and escape to Haiti, then a black republic. Vesey talked the plot up among slaves in town, including house servants, who, their owners were later shocked to learn, were not so devoted to their masters and mistresses that they did not at least listen and keep their knowledge of the plot to themselves. Vesey's chief

The Granger Collection, New York

▲ *Nat Turner's conspiracy was not discovered before the rebellion began, as Gabriel's and Vesey's were, because he deliberately informed very few trusted friends about his plans. Turner may well have been familiar with the story of Vesey's foiled uprising. It had been just 10 years, and news of such things hummed along slave grapevines.*

lieutenant, Gullah Jack, an Angolan who attended the African Methodist Church but also practiced Angolan magic, recruited soldiers on nearby plantations. Many were also native Africans; 40,000 enslaved Africans had been rushed into South Carolina in 1807, the last year it was legal to do so.

Again it is difficult to know how many people were involved; some said hundreds, some thousands. The uprising was scheduled for June 16. An informer exposed the conspiracy on June 14, and Vesey called it off. Vesey, Gullah Jack, and 33 others were hanged.

Nat Turner

Gabriel and Vesey were rational men. Neither imagined he could extirpate his enemies. Had Gabriel successfully made captives of Governor Monroe and other prominent Virginians, it is not far-fetched to imagine a negotiated resolution of the crisis, albeit not one that freed all of Virginia's slaves. Vesey was realistic to think that, in a surprise assault, his rebels could have rampaged through Charleston, seized ships, and at least begun to sail toward Haiti.

Nat Turner, whose rebellion in August 1831 was not nipped before it began, was another type altogether. He was apocalyptic; indeed, Turner was on questionable terms with reality. Turner was an ordinary field hand in Southampton County, Virginia, who had been taught to read by his first owner. (His master in 1831 was illiterate.) He was a pious if unorthodox Baptist who pored endlessly over the Bible. He had several visions of Christ, and he heard voices, which he took as God's. When there was a solar eclipse in February 1831, Turner believed it was God's go-ahead to the slaves to rise up and kill their masters. Unlike Gabriel and Vesey, Turner had no idea what he was going to do when his rebels had started killing whites. The trouble with getting military orders from God is that if there is a snag in communications, the soldiers have big problems.

Turner was, however, shrewd enough to divulge his plans to a very few trusted friends. (Did he know of the betrayal of Vesey's Rebellion?) On the night of August 21, 1831, armed with little more than farm tools, Turner and his group swept quickly across the county, killing 60 whites and recruiting supporters from among their slaves. The murders were over in a couple of days, although it was six weeks before the last of 70 rebels were rounded up. Turner and 39 others were hanged. Others, who were acquitted of shedding blood, were sold out of the state. Word of mouth had it that, in the panic of the first days, other blacks were murdered.

Turner's Rebellion terrified slave owners, especially those who lived in the parts of Louisiana, Mississippi, and South Carolina where blacks outnumbered whites. Mary Boykin Chesnut, the wife of a planter, was not offhandedly mentioning a demographic curiosity when she described her home, Mulberry, as "half a dozen whites and sixty or seventy Negroes, miles away from the rest of the world."

White belief in black inferiority meant that some southerners were unwilling to admit that blacks, left to their own devices, were capable of mounting a rebellion like Turner's. It was no coincidence, they said, that the massacre in Southampton County followed the fiery first issue of *The Liberator* by eight months. They took note of the fact that Turner knew how to read, and they blamed white abolitionists like Garrison for the tragedy.

ENTRENCHMENT OF THE SOUTH

Once Virginians decided that the Old Dominion would remain a slave state, the South stood almost alone in the Western world. The northern states had abolished the institution of slavery. The Spanish-speaking republics of the Americas had done so too. Great Britain emancipated slaves in its colonies. In the entire Christian world, slavery survived only in the Spanish colonies of Cuba and Puerto Rico, the tiny French islands of Martinique and Guadeloupe, in a few small Portuguese enclaves, and in Brazil.

After 1832, southerners began to recognize that their slavery was what they called a "peculiar institution," almost unique to them. They moved on three fronts to protect it. They attempted to insulate the South from outside ideas that threatened slavery, and they suppressed criticism of the institution at home. Slave owners ceased to doubt themselves for clinging to slavery and to regret it to outsiders as a historical tragedy or a necessary evil; they devised the argument that slavery was a positive good that benefited slave owner, slave, and southern society as a whole. Finally, they reformed the states' slave codes (the laws that governed the "peculiar institution"), both improving the material conditions under which slaves lived and instituting stricter controls over the black population.

Suppression

Most southern states passed laws forbidding the distribution of abolitionist literature. Officials screened the federal mails and seized copies of *The Liberator,* other antislavery newspapers, and books. Georgia's legislature actually offered a reward of $5,000 to any person who would bring William Lloyd Garrison into the state to stand trial for inciting rebellion.

Even if the resolutions were meant to be symbolic, a state legislature's willingness to sanction kidnapping illustrates the depth of bitterness in the South toward abolitionists. Only in border states like Maryland and Kentucky could native abolitionists like John Gregg Fee and Cassius Marcellus Clay speak their piece without fear of anything worse than heckling and harassment. Elsewhere in the South, the expression of antislavery opinions was no longer acceptable.

Even in Washington, D.C.—where slavery was legal—the expression of abolitionist ideas became unacceptable. Beginning in 1836, southern congressmen annually nagged the House of Representatives to adopt a rule providing that every petition to the House dealing with slavery be tabled (that is, set aside without discussion). Former president John Quincy Adams, now a member of Congress, argued that this gag rule violated the right to free speech. Quincy Adams considered

Pork

Southerners ate beef; so did northerners. But it was by no means the most abundant meat of the early nineteenth century, as it is today, when we consume 2 pounds of it for every pound of our second favorite, pork, including bacon and ham.

Pork was the favorite, by far. Indeed, according to *Godey's Lady's Book*—the combination *Ladies Home Journal, Ms.,* and *Vogue* of the era:

The United States of America might properly be called the great Hog-eating Confederacy, or the Republic of Porkdom. [In the] South and West . . . it is fat bacon and pork, fat bacon and pork only, and that continually morning, noon, and night, for all classes, sexes, ages, and conditions; and except the boiled bacon and collards at dinner, the meat is generally fried, and thus supersaturated with grease in the form of hog's lard.

Slaves on well-managed plantations were provided half a pound of salt pork a day. All but very poor whites surely consumed more.

Beef was less common—first of all, because it was much more expensive than it is today. Cattle had to be transported on the hoof, which meant that cities could be supplied only from the near hinterland. Farmers of such land could do better cultivating their land than leaving it in pasture. Only with the settlement of the Great Plains after the Civil War did the price of beef decline. Even then, in 1900, Americans ate as much pork as beef.

Unlike cattle, hogs flourished on wasteland—even scavenging on city streets—multiplying their weight 150 times in eight months on nuts and roots, fallen orchard fruit, whatever remained in harvested gardens and grain fields, and garbage. They required next to no attention. Indeed, American razorback hogs, those "bony, snake-headed, hairy wild beasts," needed no protection. (A farmer's fields and the farmer himself needed protection from them!)

Hogs were ideally suited to a nation where land was abundant and labor scarce, and they thrived. As early as 1705, Robert Beverley wrote in his *History of Virginia* that "hogs swarm like Vermine upon the Earth, and are often accounted such . . . [that] When an Inventory of any considerable Man's Estate is taken, the Hogs are left out." In the southern states in 1850, there were two hogs for each human being.

Hogs had another recommendation over steers. They could be slaughtered where they were raised, butchered on the spot, and cheaply preserved in salty brine in barrels, keeping for a year or more. Salt deposits were important to pioneers because of the necessity of preserving pork. Cities on the Ohio and Mississippi Rivers like Cincinnati and St. Louis owed much of their growth to their role as meat packers. The poor, certainly including slaves, owed their survival to salt pork. "I hold a family to be in a desperate way," a character in a James Fenimore Cooper novel put it, "when the mother can see the bottom of the pork barrel."

"Scraping the bottom of the barrel" is not the only catchphrase that survives from the days of the Republic of Porkdom. We still use the term "pork barrel bill" to describe those congressional acts, usually rushed through at the end of a session, that spend federal money in just about every district in which incumbents from the majority party are up for election—a highway improvement here, an agricultural station there, a defense installation somewhere else. The phrase conveys an image once familiar to every American—the none-too-attractive appearance of chunks of pork bobbing about in a barrel of scummy brine.

zealots like Walker and Garrison and most other abolitionists irresponsible and destructive. But he insisted on their constitutional right to have their opinions heard. For this, and because he criticized white southerners for quashing the right to petition Congress and be heard, the lifelong nationalist came to be lumped with the abolitionists as an enemy.

A Positive Good

Shortly after Virginia's debate on the future of slavery, a professor of economics at the College of William and Mary, Thomas Roderick Dew, published a systematic defense of slavery. He said that as a means of organizing and controlling labor, it was superior to the system of free wage workers that prevailed in the North and Europe. By 1837, southern preachers and politicians were parroting and expanding on Dew's theories. In the Senate, John C. Calhoun declared that compared with other systems by which racial and class relationships were governed, "The relation now existing in the slave holding states is, instead of an evil, a good—a positive good."

The proslavery argument incorporated religious, historical, cultural, and social proofs of the justice and beneficence of the institution. The Bible, the positive-good propagandists argued, clearly sanctioned slavery. Not only did the ancient Hebrews own slaves with God's blessing, but Christ had told a servant (a slave) who wanted to follow him that he should return to his master. It was his obligation to do so.

Dew and others pointed out that the great, universally admired civilizations of antiquity, Greece and Rome, were slaveholding societies. Hardly barbaric, slavery had served as the foundation of high cultures since the beginning of recorded time. Slavery made possible the existence of a gracious and cultured upper class that, with its leisure, preserved the highest refinements of human achievement.

Southern planters took pride in the fact that, although elementary and secondary education in the South was inferior to that provided by the public school systems of the North, more upper-class southerners were college educated than members of the northern elite were. Even as late as 1860, there were more than 6,000 college students in Georgia, Alabama, and Mississippi but fewer than 4,000 in the New England states, which were more populous.

As an aristocracy, southerners said, the planters were closer to the tradition of the gentlemanly Founding Fathers than were the vulgar, money-grubbing capitalists of the North. Because gentlemen dominated politics in the South, the section was far better governed than was the North, where demagogues won elections by playing on the whims and passions of the dregs of society. Some planters liked to think of themselves as descended from the cavaliers of seventeenth-century England. The South's favorite author was Sir Walter Scott, who spun tales of knighthood and chivalry.

George Fitzhugh, Sociologist

But did all these proofs justify denying personal freedom to human beings? Yes, answered George Fitzhugh, a Virginia lawyer, in two influential books: *A Sociology for the South* (1854) and *Cannibals All!* (1857). Fitzhugh amassed statistics and other evidence with which he argued that the southern slave lived a better life than did the northern wage worker or the European peasant.

Like Dew and Calhoun, Fitzhugh argued that, in every society, someone had to perform the drudgery. In the South, menial work was done by slaves who were cared for from cradle to grave. Not only did the slave owner feed, clothe, and house his workers, but he also supported slave children, the injured and the disabled, and the elderly—all of whom were nonproductive. Fitzhugh delighted to point out that by comparison, the northern wage worker was paid only as long as there was work to be done and the worker was fit to do it. The wage worker who was injured was cut loose to fend for

Reproduced from the Collections of the Library of Congress

▲ *Currier & Ives, publishers of prints for home decoration, was a northern company. In depicting a cotton plantation in the Deep South, the publishers presented an idyll of slaves picking cotton (and not working too hard) and a well-dressed white man (the planter) completely at ease as he explains the work to a lady. The dreamland scene would have appealed to "positive-good" southerners, and the print undoubtedly sold well in the North too.*

▲ The "quarters" of a plantation near the coast in South Carolina. The slaves' cabins are ruder than cabins on some other plantations, but much better than most, with sound walls, good roofs, and brick chimneys. In the 1840s, magazines catering to slave owners published plans for slave cabins.

himself. His children, the elderly, and the incompetent were no responsibility of capitalist employers.

Consequently, Fitzhugh said, the North was plagued by social problems unknown in the South. The North teemed with nattering reformers. The lower classes were irreligious and, in their misery, drunken and tumultuous. The free working class was tempted by socialistic, communistic, and other doctrines that threatened the social order. By comparison, Fitzhugh claimed, southern slaves were contented, indeed happy. "A merrier being does not exist on the face of the globe," Fitzhugh wrote, "than the Negro slave of the United States."

Management

Fitzhugh equated happiness with the material conditions of slave life—housing, clothing, diet—and compared them favorably with the conditions under which the poorest wage workers of the North lived. By the 1850s, when he wrote, most southern state legislatures had, in fact, defined minimum living standards as part of their slave codes. Magazines like the *Southern Agriculturalist* featured exchanges among slave owners about how well they treated their people and what kinds of improvements were desirable.

The most obvious reason for keeping slaves adequately housed, clothed, and fed was practical: a healthy slave worked more efficiently and was less likely to rebel or run away. Also underlying the trend toward improvement in the conditions of slave life after the 1830s was the South's

determination to show that the abolitionists' depiction of slavery as a life of unrelenting horror was a lie. Planters who provided decent accommodations for their slaves took pleasure in showing "the quarters," as slave communities were called, to northern or foreign visitors. They reassured themselves that they were just the beneficent patriarchs that the positive-good writers described.

Control

Less likely to be trumpeted were the measures of control that were devised in the wake of Turner's Rebellion. By 1840, the states of the Deep South had adopted laws that made it extremely difficult for a slave owner to manumit his slaves. Even Virginia, where manumission had been honored, required recently freed blacks to leave the state (although this law was impossible to enforce effectively). It was also a crime in some southern states to teach a slave to read: Gabriel, Vesey, and Turner had all been literate and, in fact, voracious readers.

County governments were required to fund and maintain slave patrols. These mounted posses of armed whites policed the roads and plantations, particularly at night. They had the legal right to break into slave cabins or demand at gunpoint that any black (or white) account for himself or herself. Usually rough, hard-bitten men who were so poor that they sorely needed the undesirable job, the "paddy-rollers" (patrollers) were brutal even with unoffending slaves. Blacks hated and feared them. Their mere presence and unbridled arrogance cast a cloud of repression over the plantation regions that few outsiders failed to notice.

Blacks who were not under the direct supervision of their masters or overseers were required by law to carry written passes that gave them permission to be abroad, even just a mile or two from their cabins. Free blacks—there were about 250,000 in the South by 1860, 1 to every 15 slaves—had to carefully protect the documentary evidence of their status. Kidnappings of free blacks and sale of them as slaves elsewhere in the South were far from unknown.

The presence of free blacks presented a serious ideological problem for slave owners. One of the most effective means of controlling slaves was to convince them that God and nature intended them to be slaves because of their race and that they should be thankful to be under the care of their masters. But if slaves saw free blacks prospering, the argument disintegrated, and slave owners knew it. Slave owners also believed that free blacks were likely to stir up discontent among slaves, and they were probably right.

Religion, which had inspired the Vesey and Turner rebellions, could also be an effective means of control. Vesey had been a member of a large, independent African Methodist Episcopal Church. After 1830, careful masters paid close attention to the kind of preaching their people heard. Some owners took their slaves to their own churches, where the minister was expected, now and then, to deliver a sermon based on biblical stories such as that of Hagar: "The angel of the Lord said unto her, return to Thy mistress, and submit thyself under her hands." Other masters permitted the blacks, who preferred an emotional Christianity peppered with vestiges of West African religion (Gullah Jack's Methodism plus magic charms), to have preachers of their own race. But these often eloquent men were instructed—specifically or indirectly—to steer clear of topics that might cast doubt on the rightness of slavery. And they were monitored.

Some toed the line. Others conveyed their protest by placing heavy emphasis on the ancient Israelites' bondage in Egypt and Babylon—and their ultimate deliverance. The idealized institution of John C. Calhoun and George Fitzhugh bore only an accidental relationship to slavery as it actually existed.

for FURTHER READING

On the South and its distinctive characteristics, see Avery O. Craven, *The Growth of Southern Nationalism, 1848–1860,* 1953; Clement Eaton, *The Growth of Southern Civilization,* 1961, and *A History of the Old South,* 1975; I. A. Newby, *The American South,* 1979; and Charles S. Sydnor, *The Development of Southern Sectionalism, 1819–1848,* 1948. Few historians today would subscribe to the conclusions in Wilbur Cash, *The Mind of the South,* 1940, and yet it contains many perceptive insights. A contemporary "travel book" about the Old South well worth reading is Frederick Law Olmstead, *The Cotton Kingdom,* 1861.

Of more specific concern but vital to understanding the subject are Edward A. Ayers, *Vengeance and Justice: Crime and Punishment in the Nineteenth-Century American South,* 1984; Dickson D. Bruce, *Violence and Culture in the Antebellum South,* 1979; Victoria E. Bynum, *Unruly Women: The Politics of Social and Sexual Control in the Old South,* 1992; William J. Cooper, *The South and the Politics of Slavery, 1828–1856,* 1978; Elizabeth Fox-Genovese, *Within the Plantation Household,* 1988; John Hope Franklin, *The Militant South,* 1956; Eugene Genovese, *The Political Economy of Slavery,* 1962, and *The World the Slave Holders Made,* 1969; Patrick Gerster and William Cords, eds., *Myth and Image in Southern History,* 1974; Lewis C. Gray, *History of Agriculture in the Southern United States to 1860,* 1933; James Oakes, *The Ruling Race: A History of American Slave Holders,* 1982; Frank Owsley, *Plain Folk of the Old South,* 1949; William R. Taylor, *Cavalier and Yankee: The Old South and American National Character,* 1961; and Gavin Wright, *The Political Economy of the Cotton South,* 1978.

 AMERICAN JOURNEY ONLINE AND INFOTRAC COLLEGE EDITION

Visit the source collections at http://ajaccess.wadsworth.com and http://infotrac.thomsonlearning.com, and use the Search function with the following key terms to explore documents, images, audio and video clips, articles, and commentary related to the material in this chapter:

Abolitionism   Nat Turner
Denmark Vesey   William Lloyd Garrison

Additional resources, exercises, and Internet links related to this chapter are available on *The American Past* Web site:
http://history.wadsworth.com/americanpast7e.

HISTORY ONLINE

Maps of Liberia 1830–1870
http://memory.loc.gov/ammem/gmdhtml/libhtml/libhome.html
Contemporary maps and other information about the early development of the African country planned to be a refuge for freed American slaves.

Turner's Rebellion
www.bigchalk.com/cgibin/WebObjects/WOPortal.woa/Homework/High_School/History/History_by_Chronology/19th_Century/Nat_Turner's_Rebellion_64167.html
Documents, sources, and links concerning Nat Turner's uprising.

THE PECULIAR INSTITUTION

Slavery as It Was Perceived and as It Was

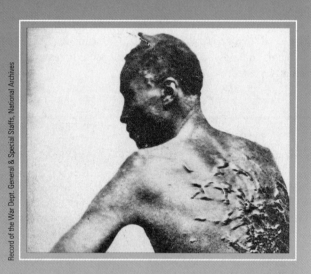

Record of the War Dept. General & Special Staffs, National Archives

Oppression has, at one stroke, deprived the descendants of the Africans of almost all the privileges of humanity. The Negro of the United States has lost all remembrance of his country; the language which his forefathers spoke is never heard around him; he abjured their religion and forgot their customs when he ceased to belong to Africa, without acquiring any European privileges. But he remains halfway between the two communities; sold by the one, repulsed by the other; finding not a spot in the universe to call by the name of country, except the faint image of a home which the shelter of his master's roof affords.

Alexis de Tocqueville

I N 1865, THE Thirteenth Amendment to the Constitution, just 43 words, wrought a more fundamental change in America than any other amendment. In stating that "neither slavery nor involuntary servitude . . . shall exist within the United States," the Thirteenth Amendment eliminated "the great exception," an institution that mocked the ideals that Americans endlessly proclaimed, made their nation special in the world: individual freedom, justice for all, and equality of opportunity.

IMAGES OF SLAVERY

Two images of slavery, one reeking of romance, the other rife with horror, contended for possession of the American mind after about 1830, when Garrison's *Liberator* and Turner's Rebellion forced most Americans to come to personal conclusions about the institution. The seeds of the romantic vision of the South were planted by the positive-good theorists and nurtured by the sentimentality that permeated American popular culture. The other image, slavery as horror, was cultivated by abolitionists who drew on their personal experiences and observations, and on information that was sometimes distorted. In a cause commissioned by God, restraint had no place, as Garrison said so vividly.

Minstrel Shows

Entertainers catering to ordinary folk—jugglers, sleight-of-hand artists, musicians, singers, dancers—worked both in cities and on tour, one-night stands in saloons and small-town theaters. Their acts were bawdy, broadly comic, and sentimental. In Louisville in 1830, one of them, Thomas D.

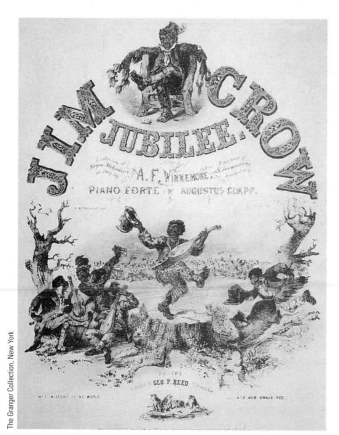

The Granger Collection, New York

▲ *Publicity for a minstrel show. The players are exuberant, simple, idle, ecstatically happy. So popular were the shows that during the 1850s, there were 100 different minstrel troupes.*

"Daddy" Rice, had a brainstorm. He imitated a dance he had seen a ragged African American perform on the street for pennies.

The dance was called "Jumpin' Jim Crow," and the audience loved it. It became the centerpiece of Daddy's act and had dozens of imitators. By the 1840s, "Ethiopian songs," sung in southern Negro dialect by white men who had blacked their faces, were so popular that a songwriter, Daniel D. Emmett, and an impresario, Edwin P. Christy, organized competing troupes of "minstrels" who put on three-act musical shows following a standardized format. Act 2 was most popular. The minstrels sat in a line across the stage. In the center was the master of ceremonies, "Mr. Interlocutor." He wore no blackface and spoke in a stilted upper-class accent, often an English accent. There were two "end men," "Brother Tambo" (he played a tambourine) and "Brother Bones" (his instrument was "the bones"—two hog ribs). Brother Tambo was a dim-witted plantation slave often called "Jim Crow." The other was a black city slicker, a dandy, called "Zip Coon." Between songs and dances by members of the ensemble, they insulted one another and Mr. Interlocutor with broad comedy.

The makeup and dialect were grotesque and are now seen as racist stereotypes of African Americans. Stereotypes they were, but the minstrel show was not vicious. The characters were good-natured, some lovable. Even Zip Coon, a con man,

was comical rather than wicked, his schemes to bilk Mr. Tambo foiled by his own bumbling. At the same time, the blackface characters were stupid, lazy, or childlike, comfortably affirming white convictions that African Americans were their inferiors. Implicitly, there was nothing in the lives of the characters on the plantations, the setting of the minstrel shows, that detracted from their carefree lives.

Stephen Foster and the Sweet Magnolia

The minstrel show depiction of African Americans was not created by proslavery southerners. Emmett and Christy were northerners. Emmett's father was a prominent abolitionist. Christy's minstrels packed a large theater in New York for 2,500 performances. Stephen Foster, who wrote more and better "Ethiopian songs" than Emmett, was from Pittsburgh and had no interest in seeing the South. In fact, Foster disliked the "trashy and really offensive words" of many blackface songs and stopped writing in dialect.

His compositions humanized slaves; there was nothing condescending about the sentiments they expressed; they were the same sentiments in the popular novels of the day. Foster's first hit, "Oh Susannah" (1849), was a nonsense song about two lovers; stripped of racial allusions, it became the anthem of the California Gold Rush. "Old Black Joe" (1860) was an old man's lament appealing to every sentimentalist over the age of 60.

Foster's contribution to the romantic myth of the plantation South lay in the fact that he did not remotely question the legitimacy of slavery and created a relationship between "Ol' Massa" and his slaves that was mutually warm and caring. In "Old Folks at Home" (1851), a slave far from "de old plantation" (a runaway?) wearily wishes he were home. In "Massa's in de Cold, Cold Ground" (1852), all the dead man's slaves are weeping that their master had been kind. The carefree "darky," the grand house, Spanish moss hanging from the oaks, the plunking of the banjo, the sweet scent of magnolia blossoms, and an easy, languid life were the ingredients of Foster's world.

Garrison on the Constitution

William Lloyd Garrison broke few, if any, laws unrelated to slavery. But his thoughts on the Constitution were less than patriotic. He called it "a covenant with death and an agreement with hell" because, however evasively, it sanctioned slavery:

A sacred compact, forsooth! We pronounce it the most heaven-daring arrangement ever made for the continuance and protection of a system of the most atrocious villainy ever exhibited on earth.

Statements like this one explain why many earnest abolitionists gave Garrison a wide berth.

Anti-Slavery Almanac.

[1840.]

"OUR *PECULIAR* DOMESTIC INSTITUTIONS."

▲ *There was nothing romantic about the South the abolitionists pictured: Slavery produced a society of torturers, brawlers, murderers, lynch mobs, drunken gamblers, duelists, and men who whipped children.*

Within a generation after the Civil War, this vision of antebellum southern life was embraced by most white Americans. In the industrial age of the late nineteenth century, paced by the relentless drive of the machine, it was consoling to dream nostalgically of a South that, however imaginary, had been its antithesis. The tradition culminated in Margaret Mitchell's novel of 1936, *Gone with the Wind,* and Hollywood's classic film based on the book.

Theodore Dwight Weld and His Converts

Abolitionists saw another slavery. To zealous black and white lecturers, journalists, and preachers who crisscrossed the northern states, the slave's world was a hell of blacksnake whips, brutal slave catchers and bloodhounds, children torn from their mothers' breasts to be sold, squalor, disease, and near starvation under callous, arrogant masters, the "slavocrats."

William Lloyd Garrison was not alone in presenting this image to northerners. Indeed, because of his rasping self-righteousness, Garrison was probably less effective in the assault on slavery than abolitionists like Theodore Dwight Weld, a white evangelical "as eloquent as an angel and powerful as thunder." No demagogue, Weld concentrated on converting prominent people to the antislavery cause. Two of his proselytes, Arthur and Lewis Tappan, were wealthy New York merchants who generously financed abolitionist institutions like Kenyon and Oberlin Colleges in Ohio, hotbeds of abolition, and the American Anti-Slavery Society, founded in 1833.

Another Weld convert was James G. Birney, an Alabama planter who freed his slaves and ran as the presidential candidate of the antislavery Liberty party in 1840 and 1844. Weld married an abolitionist who had owned slaves, Angelina Grimké of South Carolina. She and her sister Sarah instilled in him a perspective on the problem of slavery that was beyond Garrison, consideration for the moral plight of the conscientious slave owner.

Black Abolitionists

Although the abolitionist movement would have foundered without whites, its most dependable supporters were the North's free blacks. Although generally poor, African Americans contributed a disproportionate part of the money needed to publish antislavery newspapers and send antislavery lecturers on their tours.

Several of the most prominent abolitionists were black. Sojourner Truth was the name adopted by Isabella Van Wagenen, a physical giant of a woman born a slave in New York in 1797. Freed in 1827, she worked as a domestic servant, was briefly a Millerite, then burst on the abolitionist scene as one of the movement's most powerful orators. Sojourner Truth was illiterate to the end—she died in 1893, at 96—but she transfixed audiences, accompanying her speeches with songs she had herself composed.

The most distinguished of the black abolitionists was Frederick Douglass. Born a slave in Maryland, he escaped to Massachusetts, educated himself as well as Harvard educated most of its graduates, and, in 1845, wrote his autobi-

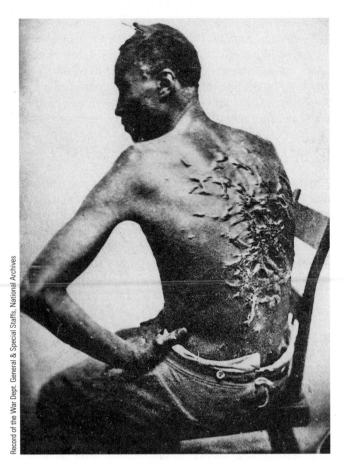

▲ *There was nothing imagined, exaggerated, or contrived in this abolitionist photograph of a slave who had been whipped.*

ography. For a while, because his former master was pursuing him, Douglass lived in England, where he furthered his education and earned enough money to pay his master off. Douglass's effectiveness stemmed from his eloquence, forthright unembellished prose, refinement, and, most of all, firsthand knowledge of life in a slave society.

Mrs. Stowe and Uncle Tom

To people of Douglass's caliber, the decisive antislavery argument was that slavery reduced human beings, God's children, to the status of livestock. That point, however, did not lend itself to emotional appeals. So, black and white abolitionists both focused on the deprivations and cruelties suffered by slaves. Some antislavery lecturers traveled with runaway slaves whose backs had been disfigured by brutal whippings.

The single most effective abolitionist shot was *Uncle Tom's Cabin, or Life Among the Lowly,* written by Harriet Beecher Stowe, the member of a distinguished family. Not only did Stowe's book sell an astonishing 300,000 copies within a year of publication (the equivalent of selling more than 3 million today), but it was adapted into plays performed by professional and amateur troupes in small towns and cities alike. So influential was Stowe's tale of Uncle Tom, a submissive and loyal old slave, that when Abraham Lincoln met her during the Civil War, he remarked, "So you are the little woman who wrote the book that made this great war."

The underlying theme of *Uncle Tom's Cabin* is that no matter how well intentioned an individual slave owner is, he cannot help but do wrong by living with an inherently evil institution. Uncle Tom's owner at the beginning is the epitome of the paternalistic planter beloved of positive-good theorists and minstrels. He genuinely loves Uncle Tom. Nevertheless, when financial troubles require him to raise money, he sells Tom. Heartbroken, he promises that, as soon as he is able, he will find Tom and buy him back. The point is that the noblest of white men sells the best of black men when the law says that he may do so.

It was not this insight that made *Uncle Tom's Cabin* so popular. The book owed its success to the lurid cruelties that Tom witnesses and suffers. Stowe herself thought that this was the book's contribution. When southerners complained that she had distorted the realities of slave life, she responded in 1853 with *A Key to Uncle Tom's Cabin,* which set out the documentary basis of her allegations in quotations from southern newspapers.

WHAT SLAVERY WAS LIKE

Which image is correct? Both and neither. Proslavery and antislavery partisans dealt with the "peculiar institution" as though it were monolithic, the same in Virginia and Texas, on cotton plantations and the New Orleans riverfront, on sprawling plantations and cramped frontier homesteads, for field hand and big-house butler. In the law—the classification of human beings as property—it was one and the same thing. The experience of slavery, however, was as diverse as the South.

Structure of the Institution: White Perspective

The census of 1860, the last taken when slavery was legal, reveals that nearly 4 million people lived in bondage, equally divided between males and females. All but a few lived in the 15 states south of the Mason-Dixon line and the Ohio River. West of the Mississippi River, Missouri, Arkansas, Louisiana, and Texas were slave states. A few Indians in Indian Territory (Oklahoma) owned slaves.

One white southern family in four owned slaves. Even when those whose living depended directly on the existence of the institution—overseers, slave traders, patrollers—are added in, only a minority of white southerners had a material stake in slavery.

The great planter class (the only slave owners in the world of the minstrels) was quite small. In 1860, only 2,200 people, less than 1 percent of the southern population, owned 100 or more slaves. Only 254 owned 200 slaves or more. Nathaniel Heyward of South Carolina was at the top of the pyramid, owning 2,000 slaves on 17 plantations.

More typical of the southern slave owner was Jacob Eaton of North Carolina. On his 160-acre farm, he worked side by side with the slave family he owned. Eaton's yeoman class—small independent farmers who owned from none to nine slaves—was the backbone of both the South and the slavery system. About 74 percent of slave owners fell into this category. Another 16 percent of slave owners owned between 10 and 20 people. A mere 10 percent of slave owners owned more than 20 slaves.

Structure of the Institution: Black Perspective

If the big plantation was rare from a white perspective, life in the shadow of the big house was more common in African American lives. By 1860, more than half the South's slaves lived on what we would think of as a plantation rather than a farm. Half a million, one in eight, belonged to members of the great planter class.

There were black slave owners. The census of 1830 revealed 3,775 free African Americans in possession of 12,760 slaves. One curious case was Dilsey Pope, a free black woman of Columbus, Georgia, who owned her husband. The two had a fierce quarrel and Mrs. Pope sold him to a white neighbor. When the couple reconciled, the new owner refused to sell Mrs. Pope's husband back. Their marriage had no standing in Georgia law, so the couple was without recourse.

There were a handful of black great planters, most in Louisiana. Andrew Durnford of New Orleans owned 77 slaves. When questioned, Durnford said that owning slaves was self-interest. It was the only way to wealth in the South. Although he contributed to the American Colonization Society, Durnford freed only four slaves during his lifetime, one other in his will.

First Light to Sundown

Few blacks enjoyed the advantages of living as domestic servants: better food, clothing, and beds. Cooks, maids, butlers, valets, and footmen made life pleasanter for the great planters who could afford them, but they did not make money for their masters. The vast majority of slaves were field hands who raised a cash crop by means of heavy labor from first light to sundown almost year-round. For a slave owner to justify investing capital in a labor force rather than hiring free laborers, it was necessary to keep the property hopping.

Cotton was by far the most important southern product—in fact, the most important American product. During the 1850s, an average annual crop of 4 million bales brought more than $190 million into the American economy from abroad. Cotton represented two-thirds of the nation's total exports and (in 1850) employed fully 1.8 million slaves out of 3.2 million. In 1860, the 12 richest counties in the United States were cotton counties. Other cash crops dependent on slave labor were tobacco (350,000 slaves); sugar (150,000 slaves); rice (125,000 slaves); and hemp (60,000 slaves), from which rope and sacking for cotton bales were made.

Southern farmers and planters strove to be self-sufficient. Therefore, slaves raised corn, vegetables, and hogs for food, and hay for fodder, as well as the cash crop. There was plenty of work to be done on a farm or plantation year-round. Thomas Jefferson heated Monticello with 10 cords of wood a month in winter: a lot of chopping. The calendar of a cotton plantation was packed with jobs, major and odd, except for a short period around Christmas, to which the slaves looked forward as "laying-by time."

▲ *The life a majority of slaves knew: picking cotton. Never was the work harder and the pressure greater; the cotton had to be under cover before the fall rains. Every slave was sent to the fields, including house servants and children barely able to walk. There was no skill involved, just hot, hard labor.*

Because slaves were expensive—by the 1850s, $2,000 for a prime field hand (a healthy male in his 20s or early 30s)—planters preferred to hire free blacks or Irish immigrants for unhealthy and dangerous jobs. Few risked their costly human property on draining swamps or working at the bottom of chutes down which 600-pound bales of cotton came hurtling at high speeds. It was a lot cheaper to give the widow of a dead employee a five-dollar gold piece.

The Rhythms of Labor

By the 1850s, a slave produced from $80 to $120 in wealth each year and cost between $30 and $50 to feed, clothe, and shelter. The margin of profit was not large enough to allow the small-scale slave owner to live without working in the fields along with his slaves.

Planters who owned 10 to 20 slaves were freed of menial tasks; but, because few slaves worked any harder than they were forced to (their share of the fruits of their labor was fixed), they had to be supervised constantly: bribed, cajoled, threatened, or whipped. If a man owned more than 20 slaves, he could afford to hire an overseer or put a slave driver (himself a slave) in charge. On the large plantations, masters had little contact with their field hands.

Slaves on large plantations worked according to the task system or the gang system. Under the task system, a specific job was assigned to each slave each day. When it was done, the slave's time was his or her own. For some planters, this was the most efficient form of organization because, when provided with an incentive, however meager, the slaves worked harder. Other planters complained that the task system resulted in slipshod work, as the slaves rushed so as to get to their own chores or recreation.

Under the gang system, slaves worked from sunrise to sundown in groups under a white overseer or black driver. Who knows how frequently they felt the sting of the whip? The lash was always in evidence, however, whether in a black hand or a white one. Frederick Douglass remarked that

The Health of Slaves

In an age when nothing was known of scientific nutrition, the slaves' diet was comparable to that of poor southern whites and free blacks, and likely better on plantations where slaves were permitted to keep gardens. The life expectancy of slaves was the same as that of free blacks and whites in the South. Statistical surveys done about 1860 showed southern slaves averaging 3 inches more in height than West Africans, 2 inches more than Trinidadians, and an inch more than British marines.

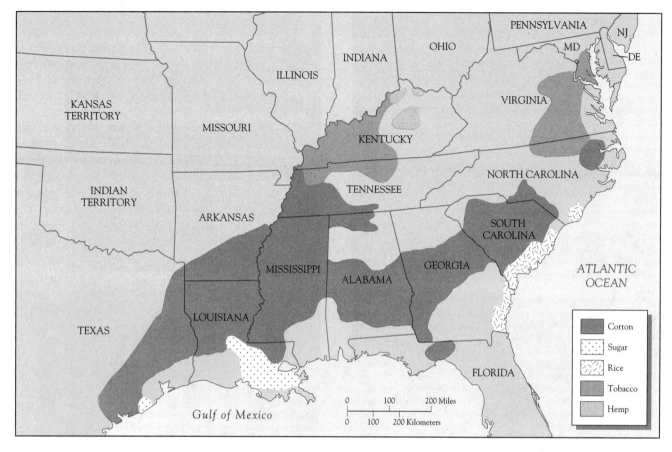

MAP 19:1 Major Crops of the South, 1860 Cotton was king in the South, but tobacco and rice were still profitable and Louisiana's sugar immensely so. Hemp (for making rope and sacking) was a minor crop, grown mostly in Kentucky and sold mostly in the cotton-growing South.

"everybody in the South wants the privilege of whipping someone else."

Slave Traders

Slaves were defined in law as chattel property—personal possessions legally much the same as cattle, hogs, a necklace, a cotton press, a chair, or a share of stock. They could be bought, sold, bartered, willed, or given away. The commerce in slaves was brisk and profitable.

Even defenders of slavery admitted that the slave trade was ugly. The slave auction was a livestock auction plus coarse sexual joking. Prospective buyers crowded around the auction block, determining the age of the slaves for sale by examining their teeth, as they would do when buying a horse. Slaves were forced to run to test their wind. Buyers wiped their bodies with rags to determine if the auctioneer had dyed gray hair black or rubbed oil into aged dry skin. If adolescent girls were for sale, sexual innuendos amused the crowd. Foreigners, northerners, and many southerners were simultaneously disgusted and fascinated by slave auctions, much as American tourists in Mexico today react to bullfights.

Masters aspiring to be patriarchs disapproved of the slave trade, describing traders as base, crude, unworthy men. Nevertheless, as Harriet Beecher Stowe and others pointed out, with-

out the slave trade, there could be no slavery. If some humans were to be property, owners had to be free to buy and sell them. Where there is trade, there are brokers.

The general flow of the commerce was "down the river"—the Mississippi—from the older, declining tobacco states to the cotton states of the Deep South. Professional slave traders purchased blacks in Virginia, Maryland, and Kentucky, and marched them, like their African ancestors, in coffles to Memphis or New Orleans, where as many as 200 companies were in the business.

LIFE IN THE QUARTERS

The slave codes of most southern states provided that slaves had no civil rights. They could not own property under the law; therefore, they could not legally buy and sell anything. They could not make contracts. They could not marry legally. (If they could, a planter could not sell a woman without her husband.) They could not testify in court against any white person (nor could free blacks in some southern states). They could not leave the plantation without written permission.

It was a crime for a slave to strike a white person under any circumstances, even to save his life. Slaves could not carry firearms. They could not congregate in more than

▲ *A slave auction in St. Louis. There is much more decorum in this depiction than there is in the accounts of northerners and foreigners who witnessed auctions. If some buyers were, no doubt, as well dressed as the gentlemen here, not everyone in attendance was.*

small groups except at religious services under white supervision. They could not be abroad at night. And in most southern states, it was a crime for a white or another black to teach a slave to read.

The slaves' rights were those to life and, under most slave codes, a minimum standard of food, clothing, and shelter.

Humans Without Human Rights

The actual experience of slave life often deviated from the letter of the slave codes. For example, a master could not legally kill his slave, but it was not considered murder when a slave died during "moderate" or "reasonable" correction, words highly debatable in court. Whipping was the most common form of corporal punishment, and 50 lashes—quite enough to kill a man—was not an uncommon punishment. This was hardly "moderate." In the end, the slaves' only guarantees against brutality at the hands of their masters were the gospel of paternalism, social expectations of the master by his peers, religious scruples, and the slaves' cash value.

There are few better guarantees of a man's good behavior than his knowledge that bad behavior will cost him money. But that applies to men who are thinking. Slave owners (and surely their overseers) flew into uncontrolled rages

and killed slaves. Because their property rights in their slaves almost always took precedence in court over the slaves' human rights, owners were rarely punished for such crimes. After an incident of hideous torture in Virginia in 1858, with a slave dying after 24 hours of beating and burning, the court punished the sadistic master by imprisoning him. But he did not forfeit ownership of the other blacks he owned.

A Diverse Institution

If the laws protecting slaves were not effective, many slave owners were moved by their religion, their sense of decency, and by their aspiration to be seen as benevolent patriarchs to care generously for their slaves, even in violation of the slave codes.

A family that owned only one or two slaves occasionally developed a relationship much like partnership with them. Some white owners and black slaves ate the same food, slept in the same cabin, and worked together intimately. However, the slave on a large plantation was likely to be better off than the slave on a small farm because of the poverty of the marginal small farmer.

After about 1840, large-scale slave owners generally provided adequate rations of cornmeal, salt pork, and molasses. It

Slave trader, Sold to Tennessee,

Arise! Arise! and weep no more dry up your tears, we Shall part no more. Come rose we go to Tennessee, that happy Shore. To old virginia never — never — return.

the Company going to Tennessee from Staunton. Augusta County, the law of virginia Suffered them to go on. I was Astonished at this boldness. the carrier Stopped a moment. then Ordered the march, I Saw the play it is Commonly in this State, with the negro's in droves Sold,

▲ *A familiar sight in the South: slaves from Virginia marching to the cotton lands of western Tennessee. The unfortunates in this watercolor by an eyewitness are, at least, not hobbled, perhaps because they are family groups. Coffles of young men—"prime field hands"—sold down the river were often chained.*

was common to allow slaves to keep their own vegetable plots of several acres and even chickens. Some masters did not keep their own gardens and coops but purchased vegetables and eggs from their slaves. They concluded, sensibly, that if both master and slave were in the vegetable and chicken businesses, no one could tell from where the slaves' dinners came. For the same reason, very few slave owners allowed slaves to raise hogs for their own use. Pork was one of the staples; the planter needed to control its production and distribution.

Some slaves were permitted to buy and sell beyond the boundaries of the plantation and to keep the money they earned. Along the Mississippi, task-system slaves working on their own time cut wood for the steamboats. Some sold chickens and eggs in towns, and here and there, a slave had a shot-

gun for hunting. One remarkable slave entrepreneur was Simon Gray, a skilled flatboat sailor whose owner paid him $8 a month to haul lumber to New Orleans. Gray commanded crews of up to 20 men, including free whites, and kept detailed accounts. He eventually bought his freedom.

A few masters permitted their slaves to save money in order to purchase their own, their spouse's, or their children's freedom, but the deal depended on the owner's decency. No contract with a slave was enforceable in most southern states (Kentucky was an exception).

A well-known example of wide-open violation of a slave code was the model plantation of Joseph Davis, brother of Jefferson Davis, the future president of the Confederate States of America. Ignoring a Mississippi state law

African Slave Traders: Defying the Law

Congress forbade the importation of slaves from abroad, "the African slave trade" in the parlance of the time, as of January 1, 1808. It was the first day the Constitution permitted Congress to do so.

The Constitution's attention to importing slaves, a specific issue more appropriate to legislation than to a frame of government, reveals several aspects of the status of slavery in America in the late 1700s. All but a few delegates to the Constitutional Convention wanted to put an end to the business. It was ugly, as anyone who saw a ship unloading slaves knew: They were invariably in wretched physical condition and terrified. Moreover, many Americans of the time saw the abolition of the foreign slave trade as a first step toward ridding the United States of the institution of slavery, which they hoped lay in the future. James Madison, the "father of the Constitution," wrote, "Happy would it be for the unfortunate Africans if an equal prospect lay before them of being redeemed from the oppression of their European brethren."

But South Carolina's and Georgia's delegates to the Constitutional Convention balked. Their states were importing a good many slaves from abroad. They made it clear that without temporary protection of the African slave trade, their states would not ratify the Constitution. So the trade was protected. The Constitution prohibited Congress from forbidding the "Importation of such Persons as any of the States now existing shall think proper to admit" for 20 years, until 1808. This provision was specifically exempted from the amendment process. It could not be changed; each state's right to two senators is the only other part of the Constitution future generations were forbidden to amend.

Attitudes toward the African slave trade were unchanged in 1807. Congress easily abolished the trade right on schedule. However, South Carolina imported more slaves during the last year it was legal to do so than in any previous year.

Enforcing the ban was difficult. Major African suppliers of slaves, like the Ashanti king, were mystified. Others were angry, saying that the termination of the business was an insult to Islam. (There were more slaves in Africa in 1807 than in all of the Americas.) The British, who also abolished the African slave trade, bore the major burden of patrolling the West African coast. By the 1840s, more than 30 naval ships were assigned to patrol the African coast, boarding vessels violating the ban and returning captives to Africa. The United States Navy assigned a squadron of up to 8 ships to Caribbean waters to search suspicious merchant vessels. Between May 1818 and November 1821, Americans freed 573 Africans bound for slavery.

From an American perspective, the term *African slave trade* was misleading. In colonial times, and illegally after 1807, very few slave traders carried captives from Africa to North America. It was the terrible nature of the business. So many captives died on the middle passage that profits depended on the voyage being kept as short as possible. The quickest crossing by far was to Brazil, a partial explanation of the fact that 40 percent of Africans sent as slaves to the Western Hemisphere went to Brazil. Slave traders bound farther north did not go to North American ports because it meant bypassing dozens of West Indian islands where their cargoes could be sold. Sailing to North America added weeks to their voyage and more deaths to their balance sheets. American slave buyers purchased their slaves in the West Indies. Almost all Africans who ended up slaves in North America spent some time in Cuba, Jamaica, or elsewhere in the West Indies.

This was even more the case after 1807, when the importation of slaves was illegal. Smugglers still risked British or French capture by buying slaves in Africa, more now from the Fulbe and Mandingo than from the Ashanti. King Gezo of Dahomey (whose bodyguard was a platoon of tall, fierce, strong women) sold 9,000 slaves annually between 1809 and 1850. The major suppliers at Sangha were an American, Paul Faber, and his African wife, Mary, who kept meticulous books, as if they were grocers. But slaves imported illegally into the United States, even those African-born, came mainly from Brazil and Cuba in vessels built for speed so they could outrun naval vessels. In 1839, two British ships brought five Spanish and Portuguese slavers flying the American flag into New York. President Van Buren asked Congress to take action against Brazilians and Cubans using the stars and stripes to evade British patrols.

He was snubbed. By 1839, many southerners and some northerners were sympathetic to the illegal slave trade. There were plenty of willing buyers, particularly in New Orleans and Charleston. The boom in cotton had sent the price of American-born slaves soaring; newly imported Africans were cheaper. Northern shipyards continued to build vessels designed for the slave trade. Of 170 slave trade expeditions identified by the British between 1859 and 1862, 74 had been outfitted in New York. The schooner *Wanderer,* ostensibly a yacht, was built for John Johnston of New Orleans in 1856. The tip-off of its real purpose was its oversized water tanks. Still, the *Wanderer* was not seized until it had successfully landed 325 slaves at Jekyll Island, South Carolina, in December 1858 (between 70 and 80 of the Africans died before arrival).

The penalties for those convicted of slave trading were harsh. The British equated slave traders with pirates. There was also a price to pay if captured by Americans and convicted. By the 1850s, however, it was difficult to get a conviction from a southern jury. In 1859, a United States warship brought the bark *Emily,* obviously a slaver, into port. The case was dismissed. In 1860, the owner of the *Wanderer* was acquitted in Savannah and permitted to buy his ship back for a quarter of its value. In the law, crewmen on a slaver were liable to be prosecuted, but they too rarely suffered more than a slap on the wrist. With such little deterrence, seamen could not ignore the fact that wages on a slave ship running from Cuba were as high as $10 a day, an astronomical sum.

forbidding the education of blacks, Joseph Davis maintained a school and teacher for the children of the quarters.

It is important to recall, however, that for every master like Joseph Davis, there were a dozen masters who kept their slaves just sound enough to work and a dozen more slave owners who, out of stupidity, ignorance, or malevolence, treated their slaves worse than they treated their mules. The editor of a southern magazine made no comment when a subscriber wrote, "Africans are nothing but brutes, and they will love you better for whipping, whether they deserve it or not."

PROTEST

Whether their master was kindly or cruel, their material circumstances adequate or deplorable, the vast majority of slaves hated their lot in life. Although some were sincerely attached to their masters, and although rebellion was rare after Nat Turner, blacks resisted slavery in various ways. When freedom became a realistic possibility during the Civil War, slaves deserted their homes by the thousands to flee to Union lines. A South Carolina planter wrote candidly after the war, "I believed these people were content, happy, and attached to their masters." That, he concluded sadly, had been "a delusion."

Malingering and Thievery

He might have been spared his disappointment had he given deeper consideration to white people's stereotypes of slaves. It was a commonly held belief that blacks were inherently lazy and irresponsible. In fact, free blacks generally worked quite hard, and the same slaves whose "laziness" was an aggravation in the cotton fields often toiled in their own gardens from dawn to dusk on Sundays and by moonlight during the week. The only incentive for a slave to work hard for the master was negative—the threat of punishment. That was often insufficient to cause men and women to ignore the blazing southern sun. When the overseer or driver was over the hill, it was nap time.

Theft was so common on plantations that whites believed blacks to be congenital thieves. Again, the only incentive not to steal a chicken, a suckling pig, or a berry pie was fear of punishment. If a slave was not caught, he had no reason to believe he had done wrong. One chicken thief who was caught in the act of eating his prize explained this point to his master: If the chicken was his master's property and he was his master's property, then the master had not lost anything because the chicken was in his belly instead of scratching around the hen yard. It is not known if his meditation saved the philosopher from a whipping.

Runaways

The clearest evidence of slave discontent was the prevalence of runaways. Only blacks who lived in the states that bordered the free states—Delaware, Maryland, Kentucky, Missouri—had a reasonable chance of escaping to permanent freedom. Some "rode" the "underground railway," rushing at night from hiding places in one abolitionist's home, most often a black abolitionist's, to another.

Harriet Tubman, who escaped from her master in 1849, returned to the South 19 times to lead other blacks to freedom. Tubman, the "Black Moses," was a hands-on and very brave abolitionist. And a shrewd one. Tubman went south only in winter, when the nights were longer and few people were out of doors. She herself never went onto a plantation; she selected a rendezvous several miles away and sent others to tell the slaves where she was.

Departure was always on Saturday night. The runaways, whom Tubman called her "cargo," would be missed Monday morning, but their master would not be alarmed until Monday evening. It was common for slaves, tired or disgusted, to disappear for a few days; the vacation was worth a whipping to many. So Tubman had a two-day head start. She moved only by night, depending on African American families known to her, free and slave, for food and shelter. (Collaborators also helped by tearing down notices of the runaways.) If Tubman had to enter a town for some reason, she approached from the north and left in a southerly direction. She was in appearance and manners "a very respectable Negro, not at all a poor fugitive."

In a dangerous business—if caught she faced serious penalties—Tubman was no sunshine-and-sugar social worker.

Uncle Remus Suggests

Because violent resistance was suicidal, it was unusual among slaves. Elders in the quarters counseled keeping one's wits and acting docile. An Uncle Remus fable recorded after the emancipation of slaves, "Why Br'er Possum Loves Peace," explains the ruse.

Mr. Dog attacks Br'er Coon and Br'er Possum. Br'er Coon fights back and drives Mr. Dog away, but at the price of serious injury. Br'er Possum "plays possum" (plays dead).

Representing blacks who fight back, Br'er Coon berates Br'er Possum for cowardice: "'I ain't runnin' wid cowards deze days,' sez Br'er Coon."

Br'er Possum replies that just because he did not fight does not mean that he is a coward: "I want no mo' skeer'd dan you is right now. . . . but I'm de most ticklish chap w'at you ever laid eyes on, en no sooner did Mr. Dog put his nose down yer 'mong my ribs dan I got ter laffin. . . . I don't mine fightin', Br'er Coon, no mo' dan you duz. . . . but I declar' ter grashus ef I kin stan' ticklin."

Note that it is Mr., not Br'er ("Brother"), Dog; the tale is about the races; the Dog was white and no brother.

Daniel Webster's Slave

Daniel Webster, representing a state that abolished slavery before he was born, bought a slave, Paul Jennings, to be his butler in Washington, D.C., where slavery was legal. Webster freed Jennings, but then again, he did not. Jennings had to sign a contract to work off Webster's expenses.

As far as Jennings was concerned, he was still a slave. In 1848, he joined other slaves to charter a sloop in which they planned to escape north. Jennings changed his mind at the last minute and dropped out of the expedition, to his good fortune. The boat was stopped in the Chesapeake, and the passengers were arrested.

▲ *Harriet Tubman (left) with a "cargo" she has led from slavery to safety. She made 19 such trips and, during the Civil War, was a spy behind Confederate lines.*

She refused to accept "cargo" she judged weak: "If he was weak enough to give out, he'd be weak enough to betray us all." She told her runaways she would shoot anyone who gave up and probably would have done so, had she carried a gun. On one occasion, to get a complainer moving, she threatened him so frighteningly that he moved.

"Let My People Go"

The culture of the quarters will never be fully understood because the slaves kept no written records. However, some reliable conjectures can be ventured based on what is known of African American religion and folklore.

By the 1850s, most slaves had embraced an emotional brand of Protestant Christianity, most commonly Baptist or Methodist in temper. Their religious services centered on animated sermons by unlettered but charismatic preachers and exuberant rhythmic singing of both hymns borrowed from the white churches and what became known as Negro spirituals.

Freedom Song
When Israel was in Egypt land
Let my people go
Oppressed so hard they could not stand
Let my people go.
Go down, Moses,
Way down in Egypt land
Tell old Pharaoh
To let my people go.

In both sermons and spirituals, the slaves explicitly identified with the ancient Hebrews. While in bondage in Babylon and Egypt, the Hebrews had been, nevertheless, in their simplicity and misery, God's chosen people. The protest—for God delivered the Hebrews from their captivity—was too obvious to be lost on whites. But as long as the whites were convinced—and the slaves obliged them—that blacks associated freedom with the afterlife, "crossing over Jordan," slave religion was not stifled.

"Bred en Bawn in a Brier Patch"

Another thinly masked form of protest were the folktales for which black storytellers became famous, particularly the Br'er Rabbit stories that were collected after the Civil War as *Uncle Remus: His Songs and Sayings.* In these yarns, elements of which have been traced back to West African folklore, the rabbit, the weakest of animals and unable to defend himself by force, survives and flourishes through wit and complex deceits.

In the most famous of the Uncle Remus stories, "How Mr. Rabbit Was Too Sharp for Mr. Fox," Br'er Fox has the rabbit in his hands and is debating with himself whether to barbecue him, hang him, drown him, or skin him. Br'er Rabbit assures the fox that he will be delighted with any of these fates just as long as the fox does not fling him into a nearby brier patch, which he fears more than anything. Of course, that is exactly what Br'er Fox does, after which Br'er Rabbit is home free. "Bred en bawn in a brier patch, Br'er Fox," Br'er Rabbit shouts back tauntingly, "bred en bawn in a brier patch." The slaves, unable to taunt their masters so bluntly, satisfied themselves with quiet trickery and coded tales about it.

It is worth noting that in the Uncle Remus stories, Br'er Rabbit now and then outsmarts himself and suffers for it. As in all social commentary of substance, the slaves were as sensitive to their own foibles as to those of their masters.

The Slave Community

Like Br'er Rabbit, slaves presented a different face to whites than to their own people. Often, individuals reinforced white beliefs in their inferiority by playing the lazy, dimwitted, comical "Sambo," devoted to "Ol' Marse" and patently incapable of taking care of himself. Observant whites noticed that Sambo was quick witted enough when they surprised him

while he was talking to other slaves or that he literally slaved in his garden and slept only when in the fields of cotton.

Recent historical research indicates that the slave family was more vital than the family among poor whites and African Americans today. Both parents were present in two-thirds of slave families, the same proportion as among European peasants at that time. Perhaps the most striking demonstration of the resiliency of African Americans, even when oppressed by slavery, is the fact that, in 1865, when slavery was abolished, there were 10 times as many blacks in the United States as had been imported from Africa and the West Indies between 1619 and 1807. The American slave population was the only slave population in the Western Hemisphere to increase as a result of natural reproduction.

for FURTHER READING

Ulrich B. Phillips, *American Negro Slavery*, 1919, and *Life and Labor in the Old South*, 1929, present romanticized portraits of slavery and yet, despite their bias, contain much valuable information. Kenneth Stampp, *The Peculiar Institution*, 1956, was an explicit response to Phillips, quite unromantic about slavery, and is quite informative.

Since the 1960s, slavery has been studied exhaustively. Just a few of hundreds of titles include Ira Berlin, *Slaves Without Masters*, 1975; John Blassingame, *The Slave Community*, 1972, and *Slave Testimony*, 1977; Carl N. Degler, *Neither Black nor White: Slavery and Race Relations in Brazil and the United States*, 1971; Stanley Elkins, *Slavery*, 1968; Robert Fogel and Stanley Engerman, *Time on the Cross*, 1974 (the findings of which are attacked in Herbert Gutman and Richard Sutch, *Slavery and the Numbers Game*, 1975); and Paul A. David et al., *Reckoning with Slavery*, 1976.

See also George M. Frederickson, *The Black Image in the White Mind*, 1971; Eugene Genovese, *The Political Economy of Slavery*, 1962, and *Roll Jordan Roll*, 1975 (perhaps the best single book about slaves); Herbert G. Gutman, *The Black Family in Slavery and Freedom, 1750–1925*, 1976; Lawrence W. Levine, *Black*

Culture and Black Consciousness: Afro-American Folk Thought from Slavery to Freedom, 1977; Gilbert Osofsky, *Puttin' On Ol' Massa*, 1969; Harold Rawick, *From Sundown to Sunup*, 1967; and R. Starobin, *Industrial Slavery in the Old South*, 1970.

On abolitionism, see Ronald Abzug, *Passionate Liberator: Theodore Dwight Weld and the Dilemma of Reform*, 1980; Anna Bontemps, *Free at Last: The Life of Frederick Douglass*, 1971; M. L. Dillon, *The Abolitionists: The Growth of a Dissenting Minority*, 1974; Aileen S. Kraditor, *Means and Ends in American Abolitionism: Garrison and His Critics on Strategy and Tactics, 1834–50*, 1967; Gerda Lerner, *The Grimké Sisters from South Carolina: Rebels Against Slavery*, 1967; Benjamin Quarles, *Black Abolitionists*, 1969; and J. B. Stewart, *Holy Warriors: The Abolitionists and American Slavery*, 1976.

On the proslavery argument, see George M. Frederickson, *The Black Image in the White Mind*, 1971; W. S. Jenkins, *Pro-Slavery Thought in the Old South*, 1935; William Stanton, *The Leopard's Spots: Scientific Attitudes Toward Race in America, 1815–1859*, 1960; and Harvey Wish, *George Fitzhugh: Propagandist of the Old South*, 1943.

 AMERICAN JOURNEY ONLINE AND INFOTRAC COLLEGE EDITION

Visit the source collections at http://ajaccess.wadsworth.com and http://infotrac.thomsonlearning.com, and use the Search function with the following key terms to explore documents, images, audio and video clips, articles, and commentary related to the material in this chapter:

Frederick Douglass	Harriet Tubman
fugitive slave	Slave trade
Grimké	Sojourner Truth
Harriet Beecher Stowe	*Uncle Tom's Cabin*

Additional resources, exercises, and Internet links related to this chapter are available on *The American Past* Web site: http://history.wadsworth.com/americanpast7e.

HISTORY ONLINE

Born in Slavery
http://memory.loc.gov/ammem/snhtml/snhome.html
Formers slaves' recollections of slave life as transcribed during the 1930s.

Slaves and the Courts
http://memory.loc.gov/ammem/sthtml/sthome.html
An extensive collection of documents revealing the legal status of slaves between 1740 and 1860.

FROM SEA TO SHINING SEA

American Expansion 1820–1848

Our manifest destiny is to overspread the continent allotted by Providence for the free development of our yearly multiplying millions.

John Louis O'Sullivan

If I were a Mexican, I would tell you, "Have you not room in your own country to bury your dead men? If you come into mine, we will greet you with bloody hands, and welcome you to hospitable graves."

Thomas Corwin

THOMAS JEFFERSON'S GENERATION believed the Louisiana Purchase had established America's boundaries for all time. In the North, the War of 1812 dashed the hopes of all reasonable people that Canada would be joined to the United States. To the west, the Rocky Mountains were as clear and as formidable a natural boundary as any in the world. The Adams-Oñis Treaty of 1819 added Florida, extending the coastline border from the Atlantic to Louisiana.

The treaty also settled on the Sabine River as the boundary between the United States and Spanish Mexico. It was the most dubious of the national frontiers. The land across the Sabine was fertile, well watered, and sparsely populated. But Spain's grip on Mexico was slipping as a popularly supported independence movement neared success. The government of the emerging Estados Unidos de Mexico was cordial to the United States of America. It was difficult to imagine conflict with a new republic that looked to the American Revolution as an inspiration.

Independent Mexico was too cordial to Americans. Within a few decades, President Porfirio Díaz would look back ruefully and lament, "Poor Mexico, so far from God, so close to the United States."

TEXAS

New Spain was the jewel of the Spanish Empire for three centuries. An elite of Spanish-born *gachupines* and Mexican-born white *criollos* monopolized the best lands, living fat off the labor of the Indians. But they were few. Mexico was not only home to the greatest of indigenous New World civilizations; it was an amalgam of Spanish and Indian cultures. The vast majority of Mexicans were, unlike the ethnically diverse Americans, a new people, *la raza* ("the race"), composed of *mestizos,* an amalgam of European and Native American blood.

Mexico's Northward Expansion

The United States expanded to the west. More slowly, for the population of New Spain was much smaller, Mexico expanded to the north. Spanish pioneers and friars planted outposts deep in what is now the American Southwest. The rivers of Texas, especially the Rio Bravo of the north (the Rio Grande), were dotted with presidios (military bases) and missions far more numerous than the old French trading posts along the Mississippi. The northernmost were at Santa Fe in the Sangre de Cristo Mountains, safe at about 75 miles south of the periodically rebellious Indian pueblo at Taos.

During the first years of American independence, a Franciscan priest, Junípero Serra, established a string of missions in California, the northernmost at Sonoma above San Francisco Bay. His plan, eventually fulfilled, made it possible for a foot traveler along the *camino real* (or "royal highway"—present-day California Highway 1 and U.S. Route 101) to shelter every night in a hospitable compound. As in New Mexico, a gracious but simple way of life evolved among the small numbers of *californios* who settled there.

The Santa Fe Trade

The Spanish had banned Americans from California and New Mexico. In 1821, independent Mexico abandoned the Spanish prohibitions on trade with the United States, and William Becknell, an alert entrepreneur in Independence, Missouri, immediately set off cross-country in a wagon packed with American manufactures: cloth, shoes, tools, and some luxury items. Feeling his way by compass and by dead reckoning across what is now Kansas, he blazed an 800-mile-long trail to Santa Fe. The 7,000 inhabitants were so remote from the Mexican heartland that they devoured Becknell's goods, paying him handsomely with furs and gold.

Annually for 14 years, a convoy of wagons rolled down the Santa Fe Trail. A few Missourians, such as Kentucky-born horse handler Christopher "Kit" Carson, settled in New Mexico, happily adapting to the gracious Spanish-Indian culture. Nevertheless, the presence of even a few *sassones* ("Saxons") in New Mexico forged a link between the country and the United States that was—no matter the flag that flew—more substantial than the link between Santa Fe and Mexico City.

The Great American Desert

Americans believed that the land the Santa Fe traders crossed, which was United States territory, was worthless. At about 100 degrees west longitude (central Nebraska and Kansas), the land gradually rises from an elevation of 2,000 feet to, at the base of the Rockies, 5,000 to 7,000 feet. These high plains lie in the rain shadow of the Rockies. Before the winds from the west reach the plains, the moisture in them is scooped out by the great mountains. Except for cottonwoods along the rivers, few trees grew on the plains. The vastness of the landscape unnerved Americans, who were accustomed to dense forests. When they gazed over the windblown buffalo grass, they thought not of farmland but of the ocean. The Santa Fe traders called their wagons

▲ *The "Great American Desert" was no desert. It was almost treeless, but once farmers broke the tough sod and dug wells, the eastern parts of the plains supported productive farms.*

Culver Pictures

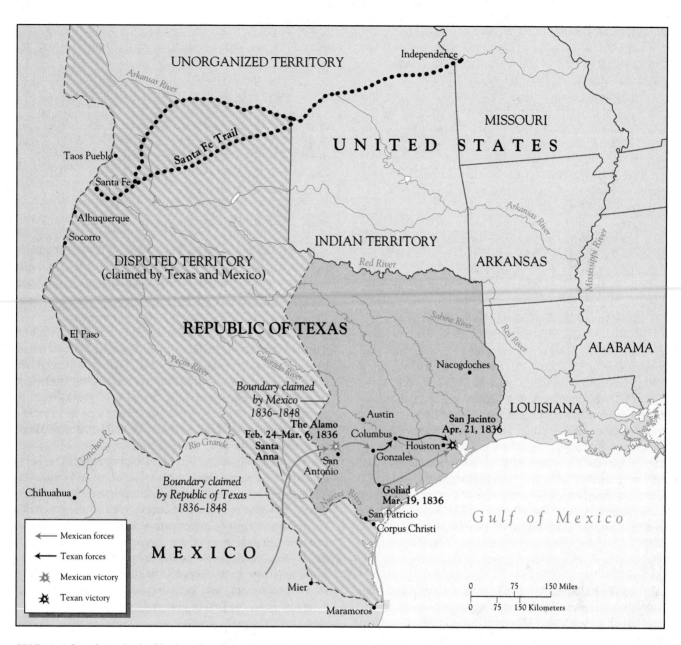

MAP 20:1 **Americans in the Mexican Borderlands, 1819–1848** The Santa Fe Trail, a commercial incursion into the Spanish borderlands, and American settlement of eastern Texas were both welcomed by the infant nation of Mexico. It was the virtual Americanization of eastern Texas that led to conflict and to the independence of Texas.

"prairie schooners." Less romantic military mapmakers labeled the country the "Great American Desert."

It was a mistake, of course, to believe that only land that grew trees naturally would support crops. However, it was true enough that the tough sod of the plains was more than a fire-tempered wood, or even cast iron, plowshare could turn over, and there was not enough rainfall to nourish grain. Travelers observed that the grass that fattened 10 million bison would fatten cattle too. However, it was difficult to imagine how such hypothetical steers might be transported to eastern markets. All agreed that the Indians of the plains, who were satisfied to exchange goods with the Santa Fe traders, were welcome to what they had.

The Texans

The Great Plains extended into Texas, a district of the Mexican state of Coahuila. There, cattle could be grazed within driving distance of the Gulf of Mexico and shipped by water to New Orleans. In 1819, a Connecticut Yankee named Moses Austin was attracted by the possibilities of a grazing economy and the suitability of eastern Texas to cotton cultivation. He proposed to the Mexicans that, in return for grants of lands, American settlers would provide a counterforce to the Comanche, raiders feared throughout the region.

Moses Austin died, but, in 1821, his son Stephen concluded the negotiations. He was licensed to settle

300 American families in Texas, each household to receive 177 acres of farmland and 13,000 acres of pastureland. The settlers would abide by Mexican law, learn the Spanish language, and observe the Roman Catholic religion.

Many of the early settlers were baptized Catholic, but most were not. Austin banned Protestant clergymen but did not force many of them to leave. Texas was far from the centers of Mexican power and culture, and the immigrants were so numerous (20,000 whites and 2,000 black slaves by 1834) that Texas was inevitably American in culture. The Texans never did bridle the Comanche (they remained free agents until the Civil War), but the Texas settlers prospered and paid taxes. Conflict was not inevitable until Mexico abolished slavery in 1829 and, in 1833, General Antonio López de Santa Anna seized power. Slavery was as vital to the economy of Texas as it was in neighboring Louisiana. Santa Anna was a less accommodating Mexican president than his predecessors had been.

Santa Anna wanted to put an end to the squabbling that had plagued Mexican politics since independence by promoting a sense of Mexican nationality. He centralized the government in a new constitution in 1835 and canceled American trading privileges in Santa Fe. Texans feared for the considerable autonomy they had enjoyed and their lucrative economic connections with the United States.

A small number of Anglo and Hispanic Texans rebelled, seizing the only military garrison in Texas, at San Antonio. At first, like the Americans of 1775, the rebels claimed that they were fighting only for the rights they had traditionally exercised. However, they had far less in common with their mother country than the rebels of 1775 had with Great Britain. Some spoke of independence from the start.

The Alamo and San Jacinto

Like George III, Santa Anna had no intention of negotiating with rebels. He welcomed the uprising in Texas as an opportunity to rally the divided Mexican people around a national cause. In 1836, he led an army of 6,000 to San Antonio, calculating he could easily defeat the 200 Texans (and a few newly arrived Americans) who were holed up in the mission compound, the Alamo (which means "cottonwood tree" in Spanish).

Among the defenders were men well known in the United States. The garrison commander was William Travis, a prominent Texan who had taken over from James Bowie, inventor of the famous double-edged knife, who was unable to rise from a sickbed. Best known in the United States was the Whig politician and humorist Davy Crockett of Tennessee, who had left the United States because of Jackson's treatment of the Cherokee.

Santa Anna could have passed the Alamo by, leaving a small detachment to contain the garrison. The real threat lay farther east, where Sam Houston, an old crony of Andrew Jackson, was frantically trying to raise an army. Houston had big problems. By no means did every Texan support the rebellion. Others, just farmers, were uneasy about confronting professional soldiers. By moving quickly, Santa Anna might easily have snuffed out the insurrection.

Instead, he sat in San Antonio for 10 days, daily more infuriated that the defenders of the Alamo, whose cause was hopeless, would not surrender. When, finally, he attacked at tremendous cost to his army, he ordered all prisoners executed. (Only a few women were spared.) Two weeks later, at Goliad, Santa Anna massacred 365 Texans who had surrendered. The atrocities rallied Texans, including many of Mexican culture, to the fight against Santa Anna.

On the banks of the Rio San Jacinto on April 21, Sam Houston's force routed the Mexican army and captured Santa Anna. In order to secure his release, Santa Anna agreed to the independence of Texas with a southern boundary at the Rio Grande rather than at the Rio Nueces, which had been the boundary of the district of Texas. As soon as he was free, Santa Anna repudiated the agreement and refused to recognize the Republic of Texas. But the demoralized Mexican army was in no condition to mount another campaign, and the Texans discreetly remained north of the Nueces.

The Lone Star Republic

In October 1836, Sam Houston was inaugurated president of a republic patterned on the United States. Texas legalized slavery and dispatched a minister to Washington, D.C. Houston hoped that his old friend Andrew Jackson would favor annexation. In his nationalistic heart, Jackson liked the idea of sewing the "lone star" of the Texas republic onto the American flag. However, Congress was embroiled in a nasty debate in which the question of slavery was being bandied about. Jackson did not want to complicate matters by proposing the admission of a new slave state. He recognized Texan independence in order to spare his successor that decision, but only on his last day in office.

President Van Buren opposed the annexation of Texas. He escaped a debate on the question when depression distracted Congress. The Texans, disappointed and worried about Mexico, looked to Europe for an ally.

Santa Anna's Legacy

Santa Anna's first presidency was ruined by Americans in Texas. However, he bore little animosity to the American people. He spent much of his exile between 1841 and 1844 in Staten Island, New York, where he helped inflict an addiction on Americans. Santa Anna chewed chicle, sap from the sapodilla tree. When, in 1844, he hurried back to Mexico, he left some in his home. The chicle fell into the hands of Thomas Adams, who, good American that he was, marketed it as an alternative to chewing tobacco, a ubiquitous habit thought filthy in polite society. Adams made a decent living from "chewing gum." It made William Wrigley Jr. rich when, in 1893, he hit on the idea of sweetening and flavoring the chicle, calling it "Juicy Fruit."

▲ *A fanciful depiction of the final moments of the defense of the Alamo. Commander Travis is at the left. The heroic figure in fringed buckskin and coonskin cap is Davy Crockett, who, if he ever wore a coon tail on his hat, did not at the Alamo. Some accounts have Crockett fighting to the end, as in this picture; some say he was shot from a distance by a sniper; yet others have him surrendering, only to be executed.*

The British were happy to oblige. They coveted Texas cotton and welcomed the opportunity to contain the expansive United States. Had the Texans not been committed to the institution of slavery, which the British had recently abolished in the empire, there might have been more than a commercial connection between the old monarchy and the new republic.

THE OREGON COUNTRY

The American government was uneasy about British influence in Texas. There was also a point of conflict between the two nations on the Pacific coast of North America in what was known as the Oregon Country. This land of mild climate, prosperous Indians, sheltered harbors, spruce and fir forests, and rich valley farmlands was not the property of

any single nation. This situation came about when two empires with claims to Oregon voluntarily withdrew.

A Distant Land

Spain's (and therefore Mexico's) claim to Oregon was never more than nominal. Spanish and Mexican influence ended just north of San Francisco, and it was nebulous there. So after 1819, when the northern boundary of Mexico was set at 42 degrees north latitude (the present California-Oregon line), the claim was itself overreaching.

The Russians had founded a string of fur-trapping stations on the Pacific coast as far south as Fort Ross, less than a hundred miles from San Francisco. However, the czars had difficulty populating Siberia. Few Russians were interested

Zorro and the Californios

Alta California—Upper California—was thinly populated when the United States seized it, but it was far from empty. Indians were more numerous in California's mild climate than in any other region except the Eastern Woodlands a century and a half earlier. Thousands of Mexicans had followed the mission fathers in the late eighteenth and early nineteenth centuries. Some of these *californios* clustered around small mercantile towns and presidios: San Diego, Los Angeles, Monterey, Yerba Buena (San Francisco), and Sonoma. Most, however, were ranchers living on vast government land grants. A few Americans and Europeans had taken out Mexican grants too.

The *californios* were rich in acres but not money. The only commodities California produced for the international market were hides and tallow, the fat of cattle and sheep cooked down for use in soap and candle manufacture. Even the richest *californios* lived in plain adobe homes of one or two stories. Furniture, iron products, and most other manufactured goods were made on the scene by Indian craftsmen. Diet was ample (plenty of beef!), but *californio* cuisine was inelegant.

Nevertheless, the *californios* at the top of the social pyramid were proud of their independence and self-sufficiency. They were hidalgos, the rightful rulers but also the benefactors of their lessers, poor Mexicans and Indians.

The *californio* community was divided down the middle by the American invasion. Some, feeling little commitment to distant Mexico, quickly made peace with the gringos and salvaged at least some of their property and social position. Others resisted and won a few small battles before being overcome.

It was less the American victory that inundated the *californios* than the great gold rush of 1849 and 1850. Spanish-speaking ranchers were literally overrun by the tens of thousands of gold seekers. Among those who were ruined was Salomon María Simeón Pico, the son of a soldier who had been granted 11 Spanish leagues (48,829 acres, 19,756 hectares) between the Tuolumne and Stanislaus Rivers. According to legend, Pico not only lost his herds and land, but his wife was raped and beaten, dying soon thereafter.

It is not possible to separate legend from fact in Pico's subsequent career. It is probable he became a masked highwayman on the *camino real* between Santa María and Santa Barbara, and may have cut an ear off each of his mostly gringo victims. (Pico, the story goes, strung his trophies and carried them on his saddle horn like a lariat.) It is less likely that he gave his loot to impoverished *californio* families, but he was a popular hero even during his lifetime. Pico moved around California with impunity for eight years, aided, no doubt, by the fact that his two brothers were the mayors of San Luis Obispo and San Jose.

Pico's most famous scrape with the law came in November 1851, when he shot the hat off the head of Los Angeles judge Benjamin Hayes. Although himself wounded, Pico escaped to Baja California where, in 1854, he was arrested by Mexican authorities and summarily executed.

In the 1920s, Pico became a popular fictional hero in the United States as Zorro ("the Fox"), a name he never used. In 1919, Johnston McCulley collected the many Pico legends, deftly adapted them for an American readership, and published them as *The Curse of Capistrano.* Pico's fictional name was Don Diego Vega, and he lived not in California's American era but earlier, when California was Mexican. His enemies were not gringos but corrupt Mexican authorities.

Don Diego was a gracious hidalgo by day who donned a mask not for the purpose of robbery but to fight for justice and something much like what was called "the American way." So admirable a gentleman could not be amputating ears. McCulley's Zorro left his trademark by cutting a Z on his victims' cheeks. Even that was too nasty for television. In the 1950s, when Zorro came into American living rooms on the small screen, he contented himself to cut Z into the bark of trees, on the sides of buildings, or (bloodlessly) on the clothing of his adversaries. Rather more remarkable, the television Zorro devoted a good deal of his time to protecting decent and well-meaning gringos from venal Mexicans.

---

in removing to permanent settlements even farther from Europe. By the 1820s, Russian trappers had looted the Pacific coves of the sea otters whose lush, warm furs had brought them there. Rather than get involved in a competition for territory they could not defend, Russia withdrew in 1825 to 54 degrees, 40 minutes north latitude, the present southern boundary of Alaska.

Between 42 degrees (the northern border of Mexico's claim) and 54 degrees, 40 minutes (the southern border of Russia's claim) lay the Oregon Country, into which some Britons and Americans had trickled. Because settlers from their nations were few in the Oregon Country, Britain and the United States easily agreed to what was called "joint occupation," putting other nations on notice that they were not welcome to snoop around.

The Mountain Men

Most of the whites in the Oregon Country were trappers in the chill creeks of the Rockies. Their prey was the beaver, prized in New York, London, and Paris both for the luxury fur and for chopping, steaming, and pressing into the best felt, a versatile fabric with a worldwide market. American and Canadian veterans of the War of 1812, the kind whose interest in home had been killed by their military experience, disappeared into the mountains for 11 months a year. The mountain men probably never numbered more than 500 in a given season. About half took Indian wives and all learned Indian ways of surviving in the ruggedest of wilderness.

At the end of each summer, the trappers brought their furs to prearranged locations on the Platte, Sweetwater, or

Big Horn Rivers. For a few weeks, buyers from the British Hudson's Bay Company and John Jacob Astor's American Fur Trading Company, mountain men, and Indians traded, drank, enjoyed a riotous orgy, and now and then bit off the ear of an old pal. Of more lasting significance was the knowledge of western geography the mountain men imparted to the folks back home, notably that although it was a long, hard trip, it was possible to cross overland to the Pacific with wagons.

Jedediah Smith opened South Pass in Wyoming, the route that would be followed by most overland emigrants. Jim Beckwourth, the son of a slave woman and a white man, discovered the pass through the Sierra Nevada that rose to the lowest elevation. Jim Bridger was a walking, talking atlas; he explored almost every nook of the Rockies. He was the first non-Indian to lay eyes on the Great Salt Lake.

The Oregon Trail

Among the first to make the six-month journey for the purpose of settling in Oregon were missionaries. In 1834, the Methodists sent Jason Lee to preach the gospel to the Indians. In 1835, four Nez Percé visited the American Board of Foreign Missions and, so the board reported, persuaded them that the gospel they wanted to hear was the Presbyterian. In 1836, Marcus and Narcissa Whitman carried it to them on foot. (The Whitmans converted a Scot, a French Canadian, and a Hawaiian, but not Indians; in 1847, Indians blamed a measles epidemic on the Whitmans and murdered them.)

The Catholic University at St. Louis sent Father Pierre-Jean de Smet to the Oregon Country.

The trek usually began at Independence, Missouri. The first great wagon train was organized there in 1843. A thousand people bound for Oregon outfitted themselves, some packing oddly chosen mementos of home: cumbersome furniture and fragile chinaware. They swore to strict rules of behavior and cooperation for the duration of the crossing and hired mountain men as guides.

The Oregon Trail crossed Kansas to the Platte River and followed that broad, shallow stream to Fort Laramie, the westernmost army outpost. The emigrants crossed the Continental Divide at South Pass and struggled through the Rockies to near the Snake River, which flows into the great Columbia and the Pacific. A wagon train covered up to 20 miles a day (or as few as none at all) depending on the terrain and the weather. At night, exhausted by the tremendous labor of moving a hundred wagons and several hundred head of cattle, horses, and mules, the emigrants drew their prairie schooners into a hollow square or circle.

The Indians of the plains and mountains did not threaten large, well-organized expeditions. Although the Indians were hardly delighted to see hordes of strangers crossing their ancestral lands (3,000 in 1845 alone), the whites were, at least, just passing through. The whites and Indians skirmished constantly with one another, but the tribes had few firearms. The Oregon-bound travelers worried less about Indian attack than about theft. Indians made a game of stealing horses that strayed too far from the caravans. They also traded with the whites and picked up the discarded trinkets that soon littered the trail. Even before the stream of wagons wore ruts into the sod and rock—which can still be seen here and there today—the Oregon Trail was marked with broken furniture, empty barrels, incapacitated wagons, the skeletons of cattle and horses, and simple grave markers. Death from accident or disease, particularly cholera, was common, but it was impossible to lose the way.

MANIFEST DESTINY

By 1845, the American population of the Columbia and Willamette Valleys had grown to 7,000. The British Hudson's Bay Company prudently moved its headquarters from the mouth of the Columbia to Vancouver Island. What is now the state of Washington was a buffer zone between British and American population centers. Still, occasional clashes threatened "joint occupation."

The Americans wanted to annex the Oregon Country to the United States. In July 1843, a group met at Champoeg and established a provisional territorial government under the American flag. A few politicians back East supported them, as much to taunt the British as for any realistic hope of affecting policy. The idea of territorial expansion was taking on a positive dignity—even, to some, the guise of a sacred duty. Increasingly, some Democratic party propagandists claimed that the United States had an obligation to increase the domain in

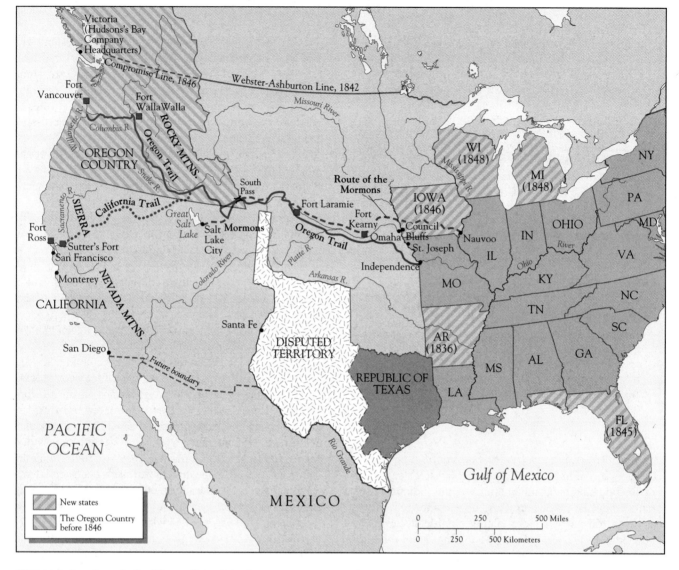

MAP 20:2 Americans in the West, 1819–1848 Britain and the United States split the Oregon Country between them in 1842, pretty much along a line reflecting the presence of the two nations. Present-day California and northern Utah were Mexican territories when Americans began to pour into the region.

which democracy and liberty held sway. It remained for a New York journalist, John O'Sullivan, to coin a phrase. It was, he said, the "manifest destiny" of the United States to expand from sea to sea.

The Texas Debate

Some southerners frankly added slavery to the list of institutions to be carried across the continent. In 1843, Secretary of State John C. Calhoun told Congress that Texas must be annexed lest growing British influence result in the abolition of slavery there. He won the support of many northern Democrats, such as Lewis Cass of Michigan, James Buchanan of Pennsylvania, and Stephen Douglas of Illinois. But, in 1844, the Senate rejected Calhoun's proposal by a two to one vote. Every Whig but one voted nay. In addition

to opposing the admission of a new slave state, most Whigs believed that absorbing Texas would almost certainly lead to a war with Mexico in which the Mexicans, not the Americans, would be in the right.

Both of the likely presidential nominees of 1844 were unhappy to see Texas shaping up as the principal issue of the campaign. Henry Clay knew that his Whig party, already strained by slavery issues, might split in two over Texas. Martin Van Buren, who commanded a majority of delegates to the Democratic nominating convention, had the same problem. The Democrats were torn between proslavery and antislavery factions. If the two old rogues took opposite stances on the question, both parties might be disarrayed. Therefore, the two men quietly met and agreed that both would oppose annexation, competing for votes on other issues.

▲ *Where the overland trail reached the Snake River, it forked—the Oregon Trail continuing along the Snake to the northwest, the California Trail branching southwest into what is now Nevada. This extraordinary photograph, with two wagon trains side by side, indicates how crowded the trail could be.*

Their bargain presented lame-duck President Tyler with an opportunity. He would be a third candidate favoring the annexation. Tyler had no party organization, so his announcement did not unduly disturb Clay and Van Buren. Then occurred one of those unlikely events that unexpectedly change the course of history. Manifest Destiny Democrats revived a neglected party rule that a presidential nominee must win the support of two-thirds of the delegates to the convention, not just a simple majority. Having declared against annexation, Van Buren was stymied. Pro-Texas Democrats numbered far more than a third of the delegates.

After eight ballots, the convention turned to a dark-horse candidate, that is, a man who was not considered a serious contender. He was James Knox Polk of Tennessee, a protégé

Show Time

During the middle years of the nineteenth century, the traveling panorama was a cheap, popular diversion. On sheets of canvas sewn end to end, painters depicted historical events or natural wonders. Paying customers walked along the tableau, sometimes with printed explanations, sometimes listening to narrators. Biblical scenes, Revolutionary War battles, and Indian massacres (and white retribution) were particularly popular.

The largest was John Banvard's "Panorama of the Mississippi," first unfurled in 1846. On canvas 12 feet high and 3 miles long (a walk of a mile and a half), Banvard depicted 1,200 miles of both banks of the Mississippi River from the mouth of the Missouri to New Orleans.

"Dark Horse"

Use of the expression "dark horse" to refer to an unexpected presidential candidate was coined by British novelist (and future prime minister) Benjamin Disraeli in *The Young Duke,* published in 1832. "A dark horse which never had been thought of," he wrote, "and which the careless St. James had never even observed in the list, rushed past the grandstand in sweeping triumph." The phrase entered racetrack lingo in the United States as well as Britain and was first applied in politics to Polk. Other dark horses elected president were James A. Garfield (1880) and Warren G. Harding (1920). Dark-horse candidates who lost were William Jennings Bryan (1896) and Wendell Willkie (1940).

▲ *A family bound overland poses, sunburned, dirty, and weary but still looking plenty tough and determined.*

of Jackson not yet 50 years old (supporters called him "Young Hickory"). Polk was a Van Buren man who personally favored annexation, a perfect compromise candidate.

The Election of 1844

"Who is Polk?" the Whigs asked scornfully when they learned who was running against their hero, Henry Clay. The sarcasm was misplaced. Polk had been governor of Tennessee and served in Congress for 14 years, several years as Speaker. His career and personality, however, were midget set beside those of Henry Clay. A frail, small man with a look of melancholy about him, Polk was priggish, sniffly disapproving of alcohol, dancing, and playing cards.

At first, Henry Clay was pleased to have Polk as his opponent. After three attempts, he would be president at last! The partyless Tyler and the colorless Polk would divide the pro-Texas vote. The anti-Texas vote, including the antislavery Democrats who would have voted for Van Buren, were his.

Then a piece of the sky fell. Tyler withdrew, and every wind brought news that manifest destiny was carrying the day. Clay began to waffle on expansion; on election day, his equivocation alienated enough anti-Texas Whigs to cost him the election. In New York State, which Polk carried (and with it, the election) by a scant 5,000 votes, long dependable Whig districts gave 16,000 votes to James G. Birney's abolitionist Liberty party. Antislavery voters cost Clay his last chance to be president.

Encouraged by the election and egged on by Calhoun, Tyler moved on the Texas question. He could not muster the two-thirds vote in the Senate that ratification of a treaty required, but he had a simple majority of both houses of Congress behind him. Three days before Polk's inauguration,

Congress approved a joint resolution annexing Texas. A few months later, the Texas Congress concurred, and Texas became the twenty-eighth state.

Polk's Promises Kept

Polk was anything but mousy. He proved to be a master politician, a shrewd diplomat, and, in terms of accomplishing what he set out to do, one of the most successful of presidents. When he took his oath of office, Polk announced he would serve only one term. During those four years, he would secure Texas to the Union; acquire New Mexico and California from Mexico; and annex as much of the Oregon Country as circumstances permitted.

Texas statehood was already in the bag. The hardworking president, who was a micromanager ("I prefer to supervise the whole operations of the government myself, rather than entrust the public business to subordinates"), immediately turned to Oregon. He embraced a chauvinistic slogan of the day: "54-40 or fight!" (referring to seizing all of the

Five States of Texas

Texas is not unique among the states because it was an independent nation before it became a state. Hawaii also was. However, by the joint resolution of the American and Texan congresses that brought Texas into the Union, Texas reserved the right to divide into five states without further congressional approval. The advisability of splitting arose periodically in Texas politics because, collectively, the states carved out of Texas would have 10 United States senators instead of 2.

▲ *Amusing in the extravagance of its imagery and symbolism today, this is a splendid representation of the exuberance of American expansion. Indians and bison flee overland emigrants in their wagon, miners, and farmers, followed by the telegraph, the overland stagecoach, and the railroad. The rider to the left of the giantess symbolizing civilization is a pony express rider.*

Oregon Country up to the southern boundary of Russian America, which was at 54 degrees, 40 minutes north latitude). This stance alarmed the British because it threatened a war neither nation wanted. Polk then presented it as a concession to Britain that he would settle for an extension of the Webster-Ashburton line, 49 degrees north latitude, as the northern boundary of American Oregon. The Oregon Country would be cut in half, with Britain retaining all of Vancouver Island. Great Britain accepted. Except for a minor adjustment of the line in the Strait of Juan de Fuca in 1872, the American-Canadian boundary was final in 1846.

Polk was candid about his designs on California and New Mexico. The United States had no legal claim in either Mexican province. Nor could Polk claim, as he could about Texas and Oregon, that California and New Mexico were peopled largely by Americans. Unassimilated gringos were few in New Mexico, and there were only about 700 Americans in California compared with 6,000 *californios*. In 1842, an American naval officer, Thomas ap Catesby Jones, somehow got it into his head that the United States was at war with Mexico and seized Monterey, the provincial capital of California. When he learned that he was mistaken, he had to run down the flag and sail off, rather the fool. But Jones was merely a few years ahead of his time. When Mexico turned down Polk's offer to buy California and New Mexico for $30 million, the president set out to take them by force.

War with Mexico

The luckless Santa Anna was back in power in Mexico City. This time, however, he moved cautiously, ordering Mexican troops not to provoke the Americans. But it was to no avail: Polk was determined to have war. He drew up an address to Congress for a declaration of war because the Mexican government owed $3 million to American banks, pretty weak stuff. Polk ordered General Zachary Taylor of Louisiana to take 1,500 men from the Nueces River in Texas to the Rio Grande. In April 1846, 16 American soldiers were killed in a skirmish with a Mexican patrol.

Affecting moral outrage, Polk rewrote his speech, declaring that because of Mexican aggression, a state of war between the two nations already existed. Constitutionally, this was nonsense; Congress alone has the power to declare war.

Gringos

The origin of the word *gringo*, once a pejorative Mexican term for Americans, now inoffensive, is obscure. One plausible theory is that it originated during the American occupation of Mexico City, when a song popular with American troops began, "Green grows the grass," which to Mexicans was gobbledygook. But they caught the first two syllables and used them to refer to the North Americans.

▲ *Neither James K. Polk nor anyone else thought Polk would ever be president, until the summer of 1844, when he was nominated by the Democratic party as a compromise candidate. Almost immediately, he excited enthusiasm because of his unabashed support for annexing Texas and the Oregon Country.*

But patriotic danders were up; both houses of Congress approved Polk's action. The Mexican army was larger than the American, but most Mexican troops were ill equipped, demoralized by endless civil war, and commanded by officers who owed their commissions to social status rather than merit. In less than two years, the Americans conquered much of the country.

In the summer of 1846, Stephen W. Kearny occupied Santa Fe without resistance. He then marched his troops to California, where he found that the Americans and a few *californio* allies already had won a nearly bloodless revolution and established the Bear Flag Republic. Kearny had only to raise the American flag and defeat a few scattered Mexican garrisons.

In September, Taylor advanced into northern Mexico, defeating Mexican armies at Matamoros and Nuevo León (also known as Monterrey). Although "Old Rough and Ready," as his men called him, showed shrewd tactical judgment, the Nuevo León garrison escaped. Polk, who disliked Taylor, used this mistake as an excuse to divert some of Taylor's troops to a command under General Winfield Scott. Nevertheless, in February 1847, Taylor became a national hero when, with his shrunken army, he was attacked at Buena Vista by Santa Anna himself and won a total victory.

The next month, March 1847, Scott landed at Vera Cruz and fought his way toward Mexico City along the ancient route of Cortés. He won a victory at Cerro Gordo and an even bigger one at Chapultepec, where he captured 3,000 men and eight generals. On September 14, 1847, Scott donned one of the gaudy uniforms he loved (his men called him "Old Fuss and Feathers") and occupied Mexico City, "the Halls of Montezuma."

By the Treaty of Guadalupe Hidalgo, signed in February 1848, Mexico ceded the Rio Grande boundary, California, and New Mexico, which included the present states of Arizona and Nevada (and the Mormon Zion in Utah). The United States paid Mexico $15 million and assumed responsibility for about $3 million that the Mexican government owed Americans. Mexico was dismembered like a carcass of beef. One-third of its territory was detached largely because the United States was strong enough to take it. Although the ineptitude of the Mexican military played a part in the national disaster, the partition of the country could not but leave a bitterness in the historical memory of the Mexican people.

The Opposition

The Mexican War was popular in the United States. The army could accept only a fraction of the young men who volunteered to fight. Most battles were American victories, and only 1,700 soldiers died in battle (11,000 soldiers, however, succumbed to disease). About 50,000 Mexicans lost their lives.

Nevertheless, the war had its critics. Many Whigs, including a young politician from Illinois named Abraham Lincoln, voted against the declaration. In New England, prominent politicians and clergymen condemned the war from platform and pulpit. Ralph Waldo Emerson and much of the Massachusetts intellectual establishment opposed it. Henry David Thoreau went to jail rather than pay a tax

▲ *General John E. Wool and his staff in Saltillo, shortly before or after the Battle of Buena Vista in 1846. This is believed to be the earliest surviving photograph of American soldiers.*

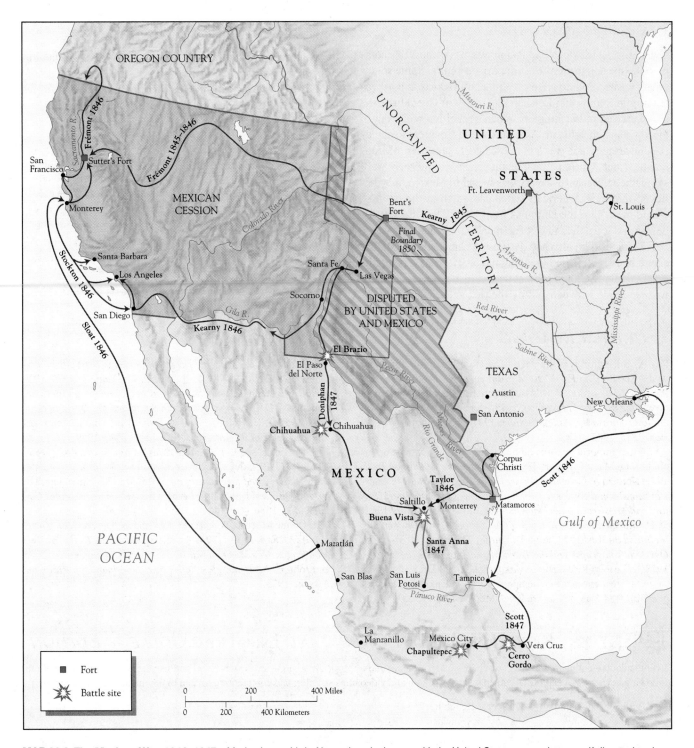

MAP 20:3 The Mexican War, 1846–1847 Mexico lost a third of its territory in the war with the United States, somewhat more if disputed territory is included.

he said would help pay for adding new slave states to the Union.

Not even the army was unanimously keen on the fight. Years later in his autobiography, then Captain Ulysses S. Grant remembered, "I was bitterly opposed to the measure, and to this day regard the war . . . as one of the most unjust ever waged by a stronger against a weaker nation. . . . Even if the annexation itself could be justified, the manner in which the . . . war was forced upon Mexico cannot."

The vote in the Senate ratifying the Treaty of Guadalupe Hidalgo was only 38 to 14. Had four senators changed their votes, the treaty would not have been approved.

Expansion Run Amok

Cynical as the Mexican acquisition was, it was moderate compared to the suggestions of some expansionists. Some southerners wanted Polk to seize even more of Mexico, and he was leaning in that direction when the Treaty of Guadalupe Hidalgo arrived in Washington. When a rebellion broke out in the Yucatán Peninsula in 1848, Polk asked Congress to authorize the army, which was still in Mexico, to take over the tropical province. Curiously, some antislavery northerners were sympathetic. Because slavery was illegal in Mexico, they believed that new American states carved from the country would come into the Union as free states. Thus did slavery obsess and warp the minds of so many Americans.

The president also had designs on Cuba, where 350,000 slaves had long excited the imagination of proslavery southerners. Polk wanted to present the Spanish government there with a choice between selling the rich sugar island or running the risk of a rebellion fomented by the United States, followed by American military intervention.

Even more bizarre was J. D. B. De Bow, an influential southern publisher. He wrote that it was the American destiny to absorb not only all of Mexico but also the West Indies, Canada, and Hawaii. And that was for appetizers. De Bow continued:

> The gates of the Chinese empire must be thrown down by the men from the Sacramento and the Oregon, and the haughty Japanese tramplers upon the cross be enlightened in the doctrines of republicanism and the ballot box. The eagle of the republic shall poise itself over the field of Waterloo, after tracing its flight among the gorges of the Himalaya or the Ural mountains, and a successor of Washington ascend the chair of universal empire.

for FURTHER READING

Ray A. Billington was the dean of western historians for many years. See his *The Far Western Frontier, 1830–1860,* 1956, and *Westward Expansion,* 1974. Also essential is Frederick Merk, *History of the Westward Movement,* 1978. More "literary" are Bernard DeVoto, *Across the Wide Missouri,* 1947, and *The Year of Decision, 1846,* 1943.

Other important works on nineteenth-century expansion include John Mack Faragher, *Women and Men on the Oregon Trail,* 1979; Norman A. Graebner, *Empire on the Pacific: A Study in American Continental Expansion,* 1955; Frederick Merk, *Manifest Destiny and Mission in American History: A Reinterpretation,* 1963; D. M. Pletcher, *The Diplomacy of Annexation: Texas, Oregon, and the Mexican War,* 1973; John D. Unruh, *The Plains Across: The Overland Emigrants and the Trans-Mississippi West, 1840–1860,* 1978; and Albert K. Weinberg, *Manifest Destiny,* 1936.

On Oregon, see the contemporary Francis Parkman, *The Oregon Trail,* 1849, as well as Frederick Merk, *The Oregon Question,* 1967, and Malcon Clark Jr., *The Eden-Seekers: The Settlement of Oregon, 1812–1862,* 1981. L. R. Duffus, *The Santa Fe Trail,* 1930, is still the standard work on that subject. On fur trappers and traders, see D. L. Morgan, *Jedediah Smith and the Opening of the West,* 1953; P. C. Phillips, *The Fur Trade,* 1961; and D. J. Wishart, *The Fur Trade of the American West, 1807–1840,* 1979.

On Texas, see E. C. Marker, *Mexico and Texas, 1821–1835,* 1928; W. C. Brinkley, *The Texas Revolution,* 1952; and Frederick Merk, *Slavery and the Annexation of Texas,* 1972. The standard biography of President Polk is Charles Sellers, *James K. Polk: Continentalist,* 1966.

On the Mexican War, see K. Jack Bauer, *The Mexican-American War, 1846–1848,* 1974; Robert W. Johnson, *To the Halls of Montezuma: The Mexican War in the American Imagination,* 1985; and John H. Schroeder, *Mr. Polk's War: American Opposition and Dissent,* 1973.

  ## AMERICAN JOURNEY ONLINE AND INFOTRAC COLLEGE EDITION

Visit the source collections at http://ajaccess.wadsworth.com and http://infotrac.thomsonlearning.com, and use the Search function with the following key terms to explore documents, images, audio and video clips, articles, and commentary related to the material in this chapter:

Battle of the Alamo   Texas Republic
Manifest Destiny   Zachary Taylor

Additional resources, exercises, and Internet links related to this chapter are available on *The American Past* Web site: http://history.wadsworth.com/americanpast7e.

HISTORY ONLINE

Mountain Men and the Fur Trade
www.xmission.com/~drudy/amm.html
Text, images, sources, and links for the mountain men.

Alamo History
http://drtl.org/History/index.asp
A detailed chronology of the mission compound that became the sacred icon of Texas.

APPLES OF DISCORD

The Poisoned Fruits of Victory 1844–1854

North Wind Picture Archives

The United States will conquer Mexico, but it will be as the man who swallows the arsenic which brings him down in turn.

Ralph Waldo Emerson

T HE VICTORY CELEBRATION was a short one. Even before the Treaty of Guadalupe Hidalgo officially transferred title of California and New Mexico to the United States, the fruits of the Mexican War proved to be apples of discord, setting northerners against southerners as bitterly as the goddesses of Greek mythology scrambled after the prize apple thrown in their midst. That was a golden apple. It was gold that inaugurated the sectional conflict of the 1850s too.

THE SECTIONAL SPLIT

Slavery was, of course, the subject of acrimonious conflict before the Mexican War. Since the 1830s, abolitionists and the defenders of slavery had hurled antagonistic, often vicious, anathemas at one another. Before the Mexican War, the debate had been between zealots and, at best, at the periphery of national politics. Most politicians of the generation of Jackson, Benton, Clay, and Webster recognized the question of slavery's morality as dangerous. They invariably tried to avoid or quash political debates in which the morality of the "peculiar institution" was at the center.

Dead Letter

It was not easy. There were extreme abolitionists in Congress and proslavery fanatics too, as prominent as John C. Calhoun. Thomas Hart Benton was so disgusted by their gratuitous injections of the slavery issue into Senate debates that he likened it to the biblical visitation of plagues on Pharaoh's Egypt:

> You could not look on the table but there were frogs. You could not sit down at the banquet table but there were frogs, you could not go to the bridal couch and lift the sheets but there were frogs! We can see nothing, touch nothing, have no measures proposed, without having this pestilence thrust before us.

Benton was himself a slave owner, although far from hysterical in his justification of the institution. His daughter married a prominent antislavery politician, again not an extremist, John C. Frémont. Benton was disgusted by politicians obsessed by slavery because, a practical man, he knew there were few points at which Congress had the authority to touch the institution of slavery. The Constitution defined slavery as a domestic institution of the states. Short of a constitutional amendment abolishing the institution, slavery was the business of state governments.

An amendment abolishing slavery was out of the question. Three-fourths of the states must agree to any change in the Constitution. During the first half of the nineteenth century, slave states were equal in number to free states. Indeed, when war was declared on Mexico in May 1846, 15 of the 28 states were slave states. Preserving slavery at home, southern state legislatures were, of course, not going to consider abolishing slavery nationally.

Small Steps Toward Abolition

The Constitution did empower Congress "to exercise exclusive legislation in all cases whatsoever" over the District of Columbia. So abolitionist congressmen regularly called for the prohibition of slaveholding in Washington or, at least, a ban on the buying and selling of slaves in the capital. Curiously, some moderate southerners were open to the latter proposal for cosmetic reasons. Slave auctions were ugly. Why put them on view in a city which almost all foreign tourists visited?

Congress also had the power to legislate concerning slaves who ran away from their masters and crossed state lines. The Fugitive Slave Act of 1793 provided that such runaways be returned to their owners. (The law was evaded or obstructed in states where antislavery sentiment was strong, and not vigorously enforced by federal officials there.) Some antislavery northern congressmen wanted to use the Constitution's interstate commerce provisions to prohibit the sale of slaves from one state to another. Southern hotheads proposed reopening the African slave trade, which Congress had the authority to do, as Congress had abolished it. President Polk had so sorely wanted to acquire Cuba because, under the American flag, Cuba would be a treasure house of slaves for sale.

These possibilities aroused the passions of extremists on both sides and vexed the moderates who wanted to keep the slavery issue off center stage. To a large extent, they succeeded—before the Mexican War.

Slavery and the Territories

Congress unambiguously had the power to legislate in regard to slavery in the territories. The Confederation Congress did just that when, in the Northwest Ordinance, it forbade slavery north of the Ohio River. The Constitutional Congress settled the issue of slavery in the Louisiana Purchase lands in the Missouri Compromise.

The Missouri Compromise was the salvation of moderate politicians who wanted to keep the subject of slavery off the floor of Congress. The Missouri bill permitted slavery in territories south of 36 degrees, 30 minutes north latitude, prohibiting it north of that line. After Arkansas was admitted as a slave state in 1836, the only territory in which slaves could legally be owned was Indian Territory (Oklahoma). In the rest of the Louisiana Purchase, slavery was "forever prohibited." There would be no more new slave states.

Then came the annexation of Texas (a slave state), Oregon, and the Mexican territories: The Missouri Compromise line did not apply to those lands. Many antislavery northerners opposed annexing Texas because it added a slave state in violation of the promise of the compromise of 1820. Proslavery southerners were keen on war with Mexico because they looked forward to new territories into which slavery could legally expand.

The Wilmot Proviso and Free Soil Party

Determined to prevent the spread of slavery into newly acquired territory, in 1846, Congressman David Wilmot of Pennsylvania attached a rider, the Wilmot Proviso, to several bills appropriating money to fight the war. The Wilmot Proviso declared that "neither slavery nor involuntary servitude shall ever exist" in any lands taken from Mexico. The House of Representatives approved the proviso in 50 bills between 1846 and 1850. Every northern Whig and all but four northern Democrats voted for it in 1846. Every northern state legislature except New Jersey's officially endorsed it. It was not that so many people were abolitionists. Only a minority of Americans were. However, like Thomas Jefferson in draft-

---

Riders

In the process of lawmaking, a *rider* is a clause, usually dealing with an unrelated matter, that is attached to a bill already under consideration in Congress or in a state assembly. The strategy of those who propose riders is to turn them into law despite considerable opposition. That is, opponents will so badly want the bill to which the rider is attached that they will pass it even with the objectionable rider. Wilmot tried to attach his antislavery rider to essential appropriations. Only because the anti-Wilmot forces in the Senate were strong enough to strike it did the Wilmot Proviso fail.

The Berrien Proviso

Another rider to a legislative bill of the era, proposed in February 1847 by Senator John M. Berrien, was less successful than David Wilmot's. The Berrien Proviso proposed that "the true intent of Congress in making this appropriation [for the army is] that the war with Mexico ought not to be prosecuted by this Government with any view to the dismemberment of that republic." Even in the northern states, Berrien's anti-expansionism was unacceptable.

ing the Northwest Ordinance, the majority clearly believed that the West should be reserved for family farmers. "Slavocrats" (the planter aristocracy) had to be kept out.

The Wilmot Proviso never became law. John C. Calhoun (naturally) led the fight against it in the Senate. The Constitution, he said, guaranteed to the citizens of all states who emigrated to the territories the same rights they had enjoyed at home. The citizens of some states could own slaves. Therefore, they had the right to take their slaves with them if they went west.

Slave state senators were equal in number (superior in a few Congresses) to free state senators. With the help of a few northern Democrats, the Senate deleted the Wilmot Proviso from every bill to which the House attached it.

When President Polk endorsed Calhoun's reasoning, a large number of northern Democrats bolted from the party and organized the Free Soil party. Some were abolitionists, but by no means all. As a party, the Free Soilers allowed that the people of the South had the constitutional right to preserve slavery at home. Most Free Soilers cared little about the injustice and suffering of African Americans. Some were vociferous racists who wanted to exclude blacks as well as slaves. There was a streak of racism in the rhetoric of many of them; a few wanted to ban free blacks as well as slaves from the western territories. (As late as 1857, Oregon prohibited the emigration of free blacks into the state.)

However, they insisted that the Mexican acquisition must be dedicated to, as their party slogan said, "Free soil! Free speech! Free men!"

The Election of 1848

Polk, as he had promised, did not stand for reelection in 1848. A hard worker, he literally wore himself out and died, at age 54, four months after leaving the White House. The Democrats nominated one of his northern supporters, the competent but gloriously dull Lewis Cass of Michigan. The Whigs, having lost once again with Clay in 1844, returned to the winning formula of 1840—a popular general whose views were unknown. They nominated the hero of Buena Vista, Zachary Taylor of Louisiana. Taylor was a southerner who owned a great many slaves. Whig strategists gambled that he would carry southern states that would otherwise be lost to the Democrats because of northern Whig support of the Wilmot Proviso.

Junk Mail
Had the leaders of the Whig party been up-to-date in 1848, they might have spared themselves the embarrassment of having Zachary Taylor refuse to pay the postage due on the letter notifying him of his presidential nomination. The previous year, 1847, the United States Post Office had begun to issue stamps that permitted the sender to pay the postage. Apparently, the idea had not yet caught on.

Taylor was a remarkable presidential candidate. "He really is a most simple-minded old man," said Whig educator Horace Mann. "Few men have ever had more contempt for learning," wrote General Winfield Scott. "He doesn't know himself from a side of sole leather in the way of statesmanship," wrote Horace Greeley. A coarse, cranky, and blunt-spoken old geezer of 64, Taylor admitted he had never bothered to vote in his life. When the letter from the Whig party announcing his nomination arrived, he refused to pay the postage due on it. When someone else did, he responded diffidently, "I will not say I will not serve if the good people were imprudent enough to elect me."

The Free Soilers put up a more distinguished and able candidate than either major party, former president Martin Van Buren. Along in years, he had announced his opposition to slavery in the territories. Little Van did not have a chance, but his name on the ballot determined the election. He won more votes in New York than Lewis Cass did, thus throwing the state's 36 electoral votes to Taylor. With New York State, as so many times, went the election.

THE CALIFORNIA CRISIS

Moderate Whigs hoped that Taylor's victory would cool southern passions aroused by the Wilmot Proviso and Free Soilers, allowing the party to use the power of government to promote orderly economic development and moral behavior nationally. But Old Rough and Ready was to know little harmony as president. Events in distant California, un-

No-Name City
In the national capital in 1850, California meant sectional crisis. However, when the first California legislature met, the delegates were more interested in making some citizens feel comfortable in the new state. The first law enacted by the legislature reduced the statute of limitations so that Californians with perhaps murky pasts back East could not easily be extradited. The second enactment made it easier for an individual to change his name.

The Gold Rush That Wasn't
In 1844, four years before Marshall's discovery, Pablo Gutiérrez discovered gold in the bed of the Bear River and immediately secured a land grant of 22,000 acres that included what he hoped would be a rich mine. When he went to Sutter's fort in Sacramento to buy mining equipment, Sutter was preoccupied with agitation and revolt near Monterey. He sent Gutiérrez there to learn what was happening, and Gutiérrez was killed by the rebels. The gold fever of 1844 died with him. His Bear River grant was sold to William Johnson, who knew nothing of Gutiérrez's gold. The Bear River was overrun in 1849 and 1850 by miners who ignored Mexican land grants, and the deposit was rediscovered.

▲ *Placer miners at Spanish Flat, California. They are using a long tom, shoveling gravel into a box through which a constant stream of water is being sluiced. With luck, there would be several ounces of gold dust in the bottom of the long tom when the sun went down. Note the rocks at the feet of the miner on the right. They were picked out of the gravel by hand.*

folding even as he was nominated and elected, caused a crisis that almost destroyed the Union in 1850.

Gold!

On the evening of January 24, 1848, a carpenter, James Marshall, took a walk along the American River where it tumbles through the foothills of the Sierra Nevada. Marshall worked for John Augustus Sutter, a Swiss adventurer who had turned a vast Mexican land grant into a feudal domain. Sutter's castle was an adobe fort on the Sacramento River, defended by cannon he had purchased from the Russians when they abandoned Fort Ross.

Marshall was building a sawmill for Sutter. Inspecting the tail race—the ditch that returned rushing water to the river after it powered the mill—he picked up a curious metallic stone. "Boys," he told the other workers, "I think I have found a gold mine."

He had, and that was that for the sawmill. Sutter's employees immediately set to shoveling gravel from the river, separating the sand and silt from what proved to be plenty of gold dust and nuggets. Briefly, Marshall's discovery was

the end of San Francisco. A town of 500 souls, it was depopulated when "everyone," including the recently arrived American military garrison, headed for the hills.

The next year—1849—80,000 people descended on California. By the end of the year, the population was about 100,000, more than in the states of Delaware and Florida. These "forty-niners" produced $10 million in gold. Californians said, plausibly enough, that their numbers and value to the nation merited immediate statehood. When Congress convened in December 1849, California's provisional constitution was on the table. In the would-be state of California, slavery was forbidden.

Trauma

The stunning rapidity of these events lay at the heart of the crisis that ensued. Polk and proslavery southerners assumed that California would be peopled slowly by, among others, southern slave owners and their slaves. When, years down the line, it was time to create a state on the Pacific, at least part of California would apply for admission as a slave state.

Now, before the Treaty of Guadalupe Hidalgo was ratified, before California was organized as a territory—work Congress expected to be doing in 1850—proslavery southerners saw their reasonable expectations pulverized by California's application for admission as a free state. The worst of it was that California statehood would mean the South's loss of equality with the northern states in the Senate. There were two more embryonic free states, Oregon and Minnesota, waiting in the wings but not a single potential slave state in sight.

Southerners were already a minority in the House of Representatives, where seats are apportioned according to population. In 1849, there were about 9 million people in the South and 14 million in the North (thus the repeated approval of the Wilmot Proviso in the House). The Senate, therefore, where each state had two members regardless of population, had assumed sacred significance to Calhoun and his like. A majority of southern congressmen immediately declared they would vote against California statehood. The North's toleration of abolitionists, they said, made it impossible for the South to trust in the goodwill of any northern senators. The South must have equality in the Senate.

Henry Clay's Last Stand

To the surprise of some, the southern intransigents discovered that President Taylor was not on their side. He would take up arms to defend his right to his hundred slaves, Taylor said, but he was a nationalist. National pride, prosperity, and security demanded that California be admitted immediately, no strings attached. He further angered southern extremists with his decision that a boundary dispute between slave state Texas and New Mexico Territory be resolved in favor of New Mexico.

How They Mined the Gold

Few American forty-niners knew even the rudiments of gold mining. Only the Mexicans, called "Sonorans" in California after the Mexican state from which most came, and the Cornish from southwestern England had been miners before they came to the gold fields. However, technological innocence was no great handicap because placer mining—recovering pure gold from the sand and gravel of creek beds—called for backbreaking toil but was quite a simple operation.

Placer mining is a mechanical process. To determine whether there was gold in a creek, a miner "panned" it. That is, he scooped up a pound or two of silt, sand, and pebbles in a sturdy, shallow pan; removed the stones by hand; and then agitated the finer contents, constantly replenishing the water in the pan so that the lighter mud and sand washed over the sides while the heavier gold dust remained.

When miners discovered enough "color" to warrant mining of a placer, they staked a claim and built a "rocker" or a "long tom," two easily constructed devices that performed the washing process on a larger scale.

The rocker was a watertight wooden box, three to five feet long and a foot or so across. It was mounted on a base like that of a rocking chair so that it could be tipped from side to side. In the bottom of the box were wooden riffles or a sheet of corrugated metal, and sometimes a fine wire mesh. These simulated the crevices in a creek bed, where the gold naturally collected. Into the rocker, by means of a sluice, also easily built, ran a stream of water. While one partner shoveled gravel and sand into the box, another rocked it and agitated the contents with a spade or a pitchfork. The lighter worthless mineral washed out (stones, again, were manually discarded), and the gold remained at the bottom to be retrieved at the end of the day, weighed, divided, and cached.

The long tom took more time to build, but it was more productive. In effect, the water-bearing sluice was extended into a long, high-sided, watertight box with riffles in the bottom. With a long tom, all the miners in a partnership could shovel gravel: no rocking.

The placer mines were known as the "poor man's diggings" because placer mining neither required much money nor gave the man with capital any advantage. The placer miner needed only a few tools and materials. Because just about everyone in California hoped to strike it rich, few were willing to work for set wages, no matter how high. The lucky discoverer of a valuable gold deposit had to take on partners if he wanted to work it efficiently.

As long as the "poor man's diggings" held out, life in the mining camps was highly democratic and egalitarian. No one was allowed to stake a claim larger than he and his partners could mine within a season or two. Law and order in the earliest mining camps was maintained by the informal common consent of the men who lived in them. Except for small military units that were plagued with desertion, there was no formal legal authority in California until late 1850 and no significant governmental presence in many of the gold fields for several years thereafter.

Not all the fruits of democracy were edifying. A man with the majority of a camp behind him could "get away with murder." Miner democracy did not extend to other than native-born Americans and immigrants from western Europe. Despite the fact that the forty-niners learned what they knew of mining from the Sonorans, they expelled the Sonorans from all but the southernmost gold fields within a year. Chileans, being Spanish speakers, came up against prejudice.

Worst treated of all were the Chinese. Because their culture was so alien and because they worked in large groups, thus spending less to live, the Chinese frightened the forty-niners. They feared that the "Celestials," as the Chinese were called, would drag down the standard of living for all. Chinese miners survived only by working deposits abandoned by white and a few African American miners as too poor. Most of the Chinese who came to the "Golden Mountain" to mine drifted into California's towns and cities and settled for other jobs.

Tempers were boiling. The election of a Speaker of the House, usually a formality, required 63 ballots. In the Senate, Henry Clay, frail and weary at 72, beyond all hope of being president, tried to cap his career as the Great Compromiser by proposing a permanent solution to the question of slavery in the territories.

Clay's Omnibus Bill was a compromise in the old tradition. It required both sides to make significant concessions in the interests of the common good, the Union. California would be admitted as a free state. The rest of the Mexican acquisition would be organized as territories with no reference to the status of slavery there. Clay meant to hold out to proslavery southerners the possibility of future slave states in what is now Utah, Nevada, New Mexico, and Arizona. Texas's border dispute with New Mexico would be resolved

as Taylor had announced (Clay certainly needed the president's blessing) but with face-saving concessions to Texas, including Congress's assumption of the state's large debts.

Clay appealed to the antislavery feelings of many northerners by proposing the abolition of the slave trade in the national capital. To compensate southerners for this symbolic rebuff, Clay included a new, stronger Fugitive Slave Act in the Omnibus Bill.

Failure

Not too many years earlier, the Omnibus Bill would have sailed through Congress amid cheers, tossed hats, and invitations to share a bottle. Texas and California changed all that. Extremists from both sections, and some congressmen

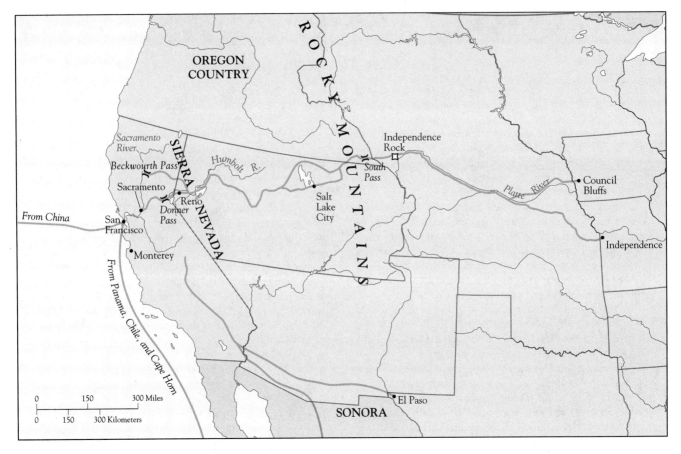

MAP 21:1 **The Gold Rush**   The route of the forty-niners was long known by mountain men, but it became a highway (some wagon wheel ruts are still visible today) only with the Gold Rush.

regarded as moderates, refused to accept the Omnibus Bill because it included concessions they regarded as morally reprehensible.

Many northerners, not just abolitionists, abhorred the Fugitive Slave Act. By allowing federal officials to arrest people who committed no crime under the laws of their states, it made slavery quasi-legal everywhere. Southern extremists could not vote to abolish the slave trade in Washington, D.C. Slavery was a positive good; they would not apologize for any aspect of it. President Taylor's friends in Congress resented compensating Texas in any way.

The spirit of compromise was dead. New York's William H. Seward called the very idea of compromise "radically wrong and essentially vicious." "Fire-eaters," militantly proslavery young southern congressmen, swore to yield nothing. John C. Calhoun, once master of cool reason and cold logic, was reduced to the sophistry of a cynical lawyer. Obsessed with his goal—the expansion of slavery and southern political power—he devised convoluted, sometimes crazy, schemes to reach it. Calhoun proposed that there should be two presidents, one from the North and one from the South, each with the power of veto over congressional acts and one another. The pathetic old man spent his last

days, dying painfully of throat cancer, surrounded by a gaggle of romantic young disciples who had, among them, half the brain he'd once had in his head.

Henry Clay plugged away among those he thought were moderates, mustering his eloquence one last time. "I have heard something said about allegiance to the South," he told the Senate. "I know no South, no North, no East, no West, to which I owe any allegiance. The Union, sir, is my country."

Because his terminal disease left him almost voiceless, Calhoun's answer had to be read for him. He was equally eloquent and more realistic about the crisis than Clay: "The cry of 'Union, Union, the glorious Union!' can no more prevent disunion than the cry of 'Health, health, glorious health!' . . . can save a patient lying dangerously ill."

Daniel Webster, the last of the Senate's aged triumvirate, had his last word too. It ranked with his greatest orations, and it destroyed him politically. Webster supported the Omnibus Bill. To save the Union, he said, he would vote even for the fugitive slave law in Clay's proposal. Webster was vilified in New England. Nothing better illustrates what the embrace of extremism does to people than the fact that New Englanders who had winked for decades at Webster's personal debauchery and panhandling of bankers now de-

MAP 21:2 Gold Rush California The gold camps (many of them actually sizable towns) were located on the western foothills of the Sierra Nevada. They were supplied through San Francisco and river towns like Marysville, Sacramento, and Stockton.

nounced him to hell for advocating compromise in a crisis that was tearing the Union apart. "The word 'honor' in the mouth of Mr. Webster," wrote Ralph Waldo Emerson, "is like the word 'love' in the mouth of a whore."

THE COMPROMISE OF 1850

The Omnibus Bill was voted down. No matter—President Taylor would have vetoed it. Stubborn and willful, Taylor was set against compensating Texas for land to which, in his view, the state had no claim. It was the most innocuous part of the Omnibus Bill. By gagging on it, Taylor demonstrated that he was no politician.

Clay left Washington, confounded and without hope. In the meantime, however, fate intervened to save his cause and to bring to the fore a resourceful young senator who would be as central in the Senate of his era as Clay was in his own.

Death of a Soldier

Zachary Taylor exited. On July 4, 1850, the president attended a ceremony on the Capitol mall where, for two hours, he sat hatless in the blazing sun listening to long-winded orators. Back at the White House, he wolfed down cherries and cucumbers and several quarts of chilled milk and ice water. A few hours later the old man took to bed with stomach cramps. Instead of leaving him alone, his doctors bled him and administered one powerful medicine after another— ipecac to make him vomit, quinine for his fever, calomel as a laxative, and opium for the pain to which they were adding. Old Rough and Ready was murder on Mexicans and Texans, but he could not handle the pharmacopeia of the nineteenth century. He died on July 9 and was succeeded by Vice President Millard Fillmore.

Fillmore is often ridiculed as the least memorable president. A New Yorker, he had flirted with radical politics early in his career. But in 1850 he was firmly within the moderate Whig camp of Clay and Webster. Although he did not declare publicly for compromise, it was generally thought he favored it.

The "Little Giant"

The senator who broke the impasse was Stephen A. Douglas of Illinois. Barely five feet in height, he was known as the "Little Giant" because of his oratorical powers and his role as tactical mastermind of the Illinois Democratic party. Only three years a senator, Douglas had mobilized contacts among both northern and southern Democrats, and he had an idea.

Instead of presenting the polarized House and Senate with a single compromise bill, parts of which offended everyone, Douglas carved Clay's package into separate bills. These he maneuvered individually through Congress by patching together a different majority for each.

Thus, Douglas could count on northern senators and representatives of both parties to vote for California statehood and the abolition of the slave trade in the District of Columbia. In the House, that was enough. In the Senate, he won the votes of just enough southern moderates from the border states to slip the bills through. He could count on a solid southern bloc for the Fugitive Slave Act and the Texas bills. To this, arguing for the necessity of preserving the Democratic party in both sections, he added enough northern Democratic votes to make a majority.

The "Compromise of 1850" was not a compromise in the sense that both sides gave a little and took a little. A majority of both northern and southern congressmen refused to yield an inch. Only four of 60 senators voted for all of Douglas's bills! Only 11 voted for five of the six bills. (Even Douglas was absent for the vote on the Fugitive Slave Act.) Only 28 of 240 representatives voted for all of the bills.

Douglas's manipulations were brilliant. He made extremely controversial bills into laws when a tiny handful of his colleagues were truly committed to the spirit of compromise. His success was popular in the nation at large, where moderation on sectional questions was probably stronger than it was under the Capitol dome. But Douglas did not extinguish the fires of sectional hostility smoldering in both Congress and the country.

▲ *The great debate of 1850. Henry Clay is making his eloquent plea for compromise in the cause of the Union. John C. Calhoun, accurately depicted as near death, is the third senator from the right. Daniel Webster, seated at the left, head in hand, would soon speak magnificently in support of Clay and be disgraced in Massachusetts.*

The Old Guard

In the Thirty-First Congress of 1849–1851, the nation's second generation of political leaders, those who had governed the country since the passing of the Founding Fathers, rubbed elbows with a third generation, a new breed. Andrew Jackson was already gone, dead in 1845. Henry Clay and Daniel Webster both passed on in 1852. Thomas Hart Benton survived until 1858, but only to discover that the new era had no place for him. Because he refused to defend slavery as a positive good and, like Webster, placed the Union above sectional prejudices, he lost his Senate seat in 1850, was defeated in a race for the House in 1856, and lost when he ran for governor of Missouri.

Calhoun would have won election after election in South Carolina had he lived to be a hundred. Alone of the giants of the Age of Jackson, he made the transition—indeed, led the transition—from commitment to Union to extreme southern sectionalism. But Calhoun did not survive to see the results of his unhappy career. He died before Douglas performed his political wizardry.

Extremists and Moderates

Shortly before his death, Calhoun croaked to one of his disciples that it was up to the young to save "the South, the poor South." With each year of the new decade, such "fire-eaters,"

so called because of the invective with which they spoke of northerners, displaced moderates in southern state legislatures, governorships, the House, and the Senate.

The southern Whig party, the refuge of moderates, dwindled. John Tyler had already led the states' rights Whigs back to the Democratic party. Compromise-minded southern Whigs left politics or, as in the case of Robert Toombs of Georgia, embraced southern extremism. Robert Toombs supported the Compromise of 1850, but within a few years, he was baiting northerners in language as torrid as any Democrat's. A few old southern Whigs were so respected as individuals that they continued to win elections under the party label or while voicing Whig principles as independents. Most of them were from the Upper South, states where the fanatical proslavery spirit burned less brightly.

In the North, abolitionists were proportionately less powerful than the fire-eaters in the South. Abolitionism remained unpopular with the majority of northerners, in part because northern whites shared the racism of southerners, in part because of the self-righteousness of some antislavery crusaders.

Nevertheless, there was a militant antislavery delegation in Congress. Among the ablest was William H. Seward of New York, a former Anti-Mason. Thaddeus Stevens of Pennsylvania was a rare, staunch believer in racial equality whom southerners hated above all other abolitionists. Charles Sumner of Massachusetts succeeded Webster as New England's

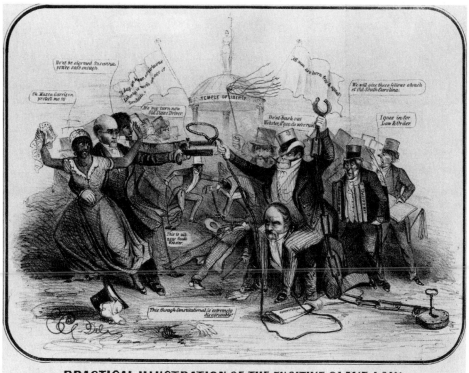

PRACTICAL ILLUSTRATION OF THE FUGITIVE SLAVE LAW.

▲ *An antislavery cartoon attacking the Fugitive Slave Act of 1850. Abolitionist William Lloyd Garrison is protecting the runaway slave woman at left (with a gun, which is curious, for Garrison was a pacifist). Daniel Webster, who voted for the law, is the mount for a stereotypical Irishman (most Irish voters were Democrats friendly to slavery) bearing chains for the woman and a noose for Garrison.*

most prominent senator. Some of the antislavery congressmen, like Salmon B. Chase of Ohio, were Free Soilers. Most were Whigs.

With the Free Soilers gone from the party, most northern Democrats were friendly to southern demands and to slavery. A few Democrats preached positive-good propaganda with the best of them. Others, notably Douglas, resembled the northern Democrats of the Age of Jackson. By no means did they look on slavery as a desirable institution. But their sensibilities were not outraged by its existence in the South. For the sake of Democratic party unity, they were willing to tolerate the spread of the institution into the territories. Northern Democrats considered themselves moderates.

THE KANSAS-NEBRASKA ACT

The United States needed a compelling, even charismatic, president committed to preserving the Union. Instead, in 1852, it got Franklin Pierce. Pierce was handsome, amiable, a good speaker, and popular both in New Hampshire and in Congress, where he served between 1833 and 1847. He left the Senate to serve in the Mexican War, then returned to New Hampshire to practice law.

Then, in 1852, the Democratic party, now tightly cinched to the two-thirds rule, deadlocked for 48 ballots. A compromise candidate, acceptable to both northern and southern

Democrats was needed. None could be found in public office. The convention turned to private citizen Pierce.

Pierce won a narrow popular vote victory over Whig candidate General Winfield Scott, but he nearly swept the electoral college. It was all a terrible mistake. As a fellow New Hampshireman commented, "Up here, where everybody knows Frank Pierce, he's a pretty considerable fellow. But come to spread him out over the whole country, I'm afraid he'll be dreadful thin in some places."

Pierce's wife, to whom he was devoted, wanted nothing to do with politics or Washington, D.C. She was an emotionally fragile woman who was completely shattered when, just before Pierce's inauguration, their young son was killed in a railroad accident. Preoccupied with his wife's distraction, Pierce leaned heavily on his personal friend, whom he named secretary of war, Jefferson Davis of Mississippi.

A Railroad to California

Davis was staunchly proslavery but not a fire-eater. With presidential ambitions of his own, he wanted to persuade northern Democrats that he was a nationally minded man, while retaining his southern political base. Of modest background—Davis was born in a log cabin in Kentucky—he looked like an aristocrat. Indeed, his brother, Joseph Davis, was one of Mississippi's richest cotton planters, and a model paternalistic slave owner.

Stephen Douglas, the "Little Giant," was too clever and manipulative a politician for his own good. He masterminded the intricate tactics that enacted the Compromise of 1850 when Henry Clay failed. Douglas also devised and passed the Kansas-Nebraska Act in the face of the opposition of a majority of northerners.

Already nationally celebrated for his bravery as an officer in the Mexican War, Davis, with the total support of the distracted Pierce, tried to revive the expansionism of the 1840s with unsuccessful attempts to annex Hawaii and Cuba. (Cuba, with its many slaves, figured prominently in southern imaginations.) He tacitly supported American filibusters, freelance adventurers, mostly southerners, who led private armies into unstable Central America in the hopes of creating personal empires.

Davis's most important project was the construction of a transcontinental railroad tying California to the old states. Everyone knew that the railroad would eventually be built. Davis wanted its eastern terminus in the South, knowing that the California trade would enrich the city that was the eastern gateway of the line. From an engineer's point of view, the best route was through Texas and along the southern boundary of the country. There were no mountains of consequence on the route until the projected railroad reached the southern New Mexico Territory, just above the Gila River. There, in order to keep the projected railroad line on the flat, it would be necessary to build in Mexico, which was unacceptable.

To remedy the problem, Davis and Pierce sent James Gadsden, a railroad man, to Mexico City. For $10 million, he purchased a 30,000-square-mile triangle of arid but level

Anthony Burns

Anthony Burns, a slave, fled Virginia for Boston in 1854. He was arrested under the Fugitive Slave Act of 1850, and a furious mob of abolitionists almost freed him. Federal troops had to be brought in to guard him and return him to his owner. In Virginia, Burns was immediately sold for $900, a very low price for a 20-year-old "prime field hand." But Burns was intelligent, self-educated, literate, and obviously determined to be free.

For northerners, the Burns case symbolized the determination of slavocrats to force slavery down their throats in the heart of New England. Bostonians raised the money to buy his freedom and sent him to Oberlin College.

Burns was a symbol for southern fire-eaters too. They rejoiced at his return to slavery. A few southerners had cooler heads. It had cost $100,000 to return one man to slavery. "A few more such victories and the South is undone," wrote the Richmond *Enquirer*.

© Corbis

land. Davis, it appeared, had plucked a juicy plum for the South that would also be a great national enterprise, big enough, perhaps, to make its chief proponent president.

Douglas's Scheme

Stephen Douglas thought so too, and he wanted the transcontinental railroad for Chicago. However, the so-called Central Route not only crossed several major mountain ranges, beyond Missouri's western border, it ran through unorganized territory, parts of the Louisiana Purchase left to the Indians. The only federal presence was a series of forts monitoring the Indians and protecting the overland trail. Southern politicians could kill the Central Route, and win the transcontinental for the South, by refusing to organize territorial governments west of Missouri.

As ingenious as he had been in 1850, Douglas came up with a scheme for seducing the southerners by offering them the possibility of spreading slavery to lands where it was forbidden by the Missouri Compromise.

In May 1854, Douglas introduced a bill to organize two new federal territories, Kansas and Nebraska. The bill explicitly repealed the section of the Missouri Compromise that prohibited slavery there. Instead, the people of the Kansas and Nebraska territories would decide for themselves whether they would allow or prohibit the institution. "Popular sovereignty," Douglas said, was the democratic solution to the problem of slavery in the territories.

Southern congressmen jumped for the bait like trout after a bad winter. None had illusions about Nebraska, through which the Central Route would run. It bordered on the free state of Iowa and would inevitably be populated by antislavery northerners. Kansas, however, abutted on Missouri, where slavery was unimportant economically but an emotionally passionate issue, even with poor whites who owned no slaves.

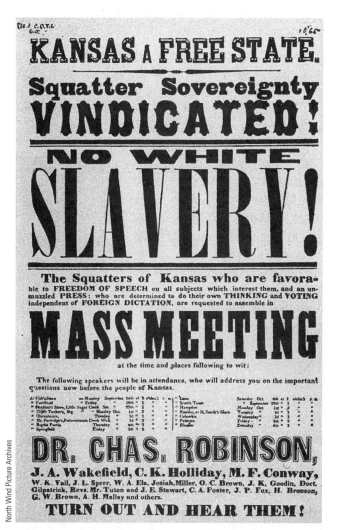

▲ *A poster announcing a rally against the Kansas-Nebraska Act. There were thousands of such meetings all over the North within weeks of Congress's enactment of the law. Rarely has there been so spontaneous a widespread protest.*

North Wind Picture Archives

Douglas's popularity soared in the South, a bonus, for he hoped to win the Democratic presidential nomination in 1856. He presented himself once again as a broker between the sections. To southerners, he was the man who opened Kansas to slavery. To northerners, he was the man who got the transcontinental railroad.

In fact, although northern Democrats supported him, Douglas was vilified by antislavery northerners as a "dough-face," a Democrat who kneaded his face into one shape in the North, another in the South—in effect, a northern man with southern principles. The epithet was also applied to Pierce and to the Democratic presidential nominee in 1856, not Douglas, but James Buchanan of Pennsylvania.

The Republican Party

The Kansas-Nebraska Act finished off the Whigs. When southern Whigs voted for it, the Whigs of the North bade them farewell. Many northern Whigs were abolitionists. Those who were not, like Abraham Lincoln of Illinois, regarded the Missouri Compromise as their party's greatest achievement. Willing to tolerate slavery in the South, unwilling to accept its expansion, the northern Whigs joined with the Free Soilers to form the new Republican party.

So spontaneous was the explosion of opposition to the Kansas-Nebraska Act that the birthplace of the new party is disputed. (Ripon, Wisconsin, has the best claim.) The fact is, the Republican party combusted and coalesced all over the North. Rather more striking, the Republican demand that the Kansas-Nebraska Act be repealed was so popular that the infant party actually captured the House of Representatives in the midterm election of 1854, months after the Kansas-Nebraska Act became law.

At first, the Republicans were a single-issue party, much like the Free Soilers, who became Republicans. But their leaders were experienced and cagey politicians with varied interests who soon worked out a comprehensive program. The Republicans stole Douglas's thunder by insisting that the transcontinental be built on the Central Route. They appealed to farmers indifferent to the question of slavery in the territories by advocating a homestead act giving western lands free to families who would actually settle and farm it.

From the Whigs, the Republicans inherited the demand for a high protective tariff, thus winning some manufacturing interests to their side. Also appealing to industrial capitalists was the Republican demand for a liberal immigration policy, which would attract cheap European labor to the United States. Also from the Whigs, Republicans inherited a

MAP 21:3 America After the Kansas-Nebraska Act The organization of Nebraska Territory caused no fuss. Proslavery southerners knew that, eventually, states formed there would be free states. Making Kansas safe for slavery, however, became a virtually sacred cause for proslavery zealots.

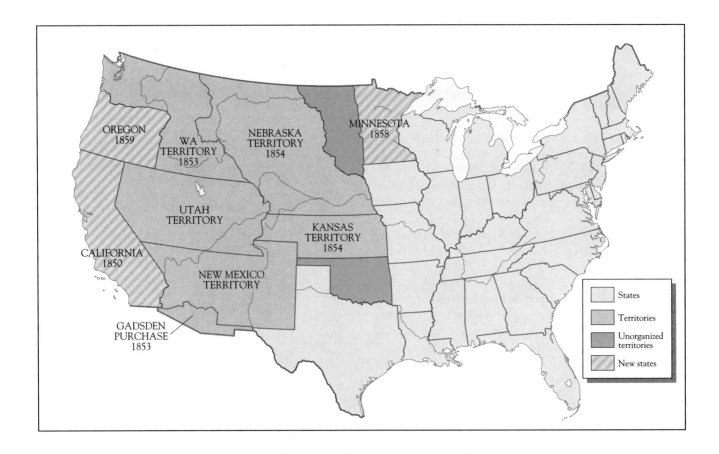

disdain for Democrats as the country's vulgar, self-serving, and ignorant. Poet Walt Whitman put it in a diatribe not to be topped. The Democrats of Washington, D.C., Whitman said, were:

> the meanest kind of bawling and blowing office-holders, office-seekers, pimps, malignants, conspirators, murderers, fancy-men, custom-house clerks, contractors, kept-editors, spaniels well-train'd to carry and fetch, jobbers, infidels, disunionists, terrorists, mail-riflers, slave-catchers, pushers of slavery, creatures of the President, creatures of would-be Presidents, spies, bribers, compromisers, lobbyers, sponges, ruin'd sports, expell'd gamblers, policy-backers, monte-dealers, duellists, carriers of conceal'd weapons, deaf men, pimpled men, scarr'd inside with vile disease, gaudy outside with gold chains made from the people's money and harlot's money twisted together; crawling serpentine men, the lousy combinings and born freedom-settlers of the earth.

The Republicans (the exact opposite on every count, of course) were not a national party, as the Whigs had been. They appealed only to northerners. They did not even put up candidates for office in most slave states. Their hopes of national victory lay in a sweep of the free states, which, indeed, would be quite enough to control the House and win the presidency. In that hope—government by a party frankly representing only one section of the Union—lay a threat to the unity of the country.

for FURTHER READING

Historians have attended to the series of events leading up to the Civil War with great care. Why did extremism triumph in the South and grow into a powerful force in the North? Why did so many Americans abandon the old spirit of compromise? At what point—with what event—did war become inevitable? Why?

See Avery O. Craven, *The Growth of Southern Nationalism, 1848–1860,* 1953 (*southern nationalism* means the sense of the South as a nation), and *The Coming of the Civil War,* 1957; William J. Cooper, *The South and the Politics of Slavery,* 1978; William W. Freehling, *The Road to Disunion,* 1990; Michael Holt, *The Political Crisis of the 1850s,* 1978; Alan Nevins, *Ordeal of the Union,* 1947; David Potter, *The Impending Crisis,* 1976; and Kenneth M. Stampp, *And the War Came,* 1950.

On the Free Soil movement, see C. W. Morrison, *Democratic Politics and Sectionalism: The Wilmot Proviso Controversy,* 1967; Eric Foner, *Free Soil, Free Labor, Free Men,* 1970; Fred J. Blue, *The Free Soilers: Third Party Politics,* 1973; and John Mayfield, *Rehearsal for Republicanism: Free Soil and the Politics of Anti-Slavery,* 1980.

On the prelude to the crisis of 1850, see Joseph G. Rayback, *Free Soil: The Election of 1848,* 1970; K. J. Bauer, *Zachary Taylor:*

Soldier, Planter, Statesman of the Old Southwest, 1985; and Holman Hamilton, *Zachary Taylor: Soldier in the White House,* 1951.

On the Gold Rush, see Rodman Paul, *California Gold: The Beginning of Mining in the Far West,* 1947; and John W. Caughey, *Gold Is the Cornerstone,* 1949. The standard study for the Compromise of 1850 is Holman Hamilton, *Prologue to Conflict: The Crisis and Compromise of 1850,* 1964. See also Richard N. Current, *Daniel Webster and the Rise of National Conservatism,* 1955; Charles M. Wiltse, *John C. Calhoun: Sectionalist,* 1951; and Robert Remini, *Henry Clay: Statesman for the Union,* 1991.

Michael Holt, *The Political Crises of the 1850s,* 1978, carries the story through the Kansas-Nebraska Act. See also James C. Malin, *The Nebraska Question: 1852–1854,* 1953; David Potter, *The South and Sectional Conflict,* 1968; and W. E. Gienapp, *The Origins of the Republican Party,* 1986. On Douglas, see G. M. Capers, *Stephen Douglas: Defender of the Union,* 1959. A sympathetic biography of Franklin Pierce is R. F. Nichols, *Young Hickory of the Granite Hills,* 1931.

  ## AMERICAN JOURNEY ONLINE AND INFOTRAC COLLEGE EDITION

Visit the source collections at http://ajaccess.wadsworth.com and http://infotrac.thomsonlearning.com, and use the Search function with the following key terms to explore documents, images, audio and video clips, articles, and commentary related to the material in this chapter:

Compromise of 1850   Kansas-Nebraska Act
Gold Rush   Stephen Douglas

Additional resources, exercises, and Internet links related to this chapter are available on *The American Past* Web site:
http://history.wadsworth.com/americanpast7e.

HISTORY ONLINE

The Mexican War
www.multied.com/wars.html
The battles of the Mexican War: maps, text.

The California Gold Country
http://malakoff.com/goldcountry/images.htm
Photographs from the earliest years of the Gold Rush.

THE COLLAPSE OF THE UNION

The Road to Secession 1854–1861

Reproduced from the Collections of the Library of Congress

Shall I tell you what this collision means? They who think it is accidental, unnecessary, the work of interested or fanatical agitators, and therefore ephemeral, mistake the case altogether. It is an irrepressible conflict between opposing and enduring forces.

William H. Seward

"A house divided against itself cannot stand." I believe this government cannot endure permanently half-slave and half-free. I do not expect the Union to be dissolved—I do not expect the house to fall—but I do expect it will cease to be divided.

Abraham Lincoln

THE KANSAS-NEBRASKA ACT was a tragedy. In devising it, Stephen A. Douglas became the Union's Pandora, the woman of Greek myth who opened a box from which woes and troubles flew. In the myth, Pandora was able to close the lid of the box before hope was lost. The Union had its hopes after 1854, but one by one, they were dashed by events directly traceable to the Kansas-Nebraska Act.

"BLEEDING KANSAS"

The Kansas Territory was a bone of contention from its creation. The southerners who voted to create it assumed that, populated by proslavery Missourians, Kansas would enter the Union as a slave state, and soon. The Republican party was sworn to repeal the Kansas-Nebraska Act and restore the prohibition of slavery in Kansas when it won control of Congress and the presidency. Abolitionists and militant Free Soilers among the Republicans would not wait. Led by New Englanders, they meant to keep slavery out of Kansas under the rules Congress had written—popular sovereignty and majority vote.

Free Soilers and Border Ruffians

Eli Thayer and other abolitionists organized the New England Emigrant Aid Company, which raised money to finance the emigration of antislavery northerners to Kansas. Their success, thanks in part to the continuing decline of New England agriculture, was extraordinary. Within two years of the Kansas-Nebraska Act, Thayer's group alone sent 2,000 people to the Kansas Territory. Undoubtedly, their propaganda—for they praised the land as if they were selling

Border Ruffians

The western counties of Missouri would have been breeding grounds for violence even without the slavery issue. Western Missouri was raw frontier, an extremely poor farming and grazing country where lawlessness was almost inevitable. In the years after the Kansas crisis, a disproportionate number of dubious characters had roots there. Western Missouri was prime recruiting ground for William C. Quantrill's notorious raiders, a Civil War unit given more to terrorist attacks on civilians than to fighting the Union army. Quantrill's right-hand man, Bloody Bill Anderson, scalped the northerners whom he killed. Future outlaws Jesse and Frank James and the Younger brothers came from western Missouri, as did the "bandit queen," Myra Belle Shirley, or Belle Starr.

yet again—this time by the stream of free staters to Kansas. The incipient slave state of Kansas might not be a slave state after all.

If few western Missourians relocated in Kansas, some of the rougher sort, egged on by southern fire-eaters, were willing to take violent action against Kansas free staters. These "border ruffians," as free staters called them, were poor and struggling men who owned few slaves. But they were intensely racist and anti-Yankee. Some of them understood that a free state of Kansas would be an attractive destination for runaway slaves and, perhaps, a place with a large free black population. Others were, no doubt, like so many adolescent males of many places and eras, hormonally excited by the prospect of making trouble. Gangs sometimes numbering in the hundreds periodically rode across the territorial line to harass northern settlers.

farms there—encouraged many other northerners to go on their own.

By contrast, few southerners seemed interested in emigrating. The fact was, no southern region was so densely populated as New England, and California still exerted more attraction with its gold than Kansas could. Western Missouri, which proslavery southerners believed would populate the new territory, was itself (outside of Independence) a thinly populated frontier. Proslavery politicians were stunned

Lawrence, Kansas, and John Brown

Kansas was, comparatively, a lawless, anarchic place. But it is not possible to tell how much of the beating, arson, robbery, and murder was prompted by the slavery controversy and how much reflected the disorder common to most American frontiers. However, two celebrated incidents were clearly motivated by the conflict over slavery. Some historians consider them the first battles of the Civil War.

▲ *"Border ruffians" in what is obviously a hostile northern depiction. Men living in western Missouri were poor and tough, but not all who harassed free staters in Kansas were frontier scum of this caliber.*

On May 21, 1856, a gang of border ruffians rode into the antislavery town of Lawrence, Kansas, shot it up and set it afire. Only one person was killed, a Missourian crushed by a falling wall, but in other incidents, probably the work of the same gang, several free-state settlers were murdered. Three days later, in an act that he announced was retribution, a Connecticut-born abolitionist named John Brown, accompanied by four of his sons, swooped down on a small settlement on Pottawatomie Creek and hacked five proslavery settlers to pieces.

Southern politicians, who had joked about proslavery violence in Kansas, howled in humanitarian anguish. Northern abolitionists who had wrung their hands over the lesser barbarism of the border ruffians were silent. A few praised John Brown.

The fact that a ritual murder was honored by people who were inclined to parade their moral rectitude indicates the degree to which the hatred between antislavery northerners and proslavery southerners had grown. Extremists on both sides no longer spoke and acted according to rational principles; they were in favor of any act done in the name of "the South, the poor South" or of the godly cause of striking the chains from the bondsmen.

Charles Sumner and Preston Brooks

Congress provided the stage for another debacle in May 1856. Senator Charles Sumner of Massachusetts, an abolitionist who found no contradiction between his pacifism and vituperative oratory, delivered a speech in the Senate called "The Crime Against Kansas."

Sumner described the harassment of free-state settlers and blamed the violence on his southern colleagues. It was pretty standard slavery debate until Sumner added some gratuitous personal insults to an elderly senator from South Carolina, Andrew Butler. Butler suffered from a physical defect that caused him to salivate when he spoke. Sumner coarsely alluded to his slobbering as an indication of the bestiality of slavocrats.

Two days later, Butler's nephew, a congressman named Preston Brooks, walked into the Senate chamber, stood behind Sumner, who was working at his desk, and proceeded to beat the senator senseless with a heavy cane. Brooks said that he was merely putting into practice the *Code Duello* of chivalry, which held that a gentleman must avenge a personal insult from an equal by challenging him to a duel but that one caned a social inferior.

In fact, Brooks's action mocked the "code of honor." He had approached Sumner from behind. (Sumner, a big man, might well have floored Brooks had they met face to face.) Instead of merely humiliating Sumner with a few sharp raps with a cane, Brooks bludgeoned the senator to within an inch of death with a club while Sumner, his legs tangled in his fallen desk, lay helpless on the floor.

Instead of disowning Brooks as a bully and coward, southerners feted him at banquets and made him gifts of dozens of gold-headed canes to replace the one he had broken. The House voted against expelling him; when Brooks resigned, his district reelected him resoundingly. Northerners forgot that Sumner had stepped beyond the bounds of senatorial courtesy and common decency in his description of Senator Butler, and they made Sumner a martyr. While Sumner recovered—it would be several years before he returned to the Senate—Massachusetts reelected him so that his empty desk would stand as a rebuke to the South.

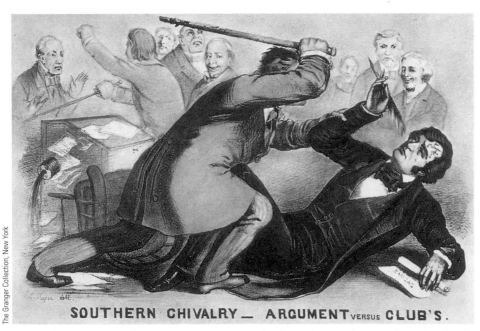

SOUTHERN CHIVALRY — ARGUMENT versus CLUB'S.

▲ *Brooks's clubbing of Charles Sumner readily lent itself to the antislavery movement's depiction of southern whites as barbarous. Note the senators in the background, ignoring or laughing at the incident.*

A HARDENING OF LINES

In normal times, politicians who argue violently in Congress often socialize cordially outside the Capitol. Even Andrew Jackson and Nicholas Biddle were capable of a civil chat at parties and balls. By 1856, this was no longer the case. Both northerners and southerners carried firearms into the congressional chambers and ceased to speak with one another even on informal occasions. Against this foreboding backdrop was held the presidential election of 1856.

The Election of 1856

Inevitably, the Democrats chose a doughface, but he was not Stephen A. Douglas. The Little Giant, a hero in the South in 1854 when he opened the territories to slavery, lost his appeal after events in Kansas indicated that the opening was purely theoretical. Indeed, Douglas told northerners not to worry about the Kansas-Nebraska Act. The concession to slavery, he said, was a symbolic gesture of goodwill to southerners. In the end, Douglas said, Kansas would be a free state because of the greater population of the North and Kansas's unsuitability to plantation agriculture. After the success of the New England Emigrant Aid Society in dispatching antislavery settlers to Kansas, his reasoning rang loudly and unpleasantly in southern ears.

Instead, the Democrats nominated James Buchanan of Pennsylvania, a man of mediocre talent and effeminate manner. (Andrew Jackson called him "Miss Nancy" behind his back.) Politically, Buchanan had been a yes-man, and he was lucky, having been out of the country serving as minister to Great Britain between 1853 and 1856. He was, therefore, not associated with the ugliness in Kansas. He was, however, congenial to southern extremists because he had, with several other diplomats, signed the Ostend Manifesto, a call for the United States to purchase Cuba, which some southerners continued to envision as a sixteenth slave state.

The Republicans chose John C. Frémont, nationally famous as "the Pathfinder," the dashing leader of two exploration parties that helped map the way to Oregon and California. Frémont was no giant of character or intellect. His greatest recommendation was his wife, Jessie Benton, the beautiful, willful, and intelligent daughter of Old Bullion Benton. But in the mood of 1856, Frémont was a logical choice for the Republicans: He was a military hero like the only two successful Whig candidates, and he believed that the western lands should be reserved for family farmers.

The Pathfinder had handicaps. He had abolitionist leanings, and he had been born out of wedlock at a time when illegitimacy carried a stain of shame. But these impediments were minor. Despite the fact he was unlisted on the ballot in every slave state, Frémont won a third of the popular vote and the electoral votes of New England and New York. But Buchanan won every slave state, enough electoral votes to match Frémont's total, plus New Jersey, Pennsylvania, Indiana, and Illinois. A third-party candidate, former president

Millard Fillmore, ran on the anti-Catholic Native American (Know-Nothing) party ticket. Curiously, he did poorly in Massachusetts, a state recently run by the Know-Nothings, but won 44 percent of the popular vote in the slave states, where there were very few Catholics.

Dred Scott

Buchanan's presidency began with a bang. In his inaugural address, he hinted that the issue of slavery in the territories would shortly be settled for all time. Two days later, March 6, 1857, Americans learned what he meant when the Supreme Court handed down its decision in the case of *Dred Scott v. Sandford.*

Dred Scott was a slave in Missouri. Most of his life, he was the valet of an army officer. In 1834, Scott accompanied his master to Illinois, where slavery was prohibited under the Northwest Ordinance. Briefly, he lived in a part of the Louisiana Purchase where slavery was illegal under the Missouri Compromise. For four years, in other words, Scott lived on free soil before returning to Missouri.

▲ *Dred Scott, his wife, and (above them) their daughters. This sympathetic presentation of the beleaguered family indicates how anger in the North toward "the slavocrat conspiracy" had spread far beyond the abolitionists. Frank Leslie's was no propaganda sheet but aimed at a broad readership.*

In 1844, Scott's owner died, bequeathing him to his widow, who was opposed to slavery. Rather than manumit him, she was persuaded by abolitionists to cooperate in a test case. Scott sued his owner (eventually a man named Sanford, spelled Sandford in the court records) for his freedom on the grounds that part of his life he was held as a slave in territory where Congress had prohibited slavery.

Missouri courts had released slaves with cases identical to Scott's, but that was before sectional animosity was so bitter. Scott lost his case on the grounds that whatever his status may have been in Illinois in 1834, he became quite legally a slave again when he returned to Missouri. The case slowly made its way to the Supreme Court.

Chief Justice Taney: The Final Solution

Although every Supreme Court justice commented individually on Scott's appeal, Chief Justice Roger B. Taney, an old Jackson henchman from Maryland, spoke for the majority when he declared that because Scott was black, he was not a citizen of Missouri, which restricted citizenship to whites. Therefore, Scott could not sue in Missouri courts.

Taney could have left the decision at that. Several justices did. The decision would have been unpopular among antislavery northerners, but not sensational. But Taney continued. With the highly irregular input of president-elect Buchanan, Taney believed he had discovered the constitutional solution to the question that was tearing the country apart—the status of slavery in the territories. In fact, the doctrine Taney propounded was pure John C. Calhoun, the extreme proslavery position.

Taney declared that the Missouri Compromise had been unconstitutional in prohibiting slavery in the territories because Congress was forbidden to discriminate against the citizens of any of the states. State legislatures could outlaw slavery, to be sure. But territorial legislatures could not do so because they were the creatures of Congress. They were, therefore, subject to the Constitution's restraints on Congress.

The Republican Panic

The Missouri Compromise was already dead, but Republicans were enraged, for their program was to restore a Missouri-type prohibition of slavery in the territories. With the Dred Scott decision, they saw the history of the question of slavery in the territories as a step-by-step whittling away of the power of the federal government to prevent the expansion of slavery.

That is, between 1820 and 1854, under the Missouri Compromise, slavery was illegal in all territories north of 36 degrees, 30 minutes. With the Kansas-Nebraska Act of 1854, slavery could be legalized in territories if the voters there chose to do so. With the Dred Scott decision of 1857, there was no way that, even by unanimous vote of the settlers in a territory, a slave owner could be forbidden to move to

that territory with a hundred slaves in a coffle. *Dred Scott v. Sandford* killed the popular sovereignty of the Kansas-Nebraska Act as dead as the Kansas-Nebraska Act had killed the Missouri Compromise.

Republicans began to speak of a "slavocratic" conspiracy, now involving the Supreme Court, to thwart the will of a majority of the American people. Their fury was fanned in October 1857 when proslavery settlers in Kansas, augmented by a good many illegal voters from Missouri, sent to Congress the Lecompton Constitution, which called for the admission of Kansas as a slave state. Although the Lecompton Constitution was obviously the work of a small group, Buchanan urged Congress to accept it.

Ever increasing arrests of runaway slaves in the North, like the celebrated case of Anthony Burns in 1854, converted more and more northerners to militant antislavery. In Milwaukee, an antislavery mob stormed a jail where a runaway slave was being held and set him free.

The Fugitive Slave Act of 1850 meant that it was no longer possible for a slave to gain freedom by escaping to a free state. Runaways had to get out of the country. Northern abolitionists, particularly free blacks, organized the "underground railroad" to spirit fugitives to Canada. This was a constantly shifting network of households, beginning at the Ohio River and Mason-Dixon line, that hid runaway slaves by day and helped them move to Canada by night.

Lincoln and Douglas: Two Northern Answers

Stephen A. Douglas did not take Taney's rebuke of popular sovereignty lying down. In a series of debates in Illinois in 1858, Douglas and a Springfield Republican who wanted Douglas's seat in the Senate, Abraham Lincoln, proposed two northern solutions to the question of slavery in the territories.

Race

Because few American whites believed in racial equality, it was in the interest of northern Democrats to accuse the Republicans of advocating race mixture. "I am opposed to Negro equality," Stephen A. Douglas said in his debate with Abraham Lincoln in Chicago. "I am in favor of preserving, not only the purity of the blood, but the purity of the government from any mixture or amalgamation with inferior races."

The Democrats' line forced Republicans to reassure their constituents that opposition to slavery did not mean a belief in the equality of the races. Lincoln replied to Douglas, "I protest, now and forever, against that counterfeit logic which presumes that because I do not want a Negro woman for a slave, I necessarily want her for a wife. . . . As God made us separate, we can leave one another alone, and do one another much good thereby."

Lincoln shrewdly took the debate back to the territorial question by saying, "Why, Judge, if we do not let them get together in the Territories, they won't mix there."

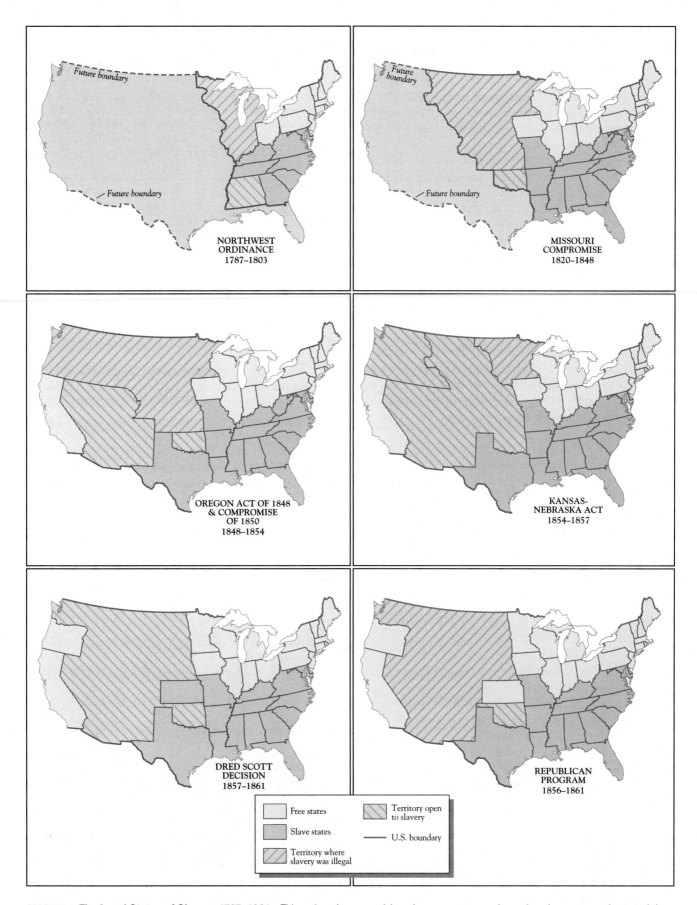

Free states

Slave states

Territory where slavery was illegal

Territory open to slavery

U.S. boundary

NORTHWEST
ORDINANCE
1787–1803

MISSOURI
COMPROMISE
1820–1848

OREGON ACT OF 1848
& COMPROMISE
OF 1850
1848–1854

KANSAS-
NEBRASKA ACT
1854–1857

DRED SCOTT
DECISION
1857–1861

REPUBLICAN
PROGRAM
1856–1861

MAP 22:1 The Legal Status of Slavery, 1787–1861 This series of maps explains why ever greater numbers of northerners were frustrated during the 1850s. Even though a majority of Americans clearly wanted no slavery in the territories, the area in which slavery was legal was increased twice within three years.

"A house divided against itself cannot stand," Lincoln said in June 1858. "I believe this government cannot endure permanently half-slave and half-free." He meant that southerners were clearly not satisfied that slavery was protected where it existed. Nor, with the clear majority of free staters in Kansas, was Douglas's popular sovereignty enough to placate the extremists. With the Fugitive Slave Act and the Dred Scott decision in their pockets, proslavery extremists were forcing the institution on people who did not want it. In their mania, southerners were forcing a showdown that, in the long run, would result in armed sectional conflict.

Douglas insisted that popular sovereignty was still alive and kicking, and was still the best solution to the problem. When Lincoln reminded him that the Supreme Court had ruled popular sovereignty unconstitutional, Douglas replied at Freeport, Illinois, in August 1858, that a territorial legislature could keep slavery out of the territory simply by failing to enact a slave code. No slave owner would dare take his valuable human property to a country where there were no laws to protect his power over his slaves. (Some slave owner forty-niners had discovered in California that their slaves simply walked away from them, even before statehood.) The Supreme Court might be able to overturn a territorial law, Douglas pointed out, but the Court could not force a territorial legislature to enact one it did not choose to enact.

The Freeport Doctrine was ingenious; Douglas was a superb lawyer. And he won reelection to the Senate, although narrowly. But events proved that Lincoln was correct about the intentions of the southern extremists to be stopped by no legal obstacle. When presented with the logic of the Freeport Doctrine, they demanded that Congress enact a national slave code that would affirmatively protect slavery in the territories. That was not in the cards. If Lincoln lost the Illinois Senate race in 1858, Republicans had a comfortable majority in the House of Representatives.

John Brown's Insurrection

John Brown dropped out of sight after the Pottawatomie murders, but he was busy and did not disappear. Moving around New England behind a newly grown beard, incognito at first, Brown persuaded several well-to-do abolitionists that the time had come to strike violently at slavery. With their financial support, he organized a band of 22 insurrectionists, including African Americans and several of his sons, at an isolated farm in Maryland. Just across the Potomac River, at the mouth of the Shenandoah, was Harpers

John Brown as Martyr
John Brown understood that although he was doomed, his death would ultimately serve the antislavery cause. Shortly before his execution, he wrote to his wife, "I have been whipped but am sure I can recover all the lost capital occasioned by that disaster by only hanging a few minutes by the neck."

John Brown's Mountains
In the Appalachians, to which John Brown planned to escape, there were nearly impenetrable places. During the Civil War, gangs of Confederate draft dodgers and deserters roamed the mountains without fear of the authorities. So isolated are some hollows that Elizabethan patterns of speech and folk ballads survived there unchanged into the twentieth century, although they had long since disappeared elsewhere in the English-speaking world.

Ferry, Virginia, site of one of the federal government's two major arsenals. Brown's plan was to seize the arsenal, capture guns and ammunition, and escape into the Appalachians, which rose steeply around Harpers Ferry.

From the mountains, his guerrilla army would swoop down on plantations, free a few slaves at a time, and enlarge the corps. Before long, Brown predicted, slave rebellions would erupt all over the South, decisively destroying the "peculiar institution."

Brown's critics later said that the scheme proved that the old man was out of his mind. Brown may well have been deranged; he was certainly not the sort one would want at a favorite daughter's wedding. But there was nothing crazy about John Brown's military thinking. His plan prefigured in many ways the theory of guerrilla warfare that twentieth-century national-liberation movements put into practice with great success: operate from a remote and shifting base; avoid big battles in which conventional military forces have the overwhelming advantage; fight only small surprise actions when

▲ *A curiously dispassionate nineteenth-century drawing of John Brown and his followers in the final hours in the roundhouse. The man in his arms is his son, who died when marines stormed the ill-chosen fortress. Brown himself was seriously wounded when he was captured. He lay on a stretcher at his trial.*

The Know-Nothing Mind

It is easy today to label the nativists, anti-Catholics, and Know-Nothings of the 1840s and 1850s as bigots and let it go at that. Self-comforting labeling is the genius of our era. It was not so simple.

There was plenty of garden-variety bigotry in the minds of those who made the Know-Nothing party briefly triumphant, but more than that. A political party (officially the American party) that won the mayor's office of New York City, the governorship and all but one seat in the assembly in Massachusetts, and 40 percent of the vote in large parts of the Upper South in 1856, and then disappeared as if a magician had waved a wand, has a more complicated story.

Hostility toward Roman Catholicism was in a corner of the American psyche from the beginning. To the Puritans, the Church of Rome was not merely mistaken; it was evil. The flood of Scotch-Irish Presbyterians who settled and dominated the slopes of the Appalachians brought with them a century of hatred of the Catholics with whom they shared the Emerald Isle.

Outside of Maryland, however, there were few flesh-and-blood targets for anti-Catholics until the 1820s. There were only about 35,000 Catholics in the United States in 1790, when John Carroll was named bishop of Baltimore. And Carroll was all-American. He endorsed separation of church and state, religious tolerance, and even spoke openly of an American church independent of the pope of Rome except as the symbolic father of the church.

Then began the immigration of Catholic Irish, which became a flood with the potato blight of the 1840s. (A million Irish died of hunger and related disease; millions more fled.) The Irish immigrants were poor and uneducated. The men, drawn to heavy labor and saloons, were tumultuous. And the women especially were profoundly deferential to their priests, the only educated people among them. In turn, Irish priests were stolid proponents of the sacred authority of the pope.

During the 1820s, an anti-Catholic tract, *The Awful Disclosures of Maria Monk,* was a sensation because it depicted convents of nuns as the dens of sexual slaves of Catholic priests. Someone has said that anti-Catholic literature was the pornography of the respectable Protestant.

The pope after 1846 was Pius IX, who inveighed against religious toleration, democracy, republican government, and the individual rights and civil liberties that were at the heart of American ideals. Pius IX took little interest in the United States; his devils were liberal Europeans who, however, often pointed to free America as their model. That was enough for American Protestants to worry, some casually, some obsessively, that Catholics, especially the ignorant, slavish Irish, were a threat to America. Calmer proponents of tolerance were not helped by the leading American bishop, John Hughes of New York, who denounced Protestantism and crowed that the Roman Catholic Church would soon displace it as America's majority religion.

In this atmosphere, a number of anti-Catholic, anti-immigrant secret societies were founded among native-born workingmen who saw the Irish as dragging wages downward. The most notable of these groups was the Order of the Star-Spangled Banner, founded in 1849. With the northern Whig party shattered the next year—"cotton Whigs" supporting the Compromise of 1850, "conscience Whigs" opposing it—many of the former drifted into the American party, the secretive Know-Nothings' public political front. In 1854, in fact, a former Whig, James Barker, became head of the party. Many Whigs followed him as their old party disintegrated. A genteel anti-Catholicism had been endemic among Whigs, not the kind that sends men into the streets to brawl (very un-Whiglike behavior!) but a distaste for the drinking and coarseness of the Irish immigrants. (The fact that almost all the Irish voted Democratic did not help their popularity among Whigs.)

The American party advocated temperance (a play for that vote), laws disqualifying Catholics from holding public office, sharp restrictions on immigration (which appealed to native-born workingmen with no particular religious animosities), and an increase in the residency requirement to 20 years for immigrants seeking citizenship. The American party tried to dodge the slavery question, as the Whigs had: New England Know-Nothings inclined to be antislavery, whereas those in the South, where presidential candidate Millard Fillmore ran strongest in 1856, did not.

After the Dred Scott decision of 1857, the slavery controversy killed the Know-Nothings more quickly than they had burst onto the political scene. The threat of slavery in the territories was far more real to northern Know-Nothings than the specter of Bishop Hughes hugging Pope Pius IX as he stepped from a ship to a New York wharf. Most of the Know-Nothings gravitated into the Republican party and voted for Lincoln despite the fact that he had several times denounced the Know-Nothings' bigotry and supported a liberal immigration policy.

In the South, anti-Catholicism and nativism never made much sense. It was a highly theoretical enthusiasm. Outside of Louisiana, Catholics were as rare in the South as polar bears. Few immigrants went South, because slaves did the menial work; Irishmen in the South competed only with free blacks (not a politically powerful group) for jobs too dangerous to be assigned to valuable slaves. Southern Know-Nothings managed to stay clear of the hated Democratic party through 1860, when they voted overwhelmingly for Constitutional Union candidate John Bell, who, like Lincoln, embraced no Know-Nothing principles.

The Know-Nothings, like the Anti-Masons, represented a whirlwind movement—the creation of a unique conjunction of circumstances only some of which, in the case of the Know-Nothings, had to do with Catholics and immigrants. There was, in fact, no Know-Nothing mind but a good many things haunting many minds in troubled times.

the odds favor the freewheeling guerrillas; and win the friendship and support of the ordinary people—in Brown's case, the slaves. The odds were never with him, but his plan was not completely hopeless.

Raid and Reaction

Better evidence of problems in Brown's mental processes was the fact that he abandoned his plan almost as soon as he got started. On October 16, 1859, his band of fighters easily captured the arsenal. Then, however, Brown either lost his nerve or deluded himself into the belief that the slaves in the area were on the verge of joining him. He forgot what Frederick Douglass had told him—what he could see all around him—that Harpers Ferry was "a perfect steel trap." Instead of making for the hills just outside the doors of the arsenal, he holed up in the locomotive roundhouse, where he was promptly surrounded by United States Marines under the command of Colonel Robert E. Lee. In two days, Lee's professional soldiers killed 10 of Brown's followers and captured Brown himself. Brown was promptly tried for treason against the state of Virginia, found guilty, and hanged in December.

Most northerners were shocked by the raid and grimly applauded the speedy trial and execution of the old man. However, most prominent abolitionists were ominously silent. Some of those who had funded Brown fled the country. A few openly praised Brown as a hero and a martyr. Ralph Waldo Emerson said that Brown's death made the gallows as holy as the Christian cross.

There was just enough of this sentiment to arouse the southern fire-eaters to a new pitch of hysteria. Brown's raid revived their deep fears of slave rebellion, and here were northerners praising a lunatic who tried to start one. Southern editors and politicians wondered how they could continue to remain under the same government as people who encouraged their massacre.

It was true that the federal government had moved quickly and efficiently to crush Brown. Southerners had few complaints with Washington. But 1860 was an election year. What was to happen if the "Black Republicans" won the presidency, thus taking control of federal police powers? Could the South still depend on protection against the John Browns, Nat Turners, Harriet Tubmans, and Ralph Waldo Emersons?

THE ELECTION OF 1860

Southern extremists declared that if the Republicans won the presidency in 1860, the southern states would secede from the Union. Then, having threatened northern voters, the same extremists not only failed to work against a Republican victory, but they guaranteed it. They split the Democratic party that had served southern interests so well. John Brown was not the only lunatic walking the streets of America.

The Democratic Split

The Democratic party was almost the last great national institution in the United States. The Methodists had split into northern and southern churches in 1844, the Baptists in 1845, the Presbyterians over the next several years. Fraternal lodges broke in two. The Whig party, the nation's nationalistic party, was a fading memory, buried by the slavery controversy. The young Republican party had an exclusively northern membership. Only within the Democratic party did

men from both sections still come together to try to settle sectional differences.

In April 1860, with the smell of the Brown affair still in the air, the Democratic convention met in Charleston. The majority of the delegates, including many southerners, supported the nomination of Stephen A. Douglas. The candidate must be a northerner, they said realistically, like Buchanan and Pierce. But the southern extremists withheld their votes. The delegations of eight southern states announced that they would support Douglas only if he repudiated the Freeport Doctrine and supported their demand for a federal slave code.

The Douglas men pointed out that to do so would ensure that many northern Democrats would vote Republican. Unmoved, the eight hard-line delegations walked out of the convention. The Douglas forces recessed without nominating their leader, hoping to talk sense into the minority.

The Democrats reassembled in Baltimore in June. The southern extremists refused to budge. Disgusted by what they considered political suicide, the regular Democrats nominated Douglas for president and a southern moderate, Herschel V. Johnson of Georgia, as his running mate. The southern Democrats then nominated John C. Breckinridge of Kentucky to represent them in the election. To give the ticket a semblance of national support, they chose an Oregon doughface, Joseph Lane, as their vice presidential candidate.

The Republican Opportunity

Meanwhile, the Republicans met in Chicago. They were optimistic but cautious. With the Democrats split, they smelled victory. But they also knew that if they ran too extreme an antislavery candidate—as they believed Frémont had been in 1856—many northern voters would back Douglas. Even worse would be winning on too extreme a platform: Southerners would make good on their threat to secede, which none but a few very extreme abolitionists wanted.

So the Republicans backed off from the sometimes radical rhetoric of previous years and rejected party stalwarts William H. Seward of New York and Salmon P. Chase of Ohio. Seward had spoken of "a higher law than the Constitution" in condemning slavery (shades of William Lloyd Garrison) and of an "irrepressible conflict" between North and South. Chase had been a militant abolitionist for more than a decade and had dozens of inflammatory remarks on his record.

Instead, the Republicans picked a somewhat obscure midwesterner, Abraham Lincoln of Illinois. Lincoln was rock solid on the fundamental Republican principle: Slavery must be banned from the territories. But he was no abolitionist; he had steered clear of the Know-Nothings, thus maintaining a good relationship with German voters; and he was moderate, humane, and ingratiating in manner. In his famous debates with Douglas in 1858 and in a speech introducing himself to eastern Republicans in New York City in February 1860, he struck a note of humility, prudence, and caution. Not only was slavery protected by the Constitution in those states where it existed, he said, but northerners ought to sympathize with slave owners rather than attack them. Lincoln himself was born in Kentucky, a slave state. He knew that a quirk of fate would have made him a slave owner; he found it easy to preach the golden rule. By choosing him, the Republicans accommodated southern sensibilities as far as they could without giving up their own principles.

The Republican platform was comprehensive: a high protective tariff, a liberal immigration policy, the construction of a transcontinental railway, and a homestead act. The platform was designed to win the votes of rather disparate economic groups often at odds with one another: eastern industrial capitalists, workers, and midwestern farmers. Moreover, by avoiding a single-issue campaign, the Republicans hoped to signal the South that they were not, as a party, antislavery fanatics. They even named a vice presidential candidate who had been a Democrat as late as 1857, Hannibal Hamlin of Maine.

The Old Man's Party

A fourth party entered the race, drawing its strength in the states of the Upper South: Maryland, Virginia, Kentucky, and Tennessee. Henry Clay's brand of Whiggery—an inclination toward compromise and a deep attachment to the Union—was strong in the border states. The platform of the new Constitutional Union party consisted, in effect, of stalling. It was a mistake, members said, to force any kind of sectional confrontation while tempers were up—better to put off the problem of slavery in the territories to a later, calmer day.

For president, the Constitutional Unionists nominated John Bell of Tennessee, a protégé of Clay. For vice president, they chose the distinguished Whig orator Edward Everett of Massachusetts. But they found little support outside the border states. Republicans and both northern and southern Democrats sneered at them as "the old man's party."

Republican Victory

Abraham Lincoln won 40 percent of the popular vote, but he carried every free state except New Jersey, which he split with Douglas. He won a clear majority in the electoral college. Breckinridge won only 18 percent of the national vote, but he was the overwhelming choice of the South, winning a plurality in 11 of the 15 slave states. Between the two, appealing to sectional feelings, they won a decisive majority of voters.

Douglas won a mere 12 electoral votes (Missouri and New Jersey), but he ran second to Lincoln in some northern states and to Breckinridge in some states in the South. John Bell carried 3 of the border states and was strong almost everywhere. Even if the Douglas and the Bell votes had been combined, however, Lincoln would have won. Nevertheless, inasmuch as many Lincoln, and some Breckinridge, supporters were more interested in making noise than, surely, in a civil war, it seems clear that most Americans wanted some kind of settlement.

The First Secession: South Carolina

They did not get their wish. Having announced that Lincoln's election meant secession, the fire-eaters of South Carolina (where there was no popular vote for presidential electors) called a convention that, on December 20, 1860, unanimously declared that "the union now subsisting between South Carolina and the other States, under the name of the 'United States of America,' is hereby dissolved."

During January 1861, the six other states of the Deep South followed suit, declaring that a Republican administration threatened their domestic institutions. Then came a glimmer of hope. The secession movement stalled when none of the other southern states approved secession ordinances. At the same time they rejected secession, however, conventions in the border states declared their opposition to any attempt by the federal government to use force against the states that had seceded. By rebuffing the big talkers on both sides, the leaders of the border states hoped to force a compromise.

The outgoing president, James Buchanan, was not the man to engineer such a compromise. No one had much respect for Old Buck, including his own advisers, mostly southern, who now betrayed him. His secretary of war, John Floyd of Virginia, transferred tons of war materiel to states that either had left the Union or were on the verge of leaving. Floyd's act skirted close to treason, but Buchanan did nothing.

Other Buchanan allies resigned their offices and left Washington, hardly pausing to remember the president who had worked on their behalf. The first bachelor ever to occupy the White House was quite alone, and he knew it. After a hand-wringing message sent to Congress in which he declared that although secession was illegal, he as president was powerless to do anything about it, Buchanan sat back to wait for the day he could go home.

HOW THE UNION BROKE

As Buchanan slumped, Senator John J. Crittenden stood up. Like many Kentuckians, Crittenden had made a career of mediating between the North and the Deep South. Now he proposed that rather than break up the Union, the territories should be divided. His proposal was to extend the Missouri Compromise line to the California border, guaranteeing slavery to the south of the line and forbidding slavery to the north of it.

Failure of the Compromisers

Because of the Dred Scott decision, Crittenden's plan could not be put into effect by congressional action; the territories could be divided only by constitutional amendment. Crittenden hoped that the specter of civil war, now chillingly real with military companies drilling in both North and South, would prompt both northern and southern state legislatures to act in haste.

With some encouragement, they might have done so. There was a flurry of enthusiasm for Crittenden's compromise

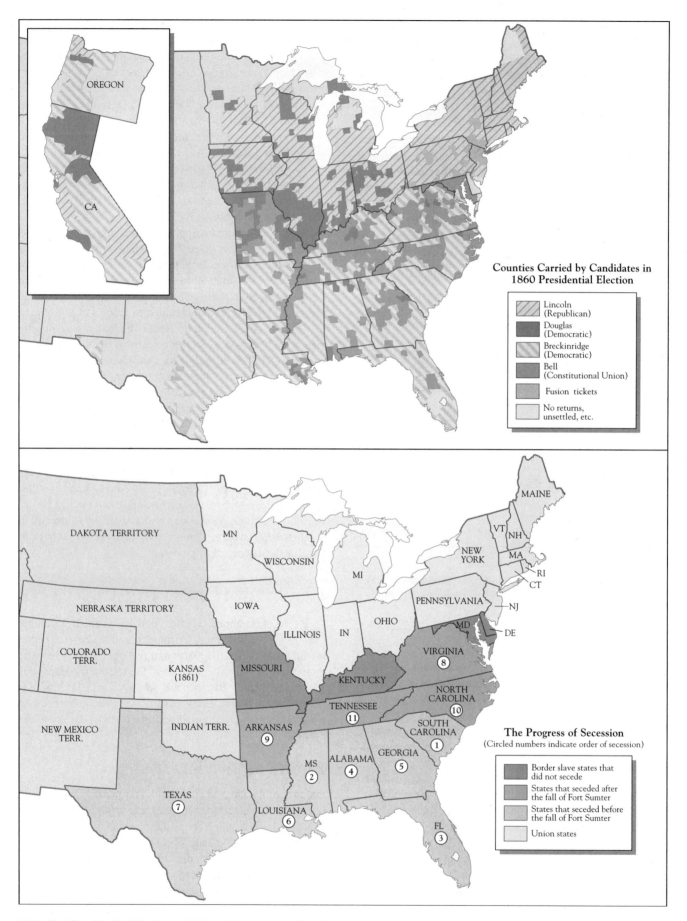

Counties Carried by Candidates in 1860 Presidential Election

- Lincoln (Republican)
- Douglas (Democratic)
- Breckinridge (Democratic)
- Bell (Constitutional Union)
- Fusion tickets
- No returns, unsettled, etc.

OREGON

CA

The Progress of Secession
(Circled numbers indicate order of secession)

- Border slave states that did not secede
- States that seceded after the fall of Fort Sumter
- States that seceded before the fall of Fort Sumter
- Union states

DAKOTA TERRITORY

MN

WISCONSIN

MI

MAINE

VT

NH

NEW YORK

MA

RI

CT

NEBRASKA TERRITORY

IOWA

PENNSYLVANIA

NJ

COLORADO TERR.

ILLINOIS

IN

OHIO

MD

DE

KANSAS (1861)

MISSOURI

KENTUCKY

VIRGINIA (8)

NEW MEXICO TERR.

INDIAN TERR.

ARKANSAS (9)

TENNESSEE (11)

NORTH CAROLINA (10)

SOUTH CAROLINA (1)

MS (2)

ALABAMA (4)

GEORGIA (5)

TEXAS (7)

LOUISIANA (6)

FL (3)

MAP 22:2 Presidential Election of 1860 and Secession   Note, in the upper map, Lincoln's sweep in the North and Breckinridge's in the South. Bell won majorities in the states that bordered the line separating slave and free states. Few counties gave Douglas a majority, but he finished second in many areas in both the North and the South.

▲ *Abraham Lincoln about the time he was elected president. He grew the beard he wore throughout his presidency between election day 1860 and his inauguration because, he said, a girl had written him that he was so homely that a beard would help.*

granted nothing the South did not already possess—and it could be overturned by constitutional amendment at a later date. By February, in fact, the secessionists had lost interest in preserving the Union. They were caught up in the excitement of creating a new nation.

The Confederate States of America

According to secessionist theory, the 7 states that left the Union were now independent republics. However, no southern leader intended his state to go it alone. Although they were disappointed that 8 of the 15 slave states refused to join them, they met in Montgomery, Alabama, shortly before Lincoln's inauguration and established the Confederate States of America.

The government of the Confederacy differed little from the one that they had rejected. All United States laws were to remain in effect until amended or repealed, and they adopted the Constitution of 1787, plus amendments, almost word for word. The changes they made reflected the South's obsession with slavery and with Calhoun's political theories, which resulted in several curious contradictions.

Thus, the Confederates defined the states as sovereign and independent but called their new government permanent. Even more oddly, the Confederates declared that individual states might not interfere with slavery, a restriction on states' rights that no prominent Republican had ever suggested.

The Confederates also modified the presidency. The chief executive was to be elected for a term of six years rather than four, but he was not permitted to run for a second term. Although this seemed to weaken the office, the Confederates allowed the president to veto parts of congressional bills rather than, as in the Union, requiring the president to accept all or nothing.

Jeff Davis

As their first president, the Confederates selected Jefferson Davis. On the face of it, he was a good choice. His bearing was regal, and he was the model slave owner, the sort that southerners liked to pretend was typical of the institution. Davis also seemed to be a wise choice because he was not closely associated with the secessionist movement. Indeed, Davis asked his fellow Mississippians to delay secession until Lincoln had a chance to prove himself. When his state overruled him, Davis delivered a moderate, eloquent, and affectionate farewell speech in the Senate. By choosing such a man, rather than a fire-eater, the Confederates demonstrated their willingness to work with southerners who opposed secession; there were plenty of them. With the respected Davis, the Confederacy could also appeal to the eight slave states that remained within the Union.

In other ways, the choice of Jefferson Davis was ill advised. It was not so much the unattractive coldness of his personality; George Washington had been icier. Davis's weakness was that despite his bearing, he lacked self-confidence and was, consequently, easily irritated and inflexible. He proved incapable of cooperating with critics, even those who differed

on both sides of the Mason-Dixon line. But before the southern extremists were forced to take a stand, Lincoln, now president-elect, quashed the plan. His reasons were political but nonetheless compelling. His Republican party was a diverse alliance of people who disagreed with one another on many issues. The one adhesive that bound them together was the principle that slavery must not expand into the territories. If Lincoln gave in on this point, he would take office with half his party sniping at him.

Lincoln also discouraged a second attempt at compromise, a peace conference held in Washington in February 1861. It was a distinguished assembly, chaired by former president John Tyler. Tyler had been a southern extremist, and, a few months later, he would support the secession of Virginia. But he worked hard for a settlement in February, proposing a series of constitutional amendments along the same lines as Crittenden's.

Once again, Lincoln drew the line on allowing slavery in the southern territories. Instead, he endorsed an amendment, passed by both houses of Congress, that would forever guarantee slavery in the states where it already existed. As he well knew, this was a purely symbolic gesture that

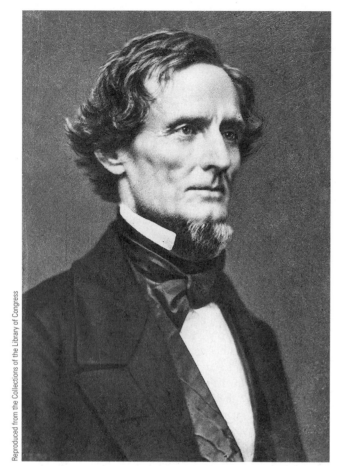

▲ *Jefferson Davis, first and only president of the Confederacy. Davis was zealously proslavery and supported every measure to expand slavery to the territories, but he tried to delay secession in Mississippi, arguing that Lincoln should be given a chance.*

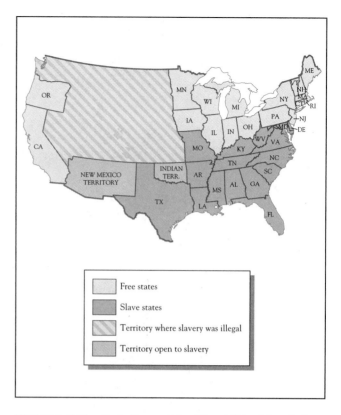

MAP 22:3 Crittenden's Compromise Plan, 1861 Crittenden's plan recognized the justice of northern anger over the Dred Scott decision (see Map 22.1 on p. 313) but provided the South with two territories likely to enter the Union as free states.

with him on minor points. He seemed to need yes-men in order to function, and, as a result, he denied his administration the services of some of the South's ablest statesmen.

Worse, Davis was a dabbler. Instead of delegating authority and presiding over the government, he repeatedly interfered in the pettiest details of administration—peering over his subordinates' shoulders, arousing personal resentments among even those who were devoted to him. He had been a good senator; he was not qualified to be the "father of his country."

Abe Lincoln

By contrast, Abraham Lincoln knew the value of unity and competent help. Rather than shun his rivals within the Republican party, he named them to his cabinet. Seward became secretary of state; Salmon P. Chase was Lincoln's secretary of the treasury. After a brief misadventure with an incompetent secretary of war, Simon Cameron, Lincoln appointed a Democrat, Edwin Stanton, to that post because his talents were obvious. Lincoln wanted able aides, not pals or toadies. Within their departments, Lincoln's cabinet officers were free to do anything that did not conflict with general

policy. As a result, a cantankerous and headstrong group of men never challenged his control of fundamentals.

Lincoln differed from Davis in other ways. Far from regal, he was an awkward, plain, even ugly man. Tall and gangling, with oversized hands and feet, he impressed those who met him for the first time as a frontier oaf. His enemies called him "the baboon." Some of his supporters snickered at his clumsiness and were appalled by his fondness for dirty jokes.

But both friends and enemies soon discovered that the president was no yokel. Lincoln had honed a sharp native intelligence on a stone of lifelong study, and he proved to be one of the three or four most eloquent chief executives. And yet, behind his brilliance was a humility born of modest background that can be found in no other American president.

Lincoln needed all his native resources. On March 4, 1861, when he was sworn in before a glum Washington crowd, the Union was in tatters. During the previous two months, the Stars and Stripes had been hauled down from every flagstaff in the South except for one at Fort Pickens in Pensacola, Florida, and another at Fort Sumter, a rocky island in the harbor of Charleston, South Carolina.

A War of Nerves

Neither of the forts threatened the security of the Confederacy. They were old installations designed for defense and

▲ *Fort Sumter, the day after it was surrendered to the Confederacy. The fort was expected only to make a symbolic resistance—it was at the mercy of the batteries in Charleston—but it took a terrific shelling as this photograph shows.*

were manned by token garrisons. But symbols take on profound importance in edgy times, and the southern fire-eaters, itching for a fight, ranted about the insulting occupation of "their country" by a "foreign power."

Davis was willing to live with the Union forts for the time being. He understood that the Confederacy could not survive as long as it consisted of seven states. His hope was to delay a confrontation with the North until he could make a foreign alliance or induce the eight slave states that remained in the Union to join the Confederacy. He feared that if he fired the first shot, the states of the Upper South might support the Union.

The fire-eaters disagreed. They believed that a battle, no matter who started it, would bring the other slave states to their side. Nevertheless, when the commander at Fort Sumter announced that he would soon have to surrender the fort for lack of provisions, Davis had his way.

Within limits, Lincoln also favored delaying confrontation. He believed that the longer the states of the Upper South did not secede, the less likely they were to go. Moreover, the leaders of Virginia, Kentucky, Tennessee, and Arkansas formally warned him against using force against the Confederacy. If the Union fired the first shot, they would secede.

First Blood

The first blood of the Civil War was not shed at Fort Sumter. No one was killed there. The first deaths of the Civil War occurred in Baltimore a week after the fall of Sumter. A mob attacked soldiers from Massachusetts on the way to Washington as they were marching from one railroad terminal to another. The soldiers fired back. Twelve members of the mob and four soldiers were killed.

Finally, Lincoln did not have the people of the North solidly behind him. Northern Democrats would not support an act of aggression, and Winfield Scott, Lincoln's chief military adviser, told him that the army was not up to a war of conquest. Some abolitionists who were also pacifists, such as Horace Greeley and William Lloyd Garrison, urged the president to "let the wayward sisters depart in peace."

Lincoln had no intention of doing that. He was determined to save the Union by peaceful means if possible, by force if necessary. He reasoned that if the Confederates fired the first shot, the border states might secede anyway, but at least the act of rebellion would unite northerners. If he delayed a confrontation indefinitely, he still might lose the border states and still have a divided, uncertain North.

This was the reasoning behind Lincoln's decision to resupply Fort Sumter. He announced that he would not use force against the state of South Carolina. There would be no arms in the relief ship, only food, medicine, and other nonmilitary supplies. He repeated his wish that the crisis be resolved peacefully. But he insisted on his presidential obligation to maintain the government's authority in Charleston Harbor.

And so the war came. When the relief ship approached the sandbar that guarded Charleston Harbor, the Confederacy attacked. On the morning of April 12, 1861, artillery under the command of General P. G. T. Beauregard opened up. The next day, Sumter surrendered. Davis was reluctant to the end. In a way, he lost control of South Carolina.

Contest for the Border States

In a way, the Battle of Fort Sumter served both Confederate and Union purposes. Although Lincoln was able to call for 75,000 volunteers and to get them, his call for troops pushed four more states into the Confederacy: Virginia, North Carolina, Tennessee, and Arkansas. In deference to Virginia's importance, the capital of the new nation was moved from Montgomery to Richmond.

Secessionist feeling was strong in the slave states of Maryland, Kentucky, and Missouri. Lincoln was able to prevent them from seceding by a combination of shrewd political maneuvers and the tactful deployment of troops. Delaware, the fifteenth slave state, never seriously considered secession.

Then, in the contest for the border states, the North won a bonus. The mountainous western part of Virginia was peopled by farmers who owned few slaves and who traditionally resented the planter aristocracy that dominated Virginia politics and was now in favor of secession. The westerners had no interest in fighting and dying to protect the human property of the rich flatlanders. In effect, the 50 western counties of Virginia seceded from the Old Dominion. By an irregular constitutional process, the Republicans provided the means for West Virginia to become a Union state in June 1863.

For the border states, the Civil War was literally a war between brothers. Henry Clay's grandsons fought on both sides. Several of President Lincoln's brothers-in-law fought for the South, and Jefferson Davis had cousins in the Union army. The most poignant case was that of Senator Crittenden of Kentucky, who had tried to head off war with a compromise. One of his sons became a general in the Union army and another a general in the Confederate army.

The Irony of Secession

However much the people of the border states disliked secession, they were not against slavery. In order to reassure them, Lincoln issued several pronouncements that the purpose of the war was to preserve the Union and not to abolish slavery. In emphasizing this war aim, he pointed up the irony of secession. Although southerners claimed that they had gone their own way in order to protect their "peculiar institution," they actually had thrown away the legal and constitutional guarantees that they had enjoyed as United States citizens.

Under the Fugitive Slave Act, slaves who ran away to the northern states were returned to their owners. In order to escape, slaves had to get to Canada, out of the country. With secession, "out of the country" was hundreds of miles closer—over the Tennessee-Kentucky or the Virginia-Maryland line. This fact was dramatized early in the war when several Union generals declared that slaves who fled to Union lines were contraband of war, subject to confiscation and therefore free. At first, Lincoln countermanded these orders so as not to antagonize the loyal slave states, especially Kentucky. But it was obvious that the South had made it easier for slaves to get away than it had been before secession.

In leaving the Union as individual states, the southerners had waived all legal rights to the territories, which were federal property. Their action was the most effective guarantee, short of a constitutional amendment, that slavery would be banned from the territories.

Some southerners had no intention of giving up the territories, of course. The Indians of Oklahoma, for example, were generally pro-Confederate. But to win the Indian lands and, perhaps, New Mexico meant launching the very war that Davis hoped to avoid. Secession was less a rational political act than it was the fruit of passion, suspicion, and sectional hatred blinding the southern extremists to reality.

for FURTHER READING

Most of the books cited here also deal with events treated in Chapter 23, particularly Avery O. Craven, *The Growth of Southern Nationalism, 1848–1860*, 1953, and *The Coming of the Civil War*, 1957; James McPherson, *Battle Cry of Freedom*, 1988; Alan Nevins, *Ordeal of the Union*, 1947; and David Potter, *The Impending Crisis, 1848–1861*, 1976. Also see Eric Foner, *Politics and Ideology in the Age of the Civil War*, 1980.

The events that promoted sectional bitterness in North and South during the 1850s are treated in Stanley W. Campbell, *The Slave-Catchers: Enforcement of the Fugitive Slave Law, 1840–1860*, 1968; James C. Malin, *John Brown and the Legend of Fifty-Six*, 1970; Truman Nelson, *The Old Man John Brown at Harpers Ferry*, 1973; Stephen Oates, *To Purge This Land with Blood: A Biography of John Brown*, 1970; Don E. Fehrenbacher, *The Dred Scott Case: Its Significance in American Law and Politics*, 1978; C. B. Swisher, *Roger B. Taney*, 1935; and R. W. Johansen, *The Lincoln-Douglas Debates*, 1965.

On the secession crisis, the standard works are Kenneth M. Stampp, *And the War Came: The North and the Secession Crisis, 1860–1861*, 1950, and W. L. Barney, *The Road to Secession*, 1972. See also Stephen A. Channing, *Crisis of Fear: Secession in South Carolina*, 1970; and R. A. Wooster, *The Secession Conventions of the South*, 1962. Don E. Fehrenbacher, *Prelude to Greatness: Lincoln in the 1850s*, 1962, is essential. Richard N. Current, *Lincoln and the First Shot*, 1963, and *The Lincoln Nobody Knows*, 1958, deal with the president's actions in 1861. For Lincoln's predecessor, see P. S. Klein, *President James Buchanan*, 1962; for his southern counterpart, see Clement Eaton, *Jefferson Davis*, 1977. See also Stephen B. Oates, *With Malice Toward None*, 1979; and Benjamin P. Thomas, *Abraham Lincoln*, 1952.

AMERICAN JOURNEY ONLINE AND INFOTRAC COLLEGE EDITION

Visit the source collections at http://ajaccess.wadsworth.com and http://infotrac.thomsonlearning.com, and use the Search function with the following key terms to explore documents, images, audio and video clips, articles, and commentary related to the material in this chapter:

Abraham Lincoln   Jefferson Davis
Dred Scott   John Brown
Fort Sumter   Lincoln-Douglas debates
Harpers Ferry

Additional resources, exercises, and Internet links related to this chapter are available on *The American Past* Web site: http://history.wadsworth.com/americanpast7e.

HISTORY ONLINE

The Dred Scott Case
www.toptags.com/aama/docs/dscott.htm
Text of pleadings in the historic Supreme Court case.

John Brown and the Valley of the Shadow
www.iath.virginia.edu/jbrown/master.html
Comprehensive coverage, with links, of Brown's raid at Harpers Ferry.

23

TIDY PLANS, UGLY REALITIES

The Civil War Through 1862

The Cooper Union Museum, New York

The first blast of civil war is the death warrant of your institution.

Benjamin Wade

Had slavery been kept out of the fight, the Union would have gone down. But the enemies of the country were so misguided as to rest their cause upon it, and that was the destruction of it and of them.

Joshua Lawrence Chamberlain

THE BOMBARDMENT OF Fort Sumter answered the big question: There would be a war. When Lincoln called for volunteers to suppress the rebellion and Davis summoned the manhood of the South to defend its honor and independence, both were flooded with recruits. By the summer of 1861, the Union had 186,000 soldiers in uniform; the Confederacy, 112,000.

But what kind of war would it be? What would battle be like? Nowhere had armies of such size clashed since the Napoleonic Wars in Europe half a century earlier. During the Mexican War, the United States had fielded no more than 10,000 men at a time. Now, just 15 years later, two American forces were faced with the challenge of feeding, clothing, sheltering, transporting, training, and controlling a mass of humanity 10 and 20 times that size.

THE ART AND SCIENCE OF WAR

The American Civil War took up where Napoleon and Wellington left off. American officers were educated in a theory of battle devised by a Swiss officer who had served both the French and the Russians, Henri de Jomini. A textbook based on Jomini's *Art of War* was the authority on tactics at West Point, where virtually all the major commanders of the Civil War learned their craft.

Position, Maneuver, and Concentration

Jomini emphasized position and maneuver as the keys to winning battle. The goal of the commanding general was to occupy high ground, ascertain the weakest point in the enemy's lines, and concentrate his power there. The general who prepared more thoroughly, better exploited the terrain, and moved his troops more skillfully than his opponent would break through the opposing line and force the enemy from the field.

The strategic object then was to capture and occupy economically important enemy cities and, best of all, the enemy's capital. The idea was that, losing what we would call a national infrastructure, the enemy had nothing for which to fight. Napoleon defeated his enemies in Europe (except Russia) when he occupied their major cities.

Jomini reduced battle situations to 12 models. Therefore, officers trained in his school (and with a brain in their heads!) knew pretty much what their adversaries had in mind at all times. As long as both sides observed the rules, there would be no long casualty lists. The general who was outfoxed knew that his duty was to disengage so that his men could fight another day under more favorable circumstances. Retreat, far from shameful, was among the most important of maneuvers because it preserved an army as a functioning machine.

The Armies

The armies of the Civil War were divided into cavalry, artillery, and infantry, with support units such as the Corps of Engineers (which constructed fortifications) and the Quartermaster Corps (entrusted with supply).

The cavalry's principal role was in reconnaissance. Horse soldiers were an army's eyes (although there would be some experimentation with anchored balloons in the Civil War). Battle plans were based on the information the cavalry brought back from sometimes spectacular rides that circled the enemy force. Because of their mobility and speed, cavalry units were also used for raids, plunging deep into hostile territory, burning and destroying what they found, sometimes seizing useful booty, and hightailing it out before they were confronted by big guns and masses of infantry.

In a pitched battle, cavalry reinforced weak points in the lines, and, if enemy troops retreated, the horse soldiers pursued, harassed, and scattered them. But cavalrymen were lightly armed by definition; for all the dash and flash, cavalry played a subsidiary role in pitched battle. Nevertheless, it was the glamorous service: the horses, the shades of the days of chivalry!

The artillery was slow to move and, with its toil, noise, and grime, notoriously unglamorous. But, as Napoleon had shown, big guns were critical to both attack and defense. Before an attacking army moved, its artillery slugged away at enemy positions with exploding shells, "softening them up." In defense, the artillery greeted attacking infantry and cavalry with grapeshot (a charge of small iron balls) and canister (projectiles that exploded and filled the air with clouds of metal). Examinations of dead soldiers after Civil War battles revealed that an attacking army suffered far more from cannon fire than from small arms. Indeed, soldiers in the field wryly joked that they fired a man's weight

▲ *Wagons of a Union supply unit in Virginia. The Union's massive resources and efficiency in supplying troops gave it an immense advantage over the Confederacy.*

in lead and iron for each enemy they killed. A Union expert found that calculation conservative; he said that 240 pounds of gunpowder and 900 pounds of lead were expended for every Confederate soldier felled.

As always, the infantry was the backbone of the army. The cavalry might worry the enemy, and the artillery weaken him, but it was the foot soldiers, squander ammunition as they did, who slogged it out face to face, took the casualties, and won and lost the battles.

The Infantry in Battle

The basic infantry unit was the brigade of 2,000 to 3,000 men. Under the command of a brigadier general, the soldiers formed double lines in defense or advanced over a front of about a thousand yards. During the first campaigns of the Civil War, captains in the front lines tried to march the men in step, as had been the practice in the Napoleonic Era. But with the greater firepower of the 1860s, so formal a charge was sensibly abandoned. It was enough that the men continued to run, trot, or simply walk into grapeshot, minié balls (conical bullets), noise like a thunderstorm in hell, and a haze of black, sulfurous smoke. Junior officers led the charge; thus, the ranks of lieutenant and captain suffered high casualties. More senior officers walked behind the lines to discourage stragglers. They carried revolvers and were authorized to shoot men who panicked and broke ranks, and they did.

If the advancing army was not forced to turn back, the final phase of battle was hand-to-hand combat. The attackers clambered over the enemy's fortifications of earth and lumber. Attackers and defenders swung their muskets at one another like the baseball bats they played with in camp until the defenders broke and ran or the attackers were killed or captured. The men had bayonets, but neither side succeeded in training the soldiers to use them very well. The importance of mastering this difficult and deadly skill was one lesson that European military observers took home with them

(as well as the opinion, lasting half a century, that Americans were afraid of cold steel).

There was plenty of shooting but not a great deal of aiming. Except for special units of sharpshooters, foot soldiers were not marksmen. There was little sense in taking on the big and expensive job of training large numbers of men in the skill of hitting small targets at great distances. With a few important exceptions (Shiloh, Antietam, Gettysburg), Civil War battles were not fought in open country. The men confronted one another in dense woods on terrain broken by hills, creeks, stone fences, and ditches. In several battles, attackers had to clamber up Appalachian cliffs on all fours. Often, opposing soldiers could not see one another until they were on the verge of touching.

Even in open country, hundreds of cannons and tens of thousands of muskets filled the air with a dense, acrid smog that, on a windless day, shrouded the battlefield. (Smokeless powder was still in the future.) Even if a soldier could shoot well, there was little he could aim at to prove it.

Billy Yank and Johnny Reb

As in all wars, the men who fought the Civil War were young, most between the ages of 17 and 25, with drummer boys of only 12. They came from every state and social class, although when both sides adopted draft laws (the Confederacy in April 1862, the Union in March 1863), the burden fell more heavily on poorer farmers and working people than on the middle and upper classes.

This was because the draft laws included exemptions favoring the well-to-do. The Confederates exempted men who owned 20 or more slaves. This was sorely resented by "Johnny Reb," the common soldier, who rarely owned one. Both the Confederate and Union draft laws allowed a man who was called to service to pay for a substitute at a price that was beyond the means of the ordinary fellow who did not want to go. In the North, a draftee could hire another to take his place or simply pay the government $300 for an exemption. In July 1863, working-class resentment of the draft led to a weeklong riot in New York City. Mobs of mostly Irish workingmen sacked draft offices, attacked rich men, and harassed and lynched blacks, whom they considered the cause of the war and a threat to their jobs. Some 60,000 people were involved, at least 400 were killed, and some $5 million in property was destroyed.

In the South, resistance to conscription took the form of thousands of draft dodgers heading west or into the Appalachians and the Ozarks, where some organized outlaw gangs, raided farms, and occasionally skirmished with Confederate troops. Most southern opposition to the war centered in the poorer mountain counties of western Virginia and North Carolina and in eastern Tennessee.

Both Union and Confederate armies were plagued by a high desertion rate, about 10 percent through most of the war. A few individuals were professional deserters, the bounty jumpers. Because some units paid cash—bounties—to men who signed up, some made a lucrative, although risky, business of enlisting, skipping out at the first opportunity, and looking for another unit offering bounties. In March 1865, Union military police arrested one John O'Connor, who was surely the champion. He confessed to enlisting, collecting a bounty, and deserting 32 times.

Shirking was not typical of either side, however. Over the course of the war, 1.5 million young men served in the Union army, and more than 1 million, from a much smaller population, with the Confederates. Whatever their resentments, ordinary people thought they had something at stake in the conflict. Despite their exemption, southern slave owners served in proportion to their numbers.

Army Life

The war they knew was not much like the war presented to the folks back home. In drawings in newspapers, masses of men moved in order across open fields amid waving flags and cloudlike puffs of white smoke. In reality, battle was a tiny part of military experience. Mostly, the war involved waiting, digging trenches, building breast works, marching, and being carted from one place to another in crowded trains.

The war meant poor food and shelter. In the South, supply was rarely efficient. Even when the Confederacy had enough uniforms, shoes, and food—which was not always—

there were problems in getting them to the soldiers. In the North, the inevitable profiteers sold the government tainted beef and shoddy blankets that fell apart in the rain. On both sides, physicians were unprepared to cope with so many patients; dysentery, typhoid, influenza, and other epidemic illnesses killed more soldiers than did enemy guns.

A Woman's War Too

A few women, although on no payroll, worked as spies during the war. The most famous Confederate agent was Rose O'Neal Greenhow, a Washington, D.C., widow with access to Washington society. During 1861, she forwarded information learned from Union officers to Richmond but was caught before the end of the year and deported through southern lines. There may have been dozens of less respectable pro-Confederate ladies in Washington, their names unknown for obvious reasons, who wheedled information from officers with whom they slept. There were plenty of Confederate sympathizers of both sexes in the city.

Harriet Tubman continued to penetrate Virginia in her role of harmless "mammy," reporting back to the Union army the disposition of rebel troops and the location of fortifications.

Female nurses were the most numerous and prominent soldiers in the cause. Shortly after Fort Sumter, Elizabeth

Wilhelmina Yank and Joanna Reb
Women fought in the Civil War, posing as men, of course. Official records list 127 female soldiers. One historian suggests the number was 400. Among them was Jennie Hodges, who fought for an Illinois regiment as Albert Cashier. Sarah Lemma Edmonds was Franklin Thompson in the Second Michigan. Passing as Lyons Wake in the 153rd Regiment of the New York State volunteers, Sarah Rosetta Wake rose to the rank of major.

The Cooper Union Museum, New York

▲ *A soldier's sketch of troops on the march. For every day a soldier spent in, preparing for, or regrouping after a battle, he spent dozens in exhausting treks, heavy labor, and training (or languishing) in camp.*

Blackwell, the first American woman to be a medical doctor, organized what became the United States Sanitary Commission, which put 3,000 nurses in army hospitals. At first, the army did not want them. Closeness to the front lines and the gore and male nakedness of the hospitals did not accord with the ideals of the gospel of true womanhood. But spokeswomen like Clara Barton (later founder of the American Red Cross) and Dorothea Dix, both women of impeccable propriety, wore the generals down. The fiercest opponents of women around the army were soon forced to admit that female nurses were infinitely superior to the disabled men who had previously assisted in army hospitals.

Hardly noticed at the time, a shortage of male workers, due to the size of the armies and full employment in industry, opened jobs in the federal bureaucracy for women, at the lowest levels. After the war, the taboo broken, the number of female civil servants steadily increased until they were a majority of federal employees in Washington.

In the South more than the North, because the Confederacy's manpower shortage was far more serious, women took heavy and dirty factory jobs. They took dangerous jobs too: An estimated 100 southern women were killed in explosions in munitions plants.

THE SOBERING CAMPAIGN OF 1861

Army life also meant drilling, day in and day out. But those who rallied to the colors in the spring of 1861 thought of the war as a great adventure, a vacation from the plow and hog trough, that would be over too soon. They trimmed themselves in gaudy uniforms. Some, influenced by pictures of Turkish soldiers in the recently concluded Crimean War, called themselves "Zouaves" (after a type of French infantry soldier) and donned fezzes and baggy pantaloons. Other units adopted names that would have been more appropriate to a boys' club. One Confederate regiment was called "The Lincoln Killers."

Manassas or Bull Run?

Early in the war, the Confederacy generally named battles after the nearest town. So they called the first battle, on July 21, 1861, "Manassas." The Union, although not consistently, named battles after the nearest waterway—thus, the "Battle of Bull Run." The Union's "Antietam" (named for a creek) was the South's "Sharpsburg" (named for a town in Maryland).

The Confederacy named armies after the state (or, in the case of Robert E. Lee's Army of Northern Virginia, part of a state) they were initially assigned to defend. The Union named its armies after rivers—for example, McClellan's Army of the Potomac. There was a Confederate "Army of Tennessee" (named after the state) and a Union "Army of *the* Tennessee" (named after the Tennessee River).

The Attempt to Take Richmond

Abraham Lincoln shared the illusion that the war would be short and painless. He waved off senior general Winfield Scott's warning that it would take three years and 300,000 men to crush the rebellion. Lincoln asked the first volunteers, mostly members of state militias, to enlist for only 90 days. That would be enough. Southerners too spoke of "our battle summer." The soldiers and civilians on the two sides disagreed only as to who would be celebrating when the leaves fell in the autumn of 1861.

These pleasant illusions were blown away on a fine July day about 20 miles outside Washington. Believing that his volunteers could take Richmond before their enlistments expired, Lincoln sent General Irvin McDowell marching directly toward the Confederate capital with 30,000 troops. Laughing and joking as they went, sometimes shooting at targets, the boys from Ohio and Massachusetts were accompanied by a parade of carriages filled with congressmen, socialites, newspaper reporters, and curiosity seekers. The crowd carried picnic lunches and discussed where in Richmond they would enjoy a late supper.

Albert Bierstadt, *Guerilla Warfare (Picket Duty in Virginia)* 1862. The Century Association

▲ *The Union rout at Manassas (Bull Run). It was a total defeat for the North, but the Confederate army had itself come so close to disintegration that a follow-up march on Washington was out of the question.*

Facing Battle

The Civil War battle experience was much the same whether a soldier wore blue or gray—except that northern troops were almost always better supplied with shelter, clothing, shoes, medicine, food, arms, and ammunition. It is difficult to say how much this meant to the outcome of the war. Cold, wet, tired, and ill soldiers are surely less effective than well-equipped ones. Confederate troops without shoes—not uncommon—were usually, but not always, exempt from charging enemy lines. Nevertheless, "Johnny Reb," the Confederate foot soldier, won the respect of both his officers and his enemies as a fighting man. As early as the second Battle of Bull Run in 1862, the commander of a unit called "Toombs's Georgians" told of leading so many barefoot men against the Yankees that they "left bloody footprints among the thorns and briars."

Johnny Reb and his Union counterpart, "Billy Yank," knew when they were going to fight. In only a few large battles was an army caught by surprise. Preparations for massive attack were so extensive that getting caught napping, as Grant's men were at Shiloh, was rare. In fact, the men who would be *defending* a position were generally prepared for battle with extra rations and ammunition earlier than the attackers, who knew when they would be moving.

Two or three days' rations were distributed before a battle. Historian Bell I. Wiley suggests that in the Confederate ranks:

this judicious measure generally fell short of its object because of Johnny Reb's own characteristics: he was always hungry, he had a definite prejudice against baggage, and he was the soul of improvidence. Sometimes, the whole of the extra rations would be consumed as soon as it was cooked, and rarely did any part of it last for the full period intended.

Such recklessness could have serious consequences because fighting was heavy labor. Tales of units incapacitated by hunger after a day's battle were common. The men learned immediately to attend to their canteens. Waiting, marching, and running in the heat, cold, and rain, and the grime and dust of battle, made everyone intolerably, constantly thirsty.

As short a time as possible before a battle, each infantryman was given 40 to 60 rounds of ammunition to stash in the cartridge box he wore on a strap slung over a shoulder. (Soldiers rarely carried much ammunition at other times because the powder so easily got damp and useless.) The Springfield repeating rifles took a round that looked like any modern cartridge. The muzzle-loading musket—which was used by all the Confederates and most of the Yankees—took a round that consisted of a ball and a charge of powder wrapped together in a piece of paper that was twisted closed at the powder end. To load the musket, a soldier bit off the twist so that the powder was exposed, pushed the cartridge into the muzzle of his gun, inserted the paper he held in his teeth to keep the ball from rolling out, and rammed a rod (attached to his gun) into the barrel to the breech. Each time he fired, he had to fall to one knee in order to reload. The times when men were reloading or retreating were far more dangerous than when troops were advancing.

On the eve or morning of a battle, the commanding general addressed his troops either personally or in written orations read by line officers. Confederate general Albert Sidney Johnston took the high road in his speech before Shiloh:

The eyes and the hope of eight millions of people rest upon you. You are expected to show yourselves worthy of your race and lineage; worthy of the women of the South, whose noble devotion in this war has never been exceeded in any time. With such incentives to brave deeds and with the trust that God is with us, your general will lead you confidently to the combat, assured of success.

Others, like General T. C. Hindman in December 1862, were demagogues:

Remember that the enemy you engage has no feeling of mercy. His ranks are made up of Pin Indians, Free Negroes, Southern Tories, Kansas Jayhawkers, and hired Dutch cutthroats. These bloody ruffians have invaded your country, stolen and destroyed your property, murdered your neighbors, outraged your women, driven your children from their homes, and defiled the graves of your kindred.

They were met by a Confederate force of about 22,000 under the command of General Beauregard, recently arrived from Fort Sumter. The rebels had hastily dug in on high ground behind a creek called Bull Run, near a railroad crossing named Manassas Junction. McDowell attacked immediately, guessing the Confederate left flank to be the weakest point in the line. He was right about that. Although his troops were shocked by the ferocity of the musket fire that greeted them, they almost cracked the southern line.

Had it cracked, the war might have been over in the Upper South. To the rear of Beauregard's line, the road to Richmond was wide open. At the critical moment, however, 9,000 Virginians commanded by Joseph E. Johnston arrived on the field after a frantic train ride from the Shenandoah Valley. A brigade under the command of Thomas J. Jackson,

a 37-year-old mathematics instructor at Virginia Military Academy, shored up the sagging Confederate left. The Union soldiers fell back and then broke in hysteria, fleeing for Washington along with the panicked spectators.

Celebrations and Recriminations

The South had a victory and a hero. At the peak of the battle, a South Carolinian rallied his men by shouting, "There stands Jackson like a stone wall." The name stuck, for it seemed appropriate to more than Thomas J. Jackson's performance on the battlefield. He was introspective and humorless, an object of mockery to his students before the war. He was a stern Scotch-Irish Presbyterian who lacked the human touch.

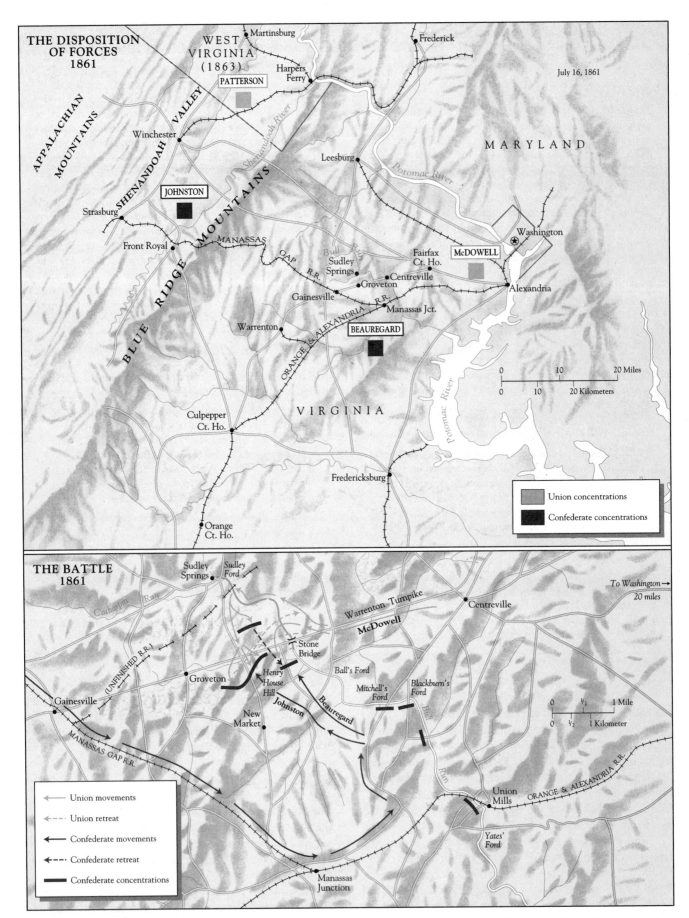

THE DISPOSITION OF FORCES 1861

WEST VIRGINIA (1863)

Martinsburg

Frederick

PATTERSON

Harpers Ferry

July 16, 1861

APPALACHIAN MOUNTAINS

SHENANDOAH VALLEY

Winchester

Shenandoah River

MARYLAND

Leesburg

Potomac River

JOHNSTON

Strasburg

BLUE RIDGE MOUNTAINS

Front Royal

MANASSAS GAP R.R.

Sudley Springs

Groveton

Gainesville

Fairfax Ct. Ho.

Centreville

Bull Run

McDOWELL

Washington

Alexandria

Warrenton

ORANGE & ALEXANDRIA R.R.

BEAUREGARD

Manassas Jct.

Culpepper Ct. Ho.

VIRGINIA

Potomac River

0   10   20 Miles

0   10   20 Kilometers

Fredericksburg

Orange Ct. Ho.

■ Union concentrations

■ Confederate concentrations

THE BATTLE 1861

Sudley Springs

Sudley Ford

Catharpin Run

Warrenton Turnpike

Centreville

McDowell

To Washington → 20 miles

(UNFINISHED R.R.)

Stone Bridge

Groveton

Henry House Hill

Ball's Ford

Johnston

Mitchell's Ford

Blackburn's Ford

Beauregard

Gainesville

New Market

MANASSAS GAP R.R.

Bull Run

Union Mills

ORANGE & ALEXANDRIA R.R.

0   ½   1 Mile

0   ½   1 Kilometer

Yates' Ford

Manassas Junction

← Union movements

←--- Union retreat

← Confederate movements

←--- Confederate retreat

━ Confederate concentrations

MAP 23:1 The Battle of Bull Run, July 21, 1861 McDowell's army advanced from Washington along the highway that led to Winchester in the Shenandoah Valley. The battle lines stretched along Bull Run, straddling the Warrenton turnpike. Confederate generals Johnston and Jackson rushed reinforcements to the scene on the Manassas Gap railroad.

▲ *Thomas J. "Stonewall" Jackson was the hero of the Confederacy's heady summer after the Battle of Manassas. He was polite at the many celebrations where he was feted but would not have enjoyed himself much. Jackson was the most morally strict and self-controlled of Presbyterians. He liked whiskey but did not drink it, for fear that he might like it too much.*

Jackson awed his soldiers because he came to life when the bullets whistled. He never yielded a line to the enemy, and he was a genius at maneuvering troops. For two years, Jackson would do what the South needed done, inserting his men in critical positions and standing like a stone wall.

By contrast, General Beauregard's reputation collapsed after Bull Run because he failed to follow up his victory by marching on Washington. He was soon replaced as Confederate commander in Virginia by Joseph E. Johnston, who had brought the troops and Stonewall Jackson from the Shenandoah Valley.

Johnston was a far superior field commander, but Beauregard was not to blame for the South's failure to capture Washington. As Johnston himself put it, "The Confederate Army was more disorganized by victory than that of the United States by defeat," and a disorganized army is no army at all. All the better generals at Bull Run, plus desk men like Robert E. Lee, who was President Davis's military adviser, emphasized the need for hard training.

The Summer Lull

Davis, who had been a pretty good junior officer, agreed. He cautioned Richmond society that there was more fighting to come. But few seemed to listen. Casualties had been minor. The soldiers were cocky and overconfident after their victory. Southern politicians spoke as though the war were over. Volunteer officers nagged their tailors to finish sewing gold braid on their dress uniforms so that they could show them off once or twice before the Union capitulated. And they bickered. At an endless round of gala parties in Richmond, old personal jealousies erupted as blustering colonels and generals blamed one another for blunders real and imaginary.

In the North, the defeat at Manassas taught a sorely needed lesson. The spectacle of McDowell's troops throwing down their guns and trotting wild-eyed into Washington, where they lay down to sleep in doorways and on the sidewalks, alarmed Lincoln and brought him around to Winfield Scott's way of thinking. The war would be no summer's pastime but a long, hard fight. Now when Lincoln asked Congress for troops, he wanted 300,000 men under three-year enlistments.

He relieved Irvin McDowell of command of what was now called the "Army of the Potomac," replacing him with George B. McClellan. The former president of the Illinois Central Railroad (for which Lincoln had been a lawyer), McClellan had a reputation as a superb organizer and administrator. In November 1861, Winfield Scott retired, and McClellan also took charge of the Union armies that were being drilled throughout the Midwest.

Northern Strategy

Although Scott was gone, living out the war at West Point, the three-part strategy that he had earlier outlined to Lincoln was effectively adopted. First, it was necessary to defend Washington with the Army of the Potomac and to maintain constant pressure on Richmond in the hope of capturing the city. This was important not only because Richmond, just 100 miles from Washington, was the Confederate capital, but because it was a railroad hub and a major industrial center, home of the Tredregar Iron Works, which was to sustain Virginia's fighting machine throughout the war.

Second—and Lincoln needed no tutoring on this—because the Ohio-Mississippi waterway was vital to the economic life of the midwestern states, Union armies would strike down the great valley. Their object was to gain complete control of the Mississippi as soon as possible in order to permit western farmers to resume the export of foodstuffs, by which they lived, and to split the Confederacy in two. The trans-Mississippi front (Arkansas and Texas) could then be left to small forces while the Union concentrated its power in the East.

Third, the Union would use its overwhelming naval superiority to blockade the South, strangling its export economy. If the Confederates were unable to sell cotton abroad, they could not buy the manufactured goods, particularly the munitions, that were essential in a lengthy war. Scott called the blockade the "Anaconda Plan" after the South American snake that slowly crushes its prey.

On the face of it, an effective blockade was out of the question. The Confederate Atlantic and Gulf coastlines were labyrinths of inlets, sheltered channels, coves, bays, bayous, salt marshes, and lonely broad beaches. It was quite impossible to prevent every vessel from reaching shore or from making a break for the high seas. Nevertheless, a national commerce could not be rowed through the surf or unloaded in swamps; the commanders of the Union navy felt confident that with time and more ships, they could bottle up the Confederate ports.

Dixie's Challenge

Southern strategy had a simpler design but a flimsier foundation. In order to win its independence, the Confederacy needed to conquer nothing. The South had only to turn back Union advances until Britain or France, both of which had expressed sympathy for the southern cause, came to the rescue or until the people of the North grew weary of fighting and forced Lincoln to negotiate. In the broadest sense, the story of the Civil War tells how these hopes were dashed and how, although long frustrated and delayed, the Union strategy succeeded.

The Confederacy's hope of foreign intervention died first. In the case of France, it may have been doomed from the beginning by the personality of the French emperor, Napoleon III. On one day a scheming power politician who recognized that an independent Confederacy might be molded into a valuable French protectorate, Napoleon III was, on the next, a flighty romantic.

At first, while leading the southerners on, he delayed when the more prudent British dithered. (Napoleon did not want to intervene in the war without British approval.) Then, when he was approached by Mexican aristocrats who, in order to defeat a mestizo and Indian revolution, offered to make an emperor of Napoleon's nephew, Maximilian of Austria, Napoleon III saw a far grander opportunity in America's tragedy than helping the South. Whereas the United States at peace might have forcefully resisted French interference in Mexico—it was not so long since some American expansionists spoke of annexing the whole country—the United States tearing itself apart was helpless to act. Anyway, what self-respecting emperor wanted a dependency of quarrelsome, headstrong cotton planters when he could tread in the footsteps of Cortés? Not Napoleon III. By the end of 1862, he was sidestepping the southern diplomats in Paris.

The pro-Confederate sentiments of the British government were solidly founded. Southern cotton fed the massive British textile industry, and British industrialists generally supported Henry Lord Palmerston's Liberal government. Moreover, many English aristocrats looked upon the southern planters, whose anglophilia and imitation of the British upper classes flattered them, as rough-cut kinsmen. Then, some strategically thinking British politicians saw an opportunity to shatter the growing power of the United States, which, they knew, was destined to eclipse Great Britain's.

The trouble was slavery. British public opinion was staunchly antislavery. In Britain, abolitionists much like America's had won their fight peacefully. British hostility toward slavery had prevented an alliance with Texas. Lord Palmerston was not willing to bear the wrath of antislavery Britons unless the Confederates demonstrated that they had a real chance of winning. Britain would not help the South fight an open-ended war of defense.

A combination of Confederate blunders in export policy, bad luck, Union diplomatic skill, and a Union victory in the Confederacy's brightest hour dashed the Confederate dream of redrawing the map of North America.

King Cotton Dethroned

The blunder was Jefferson Davis's belief he could blackmail Britain into coming to the aid of the South. In the excited solidarity of the Confederacy's first days, he prevailed on cotton shippers to keep the crop of 1860 at home, storing it in warehouses. The idea was to put the pinch on British mill owners so that they would set up a cry for a war to liberate the coveted fiber.

"Cotton diplomacy" did not work. English mill owners had anticipated the war and stockpiled huge reserves. When these supplies ran out in 1862, the price of cotton tripled, inducing farmers in Egypt and the Middle East to expand their cotton cultivation. Within a year, they were filling much of the gap created by the American war. To make matters worse, Union troops captured enough southern cotton in 1861 and 1862 to keep the mills of New England humming and even to sell some to Britain.

As the war dragged on, cotton diplomacy was completely scuttled by two successive poor grain harvests in western Europe. Fearing food shortages, monarchist Britain discovered that Union wheat was more royal than King Cotton. Blessed with bumper crops in those years, northern farmers shipped unprecedented tonnages of grain to Europe at both financial and diplomatic profit.

Diplomacy

In November 1861, a zealous Union naval officer almost ruined the northern effort to keep Britain neutral. The captain of the USS *San Jacinto* boarded a British steamer, the *Trent*, and seized two Confederate diplomats aboard, James M. Mason and John Slidell. Northern public opinion was delighted. It was refreshing to hear for a change of an American warship bullying a British vessel. But Lincoln took a dimmer view of the incident. The British minister in Washington came close to threatening war. For the president, Mason and Slidell were two hot potatoes, and he took advantage of the first lull in the public celebrations to hasten them aboard a British warship. "One war at a time," he remarked to his cabinet.

No harm was done. In France, Slidell was frustrated by Napoleon III's Mexican ambitions, and, in England, Mason proved no match for the Union minister, Charles Francis Adams, in the delicate game of diplomacy. Mason managed to see two commerce raiders, the *Florida* and the *Alabama,* constructed for the Confederacy and put to sea. But Adams cajoled and threatened the British government into preventing a sister ship and several Confederate rams from leaving port. He moved with great skill and energy through the salons of London—it ran in the family—and kept Great Britain out of the war until the North turned the tide in its direction and the possibility of British intervention quietly died.

1862 AND STALEMATE

As hopes of bringing England in dimmed, the South looked increasingly to northern sympathizers and defeatists to aid their cause. Some northerners frankly favored the South. Former president Franklin Pierce openly hoped for a Confederate victory. Prosouthern sentiment was strongest in the Union slave states of Maryland, Kentucky, and Missouri, of course, but also in the lower counties of Ohio, Indiana, and Illinois, a region with a strong southern heritage. However, these northerners who sympathized with the South, called "copperheads" (after a poisonous snake of that name that strikes without warning), were never able to mount a decisive threat to the Union war effort. They were a minority, and Lincoln played free with their civil liberties in order to silence them.

Lincoln and the Copperheads

One of the president's most controversial moves against opponents of the war was his suspension of the ancient legal right of habeas corpus, a protection against arbitrary arrest that is basic to both English and American law. At one time or another, 13,000 people were jailed, almost always briefly, because of alleged antiwar activity. Lincoln also used his control of the post office to harass, and even suppress, anti-administration newspapers.

The noisiest copperhead was Clement L. Vallandigham, a popular Democratic congressman from Ohio. His attacks on the war effort were so unsettling that, after General Ambrose Burnside jailed him, Lincoln feared he would be honored as a martyr. The president solved the problem by handing Vallandigham over to the Confederates as if he were a southern agent. Identifying Vallandigham with treason was unfair but shrewd; in 1863, he was forced to run for governor of Ohio from exile in Canada. At home, or even in prison, he might have won. But in absentia, he was defeated,

Fed Up in Dixie

By no means did all white southerners rally to the "Stars and Bars," as the Confederate flag was nicknamed. In the upland South, the foothills on both sides of the Appalachian ridge, few people owned slaves, and many of them opposed secession as the darling of the great planters, whose political and economic domination they resented. Western Virginia and eastern Tennessee voted against secession and provided thousands of soldiers for the Union army. So did many counties in western North Carolina and northern Alabama. Once the war was under way, the Confederate government's practice of expropriating crops and livestock to feed its armies aggravated the situation. When food became expensive and scarce in cities like Richmond and even in the countryside, southern women rioted to protest the war.

and when he returned to the United States the next year, he was harmless enough that Lincoln could ignore him.

More worrisome than the copperheads was defeatism, the belief that the war was not worth the expense in blood and money. Each time Union armies lost a battle, more and more northerners wondered if it would not be wiser to let the southern states go. Or, they asked, was it really impossible to negotiate? Was Lincoln's Republican administration, rather than the southern states, the obstacle to a compromise peace?

It was, in fact, impossible for Lincoln to secure reunion on any other basis than military victory. Even at the bitter end of the war, when the Confederacy was not only defeated but devastated, Jefferson Davis insisted on southern independence as a condition of peace. As long as the South was winning the battles, negotiation was out of the question.

And the South won most of the battles in 1861 and 1862. The show belonged to Stonewall Jackson and General Robert E. Lee, who succeeded Joseph Johnston as commander of the Army of Northern Virginia when, at the Battle of the Seven Pines on May 31, 1862, Johnston was seriously wounded. Time after time, Lee and Jackson halted or drubbed the Army of the Potomac. Nevertheless, even in his most triumphant hour in the summer of 1862, Lee revealed that his military genius was limited by his supreme virtue, his self-conscious image of himself as a Virginia gentleman, the scion of a distinguished old family.

Lee's cause was not so much the Confederacy as it was the dignity of "Old Virginny." He did not like slavery, the obsession of the southern hotheads. He may never have owned a slave himself and had freed his wife's slaves in 1857, when he was executor of her father's will. He did not much care for the hotheads of the Deep South, regarding them as vulgar parvenus. He had opposed Virginia's secession until it was a fact. Consequently, Lee never fully appreciated the fact that while he was defending the Old Dominion with such mastery, the southern cause was slowly throttled at sea, in the dozens of coastal enclaves Union troops occupied, and in the Mississippi Valley.

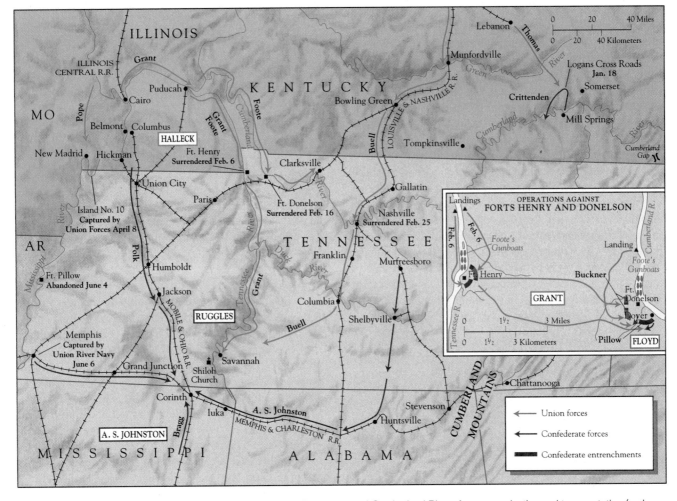

MAP 23:2 The War in the West, 1862 The importance of the Tennessee and Cumberland Rivers for communication and transportation (and thus the importance of their surrender to General Grant in February 1862) can be seen in this map. Grant's advance through Tennessee was without incident. Then came bloody Shiloh on the Mississippi border.

The Campaign in the West

Lincoln, although no military man (and himself the author of several Civil War blunders), understood the importance of the West. "We must have Kentucky," he told his cabinet. Without Kentucky—the southern bank of the Ohio River—he feared the war would be lost. Even before the army recovered from the defeat at Manassas, Lincoln approved moving a large force into the state under the command of Generals Henry Halleck and Ulysses S. Grant. In early 1862, Grant thrust into Tennessee, quickly capturing two important forts, Henry and Donelson. These forts guarded the mouths of the Tennessee and Cumberland Rivers, two waterways of infinitely greater value than muddy Bull Run. Moving on, however, General Grant fought the battle that taught both sides that they were not playing chess.

Moving up (south on) the Tennessee River unopposed, Grant intended to attack Corinth, Mississippi, in the northern part of the state. He knew that Confederate general Albert Sidney Johnston planned to defend the town, but Grant had no idea that Johnston was also prepared to attack. On April 6, 1862, while camped at Shiloh, Tennessee, Grant's soldiers were caught in their bedrolls by 40,000 rebels. Many were killed before they awoke. The others held on, but just barely. Only when Union reinforcements arrived under General Don Carlos Buell that night, did the Confederates withdraw.

Albert Sidney Johnston, regarded by some military historians as one of the Confederacy's best field commanders, was killed at Shiloh. Other southern losses numbered 11,000 of 40,000 troops engaged. The Union lost 13,000 of 60,000 men. Bodies were stacked like cordwood while massive graves were dug. Acres of ground were reddened with blood, and the stench of death sickened the survivors at their grisly job of cleaning up. Compared with the minor casualties at Bull Run—compared with the losses in most battles in any war to that date—Shiloh was a horror.

Grant was disgraced. He was accused of being drunk on the morning of the attack. Soldiers of the two armies ceased to fraternize between battles, as they had done in the woods of Tennessee, where Confederate and Union guards conversed in the night, traded tobacco for coffee, and, on at least one occasion, played a baseball game. Bull Run showed that there would be a long war; Shiloh showed that it would be bloody. Not even the success of naval officer David G. Farragut a short time after Shiloh, which put the Union in control of New Orleans, could cure the sense of melancholy that followed on the terrible battle.

The War at Sea

Confederate seamen on the commerce raiders *Florida, Alabama,* and *Shenandoah* saw quite a bit of the world. These fast, heavily armed ships destroyed or captured more than 250 northern vessels ($15 million in ships and cargo) in every corner of the seas. Sailors on the commerce raiders experienced naval warfare at its most exhilarating.

For the Union sailors assigned to the blockade, by contrast, days were long and boring, spent slowly patrolling the waters outside southern ports in scorching sun and winter winds. In 1861 and 1862, blockade duty was also frustrating. Most blockade runners, Confederate and foreign, outran the navy's ships in and out of southern ports, particularly steamers specially built for the purpose: they were low slung, so as not to be seen until within a few miles, and narrow in the beam. Blockade runners did not sail between the South and Europe. European shippers brought the goods the Confederates wanted to Bermuda or the West Indies and picked up the cotton with which southerners paid there. Blockade running was ferrying, with quick turnarounds.

The Confederates threatened to break the blockade of the Chesapeake Bay in March 1862. Out steamed an old warship, the *Merrimack,* in brand new clothes. She had been covered over with iron plates in the shape of a tent. The *Merrimack* was a ram, its prow an iron blade like a plowshare that could slice through a wooden hull. Cannonballs glanced off the sloping armor as though they were made of rubber. Within a few hours of her debut, the *Merrimack* sank several Union warships.

Left unopposed for a few weeks, this single ship might have opened the Chesapeake to trade. But the *Merrimack* did not have even a few days. The Union's experimental vessel, the even odder looking *Monitor,* was also ironclad. It resembled a cake tin on a platter skimming the waves. For five hours on March 9, 1862, the two ships had at one another, then disengaged. The battle was technically a draw but effectively a Union victory. The *Merrimack* had to retreat for repairs. In May, the Confederates destroyed the vessel so that it would not fall into Union hands.

Once again, the material disparity between the two nations told in the long run. The South never built another *Merrimack.* The *Monitor* was a prototype for a flotilla of others like it.

Williamson Art Gallery & Museum, Birkenhead, England

▲ *Confederate commerce raiders, which savaged the North's merchant fleet, under construction in Liverpool in Great Britain. Three put to sea, the most famous being the* Alabama. *Union minister Charles Francis Adams was able to persuade the British not to release others after it became clear the Union would win the war.*

The Granger Collection, New York

▲ *The Union had no better organizer and administrator than General George McClellan. But he was no good in the field—dallying and even avoiding battle either because of an innate timidity, an aversion to exposing his men to high casualties, hopes for negotiation without excessive bloodshed, or all three. Unfortunately, Union military organization did not provide for officers at the top who were "desk men" only.*

McClellan and "the Slows"

In creating the Army of the Potomac, George McClellan made an invaluable contribution to the Union cause. Not only were his men better trained than most southern troops, but they usually were better armed. Whereas the Confederates had to import or capture most of their guns, McClellan and his successors had a limitless supply of munitions and constantly improved firearms. The Springfield repeating rifle, introduced toward the end of the war, allowed Union soldiers to fire six times a minute instead of once or twice.

The problem with McClellan was that he did not exploit the tremendous edge he created. He was a man of contradictions. On the one hand, he posed, strutted, and issued bombastic proclamations in the style of Napoleon. On the other, when it came time to fight, he froze as though he were one of Napoleon's statues. It was not entirely a matter of personality. McClellan was a Democrat. He did not want to crush the South. He believed that by creating a terrifying military machine, he could persuade the Confederates to give in and negotiate a peace.

Moreover, McClellan was devoted to his soldiers. He could not bring himself to fight a battle in which the dead bodies would pile up as they had at Shiloh. Finally, he was no gambler. If there had to be a battle, he wanted overwhelming superiority. He could never get enough men to suit his conservative nature.

To Lincoln, who did not like McClellan (the feeling was mutual), it was simpler. Lincoln said that McClellan was ill; he had a bad case of "the slows."

The Peninsula Campaign

When McClellan finally moved in April 1862, he did not drive directly on Richmond. Instead, he moved by sea to the peninsula between the York and James Rivers. In a month, he had 110,000 troops poised to take Richmond from the south, bypassing the city's fortifications.

The plan was ingenious; it should have worked. The Confederate Army of Northern Virginia was outnumbered and disrupted by surprise. Having outmaneuvered the southerners, however, McClellan did not throw overwhelming force at the enemy's weakness. He sat, fiddled, and fretted. He overestimated the size of the Confederate force facing him and demanded reinforcements from Lincoln. But Lincoln refused when General Robert E. Lee, who had taken over from the injured Johnston, fooled him into thinking that Washington was in danger.

Lee set one of the traps that flummoxed northern commanders time and again. He sent Stonewall Jackson on a diversionary mission, feigning an assault on Washington that Jackson did not have the strength to bring off. The ruse was successful: Lincoln halted the movement of troops to the peninsula, and Jackson returned to reinforce the Confederates defending Richmond. By the time McClellan gave in to the president's impatient demand for massive action, Lee and Jackson had 85,000 men in position.

Seven days of nearly constant battle followed, between June 26 and July 2, 1862. Again overly cautious and outsmarted on the field, McClellan was fought to a standstill. Even then, he held a favorable position. His supply lines were intact; Confederate morale was badly shaken by the 25 percent casualties the South had suffered; and Richmond was nearly within range of bombardment. A massive Union push in the summer of 1862 might have carried the day.

It was Lincoln's turn to make a mistake. He called off the Peninsula Campaign, ordered the Army of the Potomac back to Washington, and replaced McClellan with General John Pope, who proposed to take the "safe" Manassas route to Richmond.

Pope had won several victories in the West and was a favorite with the abolitionists in Congress because of his opposition to slavery. But he was an unimaginative commander, no match for the wily Lee and Jackson. At the end of August, Lee met him on the same ground as the first Battle of Manassas and beat him back with much more ease than the Confederates had defeated McDowell.

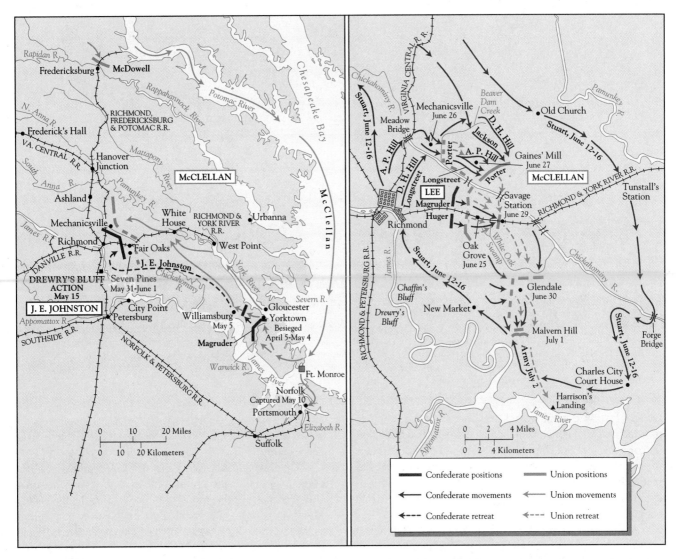

MAP 23:3 McClellan's Peninsula Campaign and the Seven Days' Battles, March 17–July 2, 1862 The Peninsula Campaign was brilliant in conception. By approaching Richmond from the southeast, virtually all the fortifications built to defend the city to the north were rendered irrelevant. But McClellan dawdled. Although his numerical advantage was overwhelming, he wanted more troops. Brilliant maneuvers by Johnston, Jackson, and Lee brought McClellan to a standstill practically within sight of the Confederate capital.

Antietam

Lincoln recalled McClellan, and the eastern theater bogged down into a stalemate that began to worry Jefferson Davis as much as it did Lincoln. Davis's critics were not satisfied with Lee's brilliant defenses; they wanted the war carried into the North. With the chances of British intervention rapidly fading, a major victory on Union soil seemed to be the only way that Britain might be brought into the war.

Unfortunately, although Lee worked defensive miracles with inferior numbers, his army of 40,000 was not up to an advance when the enemy was 70,000 strong. Moreover, he suffered a fatal stroke of bad luck when his battle plans, wrapped around a pack of cigars, fell into McClellan's hands. The Union commander caught Lee when he was least prepared to fight, at Sharpsburg, Maryland, near Antietam Creek.

The fighting was as vicious and gory as at Shiloh. Lee lost a quarter of his army, and he was in no condition to retreat in order into Virginia. Stoically, with no lines of supply, he waited for the counterattack that would destroy his army. To Lee's amazement, McClellan did not move. He was down with "the slows" again. On the second night after the battle, hardly believing his luck, Lee slipped back to the safety of Virginia.

Emancipation: A Political Masterstroke

During the first year of the war, Lincoln insisted that his aim was not the destruction of slavery but the preservation of the Union. Not only did he constantly reassure uneasy political

▲ *An unlikely subject for a landscape artist: the heaps of Confederate dead at "Bloody Lane" after the Battle of Antietam, the worst single day of the war. Their position was a road long since sunken by wagon traffic. Union troops overran the makeshift position.*

leaders from the loyal slave states, but he twice countermanded orders of generals in the field that slaves within their departments—in the Confederacy itself—were freed as acts of war. Nevertheless, Congress chipped away at the peculiar institution by declaring that those slaves employed in producing arms in the South and the slaves of people who had committed treason were free.

Antislavery feeling was growing. In August 1862, when abolitionist newspaper editor Horace Greeley publicly demanded that Lincoln move against the hated institution, the president replied, "If I could save the Union without freeing any slave, I would do it; and if I could save it by freeing all the slaves, I would do it; and if I could do it by freeing some and leaving others alone, I would also do it."

In fact, Lincoln had already decided to free some slaves. In the summer of 1862, he read the Emancipation Proclamation to his cabinet. The proclamation declared that, as of a date yet to be decided, all slaves held in territory still under the control of rebel forces were henceforth free. Secretary of State William Seward persuaded Lincoln to keep the Emancipation Proclamation in his pocket until the North could win a major victory. Otherwise, Seward argued, Lincoln's proclamation would look like an act of desperation. That major victory was Antietam. On September 22, 1862, five days after the battle, Lincoln issued his proclamation, to go into effect January 1, 1863.

A few abolitionists pointed out that Lincoln's blow against slavery did not free a single person. (It did not apply to the loyal slave states or to parts of the Confederacy occupied by Union troops.) They were unfair. The Emancipation Proclamation was a political masterstroke. It reassured loyal slave owners by allowing them to keep their slaves. Lincoln hoped it would be an inducement to Confederate slave owners to make peace before January in order to save their property.

The Emancipation Proclamation also permitted northern commanders to make use of African Americans who, once Union armies were nearby, fled to freedom by the thousands. Many young black men wanted to join the army but, so long as they were legally slaves, they could not be enlisted. Thanks to the Emancipation Proclamation, fully 150,000 blacks served in Union blue. One Billy Yank in eight was black.

African American units were usually assigned the dirtiest and most dangerous duty, heavy labor in the rear, for example, and mining tunnels under Confederate fortifications. They were paid only half a white soldier's wages, about seven dollars a month. And yet, because they were fighting for freedom rather than for an abstraction, black soldiers were said to bicker and gripe far less than whites did.

A Fight to Make Men Free

The Emancipation Proclamation served Lincoln as a trial balloon. Without committing himself either way, he was able to test northern opinion on the subject of abolition. When Union soldiers adopted Julia Ward Howe's abolitionist "Battle Hymn of the Republic" as their anthem—"let us fight to make men free"—Lincoln learned that by striking at slavery, he had improved morale. He had also ensured British neutrality. Dismayed by the Confederate defeat at Antietam, the pro-Confederates were almost completely silenced by the popularity of the Emancipation Proclamation among ordinary people.

Finally, Lincoln mollified his chief critics within the Republican party. Called the Radicals because they wanted an all-out conquest of the South and a radical remaking of its social institutions, this group controlled the Joint Committee on the Conduct of the War. The Radical leaders, Thaddeus Stevens in the House and Charles Sumner in the Senate, were not satisfied with the Emancipation Proclamation. They wanted a constitutional amendment that would abolish slavery in the Union as well as in the Confederacy. But Lincoln's action subdued them. Lincoln also played for Radical support by once again dismissing the Democrat McClellan and appointing another antislavery general, Ambrose E. Burnside, as commander of Union forces in the East.

Stalemate

Burnside did not want the job. An able corps commander, as McDowell and Pope were, he knew that he was not up to the complexities and responsibilities of directing an entire army. But he was too good a soldier to turn Lincoln down and, on December 13, led a tragic assault on an impregnable southern position on high ground near Fredericksburg, Virginia. The slaughter of 1,300 Union soldiers (10,000 wounded) shocked the hardest of men. Union general Darius Crouch exclaimed, "Oh, great God! See how our men, our poor fellows are falling!" Robert E. Lee remarked to an aide that "it is well that war is so terrible or we would grow too fond of it." Burnside retreated, in tears and broken. And the Union and Confederate armies settled down to winter quarters on either side of the Rappahannock River.

The war also bogged down in the West. After Shiloh, a Confederate force under General Braxton Bragg moved across eastern Tennessee into Kentucky in an attempt to capture that state. At Perryville on October 8, he fought to a draw against General Don Carlos Buell, decided his supply lines were overextended, and moved back into Tennessee. On the last day of 1862, Bragg fought another standoff with the Union army at Murfreesboro. Both sides went into winter quarters—neither beaten, neither within sight of victory.

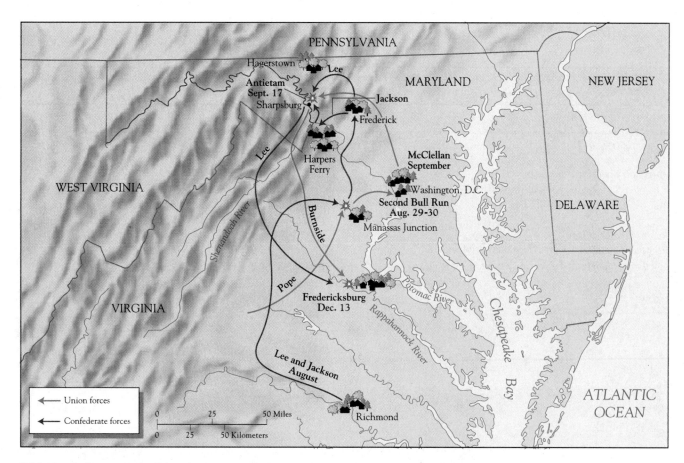

MAP 23:4 Stalemate in the East, 1862 Lee and Jackson displayed their mastery at the second Battle of Bull Run in August 1862 but were almost destroyed at Antietam, on the Maryland side of the Potomac, in September, in part because Lee's plans had fallen into McClellan's hands. Lee's reputation was restored when Union troops made an ill-advised attempt to cross the Rappahannock River at Fredericksburg at the end of 1862.

for FURTHER READING

On the Civil War, see James McPherson, *Ordeal by Fire: The Civil War and Reconstruction,* 1988. Larger, longer works are Bruce Catton, *Centennial History of the Civil War,* 3 vols., 1961–1965; Shelby Foote, *The Civil War: A Narrative,* 3 vols., 1958–1974; and Alan Nevins, *The War for the Union,* 4 vols., 1959–1971. Also see Bruce Catton, *Mr. Lincoln's Army,* 1951, and *Glory Road,* 1952.

More specialized works on the military history of the war include R. Beringer, *Why the South Lost the Civil War,* 1986; Robert Durden, *The Gray and the Black,* 1972; Herman Hattaway and Archer Jones, *How the North Won,* 1983; Frank Van Diver, *Their Tattered Flags,* 1965; and Bell I. Wiley, *The Life of Johnny Reb,* 1943, and *The Life of Billy Yank,* 1952. On black soldiers, see Dudley T. Comish, *The Sable Arm,* 1966.

On politics in the war era, see Eric Foner, *Politics and Ideology in the Age of the Civil War,* 1980; Frank L. Klement, *The Cop-* *perheads in the Middle West,* 1960; Emory Thomas, *The Confederate Nation,* 1979; and Frank Van Diver, *Jefferson Davis and the Confederate State,* 1964.

Valuable biographical studies include T. L. Connelly, *The Marble Man,* 1977 (on Lee); Clement Eaton, *Jefferson Davis,* 1977; Douglas S. Freeman, *Lee: A Biography,* 1934–1935; W. W. Hassley, *General George McClellan,* 1957; William S. McFeeley, *Grant: A Biography,* 1981; Stephen B. Oates, *With Malice Toward None,* 1979 (on Lincoln); Benjamin P. Thomas, *Abraham Lincoln,* 1952; and Frank Van Diver, *Mighty Stonewall,* 1957 (on Jackson).

Two reference works are essential: M. M. Boatner, *The Civil War Dictionary,* 1959; and E. B. Long, *The Civil War Day by Day,* 1971, a comprehensive chronicle of events.

  AMERICAN JOURNEY ONLINE AND INFOTRAC COLLEGE EDITION

Visit the source collections at http://ajaccess.wadsworth.com and http://infotrac.thomsonlearning.com, and use the Search function with the following key terms to explore documents, images, audio and video clips, articles, and commentary related to the material in this chapter:

African American soldiers
Antietam
Civil War women
Emancipation Proclamation

George B. McClellan
Robert E. Lee
Stonewall Jackson

Additional resources, exercises, and Internet links related to this chapter are available on *The American Past* Web site: http://history.wadsworth.com/americanpast7e.

HISTORY ONLINE

American Civil War Homepage
http://sunsite.utk.edu/civil-war/warweb.html
Many links to Civil War Web sites.

Index of the Civil War
Informationhttp://www.cwc.lsu.edu/cwc/civlink.htm
Another compilation of Civil War resources on the Internet.

The Valley of the Shadow
http://valley.vodh.virginia,edu
An ingenious in-depth comparison of life during the war in a northern and southern community.

DRIVING OLD DIXIE DOWN

General Grant's War of Attrition 1863–1865

The rebels now have in their ranks their last man. The little boys and old men are guarding prisoners and railroad bridges, and forming a good part of their forces, manning forts and positions, and any man lost by them cannot be replaced. They have robbed the cradle and the grave.

Ulysses S. Grant

National Park Service, Harpers Ferry Center

BY THE SPRING of 1863, the Confederacy was suffering severe shortages and an inflation of the currency just short of runaway. In the Union, the problem was frustration. Lincoln had men and money, but he could not find a general who would both fight and win. In the East, Robert E. Lee had defeated or confounded four commanders. In the West, the situation was little more encouraging. Southern Louisiana and western Tennessee were occupied, but not even Kentucky was secure from Confederate cavalry raids. In the West too, the war was at a standstill.

THE CAMPAIGNS OF 1863

The third campaign of the war began with more bad news for the Union. By the end of the year, however, the tide had unmistakably turned against the South. Lee's second invasion of the Union ended in a Confederate disaster worse than Antietam. In the West, Union armies broke the stalemate, and Lincoln found there a general who knew how to win the war.

Chancellorsville

After Burnside's debacle at Fredericksburg, his most outspoken critic was General Joseph Hooker, called "Fighting Joe" because of his aggressiveness in the Peninsula Campaign. Hooker was regularly indiscreet. He had left the military in 1853 when his bad-mouthing of fellow officers angered Winfield Scott. After Fredericksburg, he assailed even Lincoln, saying that what the country needed for the duration of the war was a dictator. In one of the most unusual commissions ever given a military officer, Lincoln told Hooker that only victorious generals could set up dictatorships. If Hooker could win the victory that the North badly needed, Lincoln would run the risk that Hooker was a Napoleon.

Hooker was no more capable than Burnside. In early May, he crossed the Rappahannock River with more than twice as many soldiers as Lee's 60,000. Lee took Hooker's measure and calculated he could gamble. He divided his army—forbidden by the rules—left his fortifications, and hit Hooker from two directions near the town of Chancellorsville.

Lee should have lost his bet, but at the moment that a Union attack would have given the battle to Hooker, Fighting Joe ordered a withdrawal. His commanders on the field were incredulous. One told the courier who delivered the order, "You are a damned liar. Nobody but a crazy man would give such an order when we have victory in sight!" General Henry Slocum rode to Hooker's headquarters to confirm the message.

▲ *Every inch an aristocrat, always impeccably tailored, and soberly dignified, Lee was "the marble man" even during his lifetime. He was a brilliant tactician but far from flawless, as would be learned at Gettysburg.*

Reproduced from the Collections of the Library of Congress

Once again, Lee had won. The Army of the Potomac suffered 11,000 casualties. Hooker was humiliated and soon relieved of command. However, the Battle of Chancellorsville also exposed a weakness in the South's fighting capacity that could only grow more serious. Lee's losses were larger than Hooker's, with a population base less than half that of the Union. If the war continued indefinitely as it had been going, with Lee winning almost all the battles, the Confederacy would run out of soldiers.

The casualty Lee noticed was his "strong right arm," Stonewall Jackson. Returning from a reconnaissance mission, Jackson was shot by his own troops and died. Lee said he could never replace Jackson and never placed the same degree of confidence that he had had in Jackson in the advice of any other general.

The Fortress of Vicksburg

In the West, the Union's object remained the control of the Mississippi River. By holding fast to a 150-mile stretch of the river between Vicksburg, Mississippi, and Port Hudson, Louisiana, the rebels were able to shuttle goods and men from one end of the Confederacy to the other. The farmers of the Midwest were unable to export their crops down the Mississippi and had to depend on railroads, which were more expensive and added to their costs.

The key to the impasse was Vicksburg. The city sat on high cliffs at a sweeping bend in the river. A Confederate force commanded by a renegade Pennsylvania Quaker, John C. Pemberton, manned heavy artillery on the top of the bluffs. Vessels passing below ran the risk of destruction. Infantry could not easily approach the city from the north, for Vicksburg was protected by rugged woodland laced by creeks and bayous—a tangle of earth, brush, and water. When Union forces approached, the Confederate garrison sallied out and repelled every assault. Vicksburg was as near and as far from the Union's western armies as Richmond was from the Army of the Potomac.

U. S. Grant

Then, within a few weeks, an unlikely candidate for the laurels of heroism broke the western stalemate. He was young General Ulysses S. Grant, just 41 years old, but with, it seemed, a century's worth of failures behind him. A West Point graduate, Grant was cited for bravery in the Mexican War but was then shunted off to duty at a lonely desert fort and then to a cold, wet, and lonelier outpost on the northern California coast. Grant took to the whiskey bottle and, after a dressing down by his superior, resigned from the army. In business and trying to farm back in Illinois, he failed. When the Civil War began, he was a clerk in a relative's store.

The Civil War was a godsend for men like Grant. Critically short of officers, the army did not quibble that Joe Hooker had been disruptive and Grant a drunk. Grant was given the command that won the first notable Union victory of the war, the capture of Forts Henry and Donelson. Then,

▲ *To say Grant's appearance was unprepossessing is an understatement. He was not slovenly, but he was careless of the state of his uniform and lacked a "soldierly bearing." But he knew what he was doing and was decisive.*

however, came Shiloh and a revived suspicion of Grant's friendship with the bottle.

Everyone who met Grant commented on his unimpressive presence. He was a dumpy man with a carelessly trimmed beard. His uniform was perpetually rumpled and often stained. From a distance, he could be mistaken for an aging corporal in danger of demotion. Up close, he struck some as listless, even stupid. But he was neither; nor was he a drunk. Grant was capable of boldness equal to that of Stonewall Jackson, and he had Lee's easy confidence with large commands. His written instructions alone should have allayed the worries of those who doubted him. Dashed off on his knee, they were superbly clear and precise.

The Siege

At Vicksburg, Grant scored a feat of old-fashioned military derring do and then sat down to an exercise in total war, not maneuvering with an army but assaulting the society that supported the enemy. First, he transferred most of his army to the western bank of the Mississippi, marched them swiftly to a few miles below Vicksburg, and then recrossed the river, ferried by gunboats that raced by night under the Confederate guns.

Having bypassed the rugged country where Pemberton had been unbeatable, Grant abandoned his lines of supply, a risky maneuver but one that confused the Confederates. He charged to the east and forced a small Confederate force under Joseph Johnston to withdraw from the area. Grant feigned a full assault on Jackson, the capital of Mississippi, and, when its defenders were holed up there, he reversed direction, turning back west to Vicksburg. The befuddled Pemberton was trounced in a series of brief battles. In a little more than two weeks, Grant won half a dozen confrontations and captured 8,000 southern troops. On May 19, with Pemberton penned up in Vicksburg, Grant sat his men down to besiege the city. Nothing was settled. Vicksburg was a natural fortress and still commanded the river below. But Union forces had broken through where they had been helpless for a year. Richmond was alarmed.

The Gettysburg Campaign

Some of Lee's advisers urged him to send part of the Army of Northern Virginia to attack Grant from the rear and lift the siege. Lee decided instead to invade Pennsylvania and threaten Washington from the north. Lincoln, he calculated reasonably enough, would be forced to call Grant's troops east. Indeed, Lee might even take the Union capital.

Had Lee succeeded, his reputation as a strategist would equal his reputation as a battlefield tactician. But he failed because, ironically, in the most famous battle of the Civil War, Lee made the most serious tactical mistake of his career.

At first, all went well. Lee's thrust into Pennsylvania (no plans wrapped around lost cigars this time) surprised the Army of the Potomac, put under the command of General George Meade when Lee's whereabouts were a mystery. An unglamorous but methodical general, Meade drifted northwest, able only to hope he would find Lee on ground favorable to his army. Forward units of both armies bumped into each other near Gettysburg, Pennsylvania, on July 1, 1863. The Confederates were looking for shoes.

Both armies descended on rolling farmland south of Gettysburg. The Confederates occupied the battlefield from the north; the Yankees, from the south. Both established strong positions on parallel ridges about half a mile apart:

Loaded Guns
Some 24,000 of 37,000 muskets and rifles that were collected from the battlefield at Gettysburg were still loaded, never fired that day. About 6,000 had between 3 and 10 charges in them. The soldiers were so excited that they continued to reload without discharging their weapons.

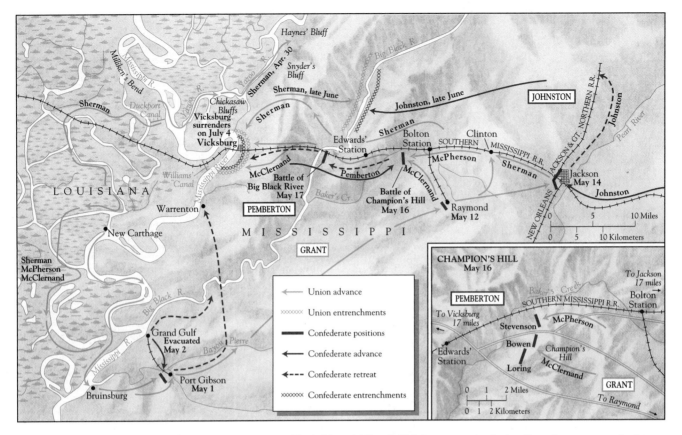

MAP 24:1 Grant's Vicksburg Campaign, May-July 1863 The boldness of Grant's Vicksburg campaign lay in taking a large army south of Vicksburg and into the heart of Mississippi with no line of supply to either the north or the south. Once Grant had penned up Confederate forces in Jackson and Vicksburg, his troops could be supplied via the Mississippi River.

the rebels on Seminary Ridge and the Union troops on Cemetery Ridge.

Deciding to move before the enemy's entrenchments were complete, Lee attacked with his left and almost won the battle on the first day. His men pushed Meade's line back until it was curled into the shape of a fishhook. Then, however, the Union soldiers held, and Lee did not have the resources with which to flank the line without exposing the rest of his army to an attack that would cut his supply lines.

On July 2, Lee attacked on his right, at the other end of the Union line, at the eye of the fishhook. Once again, the rebels came within a few yards and a few hundred men of breaking through. But when the sun set on the second day, Union troops under Joshua Lawrence Chamberlain of Maine had survived horrendous casualties to hold a bulbous knoll called Little Round Top. It was a valuable position—indeed, decisive. The troops that occupied Little Round Top—and Chamberlain was flooded with reinforcements overnight—could "enfilade" the open fields that separated the two armies. That is, they could shoot into an advancing army from the side, vastly increasing the odds of finding targets.

That night, Lee's imagination failed him. Although badly outnumbered now, he decided on a massive frontal assault on the Union center. One of his generals, James Longstreet, argued long, loudly, and late into the night against a movement that reminded Longstreet of Burnside's charge into a powerful Confederate position at Fredericksburg. Longstreet pointed out that with two days in which to dig, the Union troops would be well entrenched on Cemetery Ridge. Better, he said, that the Confederates sit tight, improve their entrenchments, and force Meade to attack. In the war to that date, the advantage always rested with the defensive position.

Pickett's Charge

Stonewall Jackson might have persuaded Lee to dig in or, alternatively, to try to turn the Union's right again. James Longstreet could not, but he was dead right. Just a few miles

"Dixie" and "The Battle Hymn"

The unofficial anthems of the Confederate and Union soldiers, "Dixie" and "The Battle Hymn of the Republic," were both stolen from the other side. "Dixie" was written for a minstrel show by Dan Emmett, the son of an abolitionist. The music to "The Battle Hymn of the Republic" (and its predecessor, "John Brown's Body") was an anonymous southern gospel song, first heard in Charleston during the 1850s.

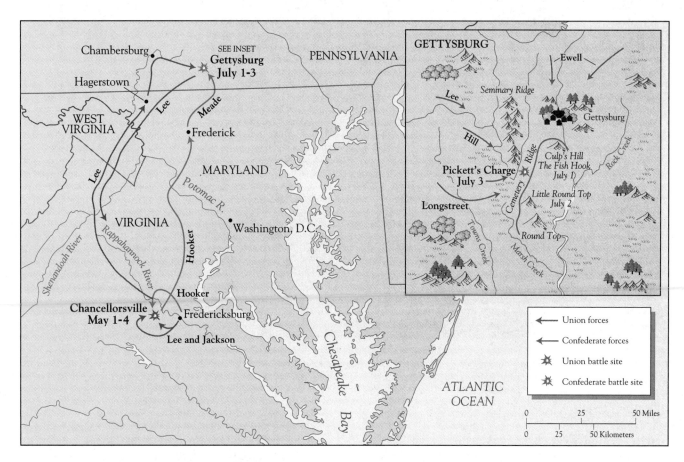

MAP 24:2 Chancellorsville and Gettysburg, May-July 1863 Almost all experts agree that General Lee's army should have been shattered at Chancellorsville. Whether he won the battle because of his brilliance or Union general Hooker's bizarre withdrawal from the field, Lee was able to make his bold foray into Pennsylvania and gain two near victories at Gettysburg before the disastrous final Confederate assault known as Pickett's Charge.

away, General Meade was betting on an assault on his center and he was ready for it. He concentrated his forces there and, on the afternoon of July 3, had the satisfaction of seeing his decision pay off. Between one and two o'clock, howling the eerie rebel yell, 15,000 men in gray began to trot across the no-man's-land. This was Pickett's Charge, somewhat of a misnomer because the angry Longstreet was in command of it. The attack was a nightmare. The men were slaughtered, first by artillery and then by minié balls. The most destructive fire came from Little Round Top.

About a hundred Virginians and North Carolinians actually reached the Union lines. There was a split second of glory, but there were too few rebels. They were surrounded by a thousand Union soldiers and killed or captured.

Pickett's Charge lasted less than an hour. When the survivors dragged themselves back to Seminary Ridge, 10,000 men were dead, wounded, or missing. Five of 20 regimental commanders were wounded; the other 15 were dead. So were two brigadier generals. Robert E. Lee rode among the survivors, restraining his tears, apologizing over and over.

On July 4, with 28,000 fewer rebels than he had led into Pennsylvania, Lee waited for the Union counterattack. It never came. Meade was still ruminating over Pickett's Charge. He would not expose his men to the horrors of cross-

ing an open field into the mouths of cannon. By nightfall, a drizzle became a downpour, making the Potomac impassable and setting up Lee's army for plucking. Defeated and huddled together, the Confederates were in a worse position than they had been in after Antietam. But the rain discouraged Meade too. He did not attack. "We had them within our grasp," Lincoln fumed in a rare display of temper. "We had only to stretch forth our hands and they were ours. And nothing I could say or do could make the Army move."

High Tide

For all Lincoln's disappointment, Gettysburg was an important victory. It ravaged southern morale. Intelligent Confederates understood that their armies would never again be capable of an offensive campaign. Lincoln was still without the decisive, relentless general who would exploit the Union's advantages. Meade was obviously not that man. But that was to change. Not long after the news of Gettysburg arrived in Washington, a spate of telegrams from the West informed the president that the siege of Vicksburg had also ended on July 4, 1863.

Literally starving, after having stripped the streets of pets and the cellars of rats, the people of Vicksburg had

▲ *The high water mark of the Confederacy: the culmination of Pickett's Charge. Miraculously, about a hundred rebels made it through the terrifying gunfire and leaped over Union fortifications. They were too few and quickly overcome. Most of the men who made the charge and were still alive were already trudging back to the Confederate line.*

surrendered. Five days later, Port Hudson, Louisiana, the last Confederate outpost on the Mississippi, gave up without a fight; Union general Nathaniel Banks took 30,000 prisoners. Within a week, the Confederacy lost several times more men than the rebels had put into the field at the first Battle of Bull Run.

The Tennessee Campaign

Worse followed bad. In September, a previously cautious Union general, William S. Rosecrans, attacked the remaining Confederate army in the West. Rosecrans pushed Braxton Bragg out of Tennessee and into northern Georgia. Union troops occupied Chattanooga, an important railroad center on the Tennessee River.

Like Grant at Shiloh, however, Rosecrans was surprised by a counterattack. On September 19, reinforced by grim Confederate veterans of Gettysburg, Bragg hit him at Chickamauga Creek. It was one of the few battles of the war in which the Confederates had the larger army, 70,000 to Rosecrans's 56,000, and the numbers made a difference. The rebels smashed through the Union right, scattering the defenders and making Chickamauga one of the bloodiest battles of the war. It would have been a total rout but for the stand on the Union left flank led by a Virginian who remained loyal to the Union, George H. Thomas, the "Rock of Chickamauga." Thanks to Thomas, the Union troops were able to retire in good order to behind the fortifications of Chattanooga.

Wisely, Bragg decided to besiege the city rather than attack it. But unlike Grant at Vicksburg, Bragg had enemies other than the army trapped inside the town. Grant himself marched his men to Chattanooga and brought 23,000 troops

from the east, also Gettysburg veterans, by rail. Late in November, he drove Bragg's Confederates from strongholds on Missionary Ridge and Lookout Mountain and back into Georgia.

The long campaign for Tennessee was over. It took two years longer than Lincoln had anticipated, but at last the Confederacy was severed in two; and the stage was set for what was hoped to be the final Union offensive. After Vicksburg and Chattanooga, there was no doubt about the man who was to lead it. Early in 1864, Lincoln promoted U. S. Grant to the rank of lieutenant general and gave him command of all Union forces. Grant turned his western command over to his "strong right arm," William Tecumseh Sherman.

TOTAL WAR

Grant had proved that he was a daring tactician of the old school. At Vicksburg, with dash and flash, he outsmarted and outmaneuvered the enemy. Now he informed Lincoln that his primary object was not the capture of Confederate flags, commanders, cities, and territory, but the total destruction of the enemy's ability to fight. Even Richmond

---

Lincoln on Grant

General Grant was on the receiving end of torrid criticism throughout his command, but Lincoln always defended him. When the president was told that Grant was a drinker, he replied, "Give me the brand, and I'll send a barrel to my other generals."

mattered to Grant because of its industry, not the Confederate government ensconced there.

The Union's numerical superiority was now overwhelming, and Grant intended to put it to work. He would force the Confederates to fight constant battles on all fronts, trading casualties that the North could bear and the South could not. At the same time, he would destroy the Confederacy's capacity to feed, shod, and arm its soldiers. He would complete on land what the naval blockade had begun: the strangulation of the South.

Grant's brand of fighting was not chivalrous. It involved making war not only on soldiers but on a society. It was left to William Tecumseh Sherman to give it a name. "War is hell," Sherman said. He was a no-nonsense man, even unpleasant in his refusal to dress up dirty work with fuss, feathers, and pretty words.

Sherman's assignment was to move from his base in Chattanooga toward Atlanta, the railroad center of the Deep South and the heart of the rich agricultural production of the black belt. Grant, with General Meade as his field commander, would personally direct the onslaught against Richmond.

Grant Before Richmond

The war of attrition—grinding down the Confederacy—began in May 1864. With 100,000 men, Grant marched into the "Wilderness," wooded country near Fredericksburg where Burnside had been defeated. There, he discovered that Lee was several cuts above any commander he had yet faced. Although outnumbered, Lee outmaneuvered Grant

and actually attacked. Although Grant's men suffered almost twice as many casualties as the southerners did, replacements rushed to the Union front. On the southern side, Lee counted his dead and sent his wounded men home.

Now it was Lee's turn to discover that he too was up against a new kind of adversary. Instead of withdrawing to Washington where his men could lick their wounds and regroup as all Union commanders had done, Grant shifted his army to the south and attacked again, at Spotsylvania Courthouse. For five days, spearheaded in places by African American troops, the Army of the Potomac assaulted the southern trenches. Grant lost 12,000 men, again almost twice Lee's casualties. Northern congressmen and editors howled. The man was a butcher! But Grant was unmoved. He sent a curt message to Washington that he intended "to fight it out on this line if it takes all summer."

It took longer. Time after time, Lee rallied his shrinking army and somehow managed to scratch together enough munitions and provisions to keep his men in the field. Time after time, he threw Grant back. At Cold Harbor, south of Spotsylvania, the two fought another gory battle. Before they charged, Union troops wrote their names on scraps of paper and pinned the tags to their uniforms. They expected to die.

Petersburg and the Shenandoah

Grant again swung south. On June 18, he attempted to capture Petersburg, a rail center that was the key to Richmond's survival. He might have succeeded immediately but for the

▲ A Union depot in Virginia. Grant's soldiers before Richmond were abundantly supplied. The troops at Petersburg were treated to a grand dinner on Thanksgiving 1864. The Confederates facing them had cornmeal mush; by the end of winter, thousands were shoeless.

© Bettmann/Corbis

The Battle of the Crater

Early in the siege of Petersburg occurred one of the war's most bizarre battles. It was Ambrose Burnside's idea, and it was a good one. Miners from Pennsylvania dug a tunnel under a salient in the Confederate lines and planted 4 tons of gunpowder beneath a critical point in the fortifications. The plan was to detonate the charge and send a massive assault force led by a crack unit of African American troops.

At the last moment, the blacks were replaced by a less experienced white unit, with the African Americans in support. Some said the reason for the change was the Union officer's fears they would be accused of using black troops as cannon fodder. (The charge had been levied before.)

In fact, Union officers were responsible for the disaster resulting in the deaths of both white and black soldiers. The explosion blasted a crater 170 feet long, 60 feet wide, and 30 feet deep—larger than expected. Confederate troops a hundreds yards on either side of the hole were killed or fled. The gap in the lines was wide enough for a brigade to crash through.

Incomprehensibly (unless he was drunk as it was said he was), the incompetent general in command waited fully an hour before ordering the troops to advance. Then he sent them not around the crater but into it! The Confederates had long since regrouped and slaughtered the Union soldiers in the trap they had created. Black soldiers who tried to surrender were murdered.

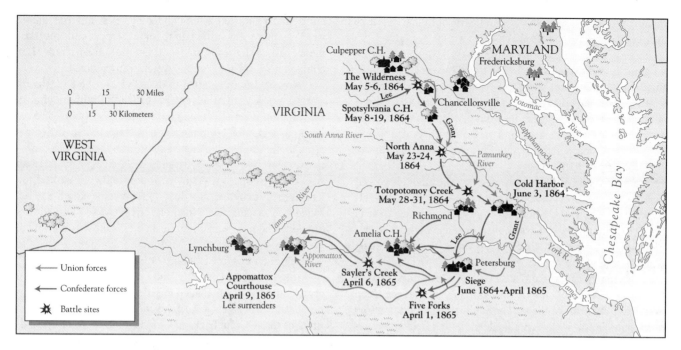

MAP 24:3 **Grant Before Richmond, 1864–1865**   Grant was a different kind of Union commander. Five times, Lee's Army of Northern Virginia repelled him after hideously bloody battles. Each time, instead of withdrawing, he attacked further south until he reached Petersburg. Lee won the battles at the cost of the reduction of his army to a near starving fraction of its size in May 1864.

failure of General Benjamin Butler, a political general in charge of 30,000 reinforcements, to join him in time. By now, Grant was as shaken by the casualties as his critics were. Some 55,000 had been lost in the campaign, more men than Lee had under arms. One unit from Maine attacked with 850 soldiers and returned to the lines with 218. Grant sat down to besiege Petersburg. The siege would last nine months, seven months longer than Vicksburg, through the harshest winter of the war.

In July, Lee tried a trick that, with Stonewall Jackson in charge, had worked in 1862. He sent General Jubal Early on a cavalry raid toward Washington designed to force Grant into weakening his army. Early was remarkably successful.

His men actually rode to within sight of the Capitol dome and some tough-talking politicians began to stutter. But Early's raid was the Confederacy's last hurrah. Grant did not panic, and, this time, neither did Lincoln. (In fact, Lincoln nearly got himself shot by a sniper when he rode out to witness the battle and did not take cover.) Grant's infantry stayed outside Petersburg, and Grant confounded Lee by sending Union cavalry under General Philip Sheridan to intercept Early, preventing him from rejoining Lee.

Sheridan chased Early into the Shenandoah Valley, the fertile country to the west of Richmond that had been an untouched Confederate sanctuary and Richmond's breadbasket for three years. Sheridan defeated Early three times. More important, he laid waste to the valley that fed the Army of Northern Virginia, burning houses, barns, and crops, and slaughtering what livestock his men did not eat. He reported that when he was done, a crow flying over the Shenandoah Valley would have to carry its own provisions.

Sherman in Georgia

General Sherman was equally destructive in scouring Georgia. He moved into the state at the same time Grant entered the Wilderness. At first, he met brilliant harassing action by Joseph E. Johnston. Then an impatient Jefferson Davis, unaware that Johnston's army was not up to a major battle, replaced him with courageous, reckless John B. Hood, whom Sherman defeated. On September 2, 1864, with Grant beginning his third month outside Petersburg, Union troops occupied Atlanta. The loss of the city was a devastating blow to the economy of the Deep South and to Confederate morale.

▲ *Trenches at Petersburg. Both armies dug in for nine months, Union troops over more than 50 miles. The static front was a glimpse into the future, to World War I, although no one could know it.*

Marching Through Georgia

In the fall of 1864, General William Tecumseh Sherman, with a battle-tempered army of 60,000, occupied Atlanta, Georgia, the most important Confederate city aside from Richmond. In order to win the prize, Sherman's men had fought a series of ugly actions, including victories that had been close calls.

But Atlanta was an insecure prize. The civilian population was fiercely hostile. A strong Confederate army, its whereabouts not precisely known, menaced Sherman. The Yankee line of supply, a jugular vein for so large an army, was fragile, 100 miles of easily raided railroad to Chattanooga, Tennessee. Sherman had reason to be apprehensive of a massive battle.

Instead, he proposed to Washington that he would evacuate Atlanta, burning it so that the city would be useless to the Confederates. "Let us . . . make it a desolation," he urged on August 10. Sherman would then "astonish" the Confederates by marching without supply lines across Georgia, "smashing things generally," and rendezvous with a naval relief force at Savannah. His men would "eat out" the country.

Sherman had more in mind than the delicacy of his isolation. He meant to savage southern society and the economy of rural Georgia, punishing the staunch Confederates of the region for sustaining four years of costly rebellion. President Lincoln was under powerful pressure to decline Sherman's proposal, but he agreed when Grant expressed confidence in Sherman's judgment and explained that Sherman's defeat in battle would mean the loss of his entire army.

On November 11, Sherman's men evacuated the burning city. So as to move quickly, lest they be caught by the Confederates, the men marched in four parallel columns, cutting a swath 30 miles, sometimes 60 miles wide, through the rich Georgia countryside. Each column usually stretched out for 5 miles when, after 15 miles of marching, it paused for the night's rest.

Sherman charged his men to "discriminate" against the rich in seizing the food, mules, horses, oxen, and hogs the army needed in order to keep moving. He told his officers to leave enough at every farm for the people who lived there to survive. They were to punish soldiers guilty of rape, and soldiers were not to "enter the dwellings of the inhabitants, or trespass."

How strict Sherman meant to be in enforcing these orders cannot be known. However, they were immediately and widely ignored, and the general shrugged off accusations of brutal behavior with the observation that his men had suffered brutality at the hands of the rebels.

In fact, crime against persons was not wholesale. Only six rapes were documented, a remarkably low figure with 60,000 young men on the loose. Georgians in Sherman's path knew that women were safe. Frequently, when Sherman's army approached, the men of plantations and farms hid, leaving their women behind to plead for mercy or glower with hatred at the Yankees. One Confederate soldier wrote that "the Federal army generally behaved very well. . . . I don't think there was ever an army in the world that would have behaved better, on a similar expedition. . . . Our army certainly wouldn't."

This was a rare southern voice. Almost every other witness of the March, Union as well as Confederate, trembled in describing the damage Sherman's army did. The typical farm or village was not hit just once but several times, first by foraging parties ("pioneers") seizing food and livestock, then by the column itself, the first comers looting, the rear guard burning or shooting the animals that were still alive. An estimated 15,000 horses, 20,000 cattle, and 100,000 hogs were seized, eaten, or simply destroyed. Half a million bushels of corn disappeared, and 100,000 bushels of just-harvested sweet potatoes.

There was little armed conflict. The Confederate army under bold but ineffective General John Hood never caught up with Sherman. The 60,000 Union soldiers were confronted only by tiny bands of guerrillas able, at most, to snipe and run.

For a century, Sherman's march across Georgia was burned into the southern psyche. Even at the time, many northerners protested. For the most part, however, Sherman's vengeance filled a deep-felt need in the hearts of northerners. They believed the war should have been ended before Sherman's men left Atlanta. General Robert E. Lee, in Virginia, was finished by the fall of 1864. By preparing for another campaign in the spring, he seemed ready to cause tens of thousands more casualties—but for what? The Confederacy was dead. Sherman's terrible rampage was emotional compensation for frustration in the Union. Indeed, Sherman's partisans said it was his march through Georgia, more than any other factor, that compelled Lee to give up in the spring of 1865 before the "campaign of 1865" began.

Sherman knew that holding the city was problematical. With a military imagination the Union had not known before the emergence of Grant, Sherman asked for approval of a march to the sea, living off the land, and "making Georgia howl" by destroying everything his army did not need. After some hesitation, Lincoln approved the daring plan.

Sherman ordered the people of Atlanta to evacuate the city and put it to the torch. He then set out in four columns to the southeast, moving quickly in order to avoid a battle that, without supplies, he could not risk. His men were instructed to destroy everything of use to the Confederacy in a swath 60 miles wide. They not only tore up the railroad between Atlanta and Savannah, but they burned the ties and twisted the iron rails around telegraph poles. "Sherman bow ties" they called them. Sherman's purpose in laying Georgia waste was to punish the people of Georgia. Those who caused and supported the war (and profited grandly from it, as Georgia had) would suffer for the suffering they had abetted. This was total war.

Sherman reached Savannah on December 10 and captured it two weeks later. Resupplied from the sea, he turned north, continuing to scorch the earth in South Carolina. He intended to join forces with Grant and fight the war's final battle.

▲ *Wounded soldiers waiting to be taken into a hospital. Many, even with less serious wounds, would die of infection.*

The Sudden End

That battle was never fought. In February 1865, Jefferson Davis sent Confederate vice president Alexander H. Stephens and two others to meet Lincoln and Secretary of State Seward on a ship off Hampton Roads, Virginia, and try to make peace with them. Absurdly, their instructions were to insist on Confederate independence as a condition of peace. Davis was out of touch with reality.

Late in March, Lee tried to draw Grant into a battle in open country. He had 54,000 men to Grant's 115,000 and was easily pushed back to Richmond. On April 2, knowing that his 37-mile-long lines were too much to man (Union lines were 53 miles long), Lee abandoned Petersburg and therefore Richmond. He plan was to make a dash west, turn south, resupply in untouched North Carolina, and link up with Johnston for a last stand. Jefferson Davis, fleeing Richmond, was able to put a happy face on the loss of the capital. "Relieved of our obligation to defend cities, we . . ."

Grant cut Lee off. Desertions had reduced the Army of Northern Virginia to 30,000 men, some of whom were shoeless. On April 9, Lee met Grant at Appomattox Courthouse in Virginia in, ironically, the home of a man who had moved there from Manassas after the first Battle of Bull Run.

Grant's terms were simple and generous. The Confederates surrendered all equipment and arms except for the officers' revolvers and swords. Grant permitted both officers and enlisted men to keep their horses for plowing. After taking an oath of loyalty to the Union, the southern troops could go home. At Lee's request, Grant provided rations for the starving southerners.

Jefferson Davis ordered Joseph Johnston to fight on. The veteran soldier, who had not fared well by Davis's whims, knew better. On April 18, he surrendered to Sherman at Durham, North Carolina. The ragged remnants of two other Confederate armies gave up over the next several weeks.

THE AMERICAN TRAGEDY

More than a third of the men who served in the two armies died in action or of disease or were wounded, maimed permanently, or captured. In some southern states, more than one-quarter of all the men of military age lay in cemeteries. The depth of the gore can best be understood by comparing the 620,000 dead (360,000 Union, 260,000 Confederate) with the population of the United States in 1860, about 30 million. Considering that half the population was female

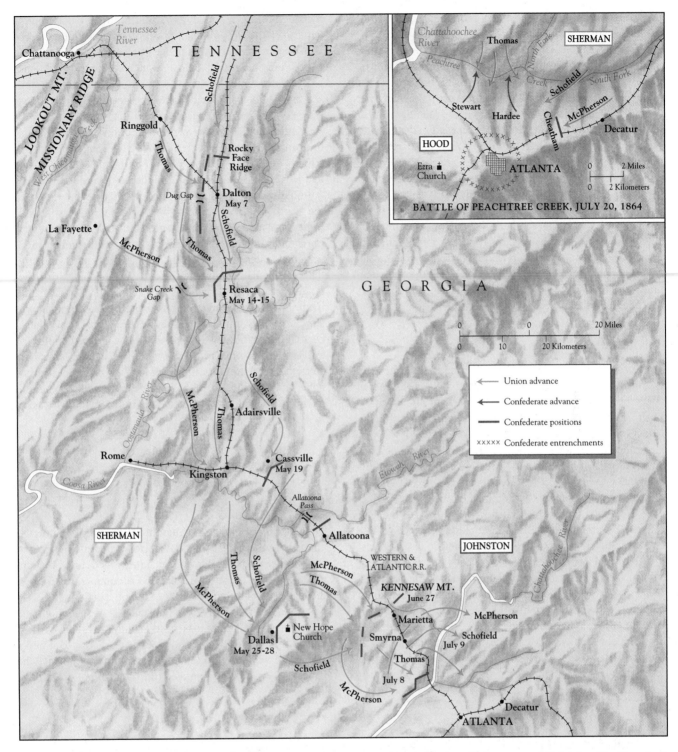

MAP 24:4 **The Campaign for Atlanta, May–September 1864** Sherman began his advance from Chattanooga to Atlanta when Grant launched his assault on Richmond. Sherman captured his objective but, with an effective Confederate army outside Atlanta, abandoned the city after burning it to the ground.

and 7 or 8 million males were either too old or too young for military service, more than 1 out of every 25 men who were "eligible" to die in the war did. Until the Vietnam War of the 1960s and 1970s added its dead to the total, more Americans were killed in the Civil War than in all other American wars combined.

Assassination

There was one more casualty to be counted. On April 14, a few days after the fall of Richmond, President Lincoln and his wife attended a play at Ford's Theater in Washington. Shortly after 10 o'clock, Lincoln was shot in the head at point-blank range by a zealous pro-Confederate, John Wilkes Booth. Lincoln died early the next morning.

Booth was one of those disturbed characters who pop up periodically to remind us of the significance of the irrational in history. An actor with delusions of grandeur, Booth organized a cabal including at least one mental defective to avenge the Confederacy by wiping out the leading officials of the Union government. Only he succeeded in the mission, although one of his gang seriously wounded Secretary of State Seward with a knife.

As he escaped the theater, Booth shouted, *"Sic semper tyrannis!"* (which means "Thus always to tyrants!")—the motto of the state of Virginia. Booth fled into Virginia; on April 26, he was cornered and killed at Bowling Green. In July, four others were hanged for Lincoln's murder, including a woman, Mary Surratt, in whose boardinghouse the plot was hatched. But vengeance did not bring the president back, and his loss proved to be inestimable, perhaps more for the South than for the North.

Father Abraham

To this day, Lincoln remains a central figure of American history. More books have been written about him than about any other American. He was the American Dream made flesh. He rose from modest frontier origins to become the leader of the nation in its greatest crisis.

Lincoln was not overwhelmingly popular as a president. The Radicals of his own party assailed him because of his reluctance to make war on slavery early in the war and his opposition to punishing the South when the war neared its end. Northern Democrats vilified him because the war dragged on and the casualties mounted to no avail. As late as September 1864, with the casualties before Petersburg at horrible levels, Lincoln expected to lose his bid for reelection to the Democratic party candidate, his old nemesis, General George McClellan. Several advisers said he should call the election off. With his religious devotion to the Constitution, Lincoln never considered it.

Lincoln weathered McClellan's threat thanks in part to political machinations; he made Nevada a state, gaining three electoral votes, although Nevada consisted of little more than a dozen mining camps of uncertain future. He directed his generals to put Republican units on furlough so they could vote on election day while he kept units thought favorable to McClellan on duty. Lincoln also appealed to prowar Democrats by dropping the name "Republican" and calling himself the "Union party" candidate. For vice president, he chose a Democrat from Tennessee, Andrew Johnson.

But Lincoln did not win the election of 1864 because of political ploys. He won because Sherman had captured Atlanta and it was obvious to everyone but Jefferson Davis and Robert E. Lee that the Confederacy was doomed. Lincoln had won the respect of the majority of the people in the North by the example of his dogged will, personal humility, and eloquent humanitarianism. In a speech dedicating a national cemetery at Gettysburg in November 1863, he stated American ideals more beautifully (and succinctly) than anyone had done since Jefferson's preamble to the Declaration of Independence. His second inaugural address, delivered in Washington a month before Lee's surrender, was simultaneously a literary masterpiece, a signal to southerners that they could lay down their arms without fear of retribution, and a plea to northerners for a compassionate settlement of the national trauma. "With malice toward none," he concluded, "with charity for all; with firmness in the right, as God gives us to see the right, let us strive on to finish the work we are in."

CONSEQUENCES OF THE CIVIL WAR

The triumph of the Union guaranteed several fundamental changes in the nature of the American republic. Once and for all, the inseparability of the states was defined beyond argument. The theories of John C. Calhoun, compelling in the abstract, were buried without honor. The United States was not a federation of sovereign states. It was a nation, one and indivisible. Politicians (mostly southerners) have called themselves "states' righters" since the Civil War. But never after 1865 would anyone suggest that a state could leave the Union if its people disapproved of a national policy.

Don't Swap Horses

Until the end of the nineteenth century, candidates for the presidency did not actively campaign. They did, however, urge on their supporters. In the wartime election of 1864, Lincoln provided his party's slogan by telling the story of the Dutch farmer who said he never swapped horses in the middle of a stream. Indeed, Americans never have changed presidents voluntarily during a war. Even during the unpopular war in Vietnam, it took the retirement of Lyndon B. Johnson in 1968 to put Republican Richard M. Nixon in the White House. With the war still on in 1972, Nixon won reelection by a landslide.

Union and Nation

Before 1861, *United States* was grammatically plural; since 1865, it has been singular. That is, before the Civil War, one said, "The United States *are . . .*" Since, we have said, "The United States *is . . .*"

Lincoln quietly charted the transformation in his speeches. In his first inaugural address (March 1861), he used the word *Union* 20 times but *nation* not once. In his first message to Congress (July 1861), he said *Union* 49 times and *nation* 3 times. In the Gettysburg Address, Lincoln never said *Union* but referred to *nation* 5 times.

A New Political Majority

The political dominance of the South was dead. Since the founding of the republic, southerners played a role in the government of the country out of all proportion to their numbers. Eight of the 15 presidents who preceded Lincoln came from slave states. At least two of the seven northerners who held the office—Pierce and Buchanan—were blatantly prosouthern in their policies. After Lincoln and Andrew Johnson, no citizen of a former Confederate state would occupy the White House until Lyndon B. Johnson in 1963, and he was more westerner than southerner. Only in 1976, with the election of Jimmy Carter of Georgia, was an unambivalent southerner accepted by the American people as their leader.

Since the Age of Jackson, southerners had dominated Congress through a combination of political skill and agrarian alliance with western farmers. In making good on the threat to secede, the southern bloc destroyed this alliance. The Democratic party remained a major force in New York and the agricultural Midwest. But the Republicans held the edge above the Mason-Dixon line; never again would an agricultural coalition dominate the federal government.

In its place, northeastern industrial and financial interests came to the fore. Businessmen had been late in joining the antislavery coalition. To bankers, great merchants, and factory owners, the Republican party was of interest more because of its economic policies than because of its hostility to slavery. With the war concluded, however, these forces held a strong position and exploited the emotional attachment of most northern voters to the "Grand Old Party."

New Economic Policies

During the war, the Republican Congress enacted a number of laws that would have been defeated had southerners been in their seats and voting. In July 1862, about the time of Antietam, both houses approved the Pacific Railways Act. As modified later in the war, this act gave 6,400 square miles of the public domain to two private companies, the Union Pacific and the Central Pacific Railroads. These corporations were authorized to sell the land and use the proceeds to construct a transcontinental railway, the ultimate internal improvement. In 1864, while Grant slogged it out with Lee before Richmond, Congress gave the Northern Pacific Railroad an even more generous subsidy. These acts revolutionized the traditional relationship between private enterprise and the federal government.

The tariff was another issue on which southern agricultural interests had repeatedly frustrated the manufacturers of the Northeast. Since 1832, with few exceptions, the Democratic party drove the taxes on imported goods ever downward. The last tariff before the war, passed in 1857 with the support of southern congressmen, set rates lower than they had been since the War of 1812.

In March 1861, even before secession was complete, the Republican Congress rushed through the Morrill Tariff, which pushed up import duties. In 1862 and 1864, rates went even higher. By 1867, the average tax on imported goods stood at 47 percent, about the same as it was under the act of 1828 that the southerners had called the "Tariff of Abominations" and that Calhoun called fit grounds for secession.

The South had long frustrated the desire of northern financial interests for a centralized banking system. Opposition to a national bank was one of the foundation stones of the old Democratic party. During the war, with no southern congressmen in Washington and with the necessity of financing the Union army looming over Congress, New York's bankers had their way.

Financing the War

The Union financed the war in three ways: by heavy taxation, by printing paper money, and by borrowing—that is, selling bonds both abroad and in the United States. The principal taxes were the tariff, an excise tax on luxury goods, and an income tax. By the end of the war, the income tax provided about 20 percent of the government's revenue.

The government authorized the printing of $450 million in paper money. These bills were not redeemable in gold. Popularly known as "greenbacks" because (like our money) they were printed on one side in green ink, they had value (again like our own money) because the federal government declared they must be accepted in the payment of debts. When the fighting went badly for the North, the greenbacks were traded at a discount. By 1865, a greenback with a face value of $1 was worth only 67 cents in gold. This inflation was minuscule compared with that in the Confederacy, where government printing presses ran amok. By 1864, a citizen of Richmond paid $25 for a pound of butter and $50 for a breakfast. By 1865, prices were even higher; many southern merchants accepted only gold or Union currency, including greenbacks!

The banking interests of the North were uncomfortable with the greenbacks. However, they profited nicely from the government's large-scale borrowing. By the end of the war, the federal government owed its own citizens and some foreigners almost $3 billion, about $75 for every person in the country. Much of this debt was held by the banks. Moreover, big financial houses, like Jay Cooke's in Philadelphia, reaped huge profits in commissions for their part in selling the bonds.

Free Land

Another momentous innovation of the Civil War years was the Homestead Act. Before the war, southern fear of new free states in the territories paralyzed every attempt to liberalize the means by which the federal government disposed of its western lands. In May 1862, the system was overhauled. The Homestead Act provided that every head of family who was a citizen or who intended to become a citizen could receive 160 acres of the public domain. There was a small filing fee, and homesteaders were required to live for five years on the land that the government gave them. Or, after six months on the land, they could buy it outright for $1.25 per acre.

A few months after approving the Homestead Act, Congress passed the Morrill Act. This law granted each loyal state 30,000 acres for each representative and senator that state sent to Congress. The states were to use the money they made from the sale of these lands to found agricultural and mechanical colleges. In subsequent years, the founding of 69 land-grant colleges greatly expanded educational opportunities, particularly in the West.

Again, it was a free-spending policy of which parsimonious southern politicians would never have approved, and the revolutionary infusion of government wealth into the economy spawned an age of unduplicated expansion—and corruption.

Free People

No consequence of the Civil War was so basic as the abolition of slavery in the United States. In a sense, the "peculiar institution" was doomed when the first shell exploded over Fort Sumter. As Congressman Ben Wade of Ohio told southerners in 1861, "The first blast of civil war is the death warrant of your institution." Slavery was not only an immoral institution; by the middle of the nineteenth century, it was

hopelessly archaic. It is the ultimate irony of wars that are fought to preserve outdated institutions that war itself is the most powerful of revolutionary forces. Precariously balanced institutions such as slavery rarely survive the disruptions of armed conflict.

Once hundreds of thousands of blacks had left their masters to flee to Union lines, once virtually all the slaves had learned of the war, it was ridiculous to imagine returning to the old ways. Even if the South had eked out a negotiated peace, even if the North had not elected to make emancipation one of its war aims, slavery would have been dead within a decade.

© Bettmann/Corbis

▲ *By the end of the war, 150,000 African Americans had donned Union uniforms, serving both in units doing menial labor (where some officers wanted to keep them) and in some of the fiercest assaults of 1864. In several instances, Confederate soldiers murdered black prisoners.*

And yet, many southerners refused to recognize this reality until the end. Several times, the Confederate Congress turned down suggestions, including one from General Lee, that slaves be granted their freedom if they enlisted in the Confederate army. Only during the last two months of the conflict did any blacks don Confederate uniforms, and those few never saw action.

On the other side of the lines, 150,000 African Americans, some free northerners, most of them runaway slaves, served in the Union army. They were less interested in preserving the Union than in freeing slaves. Their bravery won the admiration of many northerners. Lincoln confessed his surprise that blacks made such excellent soldiers, and he seems to have been revising the racist views that he shared with most white Americans.

For a time, at least, so did many Union soldiers. Fighting to free human beings, a positive goal, was better for morale than fighting to prevent secession, a negative aim at best. By 1864, as they marched into battle, Union regiments sang "John Brown's Body," an abolitionist hymn, and Julia Ward Howe's more poetic "Battle Hymn of the Republic":

> As He died to make men holy,
> Let us die to make men free.

Because the Emancipation Proclamation did not free all slaves, in February 1865, Radical Republicans in Congress proposed, with Lincoln's support, the Thirteenth Amendment to the Constitution. It provided that "neither slavery nor involuntary servitude, except as a punishment for crime . . . shall exist within the United States." Most of the northern states ratified it within a few months. Once the institution of slavery was destroyed in the United States, only Brazil, Cuba, Puerto Rico, Muslim lands, and undeveloped parts of the world continued to condone the holding of human beings in bondage.

for FURTHER READING

The works listed in "For Further Reading" in Chapter 23 are relevant to this chapter as well. See also E. D. Fite, *Social and Industrial Conditions in the North During the Civil War*, 1976; J. F. C. Fuller, *Grant and Lee*, 1957; Paul D. Gates, *Agriculture and the Civil War*, 1965; Leon F. Litwack, *Been in the Storm So Long*, 1979; Robert P. Sharkey, *Money, Class, and Party*, 1959; Hans A. Trefousse, *The Radical Republicans*, 1969; and Bell Wiley, *Southern Negroes, 1861–1865*, 1938, and *The Plain People of the Confederacy*, 1943.

 ## AMERICAN JOURNEY ONLINE AND INFOTRAC COLLEGE EDITION

Visit the source collections at http://ajaccess.wadsworth.com and http://infotrac.thomsonlearning.com, and use the Search function with the following key terms to explore documents, images, audio and video clips, articles, and commentary related to the material in this chapter:

African American soldiers
Appomattox
Gettysburg Address
Ulysses S. Grant
Vicksburg

Additional resources, exercises, and Internet links related to this chapter are available on *The American Past* Web site: http://history.wadsworth.com/americanpast7e.

HISTORY ONLINE

Civil War Treasures
http://memory.loc.gov/ammem/ndlpcoop/nhihtml/cwnyhshome.html
Documents and photographs from the New York Historical Society.

Civil War Maps
http://memory.loc.gov/ammem/gmdhtml/cwmhtml/cwmhome.html
Collection of maps used by the armies during the Civil War.

The U.S. Sanitary Commission
www.netwalk.com/~jpr/index.htm
A treasure of information on how the Union army dealt with health problems.

25

AFTERMATH

The Reconstruction of the Union 1865–1877

National Archives

Republicans gave the ballot to men without homes, money, education, or security, and then told them to use it to protect themselves. It was cheap patriotism, cheap philanthropy, cheap success.

Albion W. Tourgée

Oh, I'm a good old rebel, that's what I am,
And for this land of freedom, I don't give a damn,
I'm glad I fought ag'in her, I only wish we'd won,
And I don't axe any pardon for anything I've done.

Reconstruction Era doggerel

WHEN THE GUNS fell silent in 1865, some southern cities—Vicksburg, Atlanta, Columbia, Richmond—were flattened, eerie wastelands of charred timbers, rubble, and freestanding chimneys. Few of the South's railroads could be operated for more than a few miles. Bridges were gone. River-borne commerce had dwindled to a trickle. Old commercial ties with Europe and the North had been snapped. All the South's banks were ruined.

Even the cultivation of the soil had been disrupted. The small farms of the men who served in the ranks lay fallow by the thousands. Great planters who abandoned their fields to advancing Union armies discovered that weeds and scrub pine were more destructive conquerors than Yankees. The former slaves who had toiled in the fields were likely to be gone. If they remained in the only home they had ever known, they wondered who owned the land they had toiled over.

THE RECONSTRUCTION DEBATE

In view of the desolation and social dislocation, *reconstruction* seems to be an appropriate description of the 12-year period following the Civil War. But the word does not refer to the literal rebuilding of the South, the laying of bricks, the spanning of streams, the reclaiming of the land, and only secondarily to the rebuilding of a society.

Reconstruction refers to the political process by which the 11 rebel states were restored to a normal constitutional relationship with the national government. It was the Union, that great abstraction over which so many had died, that was to be built anew.

Blood was shed during Reconstruction too, but little glory was won. Few political reputations—northern or southern, white or black, Republican or Democratic—emerged

▲ *Richmond in ruins. Atlanta was worse. The Shenandoah Valley and northeastern Georgia were laid waste. Even areas of the South untouched by war were impoverished, dwellings and fields neglected. This was the region that had to be "reconstructed" and reintegrated into the victorious Union.*

from the era unstained. Abraham Lincoln may come down to us as a sainted figure only because he did not survive the war. Indeed, the Reconstruction policy Lincoln proposed in 1863 was repudiated by members of his own party, who would surely have fought him as they fought his successor, Andrew Johnson. Lincoln foresaw the problems that he did not live to face. He described as "pernicious" the constitutional hair-splitting with which both sides in the Reconstruction debate masked their motives and goals.

Lincoln Versus Congress

By December 1863, Union armies occupied large parts of the Confederacy. Ultimate victory, although not yet in the bag, was reasonable to assume. To provide for a rapid reconciliation after victory, Lincoln declared that as soon as 10 percent of the voters in a former Confederate state took an oath of allegiance to the Union, the people could organize a state government and elect representatives to Congress. Moving quickly, occupied Tennessee, Arkansas, and Louisiana complied.

Congress refused to recognize the new governments, returning the three states to military command. Almost all Republican congressmen were alarmed by the broad expansion of presidential powers during the war. No previous president, not even Andrew Jackson, had assumed so much authority as Lincoln had—at the expense of Congress. During a war that threatened to destroy the Union, one could swallow his anxieties. But Reconstruction was a postwar issue, and Lincoln's proposal did not involve Congress in any way.

The Radical Republicans, a minority of the party but vociferous, had another reason to reject Lincoln's proposal. Most of them were former abolitionists who hated the southern "slavocracy" and, for reasons that varied, insisted on full civil and political rights for the freedmen, as the former slaves were called. The Radicals framed the Wade-Davis Bill of July 1864, which provided that only after *50 percent* of the white male citizens of a state swore an oath of loyalty could the Reconstruction process begin. Then, in the Wade-Davis plan, Congress—not the president—would decide when former Confederate states were readmitted to the Union. Wade-Davis meant to slow down a process Lincoln wanted to speed along, and the bill aimed to put the power over approval of reconstruction of each rebel state in the hands of Congress.

Lincoln killed the Wade-Davis Bill with a pocket veto. Congress was about to adjourn and he simply did not sign it. Thus, he did not have to explain his rejection of the plan. During the final months of his life, he hinted that he was ready to compromise with Congress, even reaching out to the Radicals (whom he had never much liked) by saying he had no objection to giving the right to vote to blacks who were "very intelligent and those who have fought gallantly in our ranks." He urged the military governor of Louisiana to extend suffrage to some blacks.

Stubborn Andy Johnson

Lincoln's lifelong assumption that blacks were different from whites—inferior, in general—and his determination to reconcile southern whites to the Union quickly, made it difficult for him to accept Radical demands for the full citizenship of all African Americans. However, he let it be known he was flexible. "Saying that reconstruction will be accepted if presented in a specified way," he said, "it is not said that it will never be accepted in any other way." Andrew Johnson, his successor, was not a man of flexible positions.

Andrew Johnson of Tennessee grew up in stultifying frontier poverty. Unlike Lincoln, who taught himself to read as a boy, Johnson grew to adulthood illiterate, working as a tailor. Only then did he ask a schoolteacher in Greenville, Tennessee, to teach him to read and write. She did, later mar-

▲ *President Andrew Johnson. He was a man of integrity but inflexible and, despite his hatred of secessionists, hostile to every suggestion that the freedmen be granted civil equality.*

ried him, and encouraged Johnson to go into politics. He was a resounding success, winning elective office on every level from town councilman to congressman to senator. During the war, he was appointed governor of occupied Tennessee. No other president had so much political experience.

Experience, alas, is not the same thing as aptitude. Where Lincoln was an instinctively coy politician, sensitive to the realities of what he could and could not accomplish, Johnson was unsubtle, insensitive, willful, and stubborn—bullying when his goals were blocked. Personally, he got off to an unlucky start as Lincoln's vice president. Almost collapsing with a bad cold on inauguration day, he bolted several glasses of brandy for a pick-me-up, and took the oath of office obviously drunk. Fortunately, the ceremony was private, and Lincoln quietly told aides that Johnson was not to speak at the ceremony outside the Capitol.

The minor scandal was suppressed because Johnson had the goodwill of Lincoln's chief Republican critics, the Radicals. He had several times called for the harsh punishment of high-ranking Confederates (he wanted to hang Jefferson Davis), which was right up the Radicals' alley. But they misread him. Johnson had owned slaves as late as 1862 and considered every suggestion that the freed slaves be accorded citizenship an abomination. The Radicals' delight that he was president was short-lived. Like Lincoln, he insisted that it was the president's prerogative, and not Congress's, to decide when the rebel states were reconstructed.

Johnson: They Are Already States

Johnson based his case for presidential supervision of Reconstruction on the assumption that the southern states had never left the Union because it was constitutionally impossible to do so. The Union was one and inviolable, as Daniel Webster had said. It could not be dissolved. Johnson, the entire Republican party, and most northern Democrats held to that principle in 1861. Johnson stuck by it in 1865.

There had indeed been a war and an entity known as the Confederate States of America. But individuals fought the war and created the Confederacy. Punish individual rebels, indeed, Johnson said. He approved several confiscations of rebel-owned lands, but not the states of Virginia, Alabama, and the rest. They were still states, constitutional components of the United States of America. Seating their duly elected representatives in Congress was a purely administrative matter. Therefore, the president, the nation's chief administrator, would decide how and when to do it.

Logic Versus Horse Sense

There was nothing wrong with Johnson's logic; he was an excellent constitutionalist. The president's problem was his refusal to see beyond constitutional tidiness to the messy world of human feelings, hatreds, resentments, and flesh and blood—especially blood.

The fact was, virtually every senator and representative from the rebel states left his seat in the winter and spring of

1861. Johnson was the only senator of 22 who remained loyal. Although a rump by Johnson's reasoning, Congress had functioned constitutionally through four years of war. (Johnson's embarrassing presence in the Senate was resolved by naming him governor of Tennessee.) More than half a million people had been killed, and most northerners blamed the calamity on arrogant, destructive slave owners who, when Johnson announced he would adopt Lincoln's plan of Reconstruction (with some changes), assumed the leadership in their states that, as slavocrats, they had always held.

Nor did Johnson's reputation as a scourge of rebels hold up. By the end of 1865, he had pardoned 13,000 Confederate leaders, making them eligible to hold public office under his Reconstruction program. In elections held in the fall under Johnson's plan, southern voters sent many of these rebels to Congress: four Confederate generals, six members of Jefferson Davis's cabinet, and, as senator from Georgia, former Confederate vice president Alexander H. Stephens. It did not go down well for Americans who, for example, were buying tombstones for the menfolk they had lost.

The Radicals: They Have Forfeited Their Rights

Thaddeus Stevens, Radical leader in the House of Representatives, replied to Johnson's argument. The Confederate states had committed state suicide when they seceded, he said. They were not states. Therefore, it was within the power of Congress, and Congress alone, to admit them. Senator Charles Sumner argued that the southern states were "conquered provinces" and therefore had the same political status as the federal territories in the West.

These theories were worthy of John C. Calhoun in their ingenuity but also as contrived as Calhoun's logic-chopping. A lesser known Republican, Samuel Shellabarger of Ohio, came up with a formula that made sense constitutionally and appealed to angry, war-weary northerners, as Stevens's and Sumner's theories did: The rebel states had forfeited their identity as states.

Old Thad Stevens
Few Radical Republicans were so sincerely committed to racial equality as Thaddeus Stevens of Pennsylvania was. In his will, he insisted on being buried in a black cemetery because blacks were banned from the one where he normally would have been interred.

Nevertheless, even Stevens came to terms with the racism of northern whites who refused the vote to blacks in their own states. In order to win their support for black suffrage in the South, Stevens argued that the situation was different in the South because blacks made up the majority of loyal Union men there. "I am for negro suffrage in every rebel state," he said. "If it be just, it should not be denied; if it be necessary, it should be adopted; if it be a punishment to traitors, they deserve it."

Congress's Joint Committee on Reconstruction found that "the States lately in rebellion were, at the close of the war, disorganized communities, without civil government, and without constitutions or other forms, by virtue of which political relations could legally exist between them and the federal government." This state of affairs meant that only Congress could decide when the 11 disorganized communities might function as states of the Union.

The Radicals

Congress refused to seat the senators and representatives who came to Washington under the Johnson plan. The Radical Republicans meant to crush the southern planter class they had hated for so long and, with varying degrees of idealism, to help the freedmen who, for so long, had been victimized by their owners.

Some Radicals, like Stevens, Sumner, and Benjamin "Bluff Ben" Wade of Ohio, believed in racial equality. George W. Julian of Indiana proposed to confiscate the land of the planters and divide it, in 40-acre farms, among the freedmen. With economic independence, they could guarantee their civil freedom and political rights. Other Radicals wanted to grant the freedmen citizenship and the vote for frankly partisan purposes. Black voters would provide the core of a Republican party in the South, which did not exist before the war and was unlikely to be more than a splinter group if only southern whites voted.

The Radicals were a minority within the Republican party. However, they were able to win the support of party moderates because of Johnson's repeated blunders and a series of events in the conquered South that persuaded most northern voters that Lincolnian generosity would mean squandering the Union's hard-won military victory.

THE CRITICAL YEAR

Most southern blacks reacted to the news of their freedom by testing it. They left the plantations and farms where they had been slaves, many flocking to the cities that they associated with free blacks. Others, after a period of wandering, gathered in ramshackle camps in the countryside, eagerly discussing the rumor that each freedman's household would soon be allotted 40 acres and a mule for plowing. With no means of making a living in the stricken land, these congregations of freedmen were potentially, and in many cases in fact, dens of hunger, disease, disorder, and crime.

The Freedmen's Bureau

In order to prevent chaos in the liberated South, Congress created the Bureau of Refugees, Freedmen, and Abandoned Lands, popularly known as the Freedmen's Bureau. Administered by the army under the command of General O. O. Howard, the bureau provided relief for impoverished freedmen (and some whites) in the form of food, clothing, and

▲ *The Freedmen's Bureau was an effective federal agency, one of the few concerned with social problems before the twentieth century. Among the services it provided to African American southerners during Reconstruction, none was more important than its schools. Most of the teachers at bureau schools were idealistic white women from the North.*

shelter. The bureau attempted less successfully to find jobs for the freedmen. It set up hospitals and schools run by idealistic black and white women from the northern states, sometimes at the risk of their lives, and otherwise tried to ease the transition from slavery to freedom. When the Freedmen's Bureau Bill was first enacted, Congress assumed that properly established state governments would take over its responsibilities within a year after the end of the hostilities, a reasonable conjecture. The bureau was scheduled to expire in March 1866.

In February 1866, however, Reconstruction was at a standstill. Congress refused to recognize Johnson's state governments but had created none to its own liking. The former Confederacy was, in effect, still under military occupation. So Congress passed a bill extending the life of the Freedmen's Bureau.

Johnson vetoed it and, a month later, vetoed another act that granted citizenship to the freedmen. Once again, his constitutional reasoning was sound. The Constitution gave the states the power to rule on the terms of citizenship within their borders, and Johnson continued to insist that the state governments he had set up were legitimate and able to provide for the freedmen's needs.

He might have won his argument. Americans of the time took their constitutional fine points seriously, and Radical demands for black civil equality ran against the grain of white feelings about race. However, the refusal of many southern whites to acknowledge the simple fact that they had lost an ugly war nullified every point Johnson scored.

The Black Codes

Blacks as slaves had been the backbone of the southern economy. The Johnson southern state legislatures expected blacks to continue to bring in the crops. The freedmen certainly wanted the work. Far from providing farms for them, however, the Johnson state governments established a system of employment that scarcely acknowledged the Thirteenth Amendment. The so-called black codes defined a second-class form of citizenship for the freedmen that appeared to be more like slavery than freedom.

In some states, blacks were permitted to work only as domestic servants or in agriculture, just what they had done as slaves. Other states made it illegal for blacks to live in towns and cities, a backhanded way of keeping them in the fields. In no state were blacks allowed to vote or to bear arms. In fact, few of the civil liberties listed in the Bill of Rights were accorded them.

South Carolina said that African Americans could not sell goods. Mississippi required freedmen to sign 12-month labor contracts before January 10 of each year. Those who did not could be arrested, and their labor sold to the highest bidder in a manner that (to say the least) was strongly reminiscent of the slave auction. Dependent children could be forced to work. Blacks who reneged on their contracts were not to be paid for the work that they already had performed.

The extremism of the black codes angered many northerners who would have accepted a milder form of second-class citizenship for the freedmen. Only a few northern states allowed African Americans full civil equality. Northerners were also disturbed when whites in Memphis, New Orleans, and several smaller southern towns rioted, killing and injuring blacks, while the Johnson state governments sat passively by.

The Fourteenth Amendment

In June 1866, perceiving the shift in mood in their favor, the Radicals and moderate Republicans drew up a constitutional amendment on which to base congressional Reconstruction policy. The long and complex (and later controversial) Fourteenth Amendment banned from high federal or state office all high-ranking Confederates unless they were pardoned *by Congress*. This struck directly at many of the leaders of the Johnson governments in the South. The amendment also guaranteed that *all* "citizens of the United States and of the State wherein they reside" were to be treated equally under the laws of the states.

If ratified, the Fourteenth Amendment would preclude southern states from passing any more laws like the black codes. However, it also promised to cancel northern state laws that forbade blacks to vote, and in that aspect of the amendment Johnson saw a political opportunity. Calculating that many northerners, particularly in the Midwest, would rather have Confederates in Washington than grant full civil equality to African Americans, Johnson decided to campaign personally in the 1866 congressional election against the Radicals.

The Radicals' Triumph

The first step was to organize a political party. Johnson, conservative Republicans such as Secretary of State Seward and a few senators, and some Democrats called a convention of the "National Union party" in Philadelphia. The message of the convention was sectional reconciliation. To symbolize it, the meeting opened with a procession of northern and

Discouraging Rebellion

Among other provisions of the Fourteenth Amendment, the former Confederate states were forbidden to repay "any debt or obligation incurred in aid of insurrection or rebellion against the United States." By stinging individuals and banks that had lent money to the rebel states, the amendment was putting supporters of future rebellions on notice that there were consequences.

southern Johnson men in which couples made up of one southerner and one northerner marched arm in arm down the center aisle of the hall.

Unhappily for Johnson, the first couple on the floor was South Carolina Governor James L. Orr, a huge, fleshy man, and Massachusetts Governor John A. Andrew, a little fellow with a way of looking intimidated. When Orr seemed to drag the mousy Andrew down the length of the hall, Radical politicians and cartoonists had a field day. Johnson's National Union movement, they said, was dominated by rebels and preached in the North by their stooges.

In the fall, Johnson made things worse. He toured the Midwest seeking support—he called it his "swing around the circle"—and from the start discredited himself. Johnson had learned his oratorical skills in the rough-and-tumble, stump-speaking tradition of eastern Tennessee. There, voters liked a red-hot debate between politicians who scorched each other and ridiculed the hecklers that challenged them.

Midwesterners liked that kind of ruckus well enough, but not from their president. When Radical hecklers taunted Johnson and he responded in kind, Radicals shook their heads sadly that a man of so little dignity should be sitting in the seat of Washington and Lincoln. He was drunk again, they supposed.

The result was a landslide. Most of Johnson's candidates were defeated. The Republican party, now led by the Radicals, controlled more than two-thirds of the seats in both houses of Congress, enough to override every veto Johnson handed them.

RECONSTRUCTION REALITIES AND MYTHS

The Radical Reconstruction program was adopted in a series of laws passed by the Fortieth Congress in 1867. They dissolved the southern state governments that were organized under Johnson and partitioned the Confederacy into five military provinces, each commanded by a major general. The army would maintain order while voters were registered: blacks and those whites not specifically disenfranchised by the Fourteenth Amendment. The constitutional conventions that these voters elected were required to ratify the Thirteenth and Fourteenth Amendments and give the vote to adult black males. After Congress approved their work, the reconstructed states were admitted to the

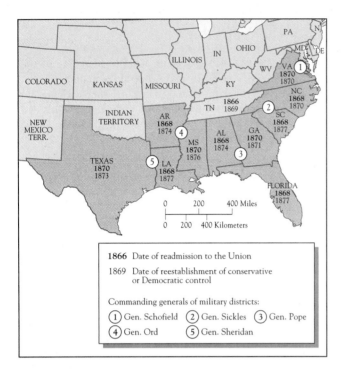

MAP 25:1 Radical Reconstruction The Radicals divided the defeated Confederacy into five military districts. The Union army supervised the establishment of state governments guaranteeing equal rights for the freedmen. Tennessee was not part of the program. The state had been occupied for much of the war by Union forces. Ironically, Tennessee had a viable state government by 1866 because of its wartime Union governor, Andrew Johnson, who, as president, opposed Radical Reconstruction.

Union, and their senators and representatives were admitted to Congress. The Radicals assumed that at least some of these congressmen would be Republicans.

Readmission

Tennessee complied immediately and was never really affected by the Radicals' plans to remake the South. Ironically, the groundwork for a stable government in Tennessee had been built by Andrew Johnson when he was military governor of Tennessee during the war.

In 1868, largely as a result of a large vote by freedmen, six more states were readmitted. Alabama, Arkansas, Florida, Louisiana, North Carolina, and South Carolina all sent Republican delegations, including some black congressmen, to Washington. In the remaining four states—Georgia, Mississippi, Texas, and Virginia—some whites obstructed every attempt to set up a government in which blacks participated. The military continued to govern them until 1870.

In the meantime, with Congress more firmly under Radical control, the Radicals attempted to establish the supremacy of the legislative over the judicial and executive branches of the government. With the Supreme Court, they were immediately successful. By threatening to reduce the size of the Court, the Radicals intimidated the justices. Chief

Justice Salmon P. Chase decided to ride out the difficult era by ignoring all cases that dealt with Reconstruction issues, exactly what the Radicals wanted.

Congress took partial control of the army away from Johnson and then struck at his right to choose his own cabinet. The Tenure of Office Act forbade the president to remove any appointed official who had been confirmed by the Senate without the Senate's approval of his dismissal. It was a step in a plot obvious to all. The Radicals wanted Johnson to violate the Tenure of Office Act so they could impeach him.

The Impeachment of Andrew Johnson

Johnson had delayed Radical Reconstruction with vetoes, which were overridden. He tried to obstruct it by urging southern whites not to cooperate, thus the late readmission of Georgia, Mississippi, Texas, and Virginia. But the strict constitutionalist in him had come to terms with the fact of the Radicals' control of Congress. He executed the duties assigned him under the Reconstruction acts. However, also because of his constitutional scruples, he defied the Tenure of Office Act. To allow Congress to decide if a president could fire a member of his own cabinet was a clear infringement of the independence of the executive branch. In February 1868, Johnson dismissed the single Radical in his cabinet, Secretary of War Edwin Stanton.

Courts may have ruled that the Tenure of Office Act did not apply to Stanton's dismissal because he had been appointed by Lincoln, not by Johnson. Nevertheless, the House of Representatives passed articles of impeachment and appointed Johnson's prosecutors, as the Constitution provides. The Senate was the jury in the trial; the chief justice presided.

A President on Trial

All but two of the 11 articles dealt with the Tenure of Office Act. As expected, Johnson's defenders in the Senate argued that it did not apply to the Stanton case and, in any event, its constitutionality was highly dubious. The other two articles condemned Johnson for disrespect of Congress. This was

▲ *A ticket to the impeachment trial, the high point of Washington's social season. The president did not attend.*

undeniably true; Johnson had spared few pungent words in describing Radicals of both houses. The president's defenders responded that sharp and vulgar language did not approach being the "high crimes and misdemeanors" the Constitution stipulates as grounds for impeachment.

Conviction of an impeached federal official—removal from office—requires a two-thirds majority of the Senate. In 1868, that meant 36 senators had to vote to convict, no more than 18 to acquit. The vote in Johnson's case was 35 to 19. He remained president by a single vote.

Actually, it was not that close. About six moderate Republican senators agreed privately that if their votes were needed to acquit, they would vote for acquittal. They did not believe that the president should be removed from office simply because he was at odds with Congress. Moreover, if Johnson were removed, his successor would be Ben Wade of Ohio, a Radical of such dubious deportment—he was notorious as a foulmouth—that by comparison, Johnson was a statesman. Finally, 1868 was an election year, and Andy Johnson's days were numbered. The immensely popular Ulysses S. Grant would be the Republican nominee. Victory in November was a sure thing. They wanted to wait for that.

But they were practical politicians. Johnson had very little support among Republican voters. If possible, the six did not want to go on record as favoring the president. It was possible, barely, and the fence-sitters were right. A Republican senator from Kansas who was thought to have cast the vote that acquitted Johnson lost his bid for reelection.

The Fifteenth Amendment

In 1868, Grant easily defeated New York governor Horatio Seymour in the electoral college, by 214 to 80. However, the popular vote was much closer, a hair's breadth in some states. Nationwide, Grant won by 300,000 votes. Some rudimentary arithmetic showed that he got 500,000 black votes in the southern states; Seymour may have been the choice of a majority of whites. Grant lost New York, the largest state, by a very thin margin. Had blacks been able to vote in New York, Grant would have carried the state easily. In Indiana, Grant won by a razor-thin margin. Had blacks been able to vote in that northern state, it would not have been close.

In a word, the future of the Republican party seemed to depend on the black man's right to vote in the northern as well as the southern states. Consequently, the Republicans, including moderates, drafted the Fifteenth Amendment. It forbade states to deny the vote to any person on the basis of "race, color, or previous condition of servitude." Because Republican governments favorable to blacks still controlled most of the southern states, the amendment was easily ratified.

Legend

By the end of the nineteenth century, a legend of Reconstruction took form in American popular consciousness. Most white people came to believe that Reconstruction was a time of degradation and humiliation for white southerners. Soldiers bullied them, and they languished under the political domination of ignorant former slaves who were incapable of good citizenship, carpetbaggers (northerners who went south in order to exploit the tragedy of defeat), and scalawags (low-class white southerners who collaborated with blacks and Yankees).

The "Black Reconstruction" governments were hopelessly corrupt. The blacks, carpetbaggers, and scalawags looted the southern state treasuries and demeaned the honor of the South. Only by heroic efforts did decent white people, through the Democratic party, redeem the southern states when they took control of them. Some versions of the legend glamorized the role of secret organizations, such as the Ku Klux Klan, in redeeming the South.

As in most legends, there was a kernel of truth in this picture of Reconstruction. The Radical governments did spend freely. There was plenty of corruption; for example, the Republican governor of Louisiana, Henry C. Warmoth, banked $100,000 during a year when his salary was $8,000. In 1869, the state of Florida spent as much on its printing bill as was spent on every function of the state's government in 1860. Sometimes theft was open and ludicrous. Former slaves in South Carolina's lower house voted a payment of $1,000 to one of their number who lost that amount in a bet on a horse race.

The Legend in Perspective

Large governmental expenditures were unavoidable in the postwar South. The southern society and economy were being built from desolation in many areas—an expensive proposition. It was the lot of the Radical state governments to provide social services—for whites as well as blacks—that had simply been ignored in the South before the Civil War. Statewide public school systems were not founded in the South until Reconstruction. Programs for relief of the destitute and handicapped were nearly unknown before the Republicans came to power.

Corrupt politicians are inevitable in times of massive government spending, no matter who is in charge. Shady deals were not peculiar to southern Republican governments during the 1860s and 1870s. The most flagrant theft of public treasuries during the period was the work of Democrats in New York, supporters of white southerners who wanted to reduce the blacks to peonage. In fact, the champion southern thieves of the era were not Radicals but white Democrats hostile to black participation in government. After a Republican administration in Mississippi ran a nearly corruption-free regime for six years, the first Democratic treasurer of the state absconded with $415,000. This paled compared to the looting done by E. A. Burke, the first post-Reconstruction treasurer of Louisiana, who took $1,777,000 with him to Honduras in 1890.

As for the carpetbaggers, the portrayal of them as low-class parasites was false. Many of them brought much-needed capital to the South. They were hot to make money, to be sure, but in the process of developing the South, not as mere exploiters. Some scalawags were "poor white trash," but the majority were respectable whites who had been opposed to secession—onetime Whigs—and some had been prominent, well-to-do Confederates.

Blacks in Government

Few of the African Americans who rose to high office in the Reconstruction governments were ignorant former field hands. Most were well-educated, refined, even rather conservative men. Moreover, whatever the misdeeds of Reconstruction, black voters could not be blamed. African Americans never ran the government of any southern state. Eighty percent of Republican voters, blacks held only a fifth of public offices. For a short time, African Americans were the majority in the legislature of South Carolina (where blacks were a large majority of the population) and filled half the seats in the legislature of Louisiana. Only two African Americans served as senators, Blanche K. Bruce and Hiram Revels, both cultivated men from Mississippi. No black ever served as a governor, although Lieutenant Governor P. B. S. Pinchback of Louisiana briefly acted in that capacity when the white governor was out of the state. Whatever Reconstruction was, its color was not black.

The crime of Reconstruction in the eyes of most southern whites was that it allowed blacks to participate in government. The experiment failed because black voters lacked the economic independence with which to guarantee their civil equality and because northerners soon lost interest in the ideals of the Civil War.

The Klan and the Redeemers

In 1866, General Nathan Bedford Forrest of Tennessee, whom Sherman thought the South's military genius, founded the Ku Klux Klan as a social club for Confederate veterans. Like other men's lodges, the Klan was replete with hocus-pocus, including white robes and titles like Kleagle and Grand Wizard. In 1868, with the triumph of the Radical Republicans in Congress, the Klan was politicized, and similar organizations, like the Knights of the White Camellia, were born.

Determined to prevent black participation in government with harassment and terrorism, Klan night riders threatened, roughed up, whipped, and killed African Americans who were politically active, who were merely deemed "impudent," or who simply refused to work for whites. They hit the South like a tornado. The federal government estimated that the Klan murdered 700 blacks in 1868. The next year was worse.

Because the Klansmen were masked, it was impossible to bring the murderers to trial. So, in 1870 and 1871, Congress passed two Ku Klux Acts, making it illegal "to go in disguise upon the public highway . . . with intent to . . . injure, oppress, threaten, or intimidate [citizens] and to prevent them from enjoying their constitutional rights."

Providing authorities and the army carte blanche to harass the Klansmen proved effective in some states. Between 1870 and 1872, Texas arrested 6,000 Klansmen and broke the organization there. It took years elsewhere in the South to end the terror. The single greatest Klan atrocity, the "Colfax Massacre," occurred in April 1873, when 100 blacks were killed.

▲ *Representative Robert Elliott of South Carolina in the House of Representatives. More African Americans were elected to the House from South Carolina during Reconstruction than from any other state.*

By then, many southern blacks had concluded that staying home on election day was a small price to pay for their families' freedom from terror. (The Klan killed women too.) Moreover, few southern blacks owned land. In order to make a living, they found that a major condition of employment was to stay away from the polls.

One by one, the Republicans lost the southern states to the Redeemers, as Democrats running frankly on a platform of "white supremacy" called themselves. Year by year, the interest of northerners in preserving the rights of southern blacks deteriorated. Never had more than a minority of northern whites been convinced that blacks were their equals. When an era of unprecedented economic expansion unfolded during the presidential administration of Ulysses S. Grant, support for Reconstruction dwindled. Albion W. Tourgée, a white northerner who fought for black civil equality in North Carolina, wrote that trying to enforce the Fourteenth and Fifteenth Amendments without federal support was "a fool's errand."

THE GRANT ADMINISTRATION

Ulysses S. Grant, only 46 years old when he took the oath of office in 1869, was the youngest man to be president up to his time. In some ways, his presence was as unimpressive as when reporters caught him whittling sticks on the battlefield. In some photographs, Grant has an odd cast to his eye as though he suspected he had risen above his capabilities. In fact, Grant disliked the duties of the presidency—the job; but he delighted in its perquisites. He took with relish to eating caviar and tournedos sauce béarnaise, and sipping the best French wines and cognac. The general whose uniform was always rumpled developed a fondness for expensive, finely tailored clothing.

Indeed, the elegant broadcloth on his back was the emblem of Grant's failure as president. Money and fame came too suddenly to a man who had struggled to pay the bills for

▲ *Ku Klux Klan night riders shoot up the house of an African American who voted or, possibly, just insisted on his dignity as a free man. In 1868 and 1869, two or three blacks were murdered each day by Klanlike terrorists.*

40 years. He and his wife were overwhelmed by the adulation heaped on them after Appomattox. When towns and counties took his name, and cities made gifts of valuable property and even cash—$100,000 from New York City— Grant accepted with a few mumbled words of thanks. He never grasped the fact that the gift givers might actually be paying in advance for future favors. Or, he saw nothing wrong in returning kindness with the resources at his disposal. Among the least of his mistakes, he gave federal jobs to any of his and his wife's relatives who asked, and they were not bashful. Worse, Grant remained as loyal to them, even after they betrayed him, as he had been loyal to junior officers in the army. In the military, backing up subordinates when they slip up is a virtue, essential to morale. Grant never learned that, in politics, backing up subordinates who consciously steal is quite another thing.

Black Friday

Grant's friends, old and new, wasted no time in stealing. Unlucky in business himself, the president luxuriated in the flattery lavished on him by wealthy men. In 1869, two unscrupulous speculators, Jay Gould and Jim Fisk, made it a point to be seen in public with the president while they schemed secretly with Grant's brother-in-law, Abel R. Corbin. The stakes were high: Gould and Fisk planned to corner the nation's gold supply.

With Corbin's assurance he would keep Grant from selling government gold, Gould and Fisk bought up as much

gold and gold futures (commitments to buy gold at a future date at a set price) as they could find on the market. The immediate sale of so much gold sent its price soaring. By September 1869, gold was bringing $162 an ounce. Gould and Fisk's plan was to push the price a bit higher, dump their holdings, and pocket a fortune.

Finally grasping that he was an accomplice to the scheme, on Friday, September 24, Grant put $4 million in government gold on the market. The price collapsed, but Gould and Fisk suffered little. Jim Fisk simply refused to honor his futures commitments and hired thugs to threaten sellers who insisted. (High finance could be highly exercising during the Grant years.) But businessmen who needed gold to pay debts and wages were ruined by the hundreds; thousands of workingmen lost their jobs. The luster of a great general's reputation was tarnished before he was president for a year.

Other Scandals

During the construction of the Union Pacific Railway, the directors of the UP set up a dummy construction corporation called the "Crédit Mobilier." It charged the Union Pacific some $5 million for work that the Crédit Mobilier paid subcontractors $3 million to perform. The difference went into the pockets of Union Pacific executives. Because the Union Pacific was heavily subsidized by the federal government, and therefore under scrutiny, key members of Congress were cut in on the loot. Among the beneficiaries was

Black Politicos

Better a white crook than a black crook; better a white grafter than a black of stature and probity. Such was the view of the "Redeemers," white Democrats who wrested control of southern state governments from the Republican party during Reconstruction. They depicted black officials as incompetent, corrupt, and uninterested in the welfare of the South as a whole. With most southern whites contemptuous of the freedmen, it was an effective appeal. Other issues paled nearly into invisibility in what seemed the blinding urgency of asserting "white supremacy."

At low levels, some black officials were incompetent and self-serving. A few high officials were venal grafters. That their Redeemer challengers were no better and often worse did not, however, lead to reflection among southern Democrats. Race was all.

As a group, the African Americans who sat in Congress during Reconstruction and, in a few cases, beyond, were as able and worthy as any other identifiable category of congressmen of any era. Between 1869 and 1901, 20 blacks served in the House, two in the Senate. South Carolina sent eight; North Carolina, four; Alabama, three; and Virginia, Georgia, Florida, Louisiana, and Mississippi, one each. Both black senators, Hiram K. Revels and Blanche K. Bruce, represented Mississippi, where potential black voters outnumbered whites.

Thirteen of the 22 African Americans in Congress had been slaves; the others were lifelong free blacks. Their educational attainment compared well with that of Congress as a whole. Ten of the black congressmen had gone to college, and five had graduated. Six were lawyers; three were preachers; four were farmers. Most of the others were skilled artisans.

Hiram Revels was a Methodist pastor. He was born in North Carolina in 1822 but, as a free black, prudently moved to Indiana and Ohio, where, during the Civil War, he organized a black regiment. The end of the war found him in Natchez, Mississippi where his cultivated and conservative demeanor (and a willingness to defer to white Republicans) made him an attractive candidate for the Senate.

Blanche K. Bruce was born a slave in 1841, but he was well educated: His owner leased him to a printer. In 1861, he escaped from his apparently lackadaisical master and, in the wake of the Union army, moved to Mississippi. His record in the Senate was conservative.

The most durable of the black congressmen was J. H. Rainey of South Carolina. He sat in Congress between 1869 and 1879, winning his last election in the year of the Hayes-Tilden debacle. In most of his district, blacks outnumbered whites by six to one. He was retired in the election of 1878 only as a consequence of widespread economic reprisals against black voters and some Klan-type violence.

Rainey's parents had bought their freedom long before the Civil War, but, in 1862, he was drafted to work on the fortifications in Charleston Harbor, a condition tantamount to enslavement. He escaped to the West Indies and worked his way to the North, returning to his home state during the early part of Re-construction. Rainey was vindictive toward the white South. He exploited racial hostilities as nastily as any Redeemer. He was, unsurprisingly, preoccupied with civil rights issues. However, Rainey was not oblivious to other political problems. By the end of the 1870s, he used his seniority to work for southern economic interests that transcended the color line. He defended the rights of Chinese in California on "probusiness" Republican, as well as racial, grounds and attempted to improve relations with the black republic of Haiti.

George H. White was the last African American from a southern state to sit in Congress before the passage of the Civil Rights Act of 1964. Born a slave in 1852, after the war, he attended Howard University in Washington and practiced law in North Carolina. In 1896, he won election to the House of Representatives by adding white Populist votes to the black Republican bloc still enfranchised in North Carolina. Some southern Populists, like Thomas Watson of Georgia, preached interracial political cooperation in an attempt to build a solid agrarian front against the "Bourbons" into which the Redeemers had been transformed.

Populist support put White in an impossible situation, for the national Republican party was staunchly anti-Populist. If he were not to be shut out of the party in Washington, he had to support the policies of the McKinley administration, such as a high protective tariff, the Spanish-American War, and imperialism. Inevitably, his positions alienated those whites who had helped elect him. Moreover, southern Populism was undergoing a momentous transformation during the late 1890s. Democratic party politicians like Benjamin "Pitchfork Ben" Tillman of neighboring South Carolina combined populist appeals to poor whites with an incendiary hatred of blacks.

Conservative party-line Republicans like White were easy targets. In 1898, the North Carolina Populists switched sides, supporting the Democratic candidate and almost ousting White after only one term. He knew his political future was doomed and spoke out loudly about what was happening to African Americans in the South. The only black in Congress, he described himself as "the representative on this floor of 9,000,000 of the population of these United States."

By 1900, black voters in White's district had been reduced to a fragment. He did not even bother to stand for reelection. Instead, in his farewell speech in Washington in 1901, he delivered his finest oration, an eloquent speech that served as the coda to Reconstruction's failure to integrate blacks into American society:

> These parting words are in behalf of an outraged, heart-broken, bruised and bleeding, but God-fearing people, faithful, industrial, loyal people, rising people, full of potential force. The only apology that I have to make for the earnestness with which I have spoken is that I am pleading for the life, the liberty, the future happiness, and manhood suffrage for one-eighth of the entire population of the United States.

Schuyler Colfax, Grant's vice president. Speaker of the House James A. Garfield also accepted a "stipend."

Three of Grant's cabinet were involved in corruption. Carriers under contract to the Post Office Department paid kickbacks in return for exorbitant payments for their services. The secretary of war, William W. Belknap, took bribes from companies that operated trading posts in Indian reservations under his authority. He and his subordinates shut their eyes while the traders defrauded the tribes of goods they were due under the terms of federal treaties. Grant insisted that Belknap resign but refused to bring charges against him.

Nor did Grant punish his secretary of the treasury, Benjamin Bristow, or his personal secretary, Orville E. Babcock, when he learned that they sold excise stamps to whiskey distillers in St. Louis. Whenever the president came close to losing his patience (which was considerable), Roscoe Conkling or another stalwart Republican reminded him of the importance of party loyalty. Better a few scoundrels escape than party morale be damaged and the Democrats take over.

The Liberal Republicans

Although the full story of the Grant scandals was known only later, enough was suspected in 1872 that a number of prominent Republicans broke with the president. Charles Sumner of Massachusetts, a senator since 1851 and chairman of the Senate Foreign Relations Committee, fought the president fiercely over Grant's determination to annex Santo Domingo (now the Dominican Republic).

Senator Carl Schurz of Missouri and the editor of *The Nation* magazine, E. L. Godkin, were appalled by the atmosphere of corruption in Washington and the treatment of public office as a way of making a living rather than as a public service. Schurz and Godkin (although not Sumner) had also given up on Radical Reconstruction, which Grant enforced. Although not necessarily convinced that blacks were inferior to whites, they concluded that the protection of African Americans' civil rights was not worth the instability chronic in the South or the continued presence of troops in several southern states. Better to allow the white Redeemers to return to power.

The Election of 1872

This was also the position of the man whom the Liberal Republicans named to run for president in 1872, the editor of the *New York Tribune,* Horace Greeley. He described southern blacks as "simple, credulous, ignorant men," and the carpetbaggers he had once encouraged "as stealing and plucking, many of them with both arms around negroes, and their hands in their rear pockets." The freedmen, Greeley and others thought, needed the guidance of selfless gentlemen like himself or even responsible southern whites.

Greeley was a terrible choice as a presidential nominee, for he was a lifelong eccentric. Throughout his 61 years, Greeley clambered aboard almost every reform or fad from

abolitionism and women's rights to vegetarianism, spiritualism (communicating with the dead), and phrenology (reading a person's character in the bumps on his or her head).

His appearance invited ridicule. He looked like a crackpot, with his round, pink face exaggerated by close-set, beady eyes and a wispy white fringe of chin whiskers. He wore an ankle-length overcoat on the hottest days and carried a brightly colored umbrella on the driest. Republican cartoonists like Thomas Nast had an easy time making fun of Greeley.

To make matters worse, Greeley needed the support of the Democrats to make a race of it. He proposed to "clasp hands across the bloody chasm" between North and South. This was asking too much of Republican party regulars. Many who disapproved of Grant disapproved much more of southern Democrats.

Moreover, throughout his editorial career, Greeley had printed just about every printable vilification of the Democrats—particularly southerners—that the English language offered. The Democrats did give him their nomination, but southern whites found it difficult to support him. A large African American vote for Grant in seven southern states helped give the president a 286 to 66 victory in the electoral college.

Culver Pictures, Inc.

▲ *Horace Greeley, a celebrated newspaperman but a hopeless eccentric. Even if all the Grant administration scandals had been known in 1872, it is unlikely that the easily mocked Greeley could have defeated Grant.*

THE TWILIGHT OF RECONSTRUCTION

The liberals returned to the Republican party. For all their loathing of President Grant, the liberals found their fling with the Democrats humiliating. Of the bunch, only Charles Sumner remained true to the cause of the southern blacks. His Civil Rights Act of 1875 (passed a year after his death) guaranteed equal accommodations for blacks in public facilities such as hotels and theaters and forbade the exclusion of blacks from juries. Congress quietly dropped another provision forbidding schools segregated by race.

The Civil Rights Act of 1875 was the last significant federal attempt to enforce equal rights for 80 years. Not only had northerners lost interest in Civil War idealism, but southern white Democrats had "redeemed" most of the former Confederacy. By the end of 1875, only three states remained Republican: South Carolina, Florida, and Louisiana.

The Disputed Election

The Democratic candidate in 1876, New York governor Samuel J. Tilden, said he would remove the troops from these three states, which would mean a decline in black voting, bringing the white supremacy Democrats to power. The Republican candidate, Governor Rutherford B. Hayes of Ohio, ran on a platform that guaranteed African Americans rights in the South, but Hayes, personally, was known to be skeptical of black capabilities and a personal friend of several white southern politicians.

When the votes were counted, Hayes's opinions seemed beside the point. Tilden won a close popular vote and appeared to have won the electoral college 204 to 165. However, Tilden's margin of victory included the electoral votes of South Carolina, Florida, and Louisiana, where Republicans still controlled the state governments. On instructions from Republican leaders in New York, officials there declared that Hayes had carried their states. According to this set of returns, Hayes eked out a 185 to 184 electoral vote victory.

It was not that easy. When the returns reached Washington, there were two sets from each of the three disputed states—one set for Tilden and one for Hayes. Because the Constitution did not provide for such an occurrence, a special commission was established to decide which returns were valid. Five members of each house of Congress and five members of the Supreme Court sat on the panel. Seven of them were Republicans; seven were Democrats; one, David Davis of Illinois, a Supreme Court justice and once Abraham Lincoln's law partner, was known to be an independent. No one was interested in determining the case on its merits; each commissioner intended to vote for his party's candidate no matter what documents were set before him. The burden of naming the next president of the United States fell on David Davis.

He did not like it. No matter how conscientious and honest he was, half the nation's voters would call for his scalp. Davis prevailed on friends in Illinois to get him off the hook by naming him to a vacant Senate seat. He resigned from the Court and, therefore, from the commission. His replacement was a Republican justice, and the stage was set for the Republicans to steal the election.

The Compromise of 1877

The commission voted on strict party lines, eight to seven, to accept the Hayes returns from Louisiana, Florida, and South Carolina—giving Rutherford B. Hayes the presidency by a single electoral vote. Had that been all there was to it, there might well have been violence. At a series of meetings, however, a group of prominent northern and southern politicians and businessmen came to an informal agreement that was satisfactory to the political leaders of both sections.

The "Compromise of 1877" involved several commitments, not all of them honored, for northern investments in the South. Also not honored was a vague agreement on the part of conservative southerners to build a white Republican party in the South based on the economic and social views that they shared with northern conservatives.

As to the disputed election, Hayes would move into the White House without resistance by either northern or southern Democrats. In return, he would withdraw the troops from South Carolina, Florida, and Louisiana, thus allowing the Democratic party in these states to oust the Republicans and eliminate African American political power.

for FURTHER READING

James McPherson, *Ordeal by Fire: The Civil War and Reconstruction*, 1982, is the best recent account of Reconstruction. Also see Eric Foner, *Reconstruction: America's Unfinished Revolution*, 1988. See William A. Dunning, *Reconstruction: Political and Economic*, 1907, for the old, harshly critical view of the era's policies that dominated American historical thinking for half a century. For a rejoinder, see W. E. B. Du Bois, *Black Reconstruction*, 1935. John Hope Franklin, *Reconstruction After the Civil War*, 1961, provides a more brief, objective account, as does Herman Belz, *Reconstructing the Union*, 1969. A splendid account of the reaction of blacks to freedom is Leon F. Liwack, *Been in the Storm So Long*, 1979.

Valuable studies of special topics include Richard N. Current, *Three Carpetbag Governors*, 1967; Stanley Kutler, *Judicial Power and Reconstruction Politics*, 1968; Eric McKitrick, *Andrew Johnson and Reconstruction*, 1960; Robert C. Morris, *Reading, 'Riting, and Reconstruction: The Education of Freedmen in the South, 1861–1870*, 1981; Willie Lee Rose, *Rehearsal for Reconstruction*, 1964; Hans A. Trefousse, *The Radical Republicans*, 1969; A. W. Trelease, *KKK: The Ku Klux Klan Conspiracy and Southern Reconstruction*, 1971; and C. Vann Woodward, *Reunion and Reaction: The Compromise of 1877 and the End of Reconstruction*, 1951.

Visit the source collections at http://ajaccess.wadsworth.com and http://infotrac.thomsonlearning.com, and use the Search function with the following key terms to explore documents, images, audio and video clips, articles, and commentary related to the material in this chapter:

Andrew Johnson
Freedmen's Bureau
Reconstruction

Additional resources, exercises, and Internet links related to this chapter are available on *The American Past* Web site:
http://history.wadsworth.com/americanpast7e.

HISTORY ONLINE

The Andrew Johnson Impeachment Trial
http://law.umkc.edu/faculty/projects/ftrials/impeach/impreachmt.htm
A thoroughgoing analysis of America's first presidential impeachment trial.

African American Perspectives
http://memory.loc.gov/ammem/aap/aaphome.html
African American pamphlets from the abolitionist period through 1907.

KKK
http://blackhistorypages.com/reconstruction
Freedmen's Bureau reports about Ku Klux Klan activities in North Carolina and Alabama.

APPENDIX

The Declaration of Independence

The Constitution of the United States of America

Admission of States

Population of the United States

Presidential Elections

Presidents, Vice Presidents, and Major Cabinet Officers

Cabinet Level Departments

Justices of the U.S. Supreme Court

Political Party Affiliations in Congress and the Presidency

The Declaration of Independence

The Unanimous Declaration of the Thirteen United States of America,

When in the Course of human events it becomes necessary for one people to dissolve the political bands which have connected them with another, and to assume among the Powers of the earth, the separate and equal station to which the Laws of Nature and of Nature's God entitle them, a decent respect to the opinions of mankind requires that they should declare the causes which impel them to the separation.

We hold these truths to be self-evident, that all men are created equal, that they are endowed by their Creator with certain unalienable Rights, that among these are Life, Liberty and the pursuit of Happiness. That to secure these rights, Governments are instituted among Men, deriving their just Powers from the consent of the governed. That whenever any Form of Government becomes destructive of these ends, it is the Right of the People to alter or to abolish it, and to institute new Government, laying its foundation on such principles and organizing its Powers in such form, as to them shall seem most likely to effect their Safety and Happiness. Prudence, indeed, will dictate that Governments long established should not be changed for light and transient causes; and accordingly all experience hath shewn, that mankind are more disposed to suffer, while evils are sufferable, than to right themselves by abolishing the forms to which they are accustomed. But when a long train of abuses and usurpations, pursuing invariably the same Object evinces a design to reduce them under absolute Despotism, it is their right, it is their duty, to throw off such Government, and to provide new Guards for their future security. Such has been the patient sufferance of these Colonies; and such is now the necessity which constrains them to alter their former Systems of Government. The history of the present King of Great Britain is a history of repeated injuries and usurpations, all having in direct object the establishment of an absolute Tyranny over these States. To prove this, let Facts be submitted to a candid world.

He has refused his Assent to Laws, the most wholesome and necessary for the public good.

He has forbidden his Governors to pass Laws of immediate and pressing importance, unless suspended in their operation till his Assent should be obtained; and when so suspended, he has utterly neglected to attend to them.

He has refused to pass other Laws for the accommodation of large districts of people, unless those people would relinquish the right of Representation in the Legislature, a right inestimable to them and formidable to tyrants only.

He has called together legislative bodies at places unusual, uncomfortable, and distant from the depository of their Public Records, for the sole Purpose of fatiguing them into compliance with his measures.

He has dissolved Representative Houses repeatedly, for opposing with manly firmness his invasions on the rights of the People.

He has refused for a long time, after such dissolutions, to cause others to be elected; whereby the Legislative Powers, incapable of Annihilation, have returned to the People at large for their exercise; the State remaining in the mean time exposed to all the dangers of invasion from without, and convulsions within.

He has endeavoured to prevent the Population of these States; for that purpose obstructing the Laws for Naturalization of Foreigners; refusing to pass others to encourage their migrations hither, and raising the conditions of new Appropriations of Lands.

He has obstructed the Administration of Justice, by refusing his Assent to Laws for establishing Judiciary Powers.

He has made Judges dependent on his Will alone, for the tenure of their offices, and the amount and payment of their salaries.

He has erected a multitude of New Offices, and sent hither swarms of Officers to harass our People, and eat out their substance.

He has kept among us, in times of peace, Standing Armies without the Consent of our legislatures.

He has affected to render the Military independent of and superior to the Civil Power.

He has combined with others to subject us to a jurisdiction foreign to our constitution, and unacknowledged by our laws; giving his Assent to their Acts of pretended Legislation:

For Quartering large bodies of armed troops among us:

For protecting them, by a mock Trial, from Punishment for any Murders which they should commit on the Inhabitants of these States:

For cutting off our Trade with all parts of the world:

For imposing Taxes on us without our Consent:

For depriving us in many cases, of the benefits of Trial by Jury:

For transporting us beyond Seas to be tried for pretended offences:

For abolishing the free System of English Laws in a neighbouring Province, establishing therein an Arbitrary government, and enlarging its Boundaries so as to render it at once an example and fit instrument for introducing the same absolute rule into these Colonies:

Text is reprinted from the facsimile of the engrossed copy in the National Archives. The original spelling, capitalization, and punctuation have been retained. Paragraphing has been added.

For taking away our Charters, abolishing our most valuable Laws, and altering fundamentally the Forms of our Governments:

For suspending our own Legislatures, and declaring themselves invested with Power to legislate for us in all cases whatsoever.

He has abdicated Government here, by declaring us out of his Protection, and waging War against us.

He has plundered our seas, ravaged our Coasts, burnt our towns, and destroyed the lives of our people.

He is at this time transporting large Armies of foreign Mercenaries to compleat the works of death, desolation and tyranny, already begun with circumstances of Cruelty and perfidy scarcely paralleled in the most barbarous ages, and totally unworthy the Head of a civilized nation.

He has constrained our fellow Citizens taken Captive on the high Seas to bear Arms against their Country, to become the executioners of their friends and Brethren, or to fall themselves by their Hands.

He has excited domestic insurrections amongst us, and has endeavoured to bring on the inhabitants of our frontiers, the merciless Indian Savages, whose known rule of warfare, is an undistinguished destruction of all ages, sexes and conditions.

In every stage of these Oppressions We have Petitioned for Redress in the most humble terms: Our repeated Petitions have been answered only by repeated injury. A Prince, whose character is thus marked by every act which may define a Tyrant, is unfit to be the ruler of a free People.

Nor have We been wanting in attentions to our British brethren. We have warned them from time to time of attempts by their legislature to extend an unwarrantable jurisdiction over us. We have reminded them of the circumstances of our emigration and settlement here. We have appealed to their native justice and magnanimity, and we have conjured them by the ties of our common kindred to disavow thee usurpations, which, would inevitably interrupt our connections and correspondence. They too have been deaf to the voice of justice and of consanguinity. We must, therefore, acquiesce in the necessity, which denounces our Separation, and hold them, as we hold the rest of mankind, Enemies in War, in Peace Friends.

WE, THEREFORE, the Representatives of the UNITED STATES OF AMERICA, in General Congress, Assembled, appealing to the Supreme Judge of the world for the rectitude of our intentions, do, in the Name, and by Authority of the good People of these Colonies, solemnly publish and declare, That these United Colonies are, and of Right ought to be FREE AND INDEPENDENT STATES; that they are Absolved from all Allegiance to the British Crown, and that all political connection between them and the State of Great Britain, is and ought to be totally dissolved; and that, as Free and Independent States, they have full Power to levy War, conclude Peace, contract Alliances, establish Commerce, and to do all other Acts and Things which Independent States may of right do. And for the support of this Declaration, with a firm reliance on the protection of divine Providence, we mutually pledge to each other our Lives, our Fortunes and our sacred Honor.

The Constitution of the United States of America

We the People of the United States, in Order to form a more perfect Union, establish Justice, insure domestic Tranquility, provide for the common defence, promote the general Welfare, and secure the Blessings of Liberty to ourselves and our Posterity, do ordain and establish this Constitution for the United States of America.

Article. I.

SECTION. 1. All legislative Powers herein granted shall be vested in a Congress of the United States, which shall consist of a Senate and House of Representatives.

SECTION. 2. The House of Representatives shall be composed of Members chosen every second Year by the People of the several States, and the Electors in each State shall have the Qualifications requisite for Electors of the most numerous Branch of the State Legislature.

No Person shall be a Representative who shall not have attained to the Age of twenty five Years, and been seven Years a Citizen of the United States, and who shall not, when elected, be an Inhabitant of that State in which he shall be chosen.

Representatives and direct Taxes[1] shall be apportioned among the several States which may be included within this Union, according to their respective Numbers, which shall be determined by adding to the whole Number of free Persons, including those bound to Service for a Term of Years, and excluding Indians not taxed, three fifths of all other Persons.[2] The actual Enumeration shall be made within three Years after the first Meeting of the Congress of the United States, and within every subsequent Term of ten Years, in such Manner as they shall by Law direct. The Number of Representatives shall not exceed one for every thirty Thousand, but each State shall have at Least one Representative; and until such enumeration shall be made, the State of New Hampshire shall be entitled to chuse three; Massachusetts eight; Rhode Island and Providence Plantations one; Connecticut five; New York six; New Jersey four; Pennsylvania eight; Delaware one; Maryland six; Virginia ten; North Carolina five; South Carolina five; and Georgia three.

When vacancies happen in the Representation from any State, the Executive Authority thereof shall issue Writs of Election to fill such Vacancies.

The House of Representatives shall chuse their Speaker and other Officers; and shall have the sole Power of Impeachment.

SECTION. 3. The Senate of the United States shall be composed of two Senators from each State, chosen by the Legislature thereof, for six Years; and each Senator shall have one Vote.[3]

Immediately after they shall be assembled in Consequence of the first Election, they shall be divided as equally as may be into three Classes. The Seats of the Senators of the first Class shall be vacated at the Expiration of the second Year, of the second Class at the Expiration of the fourth Year, and of the third Class at the Expiration of the sixth Year, so that one third may be chosen every second Year; and if Vacancies happen by Resignation, or otherwise, during the Recess of the Legislature of any State, the Executive thereof may make temporary Appointments until the next Meeting of the Legislature, which shall then fill such Vacancies.[4]

No Person shall be a Senator who shall not have attained to the Age of thirty Years, and been nine Years a Citizen of the United States, and who shall not, when elected, be an Inhabitant of that State for which he shall be chosen.

The Vice President of the United States shall be President of the Senate, but shall have no Vote, unless they be equally divided.

The Senate shall chuse their other Officers, and also a President pro tempore, in the Absence of the Vice President, or when he shall exercise the Office of President of the United States.

The Senate shall have the sole Power to try all Impeachments. When sitting for that Purpose, they shall be on Oath or Affirmation. When the President of the United States is tried, the Chief Justice shall preside: And no Person shall be convicted without the Concurrence of two thirds of the Members present.

Judgment in Cases of Impeachment shall not extend further than to removal from Office, and disqualification to hold and enjoy any Office of honor, Trust or Profit under the United States: but the Party convicted shall nevertheless be liable and subject to Indictment, Trial, Judgment and Punishment, according to Law.

SECTION. 4. The Times, Places and Manner of holding Elections for Senators and Representatives, shall be prescribed in each State by the Legislature thereof, but the Congress may at any time by Law make or alter such Regulation, except as to the Places of chusing Senators.

The Congress shall assemble at least once in every Year, and such Meeting shall be on the first Monday in December, unless they shall by Law appoint a different Day.[5]

Text is from the engrossed copy in the National Archives. Original spelling, capitalization, and punctuation have been retained.

[1] Modified by the Sixteenth Amendment.

[2] Replaced by the Fourteenth Amendment.

[3] Superseded by the Seventeenth Amendment.

[4] Modified by the Seventeenth Amendment.

[5] Superseded by the Twentieth Amendment.

SECTION. 5. Each House shall be the Judge of the Elections, Returns and Qualifications of its own Members, and a Majority of each shall constitute a Quorum to do Business; but a smaller Number may adjourn from day to day, and may be authorized to compel the Attendance of absent Members, in such Manner, and under such Penalties as each House may provide.

Each House may determine the Rules of its Proceedings, punish its Members for disorderly Behaviour, and, with the Concurrence of two thirds, expel a Member.

Each House shall keep a Journal of its Proceedings, and from time to time publish the same, excepting such Parts as may in their Judgment require Secrecy; and the Yeas and Nays of the Members of either House on any question shall, at the Desire of one fifth of those Present, be entered on the Journal.

Neither House, during the Session of Congress, shall, without the Consent of the other, adjourn for more than three days, nor to any other Place than that in which the two Houses shall be sitting.

SECTION. 6. The Senators and Representatives shall receive a Compensation for their Services, to be ascertained by Law, and paid out of the Treasury of the United States. They shall in all Cases, except Treason, Felony and Breach of the Peace, be privileged from Arrest during their Attendance at the Session of their respective Houses, and in going to and returning from the same; and for any Speech or Debate in either House, they shall not be questioned in any other Place.

No Senator or Representative shall, during the Time for which he was elected, be appointed to any civil Office under the Authority of the United States, which shall have been created, or the Emoluments whereof shall have been encreased during such time; and no Person holding any Office under the United States, shall be a Member of either House during his Continuance in Office.

SECTION. 7. All Bills for raising Revenue shall originate in the House of Representatives; but the Senate may propose or concur with Amendments as on other Bills.

Every Bill which shall have passed the House of Representatives and the Senate shall, before it become a Law, be presented to the President of the United States; If he approve he shall sign it, but if not he shall return it, with his Objections to that House in which it shall have originated, who shall enter the Objections at large on their Journal, and proceed to reconsider it. If after such Reconsideration two thirds of that House shall agree to pass the Bill, it shall be sent, together with the Objections, to the other House, by which it shall likewise be reconsidered, and if approved by two thirds of that House, it shall become a Law. But in all such Cases the Votes of both Houses shall be determined by yeas and Nays, and the Names of the Persons voting for and against the Bill shall be entered on the Journal of each House respectively. If any Bill shall not be returned by the President within ten Days (Sundays excepted) after it shall have been presented to him, the Same shall be a Law, in like Manner as if he had signed it, unless the Congress by their Adjournment prevent its Return, in which Case it shall not be a Law.

Every Order, Resolution, or Vote to which the Concurrence of the Senate and House of Representatives may be necessary (except on a question of Adjournment) shall be presented to the President of the United States; and before the Same shall take Effect, shall be approved by him, or being disapproved by him shall be repassed by two thirds of the Senate and House of Representatives, according to the Rules and Limitations prescribed in the Case of a Bill.

SECTION. 8. The Congress shall have power To lay and collect Taxes, Duties, Imposts and Excises, to pay the Debts and provide for the common Defence and general Welfare of the United States; but all Duties, Imposts and Excises shall be uniform throughout the United States;

To borrow Money on the credit of the United States;

To regulate Commerce with foreign Nations, and among the several States, and with the Indian Tribes;

To establish an uniform Rule of Naturalization, and uniform Laws on the subject of Bankruptcies throughout the United States;

To coin Money, regulate the Value thereof, and of foreign Coin, and fix the Standard of Weights and Measures;

To provide for the Punishment of counterfeiting the Securities and current Coin of the United States;

To establish Post Offices and post Roads;

To promote the Progress of Science and useful Arts, by securing for limited Times to Authors and Inventors the exclusive Right to their respective Writings and Discoveries;

To constitute Tribunals inferior to the Supreme Court;

To define and punish Piracies and Felonies committed on the high Seas, and Offences against the Law of Nations;

To declare War, grant Letters of Marque and Reprisal, and make Rules concerning Captures on Land and Water;

To raise and support Armies, but no Appropriation of Money to that Use shall be for a longer Term than two Years;

To provide and maintain a Navy;

To make Rules for the Government and Regulation of the land and naval Forces;

To provide for calling forth the Militia to execute the Laws of the Union, suppress Insurrections and repel Invasions;

To provide for organizing, arming, and disciplining, the Militia, and for governing such Part of them as may be employed in the Service of the United States, reserving to the States respectively, the Appointment of the Officers, and the Authority of training the Militia according to the discipline prescribed by Congress;

To exercise exclusive Legislation in all Cases whatsoever, over such District (not exceeding ten Miles square) as may, by Cession of particular States, and the Acceptance of Congress, become the Seat of the Government of the United States, and to exercise like Authority over all Places purchased by the Consent of the Legislature of the State in which the Same shall be, for the Erection of Forts, Magazines, Arsenals, dock-Yards, and other needful Buildings;—And

To make all Laws which shall be necessary and proper for carrying into Execution the foregoing Powers, and all other Powers vested by this Constitution in the Government of the United States, or in any Department or Officer thereof.

SECTION. 9. The Migration or Importation of such Persons as any of the States now existing shall think proper to admit, shall not be prohibited by the Congress prior to the Year one thousand eight hundred and eight, but a Tax or duty may be imposed on such Importation, not exceeding ten dollars for each Person.

The Privilege of the Writ of Habeas Corpus shall not be suspended, unless when in Cases of Rebellion or Invasion the public Safety may require it.

No Bill of Attainder or ex post facto Law shall be passed.

No Capitation, or other direct, Tax shall be laid, unless in Proportion to the Census or Enumeration herein before directed to be taken.

No Tax or Duty shall be laid on Articles exported from any State.

No Preference shall be given by any Regulation of Commerce or Revenue to the Ports of one State over those of another: nor shall Vessels bound to, or from, one State, be obliged to enter, clear, or pay Duties in another.

No Money shall be drawn from the Treasury, but in Consequence of Appropriations made by Law, and a regular Statement and Account of the Receipts and Expenditures of all public Money shall be published from time to time.

No Title of Nobility shall be granted by the United States: And no Person holding any Office of Profit or Trust under them, shall, without the Consent of the Congress, accept of any present, Emolument, Office, or Title, of any kind whatever, from any King, Prince, or foreign State.

SECTION. 10. No State shall enter into any Treaty, Alliance, or Confederation; grant Letters of Marque and Reprisal; coin Money; emit Bills of Credit; make any Thing but gold and silver Coin a Tender in Payment of Debts; pass any Bill of Attainder, ex post facto Law, or Law impairing the Obligation of Contracts, or grant any Title of Nobility.

No State shall, without the Consent of the Congress, lay any Imposts or Duties on Imports or Exports, except what may be absolutely necessary for executing its inspection Laws: and the net Produce of all Duties and Imposts, laid by any State on Imports or Exports, shall be for the Use of the Treasury of the United States; and all such Laws shall be subject to the Revision and Controul of the Congress.

No State shall, without the Consent of Congress, lay any Duty of Tonnage, keep Troops, or Ships of War in time of Peace, enter into any Agreement or Compact with another State, or with a foreign Power, or engage in War, unless actually invaded, or in such imminent Danger as will not admit of delay.

Article. II.

SECTION. 1. The executive Power shall be vested in a President of the United States of America. He shall hold his Office during the Term of four Years, and, together with the Vice President, chosen for the same Term, be elected, as follows:

Each State shall appoint, in such Manner as the Legislature thereof may direct, a Number of Electors, equal to the whole Number of Senators and Representatives to which the State may be entitled in the Congress: but no Senator or Representative, or Person holding an Office of Trust or Profit under the United States, shall be appointed an Elector.

The Electors shall meet in their respective States, and vote by Ballot for two Persons, of whom one at least shall not be an Inhabitant of the same State with themselves. And they shall make a List of all the Persons voted for, and of the Number of Votes for each; which List they shall sign and certify, and transmit sealed to the Seat of the Government of the United States, directed to the President of the Senate. The President of the Senate shall, in the Presence of the Senate and House of Representatives, open all the Certificates, and the Votes shall then be counted. The Person having the greatest Number of Votes shall be the President, if such Number be a Majority of the whole Number of Electors appointed; and if there be more than one who have such Majority, and have an equal Number of Votes, then the House of Representatives shall immediately chuse by Ballot one of them for President; and if no Person have a Majority, then from the five highest on the List the said House shall in like Manner chuse the President. But in chusing the President, the Votes shall be taken by States, the Representation from each State having one Vote; A quorum for this Purpose shall consist of a Member or Members from two thirds of the States, and a Majority of all the States shall be necessary to a Choice. In every Case, after the Choice of the President, the Person having the greatest Number of Votes of the Electors shall be the Vice President. But if there should remain two or more who have equal Votes, the Senate shall chuse from them by Ballot the Vice President.[6]

The Congress may determine the Time of chusing the Electors, and the Day on which they shall give their Votes; which Day shall be the same throughout the United States.

No Person except a natural born Citizen, or a Citizen of the United States, at the time of the Adoption of this Constitution, shall be eligible to the Office of President, neither shall any Person be eligible to that Office who shall not have attained to the Age of thirty five Years, and been fourteen Years a Resident within the United States.

In Case of the Removal of the President from Office, or of his Death, Resignation, or Inability to discharge the Powers and Duties of the said Office, the Same shall devolve on the Vice President, and the Congress may by Law provide for the Case of Removal, Death, Resignation or Inability, both of the President and Vice President, declaring what Officer shall then act as President, and such Officer shall act accordingly, until the Disability be removed, or a President shall be elected.[7]

The President shall, at stated Times, receive for his Services, a Compensation, which shall neither be increased nor diminished during the Period for which he shall have been elected, and he shall not receive within that Period any other Emolument from the United States, or any of them.

---

[6]Superseded by the Twelfth Amendment.

[7]Modified by the Twenty-fifth Amendment.

Before he enter on the Execution of his Office, he shall take the following Oath or Affirmation:—"I do solemnly swear (or affirm) that I will faithfully execute the Office of President of the United States, and will to the best of my Ability, preserve, protect and defend the Constitution of the United States."

SECTION. 2. The President shall be Commander in Chief of the Army and Navy of the United States, and of the Militia of the several States, when called into the actual Service of the United States; he may require the Opinion, in writing, of the principal Officer in each of the executive Departments, upon any Subject relating to the Duties of their respective Offices, and he shall have Power to grant Reprieves and Pardons for Offences against the United States, except in Cases of Impeachment.

He shall have Power, by and with the Advice and Consent of the Senate, to make Treaties, provided two thirds of the Senators present concur; and he shall nominate, and by and with the Advice and Consent of the Senate, shall appoint Ambassadors, other public Ministers and Consuls, Judges of the supreme Court, and all other Officers of the United States, whose Appointments are not herein otherwise provided for, and which shall be established by Law: but the Congress may by Law vest the Appointment of such inferior Officers, as they think proper, in the President alone, in the Courts of Law, or in the Heads of Departments.

The President shall have Power to fill up all Vacancies that may happen during the Recess of the Senate, by granting Commissions which shall expire at the End of their next Session.

SECTION. 3. He shall from time to time give the Congress Information of the State of the Union, and recommend to their Consideration such Measures as he shall judge necessary and expedient; he may, on extraordinary Occasions, convene both Houses, or either of them, and in Case of Disagreement between them, with Respect to the Time of Adjournment, he may adjourn them to such Time as he shall think proper; he shall receive Ambassadors and other public Ministers; he shall take Care that the Laws be faithfully executed, and shall Commission all the Officers of the United States.

SECTION. 4. The President, Vice President and all civil Officers of the United States, shall be removed from Office on Impeachment for, and Conviction of, Treason, Bribery, or other high Crimes and Misdemeanors.

Article. III.

SECTION. 1. The judicial Power of the United States, shall be vested in one supreme Court, and in such inferior Courts as the Congress may from time to time ordain and establish. The Judges, both of the supreme and inferior Courts, shall hold their Offices during good Behaviour, and shall, at stated Times, receive for their Services, a Compensation, which shall not be diminished during their Continuance in Office.

SECTION. 2. The judicial Power shall extend to all Cases, in Law and Equity, arising under this Constitution, the Laws of the United States, and Treaties made, or which shall be made, under their Authority;-to all Cases affecting Ambassadors, other public Ministers and Consuls;—to all Cases of admiralty and maritime Jurisdiction;—to Controversies to which the United States shall be a Party;—to Controversies between two or more States;—between a State and Citizens of another State;[8]—between Citizens of different States,—between Citizens of the same State claiming Lands under Grants of different States, and between a State, or the Citizens thereof, and foreign States, Citizens or Subjects.

In all Cases affecting Ambassadors, other public Ministers and Consuls, and those in which a State shall be Party, the supreme Court shall have original Jurisdiction. In all the other Cases before mentioned, the supreme Court shall have appellate Jurisdiction, both as to Law and Fact, with such Exceptions, and under such Regulations as the Congress shall make.

The Trial of all Crimes, except in Cases of Impeachment, shall be by Jury; and such Trial shall be held in the State where the said Crimes shall have been committed; but when not committed within any State, the Trial shall be at such Place or Places as the Congress may by Law have directed.

SECTION. 3. Treason against the United States, shall consist only in levying War against them, or in adhering to their Enemies, giving them Aid and Comfort. No Person shall be convicted of Treason unless on the Testimony of two Witnesses to the same overt Act, or on Confession in open Court.

The Congress shall have Power to declare the Punishment of Treason, but no Attainder of Treason shall work Corruption of Blood, or Forfeiture except during the Life of the Person attainted.

Article. IV.

SECTION. 1. Full Faith and Credit shall be given in each State to the public Acts, Records, and judicial Proceedings of every other State. And the Congress may by general Laws prescribe the Manner in which such Acts, Records and Proceedings shall be proved, and the Effect thereof.

SECTION. 2. The Citizens of each State shall be entitled to all Privileges and Immunities of Citizens in the several States.

A Person charged in any State with Treason, Felony, or other Crime, who shall flee from Justice, and be found in another State, shall on Demand of the executive Authority of the State from which he fled, be delivered up, to be removed to the State having Jurisdiction of the Crime.

No Person held to Service or Labour in one State, under the Laws thereof, escaping into another, shall, in Consequence of any Law or Regulation therein, be discharged from such Service or Labour, but shall be delivered up on Claim of the Party to whom such Service or Labour may be due.

SECTION. 3. New States may be admitted by the Congress into this Union; but no new State shall be formed or erected within the Jurisdiction of any other State, nor any State be

---

[8]Modified by the Eleventh Amendment.

formed by the Junction of two or more States, or Parts of States, without the Consent of the Legislatures of the States concerned as well as of the Congress.

The Congress shall have Power to dispose of and make all needful Rules and Regulations respecting the Territory or other Property belonging to the United States; and nothing in this Constitution shall be so construed as to Prejudice any Claims of the United States, or of any particular State.

SECTION. 4. The United States shall guarantee to every State in this Union a Republican Form of Government, and shall protect each of them against Invasion; and on Application of the Legislature, or of the Executive (when the Legislature cannot be convened) against domestic Violence.

Article. V.

The Congress, whenever two thirds of both Houses shall deem it necessary, shall propose Amendments to this Constitution, or, on the Application of the Legislatures of two thirds of the several States, shall call a Convention for proposing Amendments, which, in either Case, shall be valid to all Intents and Purposes, as Part of this Constitution, when ratified by the Legislatures of three fourths of the several States, or by Conventions in three fourths thereof, as the one or the other Mode of Ratification may be proposed by the Congress; Provided that no Amendment which may be made prior to the Year One thousand eight hundred and eight shall in any Manner affect the first and fourth Clauses in the Ninth Section of the first Article; and that no State, without its Consent, shall be deprived of its equal Suffrage in the Senate.

Article. VI.

All Debts contracted and Engagements entered into, before the Adoption of this Constitution, shall be as valid against the United States under this Constitution, as under the Confederation.

This Constitution, and the Laws of the United States which shall be made in Pursuance thereof; and all Treaties made, or which shall be made, under the Authority of the United States, shall be the supreme Law of the Land; and the Judges in every State shall be bound thereby, any Thing in the Constitution or Laws of any State to the Contrary notwithstanding.

The Senators and Representatives before mentioned, and the Members of the several State Legislatures, and all executive and judicial Officers, both of the United States and of the several States, shall be bound by Oath or Affirmation, to support this Constitution; but no religious Test shall ever be required as a Qualification to any Office or public Trust under the United States.

Article. VII.

The Ratification of the Conventions of nine States, shall be sufficient for the Establishment of this Constitution between the States so ratifying the Same.

Done in Convention by the Unanimous Consent of the States present the Seventeenth Day of September in the Year of our Lord one thousand seven hundred and Eighty seven and of the Independence of the United States of America the Twelfth. **In witness** whereof We have hereunto subscribed our Names,

Articles in Addition to, and Amendment of, the Constitution of the United States of America, Proposed by Congress, and Ratified by the Legislatures of the Several States, Pursuant to the Fifth Article of the Original Constitution.

Amendment I[9]

Congress shall make no law respecting an establishment of religion, or prohibiting the free exercise thereof; or abridging the freedom of speech, or of the press; or the right of the people peaceably to assemble, and to petition the Government for a redress of grievances.

Amendment II

A well regulated Militia, being necessary to the security of a free State, the right of the people to keep and bear Arms shall not be infringed.

Amendment III

No Soldier shall, in time of peace, be quartered in any house, without the consent of the Owner, nor in time of war, but in a manner to be prescribed by law.

Amendment IV

The right of the people to be secure in their persons, houses, papers, and effects, against unreasonable searches and seizures, shall not be violated, and no Warrants shall issue, but upon probable cause, supported by Oath or affirmation, and particularly describing the place to be searched, and the persons or things to be seized.

Amendment V

No person shall be held to answer for a capital or otherwise infamous crime, unless on a presentment or indictment of a Grand Jury, except in cases arising in the land or naval forces, or in the Militia, when in actual service in time of War or public danger; nor shall any person be subject for the same offence to be twice put in jeopardy of life or limb; nor shall be compelled in any criminal case to be a witness against himself, nor be deprived of life, liberty, or property, without due process of law; nor shall private property be taken for public use, without just compensation.

---

[9]The first ten amendments were passed by Congress September 25, 1789. They were ratified by three-fourths of the states December 15, 1791.

Amendment VI

In all criminal prosecutions, the accused shall enjoy the right to a speedy and public trial, by an impartial jury of the State and district wherein the crime shall have been committed, which district shall have been previously ascertained by law, and to be informed of the nature and cause of the accusation; to be confronted with the witnesses against him; to have compulsory process for obtaining witnesses in his favor, and to have the Assistance of Counsel for his defence.

Amendment VII

In suits at common law, where the value in controversy shall exceed twenty dollars, the right of trial by jury shall be preserved, and no fact tried by a jury, shall be otherwise re-examined in any Court of the United States, than according to the rules of the common law.

Amendment VIII

Excessive bail shall not be required, nor excessive fines imposed, nor cruel and unusual punishments inflicted.

Amendment IX

The enumeration in the Constitution, of certain rights, shall not be construed to deny or disparage others retained by the people.

Amendment X

The powers not delegated to the United States by the Constitution; nor prohibited by it to the States, are reserved to the States respectively, or to the people.

Amendment XI[10]

The Judicial power of the United States shall not be construed to extend to any suit in law or equity, commenced or prosecuted against one of the United States by Citizens of another State, or by Citizens or Subjects of any Foreign State.

Amendment XII[11]

The Electors shall meet in their respective States and vote by ballot for President and Vice-President, one of whom, at least, shall not be an inhabitant of the same State with themselves; they shall name in their ballots the person voted for as President, and in distinct ballots the person voted for as Vice-President, and they shall make distinct lists of all persons voted for as President, and of all persons voted for as Vice-President, and of the number of votes for each, which lists they shall sign and certify, and transmit sealed to the seat of the government of the United States, directed to the President of the Senate;—The President of the Senate shall, in the presence of the Senate and House of Representatives, open all the certificates and the votes shall then be counted;—The person having the greatest number of votes for President, shall be the President, if such number be a majority of the whole number of Electors appointed; and if no person have such majority, then from the persons having the highest numbers not exceeding three on the list of those voted for as President, the House of Representatives shall choose immediately, by ballot, the President. But in choosing the President, the votes shall be taken by states, the representation from each state having one vote; a quorum for this purpose shall consist of a member or members from two-thirds of the states, and a majority of all the states shall be necessary to a choice. And if the House of Representatives shall not choose a President whenever the right of choice shall devolve upon them, before the fourth day of March next following, then the Vice-President shall act as President, as in the case of the death or other constitutional disability of the President.—The person having the greatest number of votes as Vice-President, shall be the Vice-President, if such number be a majority of the whole number of Electors appointed, and if no person have a majority, then from the two highest numbers on the list, the Senate shall choose the Vice-President; a quorum for the purpose shall consist of two-thirds of the whole number of Senators, and a majority of the whole number shall be necessary to a choice. But no person constitutionally ineligible to the office of President shall be eligible to that of Vice-President of the United States.

Amendment XIII[12]

SECTION 1. Neither slavery nor involuntary servitude, except as a punishment for crime whereof the party shall have been duly convicted, shall exist within the United States, or any place subject to their jurisdiction.
SECTION 2. Congress shall have power to enforce this article by appropriate legislation.

Amendment XIV[13]

SECTION 1. All persons born or naturalized in the United States, and subject to the jurisdiction thereof, are citizens of the United States and of the State wherein they reside. No State shall make or enforce any law which shall abridge the privileges or immunities of citizens of the United States; nor shall any State deprive any person of life, liberty, or property, without due process of law; nor deny to any person within its jurisdiction the equal protection of the laws.
SECTION 2. Representatives shall be apportioned among the several States according to their respective numbers, counting

---

[10]Passed March 4, 1794. Ratified January 23, 1795.

[11]Passed December 9, 1803. Ratified June 15, 1804.

[12]Passed January 31, 1865. Ratified December 6, 1865.

[13]Passed June 13, 1866. Ratified July 9, 1868.

the whole number of persons in each State, excluding Indians not taxed. But when the right to vote at any election for the choice of electors for President and Vice-President of the United States, Representatives in Congress, the Executive and Judicial officers of a State, or the members of the Legislature thereof, is denied to any of the male inhabitants of such State, being twenty-one years of age, and citizens of the United States, or in any way abridged, except for participation in rebellion, or other crime, the basis of representation therein shall be reduced in the proportion which the number of such male citizens shall bear to the whole number of male citizens twenty-one years of age in such State.

SECTION 3. No person shall be a Senator or Representative in Congress, or elector of President and Vice-President, or hold any office, civil or military, under the United States, or under any State, who, having previously taken an oath, as a member of Congress, or as an officer of the United States, or as a member of any State legislature, or as an executive or judicial officer of any State, to support the Constitution of the United States, shall have engaged in insurrection or rebellion against the same, or given aid or comfort to the enemies thereof. But Congress may by a vote of two-thirds of each House, remove such disability.

SECTION 4. The validity of the public debt of the United States, authorized by law, including debts incurred for payment of pensions and bounties for services in suppressing insurrection or rebellion, shall not be questioned. But neither the United States nor any State shall assume or pay any debt or obligation incurred in aid of insurrection or rebellion against the United States, or any claim for the loss or emancipation of any slave; but all such debts, obligations, and claims shall be held illegal and void.

SECTION 5. The Congress shall have the power to enforce, by appropriate legislation, the provisions of this article.

Amendment XV[14]

SECTION 1. The right of citizens of the United States to vote shall not be denied or abridged by the United States or by any State on account of race, color, or previous conditions of servitude—

SECTION 2. The Congress shall have power to enforce this article by appropriate legislation.

Amendment XVI

The Congress shall have power to lay and collect taxes on incomes, from whatever source derived, without apportionment among the several States, and without regard to any census or enumeration.

Amendment XVII[15]

The Senate of the United States shall be composed of two Senators from each State, elected by the people thereof, for six years; and each Senator shall have one vote. The electors in each State shall have the qualifications requisite for electors of the most numerous branch of the State legislatures.

When vacancies happen in the representation of any State in the Senate, the executive authority of such State shall issue writs of election to fill such vacancies: Provided, That the legislature of any State may empower the executive thereof to make temporary appointments until the people fill the vacancies by election as the legislature may direct.

This amendment shall not be so construed as to affect the election or term of any Senator chosen before it becomes valid as part of the Constitution.

Amendment XVIII[16]

SECTION 1. After one year from the ratification of this article the manufacture, sale, or transportation of intoxicating liquors within, the importation thereof into, or the exportation thereof from the United States and all territory subject to the jurisdiction thereof for beverage purposes is hereby prohibited.

SECTION 2. The Congress and the several States shall have concurrent power to enforce this article by appropriate legislation.

SECTION 3. This article shall be inoperative unless it shall have been ratified as an amendment to the Constitution by the legislatures of the several States, as provided in the Constitution, within seven years from the date of the submission hereof to the States by the Congress.

Amendment XIX[17]

The right of citizens of the United States to vote shall not be denied or abridged by the United States or by any State on account of sex.

Congress shall have power to enforce this article by appropriate legislation.

Amendment XX[18]

SECTION 1. The terms of the President and Vice-President shall end at noon on the 20th day of January, and the terms of Senators and Representatives at noon on the 3d day of January, of the years in which such terms would have ended if this article had not been ratified; and the terms of their successors shall then begin.

SECTION 2. The Congress shall assemble at least once in every year, and such meeting shall begin at noon on the 3d day of January, unless they shall by law appoint a different day.

SECTION 3. If, at the time fixed for the beginning of the term of the President, the President elect shall have died the Vice-

---

[14]Passed February 26, 1869. Ratified February 2, 1870.

[15]Passed May 13, 1912. Ratified April 8, 1913.

[16]Passed December 18, 1917. Ratified January 16, 1919.

[17]Passed June 4, 1919. Ratified August 18, 1920.

[18]Passed March 2, 1932. Ratified January 23, 1933.

President elect shall become President. If a President shall not have been chosen before the time fixed for the beginning of his term, or if the President elect shall have failed to qualify, then the Vice-President elect shall act as President until a President shall have qualified; and the Congress may by law provide for the case wherein neither a President elect nor a Vice-President elect shall have qualified, declaring who shall then act as President, or the manner in which one who is to act shall be selected, and such person shall act accordingly until a President or Vice-President shall have qualified.

SECTION 4. The Congress may by law provide for the case of the death of any of the persons from whom the House of Representatives may choose a President whenever the right of choice shall have devolved upon them, and for the case of the death of any of the persons from whom the Senate may choose a Vice-President whenever the right of choice shall have devolved upon them.

SECTION 5. Sections 1 and 2 shall take effect on the 15th day of October following the ratification of this article.

SECTION 6. This article shall be inoperative unless it shall have been ratified as an amendment to the Constitution by the legislatures of three-fourths of the several States within seven years from the date of its submission.

Amendment XXI[19]

SECTION 1. The eighteenth article of amendment to the Constitution of the United States is hereby repealed.

SECTION 2. The transportation or importation into any State, Territory, or possession of the United States for delivery or use therein of intoxicating liquors, in violation of the laws thereof, is hereby prohibited.

SECTION 3. This article shall be inoperative unless it shall have been ratified as an amendment to the Constitution by conventions in the several States, as provided in the Constitution, within seven years from the date of the submission hereof to the States by the Congress.

Amendment XXII[20]

No person shall be elected to the office of the President more than twice, and no person who has held the office of President, or acted as President, for more than two years of a term to which some other person was elected President shall be elected to the office of the President more than once.

But this Article shall not apply to any person holding the office of President when this Article was proposed by the Congress, and shall not prevent any person who may be holding the office of President, or acting as President, during the term within which this Article becomes operative from holding the office of President or acting as President during the remainder of such term.

Amendment XXIII[21]

SECTION 1. The District constituting the seat of Government of the United States shall appoint in such manner as the Congress may direct:

A number of electors of President and Vice President equal to the whole number of Senators and Representatives in Congress to which the District would be entitled if it were a State, but in no event more than the least populous State; they shall be in addition to those appointed by the States, but they shall be considered, for the purposes of the election of President and Vice President, to be electors appointed by the State; and they shall meet in the District and perform such duties as provided by the twelfth article of amendment.

SECTION 2. The Congress shall have power to enforce this article by appropriate legislation.

Amendment XXIV[22]

SECTION 1. The right of citizens of the United States to vote in any primary or other election for President or Vice President, or for Senator or Representative in Congress, shall not be denied or abridged by the United States or any State by reason of failure to pay any poll tax or other tax.

SECTION 2. The Congress shall have power to enforce this article by appropriate legislation.

Amendment XXV[23]

SECTION 1. In case of the removal of the President from office or of his death or resignation, the Vice President shall become President.

SECTION 2. Whenever there is a vacancy in the office of the Vice President, the President shall nominate a Vice President who shall take office upon confirmation by a majority vote of both Houses of Congress.

SECTION 3. Whenever the President transmits to the President pro tempore of the Senate and the Speaker of the House of Representatives his written declaration that he is unable to discharge the powers and duties of his office, and until he transmits them a written declaration to the contrary, such powers and duties shall be discharged by the Vice President as Acting President.

SECTION 4. Whenever the Vice President and a majority of either the principal officers of the executive department or of such other body as Congress may by law provide, transmit to the President pro tempore of the Senate and the Speaker of the House of Representatives their written declaration that the President is unable to discharge the powers and duties of his office, the Vice President shall immediately assume the powers and duties of the office of Acting President.

---

[19]Passed February 20, 1933. Ratified December 5, 1933.

[20]Passed March 12, 1947. Ratified March 1, 1951.

[21]Passed June 16, 1960. Ratified April 3, 1961.

[22]Passed August 27, 1962. Ratified January 23, 1964.

[23]Passed July 6, 1965. Ratified February 11, 1967.

Thereafter, when the President transmits to the President pro tempore of the Senate and the Speaker of the House of Representatives his written declaration that no inability exists, he shall resume the powers and duties of his office unless the Vice President and a majority of either the principal officers of the executive department or of such other body as Congress may by law provide, transmit within four days to the President pro tempore of the Senate and the Speaker of the House of Representatives their written declaration that the President is unable to discharge the powers and duties of his office. Thereupon Congress shall decide the issue, assembling within forty-eight hours for that purpose if not in session. If the Congress, within twenty-one days after receipt of the latter written declaration, or, if Congress is not in session, within twenty-one days after Congress is required to assemble, determines by two-thirds vote of both Houses that the President is unable to discharge the powers and duties of his office, the Vice President shall continue to discharge the same as Acting President; otherwise, the President shall resume the powers and duties of his office.

Amendment XXVI[24]

SECTION 1. The right of citizens of the United States, who are eighteen years of age or older, to vote shall not be denied or abridged by the United States or by any State on account of age.
SECTION 2. The Congress shall have power to enforce this article by appropriate legislation.

Amendment XXVII[25]

No law, varying the compensation for the service of the Senators and Representatives, shall take effect, until an election of Representatives shall have intervened.

---

[24]Passed March 23, 1971. Ratified July 5, 1971.

[25]Passed September 25, 1989. Ratified May 7, 1992.

Admission of States

Order of admission	State	Date of admission	Order of admission	State	Date of admission
1	Delaware	December 7, 1787	26	Michigan	January 26, 1837
2	Pennsylvania	December 12, 1787	27	Florida	March 3, 1845
3	New Jersey	December 18, 1787	28	Texas	December 29, 1845
4	Georgia	January 2, 1788	29	Iowa	December 28, 1846
5	Connecticut	January 9, 1788	30	Wisconsin	May 29, 1848
6	Massachusetts	February 6, 1788	31	California	September 9, 1850
7	Maryland	April 28, 1788	32	Minnesota	May 11, 1858
8	South Carolina	May 23, 1788	33	Oregon	February 14, 1859
9	New Hampshire	June 21, 1788	34	Kansas	January 29, 1861
10	Virginia	June 25, 1788	35	West Virginia	June 20, 1863
11	New York	July 26, 1788	36	Nevada	October 31, 1864
12	North Carolina	November 21, 1789	37	Nebraska	March 1, 1867
13	Rhode Island	May 29, 1790	38	Colorado	August 1, 1876
14	Vermont	March 4, 1791	39	North Dakota	November 2, 1889
15	Kentucky	June 1, 1792	40	South Dakota	November 2, 1889
16	Tennessee	June 1, 1796	41	Montana	November 8, 1889
17	Ohio	March 1, 1803	42	Washington	November 11, 1889
18	Louisiana	April 30, 1812	43	Idaho	July 3, 1890
19	Indiana	December 11, 1816	44	Wyoming	July 10, 1890
20	Mississippi	December 10, 1817	45	Utah	January 4, 1896
21	Illinois	December 3, 1818	46	Oklahoma	November 16, 1907
22	Alabama	December 14, 1819	47	New Mexico	January 6, 1912
23	Maine	March 15, 1820	48	Arizona	February 14, 1912
24	Missouri	August 10, 1821	49	Alaska	January 3, 1959
25	Arkansas	June 15, 1836	50	Hawaii	August 21, 1959

Population of the United States
(1790–1999)

Year	Total population (in thousands)	Number per square mile of land area (continental United States)	Year	Total population (in thousands)	Number per square mile of land area (continental United States)
1790	3,929	4.5	1829	12,565	
1791	4,056		1830	12,901	7.4
1792	4,194		1831	13,321	
1793	4,332		1832	13,742	
1794	4,469		1833	14,162	
1795	4,607		1834	14,582	
1796	4,745		1835	15,003	
1797	4,883		1836	15,423	
1798	5,021		1837	15,843	
1799	5,159		1838	16,264	
1800	5,297	6.1	1839	16,684	
1801	5,486		1840	17,120	9.8
1802	5,679		1841	17,733	
1803	5,872		1842	18,345	
1804	5,065		1843	18,957	
1805	6,258		1844	19,569	
1806	6,451		1845	20,182	
1807	6,644		1846	20,794	
1808	6,838		1847	21,406	
1809	7,031		1848	22,018	
1810	7,224	4.3	1849	22,631	
1811	7,460		1850	23,261	7.9
1812	7,700		1851	24,086	
1813	7,939		1852	24,911	
1814	8,179		1853	25,736	
1815	8,419		1854	26,561	
1816	8,659		1855	27,386	
1817	8,899		1856	28,212	
1818	9,139		1857	29,037	
1819	9,379		1858	29,862	
1820	9,618	5.6	1859	30,687	
1821	9,939		1860	31,513	10.6
1822	10,268		1861	32,351	
1823	10,596		1862	33,188	
1824	10,924		1863	34,026	
1825	11,252		1864	34,863	
1826	11,580		1865	35,701	
1827	11,909		1866	36,538	
1828	12,237		1867	37,376	

Figures are from *Historical Statistics of the United States, Colonial Times to 1957* (1961), pp. 7, 8; *Statistical Abstract of the United States:* 1974, p. 5, Census Bureau for 1974 and 1975; and *Statistical Abstract of the United States:* 1988, p. 7.

(continued)

Population of the United States *(continued)*
(1790–1999)

Year	Total population (in thousands)	Number per square mile of land area (continental United States)	Year	Total population (in thousands)[1]	Number per square mile of land area (continental United States)
1868	38,213		1907	87,000	
1869	39,051		1908	88,709	
1870	39,905	13.4	1909	90,492	
1871	40,938		1910	92,407	31.0
1872	41,972		1911	93,868	
1873	43,006		1912	95,331	
1874	44,040		1913	97,227	
1875	45,073		1914	99,118	
1876	46,107		1915	100,549	
1877	47,141		1916	101,966	
1878	48,174		1917	103,414	
1879	49,208		1918	104,550	
1880	50,262	16.9	1919	105,063	
1881	51,542		1920	106,466	35.6
1882	52,821		1921	108,541	
1883	54,100		1922	110,055	
1884	55,379		1923	111,950	
1885	56,658		1924	114,113	
1886	57,938		1925	115,832	
1887	59,217		1926	117,399	
1888	60,496		1927	119,038	
1889	61,775		1928	120,501	
1890	63,056	21.2	1929	121,700	
1891	64,361		1930	122,775	41.2
1892	65,666		1931	124,040	
1893	66,970		1932	124,840	
1894	68,275		1933	125,579	
1895	69,580		1934	126,374	
1896	70,885		1935	127,250	
1897	72,189		1936	128,053	
1898	73,494		1937	128,825	
1899	74,799		1938	129,825	
1900	76,094	25.6	1939	130,880	
1901	77,585		1940	131,669	44.2
1902	79,160		1941	133,894	
1903	80,632		1942	135,361	
1904	82,165		1943	137,250	
1905	83,820		1944	138,916	
1906	85,437		1945	140,468	

[1]Figures after 1940 represent total population including armed forces abroad, except in official census years.

(continued)

Population of the United States (continued)
(1790–1999)

Year	Total population (in thousands)	Number per square mile of land area (continental United States)	Year	Total population (in thousands)[1]	Number per square mile of land area (continental United States)
1946	141,936		1973	211,909	
1947	144,698		1974	213,854	
1948	147,208		1975	215,973	
1949	149,767		1976	218,035	
1950	150,697	50.7	1977	220,239	
1951	154,878		1978	222,585	
1952	157,553		1979	225,055	
1953	160,184		1980	227,225	64.0
1954	163,026		1981	229,466	
1955	165,931		1982	232,520	
1956	168,903		1983	234,799	
1957	171,984		1984	237,001	
1958	174,882		1985	239,283	
1959	177,830[2]		1986	241,596	
1960	180,671	60.1	1987	234,773	
1961	186,538		1988	245,051	
1962	189,242		1989	247,350	
1963	189,197		1990	250,122	
1964	191,889		1991	254,521	
1965	194,303		1992	245,908	
1966	196,560		1993	257,908	
1967	198,712		1994	261,875	
1968	200,706		1995	263,434	
1969	202,677		1996	266,096	
1970	205,052	57.52	1997	267,744	
1971	207,661		1998	270,299	
1972	209,896		1999	274,114	

[1]Figures after 1940 represent total population including armed forces abroad, except in official census years.

[2]Figures after 1959 include Alaska and Hawaii.

Presidential Elections
(1789–1832)

Year	Number of states	Candidates[1]	Parties	Popular vote	Electoral vote	Percentage of popular vote[2]
1789	**11**	**George Washington***	**No party designations**		**69**	
		John Adams			34	
		Minor Candidates			35	
1792	**15**	**George Washington**	**No party designations**		**132**	
		John Adams			77	
		George Clinton			50	
		Minor Candidates			5	
1796	**16**	**John Adams**	**Federalist**		**71**	
		Thomas Jefferson	Democratic-Republican		68	
		Thomas Pinckney	Federalist		59	
		Aaron Burr	Democratic-Republican		30	
		Minor Candidates			48	
1800	**16**	**Thomas Jefferson**	**Democratic-Republican**		**73**	
		Aaron Burr	Democratic-Republican		73	
		John Adams	Federalist		65	
		Charles C. Pinckney	Federalist		64	
		John Jay	Federalist		1	
1804	**17**	**Thomas Jefferson**	**Democratic-Republican**		**162**	
		Charles C. Pinckney	Federalist		14	
1808	**17**	**James Madison**	**Democratic-Republican**		**122**	
		Charles C. Pinckney	Federalist		47	
		George Clinton	Democratic-Republican		6	
1812	**18**	**James Madison**	**Democratic-Republican**		**128**	
		DeWitt Clinton	Federalist		89	
1816	**19**	**James Monroe**	**Democratic-Republican**		**183**	
		Rufus King	Federalist		34	
1820	**24**	**James Monroe**	**Democratic-Republican**		**231**	
		John Quincy Adams	Independent Republican		1	
1824	**24**	**John Quincy Adams**	**Democratic-Republican**	**108,740**	**84**	**30.5**
		Andrew Jackson	Democratic-Republican	153,544	99	43.1
		William H. Crawford	Democratic-Republican	46,618	41	13.1
		Henry Clay	Democratic-Republican	47,136	37	13.2
1828	**24**	**Andrew Jackson**	**Democratic**	**647,286**	**178**	**56.0**
		John Quincy Adams	National Republican	508,064	83	44.0
1832	**24**	**Andrew Jackson**	**Democratic**	**687,502**	**219**	**55.0**
		Henry Clay	National Republican	530,189	49	42.4
		William Wirt	Anti-Masonic		7	
		John Floyd	National Republican	33,108	11	2.6

[1]Before the passage of the Twelfth Amendment in 1804, the Electoral College voted for two presidential candidates; the runner-up became vice president. Figures are from *Historical Statistics of the United States, Colonial Times to 1957* (1961), pp. 682–83; and the U.S. Department of Justice.

[2]Candidates receiving less than 1 percent of the popular vote have been omitted. For that reason the percentage of popular vote given for any election year may not total 100 percent.

*Note: Boldface indicates the winner of each election.

Presidential Elections
(1836–1888)

Year	Number of states	Candidates	Parties	Popular vote	Electoral vote	Percentage of popular vote[1]
1836	**26**	**Martin Van Buren**	**Democratic**	**765,483**	**170**	**50.9**
		William H. Harrison	Whig		73	
		Hugh L. White	Whig		26	
		Daniel Webster	Whig	739,795	14	
		W. P. Mangum	Independent		11	
1840	**26**	**William H. Harrison**	**Whig**	**1,274,624**	**234**	**53.1**
		Martin Van Buren	Democratic	1,127,781	60	46.9
1844	**26**	**James K. Polk**	**Democratic**	**1,338,464**	**170**	**49.6**
		Henry Clay	Whig	1,300,097	105	48.1
		James G. Birney	Liberty	62,300		2.3
1848	**30**	**Zachary Taylor**	**Whig**	**1,360,967**	**163**	**47.4**
		Lewis Cass	Democratic	1,222,342	127	42.5
		Martin Van Buren	Free Soil	291,263		10.1
1852	**31**	**Franklin Pierce**	**Democratic**	**1,601,117**	**254**	**50.9**
		Winfield Scott	Whig	1,385,453	42	44.1
		John P. Hale	Free Soil	155,825		5.0
1856	**31**	**James Buchanan**	**Democratic**	**1,832,955**	**174**	**45.3**
		John C. Frémont	Republican	1,339,932	114	33.1
		Millard Fillmore	American	871,731	8	21.6
1860	**33**	**Abraham Lincoln**	**Republican**	**1,865,593**	**180**	**39.8**
		Stephen A. Douglas	Democratic	1,382,713	12	29.5
		John C. Breckinridge	Democratic	848,356	72	18.1
		John Bell	Constitutional Union	592,906	39	12.6
1864	**36**	**Abraham Lincoln**	**Republican**	**2,206,938**	**212**	**55.0**
		George B. McClellan	Democratic	1,803,787	21	45.0
1868	**37**	**Ulysses S. Grant**	**Republican**	**3,013,421**	**214**	**52.7**
		Horatio Seymour	Democratic	2,706,829	80	47.3
1872	**37**	**Ulysses S. Grant**	**Republican**	**3,596,745**	**286**	**55.6**
		Horace Greeley	Democratic	2,843,446	[2]	43.9
1876	**38**	**Rutherford B. Hayes**	**Republican**	**4,036,572**	**185**	**48.0**
		Samuel J. Tilden	Democratic	4,284,020	184	51.0
1880	**38**	**James A. Garfield**	**Republican**	**4,453,295**	**214**	**48.5**
		Winfield S. Hancock	Democratic	4,414,082	155	48.1
		James B. Weaver	Greenback-Labor	308,578		3.4
1884	**38**	**Grover Cleveland**	**Democratic**	**4,879,507**	**219**	**48.5**
		James G. Blaine	Republican	4,850,293	182	48.2
		Benjamin F. Butler	Greenback-Labor	175,370		1.8
		John P. St. John	Prohibition	150,369		1.5
1888	**38**	**Benjamin Harrison**	**Republican**	**5,477,129**	**233**	**47.9**
		Grover Cleveland	Democratic	5,537,857	168	48.6
		Clinton B. Fisk	Prohibition	249,506		2.2
		Anson J. Streeter	Union Labor	146,935		1.3

[1]Candidates receiving less than 1 percent of the popular vote have been omitted. For that reason the percentage of popular vote given for any election year may not total 100 percent.

[2]Greeley died shortly after the election; the electors supporting him then divided their votes among minor candidates.

Presidential Elections
(1892–1932)

Year	Number of states	Candidates	Parties	Popular vote	Electoral vote	Percentage of popular vote[1]
1892	**44**	**Grover Cleveland**	**Democratic**	**5,555,426**	**277**	**46.1**
		Benjamin Harrison	Republican	5,182,690	145	43.0
		James B. Weaver	People's	1,029,846	22	8.5
		John Bidwell	Prohibition	264,133		2.2
1896	**45**	**William McKinley**	**Republican**	**7,102,246**	**271**	**51.1**
		William J. Bryan	Democratic	6,492,559	176	47.7
1900	**45**	**William McKinley**	**Republican**	**7,218,491**	**292**	**51.7**
		William J. Bryan	Democratic; Populist	6,356,734	155	45.5
		John C. Wooley	Prohibition	208,914		1.5
1904	**45**	**Theodore Roosevelt**	**Republican**	**7,628,461**	**336**	**57.4**
		Alton B. Parker	Democratic	5,084,223	140	37.6
		Eugene V. Debs	Socialist	402,283		3.0
		Silas C. Swallow	Prohibition	258,536		1.9
1908	**46**	**William H. Taft**	**Republican**	**7,675,320**	**321**	**51.6**
		William J. Bryan	Democratic	6,412,294	162	43.1
		Eugene V. Debs	Socialist	420,793		2.8
		Eugene W. Chafin	Prohibition	253,840		1.7
1912	**48**	**Woodrow Wilson**	**Democratic**	**6,296,547**	**435**	**41.9**
		Theodore Roosevelt	Progressive	4,118,571	88	27.4
		William H. Taft	Republican	3,486,720	8	23.2
		Eugene V. Debs	Socialist	900,672		6.0
		Eugene W. Chafin	Prohibition	206,275		1.4
1916	**48**	**Woodrow Wilson**	**Democratic**	**9,127,695**	**277**	**49.4**
		Charles E. Hughes	Republican	8,533,507	254	46.2
		A. L. Benson	Socialist	585,113		3.2
		J. Frank Hanly	Prohibition	220,506		1.2
1920	**48**	**Warren G. Harding**	**Republican**	**16,143,407**	**404**	**60.4**
		James N. Cox	Democratic	9,130,328	127	34.2
		Eugene V. Debs	Socialist	919,799		3.4
		P. P. Christensen	Farmer-Labor	265,411		1.0
1924	**48**	**Calvin Coolidge**	**Republican**	**15,718,211**	**382**	**54.0**
		John W. Davis	Democratic	8,385,283	136	28.8
		Robert M. La Follette	Progressive	4,831,289	13	16.6
1928	**48**	**Herbert C. Hoover**	**Republican**	**21,391,993**	**444**	**58.2**
		Alfred E. Smith	Democratic	15,016,169	87	40.9
1932	**48**	**Franklin D. Roosevelt**	**Democratic**	**22,809,638**	**472**	**57.4**
		Herbert C. Hoover	Republican	15,758,901	59	39.7
		Norman Thomas	Socialist	881,951		2.2

[1]Candidates receiving less than 1 percent of the popular vote have been omitted. For that reason the percentage of popular vote given for any election year may not total 100 percent.

Presidential Elections
(1936–2000)

Year	Number of states	Candidates	Parties	Popular vote	Electoral vote	Percentage of popular vote[1]
1936	**48**	**Franklin D. Roosevelt**	**Democratic**	**27,752,869**	**523**	**60.8**
		Alfred M. Landon	Republican	16,674,665	8	36.5
		William Lemke	Union	882,479		1.9
1940	**48**	**Franklin D. Roosevelt**	**Democratic**	**27,307,819**	**449**	**54.8**
		Wendell L. Willkie	Republican	22,321,018	82	44.8
1944	**48**	**Franklin D. Roosevelt**	**Democratic**	**25,606,585**	**432**	**53.5**
		Thomas E. Dewey	Republican	22,014,745	99	46.0
1948	**48**	**Harry S Truman**	**Democratic**	**24,105,812**	**303**	**49.5**
		Thomas E. Dewey	Republican	21,970,065	189	45.1
		J. Strom Thurmond	States' Rights	1,169,063	39	2.4
		Henry A. Wallace	Progressive	1,157,172		2.4
1952	**48**	**Dwight D. Eisenhower**	**Republican**	**33,936,234**	**442**	**55.1**
		Adlai E. Stevenson	Democratic	27,314,992	89	44.4
1956	**48**	**Dwight D. Eisenhower**	**Republican**	**35,590,472**	**457**	**57.6**
		Adlai E. Stevenson	Democratic	26,022,752	73	42.1
1960	**50**	**John F. Kennedy**	**Democratic**	**34,227,096**	**303**	**49.9**
		Richard M. Nixon	Republican	34,108,546	219	49.6
1964	**50**	**Lyndon B. Johnson**	**Democratic**	**43,126,506**	**486**	**61.1**
		Barry M. Goldwater	Republican	27,176,799	52	38.5
1968	**50**	**Richard M. Nixon**	**Republican**	**31,785,480**	**301**	**43.4**
		Hubert H. Humphrey	Democratic	31,275,165	191	42.7
		George C. Wallace	American Independent	9,906,473	46	13.5
1972	**50**	**Richard M. Nixon**	**Republican**	**47,169,911**	**520**	**60.7**
		George S. McGovern	Democratic	29,170,383	17	37.5
1976	**50**	**Jimmy Carter**	**Democratic**	**40,827,394**	**297**	**50.0**
		Gerald R. Ford	Republican	39,145,977	240	47.9
1980	**50**	**Ronald W. Reagan**	**Republican**	**43,899,248**	**489**	**50.8**
		Jimmy Carter	Democratic	35,481,435	49	41.0
		John B. Anderson	Independent	5,719,437		6.6
		Ed Clark	Libertarian	920,859		1.0
1984	**50**	**Ronald W. Reagan**	**Republican**	**54,281,858**	**525**	**59.2**
		Walter F. Mondale	Democratic	37,457,215	13	40.8
1988	**50**	**George H. Bush**	**Republican**	**47,917,341**	**426**	**54**
		Michael Dukakis	Democratic	41,013,030	112	46
1992	**50**	**William Clinton**	**Democratic**	**44,908,254**	**370**	**43.0**
		George H. Bush	Republican	39,102,343	168	37.4
		Ross Perot	Independent	19,741,065		18.9
1996	**50**	**William Clinton**	**Democratic**	**47,402,357**	**379**	**49**
		Robert J. Dole	Republican	39,198,755	159	41
		H. Ross Perot	Reform	8,085,402		8
2000	**50**	**George W. Bush**	**Republican**	**50,456,062**	**271**	**47.9**
		Albert Gore	Democratic	50,996,582	266	48.4
		Ralph Nader	Green	2,858,843		2.7

[1]Candidates receiving less than 1 percent of the popular vote have been omitted. For that reason the percentage of popular vote given for any election year may not total 100 percent.

Presidents, Vice Presidents, and Major Cabinet Officers

President	Vice President	State	Treasury	War	Justice (Attorney General)
George Washington 1789–1797	John Adams 1789–1797	Thomas Jefferson 1789–1794	Alexander Hamilton 1789–1795	Henry Knox 1789–1795	Edmund Randolph 1789–1794
		Edmund Randolph 1794–1795 Timothy Pickering 1795–1797	Oliver Wolcott 1795–1797	Timothy Pickering 1795–1796 James McHenry 1796–1797	William Bradford 1794–1795 Charles Lee 1795–1797
John Adams 1797–1801	Thomas Jefferson 1797–1801	Timothy Pickering 1797–1800 John Marshall 1800–1801	Oliver Wolcott 1797–1801 Samuel Dexter 1801	James McHenry 1797–1800 Samuel Dexter 1800–1801	Charles Lee 1797–1801
Thomas Jefferson 1801–1809	Aaron Burr 1801–1805 George Clinton 1805–1809	James Madison 1801–1809	Samuel Dexter 1801 Albert Gallatin 1801–1809	Henry Dearborn 1801–1809	Levi Lincoln 1801–1805 John Breckinridge 1805–1807 Caesar Rodney 1807–1809
James Madison 1809–1817	George Clinton 1809–1813 Elbridge Gerry 1813–1817	Robert Smith 1809–1811 James Monroe 1811–1817	Albert Gallatin 1809–1814 George Campbell 1814 Alexander Dallas 1814–1816 William Crawford 1816–1817	William Eustis 1809–1813 John Armstrong 1813–1814 James Monroe 1814–1815 William Crawford 1815–1817	Caesar Rodney 1809–1811 William Pinkney 1811–1814 Richard Rush 1814–1817
James Monroe 1817–1825	Daniel D. Tompkins 1817–1825	John Quincy Adams 1817–1825	William Crawford 1817–1825	George Graham 1817 John C. Calhoun 1817–1825	Richard Rush 1817 William Wirt 1817–1825
John Quincy Adams	John C. Calhoun 1825–1829	Henry Clay 1825–1829	Richard Rush 1825–1829	James Barbour 1825–1829 Peter B. Porter 1828–1829	William Wirt 1825–1829

(continued)

Presidents, Vice Presidents, and
Major Cabinet Officers *(continued)*

President	Vice President	State	Treasury	War	Justice (Attorney General)
Andrew Jackson 1829–1837	John C. Calhoun 1829–1833 Martin Van Buren 1833–1837	Martin Van Buren 1829–1831 Edward Livingston 1831–1833 Louis McLane 1833–1834 John Forsyth 1834–1837	Samuel Ingham 1829–1831 Louis McLane 1831–1833 William Duane 1833 Roger B. Taney 1833–1834 Levi Woodbury 1834–1837	John H. Eaton 1829–1831 Lewis Cass 1831–1837 Benjamin Butler 1837	John M. Berrien 1829–1831 Roger B. Taney 1831–1833 Benjamin Butler 1833–1837
Martin Van Buren 1837–1841	Richard M. Johnson 1837–1841	John Forsyth 1837–1841	Levi Woodbury 1837–1841	Joel R. Poinsett 1837–1841	Benjamin Butler 1837–1838 Felix Grundy 1838–1840 Henry D. Gilpin 1840–1841
William H. Harrison 1841	John Tyler 1841	Daniel Webster 1841	Thomas Ewing 1841	John Bell 1841	John J. Crittenden 1841
John Tyler 1841–1845		Daniel Webster 1841–1843 Hugh S. Legaré 1843 Abel P. Upshur 1843–1844 John C. Calhoun 1844–1845	Thomas Ewing 1841 Walter Forward 1841–1843 John C. Spencer 1843–1844 George M. Bibb 1844–1845	John Bell 1841 John C. Spencer 1841–1843 James M. Porter 1843–1844 William Wilkins 1844–1845	John J. Crittenden 1841 Hugh S. Legaré 1841–1843 John Nelson 1843–1845
James K. Polk 1845–1849	George M. Dallas 1845–1849	James Buchanan 1845–1849	Robert J. Walker 1845–1849	William L. Marcy 1845–1849	John Y. Mason 1845–1846 Nathan Clifford 1846–1848 Isaac Toucey 1848–1849
Zachary Taylor 1849–1850	Millard Fillmore 1849–1850	John M. Clayton 1849–1850	William M. Meredith 1849–1850	George W. Crawford 1849–1850	Reverdy Johnson 1849–1850
Millard Fillmore 1850–1853		Daniel Webster 1850–1852 Edward Everett 1852–1853	Thomas Corwin 1850–1853	Charles M. Conrad 1850–1853	John J. Crittenden 1850–1853
Franklin Pierce 1853–1857	William R. King 1853–1857	William L. Marcy 1853–1857	James Guthrie 1853–1857	Jefferson Davis 1853–1857	Caleb Cushing 1853–1857

(continued)

Presidents, Vice Presidents, and Major Cabinet Officers *(continued)*

President	Vice President	State	Treasury	War	Justice (Attorney General)
James Buchanan 1857–1861	John C. Breckinridge 1857–1861	Lewis Cass 1857–1860 Jeremiah S. Black 1860–1861	Howell Cobb 1857–1860 Philip F. Thomas 1860–1861 John A. Dix 1861	John B. Floyd 1857–1861 Joseph Holt 1861	Jeremiah S. Black 1857–1860 Edwin M. Stanton 1860–1861
Abraham Lincoln 1861–1865	Hannibal Hamlin 1861–1865 Andrew Johnson 1865	William H. Seward 1861–1865	Salmon P. Chase 1861–1864 William P. Fessenden 1864–1865 Hugh McCulloch 1865	Simon Cameron 1861–1862 Edwin M. Stanton 1862–1865	Edward Bates 1861–1864 James Speed 1864–1865
Andrew Johnson 1865–1869		William H. Seward 1865–1869	Hugh McCulloch 1865–1869	Edwin M. Stanton 1865–1867 Ulysses S. Grant 1867–1868 John M. Schofield 1868–1869	James Speed 1865–1866 1865 Henry Stanbery 1866–1868 O. H. Browning 1866–1869
Ulysses S. Grant 1869–1877	Schuyler Colfax 1869–1873 Henry Wilson 1873–1877	Elihu B. Washburne 1869 Hamilton Fish 1869–1877	George S. Boutwell 1869–1873 William A. Richardson 1873–1874 Benjamin H. Bristow 1874–1876 Lot M. Morrill 1876–1877	John A. Rawlins 1869 William T. Sherman 1869 William W. Belknap 1869–1876 Alphonso Taft 1876 James D. Cameron 1876–1877	Ebenezer R. Hoar 1869–1870 Amos T. Akerman 1870–1871 G. H. Williams 1871–1875 Edwards Pierrepont 1875–1876 Alphonso Taft 1876–1877
Rutherford B. Hayes 1877–1881	William A. Wheeler 1877–1881	William M. Evarts 1877–1881	John Sherman 1877–1881	George W. McCrary 1877–1879 Alexander Ramsey 1879–1881	Charles Devens 1877–1881
James A. Garfield 1881	Chester A. Arthur 1881	James G. Blaine 1881	William Windom 1881	Robert T. Lincoln 1881	Wayne MacVeagh 1881
Chester A. Arthur 1881–1885		F. T. Frelinghuysen 1881–1885	Charles J. Folger 1881–1884 Walter Q. Gresham 1884 Hugh McCulloch 1884–1885	Robert T. Lincoln 1881–1885	B. H. Brewster 1881–1885

(continued)

Presidents, Vice Presidents, and Major Cabinet Officers (continued)

President	Vice President	State	Treasury	War	Justice (Attorney General)
Grover Cleveland 1885–1889	T. A. Hendricks 1885	Thomas F. Bayard 1885–1889	Daniel Manning 1885–1887 Charles S. Fairchild 1887–1889	William C. Endicott 1885–1889	A. H. Garland 1885–1889
Benjamin Harrison 1889–1893	Levi P. Morton 1889–1893	James G. Blaine 1889–1892 John W. Foster 1892–1893	William Windom 1889–1891 Charles Foster 1892–1893	Redfield Procter 1889–1891 Stephen B. Elkins 1891–1893	W. H. H. Miller 1889–1893
Grover Cleveland 1893–1897	Adlai E. Stevenson 1893–1897	Walter Q. Gresham 1893–1895 Richard Olney 1895–1897	John G. Carlisle 1893–1897	Daniel S. Lamont 1893–1897	Richard Olney 1893–1897 Judson Harmon 1895–1897
William McKinley 1897–1901	Garret A. Hobart 1897–1899 Theodore Roosevelt 1901	John Sherman 1897–1898 William R. Day 1898 John Hay 1898–1901	Lyman J. Gage 1897–1901	Russell A. Alger 1897–1899 Elihu Root 1899–1901	Joseph McKenna 1897–1898 John W. Griggs 1898–1901 Philander C. Knox 1901
Theodore Roosevelt 1901–1909	Charles Fairbanks 1905–1909	John Hay 1901–1905 Elihu Root 1905–1909 Robert Bacon 1909	Lyman J. Gage 1901–1902 Leslie M. Shaw 1902–1907 George B. Cortelyou 1907–1909	Elihu Root 1901–1904 William H. Taft 1904–1908 Luke E. Wright 1908–1909	Philander C. Knox 1901–1904 William H. Moody Charles J. Bonaparte 1906–1909
William H. Taft 1909–1913	James S. Sherman 1909–1913	Philander C. Knox 1909–1913	Franklin MacVeagh 1909–1913	Jacob M. Dickinson 1909–1911 Henry L. Stimson 1911–1913	G. W. Wickersham 1909–1913
Woodrow Wilson 1913–1921	Thomas R. Marshall 1913–1921	William J. Bryan 1913–1915 Robert Lansing 1915–1920 Bainbridge Colby 1920–1921	William G. McAdoo 1913–1918 Carter Glass 1918–1920 David F. Houston 1920–1921	Lindley M. Garrison 1913–1916 Newton D. Baker 1916–1921	J. C. McReynolds 1913–1914 T. W. Gregory A. Mitchell Palmer 1919–1921

(continued)

Presidents, Vice Presidents, and Major Cabinet Officers *(continued)*

President	Vice President	State	Treasury	War	Justice (Attorney General)
Warren G. Harding 1921–1923	Calvin Coolidge 1921–1923	Charles E. Hughes 1921–1923	Andrew W. Mellon 1921–1923	John W. Weeks 1921–1923	H. M. Daugherty 1921–1923
Calvin Coolidge 1923–1929	Charles G. Dawes 1925–1929	Charles E. Hughes 1923–1925 Frank B. Kellogg 1925–1929	Andrew W. Mellon 1923–1929	John W. Weeks 1923–1925 Dwight F. Davis 1925–1929	H. M. Daugherty 1923–1924 Harlan F. Stone 1924–1925 John G. Sargent 1925–1929
Herbert C. Hoover 1929–1933	Charles Curtis 1929–1933	Henry L. Stimson 1929–1933	Andrew W. Mellon 1929–1932 Ogden L. Mills 1932–1933	James W. Good 1929 Patrick J. Hurley 1929–1933	J. D. Mitchell 1929–1933
Franklin Delano Roosevelt 1933–1945	John Nance Garner 1933–1941 Henry A. Wallace 1941–1945 Harry S Truman 1945	Cordell Hull 1933–1944 E. R. Stettinius, Jr. 1944–1945	William H. Woodin 1933–1934 Henry Morgenthau, Jr. 1934–1945	George H. Dern 1933–1936 Harry H. Woodring 1936–1940 Henry L. Stimson 1940–1945	H. S. Cummings 1933–1939 Frank Murphy 1939–1940 Robert Jackson 1940–1941 Francis Biddel 1944–1945
Harry S Truman 1945–1953	Alben W. Barkley 1949–1953	James F. Byrnes 1945–1947 George C. Marshall 1947–1949 Dean G. Acheson 1949–1953	Fred M. Vinson 1945–1946 John W. Snyder 1946–1953	Robert P. Patterson 1945–1947 Kenneth C. Royall 1947 <u>Secretary of Defense</u> James V. Forrestal 1947–1949 Louis A. Johnson 1949–1950 George C. Marshall 1950–1951 Robert A. Lovett 1951–1953	Tom C. Clark 1945–1949 J. H. McGrath 1949–1952 James P. McGranery 1952–1953
Dwight D. Eisenhower 1953–1961	Richard M. Nixon 1953–1961	John Foster Dulles 1953–1959 Christian A. Herter 1957–1961	George M. Humphrey 1953–1957 Robert B. Anderson 1957–1961	Charles E. Wilson 1953–1957 Neil H. McElroy 1957–1961 Thomas S. Gates 1959–1961	H. Brownell, Jr. 1953–1957 William P. Rogers 1957–1961

(continued)

Presidents, Vice Presidents, and
Major Cabinet Officers *(continued)*

President	Vice President	State	Treasury	Defense	Justice (Attorney General)
John F. Kennedy 1961–1963	Lyndon B. Johnson 1961–1963	Dean Rusk 1961–1963	C. Douglas Dillon 1961–1963	Robert S. McNamara 1961–1963	Robert F. Kennedy 1961–1963
Lyndon B. Johnson 1963–1969	Hubert H. Humphrey 1965–1969	Dean Rusk 1963–1969	C. Douglas Dillon 1963–1965 Henry H. Fowler 1965–1968 Joseph W. Barr 1968–1969	Robert S. McNamara 1963–1968 Clark M. Clifford 1968–1969	Robert F. Kennedy 1963–1965 N. deB. Katzenbach 1965–1967 Ramsey Clark 1967–1969
Richard M. Nixon 1969–1974	Spiro T. Agnew 1969–1973 Gerald R. Ford 1973–1974	William P. Rogers 1969–1973 Henry A. Kissinger 1973–1974	David M. Kennedy 1969–1970 John B. Connally 1970–1972 George P. Schultz 1972–1974 William E. Simon 1974	Melvin R. Laird 1969–1973 Elliot L. Richardson 1973 James R. Schlesinger 1973–1974	John M. Mitchell 1969–1972 Richard G. Kleindienst 1972–1973 Elliot L. Richardson 1973 William B. Saxbe 1974
Gerald R. Ford 1974–1977	Nelson A. Rockefeller 1974–1977	Henry A. Kissinger 1974–1977	William E. Simon 1974–1977	James R. Schlesinger 1974–1975 Donald H. Rumsfeld 1975–1977	William B. Saxbe 1974–1975 Edward H. Levi 1975–1977

(continued)

Presidents, Vice Presidents, and Major Cabinet Officers *(continued)*

President	Vice President	State	Treasury	Defense	Justice (Attorney General)
Jimmy Carter 1977–1981	Walter F. Mondale 1977–1981	Cyrus R. Vance 1977–1980 Edmund S. Muskie 1980–1981	W. Michael Blumenthal 1977–1979 G. William Miller 1979–1981	Harold Brown 1977–1981	Griffin Bell 1977–1979 Benjamin R. Civiletti 1979–1981
Ronald W. Reagan 1981–1989	George H. Bush 1981–1989	Alexander M. Haig, Jr. 1981–1982 George P. Shultz 1982–1989	Donald T. Regan 1981–1985 James A. Baker 1985–1988 Nicholas F. Brady 1988–1989	Caspar W. Weinberger 1981–1987 Frank C. Carlucci 1987–1989	William French Smith 1981–1985 Edwin Meese 1985–1988 Richard Thornburgh 1988–1989
George H. Bush 1989–1992	J. Danforth Quayle 1989–1992	James A. Baker 1989–1992 Lawrence S. Eagleburger 1992	Nicholas F. Brady 1989–1992	Richard Cheney 1989–1992	Richard Thornburgh 1989–1990 William Barr 1990–1992
William Clinton 1993–2001	Albert Gore 1993–2001	Warren M. Christopher 1993–1996 Madeleine K. Albright 1997–2001	Lloyd Bentsen 1993–1994 Robert E. Rubin 1994–1999 Lawrence H. Summers 1999–2001	Les Aspin 1993–1994 William J. Perry 1994–1997 William S. Cohen 1997–2001	Janet Reno 1993–2001
George W. Bush 2001–	Richard Cheney 2001–	Colin L. Powell 2001–	Paul H. O'Neill 2001–2003 John W. Snow 2003–	Donald H. Rumsfeld 2001–	John Ashcroft 2001–

Cabinet Level Departments

(The heads of cabinet level departments are known as the Secretary of the Department except for the head of the Justice Department, the Attorney General, and until 1971, the head of the Post Office, the Postmaster General.)

Department	Year Established	Modifications
State	1789	
Treasury	1789	
War	1789	In 1947, the War Department became a sub-cabinet level division of the Department of Defense.
Justice	1789	
Post Office	1789	In 1971, the Post Office became the United States Postal Service, an independent agency; the head of the USPS did not sit in the president's cabinet.
Navy	1798	In 1947, the Navy Department became a sub-cabinet level division of the Department of Defense.
Interior	1849	
Agriculture	1889	
Commerce and Labor	1903	In 1913, the Department was divided into two cabinet-level departments—Commerce and Labor.
Commerce	1913	
Labor	1913	
Defense	1947	
Health, Education, and Welfare	1953	In 1980, the Department was divided into two cabinet-level departments—Health and Human Services, and Education.
Housing and Urban Development	1966	
Transportation	1966	
Energy	1977	
Health and Human Services	1980	
Education	1980	
Veterans' Affairs	1989	
Homeland Security	2003	

Justices of the U.S. Supreme Court

Chief Justices appear in bold type

	Term of Service	Years of Service	Appointed by
John Jay	1789–1795	5	Washington
John Rutledge	1789–1791	1	Washington
William Cushing	1789–1810	20	Washington
James Wilson	1789–1798	8	Washington
John Blair	1789–1796	6	Washington
Robert H. Harrison	1789–1790	—	Washington
James Iredell	1790–1799	9	Washington
Thomas Johnson	1791–1793	1	Washington
William Paterson	1793–1806	13	Washington
John Rutledge[1]	1795	—	Washington
Samuel Chase	1796–1811	15	Washington
Oliver Ellsworth	1796–1800	4	Washington
Bushrod Washington	1798–1829	31	J. Adams
Alfred Moore	1799–1804	4	J. Adams
John Marshall	1801–1835	34	J. Adams
William Johnson	1804–1834	30	Jefferson
H. Brockholst Livingston	1806–1823	16	Jefferson
Thomas Todd	1807–1826	18	Jefferson
Joseph Story	1811–1845	33	Madison
Gabriel Duval	1811–1835	24	Madison
Smith Thompson	1823–1843	20	Monroe
Robert Trimble	1826–1828	2	J. Q. Adams
John McLean	1829–1861	32	Jackson
Henry Baldwin	1830–1844	14	Jackson
James M. Wayne	1835–1867	32	Jackson
Roger B. Taney	1836–1864	28	Jackson
Philip P. Barbour	1836–1841	4	Jackson
John Catron	1837–1865	28	Van Buren
John McKinley	1837–1852	15	Van Buren
Peter V. Daniel	1841–1860	19	Van Buren
Samuel Nelson	1845–1872	27	Tyler
Levi Woodbury	1845–1851	5	Polk
Robert C. Grier	1846–1870	23	Polk
Benjamin R. Curtis	1851–1857	6	Fillmore
John A. Campbell	1853–1861	8	Pierce
Nathan Clifford	1858–1881	23	Buchanan
Noah H. Swayne	1862–1881	18	Lincoln
Samuel F. Miller	1862–1890	28	Lincoln
David Davis	1862–1877	14	Lincoln
Stephen J. Field	1863–1897	34	Lincoln
Salmon P. Chase	1864–1873	8	Lincoln
William Strong	1870–1880	10	Grant
Joseph P. Bradley	1870–1892	22	Grant
Ward Hunt	1873–1882	9	Grant

[1] Acting Chief Justice; Senate refused to confirm appointment.

(continued)

Justices of the U.S. Supreme Court *(continued)*

Chief Justices appear in bold type

	Term of Service	Years of Service	Appointed by
Morrison R. Waite	1874–1888	14	Grant
John M. Harlan	1877–1911	34	Hayes
William B. Woods	1880–1887	7	Hayes
Stanley Matthews	1881–1889	7	Garfield
Horace Gray	1882–1902	20	Arthur
Samuel Blatchford	1882–1893	11	Arthur
Lucius Q. C. Lamar	1888–1893	5	Cleveland
Melville W. Fuller	1888–1910	21	Cleveland
David J. Brewer	1890–1910	20	B. Harrison
Henry B. Brown	1890–1906	16	B. Harrison
George Shiras, Jr.	1892–1903	10	B. Harrison
Howell E. Jackson	1893–1895	2	B. Harrison
Edward D. White	1894–1910	16	Cleveland
Rufus W. Peckham	1895–1909	14	Cleveland
Joseph McKenna	1898–1925	26	McKinley
Oliver W. Holmes, Jr.	1902–1932	30	T. Roosevelt
William R. Day	1903–1922	19	T. Roosevelt
William H. Moody	1906–1910	3	T. Roosevelt
Horace H. Lurton	1910–1914	4	Taft
Charles E. Hughes	1910–1916	5	Taft
Willis Van Devanter	1911–1937	26	Taft
Joseph R. Lamar	1911–1916	5	Taft
Edward D. White	1910–1921	11	Taft
Mahlon Pitney	1912–1922	10	Taft
James C. McReynolds	1914–1941	26	Wilson
Louis D. Brandeis	1916–1939	22	Wilson
John H. Clarke	1916–1922	6	Wilson
William H. Taft	1921–1930	8	Harding
George Sutherland	1922–1938	15	Harding
Pierce Butler	1922–1939	16	Harding
Edward T. Sanford	1923–1930	7	Harding
Harlan F. Stone	1925–1941	16	Coolidge
Charles E. Hughes	1930–1941	11	Hoover
Owen J. Roberts	1930–1945	15	Hoover
Benjamin N. Cardozo	1932–1938	6	Hoover
Hugo L. Black	1937–1971	34	F. Roosevelt
Stanley F. Reed	1938–1957	19	F. Roosevelt
Felix Frankfurter	1939–1962	23	F. Roosevelt
William O. Douglas	1939–1975	36	F. Roosevelt
Frank Murphy	1940–1949	9	F. Roosevelt
Harlan F. Stone	1941–1946	5	F. Roosevelt
James F. Byrnes	1941–1942	1	F. Roosevelt
Robert H. Jackson	1941–1954	13	F. Roosevelt
Wiley B. Rutledge	1943–1949	6	F. Roosevelt

(continued)

Justices of the U.S. Supreme Court *(continued)*

Chief Justices appear in bold type

	Term of Service	Years of Service	Appointed by
Harold H. Burton	1945–1958	13	Truman
Fred M. Vinson	1946–1953	7	Truman
Tom C. Clark	1949–1967	18	Truman
Sherman Minton	1949–1956	7	Truman
Earl Warren	1953–1969	16	Eisenhower
John Marshall Harlan	1955–1971	16	Eisenhower
William J. Brennan, Jr.	1956–1990	34	Eisenhower
Charles E. Whittaker	1957–1962	5	Eisenhower
Potter Stewart	1958–1981	23	Eisenhower
Byron R. White	1962–1993	31	Kennedy
Arthur J. Goldberg	1962–1965	3	Kennedy
Abe Fortas	1965–1969	4	Johnson
Thurgood Marshall	1967–1994	24	Johnson
Warren E. Burger	1969–1986	18	Nixon
Harry A. Blackmun	1970–1994	24	Nixon
Lewis F. Powell, Jr.	1971–1987	15	Nixon
William H. Rehnquist[2]	1971–	—	Nixon
John P. Stevens III	1975–	—	Ford
Sandra Day O'Connor	1981–	—	Reagan
Antonin Scalia	1986–	—	Reagan
Anthony M. Kennedy	1988–	—	Reagan
David Souter	1990–	—	Bush
Clarence Thomas	1991–	—	Bush
Ruth Bader Ginsburg	1993–	—	Clinton
Stephen G. Breyer	1994–	—	Clinton

[2]Chief Justice from 1986 (Reagan administration).

Political Party Affiliations in Congress and the Presidency, 1789–2003*

Congress	Year	House* Majority Party	House* Principal Minority Party	House* Other (except Vacancies)	Senate* Majority Party	Senate* Principal Minority Party	Senate* Other (except Vacancies)	President and Party
1st	1789–1791	Ad-38	Op-26	—	Ad-17	Op-9	—	F (Washington)
2nd	1791–1793	F-37	DR-33	—	F-16	DR-13	—	F (Washington)
3rd	1793–1795	DR-57	F-48	—	F-17	DR-13	—	F (Washington)
4th	1795–1797	F-54	DR-52	—	F-19	DR-13	—	F (Washington)
5th	1797–1799	F-58	DR-48	—	F-20	DR-12	—	F (John Adams)
6th	1799–1801	F-64	DR-42	—	F-19	DR-13	—	F (John Adams)
7th	1801–1803	DR-69	F-36	—	DR-18	F-13	—	DR (Jefferson)
8th	1803–1805	DR-102	F-39	—	DR-25	F-9	—	DR (Jefferson)
9th	1805–1807	DR-116	F-25	—	DR-27	F-7	—	DR (Jefferson)
10th	1807–1809	DR-118	F-24	—	DR-28	F-6	—	DR (Jefferson)
11th	1809–1811	DR-94	F-48	—	DR-28	F-6	—	DR (Madison)
12th	1811–1813	DR-108	F-36	—	DR-30	F-6	—	DR (Madison)
13th	1813–1815	DR-112	F-68	—	DR-27	F-9	—	DR (Madison)
14th	1815–1817	DR-117	F-65	—	DR-25	F-11	—	DR (Madison)
15th	1817–1819	DR-141	F-42	—	DR-34	F-10	—	DR (Monroe)
16th	1819–1821	DR-156	F-27	—	DR-35	F-7	—	DR (Monroe)
17th	1821–1823	DR-158	F-25	—	DR-44	F-4	—	DR (Monroe)
18th	1823–1825	DR-187	F-26	—	DR-44	F-4	—	DR (Monroe)
19th	1825–1827	Ad-105	J-97	—	Ad-26	J-20	—	C (J. Q. Adams)
20th	1827–1829	J-119	Ad-94	—	J-28	Ad-20	—	C (J. Q. Adams)
21st	1829–1831	D-139	NR-74	—	D-26	NR-22	—	D (Jackson)
22nd	1831–1833	D-141	NR-58	14	D-25	NR-21	2	D (Jackson)
23rd	1833–1835	D-147	AM-53	60	D-20	NR-20	8	D (Jackson)
24th	1835–1837	D-145	W-98	—	D-27	W-25	—	D (Jackson)
25th	1837–1839	D-108	W-107	24	D-30	W-18	4	D (Van Buren)
26th	1839–1841	D-124	W-118	—	D-28	W-22	—	D (Van Buren)
27th	1841–1843	W-133	D-102	6	W-28	D-22	2	W (Harrison) W (Tyler)
28th	1843–1845	D-142	W-79	1	W-28	D-25	1	W (Tyler)
29th	1845–1847	D-143	W-77	6	D-31	W-25	—	D (Polk)
30th	1847–1849	W-115	D-108	4	D-36	W-21	1	D (Polk)
31st	1849–1851	D-112	W-109	9	D-35	W-25	2	W (Taylor) W (Fillmore)
32nd	1851–1853	D-140	W-88	5	D-35	W-24	3	W (Fillmore)
33rd	1853–1855	D-159	W-71	4	D-38	W-22	2	D (Pierce)
34th	1855–1857	R-108	D-83	43	D-40	R-15	5	D (Pierce)
35th	1857–1859	D-118	R-92	26	D-36	R-20	8	D (Buchanan)
36th	1859–1861	R-114	D-92	31	D-36	R-26	4	D (Buchanan)
37th	1861–1863	R-105	D-43	30	R-31	D-10	8	R (Lincoln)
38th	1863–1865	R-102	D-75	9	R-36	D-9	5	R (Lincoln)
39th	1865–1867	U-149	D-42	—	U-42	D-10	—	R (Lincoln) R (Johnson)
40th	1867–1869	R-143	D-49	—	R-42	D-11	—	R (Johnson)
41st	1869–1871	R-149	D-63	—	R-56	D-11	—	R (Grant)
42nd	1871–1873	R-134	D-104	5	R-52	D-17	5	R (Grant)
43rd	1873–1875	R-194	D-92	14	R-49	D-19	5	R (Grant)
44th	1875–1877	D-169	R-109	14	R-45	D-29	2	R (Grant)
45th	1877–1879	D-153	R-140	—	R-39	D-36	1	R (Hayes)
46th	1879–1881	D-149	R-130	14	D-42	R-33	1	R (Hayes)
47th	1881–1883	R-147	D-135	11	R-37	D-37	1	R (Garfield) R (Arthur)
48th	1883–1885	D-197	R-118	10	R-38	D-36	2	R (Arthur)

*Letter symbols for political parties. Ad—Administration; AM—Anti-Masonic; C—Coalition; D—Democratic; DR—Democratic-Republican; F—Federalist; J—Jacksonian; NR—National—Republican; Op—Opposition; R—Republican; U—Unionist; W—Whig.

Source: *Historical Statistics of the United States: Colonial Times to the Present,* Various eds. Washington, D.C.: GOP.

(continued)

Political Party Affiliations in Congress and the Presidency, 1789–2003 *(continued)*

Congress	Year	House			Senate			President and Party
		Majority Party	Principal Minority Party	Other (except Vacancies)	Majority Party	Principal Minority Party	Other (except Vacancies)	
49th	1885–1887	D-183	R-140	2	R-43	D-34	—	D (Cleveland)
50th	1887–1889	D-169	R-152	4	R-39	D-37	—	D (Cleveland)
51st	1889–1891	R-166	D-159	—	R-39	D-37	—	R (B. Harrison)
52nd	1891–1893	D-235	R-88	9	R-47	D-39	2	R (B. Harrison)
53rd	1893–1895	D-218	R-127	11	D-44	R-38	3	D (Cleveland)
54th	1895–1897	R-244	D-105	7	R-43	D-39	6	D (Cleveland)
55th	1897–1899	R-204	D-113	40	R-47	D-34	7	R (McKinley)
56th	1899–1901	R-185	D-163	9	R-53	D-26	8	R (McKinley)
57th	1901–1903	R-197	D-151	9	R-55	D-31	4	R (McKinley) R (T. Roosevelt)
58th	1903–1905	R-208	D-178	—	R-57	D-33	—	R (T. Roosevelt)
59th	1905–1907	R-250	D-136	—	R-57	D-33	—	R (T. Roosevelt)
60th	1907–1909	R-222	D-164	—	R-61	D-31	—	R (T. Roosevelt)
61st	1909–1911	R-219	D-172	—	R-61	D-32	—	R (Taft)
62nd	1911–1913	D-228	R-161	1	R-51	D-41	—	R (Taft)
63rd	1913–1915	D-291	R-127	17	D-51	R-44	1	D (Wilson)
64th	1915–1917	D-230	R-196	9	D-56	R-40	—	D (Wilson)
65th	1917–1919	D-216	R-210	6	D-53	R-42	—	D (Wilson)
66th	1919–1921	R-240	D-190	3	R-49	D-47	—	D (Wilson)
67th	1921–1923	R-301	D-131	1	R-59	D-37	—	R (Harding)
68th	1923–1925	R-225	D-205	5	R-51	D-43	2	R (Coolidge)
69th	1925–1927	R-247	D-183	4	R-56	D-39	1	R (Coolidge)
70th	1927–1929	R-237	D-195	3	R-49	D-46	1	R (Coolidge)
71st	1929–1931	R-267	D-167	1	R-56	D-39	1	R (Hoover)
72nd	1931–1933	D-220	R-214	1	R-48	D-47	1	R (Hoover)
73rd	1933–1935	D-310	R-117	5	D-60	R-35	1	D (F. Roosevelt)
74th	1935–1937	D-319	R-103	10	D-69	R-25	2	D (F. Roosevelt)
75th	1937–1939	D-331	R-89	13	D-76	R-16	4	D (F. Roosevelt)
76th	1939–1941	D-261	R-164	4	D-69	R-23	4	D (F. Roosevelt)
77th	1941–1943	D-268	R-162	5	D-66	R-28	2	D (F. Roosevelt)
78th	1943–1945	D-218	R-208	4	D-58	R-37	1	D (F. Roosevelt)
79th	1945–1947	D-242	R-190	2	D-56	R-38	1	D (Truman)
80th	1947–1949	R-245	D-188	1	R-51	D-45	—	D (Truman)
81st	1949–1951	D-263	R-171	1	D-54	R-42	—	D (Truman)
82nd	1951–1953	D-243	R-199	1	D-49	R-47	—	D (Truman)
83rd	1953–1955	R-221	D-211	1	R-48	D-47	1	R (Eisenhower)
84th	1955–1957	D-232	R-203	—	D-48	R-47	1	R (Eisenhower)
85th	1957–1959	D-233	R-200	—	D-49	R-47	—	R (Eisenhower)
86th	1959–1961	D-283	R-153	—	D-64	R-34	—	R (Eisenhower)
87th	1961–1963	D-263	R-174	—	D-65	R-35	—	D (Kennedy)
88th	1963–1965	D-258	R-177	—	D-67	R-33	—	D (Kennedy) D (Johnson)
89th	1965–1967	D-295	R-140	—	D-68	R-32	—	D (Johnson)
90th	1967–1969	D-247	R-187	1	D-64	R-36	—	D (Johnson)
91st	1969–1971	D-243	R-192	—	D-58	R-42	—	R (Nixon)
92nd	1971–1973	D-255	R-180	—	D-54	R-44	2	R (Nixon)
93rd	1973–1975	D-242	R-192	1	D-56	R-42	2	R (Nixon, Ford)
94th	1975–1977	D-291	R-144	—	D-61	R-37	2	R (Ford)
95th	1977–1979	D-292	R-143	—	D-61	R-38	1	D (Carter)
96th	1979–1981	D-277	R-158	—	D-58	R-41	1	D (Carter)
97th	1981–1983	D-242	R-192	—	R-54	D-45	1	R (Reagan)
98th	1983–1985	D-266	R-167	2	R-55	D-45	—	R (Reagan)
99th	1985–1987	D-252	R-183	—	R-53	D-47	—	R (Reagan)
100th	1987–1989	D-258	R-177	—	D-55	R-45	—	R (Reagan)
101st	1989–1991	D-262	R-173	—	D-57	R-43	—	R (Bush)
102nd	1991–1993	D-267	R-167	1	D-57	R-43	—	R (Bush)
103rd	1993–1995	D-256	R-178	1	D-56	R-44	—	D (Clinton)

(continued)

Political Party Affiliations in Congress
and the Presidency, 1789–2003 (continued)

| Congress | Year | House | | | Senate | | | President |
		Majority Party	Principal Minority Party	Other (except Vacancies)	Majority Party	Principal Minority Party	Other (except Vacancies)	and Party
104th	1995–1997	R-230	D-204	1	R-52	D-48	—	D (Clinton)
105th	1997–1999	R-228	D-206	1	R-55	D-45	—	D (Clinton)
106th	1999–2001	R-223	D-211	1	R-55	D-45	—	D (Clinton)
107th	2001–2003	R-221	D-212	2	D-50	R-49*	1	R (Bush)
108th	2003–2005	R-229	D-205	1	R-51	D-48	1	R (Bush)

*Senator James M. Jeffords of Vermont, a Republican when the 107th Congress convened, changed his party identification to Independent and voted with the Democrats in organizing the Senate.

CREDITS

INDEX

Manufacturing: American System of, 189; Hamilton on, 153; mercantilism and, 46

Manumission, 135, 258, 266

Mapmaker: Columbus as, *11*

Marbury, William, 166

Marbury v. Madison, 166–167, 200

Marie Antoinette (France), 122, 154

Mariner's Almanac, 51

Marion, Francis, *129, 197*

Marquette, Jacques, *66,* 67

Marriage: Indian-white, 62

Marryat, Frederick, 250

Marshall, James, 298

Marshall, John, 135, 161, 224, 259; Burr trial and, 170; as Chief Justice, 200; on Constitution, 143; *Marbury v. Madison* and, 166

Martineau, Harriett, 250

Martinique, 92, 167

Martin v. Hunter's Lessee, 200

Martyr, Peter, 1

Mary I Tudor (England), 19

Maryland, 39, 47, 49–50, 217

Mason, James M., 332–333

Mason-Dixon line, 81, 210, 271

Masons: politics and, 218

Massachusetts: charter revoked in, 55; Coercive Acts and, 111; independence in, 55; as royal colony, 55; Shays's Rebellion in, 142; Sunday activities in, 41

Massachusetts Bay: Plymouth Plantation at, 32

Massachusetts Bay colony, 34, 35

Massachusetts Bay Company: charter of, 34

Massachusetts Committee of Safety, 114

Mastodons: Paleo-Indians and, 2

Matamoros: battle at, 292

Maternal descent: in Africa, 73

Mathew, Theobald, 253

Matriarchy: of Iroquois, 94

Mayans, 3, *3, 4,* 5

Mayer, Tobias, 51

Mayflower (ship), 32

Mayflower Compact, 33

Maysville Road veto, 223

Mazzei, Filippo, 165

McAdam, John, 205

McClellan, George B., 352; in Civil War, 331, 336, *336, 337, 337,* 339

McCrea, Jane, 125

McCulley, Johnston, 286

McCulloch v. Maryland, 200

McDowell, Irvin, 328, *329,* 331

McGready, James, 243

McHenry, Fort, 176

McKenney, Thomas L., 223

Meade, George, 343–344

Measles, 15

Mechanics: workingmen's parties and, 217

Medicine: birthing and, 151; in prehistoric America, 2–3

Meetinghouse: in Massachusetts, 41

Melville, Herman, 213, 249

Memphis: race riot in, 361

Men: college education for, 234; in Indian tribes, 60; Iroquois, 94; voting rights of, 79. *See also* Gender

Menéndez de Avilés, Pedro, 29

Mennonites, 78

Mercantilism, 46–57; counting room and, *46;* in New England, 53–54; protective tariff and, 153; in South, 47–52

Mercenaries, 119, 126–127

Merchants: as adventurers, 24–25; as Loyalists, 121; in Middle Colonies, 57

Merrimack (ironclad ship), 335

"Merrymount," *32, 33*

Mesoamerica, 2; astronomy in, 5, *5;* civilization in, 3–4; pyramids in, *3;* warfare in, 4

Mestizos, 281

Metacomet (Wampanoag), 65

Methodists, 243, 279; slavery and, 244, 257–258, 316

Mexica: Aztecs as, 5

Mexican territories: annexation of, 296

Mexican War, 291–293; battles in, *293*

Mexico, 2; Americans in borderlands of (1819-1848), *283;* under Aztecs, *6;* boundary with U.S., 281; civilization in, 3–4; Cortés in, 11–12; horses and, 14–15; northward expansion of, 282; Texas as district of, 283–284; U.S. offer to buy California and New Mexico, 291

Mexico City: occupation of, 292

Miami Indians, 158, 175

Michigan, 138, 181

Middle Colonies, 47, 56–57; life expectancy in, 77; Queen Anne's War and, 84

Middle passage, 72, 277

Midnight judges, 166

Midwest: growth of, 181

Midwives, 151

Migration: of early peoples, 1; of Mormons, 246. *See also* Immigrants and immigration; Westward movement

Milan decree (Napoleon), 171

Military: medals of, *149;* music of, 122; Washington, George, and, 130. *See also* Armed forces

Military districts: in Reconstruction South, 361, *362*

Military draft. *See* Draft (military)

Militia: colonial, 112–113; in Revolutionary War, 120

Miller, Peter, 151

Miller, Samuel, 234

Miller, William, 245, *245*

Millerites, 270. *See also* Adventists

Milling device: for muskets, 203–204

Mills: Lowell system and, 206–207; machine technology for, 203; power for, 202, *202,* 204

Mill towns, *202*

Mining and mining industry: gold and silver rushes and, 299

Mining camps: in California gold rush, *301;* democracy and egalitarianism in, 299

Minnesota, 298

Minstrel shows, 268–269, *269*

Minuit, Peter, 40, 64

Minutemen, 114

Miscegenation, 62

Missions and missionaries: in California, 282; conversion of Catholics and, 254–255; Franciscan, 29; French, 68; in Hawaii, 255; in Oregon Country, 287; Protestant, 67

Mississippi, 217

Mississippi Colonization Society, 259

Mississippi River region, 13; in Civil War, 342; Louisiana Purchase and, 167; Marquette and Joliet in, *66;* Pinckney's Treaty and, 156; trade in, 139

Mississippi River system: shipping on, 192; steamboats and, 193–194

Missouri, 181, 309

Missouri Compromise (1820), 209–211, *210;* demarcation line permitting slavery, 296; Kansas-Nebraska Act and, 305; legal status of slavery and, *313;* Supreme Court on, 312

Missouri Territory: slavery and, 210–211

Mitchell, Margaret, 270

Mixed government: in Constitution (U.S.), 144

Mobility: social, 79–80. *See also* Immigrants and immigration; Migration

Moctezuma II (Aztecs), 6; Cortés and, 11–12, *12*

Mohawk Indians, 121; Five Nations of the Iroquois and, 62, 94; scalping by, 64; use of name, 60

Mohican Indians, 65, 66

Molasses: sugar industry and, 92

Molasses Act (1733), 84–85, 96–97

Money: under Articles of Confederation, 139, *139;* "buck" as, 152; dollar and, 152; New England trade and, 54–55; pound sterling as, 96

Moneymaking: in proprietary colonies, 38–39

Money supply: Bank of the United States and, 231

Monitor (ironclad), 335

Monotheism: of Indians, 61

Monroe, James, 167, 259; biography of, 197–198; election of 1816 and, 198; Missouri Compromise and, 305

Monroe Doctrine, 199–200

Monrovia, Liberia, 258, 259, *260*

Montcalm, Louis de, 89

Monterey: seizure of, 291

Montesinos, Antonio de, 13

Monticello, 164, 165, *165*

Moors: in Spain, 10

Morality: of slavery, 260–261, 295

Moral suasionists: teetotalers and, 253

Moravians, 78

Morgan, Henry, 82

Morgan, William, 217–218

Mormons, 245; in "Deseret," 246; migration to Utah, 246; persecution of, 245–246

Morrill Act (1862), 354

Morrill Tariff (1861), 353

Morris, Gouverneur, 149, 159

Morris, Robert, 116

Morse, Samuel F. B., 254

Morton, Thomas, 31, 32

Mosell (steamboat), 194

Mott, Lucretia Coffin, 255, 256

Mound Builders, 2, *3*

Mountain men: gold rush and, *300;* in Oregon Country, 286–287

Mount Vernon, 272

Mulberry Plantation: slaves' cabins at, *74*

Mullins, Priscilla, 32

Mun, Thomas, 46

Murfreesboro: battle at, 339

Muscovy Company, 25

Music: Civil War anthems and, 344; "Ethiopian songs" and, 269; of Foster, Stephen, 269; military, 122; Negro spirituals as, 279; patriotic, 197

Muskets, 204

Muskogean languages, 62

Muslims: trade and, 8

Napoleon I Bonaparte (France), 167, 171; Berlin and Milan decrees of, 171; Louisiana Purchase and, 167; trade with, 173

Napoleon III: Civil War (U.S.) and, 332, 333

Narragansett Indians, 65, 66; Williams and, 37

Nast, Thomas, 368

Nation, The (magazine), 368

National anthem: "Star-Spangled Banner, The" as, 176

National debt, 231

National government. *See* Federal government; Government (U.S.)

Nationalism: of Clay, 189; Iberian, 9

Nationalist: Taylor, Zachary, as, 298

National Republicans (Whigs), 213, 232

National road, 188

National Union party, 361

Native American party. *See* Know-Nothings

Native Americans, 1, 2; in Chesapeake region, 26; during Civil War, 332; concept of "Indian-ness" and, 65–66; conversions of, 67–68; Cortés and, 11; of Eastern Woodlands, 60, 61–62, 158; English colonists and, 22; enslavement of, 27, 62; European perception of, *14,* 65; freedoms for, 135; French and, 67; in French and Indian War, *89;* in French Canada, 29; in Great Plains, 158; of Hispaniola, 14; intertribal wars of, 29; Jackson and, 222–223; land of, 63, 158; languages of, 61; Lewis and Clark expedition and, 169; in Mexico, 281; mountain men and, 286, 287; of North America, 59–66; Oregon-bound settlers and, 287; of Plains, 283; Pontiac's conspiracy and, 94–95; Proclamation of 1763 and, 95; removal policy and, 223, 224–225, *225;* Scots-Irish and, 78; Sequoya and, 224; 1650-1750, *60;* in Spanish America, 13–14; in Tidewater and Piedmont, 48–49; Trail of Tears and, 224–225; tribal names of, 60; War of 1812 and, 175; wars among, 64–65; wars in Northwest Territory, *157;* as wives of mountain men, 286, 287

Nativism, 315. *See also* Know-Nothings

Natural resources: industrialization and, 204

Nautilus (submarine), 168

Nauvoo, Illinois: Mormons in, 245–246

Nauvoo Legion, 246, *246*

Navajo Indians, 14

Navigation, 51; Henry the Navigator and, 9; trade and, 8

Navigation Acts (1660-1663), 45, 46–47; molasses and, 92

Navy: English, 154; French, 154; trade and, 8

Navy (U.S.): during Civil War, 335; in Revolution, 120, 126

Nebraska Territory, *306*

Necessity, Fort, 88

Negative campaigning: in 1828, 221

Negro spirituals, 279

Neolin (Delaware), 95

Netherlands: New Netherland and, 40

Neutrality: French-British war and, 171–172; in French Revolution, 154; Rule of 1756 in shipping and, 155

Nevada, 299, 352

New Amsterdam, 40

Newburgh, New York: Continental Army in, 130

New England, *25,* 47, 52–56; Connecticut and, 38; Dominion of, 55; establishment of, 31–36; expansion in, 36–38; gender of settlers, 62; geography of, 52–53; housing in, *37;* independence in, 55; King Philip's War in, 65; land in, *53;* life expectancy in, 77; Massachusetts Bay colony and, 34; New Hampshire and, 38; Plymouth Plantation and, 32–33; Rhode Island and, 36–38; self-government in, 33; society in, 36; tariffs and, 206; textile industry in, 204

New England Emigrant Aid Society, 308–309, 311

Newfoundland, 7, 18, 20, 21, 25; fishing rights and, 129

New France, 29, 66–68, *88;* end of, 87–90; French and Indian War and, 88–89; representative government and, 94

Population: blacks in North, 258; blacks in South, 258; in California, gold rush and, 298; density of (1790-1820), *181*; English colonization and, 23–24; growth of, 181; of Indians of Hispaniola, 14; of Jamestown, 26; of New France, 66; of New Netherland, 40; of slaves, 271; in South, 209; of Teotihuacán, 3–4; of Virginia, 26
Populism and populists: African Americans and, 367
Pore, Tryal, 35
Pork: in early 19th century diet, 264, 265
"Pork-barrel" bills, 264
Port Hudson, 346
Port Royal, 83
Portugal, 8–10, *9*, 11
Positive good: slavery as, 264, *265*
Post Office Department: corruption in, 368
Potatoes, 15
Potlatches, 61
Pottawatomie Creek massacre, 310
Pottawottamie Indians, 175
Pound sterling, 96
Power (energy): for textile machines, 202
Power (political): Congress under Articles of Confederation and, 136; reserved to states, 147
Power loom, 203
Power of the purse, 85–86
Powhatan (Chief), 28, 59
Powhatan Confederacy, 26; Jamestown Massacre and, *28, 28–29*
Powhatan Indians, 25, 26. *See also* Powhatan Confederacy
Practical science, 204
Prairie schooner wagons, 283, 287. *See also* Conestoga wagon
Pre-Columbian explorers, 7
Predestination, 242
Preemption Act (1841), 239
Prehistory, 2
Presbyterians, 134, 242, 287; slavery issue and, 244, 316
Prescott, Samuel, 113
Presidency: of Confederacy, 319
Presidential elections. *See* Elections
Presidential powers: during Civil War, 357
President of United States: dark horse candidates for, 289; electoral college selection of, 145; title of, 148; Twelfth Amendment and, 162; two-term tradition for, 172; Virginia Dynasty of, 214; Washington as, 148–149
Presidios, 282
Press gangs. *See* Impressment
Prester John, 7
Primogeniture: laws of, 79
Princeton: battle at, 124
Princeton University, 87
Principal Navigations, Voyages, Traffiques, and Discoveries of the English Nation (Hakluyt), 22
Principia Mathematica (Newton), 87
Private enterprise: colonization and, 24–25
Privateering, 18, *82*, 82–83; French, 173; Genet and, 155–156
Proclamation of 1763, 95
Prohibition: vs. moderation in temperance movement, 253
Property laws, 79; lower orders and, 80–81
Property qualification: for voting, 134
Property rights: slaves and, 275
Prophet. *See* Tenskwatawa (the Prophet)
Proprietary colonies: Delaware as, 42; government structure in, 38; headright system and quitrents in, 39; Maryland and, 55; New Jersey as, 42; New York as, 40; royal colonies and, 38–43
Proslavery arguments, 264
Prosser, Gabriel, 262
Prostitution, 342
Protective tariffs, 153, 306
Protest(s): Adams, Samuel, and, 110; against Stamp Act, 98–99, *100*; against Sugar Act, 97
Protestant Episcopal Church, 242. *See also* Episcopal Church
Protestantism, 19; of Elizabeth I, 20; in England, 19–20; Episcopal Church and, 134; Huguenots and, 29; in Maryland, 39
Protestant Reformation, 19
Protests and protest movements: of slaves, 278–280
Providence, 37
Public schools: in South, 364. *See also* Education; Schools
Pueblo Indians, 61
Puerperal fever (childbirth fever), 151
Pulaski, Casimir, 126–127

Punishment: for crimes, 251, *252*; by Puritans, *35*, 35–36
Puritans and Puritanism, 20, 34, 67–68, 86–87, 242; city upon a hill of, 35; commonwealth of, 35; justification of land seizures by, 63; meetinghouse services of, 41; names of, 36; society of, 36
Putting-out system, 201–202
Pyramids: Aztec, *3*, 4, 6; Mayan, *3*, 4

Quakers, 40–42, 78–79, 242, 247; pacifism of, 78; slavery and, 257, 260; "Walking Purchase" and, 63
Quantrill, William C., 309
Quartering Act (1765), 95, 106
Quarters: dollar divided into, 152
Quebec, 29, 66; battle at, 89, *89*
Quebec Act (1774), 111
Queen Anne's War, 83–84
Queen's College (Rutgers), 87
Quetzlcoatl, 11
Quincy, Edmund, 238
Quitman, John A., 305
Quitrents, 39

Race and racism: abolition in South and, 258; Bible and, 265; limitations by, 135; minstrel shows and, 269; racial equality and, 312; of runaways, 71–72; Stevens, Thaddeus, and, 359; in territories, 297. *See also* African Americans; Immigrants and immigration
Race riots: after Civil War, 361
Radical Reconstruction, 361–362, *362*
Radical Republicans, 339, 355, 361; Lincoln's reconstruction plan and, 357–358; reconstruction views of, 359
Railroads, 191–192, *192*; construction costs for, 192; 1850-1860, *193*; land grants to, 353; transcontinental, 304. *See also* Transcontinental railroads
Rainey, J. H., 367
Raleigh, Walter, 20, *22, 23*; colonization by, 21–22
Ranching. *See* Cattle and cattle industry
Randolph, Edmund, 146, 150, *150*; Bill of Rights and, 147
Randolph, John, 167, 215, 220, 258
Randolph, Peyton, 112
Rape, 80
Ratification: of Constitution, 145–147
Rebellions. *See* Revolts and rebellions
Reconstruction, 356–369; black codes and, 360–361; blacks and, 364; Civil Rights Act (1875) and, 369; congressional plan (Radical), 359; end of, 368; Fifteenth Amendment and, 363; Fourteenth Amendment and, 361; legend of, 363–364; Lincoln's plan for, 357–358; presidential, 358–359; Radical program for, 361–362, *362*
Rectangular survey: of Northwest Territory, 138, *138*
Redcoats, 106–107, *107*; Boston Massacre and, 106; garrison in Canada and along frontier, 95; number in Revolutionary War, 119
Redeemers, 365, 367, 368
Redemptioners, 70
Reform and reform movements: for blind, 250; for deaf, 249–250; of insane asylums, 250–251; missionary activity and, 255; of penitentiaries, 251–252; prohibition and, 253; temperance movement and, 252. *See also* Protest(s)
Reformation: Protestant, 19
Regions. *See* Sectionalism
Regulators, 108
Reign of Terror (France), 154, 155
Religion(s): Adventists and, 245; camp meetings and, 243; circuit riders and, 243–244; in colonies, 86; Cortés and, 11–12; in early 19th century, 242–243; First Great Awakening and, 86–87; French Revolution and, 154; French vs. English, 67–68; of Iroquois Confederacy members, 94; Know-Nothings and, 315; in Massachusetts, 41; as means to control slaves, 267; Mormons and, 245; neutrality of, 134; in New France, 66; revivalism and, 243–244; Second Great Awakening and, 244; slavery and, 279, 316; of Tenskwatawa (the Prophet), 175; warfare and, 4. *See also* Puritans and Puritanism
Religious toleration: in Maryland, 39; in Middle Colonies, 57
Rensselaer Polytechnic Institute, 204
"Report on Manufactures" (Hamilton), 153
Representative government: British vs. American concepts of, 100–101; in New France, 94; principle of, 100
Republican party: election of 1860 and, 316–317; formation of, 306–307; Liberal Republicans and,

368, 369; northern appeal of, 307; Radicals in, 339; slavery and, *313*; in South, 368. *See also* Elections; Jefferson Republicans
Republic of Texas, *283*, 284
Resistance: to British policy, 108. *See also* Revolts and rebellions; Revolutions
Revels, Hiram K., 367
Revenues: British, 95–97
Revere, Paul, 113–114, 197; Boston Massacre and, 106, *106*
Revivalism, 243–244; in Great Awakening, 86–87; sermons and, 244
Revolts and rebellions: by Anglo and Hispanic Texans, 284; by Bacon, 49; of blacks on *Creole*, 240; by Culpeper, 42; Dorr's Rebellion, 217; in early 19th century colleges, 234; by Gabriel, 262; by Pontiac, 94–95; Shays's, *141*, 142; slave, 81; slave in Saint-Domingue, 261; by Turner, Nat, *262*, 263, 266, 267; by Vesey, Denmark, 262–263, 267; Whiskey Rebellion, 158. *See also* Protest(s); Resistance
Revolutionary War: battles in (1776-1777), *123*; debt payment after, 151–152; events leading to, 111–113; first battles of (1775-1776), *115*; France and, 122; mercenaries in, 126–127; patriots, Loyalists, and neutral individuals, 120–121, 131; in 1777, 125; Treaty of Paris and, 129; Yorktown battle and, 128
Revolutions: French, 154
Rhode Island, 37, 55
Rhode Island and Providence Plantations, 36–37
"Rhodora, The" (Emerson), 248
Ribault, Jean, 29
Rice, 51–52; in Carolinas, 42; indigo and, 81
Rice, Thomas D. ("Daddy"), 268–269
Richmond, Virginia: in Civil War, 336, *337*; as Confederate capital, 322
Rider: in lawmaking process, 296
Rifles: Hawkens, 287
Rights: in Bill of Rights, 146–147; of British subjects, 97; in Declaration of Independence, 117; French Revolution and, 154; to levy taxes, 97; in state constitutions, 134; to trial by jury, 98; of women, 134–135
Rio Bravo, 282
Rio Grande region, 282; Spanish in, 29; as U.S./Mexico boundary, 284, 292
Riot(s): draft, 326; food, 333; between Irish-Orangemen and Irish-Catholics, 253, 254, *254*; against Stamp Act, 99. *See also* Race riots
Ripon, Wisconsin, 306
"Rip Van Winkle" (Irving), 250
Ritchie, Thomas, 262
River(s): transportation on (1825-1860), *190*
River Farm, 272
Roads and highways: in backcountry, 131; *camino real*, 282, 286; Clay and, 187; development of, 205; in 1825-1860, *190*; federal financing for, 187–189; Gold Rush route to California, *300*
Roanoke Island: Raleigh on, 21–22
Robespierre, Maximilien, 154
Rochambeau, Jean-Baptiste, comte de, 127, 128
Rockingham, Marquis of, 102, 121, 129
Rocky Mountains, 168, 281, 282; Oregon Trail through, 287
Rodney, Caesar, 116
Rolfe, John, 25, 26, 28, *28*, 62
Roman Catholic Church. *See* Catholicism
Roosevelt, Franklin D.: two-term presidency tradition and, 172
Roosevelt, Theodore: as vice president, 160
Rosecrans, William S., 346
Ross: Fort, 199, 200, 285
Rousseau, Jean-Jacques, 122
Royal colonies: government structure in, 38; Massachusetts as, 55; North and South Carolina as, 42; proprietary colonies and, 38–43; Virginia as, 29
Royal Navy (England), 154; Anglo-French conflict and, 171–172; impressment by, 155–156, 172, *172*
Royal Observatory at Greenwich, 51
Rule of 1756: neutral shipping and, 155
Rum: in colonial lifestyle, 107–108; molasses and, 92
Runaways: race of, 71–72; servants as, 71; as slave protest, 278–279. *See also* Fugitive slaves
Rural areas: industrialization and population of, 201
Rush, Benjamin, 252
Rush-Bagot Agreement (1817), 199
Russia: Muscovy Company from, 25; Oregon Country and, 285–286; on Pacific Coast, 199, 200
Rutgers University, 87

United States: French recognition of, 126; as grammatically singular, 352; Ponce de León in, 13; in 1792, 153
United States Post Office: creation of stamps to pay postage, 297
United States Sanitary Commission, 328
U.S. Supreme Court. *See* Supreme Court (U.S.)
Universal human rights: in Declaration of Independence, 117
Universities and colleges: abolitionism in, 270; in early nineteenth century, 234; Harvard College, 29; Morrill Act and, 354; New Light founding of, 87; in South, 51; southerners in, 264–265
Upper Canada, 174–175
Ursuline convent: burning of, 254
Utah, 299; as Mexican territory, *288*; Mormons in, 246
Utopian communities, 246–248, *248*
Utrecht, Treaty of, 23

Vallandigham, Clement L., 333
Valley Forge: Washington at, 125, 127, *128*
Van Arsdale, Jans, 79
Van Buren, Martin, 216, *230*; annexation of Texas and, 284; depression of 1838 and, 237; Eaton affair and, 230; election of 1836 and, 236–237, *237*; election of 1840 and, 238–239, *239*; election of 1844 and, 288–289; election of 1848 and, 297; laissez-faire attitude of, 237; Maine-New Brunswick boundary dispute and, 240; as vice president, 231; Whig depiction of, 238
Vancouver, George, 168
Vancouver Island, 168, 287, 291
Van Rensselaer, Stephen, 215
Van Rensselaerswyck, 40
Van Wagenen, Isabella. *See* Truth, Sojourner
Venereal disease: Columbian Exchange and, 15, 16
Vera Cruz, 11; battle at, 292
Vergennes, Charles, comte de, 122, 125; United States recognized by, 126
Vermont: abolition of slavery in, 135
Verrazano, Giovanni, 18
Vesey, Denmark, 262
Vesey's Rebellion, 262–263, 267
Vespucci, Amerigo, 10
Vetoes: by Jackson, 232; by Tyler, 239
Vice admiralty courts: trial by jury and, 98
Vice president: role of, 160
Viceroys: in Spanish America, 13
Vicksburg: siege of, 342, 343, *344*, 345–346
Vikings, 7
Vindication of the Rights of Women (Wollstencroft), 134–135
Vinland, 7
Violence: anti-Catholic, 253–254, *254*; caning of Sumner in Senate, 310, *310*; in early 1770s, 105–106; along frontier, 186; by Ku Klux Klan, 364–365, *366*
Virginia, 21, *25*, 47; backcountry of, 48–49; Bacon's Rebellion in, 49; Berkeley in, 48–49; black slaves in, 72; colony in, 25–29; constitutional rights in, 134; in French and Indian War, 88; lifestyle in, 26; manumission in, 135; planters in, 49–50, 112; plan to end slavery in, 259–260; population of, 26; rights in constitution of, 134; as royal colony, 29, 38; secession of, 321–322; slavery in, 27; tobacco in, 26–27, *27*
Virginia and Kentucky Resolutions, 161–162, 165
Virginia Dynasty: of presidents, 214
Virtual representation, 100–101
Volunteers: for Civil War, 321, 324; for Mexican War, 292
Voting and voting rights: democratization of, 217; in 1816, 199; Fifteenth Amendment and, 363; for men, 79; qualifications for, 134; religion and, 134; representation and, 100; in Virginia, 112
Voyages of Sir Marco Polo, 7

Wade, Benjamin ("Bluff Ben"), 324, 354, 359
Wade-Davis Bill (1864), 357–358
Wagon trains, 182, *182*, 287, *289*
Wake, Lyons (Sarah Rosetta Wake), 327
Walden (Thoreau), 249
Walden Pond, 249
Waldo, Albigence, 127
Walker, William, 305
"Walking Purchase": in Pennsylvania, 63
Walpole, Robert, 84, 95–96, 103
Wampanoag Indians, 65
Wanderer (schooner), 277
War crimes: in Revolutionary War, 125

Ward, Artemus, 34
War for Independence. *See* Revolutionary War
War Hawks: Clay as, 187; in War of 1812, 173–175
Warmoth, Henry C., 364
War of 1812, 173–179, *177,* 281; "Star-Spangled Banner, The" and, 176
War of Jenkins' Ear, 87–88
War of the Austrian Succession. *See* King George's War
War of the League of Augsburg. *See* King William's War
Warren, Mercy Otis, 146
Warrior's path, 131
Wars and warfare: in 18th century, 113; European (1689–1763), 81–84; guerrilla, 314–315; intertribal, 29, 64–65; in Mesoamerica, 4. *See also* Draft (military); specific battles and wars
Warships: in Revolutionary War, 120
Washington, Bushrod, 161
Washington, D.C.: abolition and, 263–264; assumption and, 152; burning of, 176; capital in, 166; during Civil War, 331; in War of 1812, 178
Washington, Fort, 123
Washington, George, 133, *142,* 205; at Constitutional Convention, 143; Continental Army and, 120; at Continental Congress, 111; death of, 162; dislike for, 159; farewell address of, 153; as "father of his country," 130; inauguration of, *149*; inheritance by, 79; manumission and, 258; in Ohio region, 88; pottery statuettes of, *102*; as president, 148–149; on Proclamation Line, 95; reelection of, 153; as slave owner, 272; two-term presidency and, 172; at Valley Forge, 125, 127, *128*; virtual representation and, 101
Washington, Lawrence, 79
Washington, Martha, 79, 272
Washington Temperance Society, 252
Waterways. *See* Canals
Watson, Thomas, 367
Watt, James, 193
Wayne, Anthony ("Mad Anthony"): Indian battles with, 158
Wealth: exploration and, 7; Levantine and Italian, 8; Spanish, 23; from Spanish America, 13
Wealthy, 79; as Federalists, 159; in South, 47; trade goods and, 47; women as, 80
Weapons: in Civil War, 325–326, 330; colonial, 113; Indian trade for, 64; Kentucky long rifle as, 183; submarine warfare and, 547
Webster, Daniel, 148, 206, 228, 235–236, 239, 240, 302, *302, 303*; Clay's Omnibus Bill and, 300–301; election of 1836 and, 237, *237*; on liberty and union, 236; as slave owner, 278
Webster, Noah, 76, 251; Americanization of English language by, 197; Bible of, 197
Webster-Ashburton line, 291
Webster-Ashburton Treaty, 240
Webster-Hayne debate, 236, *236*
Weed, Thurlow, 218, 238
Weems, Mason Locke, 197
Weld, Theodore Dwight: antislavery view of, 270
West: Americans in (1819-1848), *288*; Civil War in, *334,* 334–335; Clay and, 187; development of, 180–182; growth of, *184*; settlement of, 182–185
West, Thomas (Baron De La Warr), 26
West Africa: Ashanti Confederation in, 72; roots of slavery in, 72–73, *73*
Western lands: under Articles of Confederation, 136; state claims over, *137. See also* West
Western reserve, 136
West Indies: life expectancy in, 77; Napoleon and, 167; sugar planters of, 92; trade with, 126
West Point, 127
West Virginia: creation of, 322
Westward movement, 180–182; to Oregon Country, 285–288; speculators and, 183–184; to Texas, 281–285; wagon trains and, *182*; west of Appalachians, 157. *See also* West
Wethersfield, 38
Whaling: in New England, 54
Wheelwright, John, 38
Whig party (U.S.), 233; diversity of, 235; election of 1836 and, 236–237, *237*; election of 1840 and, 238–239, *239*; election of 1844 and, 288–289; Kansas-Nebraska Act and, 306; in Thirty-First Congress, 302–303
Whigs: in England, 101
Whiskey, 158
Whiskey Rebellion, 158
White, George H., 367
White, Hugh Lawson: election of 1836 and, 237, *237*
White, John, 21–22, *22*; on Secotan village, *61*

Whitefield, George, *86,* 87
White House: burning of, 178
White potatoes, 15
Whites: Indians and, 62, 63–64
White supremacy: in Reconstruction South, 365
Whitman, Marcus and Narcissa, 287
Whitman, Walt: on Democrats, 307
Whitney, Eli, 203–204
Whittier, John Greenleaf, 245
"Wildcat banks," 184, 185
Wilderness: Battle of, 347
Wilderness Road, 131, 205
Wiley, Bell I., 330
Wilkes, John, 101, 121
Wilkinson, James: Burr and, 170
Willamette Valley, 287
William III (England), 82, 97
William and Mary (England), 55
William and Mary, College of, 51
William of Orange. *See* William III (England); William and Mary (England)
Williams, Margaret, 70
Williams, Roger, 36–37, 63, 67
Williamsburg, 50
Willkie, Wendell, 289
Wilmot, David, 296
Wilmot Proviso, 296–297, 298
Wilson, James, 143
Wilson, Woodrow, 164
Wines: Jefferson and, 165
Winthrop, John, 31, 35, 36, 37, *38,* 86–87
Wirt, William, 197, 218
Wisconsin, 138
Witchcraft: in Salem, 55–56, *56*; women's crimes and, 80
Wives: Native American, of mountain men, 286, 287
Wolcott, Oliver, 91
Wolfe, James, 89, *89,* 90, 113
Wollstencroft, Mary, 134–135
Women: in Civil War, 327–328; dowries for, 79; higher education and, 234; Indian, 60, 62; Indian capture of European, 62; as industrialists, 200; Iroquois, 94; Jackson's attitude toward, 222; in Massachusetts meetinghouses, 41; as mill workers, 206–207, *207*; in nursing, 327–328; reform movements and, 255; Salem witchcraft and, 55–56, *56*; social status of, 80; voting and, 134, *135*; in West Africa, 73. *See also* Feminism; Gender
Women's movement: vs. abolition, 255; Seneca Falls convention and, 255–256
Women's rights: Garrison and, 261; after Revolution, 134
Wool, John E., 225, 292
Woolen mills, 203
Woolman, John, 260
Wool trade: mercantilism and, 46
Worcester v. Georgia, 224
Workers: industrialization and, 202
Workforce: blacks in, 258; slaves as, 72
Working class: Civil War draft and, 326; industrial, 202
Workingmen's parties, 217
Worldview: of Europeans and Indians, 62–63
Wright, Frances "Franny," 217, 218
Wrigley, William, Jr., 284
Writers: Franklin as, 76
Writing: Mesoamerican, 3
Wythe, George, 258

XYZ Affair, 161

Yahi Indians, 60
Yale, 87
Yancey, William L., 220
Yankee(s): English perspective on, 55; origins of term, 40; as traders, 54–55
Yaws, 15
Yellow fever, 52
Yeoman farmers: as slave owners, 272
York (slave): in William and Clark expedition, 168, 169, *169*
York, Canada. *See* Toronto, Canada
Yorktown, Battle of, 127, 128, *129*; British surrender at, *130*; Treaty of Paris and, 130
Young, Brigham, 246
Young Duke, The (Disraeli), 289
"Young Hickory": Polk as, 290
Yucatán Peninsula, *4,* 11, 294

Zorro (fictional character), 286
Zouaves, 328